# Dictionary of Literary Biography

## *Dictionary of Literary Biography Documentary Series*

# Dictionary of Literary Biography Yearbooks

1980 edited by Karen L. Rood, Jean W. Ross, and Richard Ziegfeld (1981)

1981 edited by Karen L. Rood, Jean W. Ross, and Richard Ziegfeld (1982)

1982 edited by Richard Ziegfeld; associate editors: Jean W. Ross and Lynne C. Zeigler (1983)

1983 edited by Mary Bruccoli and Jean W. Ross; associate editor Richard Ziegfeld (1984)

1984 edited by Jean W. Ross (1985)

1985 edited by Jean W. Ross (1986)

1986 edited by J. M. Brook (1987)

1987 edited by J. M. Brook (1988)

1988 edited by J. M. Brook (1989)

1989 edited by J. M. Brook (1990)

1990 edited by James W. Hipp (1991)

1991 edited by James W. Hipp (1992)

1992 edited by James W. Hipp (1993)

1993 edited by James W. Hipp, contributing editor George Garrett (1994)

1994 edited by James W. Hipp, contributing editor George Garrett (1995)

1995 edited by James W. Hipp, contributing editor George Garrett (1996)

1996 edited by Samuel W. Bruce and L. Kay Webster, contributing editor George Garrett (1997)

1997 edited by Matthew J. Bruccoli and George Garrett, with the assistance of L. Kay Webster (1998)

1998 edited by Matthew J. Bruccoli, contributing editor George Garrett, with the assistance of D. W. Thomas (1999)

1999 edited by Matthew J. Bruccoli, contributing editor George Garrett, with the assistance of D. W. Thomas (2000)

2000 edited by Matthew J. Bruccoli, contributing editor George Garrett, with the assistance of George Parker Anderson (2001)

# Concise Series

**Concise Dictionary of American Literary Biography,** 7 volumes (1988-1999): *The New Consciousness, 1941-1968; Colonization to the American Renaissance, 1640-1865; Realism, Naturalism, and Local Color, 1865-1917; The Twenties, 1917-1929; The Age of Maturity, 1929-1941; Broadening Views, 1968-1988; Supplement: Modern Writers, 1900-1998.*

**Concise Dictionary of British Literary Biography,** 8 volumes (1991-1992): *Writers of the Middle Ages and Renaissance Before 1660; Writers of the Restoration and Eighteenth Century, 1660-1789; Writers of the Romantic Period, 1789-1832; Victorian Writers, 1832-1890; Late-Victorian and Edwardian Writers, 1890-1914; Modern Writers, 1914-1945; Writers After World War II, 1945-1960; Contemporary Writers, 1960 to Present.*

**Concise Dictionary of World Literary Biography,** 10 volumes projected (1999-    ): *Ancient Greek and Roman Writers; German Writers; African, Caribbean, and Latin American Writers; South Slavic and Eastern European Writers.*

# Twentieth-Century Western Writers
## Third Series

Dictionary of Literary Biography® • Volume Two Hundred Fifty-Six

# Twentieth-Century Western Writers
## Third Series

Edited by
Richard H. Cracroft
*Brigham Young University*

A Bruccoli Clark Layman Book
The Gale Group
Detroit • San Francisco • London • Boston • Woodbridge, Conn.

Advisory Board for
DICTIONARY OF LITERARY BIOGRAPHY

John Baker
William Cagle
Patrick O'Connor
George Garrett
Trudier Harris
Alvin Kernan
Kenny J. Williams

Matthew J. Bruccoli and Richard Layman, Editorial Directors
Karen L. Rood, Senior Editor

Printed in the United States of America

The paper used in this publication meets the minimum requirements
of American National Standard for Information Sciences–Permanence
Paper for Printed Library Materials, ANSI Z39.48-1984. ∞™

10 9 8 7 6 5 4 3 2 1

*To Don D. Walker (1918–2000)*
*His Western vision enlightened a generation of Western scholars.*

# Contents

# Plan of the Series

*. . . Almost the most prodigious asset of a country, and perhaps its most precious possession, is its native literary product— when that product is fine and noble and enduring.*

Mark Twain*

The advisory board, the editors, and the publisher of the *Dictionary of Literary Biography* are joined in endorsing Mark Twain's declaration. The literature of a nation provides an inexhaustible resource of permanent worth. Our purpose is to make literature and its creators better understood and more accessible to students and the reading public, while satisfying the needs of teachers and researchers.

To meet these requirements, *literary biography* has been construed in terms of the author's achievement. The most important thing about a writer is his writing. Accordingly, the entries in *DLB* are career biographies, tracing the development of the author's canon and the evolution of his reputation.

The purpose of *DLB* is not only to provide reliable information in a usable format but also to place the figures in the larger perspective of literary history and to offer appraisals of their accomplishments by qualified scholars.

The publication plan for *DLB* resulted from two years of preparation. The project was proposed to Bruccoli Clark by Frederick G. Ruffner, president of the Gale Research Company, in November 1975. After specimen entries were prepared and typeset, an advisory board was formed to refine the entry format and develop the series rationale. In meetings held during 1976, the publisher, series editors, and advisory board approved the scheme for a comprehensive biographical dictionary of persons who contributed to literature. Editorial work on the first volume began in January 1977, and it was published in 1978. In order to make *DLB* more than a dictionary and to compile volumes that individually have claim to status as literary history, it was decided to organize volumes by topic, period, or

*From an unpublished section of Mark Twain's autobiography, copyright by the Mark Twain Company*

genre. Each of these freestanding volumes provides a biographical-bibliographical guide and overview for a particular area of literature. We are convinced that this organization—as opposed to a single alphabet method— constitutes a valuable innovation in the presentation of reference material. The volume plan necessarily requires many decisions for the placement and treatment of authors. Certain figures will be included in separate volumes, but with different entries emphasizing the aspect of his career appropriate to each volume. Ernest Hemingway, for example, is represented in *American Writers in Paris, 1920–1939* by an entry focusing on his expatriate apprenticeship; he is also in *American Novelists, 1910–1945* with an entry surveying his entire career, as well as in *American Short-Story Writers, 1910– 1945, Second Series* with an entry concentrating on his short fiction. Each volume includes a cumulative index of the subject authors and articles.

Since 1981 the series has been further augmented by the *DLB Yearbooks,* which update published entries, add new entries to keep the *DLB* current with contemporary activity, and provide articles on literary history. There have also been nineteen *DLB Documentary Series* volumes which provide illustrations, facsimiles, and biographical and critical source materials for figures, works, or groups judged to have particular interest for students. In 1999 the *Documentary Series* was incorporated into the *DLB* volume numbering system beginning with *DLB 210: Ernest Hemingway.*

We define literature as the *intellectual commerce of a nation:* not merely as belles lettres but as that ample and complex process by which ideas are generated, shaped, and transmitted. *DLB* entries are not limited to "creative writers" but extend to other figures who in their time and in their way influenced the mind of a people. Thus the series encompasses historians, journalists, publishers, book collectors, and screenwriters. By this means readers of *DLB* may be aided to perceive literature not as cult scripture in the keeping of intellectual high priests but firmly positioned at the center of a nation's life.

*DLB* includes the major writers appropriate to each volume and those standing in the ranks behind them. Scholarly and critical counsel has been sought in deciding which minor figures to include and how full their entries should be. Wherever possible, useful references are made to figures who do not warrant separate entries.

Each *DLB* volume has an expert volume editor responsible for planning the volume, selecting the figures for inclusion, and assigning the entries. Volume editors are also responsible for preparing, where appropriate, appendices surveying the major periodicals and literary and intellectual movements for their volumes, as well as lists of further readings. Work on the series as a whole is coordinated at the Bruccoli Clark Layman editorial center in Columbia, South Carolina, where the editorial staff is responsible for accuracy and utility of the published volumes.

One feature that distinguishes *DLB* is the illustration policy—its concern with the iconography of literature. Just as an author is influenced by his surroundings, so is the reader's understanding of the author enhanced by a knowledge of his environment. Therefore *DLB* volumes include not only drawings, paintings, and photographs of authors, often depicting them at various stages in their careers, but also illustrations of their families and places where they lived. Title pages are regularly reproduced in facsimile along with dust jackets for modern authors. The dust jackets are a special feature of *DLB* because they often document better than anything else the way in which an author's work was perceived in its own time. Specimens of the writers' manuscripts and letters are included when feasible.

Samuel Johnson rightly decreed that "The chief glory of every people arises from its authors." The purpose of the *Dictionary of Literary Biography* is to compile literary history in the surest way available to us—by accurate and comprehensive treatment of the lives and work of those who contributed to it.

The *DLB* Advisory Board

# Introduction

Frederick Jackson Turner, speaking before a meeting of the American Historical Association in Chicago in July 1893, told his fellow historians what they and the American people had been sensing for a long time—that the American endeavor that Theodore Roosevelt had called the "winning of the West" had not only been central to shaping the history of the still-youthful nation but also in formulating that defining sense of optimism, meliorism, and Manifest Destiny that many Americans shared. As the twentieth century dawned, Americans were beginning to realize that something big and important had occurred and was still occurring in the great westward movement of the American peoples. As the Atlantic seaboard filled up with the flood of European immigrants who agreed with Johann Wolfgang von Goethe that *"Amerika, du hast es besser!"* (America, you have it better!), restless inhabitants of the young nation were still heeding Horace Greeley's advice, "Go west, young man, and grow up with the country." Having gone west to realize their individual American dreams, hundreds of thousands agreed with Brigham Young's affirmation on first gazing upon the Great Salt Lake Valley: "This is the place."

In the vast and borderless region loosely located "west of the one hundredth meridian," there lay—in reality as well as in the imaginations of people of many nations—an arid region of mountains, valleys, deserts, and plains that Robert Frost in "The Gift Outright" called the "land vaguely realizing westward, / But still unstoried, artless, unenhanced, / Such as she was, such as she would become." The story of a westering people—told by the men and women who lived it and then rendered imaginatively by their children and grandchildren in fiction, memoir, drama, and verse—is an exciting story of the indomitable human spirit in confrontation with an awesome land. Perhaps such a sequence of events has happened before in human history, but it has never been so well chronicled or so well told by and about the common men and women in a democratic country in which the national ruler would doff his hat to the common citizen, and the domestic servant would take tea with her employer. The Westward Movement is the story of European civilization under new management and at work humanizing, subduing, and harnessing a virgin wilderness; it is a story that has had both happy and—in the uneven, "might makes right" confrontation of European Americans with native peoples—tragic consequences.

*Volume 256: Twentieth-Century American Western Writers, Third Series* of *The Dictionary of Literary Biography* is the final part of a three-volume set and continues the story of Western American literature from where *DLB 186: Nineteenth-Century American Western Writers* leaves off. *DLB 256* presents entries for twentieth-century writers of American Western literature who, individually and collectively, demonstrate that the West is no longer, in Robert Frost's words in "The Gift Outright," "vaguely realizing," "unstoried," "artless," or "unenhanced." These biographical essays show, as well, that at the end of the rough-and-tumble twentieth century—which continued the rough-and-tumble nineteenth century—the American West was still a vital and vibrant land, still packed with the stuff of literature. In the hopeful works of Wallace Stegner, whose own Western life spanned much of the twentieth century and who participated in the battle to stave off destruction of the Western wilderness, "the West remains unique as a region of American possibilities and imagination, 'the last, best place'" that offers "a geography of hope," and a rich and diverse literature to match its variegated splendor.

Common to the thirty-one authors presented in *DLB 256* and to all Western writers are their awe before the immensity of Western space, land, and landscape and their affection for the harsh and gentle contrasts of Western beauty. The compelling attraction of Western space—"big sky country"—and landscape arises primarily from Western aridity. This "incorrigible aridity," as Wallace Stegner calls it in *Where the Bluebird Sings to the Lemonade Springs: Living and Writing in the West* (1992)—what he calls the "visible, pervasive fact of Western space"—and its effects upon topography, air, light, and life make the American West unique among North American regions. Individually and collectively, the Western authors featured in this volume suggest the enormous diversity, vision, and possibilities of the peoples of the North American West. They exhibit, as well, a wide range of individual, cultural, and ethical literary responses to the nature and meaning of the Western American experience. This volume includes not only the perspectives of European Americans but also those of Native Americans and Hispanic Americans. Each writer portrays the struggle, early and late in American history, to realize the West as "the last, great hope for humanity," as Stegner calls it.

As *DLB 186* makes clear, much of the literary response to the West in the twentieth century was rooted in that near-mythical era of discovery, exploration, and adventure that lasted from the Meriwether Lewis and William Clark Expedition of 1804–1806 and the Zebulon Montgomery Pike Expedition of 1806–1807 through John C. Frémont's three expeditions in the 1840s and John Wesley Powell's explorations of the Colorado River in the 1870s. Since that era of discovery, American—and world—consciousness about the West has been shaped by an awareness of its history, including the great westward emigrations; the Mexican War, the Civil War, and the Indian wars; the gold and silver rushes that drove people along the Oregon, Mormon, California, and Santa Fé Trails; the transcontinental railroad that linked the eastern and western United States at Promontory Point, Utah, in 1869; the great cattle drives and the ensuing range wars; and the land rushes of eager settlers. In the creation of the first national parks, Yellowstone and then Yosemite, Grand Canyon, and Zion, the United States recognized the West as a land to cherish and preserve; yet, by building reservoirs and huge dams after the turn of the century, the nation showed its determination not to allow romantic notions of wilderness to interfere with progress—and the exploitation of seemingly unlimited natural resources.

Meanwhile, the American people living in the West finally stopped looking, Daniel-Boone-like, beyond the next hill; they sank roots, planted crops, built homes and schools and churches, and busied themselves with making "the desert blossom as the rose." The nineteenth century ended, and the children of the settlers of the Old West, coming of age in the twentieth century, found themselves living in a New West. Some left the land for a time to study at midwestern or eastern schools, where they gained distance and thus a fresh perspective on the nature and meaning of their Western experience. Returning home, they began to write, and the fiction, poetry, memoirs, and drama they produced—decidedly Western American—provided, throughout the twentieth century and into the early twenty-first, a rich and refreshing literary examination and expression of that which is unique and universal in the Western American experience.

The authors who came of age early in the twentieth century sought to render and understand their par-

ents' and grandparents' experience of settling the frontier. They dramatized the confrontations of ordinary westering Americans with the magnificent but often terrifying plains, mountains, deserts, canyons, valleys, and arroyos of the arid West. They vivified the real and imagined lives of mountain men, Nez Perce and Blackfoot warriors, California gold miners, Wyoming schoolteachers, Mexican farmers, U.S. cavalrymen, Hispanic priests, Apache war chiefs, French fathers, good-hearted (and not-so-good-hearted) cowboys, Mormon mothers, Lakota Sioux medicine men, Texas ranchers, Nebraska sodbusters, Kansas squatters, Taos freighters, dam builders, and exploitive politicos—all of whom had attempted to carve out their respective niches amid Western fastnesses, harsh extremes, and hardship to shape worthwhile lives worth remembering and worth recording.

*DLB 256* includes the biographies of several writers who, born in the nineteenth century or early in the twentieth century, made their contributions to the canon of Western American literature during the first three decades of the twentieth century. Owen Wister, generally conceded to be the founder of Western literature, collected his Western series as *Red Men and White* (1896) and *Lin McLean* (1898) and transformed them into the novel *The Virginian: A Horseman of the Plains* (1902), and forever changed the course of Western fiction by creating the prototype of the Western hero. Later, Eugene Manlove Rhodes, regarded by many of his contemporaries as the best Western fiction writer (and not, he insisted, a writer of Westerns), put New Mexico on the literary map with his dozens of Western stories and novels, most notably *Once in the Saddle, and Pasó por Aquí* (1927). Far different from the works of these classic Western writers are the works of Laura Ingalls Wilder. In her "Little House on the Prairie" series, Wilder recounts vividly her personal experiencing of "all the successive phases of the frontier, first the frontiersman, then the pioneer, then the farmers, and the towns." Willa Cather, in her *O Pioneers!* (1913), *My Ántonia* (1918), and *Death Comes for the Archbishop* (1927), renders and interprets the experiences of Nebraska homesteaders and French Catholic priests ministering among the native inhabitants of New Mexico and brings the American Western novel to an artistic high. Bernard DeVoto, who crafted a handful of literary novels and a landmark study of Samuel Langhorne Clemens (Mark Twain), earned his secure niche in Western letters with his trilogy of Western history—*The Year of Decision: 1846* (1942), *Across the Wide Missouri* (1947), and *The Course of Empire* (1952)—and thereby put his mark on virtually every Western writer since. Herbert Arthur Krause recounts in three novels—*Wind Without Rain* (1939), *The Thresher* (1946), and *The Oxcart Trail*

(1954)–the cost in human suffering of settling the frontier and the subsequent socioeconomic difficulties encountered as the country grew.

John G. Neihardt appears in this volume as the Western writer who fits comfortably into several genres: as biographer of mountain man Jedediah Strong Smith in *The Splendid Wayfaring* (1920); as editor of a spiritual/cultural autobiography of Black Elk, an Oglalah Sioux, in *Black Elk Speaks* (1932), which some have called "the Indian Bible"; as epic poet of *The Song of Hugh Glass* (1915), *The Song of Three Friends* (1919), *The Song of the Indian Wars* (1925), *The Song of the Messiah* (1935), and *The Song of Jed Smith* (1941). With *Black Elk Speaks* Neihardt shaped a new image of the American Indian and helped to open the door for Native American writers such as James Welch in his novels *Winter in the Blood* (1974), *The Death of Jim Loney* (1979), *Fools Crow* (1986), and in a history, *Killing Custer: The Battle of the Little Bighorn and the Fate of the Plains Indians* (1994); and for N. Scott Momaday, in his landmark novel *House Made of Dawn* (1968) and his cultural narrative, *The Way to Rainy Mountain* (1969); and for the poetry and novels of Leslie Marmon Silko: *Laguna Woman: Poems* (1974), *Ceremony* (1977), *Almanac of the Dead* (1991), and *Gardens in the Dunes* (1999); and for the several poetry collections–*Going for the Rain* (1976), *A Good Journey* (1977), *A Poem Is a Journey* (1981)–of Simon J. Ortiz, a Native American who grew up on the Acoma Indian Reservation in New Mexico. Richard Rodriguez treats issues facing Hispanic Americans in his highly autobiographical *Hunger of Memory: The Education of Richard Rodriguez* (1982) and *Days of Obligation: An Argument with My Mexican Father* (1992).

In addition to Neihardt, Silko, and Ortiz, other Western poets who are featured in *DLB 256* are Leslie Norris of Wales–but, in the last two decades, of the United States–whose *Collected Poems* (1996) and *Collected Stories* (1996) introduce images from the American West and Utah into the English and Welsh ambience of his *The Hawk's Eye* (1988) and *A Sea in the Desert* (1989); Clinton F. Larson, whose cosmic Mormonism illuminates plays such as *The Mantle of the Prophet* (1966) and collections of his poetry–*The Lord of Experience* (1967) and *Selected Poems* (1988); David Wagoner, student of Theodore Roethke and author of more than a dozen books of poems, including *Collected Poems (1956–1976)* (1976) and *Through the Forest: New and Selected Poems, 1977–1987* (1987), and ten novels; William Studebaker, whose keen sense of Idaho speaks to readers in *Everything Goes without Saying* (1978) and *The Rat Lady at the Company Dump* (1990); Ron McFarland, poet–*Composting at Forty* (1984), *Stranger in Town: New and Selected Poems* (2000)–and biographer of David Wagoner, Norman Maclean, Tesa Gallagher, and

James Welch; and Robert Wrigley, whose westerly migration culminates in his collection of poems *In the Bank of Beautiful Sins* (1995), set in Idaho.

Between the startling transformation brought about by World War II and the still reverberating cultural shocks of the late 1960s, the literature of the West underwent its own transformation. As elsewhere in the nation, the peoples of the region began to look at the modern world through lenses tinctured by gender, race, and culture. Linda Hasselstrom, in *Windbreak: A Woman Rancher on the Northern Plains* (1987), *Dakota Bones: The Collected Poems of Linda Hasselstrom* (1993), and *Roadside History of South Dakota* (1994), has undertaken to educate others about the practical, communal, historical, and spiritual dimensions of what it means to be a woman rancher on the plains of South Dakota. Mary Clearman Blew looks in short fiction at the harsh realities of ranch life in northern Montana from 1940 through the rest of the twentieth century, *Runaway* (1990); essays, *All But the Waltz* (1991); and a novella, *Sister Coyote* (2000). Judith Freeman, in several striking novels–*The Chinchilla Farm* (1989), *Set for Life* (1991), and *A Desert of Pure Feeling* (1996)–undertakes to trace the processes of self-discovery and self-creation in several Western women and men characters living in the mountainous West. Ursula K. Le Guin, in *Always Coming Home* (1985), sets her most ambitious Western work in the extreme distant future country of Napa Valley, which she populates with the Kesh, her imaginary "'new' ancients"; in *Buffalo Gals and Other Animal Presences* (1987) she turns her brilliant accomplishment as a writer of fantasy, science fiction, and children's books to the alternative reality of Native American legends and myths; in *Searoad: Chronicles of Klatsand* (1991) and *Unlocking the Air* (1996) she tells mainstream stories about a tiny Oregon coastal village. Le Guin has also added eight collections of poetry to American Western letters. Douglas Thayer, in *Under the Cottonwoods and Other Mormon Stories* (1977), examines life in the Mormon West, and in *Mr. Wahlquist in Yellowstone and Other Stories* (1989) he universalizes his Western vision. Edward Abbey, in fiction–*The Brave Cowboy* (1956) and *The Monkey Wrench Gang* (1975)–and in exposition, in *Desert Solitaire* (1968), has unleashed his guerilla-style environmentalism against those who threaten the lifestyle, land, and water of the Southwest. Barry Lopez reports his ecological vision of the natural Western world in *Of Wolves and Men* (1978), *Arctic Dreams: Imagination and Desire in a Northern Landscape* (1986), and *The Rediscovery of North America* (1990).

Larry McMurtry, in twenty-one novels, two books of nonfiction, two collaborative novels, several screenplays, and dozens of essays, became the best-known Texas writer of the twentieth century, and his fictional Thalia and Hardtop Counties are as familiar to readers of Western American literature as William Faulkner's Jefferson and Yoknapatawpha County are to readers of Southern fiction. From *Horseman, Pass By* (1961), *Leaving Cheyenne* (1963), and *Lonesome Dove* (1985) to *Streets of Laredo* (1993), *Dead Man's Walk* (1995), and *Comanche Moon* (1997), McMurtry, a student of Wallace Stegner, manifests his love for the land and the people that nourished him; in his urban Western novels, *The Last Picture Show* (1966) and *Terms of Endearment* (1975), he shows his aversion to the narrow-minded elements and the modern ugliness of his Texas heritage. The novels of Cormac McCarthy, hailed by critics as one of the finest American writers of the twentieth century, have been compared to the works of Herman Melville, Faulkner, Twain, and William Shakespeare. *All the Pretty Horses* (1992) won the National Book Award and the National Book Critics Circle Award. *The Crossing* (1994) and *Cities of the Plain* (1998) complete his *Border Trilogy* (1999) and secure McCarthy's place at the forefront of American Western writers at the turn of the new century. In *The River Why* (1983), a novel about "fly-fishing and spiritual questing in western Oregon," David James Duncan shows himself as a writer of potential, and he proves his worth in *The Brothers K* (1992) and *River Teeth: Stories and Writings* (1995).

Running through the continuing fascination for Western literature is the Popular Western, represented in this volume by Frederick D. Glidden (Luke Short), whose several dozen violent Westerns rode high in the saddle across five decades, from *The Feud at Single Shot* (1936) to *Trouble Country* (1976); by Frederick Schiller Faust (Max Brand), whose 196 novels, 226 novelettes, and hundreds of short stories almost certainly make him one of the most prolific writers of all time and whose *The Untamed* (1919) and *Destry Rides Again* (1930) seem to be the quintessential Westerns in paperback and motion picture; and by Benjamin Capps, who reinvented the southern Great Plains in recounting fictionalized history in his tales, novels, and histories of cowboys, gunfighters, ranchers, and Indians in *Hanging at Comanche Wells* (1962), *A Woman of the People* (1966), and *Tales of the Southwest* (1991). A recent producer of Popular Westerns is Elmer Kelton, whose more than forty Westerns have won him several literary prizes for works such as *Buffalo Wagons* (1956), *The Day the Cowboys Quit* (1971), *The Time It Never Rained* (1973), and *The Good Old Boys* (1973). The Popular Western, despite recent decline in readership, keeps on sounding the call of the "right" perspective on the West as the battleground of good and evil, where all wrongs are righted, all tears dried, and all (clearly delineated) villains and heroes given their just deserts.

*DLB 256: Twentieth-Century American Western Writers, Third Series,* gathers into one volume a plentiful harvest of biographies that, at the beginning of the twenty-first century, with the era of Western discovery and adventure now in the remote past, reveals much about the history as well as the future of Western American letters. Some twenty-one of the thirty-one writers whose lives and works are treated in this book are still alive and productive in the year A.D. 2002. Their works in progress suggest not only the continuation of a vital and influential Western literature, with its expansive take on the American experience, but also of a region still vigorous and growing in both the American and world imagination as a place where human beings will continue to engage with rugged wilderness, fellow beings, and themselves, whether in a real landscape, on an imaginary frontier, or in a morally unambiguous never-never land. Whatever one's taste, there is—and will probably continue to be, in a new century and millennium—exciting fare.

*–Richard H. Cracroft*

## Acknowledgments

This book was produced by Bruccoli Clark Layman, Inc. Penelope M. Hope and Patricia M. Hswe were the in-house editors.

Production manager is Philip B. Dematteis.

Administrative support was provided by Ann M. Cheschi, Amber L. Coker, Linda Dalton Mullinax, and Angi Pleasant.

Accountant is Ann-Marie Holland.

Copyediting supervisor is Sally R. Evans. The copyediting staff includes Phyllis A. Avant, Brenda Carol Blanton, Melissa D. Hinton, Charles Loughlin, Rebecca Mayo, Nancy E. Smith, and Elizabeth Jo Ann Sumner. Freelance copyeditor is Jennie Williamson.

Editorial associates are Michael S. Allen, Michael S. Martin, and Pamela A. Warren.

Permissions editor is Jason Paddock.

Indexer is Alex Snead.

Database manager is José A. Juarez.

Layout and graphics supervisor is Janet E. Hill. The graphics staff includes Karla Corley Brown and Zoe R. Cook.

Office manager is Kathy Lawler Merlette.

Photography supervisor is Paul Talbot. Photography editor is Scott Nemzek.

Digital photographic copy work was performed by Joseph M. Bruccoli.

Systems manager is Marie L. Parker.

Typesetting supervisor is Kathleen M. Flanagan. The typesetting staff includes Jaime All, Patricia Marie

Flanagan, Mark J. McEwan, and Pamela D. Norton. Freelance typesetter is Wanda Adams.

Walter W. Ross did library research. He was assisted by Jaime All and the following librarians at the Thomas Cooper Library of the University of South Carolina: circulation department head Tucker Taylor; reference department head Virginia W. Weathers; Brette Barclay, Marilee Birchfield, Paul Cammarata, Gary Geer, Michael Macan, Tom Marcil, Rose Marshall, and Sharon Verba; interlibrary loan department head John Brunswick; and interlibrary loan staff Robert Arndt, Hayden Battle, Barry Bull, Jo Cottingham, Marna Hostetler, Marieum McClary, Erika Peake, and Nelson Rivera.

The editor is indebted to the distinguished scholars whose contributions comprise this volume: their scholarly and literary acumen, responsible professional manner, and kindly cooperation have been for me a source of personal pleasure and pride in the profession of letters. I am particularly grateful to James H. Maguire, John P. O'Grady, and Thomas Trusky of Boise State University, for their inestimable assistance in winnowing and sifting the authors to be included in Series 1, 2, and 3;

and to Ron McFarland of the University of Idaho, poet and scholar, who, along with Jim Maguire, kindly steered me to many of those who have contributed to this volume. I am also indebted to Robert L. Gale, University of Pittsburgh professor emeritus, esteemed scholar, and editor of *DLB 186: Nineteenth-Century American Western Writers*. Bob first headed me down this particular trail, and his example, counsel, and suggestions, as both "my editor" and professional friend, have been vital to this work. Finally, I thank Janice Alger Cracroft, my wife of more than forty-two years, for her careful attention to detail—and to me, our children, and our grandchildren.

I dedicate this volume to the late Don D. Walker, professor emeritus of English, and of American Studies, University of Utah, who passed away as this volume was being completed. Don Walker has been a career-long blessing to me and to many of us in the Western Literature Association. He was an exemplary gentleman and inspiring scholar, exacting teacher, kindly graduate adviser, generous mentor, friend, and dutch-oven cook.

Dictionary of Literary Biography® • Volume Two Hundred Fifty-Six

# Twentieth-Century Western Writers
## Third Series

# Dictionary of Literary Biography

# Edward Abbey
*(29 January 1927 – 14 March 1989)*

Russell Burrows
*Weber State University*

BOOKS: *Jonathan Troy* (New York: Dodd, Mead, 1954);

*The Brave Cowboy: An Old Tale in a New Time* (New York: Dodd, Mead, 1956);

*Fire on the Mountain* (New York: Dial, 1962; London: Eyre & Spottiswoode, 1963);

*Desert Solitaire: A Season in the Wilderness* (New York: McGraw-Hill, 1968);

*Appalachian Wilderness: The Great Smoky Mountains,* text by Abbey and photographs by Eliot Porter (New York: Dutton, 1970);

*Slickrock: The Canyon Country of Southeast Utah,* text by Abbey and photographs by Philip Hyde (New York: Sierra Club/Scribners, 1971);

*Black Sun* (New York: Simon & Schuster, 1971);

*Cactus Country,* by Abbey and the editors of Time-Life Books (New York: Time-Life Books, 1973);

*The Monkey Wrench Gang* (Philadelphia: Lippincott, 1975);

*The Hidden Canyon: A River Journey,* text by Abbey and photographs by John Blaustein (New York: Viking, 1977);

*The Journey Home: Some Words in Defense of the American West* (New York: Dutton, 1977);

*Abbey's Road* (New York: Dutton, 1979);

*Desert Images: An American Landscape,* text by Abbey and photographs by David Muench (New York: Harcourt Brace Jovanovich, 1979);

*Good News* (New York: Dutton, 1980);

*Down the River with Henry David Thoreau and Friends* (New York: Dutton, 1982);

*Beyond the Wall: Essays from the Outside* (New York: Holt, Rinehart & Winston, 1984);

*Edward Abbey ( photograph by Jay Dusard; from the dust jacket for* Hayduke Lives! *1990)*

*Slumgullion Stew: An Edward Abbey Reader* (New York: Dutton, 1984); republished as *The Best of Edward Abbey* (San Francisco: Sierra Club, 1988);

*In Praise of Mountain Lions,* text by Abbey and photographs by John Nichols (Albuquerque, N.Mex.: Albuquerque Sierra Club, 1984);

*Confessions of a Barbarian* (Santa Barbara: Capra Press, 1986);

*The Fool's Progress: An Honest Novel* (New York: Holt, 1988);

*One Life at a Time, Please* (New York: Holt, 1988);

*Vox Clamantis in Deserto: Some Notes from a Secret Journal* (Santa Fe: Rydal Press, 1989); republished as *A Voice Crying in the Wilderness: Notes from a Secret Journal* (New York: St. Martin's Press, 1990);

*Hayduke Lives!* (Boston: Little, Brown, 1990);

*Confessions of a Barbarian: Selections from the Journals of Edward Abbey, 1951–1989* (Boston: Little, Brown, 1994);

*Journals of Edward Abbey* (Boston: Little, Brown, 1994);

*Earth Apples = (Pommes des terre): The Poetry of Edward Abbey,* edited by David Peterson (New York: St. Martin's Press, 1994).

Edward Abbey's nickname might just as well have been "the Monkey Wrench" instead of "Cactus Ed." Abbey breathed new life into the Luddites' notorious sabotage of technology–their tossing wrenches into new machinery; however, he aimed his sabotage at those who were threatening the land and water of the Southwestern states. Abbey's was a guerrilla-style environmentalism, which inspired the radical Earth First, a Tucson-based underground that made news for wrecking such things as logging trucks, ski lodges, and power lines.

This "monkey wrenching" was already a fully developed theme in Abbey's first best-seller, a fast-paced piece of exposition called *Desert Solitaire: A Season in the Wilderness* (1968). Then, in a novel that Abbey actually titled *The Monkey Wrench Gang* (1975), his theme assumes its largest and perhaps most enduring form as Abbey's unlikely collection of characters load houseboats with explosives and try to float their armada against the 792,000-ton, $750,000,000 Glen Canyon Dam. Abbey's dam-busting idea simply will not die. In recent years, however, it has taken the milder form of a referendum that calls for draining Lake Powell, not blowing up its dam. Nevertheless, this possibility of returning the Colorado once more to a free and wild river continues to come around every two or three years. Each time, the proposition stirs deep wells of hatred in the region. It has also tempted Hollywood producers, who have speculated on the potential of the original story for an action-packed movie.

Edward Paul Abbey was born on 29 January 1927 to Mildred Postlewaite Abbey, a schoolteacher, who influenced her son's interest in literature and music, and Paul Revere Abbey, who had been associated with the Wobblies in the logging camps and whose name seems to have fit the populist politics that–with a 1960s twist–his son adapted to Southwestern themes and settings. Abbey was born near the rural Pennsylvania towns of Home and Indiana, but he usually gave Home, Pennsylvania, as his birthplace and played on the name to make himself seem a lost soul who had strayed from "home." Edward Abbey's adopted home of the Sonoran Desert seems an unlikely choice for one who grew up in the lush Allegheny Mountains of Pennsylvania.

The formative experience of Abbey's boyhood, chronicled in "Hallelujah on the Bum," in the collection *The Journey Home: Some Words in Defense of the American West* (1977), was a huge, looping excursion he took alone in the summer of 1944. The journey took Abbey, then a high-school student, high into the Northwest, then down the coast, and finally back across the Southwest to Home. He traveled by hitchhiking–a slow method during World War II because of gas rationing; by hopping trains with the hoboes; and, on the return leg of the journey, by bus. Except for $20 his father had given him, the seventeen-year-old earned his way by picking fruit and by packing in a cannery. Arrested once for vagrancy, he spent a rough night on the floor of a drunk tank in Flagstaff, Arizona. But neither that foul time nor the occasional heat and hunger of his travels much deterred him in a private rite of passage–that of falling thoroughly in love with the red rock deserts of the Southwest.

Abbey had found the subject that lasted his lifetime. But his last year of high school and his two-year stint in the army–as a military policeman in Italy–that immediately followed, delayed his return to the region. The army was important to the forming of Abbey's philosophy because he recoiled from its stiff dose of authority and moved further toward an anarchism that he hoped to work out in the still relatively open West. Thus, by the time he enrolled in the University of New Mexico to seek degrees in philosophy and English, he had already mailed back his discharge papers marked "Return to Sender" and had helped to organize a draft-card burning–two acts that attracted the notice of the Federal Bureau of Investigation.

Abbey next attracted the notice of his college officials when he played a prank with the college literary magazine, *The Thunderbird*. As the student editor, Abbey reprinted one of Voltaire's epigrams: "Man will never be free until the last king is strangled with the entrails of the last priest." The mischief angered school and church officials of Albuquerque, and not the least of their outrage was that Abbey had attributed the line to Louisa May Alcott. But eventually, Abbey put a finishing touch on approximately ten years of on-again, off-again schooling by submitting in 1956 a master's thesis under the title "Anarchy and the Morality of Violence."

The philosophy Abbey followed in his thesis was practically the same one he was simultaneously exploring in two poorly received novels. The first of these school-era novels was *Jonathan Troy* (1954). Something of a bildungsroman, the story tells of a nineteen-year-old Pennsylvanian who finally realizes his dream of escaping to the West. The many problems Jonathan Troy has to overcome in his coming-to-awareness might have swamped an ordinary boy. The greatest difficulty is the loss of his anarchist father, Nat, killed when he pulled a gun on some drunks who demanded that he kiss the flag. But Nat did not pull the trigger, nor had any in the mob done so; it had been a rookie cop, who misread the encounter. Another difficulty is Jonathan's dalliance with a shallow young woman who tries to trap him into marriage. Still another problem is Jonathan's friendship with his English teacher, who keeps reinforcing in him his father's radical politics. Jonathan experiences some pain in breaking with this teacher, who had directed the boy in the school production of *Macbeth*, and more pain in breaking with a girl who, in a different time and place, might have been good for him. Ultimately, Jonathan sees that his Eastern home has become impossible. His birth and childhood had been in the West, in a time before his father had discovered his radical anarchism, and the story ends with the myth of the West beckoning the boy.

That a first novel would flop—especially an undergraduate's first novel—is no surprise. But both Ann Ronald and Garth McCann have seen *Jonathan Troy* as a qualified success. The strong parts are Abbey's descriptions of an industrial wreckage visited on the Pennsylvania coal country. These descriptions are important because they mark the first expressions of Abbey's environmental awareness. The dialogue is the weak element of the novel, particularly Jonathan's ponderous interior monologues, which were influenced by the philosophies of William Godwin, Pierre-Joseph Proudhon, Karl Marx, and Michael Bakunin—all of whose works Abbey read for his master's thesis.

The evident lack of polish of *Jonathan Troy* can be attributed to Abbey's hectic school days during which he wrote by fits and starts, as class work allowed. To his credit, he managed to be enough of a student to win a Fulbright fellowship to Edinburgh, Scotland. With Edinburgh as a base, Abbey spent virtually every weekend exploring Europe, an extension of his constant explorations of the desert in the

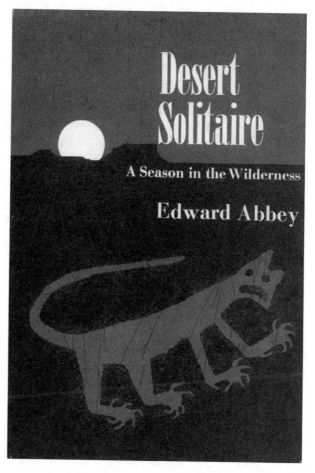

*Dust jacket for Abbey's philosophical 1968 account of his experiences as a park ranger at Arches National Monument in Utah*

American West. Edward Hoagland, a nature writer who had camped with Abbey, has remarked that Abbey probably had "slept out more nights under the stars than all of his competitors combined." Abbey deliberately took time away from school to gather the wilderness experiences out of which he made his books.

Another interesting but negative by-product of Abbey's school days was his legendary carousing, which provided some of the literary raw material for "Drunk in the Afternoon" and other essays included in *The Serpents of Paradise: A Reader* (1995). Abbey apparently also went through a beatnik phase, when such behavior was all but unheard-of in Albuquerque, but he did not mine this experience for his writing. Nor did he touch more than tangentially on his chaotic marriages and constant womanizing. He married Jean Schmechalon on 5 August 1950, but a year later, while he was polishing the manuscript of *Jonathan Troy*, she walked out on him, leaving him in Edinburgh. An apparent friction in this first marriage—he ultimately married five times—was Abbey's ongoing entanglement with Rita Deanin, whom he subsequently married on 20 November 1952. With her, Abbey had the first two of his five children—Joshua Nathanael, born 12 April 1956, and Aaron Paul, born 28 May 1959. Abbey and Deanin divorced 25 August 1965. Meanwhile, in the fall of 1953 Abbey attempted a Ph.D. program in philosophy at Yale, but after two weeks he withdrew, complaining he could not fathom symbolic logic. The wonder is, considering all these distractions, that he managed to write any kind of novel at all.

From the second novel he had started while still in school, however, he realized a large measure of success. *The Brave Cowboy: An Old Tale in a New Time* (1956) follows the adventures of Jack Burns, as anachronistic a character as Abbey ever created. Burns rides his horse into modern Duke City, intent on helping his friend Paul Bondi, a draft resister serving a jail term. Burns undertakes this rescue by hiding a file on himself and then getting arrested. The plot complication is that Bondi, who has scruples, will not follow Burns into the night and to freedom.

So bidding one another *adios, buena suerte* (good-bye, good luck), Burns rides hell-for-leather toward Mexico. The ensuing chase is compelling, with Burns cutting fence lines and using the tree lines and ridge lines for cover. A high point comes when he pulls out a .30–30 saddle rifle—a small bore by modern standards—and brings down a helicopter.

The figurative action, meanwhile, turns heavy-handedly scatological. This element becomes apparent as the story flashes repeatedly to its subplot, in which a long-haul trucker pulls a load of toilets. The two plots come together disastrously for the cowboy. In the dark, with only one more road to cross, the trucker hits Burns. In the last scene, Burns's horse is shot, while the cowboy lies bleeding on a Navaho rug that some passerby presses into use as first-aid. The implication is that the modern world has neither the room nor the tolerance for individual heroism.

While *The Brave Cowboy* generally sold well, the far more interesting development was Kirk Douglas's turning the novel into the movie *Lonely Are the Brave* (1962). The opportunity for the movie arose when Douglas resorted to a clause in his studio contract that allowed him to make a "disapproved" picture so long as he could bring it in under a $3 million budget. Douglas, much taken by the novel, later called his part in the movie adaptation his favorite role. The motion picture also starred Walter Matthau, Michael Kane, and Carroll O'Connor, and garnered Abbey a bit part as a cop, an additional scouting fee for looking around Albuquerque, and the story rights for a modest $7,500.

*Lonely Are the Brave* did splendidly after its release in 1962, actually breaking an attendance record in London. This success was all the more remarkable since the movie ran without advertising, without playing in first-run theaters, and without press screenings. But after two weeks of success, the studio executives pulled it from the market. Douglas seethed that human vanity "wouldn't let [the executives] admit they had made a mistake. . . . They just dropped the picture flat." *Lonely Are the Brave* has since occasionally run on television, earning a good deal of approval, although few seem to have associated its story with the name of Edward Abbey.

In 1957 Abbey turned an important corner in his career when, after earning an M.A. degree in philosophy, he started work with the National Park Service, mostly on summer assignments at Western posts. Such was the arrangement, for instance, when he wrote *Desert Solitaire:* he spent his summers in the Utah desert and wintered in Hoboken, New Jersey, where he was a caseworker for a welfare department and where he tried to hold his marriage with Rita Deanin together. But Abbey's literary interest clearly lay out West in his park outposts. Over the years, his positions included such choice locations as Arches National Monument, Glacier National Park, Organ Pipe National Monument, the Coronado National Forest, and the North Rim of the Grand Canyon. The chance to live in and to write about these inspiringly beautiful places was, in the words of Abbey's biographer, James Bishop Jr., "the beginning of a life-style, and a legend."

*Fire on the Mountain* (1962), Abbey's third novel and his first since taking his graduate degree, turned out to be one of his weakest pieces of writing, although it was the first novel Abbey completed after passing through the intense training of a Wallace Stegner Fellowship in Creative Writing at Stanford in 1957. *Fire on the Mountain* pits Grandfather Vogelin against the bureaucrats in charge of the atomic test range in New Mexico, who want Vogelin's ranch. Their struggle ends with the old man's death, after which his relatives and friends lay his body in his cabin and burn it as a funeral pyre. Vogelin is, again, the Old West anarchist around whose philosophy the action is supposed to turn. But, bent with age, Vogelin can sustain no credible chase scene, the spark that so enlivened *The Brave Cowboy.*

*Desert Solitaire,* published in 1968 and undoubtedly Abbey's best book, has attracted the most critical attention and is one on which his reputation rests. Both the substance and tone of this book are so strong that a nearly universal judgment calls it the twentieth-century update of Henry David Thoreau's

*Walden* (1854). Subtitled *A Season in the Wilderness,* Abbey's book is a distillation of the journals he kept while working for three summers as a ranger at Arches National Monument (since made a national park), near the city of Moab in southeastern Utah.

Abbey's first-person account of the many things he saw, felt, and thought at Arches National Monument at first reveals no apparent organization. But as Paul T. Bryant has shown in his essay "The Structure and Unity of *Desert Solitaire*" in *Western American Literature* (May 1993), Abbey's rhetoric aimed at the Latin proverb "*Ars est celare artem*" (art lies in concealing art). Abbey's art includes a complex persona who tends to operate as one typically does in fiction; the leitmotiv of exquisitely painted desert images; and an Aristotelian sense of the unities of time and place. Abbey liked to claim that he had slapped the book together, but a careful look reveals his serious craftsmanship.

There has been considerable debate about the apparent lack of coherence or logical consistency of the Abbey persona in *Desert Solitaire.* One way to reduce the problem is to recall Abbey's formal training in philosophy and to look for his chapter-to-chapter alternations between the viewpoints of ontology and epistemology. He begins with an ontological chapter, "The First Morning," which questions existence: what does it mean when humans say that they live—that they are? Abbey pursues these questions in each odd-numbered chapter of the book: "The Serpents of Paradise" and "The Moon-Eyed Horse" delve into the meaning of the animals' existence, while "The Heat of Noon: Rock and Tree and Cloud" and "The Dead Man at Grandview Point" question the possible meanings of death.

At the same time, the even-numbered chapters pursue the complementary philosophy of epistemology—the question of how do humans know what they know? Abbey wrote these chapters from the disciplines of botany in "Cliffrose and Bayonets," geology in "Rocks," hydrology in "Water," and geography in "Terra Incognita."

Everywhere, the writing features the theme of experimentation. The Abbey persona is an inveterate experimenter: his epistemological self is a thoroughgoing empiricist, while his ontological self engages in thought experiments. The dynamic mix of these perspectives imparts a sense of totality of experience. Readers find themselves not only intimately acquainted with a powerfully reflective persona but also richly educated about the flora and fauna of the desert.

Abbey married his third wife, Judy Pepper, on 16 October 1965, and they had a daughter, Susannah Mildred, on 28 August 1968. But this third marriage did not last: Judy Pepper died of leukemia on 4 July

Dust jacket for Abbey's 1975 novel, about an eccentric group of ecoterrorists

1970, leaving Abbey badly shaken. He had just enough energy to resort to the first of his colorful, large-format, slick-paper "coffee-table" books—the photo essay *Appalachian Wilderness: The Great Smoky Mountains* (1970). Eliot Porter supplied the photography, and together Abbey and Porter chronicled the ecological dangers overtaking the broad-leafed forests of the East.

During the next few years Abbey was busy with similar photo projects, though set in the West. The first of these was *Slickrock: The Canyon Country of Southeast Utah* (1971), for which the photographer was Philip Hyde, and of which the ecological message was identical to that of *Desert Solitaire,* only packaged much more richly in hopes of reaching a different audience. The second book, *Cactus Country* (1973), was published by the Time-Life nature series and is clearly educational in design. These coffee-table books gave Abbey little opportunity to use his muscular rhetoric, since the assignments called primarily for factual descriptions of the Sonoran Desert.

Abbey's attempt at fiction during the early 1970s was the mediocre novel *Black Sun* (1971). This book details the story of Will Gatlin, something of a somnambulist in his unwillingness to interact with others, whose only desire is to "stare at the sun until it goes . . . black" and thus to transcend his human nature. But this wish does not go so far as to leave sex behind. Quite clearly, Abbey lingered over the scenes in which Gatlin initiates the much younger Sandy MacKenzie into the delights of the flesh. In response, her fiancé, a cadet in the air force, comes near to using a jet fighter to make good on his threats against Gatlin. But this conflict between the two men is not resolved, because Sandy mysteriously disappears in the forest surrounding the tower from which Gatlin keeps his fire lookout. No one ever finds her body, and since not much else changes in the plot, critics have wondered if Abbey wrote the novel primarily from his sexual fantasies. On 10 February 1974 Abbey married the much younger Renée Downing, his fourth wife. The marriage was an unhappy one, and the couple divorced in 1980.

No such trouble intrudes on *The Monkey Wrench Gang,* which, if it is not Abbey's best book, is certainly his most popular one. Its energy comes in large part from its madcap collection of ecoterrorist characters—Doc A. K. Sarvis of Albuquerque; his gorgeous and spirited secretary, Bonnie Abbzug; a cohabitating, jack-Mormon river guide, Seldom Seen Smith; and a shell-shocked Vietnam veteran, George Washington Hayduke. Each brings an anarchist's heart into the story, but teamed together they find themselves capable of taking action against some of the agents—the bulldozers and graders, and the power stations and transmission lines—of industrialized civilization. The characters score some hits against these targets but miss others and are eventually jailed for their capers. Unlike many of Abbey's previous characters, they exhibit a degree of growth by giving up their lives of crime. Despite their considerable age difference, Doc and Bonnie marry and settle down to a law-abiding practice of medicine. Smith, a descendant of Joseph Smith, the founding prophet of the Mormon Church, finds a third wife after his other two wives divorce him. And Hayduke, it turns out, has not died in one of the bombings of his industrialized enemies. Of these characters only Hayduke, under a new disguise, runs off in search of more eco-sabotage. With him, the fight goes on.

A second source of the energy in the story comes from a theme that, in its way, is as large as was Herman Melville's whale in *Moby-Dick* (1851). In *The Monkey Wrench Gang,* evil enters with the building of Glen Canyon Dam. Located nearly sixty miles upriver from the Grand Canyon, Glen Canyon was, before its 1963 immersion by the dammed waters of the Colorado, a jewel in the region, the loss of which has been deeply regretted. Wallace Stegner, often called the dean of Western American literature, had rafted through Glen Canyon in 1955 and was speaking of it as better than Dinosaur Park, a place higher on the river that he was working to save from dam building. Stegner's view was that sacrificing Glen Canyon in exchange for Dinosaur Park had been a terrible move, even though the action had been sanctioned by the Sierra Club. Barry Goldwater, a senator from Arizona, likewise recanted his earlier enthusiasm for Glen Canyon Dam: "I think of that river as it was when I was a boy. And that is the way I would like to see it again." One of the last to have gone kayaking through Glen Canyon, Abbey recognized in its tranquility and diversity of life why the Indians had taken it as their sacred place. Abbey regarded it as his sacred place, as well, and about a decade later he redressed the violation of the canyon—albeit imaginatively—by sending his cast of characters to test the possibilities of blowing up the dam.

So compelling has this fictional scenario proven that many have read *The Monkey Wrench Gang* less as a novel than as a terrorist's tract. The Earth Firsters as a group have fallen into the myopic, literalist fallacy of acting out the characters' antiheroic roles. As a consequence, Abbey found himself promoted to the head of a counterculture that would, given leadership, revolt from industrialized life. But Abbey was never willing to lead. When a television interviewer once pressed him to declare himself, Abbey diffidently said that he would not use the broadcast to advocate the destruction of property. When a group of college students tried to draw him out, he replied that he would not bomb the dam, but he added, with a characteristic touch of humor, ". . . if someone else wanted to do it, I'd be there holding a flashlight." But he might not have, for Abbey—at least the serious side of him—had won a Guggenheim Fellowship on 21 March 1975. He often said that *The Monkey Wrench Gang* had simply been one of his novels, and shortly before he died, he attempted a final word on this problematic work, explaining that he had written out of an "indulgence of spleen and anger from a position of safety behind my typewriter. But that was a tertiary motive. Mainly I wanted to entertain and amuse." Perhaps, then, the best that could follow any such "amusement" would be this conclusion: the novel takes its readers on an intellectual and emotional adventure the real-world consequences of which none should actually want to shoulder. But the premise of the story, if gathered and focused into

*Abbey shortly before his death in 1989, with his wife, Clarke Cartwright Abbey, and their children, Benjamin and Rebecca*

a political resolve, might well result in some effective and also lawful means of defending nature.

So much did *The Monkey Wrench Gang* establish a reputation for Abbey in what is called eco-fiction that now *The Bear Essential* magazine of Portland, Oregon, annually awards "The Abbey" for work in this new and popular genre. However, by many counts, *The Monkey Wrench Gang* also marked the beginning of Abbey's decline. While he may have had other books in him, most of his later ones rework and attempt to refine his two best—*Desert Solitaire* and *The Monkey Wrench Gang*. Such revision is apparent in *The Journey Home: Some Words in Defense of the American West* (1977). This book is a collection of twenty-three essays, whose tone is typically curmudgeonly—and splendidly so: "Every Boy Scout troop deserves a forest to get lost, miserable, and starving in." And the central theme is, again, monkey-wrenching: "I see the preservation of wilderness as one sector of the front in the war against the encroaching industrial state." The ease with which Abbey seems to have written these essays is apparent in his having brought out another of his coffee-table

books during that same year—*The Hidden Canyon: A River Journey* (1977), with John Blaustein supplying the photography.

Two years later, Abbey published *Abbey's Road* (1979), another collection of the essays that extend the reach of *Desert Solitaire*. These are Abbey's usual mix of travel essays, wilderness polemics, and American jeremiads. But they do seem to rise to higher levels of Abbey's irreverent and bawdy humor. A mild example is his limerick: "A modest young fellow named Morgan / Had an awesome sexual organ; / It resembled a log / Dredged up from a bog / With a head on it fierce as a Gorgon." "Death Valley Junk," the seventeenth chapter of *Abbey's Road,* also offers a glimpse beyond his drinking and into his experiments with LSD while in Death Valley, a setting appropriate to such dabbling. Repeating a pattern of his essay writing, Abbey complemented his *Abbey's Road* collection by simultaneously publishing his fifth picture book, *Desert Images: An American Landscape* (1979), with David Muench supplying the photography.

In *Good News* (1980) Abbey returned to fiction and brought back Jack Burns of *The Brave Cowboy,* who rides through an apocalyptic vision of a destroyed Phoenix, fighting an ecological war much expanded from that in *The Monkey Wrench Gang*. While in his exposition, Abbey had been earning some of his living with magazine pieces, and as his reputation grew, he found that he could gather his occasional pieces into profitable volumes; *Down the River with Henry David Thoreau and Friends* (1982) and *Beyond the Wall: Essays from the Outside* (1984) fall into this category of his work. *Beyond the Wall* is a collection of ten articles that Abbey dedicated to Clarke Cartwright, to whom he was married at the time of his death. They were married on 5 May 1982 and had two children—Rebecca Claire, born on 14 October 1983, and Benjamin Cartwright, born on 19 March 1987.

The three remaining Abbey collections broke little new ground. Edited by David Petersen, *Confessions of a Barbarian* (1986) is a sampling of the journal that Abbey kept from 1951 to 1989. *One Life at a Time, Please* (1988) and *Vox Clamantis in Deserto: Some Notes from a Secret Journal* (1989), republished as *A Voice Crying in the Wilderness: Notes from a Secret Journal* (1990), are similar gleanings. In them, Abbey demonstrates that he had always been a gifted phrasemaker: his "damnation" of free-flowing rivers and his "Californicate" for land development repeatedly showed up in his journal writing as well as in his finished pieces and thus gradually became environmental commonplaces. Perhaps Abbey's most famous line applied to a sane pace for economic development: "Growth for the sake of growth is the ideology of the cancer cell." He made this statement first in *Desert Solitaire* and kept repeating variations of it throughout his career.

One of the most generous, if not also most intelligent, assessments of Abbey's career is Wendell Berry's "A Few Words in Favor of Edward Abbey" in *What Are People For?* (1990). Beginning his essay with something of a cliché, Berry painted Abbey as "a horse of a different color," a gadfly "iconoclast" whose value has been his rare ability to engage his readers in fruitful arguments. To the many charges that Abbey had been in one way or another untrue to conservation, Berry replies that Abbey seldom wrote purely as an environmentalist nor as any other kind of "-ist." He was primarily an "autobiographer" whose "work [was] self-defense." His was thus a conservation of the highest order, and he was a writer intent on conserving "himself as a human being," a goal that necessarily demanded that he conserve much else besides. Berry's reminder in this essay may echo Ralph Waldo Emerson's famous assertion that "A foolish consistency is the hobgoblin of little minds. . . ." Abbey bragged of

littering roadsides with his beer cans but defended himself by arguing that hard roads are themselves a desecration of the earth and thus his trash mattered not at all. He was also passionate about zero population growth but fathered five children. These are by no means all the contradictions of Edward Abbey. But his writing was in its way truthful and was also an "antidote to despair."

Abbey's last act contributed immeasurably to his legend. When he knew he was dying, he left the care of his doctors and checked himself out of the hospital. He went into the desert with his wife, Clarke, and his friends Jack Loeffler, Dave and Nancy Foreman, and Doug and Lisa Peacock. They built a campfire and made Abbey comfortable in his sleeping bag. When he did not die that night, they carried him back to his writing cabin, beside his home, where he died on 14 March 1989. The centrality of *Desert Solitaire* to Abbey's achievement is seen in the memorial service held at Arches Park after his death. The celebration of his life and work began as a sunrise service on a Saturday, 20 March 1989. But any sort of "commemoration" would be an inadequate expression for the wake/square dance/beer bust that actually unfolded throughout that day and night. Advertised with a postcard that enjoined, "Please join us for a gathering of the tribe," the "mourners" followed the older, abandoned, dirt road into Arches Park, where nearly a thousand people filled a natural amphitheater of the famous slickrock sandstone. Speakers included Sleight and Doug Peacock, who had served as models for the *Monkey Wrench* characters Seldom Seen Smith and George Washington Hayduke; Dave Foreman, an alleged cofounder of Earth First; and nature writers Barry Lopez, Ann Zwinger, Wendell Berry, and Terry Tempest Williams. The starkest incongruity was the celebration of Abbey's well-known love of classical music by an orchestral string ensemble from the University of Utah, who performed in formal black dress on the desert slickrock. The impromptu gathering then adjourned to Sleight's Pack Creek Ranch in the nearby LaSal Mountains for a bacchanalian phase. These "services" were entirely in keeping with the spirit Abbey had infused into his writing, and the measure of his personal and literary influence is that no other death of a Western writer has turned so many into pilgrims as did Abbey's untimely passing from the internal bleeding from which he had long suffered. Following his instructions, set down years earlier in his journal, his friends illegally buried Abbey's body deep in a wilderness. They brought back word of having piled rocks on the grave, in the fashion of Native Americans, to keep coyotes off. His friends have kept the location of the grave a secret, and so that it might remain concealed, his friends have since piled up many false graves throughout the South-west.

**Interviews:**

Dave Solheim and Rob Levin, "*Bloomsbury Review* Interview," *Bloomsbury Review,* 1, no. 1 (November/December 1980): 17–21; reprinted in *Resist Much, Obey Little: Some Notes on Edward Abbey,* edited by James Hepworth and Gregory McNamee (Salt Lake City, Utah: Dream Garden, 1985), pp. 79–91;

Kay Jimerson, "Edward Abbey: Interview," in *This Is about Vision: Interviews with Southwestern Writers,* edited by William Balassi, John F. Crawford, and Annie O. Eysturoy (Albuquerque: University of New Mexico Press, 1990);

Lyman Hafen and Milo McCowan, *Edward Abbey: An Interview at Pack Creek Ranch* (Santa Fe, N.Mex.: Vinegar Tom, 1991).

**Biography:**

James M. Cahalan, *Edward Abbey: A Life* (Tucson: University of Arizona Press, 2001).

**References:**

Wendell Berry, "A Few Words in Favor of Edward Abbey," in *What Are People For?* (San Francisco: North Point, 1990), pp. 36–47;

James Bishop Jr., *Epitaph for a Desert Anarchist: The Life and Legacy of Edward Abbey* (New York: Atheneum, 1994);

Paul T. Bryant, "The Structure and Unity of *Desert Solitaire,*" *Western American Literature,* 28 (May 1993): 3–19;

James Hepworth and Gregory McNamee, eds., *Resist Much, Obey Little: Some Notes on Edward Abbey* (Salt Lake City, Utah: Dream Garden, 1985);

Edward Hoagland, "Standing Tough in the Desert," *New York Times Review of Books,* 7 (7 May 1989): 44;

Garth McCann, *Edward Abbey,* Boise State University Western Writers Series, no. 29 (Boise, Idaho: Boise State University Press, 1977);

Peter Quigley, ed., *Coyote in the Maze: Tracking Edward Abbey in a World of Words* (Salt Lake City: University of Utah Press, 1998);

Ann Ronald, *The New West of Edward Abbey* (Albuquerque: University of New Mexico Press, 1982);

Wallace Stegner and Richard W. Etulain, *Conversations with Wallace Stegner on Western History and Literature,* revised edition (Salt Lake City: University of Utah Press, 1990).

**Papers:**

The Edward Abbey papers are in the University of Arizona Library, Special Collections.

# Mary Clearman Blew

*(10 December 1939 – )*

Ron McFarland
*University of Idaho*

BOOKS: *Lambing Out and Other Stories,* as Mary Clearman (Columbia: University of Missouri Press, 1977);

*Runaway: A Collection of Stories* (Lewiston, Idaho: Confluence Press, 1990);

*All But the Waltz: Essays on a Montana Family* (New York: Viking, 1991); republished as *All But the Waltz: A Memoir of Five Generations in the Life of a Montana Family* (New York: Penguin, 1992);

*Balsamroot: A Memoir* (New York: Viking, 1994);

*Bone Deep in Landscape: Writing, Reading, and Place* (Norman: University of Oklahoma Press, 1999);

*Sister Coyote: Montana Stories* (New York: Lyons, 2000).

OTHER: *Circle of Women: An Anthology of Contemporary Western Women Writers,* edited by Blew and Kim Barnes (New York: Penguin, 1994);

*Written on Water: Essays on Idaho Rivers by Idaho Writers,* compiled and edited by Blew (Moscow: University of Idaho Press, 2001);

Margaret Bell, *When Montana and I Were Young: A Frontier Childhood,* edited by Blew (Lincoln: University of Nebraska Press, 2002).

*Mary Clearman Blew (courtesy of the author)*

In fiction and nonfiction Mary Clearman Blew, the great-granddaughter of homesteaders in northern Montana, has written a vivid and moving record of ranch life in the decades between 1940 and 2000. Her short fiction has been included in the O. Henry Prize and Best American Short Stories anthologies, and two of her books, *Runaway: A Collection of Stories* (1990) and *All But the Waltz: Essays on a Montana Family* (1991), have garnered Pacific Northwest Booksellers Awards. Blew is the recipient of two Montana Awards in the Humanities and the H. G. Merriam Award for Distinguished Contribution to Montana Literature. In 1997 she received an honorary doctorate from Carroll College in Helena, Montana. Along with fellow Montana writers such as James Welch, Ivan Doig, William Kittredge, and Linda M. Hasselstrom, Blew is among the notable writers from the inland Northwest whose work has drawn national attention. Credit for that attention, which has increased over the past thirty years, is often attributed to the influence of diverse writers such as Richard Hugo, a Seattle native who taught creative writing—mostly poetry—at the University of Montana in Missoula between 1964 and his death in 1982, and A. B. Guthrie Jr., whose novels appeared in the decades spanning the 1940s through the 1980s.

Born on 10 December 1939 in Lewistown, Montana, to Albert "Jack" Hogeland, a rancher, and Doris

Welch Hogeland, Mary grew up with her brother and sister on the family ranch in central Montana. As Kate, the protagonist in the title story "Runaway" observes, "It was a great country for men and dogs . . . but hell on women and horses." As Blew expressed the thought in an interview with Gregory L. Morris: "To grow up female in Charlie Russell country is to grow up in the context of a myth of the West in which women are idealized, if they exist at all." Mary Blew is definitely a Westerner; she grew up with a love of horses, and she still rides frequently. Mary was treated like a boy as she was growing up, and issues of conflicted gender identity inform much of her writing. Married to Ted T. Clearman and pregnant at the age of eighteen, Mary Clearman was still able to complete her college education, partly because of loans from her namesake grandmother, Mary Welch, who taught in one-room schools in Montana during the 1920s. Clearman's favorite aunt, Imogene, subject of the memoir *Balsamroot* (1994), also taught in the public schools. Following the births of her son, Jack, in 1959 and daughter Elizabeth in 1961, Clearman graduated with honors in English and Latin from the University of Montana in 1962 and stayed to pursue a master's degree, which she completed in 1963. Between 1963 and 1969 she taught as an instructor in the English department at the University of Missouri in Columbia, where she completed her doctorate in 1969. Her dissertation was titled "Aspects of Juvenal in Ben Jonson's Comical Satyres."

Clearman's first published story, "Lambing Out," appeared in the summer 1970 issue of the *North American Review* and was reprinted in the volume of O. Henry Award stories for 1972, the same year her marriage ended in divorce. By then she was chairwoman of the English department at Northern Montana College in Havre, where she taught for ten years (1969–1979) and served as dean of the School of Arts and Sciences for another eight years (1979–1987). Reviewers generally overlooked Clearman's first book, *Lambing Out and Other Stories,* which appeared in 1977 in the Breakthrough Series of the University of Missouri Press. Cast in the realist vein of Mildred Walker Schemm, who turned out more than a dozen novels between the 1930s and the 1950s—several of them set in Montana—all but one of Clearman's seven stories are located in Montana, and most of those concern ranch life.

The four stories in which women are protagonists suggest the high price exacted of women by the harsh weather and, more important, by the traditional, patriarchal Code of the West. Nettie Evans, the main character in the title story, misses a day of school because of a snowstorm and because her father needs her help tending the ewes, some of which survive while others do not. Presumably, Nettie will not be joining her fel-

low seniors in applying for college. The "daddy's girl" Johnnie MacReady of "Reining Pattern" conquers her envy of her more feminine cousin by winning the reining competition in the county horse show; but in the process she defers marriage to Marty, effectually reining in her conventional womanly impulses. In "Slightly Broken," Rita overcomes her fear of flying, but more significantly her bitterness about her philandering husband, when she struggles with a Cessna Skyhawk in stormy weather on the Montana Highline. Although she ends up circling back to the airport at Havre, she proves equal to the sneering challenge of one of the men: "You women always like to let on you can do anything." When her angry husband tries to play on her fear at the end of the story, Rita insists that she will take the driving test for her license anyway.

The harshness of a woman's life in the rural West is most strikingly detailed in the last story of the book, "Monsters," which features a male protagonist, an Indian named Gary Jeanmaire, whose assistance with the birthing of a two-headed calf is interrupted by an appeal from the sheriff for help with a supposed kidnapping. What has really happened is that Gary's former girlfriend, Shelley, has killed her baby, whose father is another man, and stuffed it into a culvert in a pathetic attempt, she declares hysterically, to "put it back."

A year after the publication of her first book, Clearman married Robert Blew on 18 August 1978, a high roller of sorts, a "Marlboro man" who made his money in oil and other speculative ventures. Their child, Rachel, was born nearly twenty years after the birth of Clearman's first child. In the title essay of *All But the Waltz* Mary Blew recounts the uneasy marriage, which ended with separation and her departure from Montana in 1987. She began teaching at Lewis-Clark State College in Lewiston, Idaho, that year, and in 1990 her second collection of short stories, *Runaway,* was published by Confluence Press. C. L. Rawlins, reviewing *Runaway* for *Western American Literature* (Fall 1991), described the collection of fourteen stories as "full of penetrating wisdom . . . delivered in strong, modest prose that illuminates character while staying out of the reader's way." The stories are evenly divided between first-person and third-person narrators, and in ten of the stories the main character is female. Teachers figure prominently in the stories, all of which are set in central Montana.

In "Album," a retitled version of "Paths unto the Dead" from *Lambing Out and Other Stories*—it also appeared in *Best American Short Stories 1975*—a young woman named Jean sits with her great-aunts after her grandmother's funeral. Like Blew's grandmother and namesake, Jean's grandmother Lavinia taught school at Bally-Dome. Jean rebels against the stultifying

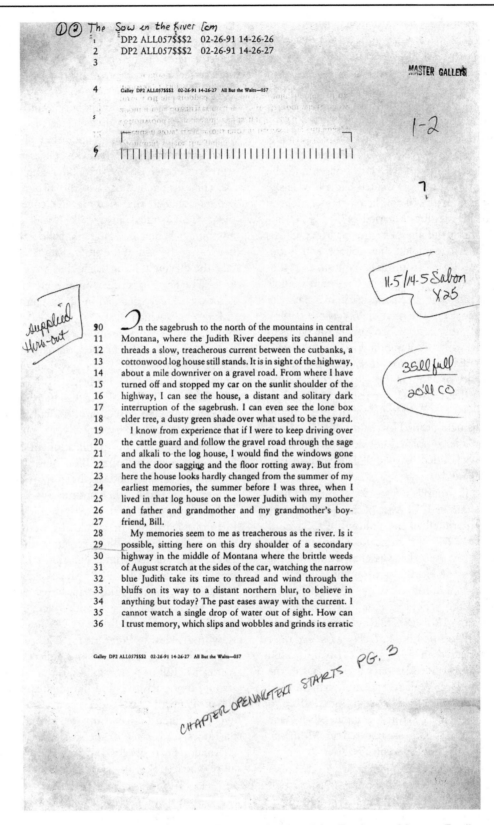

On the sagebrush to the north of the mountains in central Montana, where the Judith River deepens its channel and threads a slow, treacherous current between the cutbanks, a cottonwood log house still stands. It is in sight of the highway, about a mile downriver on a gravel road. From where I have turned off and stopped my car on the sunlit shoulder of the highway, I can see the house, a distant and solitary dark interruption of the sagebrush. I can even see the lone box elder tree, a dusty green shade over what used to be the yard.

I know from experience that if I were to keep driving over the cattle guard and follow the gravel road through the sage and alkali to the log house, I would find the windows gone and the door sagging and the floor rotting away. But from here the house looks hardly changed from the summer of my earliest memories, the summer before I was three, when I lived in that log house on the lower Judith with my mother and father and grandmother and my grandmother's boyfriend, Bill.

My memories seem to me as treacherous as the river. Is it possible, sitting here on this dry shoulder of a secondary highway in the middle of Montana where the brittle weeds of August scratch at the sides of the car, watching the narrow blue Judith take its time to thread and wind through the bluffs on its way to a distant northern blur, to believe in anything but today? The past eases away with the current. I cannot watch a single drop of water out of sight. How can I trust memory, which slips and wobbles and grinds its erratic

*Page from the galley proofs for the first piece in Blew's* All But the Waltz: Essays on a Montana Family, *published in 1991 (Collection of Mary Clearman Blew)*

harshness of the ranch, which she sees as having destroyed any of the "prettiness" the aunts once had; but in a deftly handled scene at the end of the story, one of the aunts reveals her romantic attachment to a sheepherder named Jesse MacGregor. Just as Lavinia reappears, albeit much altered, as Mary Welch in an essay in *All But the Waltz,* so Jesse MacGregor shows up again in *Balsamroot* in the person of Aunt Imogene's suitor, Lud. Blew's subsequent autobiographical writing reveals such echoes fairly often. The character Juley, for example, who figures in four of the stories, most notably in "Granddaughters," appears at her cousin Caroline's wedding as a thirty-five-year-old divorcée who has proven "too strong" and "too tough" for her husband. Blew underwent a divorce at about the same age as Juley and appears to speak through Juley, who takes pride in the "extra dose of stubbornness" inherited from her grandmother along with "a determination to hold out against the claims of a dearly-built world."

Perhaps the most memorable story in the book is "The Snowies, the Judiths"—both mountain ranges in the vicinity of the ranches where Blew grew up—in which a disgruntled student shoots and kills one teacher and wounds another along with a classmate. The story seems prophetic of the shootings that occurred in the public schools in the late 1990s. Fourteen-year-old Mary Dare's parents had actually moved from Portland back to Montana for safety. When Mary is asked repeatedly at the end of the story whether she has seen anything, she says she has not; but in fact she has seen quite a bit, and when her father angrily derides some young people who have come to the basketball tournament, Mary is tempted to revolt against her father's authority and say it is her parents who are the "pack of fools." In the last sentence, the supposedly protective mountains are reduced to insignificance: "Far out in the circle of the mountains their glowing outlines fell to ash."

Blew's most important and most favorably reviewed book to date is *All But the Waltz,* published in 1991. As Barbara Howard Meldrum has observed in "Creative Cowgirl: Mary Clearman Blew's Herstory," an article that appeared in the *South Dakota Review* (Spring 1993), the collection of eleven essays is not arranged chronologically but in a sequence that "moves from male domination to a more female-centered configuration." Meldrum also points out some similarities and differences between Blew's work and that of Doig. Writing for the *Smithsonian* (October 1991), Donald Dale Jackson praised Blew's style for being "spare and plain in the Western manner, often understated, the words bitten off sharply the way cowboys sometimes speak." In the opening

essay, "The Sow in the River," Blew asserts, "My memories seem to me as treacherous as the river"—hardly the sort of statement one expects from a writer of memoir. But as Blew indicates in "The Art of Memoir" in *Bone Deep in Landscape: Writing, Reading, and Place* (1999), she struggles as all memoirists do with "the conflicting claims of the exact truth of the story and its emotional truth as I perceive it." She is among the writers who have embraced the still rather nebulous genre of creative nonfiction, of which she writes in the essay on writing memoirs: "The boundaries of creative nonfiction will always be as fluid as water." In the flooded waters of the Judith River, which Blew recalls from age three, she finds herself remembering vividly that several pigs were stranded on an island, but the recollection and logic of her father appear to persuade her otherwise.

Having firmly established the unreliability of memory, Blew uses historical documents, including photographs and letters, in the next essay to write of her great-grandparents, Abraham and Mary Hogeland, who came to Montana from Pennsylvania in 1882. According to Blew, Abraham Hogeland came to Montana as a surveyor for the Pacific Northern Railroad "to convert landscape into property." Although she is fascinated by his carefully revised letters, composed as if intended for eventual publication, Blew considers his accounts too linear and his voice overly patriarchal, reminiscent of her father, whose italicized scolding comes back to her "like an unwanted legacy": *"Somewhere you got the idea in your head that you know something, but you don't know a goddamned thing."* It could be argued that this book is Blew's response to her father and to patriarchal authority in general. The next essay, "Dirt Roads," concerns her father's fascination with the "romantic and despairing mythology" of the West as embodied in the writings of Guthrie, Zane Grey, and Louis L'Amour. Having no sons, Jack Hogeland "raised his daughters as though they were boys," a circumstance that inevitably led them to undervalue being women. In 1983, at age seventy, Hogeland disappeared; his body showed up days later—he apparently died of natural causes—a couple of hundred miles to the southeast.

Blew saves the three most poignant essays in *All But the Waltz* for the last quarter of the book, by which time the women in her family dominate the text. In the context of Blew's first pregnancy in 1958, "The Unwanted Child" reflects on her mother's bitterness over being made to feel unwanted. "January 1922" is an account of Mary Welch's struggle to survive in Montana during a disastrous drought that drove her husband over the edge. The title essay, the last in the book, recounts Blew's second marriage,

*Dust jacket for Blew's memoirs of her ancestors and her own unhappy marriage*

her third pregnancy, and the disintegration of the marriage in 1983 after her husband, sick with pulmonary fibrosis, became erratic in his business dealings and fled to Kansas to avoid his creditors. By the time he died in 1987, Mary Blew had left Montana for Idaho. The book ends with Blew and her seven-year-old daughter, Rachel, attending Robert Blew's funeral in Kansas.

Blew's fourth book, *Balsamroot,* published in 1994, is a memoir devoted to her Aunt Imogene, who also had appeared prominently in an essay titled "Auntie" in *All But the Waltz.* Imogene left Montana for a teaching job in Port Angeles, on the Olympic Peninsula in Washington, after suffering an ankle injury in a mowing accident in 1942. Blew remembers her as the easygoing, tolerant, fun-loving aunt who taught her to swim and became something of a surrogate mother. In the fall of 1989 Imogene, aged seventy-nine, decided to sell her home in Port Angeles and move near her favorite niece in Lewiston, Idaho. "Even today," Blew writes, "Idaho is like an opposite facet of Montana, a kept secret in the shadow of Montana's glamour." The book, which Susan Allen Toth praised in *The New York Times Book Review* (8 December 1991) as "lucid, candid, haunting," negotiates several subjects: Imogene's struggle with dementia and Alzheimer's disease; Blew's experiences as a single mother of a seven-year-old (Rachel) and a twenty-eight-year-old (Elizabeth), who was preparing for veterinary school at Washington State University and for marriage; and, after Imogene is placed in a nursing home, Blew's reconstruction of Imogene's life, partly through a diary that begins in 1933. The book ends with a remarkable scene of reconciliation between Elizabeth and Blew as they ride horseback on a hill above the Snake River: "I think of Yellow Wolf and the emptiness he saw here, and I know I am as transitory as he, a fleeting glimpse of a bay horse and a rider before the light fades." As Cathy Downs observed in *Western American Literature* (Fall 1995), "Blew's lyrical prose is compelling and gentle."

In the fall of 1994 Blew began teaching at the University of Idaho in Moscow, about thirty-five miles north of Lewiston, where, as director of creative writing (1996–1999), she helped establish the new Master of Fine Arts program. She has edited two anthologies of Western writing—*Circle of Women: An Anthology of Contemporary Western Women Writers* (1994), with Kim Barnes, and *Written on Water: Essays on Idaho Rivers by Idaho Writers* (2001). In 1999 her collection *Bone Deep in Landscape* appeared—thirteen essays on the subjects of writing, notably of memoir, and place. The initial essay, "The Art of Memoir," proceeds from Blew's love of quilting, which, along with horseback riding, is a favorite avocation. Submitting that "when I write about myself, I transform myself just as I do the past," she concludes, "I experience a detachment from the finished essay because I have come to exist in it as a character, as separate from myself as any fictional character." The essays take the reader on a visit to an ancient Indian buffalo jump near Havre, Montana; across the Continental Divide into Idaho in the summer of 1987; back to Fergus County in central Montana; up to Fort Assiniboine on the Montana Highline, built in 1879 and abandoned in 1911; into the fictional world of an all-but-lost Montana novelist of the turn of the century, Bertha Muzzy Bower; and back to Lewiston, Idaho, where Blew observes of her newly adopted state, "Idaho remains largely uninvented" but urges its writers to "emerge from their enclaves" and join the community "as the respite that every solitary writer needs."

Blew's next collection, *Sister Coyote: Montana Stories* (2000), comprises the title piece—a novella that covers nearly a hundred pages and is her most ambitious effort in fiction to date—and six short stories, one of which, "Hunter Safety," is a revision of "A Lesson in Hunter Safety," which appeared in *Runaway*. All but the final story are set in Montana, and only one story features a male narrator. A character known as Laura appears centrally in the first two stories, as a fourteen-year-old hunting deer illegally with boys in "Kids in the Dark" and as a lawyer and single mother of a thirteen-year-old son in "Hunter Safety." She appears more peripherally in two other stories. The title novella, *Sister Coyote,* is set a few days before Christmas 1972 in Versailles, a town that closely resembles Havre. The main character, Beth Anne Vanago—a pathetic, overweight divorcée and mother of four—attempts to struggle through college as she deals with various forms of domestic abuse, some of which she appears to bring on herself in the form of self-destructive barhopping and binge eating.

Deftly woven into the main plot of the novella are subplots involving a young woman traveling at

*Dust jacket for Blew's 2000 fiction collection, which includes the title novella and six short stories*

night through the snow, north to Versailles to take a teaching job at the college, and a young coyote—a dominant female—traveling across country from Alberta south toward Versailles. Meanwhile, a pack of coyotes attacks a flock of lambs. Beth Anne, however, is akin to the lone female coyote that is hunted from a plane by men who are shooting the animals for their pelts. The teacher survives a close call when she goes into a skid trying to avoid the shadow of some animal, presumably a coyote, and she continues toward her job with renewed confidence in her independence—a quality the hapless Beth Anne seems unable to acquire. Failing in her effort to confront her estranged husband with a pistol at a restaurant, Beth Anne turns herself in to the police, claiming she intends to shoot her children. She is disarmed by the coyote hunter.

Beth Anne could be said to embody all of the negative traits of the Western myth, both as the victim of men who follow it and as a would-be advocate. When she attempts to resort to the kind of violence that has been wreaked on her and that the reader sees aimed at the coyotes, she fails. But if Beth Anne represents a worst-case scenario, the protagonist in the final story of the collection, "Varia's Revenge," might be said to represent her anti-type, at least to a point. Set in northern Idaho at the opening of deer season, this humorous story features a business executive who has opted for early retirement on acreage where she can enjoy solitude, nature, and her two horses. When a careless young hunter kills her beloved old mare, Varia finds herself holding the young man's deer rifle on him and locking him up in a neighbor's outhouse. In none of her other writings does Blew demonstrate the comic sensibility she exhibits in this story. Although her neighbor argues that nothing is likely to come of the episode, given the local prejudice against out-of-state hunters and the young hunter's embarrassment at having been disarmed by an elderly lady, Varia has sufficient maturity and perspective to insist on reporting the incident to the sheriff. In effect, she refuses to yield to the myth, or even to the rage or righteous indignation that prompted her temporary conformity to its outlines.

As Krista Comer has observed, against the male myth of rugged individualism, self-reliance, and independence that tends to conform to the distances and isolation of the Western landscape, Blew argues for such "women's values" as community, interdependence, culture, and education. In the New West, after all, those distances and that isolation are vanishing. Under pressure, Varia finds herself role-playing a mythic male of the Old West, but she walks away from that part at the end of the drama.

Mary Clearman Blew was nearly forty years old when her first book was published, and her acclaim has come only since the publication of *All But the Waltz,* but she has a deep commitment to the craft of writing and revises her work rigorously. Although a full critical appreciation of her achievement has not yet come, hers is an authentic and appealing voice of the contemporary West, and the fellow writers who have contributed blurbs to her book covers have indicated an array of qualities that accurately reflects the nature of her writing—clarity, candor, precision, honesty, inner toughness, affection, and sympathy. Her own self-description is less flattering, but it fulfills the promise of candor: "I am a white woman, born and bred in the West, loaded with the baggage of my upbringing, which includes an unforgiving work ethic, a prairie stoicism, and a suspicion of all that is manicured, polished, decorated, or mannered."

**Interview:**

Gregory L. Morris, "Mary Clearman Blew," in his *Talking Up a Storm: Voices of the New West* (Lincoln: University of Nebraska Press, 1994), pp. 25–32.

**References:**

Krista Comer, *Landscapes of the New West: Gender and Geography in Contemporary Women's Writing* (Chapel Hill: University of North Carolina Press, 1999);

Barbara Howard Meldrum, "Creative Cowgirl: Mary Clearman Blew's Herstory," *South Dakota Review,* 31 (Spring 1993): 63–72.

# Benjamin Capps
*(11 June 1922 –    )*

Lawrence Clayton
*Hardin-Simmons University*

BOOKS: *Hanging at Comanche Wells* (New York: Ballantine, 1962);

*The Trail to Ogallala* (New York: Duell, Sloan & Pearce, 1964);

*Sam Chance* (New York: Duell, Sloan & Pearce, 1965);

*A Woman of the People* (New York: Duell, Sloan & Pearce, 1966);

*The Brothers of Uterica* (New York: Meredith Press, 1967);

*The White Man's Road* (New York: Harper & Row, 1969; London: Tandem, 1975);

*The True Memoirs of Charley Blankenship* (Philadelphia: Lippincott, 1972);

*The Indians* (New York: Time-Life Books, 1973; revised, 1975, 1979);

*The Warren Wagontrain Raid: The First Complete Account of an Historic Indian Attack and Its Aftermath* (New York: Dial, 1974); republished with an "Apologia" by Capps (Dallas: Southern Methodist University Press, 1989);

*The Great Chiefs* (New York: Time-Life Books, 1975; revised, 1976, 1982);

*Woman Chief* (Garden City, N.Y.: Doubleday, 1979);

*The Heirs of Franklin Woodstock* (Fort Worth: Texas Christian University Press, 1989);

*Tales of the Southwest* (New York: Doubleday, 1991).

**Editions**: *The Trail to Ogallala,* Texas Tradition Series, no. 3 (Fort Worth: Texas Christian University Press, 1985);

*A Woman of the People* (Albuquerque: New Mexico University Press, 1985);

*Sam Chance,* Southwest Life and Letters Series (Dallas: Southern Methodist University Press, 1987);

*The Brothers of Uterica,* Southwest Life and Letters Series (Dallas: Southern Methodist University Press, 1988);

*The White Man's Road,* Southwest Life and Letters Series (Dallas: Southern Methodist University Press, 1988);

*Benjamin Capps (photograph by John D. Jackson; from the dust jacket for* Woman Chief, *1979)*

*The Warren Wagontrain Raid: The First Complete Account of an Historic Indian Attack and Its Aftermath,* Southwest Life and Letters Series (Dallas: Southern Methodist University Press, 1989);

*A Woman of the People,* Texas Tradition Series, no. 26 (Fort Worth: Texas Christian University Press, 1999).

OTHER: *Fodor's South Central States,* introduction by Capps, edited by Eugene Fodor, Robert C.

Fisher, and Barnett D. Laschever (New York: McKay, 1966), pp. 11–18;

*Duncan Robinson: Texas Teacher and Humanist,* edited by Capps and Thomas Sutherland (Arlington: Texas at Arlington University Press, 1976);

"Law Comes to the Old West: Do-It-Yourself Justice," in *Fodor's Old West: A Practical Guide to Where the West Was Won,* edited by Fodor and Fisher (New York: McKay, 1976), pp. 78–92;

*Fodor's South-West,* introduction by Capps, edited by Fisher and Leslie Brown (New York: McKay, 1979), pp. 1–8;

"The Disgraceful Affair of Turpentine Jackson," in *Roundup,* edited by Stephen Overholser (Garden City, N.Y.: Doubleday, 1982), pp. 52–57;

*"Centennial!" Texas, Our Texas: 150 Moments That Made Us the Way We Are* (Austin: Texas Monthly Press, 1986), p. 151.

SELECTED PERIODICAL PUBLICATIONS–UNCOLLECTED: "A Critical Look at a Classic Western Novel," *Roundup,* 22 (June 1964): 2, 4;

"The Promise of Western Fiction, Part 1," *Roundup,* 17 (October 1969), pp. 1–2, 20; "Part 2," *Roundup,* 17 (November 1969): 2, 4, 14; "Part 3," *Roundup,* 17 (December 1969): 6, 8, 24.

Benjamin Capps's work is balanced between the genres of fictionalized history and historical fiction. Capps wrote of cowboys, gunfighters, and ranchers as well as Indians, creating a series of successful characterizations. He chronicled some of the most interesting historical episodes in the saga of the American West, ranging from the days before European intrusion on into the early twentieth century.

Benjamin Franklin Capps was born on 11 June 1922 in Dundee, a small town in Archer County in north Texas. Capps's grandfather was a cowboy who later supplemented his income by capturing and breaking mustangs to sell to settlers. Capps's father, who carried the same name as the son, was born in a dugout in Archer County and followed in his father's footsteps as a cowboy and horseman. Later he went to work in the oil fields in that region. Following service in World War I, he returned home, married Ruth Kathleen Rice, fathered three sons, and died of a stomach ailment in 1926. This frontier heritage, typified in many ways by his father and grandfather, influenced and focused Capps's thinking as he later turned to writing.

Capps's early education came from his mother, who had been a schoolteacher before marrying. Her first job after her husband's death was at Anarene, a small village eight miles south of Archer City, Texas. The school consisted of two rooms, one a classroom and the other the living quarters for the family. Capps's mother later married a rancher who lived about three miles away, and the boys rode their horses to school. A bookish child, Capps found comfort in reading. Although he was isolated from much of society, his voracious and eclectic reading habits kept him from feeling deprived or lonely. When he lived at the school, he had access to books and early on began to make up stories to entertain his brothers. Other pastimes included walking or riding horseback to the post office once a week and to a neighbor's house to listen to radio programs such as *The Grand Old Opry.*

Capps graduated from Archer City High School as salutatorian in 1938 and entered Texas Technological College (now Texas Tech University) in Lubbock that fall. He had earned money during the summer by helping to deliver bottled soft drinks on a route that took him through small towns north of his home; but expenses soon depleted his resources, despite his job sweeping classrooms as part of the National Youth Agency. Capps had started his higher education in the burgeoning science of agriculture, a course of study that soon bored him. His courses in English, chemistry, and botany, not poultry husbandry, were the most rewarding. After the first year, he dropped out of college. He thought of studying law but was also interested in writing. He believed, however, that the writers he had been reading were from far more interesting places than he was, so he doubted that becoming a writer was possible for him.

From 1939 to 1940 he worked for the Civilian Conservation Corps in Colorado. In 1940 he took a job with the U.S. Corps of Engineers at Grand Junction, Colorado, but by 1942 he was back in North Texas helping survey an airport at Greenville. On his twentieth birthday he traveled to Dallas to take the test for aviation cadet in the U.S. Army Air Corps. He passed the test, but his entry was delayed for eight months because of a lack of space in the training program for new cadets. Meanwhile, to earn money, he took a job surveying on the site of the project that resulted in Lake Texoma. He recalls that one evening as he sat in his room at Miller's Boarding House in Denison, Texas, he vowed to become a writer if he lived through the war. Since truck drivers made twice what he was making, he took the driving test, passed, and began driving a huge truck hauling rock and dirt for the project. Unable to negotiate a turn one day, he suffered an accident that resulted in a skull fracture along with several broken

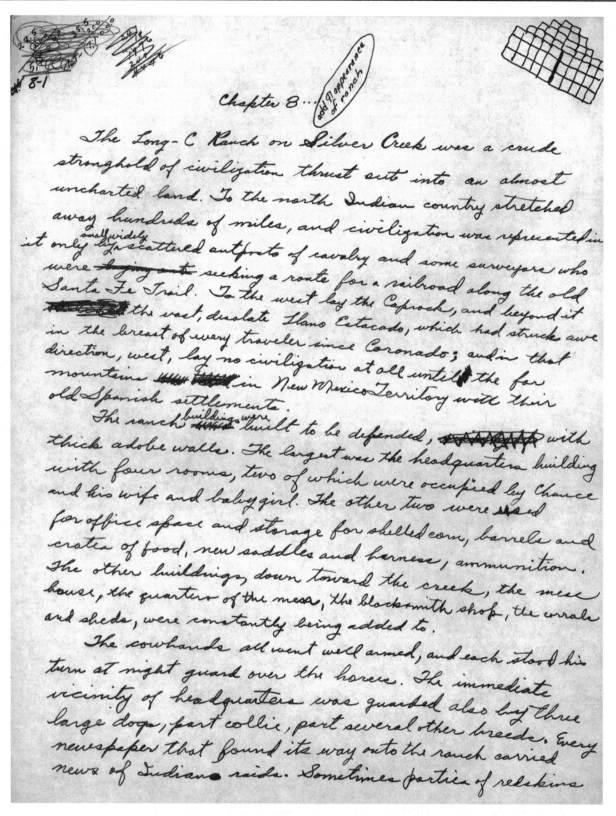

Chapter 8 ... add appearance of ranch

The Long-C Ranch on Silver Creek was a crude stronghold of civilization thrust out into an almost uncharted land. To the north Indian country stretched away hundreds of miles, and civilization was represented in it only small widely scattered outposts of cavalry and some surveyors who were trying out seeking a route for a railroad along the old Santa Fe Trail. To the west lay the Caprock, and beyond it the vast, desolate Llano Estacado, which had struck awe in the breast of every traveler since Coronado; and in that direction, west, lay no civilization at all until the far mountains in New Mexico Territory with their old Spanish settlements.

The ranch buildings were built to be defended, with thick adobe walls. The largest was the headquarters building with four rooms, two of which were occupied by Chance and his wife and baby girl. The other two were used for office space and storage for shelled corn, barrels and crates of food, new saddles and harness, ammunition. The other buildings, down toward the creek, the mess house, the quarters of the men, the blacksmith shop, the corrals and sheds, were constantly being added to.

The cowhands all went well armed, and each stood his turn at night guard over the horses. The immediate vicinity of headquarters was guarded also by three large dogs, part collie, part several other breeds. Every newspaper that found its way onto the ranch carried news of Indian raids. Sometimes parties of redskins

*Page from the first draft of the manuscript for Capps's 1965 novel, Sam Chance
(Special Collections Division, University of Texas at Arlington Libraries)*

bones. These serious injuries further delayed his entry into military service. He had been corresponding with a young woman named Millie Marie Thompson, and during his convalescence he married her in Ardmore, Oklahoma, in 1943, ten days before she turned sixteen years of age; he was twenty-one. Recovered from his injuries, Capps entered military service in 1943 and served in the Pacific theater as a navigator on a B-24 bomber in the Seventh Air Force, 11th Bomb Group, 26th Squadron. At the end of the war Capps was discharged with the rank of first lieutenant.

Like many other veterans, Capps was able to resume his college education with the help of the GI Bill. Spurning agriculture, he turned his efforts to becoming a writer by enrolling at the University of Texas in Austin, a school known for its excellent writing program. He earned a bachelor's degree in English and journalism in 1948, along with a Phi Beta Kappa key. His mentors at the university were Dewitt Reddick in journalism and Harry Ransom in the English department. During his years at the university, Capps published several non-Western pieces, some fiction, and other nonfiction in such outlets as *The Daily Texan*. He later published three pieces in *Lariat Story Magazine*, two in *Texas Literary Quarterly*, one in *Sir!*, and one in *Alfred Hitchcock's Mystery Magazine*. In addition, he won some local prizes for short pieces that attested to his dedication to the writer's craft as an undergraduate student. Indeed, some of the pieces were good enough to include later in his *Tales of the Southwest* (1991).

At first Capps contemplated an academic career and completed a master's degree in English in 1949. Encouraged by Mody C. Boatright, a renowned folklorist at the university, Capps wrote a novel titled "Mesquite Country" for his thesis. The work never found a publisher despite several revisions by the author. He produced three other unpublished novels: "Ethel May," "Movers of Earth," and "Hell, Fire, and Drinking Water." Capps's only teaching appointment was a two-year stint at Northeastern State College in Tahlequah, Oklahoma. Although Native American students he met there prompted his thinking about them and their role in American life, he decided that academic life was detrimental to his development as a writer, and he quit his position.

In 1951 he moved to Paris, Texas, where he tried writing full-time but failed to turn out a publishable work. By then he and Marie had two children—Benjamin Franklin Jr. and Kathleen Marie. In 1952, his savings gone and his wife expecting their third child, Mark Victor, they moved to Grand Prairie, located between Dallas and Fort Worth, which he

has since called home. In Grand Prairie he began a career as a tool-and-die maker, mistakenly thinking that he could earn a living in this line of work without exhausting his creativity. Unable to produce publishable work under these circumstances, however, he quit in 1961 to write full-time.

Capps set his course as a writer with the 1962 publication of his first novel, *Hanging at Comanche Wells*. The experience launched Capps into writing serious, interpretive books about the West and enabled him to abandon the format of the formula Western. In his introduction to *Tales of the Southwest* he wrote, "I had not been much interested in the standard, or formula, Western; it seems too simple and repetitious." While this decision may have cost him dollars and readers over the years, it also prompted him to produce some of the best interpretive writing, both historical fiction and fictionalized history, written about the West. Capps produced six more novels, a volume of short stories, two books on Indians for the Time-Life series, and a fictionalized history of an Indian raid in North Texas. He not only developed a series of significant characterizations but also explored the problems that settlement patterns in the West raised for both the Indians and the Europeans. Taking the broader view, Capps saw the conflicts in these books as archetypal of conflicts throughout world history, and he realized that conquest had long dominated human activity, whether it was Indian versus Indian, Anglo versus Indian, or Anglo versus Anglo. While he sympathized with the plight of people caught up in these wars, he was unsparing in his realistic and authentic depiction of events. He closes his introduction to *Tales of the Southwest* with this pronouncement: "I believe the fiction writer serves an important moral function in showing the basic humanity in strange or unfamiliar human beings." In addition, he wrote several commissioned works for *Fodor's Travel Guides* as well as articles for such publications as *The Roundup* and *The Dallas Times-Herald*. He also wrote more than a hundred book reviews in newspapers, magazines, and journals.

According to Capps, *Hanging at Comanche Wells*, his first book, incorporates the story of Tom Horn, a deputy sheriff and Pinkerton detective who turned killer-for-hire for cattlemen in Wyoming near the turn of the century. Capps's story depicts a time when Wyoming was struggling to establish a culture that ran counter to wishes of cattlemen there. The figure based on the historic Horn is William Ivey, one of the villains in the novel, who, like Horn, is in jail awaiting hanging for killing a boy. The other villain is the man who hired Ivey, Stephen Pendergrass, a rancher intent on dominating the region at any cost. The cast of characters also includes Bart Youngblood, a young deputy sheriff with a pregnant wife; Sheriff Bell, an aging servant of the law; and Judge Pendergrass, the brother of the rancher. The judge, who was crippled early in his life when a horse fell on his leg, has damaged his professional life by opposing secession of Texas from the Union during the Civil War and has been relegated to this remote judgeship on the frontier.

The novel concentrates on that transitional moment when frontier life has outlived itself, and law and order must be painfully brought to Comanche Wells. The central issue, then, is whether the forces of law and order can keep Ivey, who has been duly convicted of his crime, in jail and execute him according to the judge's schedule. That crucial moment has been the center of many Western stories such as Stephen Crane's "The Bride Comes to Yellow Sky" (1898) and Jack Schaefer's *Shane* (1949) as well as the movies *High Noon* (1952) and *High Plains Drifter* (1972). The novel incorporates the End-of-the-West motif, but not in the negative sense later used by Larry McMurtry in much of his work, especially *Horseman, Pass By* (1961) and *Lonesome Dove* (1985). In critiquing *Hanging at Comanche Wells,* James Ward Lee in *Fifty Western Writers* (1982) notes that it stands somewhere between the formula Western and serious fiction. The novel reads well and has its moments of excitement—especially the tense events building to the hanging, when Stephen Pendergrass rides into town on his huge black horse at the head of his band of death angels, but fails to accomplish his purpose. The further suspense of the pending birth of Youngblood's child is almost anticlimactic in this strongly masculine novel.

Capps found his stride in his second novel, *The Trail to Ogallala* (1964). He explained in a letter to Boatright that in this novel he hoped to capture the true action and spirit of trail driving from Texas to the Northern Plains. The book invites favorable comparison with such firsthand accounts as Andy Adams's *Log of a Cowboy* (1903) and Emerson Hough's *North of 36* (1923). In a personal interview Capps said he wanted to be "more deliberate than Adams, more realistic than Hough." In his penchant for selecting historical figures after which to pattern at least one of his characters, Capps chose the story and personality of Achilles, the great Greek warrior who, though a superior fighter, was not in charge of the army at Troy. Like Achilles, Billy Scott, a young but seasoned cowboy and trail driver, is denied his promised role as leader of the cattle drive because of the death of Lawson, one of the owners, and the hir-

*Dust jacket for Capps's 1969 novel, about a Comanche youth's coming of age on the reservation at Fort Sill in what is now Oklahoma*

ing by Lawson's widow of Colonel Horace Kittredge, an old friend and experienced drover. Scott is not even second in command, *segundo,* a job given to the inept but hot-tempered Blackie. At the insistence of two other owners of the herd, Brown and Greer, Scott agrees to make the drive anyway, but he quickly runs afoul of Kittredge's practices and questionable decisions. The action in the novel is archetypal of trail driving, with stampedes, trouble with rustlers, storms, and death. Kittredge is killed on the drive, and Blackie takes charge, though his actions threaten the success of the venture. Scott must run the drive, however, and he eventually does so through Blackie.

A pronounced success, *The Trail to Ogallala* has been republished by New American Library and Ace Books, and in a scholarly edition by Texas Christian University Press (1985). In a letter to Capps, Boatright wrote that the work compares favorably with that of Adams and praised the characterizations of Scott, Kittredge, and Blackie as being particularly strong. Other characters in the novel show the diversity of frontier types ranging from Civil War veterans and a Mexican fleeing a past murder to an ill-tempered cook. In *The Trail to Ogallala* Capps exceeds the limited success of his first book and emerges as a novelist to be reckoned with. Lee, in his *Classics of Texas Fiction* (1987), praises the book as superior to Adams's *Log of a Cowboy,* because Adams's is history and Capps's is fiction—and Aristotle noted that literature is superior to history. Don Graham praises, for example, the "convincing psychological growth" that Scott undergoes in the novel.

Capps followed this success with what may well be his best novel, *Sam Chance* (1965), the story of a man who helped settle the West but lived long enough to see his philosophy and tactics become unacceptable, much as Natty Bumppo does in James Fenimore Cooper's *The Pioneers* (1823). Lou Rodenberger calls *Sam Chance* "the most perceptive chronicle exploring the evolution of the Civil War soldier into Texas cowboy and finally cattleman who became a legend in his own time." If there is an historical model, one would suspect the famous cattleman Charles Goodnight; but in a letter to Boatright, Capps cites differences between the two, such as Goodnight's not being from Tennessee, not serving in the regular Confederate army, and his being in Texas prior to the end of the war. The two also ranched in different areas of Texas. In a letter to scholar Ernest Speck, however, Capps admits that similarities exist, even "more than I intended." Capps acknowledges that Chance evidences too many positive traits for one man and concludes that "Chance is . . . too much the polemicist, too articulate."

The novel is organized as an epic, similar to Homer's *Odyssey,* in which the hero leaves the scene of battle and has a long and adventurous life. Strongly aware of the history and folklore of this part of northwest Texas, Capps covers almost too many facets of the development. Chance's adventures include those of a buffalo hunter, cowboy, trail driver, water conservator, railroad advocate, and even defender of Indian rights. Especially vivid is the depiction of the dying off of cattle in the disastrous 1886–1888 period. Capps's treatment of the negative response of Martha, Chance's wife, to the isolation and desolation of northwest Texas typifies many women's reaction to the treeless plains, dust, and danger.

The one major flaw in Chance is that he is unable to accommodate the change necessary to adjust to the new kind of life in the area he helped settle; it is the problem of one who lives so long that life passes him by and people come to disdain the former hero. The major success of this novel, however, is apparent in its several subsequent republications, including an edition from Southern Methodist University Press in 1987.

In his next novel, *A Woman of the People* (1966), Capps changed his direction and loosely followed the best-known Indian captivity story in Texas—that of Cynthia Ann Parker. As usual, however, Capps put his special touch on the story to make it his own. The plot is typical of many other Indian captivity narratives, in which a young girl and her sister are taken by Indians who kill the other members of the family. Capps deals sympathetically with the older girl, Helen Morrison, who constantly reminds her sister, Katy, that they will escape and return home, only to realize later that there is no home to go back to. Helen is almost killed because of her unwillingness to adjust, but she eventually takes on the Indian name Tehanita, marries a warrior named Burning Hand, and gives birth to their son. Later Burning Hand becomes the chief of the tribe. As the years pass and the Indians must give way to encroaching whites, Tehanita becomes her husband's spiritual guide in making the transition. Burning Hand, who feels he has never received his spiritual vision, comes to find that source of wisdom in his wife.

*A Woman of the People* is certainly one of Capps's best. Lee, in his afterword to the 1985 edition, praises the prose as "simple and unadorned." The focus on Helen is maintained throughout the novel, and Capps avoids the sensationalism, bloodshed, and rape often found in these narratives. Instead, he presents the Indians as thinking, caring people who willingly give their lives to maintain their traditions, until it becomes evident that annihilation is all that awaits them if they persist in their efforts to live their traditional nomadic life.

In his next novel Capps produced a work atypical of his canon. While *The Brothers of Uterica* (1967) is set in the West, it is not a Western. Rather, the novel treats fictionally the experiences of La Reunion, a socialist colony in the 1840s that was located in what is now downtown Dallas. One of the principal figures is Reverend Langley, a Methodist minister and teacher who is determined to give the commune a chance. The central figure is Jean Charles Bossereau, a Frenchman in his sixties, who has come to the United States with experience and fervor sparked by the French Revolution. As Martin Bucco pointed out in his review of the book for *Western American Literature* (1969), Bossereau is "too innocent to realize his glorious plan." The cast of characters includes a diverse mix of personalities: Bossereau's daughter, Jeanette; a feminist named

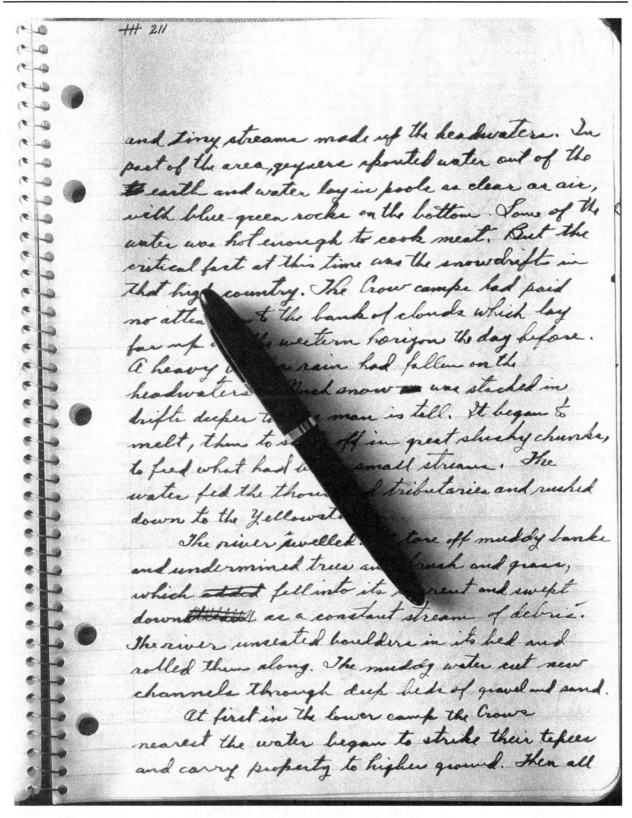

HH 211

and tiny streams made up the headwaters. In part of the area, geysers spouted water out of the earth and water lay in pools as clear as air, with blue-green rocks on the bottom. Some of the water was hot enough to cook meat. But the critical fact at this time was the snowdrift in that high country. The Crow camps had paid no attention to the bank of clouds which lay far up on the western horizon the day before. A heavy winter rain had fallen on the headwaters. Much snow was stacked in drifts deeper than a man is tall. It began to melt, then to slip off in great slushy chunks, to feed what had been small streams. The water fed the thousand tributaries and rushed down to the Yellowstone.

The river swelled, tore off muddy banks and undermined trees and brush and grass, which added fell into its current and swept down as a constant stream of debris. The river unseated boulders in its bed and rolled them along. The muddy water cut new channels through deep beds of gravel and sand.

At first in the lower camp the Crows nearest the water began to strike their tepees and carry property to higher ground. Then all

*Page from the manuscript for* Woman Chief *(photograph by C. W. Smith,*
The Dallas Times Herald; *Collection of Benjamin F. Capps)*

*Dust jacket for Capps's novel about a Crow Indian who rises from enslavement to become the leader of the tribe that kidnapped her as a child*

Harriet Edwards; Dr. Valentin, a totalitarian; a physician named Sockwell; a Unitarian named Brother Adams; and the troublemaker Deveraux.

In his preface to the 1988 Southern Methodist University Press edition of the novel, Capps notes that in Utopian societies the false assumption is that "human life can be well ordered by human reason." Capps's fictional colony failed, as did the other more than sixty communal societies he researched in writing the book. He correctly concludes that this subject has been hardly touched on in the literature of the West. *The Brothers of Uterica* itself was not a commercial success, probably because it deviated so far from traditional Western subject matter. Still, Capps proves in this book that he will not confine himself to any form or genre and will write only what appeals to him. C. W. Smith praised the novel and found the characterizations strong.

In his second novel about Comanches, *The White Man's Road* (1969), Capps chose a period after the heyday of the tribe as rulers of the South Plains. Likely influenced by the lives of the students he had taught and talked with during his brief tenure as a university professor, he depicts a time after the Comanches had been moved to the reservation at Fort Sill in present-day Oklahoma. Through his protagonist, Joe Cowbone, Capps depicts the agony of young Indians coming of age but denied the tribal rituals of becoming warriors and forced, instead, to travel the "White Man's Road," not the Indian Way. The various routes open to him range from the pointless path of the older Indians, the equally useless life of young Indians, and right-wing Christianity. Cowbone follows the road that incorporates both Indian and Anglo traditions in a way that best helps him cope with life.

*The White Man's Road* represents Capps at his best. Not a traditional Western, the book deals, rather, with the way this once-proud people must cope with a world dominated by the white man. One of the most telling incidents in the book involves a group of young Indians, including Cowbone, who steal horses from the army. The raid is a travesty of the well-organized forays for which Comanches were famous, but while the young men eventually lose the stolen horses to the army, they are not apprehended. Later, to please Lottie Manybirds, whom he marries in a Christian ceremony, Cowbone gives himself up to the military authorities. One of the ludicrous episodes of the novel is the lecture on the evils of stealing given to Cowbone by a white officer: the officer does not realize that traditional Comanche warriors prove their manhood through theft. This event underscores the lack of understanding between white and Indian.

Capps's next novel is an open-ended picaresque tale of a frontier "character" whose exploits cover the fullest range possible. *The True Memoirs of Charley Blankenship* (1972) canvasses the frontier experience in Missouri, Texas, Wyoming, Arizona, New Mexico, Colorado, Nebraska, and other areas. The vehicle for relating the adventures is the journey motif, as Charley sets off to find his brother Buck. Charley's adventures take him to whorehouses, saloons, and even the buffalo ranges, where Charley mainly picks up bones to sell. Like Huckleberry Finn, he meets scoundrels and charlatans and usually comes out on the short end of the count, as when he gives money to a prostitute who pleads her case but does not even recognize him when they next meet. In his introduction to the work, Capps identifies Blankenship as a "typical American cowboy" who ran away from

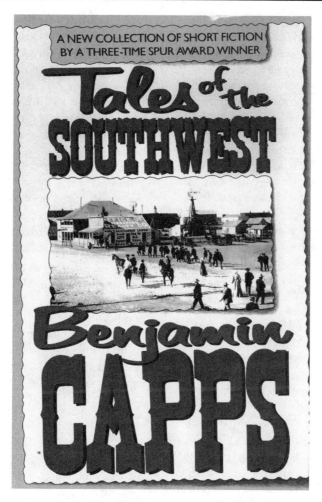

Dust jacket for Capps's final book, published two years before a 1993 stroke ended his writing career

home to seek his fortune and ended up working on ranches along the Powder River in Wyoming, the Pecos in New Mexico, and the Matador and XIT in northwestern Texas. Capps is aware of the correct gear and tack for the cowboy, and he is quite attentive to folk speech patterns and sayings, a pattern of detail he established in *The Trail to Ogallala*. While *The True Memoirs of Charley Blankenship* is not one of Capps's better-known works, it is his most humorous because of the title character's antics. The novel has not been republished; but, after *Hanging at Comanche Wells*, it is the closest Capps came to writing a formula Western.

Capps followed *The True Memoirs of Charley Blankenship* with a largely historical account of Indians in the Time-Life series on the West. *The Indians* (1973) adheres to the typical format of such books and adds little new knowledge on the subject. The purpose of this book, and of his *Great Chiefs* (1975), is to present in palatable form much of the known material on North American Indians. Capps relates the general history of Indians in North America from the time before European intrusion up to the high point of Indian history, the defeat of General George Armstrong Custer at Little Big Horn. His careful descriptions of Indian clothing, jewelry, horse gear, and weapons are admirable, as is other anthropological information about training horses, hunting buffalo, making arrows, cooking and drying meat, and naming children. Capps studies, as well, religious ritual and the effect of Manifest Destiny on the Indians. Although books of this sort rarely enhance a novelist's reputation, the research prepared Capps for two outstanding later books that demonstrate his excellence as a professional writer.

Capps's next book is a history heavily fictionalized through the author's imaginative dialogue in the mouths of historically authentic characters. *The Warren Wagontrain Raid: The First Complete Account of an Historic Indian Attack and Its Aftermath* (1974) lives up to its title. The raid, which took place near Capps's home in Archer County, was historically significant in shaping U.S. policy toward Indians. General William Tecumseh Sherman, then traveling in the West to determine the appropriate response to the Indian problem, barely missed coming under Indian attack, only to learn of the brutal massacre of some white wagoneers by Kiowa Indians from the reservation in Oklahoma. Because of this experience, Sherman influenced the U.S. policy change to genocide. Carefully researched and copiously documented, the book nonetheless drew serious objection from formal historians because of Capps's invented dialogue. For a 1989 edition of the book, Capps wrote an "Apologia" in which he responded to criticism that he fictionalized the historical account. He insisted that he was not altering history but "merely adding fiction elements which seem true." *The Warren Wagontrain Raid* remains the definitive account of the battle and its aftermath, in which the Indians were arrested, tried in a civilian court, and sentenced to prison in Huntsville, Texas. One of the three leaders, Satank (Sitting Bear), did not stand trial because he prompted his own death in battle as his wagon was leaving Fort Sill for Jacksboro.

*The Great Chiefs,* a continuation of the work Capps did in his first book in the Time-Life series, concentrates on Kiowa chiefs White Bear and Sitting Bear, the Apache chief Cochise and their famous warrior Geronimo, the Comanche chief Quanah Parker, the Eastern Shoshone chief Washakie, the Nez Percé chief Joseph, and the Sioux chief Sitting Bull, among other less well-known leaders. The volume, typical of the series, includes some fictionalizing as Capps depicts some of the events through the imagined conversations of Indians, conveying information to which he was not privy but which lent itself to use by Capps the storyteller.

Set along the Yellowstone River in Wyoming, *Woman Chief* (1979) is a novel about a Crow woman based, Capps says in the preface, on an actual woman who lived a "century and a half ago." Atypically for Indian fiction, *Woman Chief* takes place at a time when Anglo intrusion is not yet an issue for the Indians, who are fighting among themselves. The novel is a bildungsroman of the woman, who begins as "Slave Girl," becomes "Horse Tender," and eventually becomes "Woman Chief." Mistaken for a male child by Antelope Man, one of the raiders of her village, she is taken into his tribe as a slave. As an orphan, the girl is accustomed to having to adapt and does so; but the path is long and arduous because of hostility from Antelope Man's two wives. She becomes the friend and then the lover of Ride Away,

the grandson of One Good Eye, a medicine man. From an early age the girl takes intense interest in horses and weapons of war, and she becomes a great hunter and successful warrior, stealthily accompanying a punitive raid against an enemy and earning recognition by exacting vengeance on the enemy chief. After she has served as chief, a remarkable honor for an adopted woman, she attends a peace conference and is slain. *Woman Chief* is a straightforward narrative that has historical precedent among such Indian tribes as the Apache and Comanche. While the reception of the book was not particularly strong, its unusual setting and action separate it from Western formula fiction and secure for it an important place among Capps's works.

*The Heirs of Franklin Woodstock* (1989), Capps's last published novel, was written earlier and published at the end of his productive years. Set in contemporary times, the novel follows a fiercely independent but terminally ill elderly man, Franklin Woodstock, who has "escaped" from a nursing home in order to die on his own terms. While the title character never appears in the text, his spirit permeates the story. His children include George, a machinist living in the Dallas area; Walter, a graduate of the Harvard School of Business and a typical business tycoon; Irma, a religious fanatic whose son Wilbur is becoming a fundamentalist preacher; and Clarence, an English professor from California. In these people and their various plans for the ranch properties, Capps epitomizes the foibles of developers, tycoons, religious fanatics, and intellectuals. In the end all of the plans are foiled because the father has left the ranch to his Mexican wife, Izzy, and late-life son Johnny, who want to keep the property a working ranch. The rest of the family know nothing of the father's marriage to Izzy and the existence of Johnny. The older children assumed that Izzy was just a housekeeper for the father.

*The Heirs of Franklin Woodstock* probes pressing modern social issues, especially the plight of the elderly. Also of interest is the amount of autobiographical material in the book. Capps's wife worked in nursing homes, and Capps likely became aware through her of many aging men who once lived independent lives but found themselves confined and forced to follow institutional rules, against which they rebelled. The story is a declaration of independence of the elderly. The focus of the work, however, is on the disparate lives of the older Woodstock children. Not a commercial success, the novel is nonetheless well-done and further enlarges the scope of Capps's canon.

*Shelf of Capps's fiction and nonfiction books (photograph courtesy of the author)*

Capps's last book is a short-story collection, titled *Tales of the Southwest* and published in 1991. Included are several stories from his early work at the University of Texas, such as "A Secret of Military Significance" and "The Last Bearden." "Ethel May Is That Kind" echoes the title of one of his unpublished novels, and "Your Grandpa Was a Supporting Man" is lifted from "Mesquite Country." In the introduction Capps says, "I still have a real fondness for the short story. It's somewhere between the novel and lyric poetry. It's more concentrated than longer fiction and should have a single theme or impression or revelation about human life." Capps's affection for the form is apparent in his admission in the introduction that by 1961 he had written sixty-one short stories, of which only one was published. Published in hardcover by Double D Westerns, a leading series, *Tales of the Southwest* turned out to be Capps's last work, for a stroke in 1993 ended his productivity as a writer.

Benjamin Capps's output won him several prizes, including three Spur Awards and two Wrangler Awards from the National Cowboy Hall of Fame. Three of his novels were finalists for the Western Writers of America Award. He also was honored with membership in the Texas Institute of Letters and a lifetime membership in Western Writers of America. A serious student of life in the West, in a broad sense, and a talented creator of plausible characters, he nonetheless remained a retiring figure unwilling to speak on his own behalf, even when invited. He told Speck in a letter, on turning down an invitation to deliver the main address at the annual meeting of the Texas Folklore Society, that such appearances crippled his writing and caused him such stress as to be not worth the effort. He was active in Western Writers of America, however, and accepted a position as writer-in-residence at the University of Texas at Arlington in the spring and summer of 1976. What the passing of time and new readers of Capps's work will do for his critical reputation will be interesting to watch.

**References:**

Martin Bucco, "The Brothers Uterica," *Western American Literature,* 3 (1969): 308–310;

Lawrence Clayton, *Benjamin Capps and the South Plains: A Literary Relationship* (Denton: University of North Texas Press, 1990);

Don Graham, "Old and New Cowboy Classics," *Southwest Review,* 65 (1980): 293–303;

James Ward Lee, Afterword, in Capps's *The White Man's Road* (Dallas: Southern Methodist University Press, 1988), pp. 187–188;

Lee, Afterword, in Capps's *A Woman of the People* (Albuquerque: University of New Mexico Press, 1985), pp. 311–316;

Lee, "Benjamin Capps," in *Fifty Western Writers: A Bio-Bibliographical Sourcebook,* edited by Fred Erisman and Richard Etulain (Westport, Conn.: Greenwood Press, 1982), p. 43;

Lee, "Benjamin Capps," in *A Literary History of the American West,* edited by Thomas Lyon and others (Fort Worth: Texas Christian University Press, 1986), pp. 597–603;

Lee, *Classics of Texas Fiction* (Dallas: E-Heart, 1987);

William T. Pilkington, "The Recent Southwestern Novel," *Southwestern American Literature,* 1 (1971): 12–15;

Richard C. Poulson, "The Trail Drive Novel: A Matter of Balance," *Southwestern American Literature,* 4 (1974): 53–61;

Lou Rodenberger, "The 'Gen-u-wine Stuff': Character Makes the Difference in Trail-Drivin' Novel," *Heritage of Kansas,* 11 (1978): 3–12;

Rodenberger, "The Novel of the Cowboy," in *A Literary History of the American West,* edited by Thomas J. Lyon and others (Fort Worth: Texas Christian University Press, 1987), pp. 523–533;

Mary Simpson, "Benjamin Capps and the Sacajawea Plagiarism Case," master's thesis, North Texas State University, 1986;

C. W. Smith, "A Novelist of the Frontier," *Sunday Dallas Times Herald Magazine,* 2 March 1980: 4–9;

C. L. Sonnichsen, Afterword, in Capps's *The Brothers of Uterica* (Dallas: Southern Methodist University Press, 1988), pp. 311–314;

Sonnichsen, *From Hopalong to Hud: Thoughts on Western Fiction* (College Station: Texas A & M University Press, 1978);

Sonnichsen, "The New Style Western," *South Dakota Review,* 4 (1966): 22–28;

Ernest Speck, *Benjamin Capps,* Western Writers Series (Boise, Idaho: Boise State University, 1981);

Carlton Stowers, "The Old West of Benjamin Capps," *Southwestern American Literature,* 2 (1972): 150–152.

**Papers:**
The papers of Benjamin Capps are in the library of the University of Texas at Arlington.

# Willa Cather

*(7 December 1873 – 24 April 1947)*

John J. Murphy
*Brigham Young University*

See also the Cather entries in *DLB 9: American Novelists, 1910–1945; DLB 54: American Poets, 1880–1945, Third Series;* and *DLB 78: American Short-Story Writers, 1880–1910.*

BOOKS: *April Twilights* (Boston: Badger, 1903; enlarged edition, edited by Bernice Slote, Lincoln: University of Nebraska Press, 1968);

*The Troll Garden* (New York: McClure, Phillips, 1905);

*Alexander's Bridge* (Boston & New York: Houghton Mifflin, 1912); republished as *Alexander's Bridges* (London: Heinemann, 1912);

*O Pioneers!* (Boston & New York: Houghton Mifflin, 1913; London: Heinemann, 1913);

*The Song of the Lark* (Boston & New York: Houghton Mifflin, 1915; London: Murray, 1916; revised edition, Boston: Houghton Mifflin, 1937; London: Cassell, 1938);

*My Ántonia* (Boston & New York: Houghton Mifflin, 1918; London: Heinemann, 1919);

*Youth and the Bright Medusa* (New York: Knopf, 1920; London: Heinemann, 1921);

*One of Ours* (New York: Knopf, 1922; London: Heinemann, 1923);

*April Twilights and Other Poems* (New York: Knopf, 1923; London: Heinemann, 1924; enlarged edition, New York: Knopf, 1933); abridged in volume 3 of *The Novels and Stories of Willa Cather* (Boston: Houghton Mifflin, 1937);

*A Lost Lady* (New York: Knopf, 1923; London: Heinemann, 1924);

*The Professor's House* (New York: Knopf, 1925; London: Heinemann, 1925);

*My Mortal Enemy* (New York: Knopf, 1926; London: Heinemann, 1928);

*Death Comes for the Archbishop* (New York: Knopf, 1927; London: Heinemann, 1927);

*Shadows on the Rock* (New York: Knopf, 1931; London: Cassell, 1932);

*Obscure Destinies* (New York: Knopf, 1932; London: Cassell, 1932);

*Willa Cather*

*Lucy Gayheart* (New York: Knopf, 1935; London: Cassell, 1935);

*Not Under Forty* (New York: Knopf, 1936; London: Cassell, 1936);

*Sapphira and the Slave Girl* (New York: Knopf, 1940; London: Cassell, 1941);

*The Old Beauty and Others* (New York: Knopf, 1948; London: Cassell, 1956);

*Willa Cather on Writing* (New York: Knopf, 1949);

*Writings from Willa Cather's Campus Years,* edited by James R. Shively (Lincoln: University of Nebraska Press, 1950);

*Willa Cather in Europe,* edited by George N. Kates (New York: Knopf, 1956);

*Willa Cather's Collected Short Fiction, 1892–1912,* edited by Virginia Faulkner (Lincoln: University of Nebraska Press, 1965; revised, Lincoln & London: University of Nebraska Press, 1970);

*The Kingdom of Art: Willa Cather's First Principles and Critical Statements, 1893–1896,* edited by Slote (Lincoln: University of Nebraska Press, 1966);

*The World and the Parish: Willa Cather's Articles and Reviews, 1893–1902,* 2 volumes, edited by William M. Curtin (Lincoln: University of Nebraska Press, 1970);

*Uncle Valentine and Other Stories,* edited by Slote (Lincoln: University of Nebraska Press, 1973).

**Editions and Collections:** *The Novels and Stories of Willa Cather,* Autograph Edition, 13 volumes (Boston: Houghton Mifflin, 1937–1941);

*The Troll Garden,* edited by James Woodress, variorum edition (Lincoln & London: University of Nebraska Press, 1983);

*O Pioneers!* edited by Susan J. Rosowski and others, Willa Cather Scholarly Edition (Lincoln & London: University of Nebraska Press, 1992);

*My Ántonia,* edited by Charles W. Mignon and others, Willa Cather Scholarly Edition (Lincoln & London: University of Nebraska Press, 1994);

*A Lost Lady,* edited by Mignon and others, Willa Cather Scholarly Edition (Lincoln & London: University of Nebraska Press, 1997);

*Obscure Destinies,* edited by Kari A. Ronning and others, Willa Cather Scholarly Edition (Lincoln & London: University of Nebraska Press, 1998);

*Death Comes for the Archbishop,* edited by John J. Murphy and others, Willa Cather Scholarly Edition (Lincoln & London: University of Nebraska Press, 1999);

*The Professor's House,* edited by Frederick M. Link and others, Willa Cather Scholarly Edition (Lincoln & London: University of Nebraska Press, 2002).

OTHER: Georgine Milmine, *The Life of Mary G. Baker Eddy,* edited by Cather (New York: Doubleday, Page, 1909; London: Hodder & Stoughton, 1909);

S. S. McClure, *My Autobiography,* ghostwritten by Cather (New York: Stokes, 1914; London: Murray, 1914).

During the 1973 Willa Cather centennial seminar in Lincoln, Nebraska, Leon Edel—the Henry James biographer who collaborated with E. K. Brown on the first important biographical study of Cather—put himself "out on a limb" by announcing that "the time will come when [Cather will] be ranked above Hemingway. . . . But I've got her below Faulkner." Although arguable, Edel's statement accords with the recent explosion of interest in Cather and her fiction in contemporary scholarly circles as well as in high school and college classrooms. Cather has dominated American Western literary studies—as William Faulkner does Southern—for some time and is being recognized as an experimental modernist and a touchstone of twentieth-century American and world civilization. Her Jamesian commitment to fictional technique served thematic interests embracing immigration, cultural blending, and turn-of-the-century spiritual aridity, as well as a search for cosmic integrity that ultimately brought her, like Henry Adams, to medieval France.

Wilella (Willa) Cather was born in Back Creek Valley (now Gore), Virginia, on 7 December 1873, the first of Charles and Mary Virginia Boak Cather's seven children. Cather later added Sibert, after her maternal grandmother, as a middle name. In April 1883 the Charles Cathers joined other family members who had immigrated to Webster County in south-central Nebraska. The uprooting was undoubtedly Cather's primary formative experience. She told interviewers in 1913 and 1921 that, having been thrown upon land "as bare as a piece of sheet iron," she felt "a kind of erasure of personality" but determined to have it out with the land and that "by the end of autumn the shaggy grass country had gripped me with a passion I have never been able to shake. It has been the happiness and curse of my life." Cather dramatized this experience almost autobiographically in *My Ántonia* (1918). Landscape, first the prairies of Nebraska and later the Southwestern deserts, remained the emotional center of both Cather's life and her art beginning with her years as a University of Nebraska undergraduate—when she published her first stories and launched a long career in editing and reviewing—through her gradual substitution of the landscapes of the Northeast, Virginia, and France for those of the American West during the mid 1920s until her death in 1947.

The issue of lesbianism, as inconclusive as it is in Cather's case, needs to be clarified at the outset, since it has become an expressed presumption in the opening paragraphs of many contemporary introductions to her fiction. Because Cather never married and few contemporary theorists are willing to accept as marriages her dedication either to landscape or to art, although she eulogized the first as "something complete and great" into which one desires "to be dissolved" and the second as a master more exacting than Jehovah in demanding "human sacrifices," a significant body of recent criticism claims or presumes lesbianism as the impetus of her art. Some of these studies have been reasonable, but

*Cather's parents, Charles and Mary Virginia Boak Cather (Nebraska State Historical Society)*

others seem designed to titillate against accepted views of the "wholesomeness" of Cather's subjects and exaggerate as evidence several aspects of Cather's life and art. For example, as a teenager Cather cross-dressed and cut her hair short; later, she developed intimate friendships with several women; and as a novelist she wrote from male perspectives and used male narrators. While Cather texts are now customarily read as narcissistic psychoallegories covertly expressing erotic female attachments, more restrained lesbian-oriented critics such as Sharon O'Brien caution readers against facile presumptions that male characters are always masks rather than opposite-sex characters. Cather's most informed biographer, James Woodress, refuses to accept the lesbian label unless it is qualified by Lillian Faderman's generic definition as including strong emotional attachments that need not involve physical contact. Cynthia Griffin Wolff has dismissed the "male" haircut as the result of head lice and the cross-dressing as a turn-of-the-century fad popular with actresses and their groupies. James E. Miller's response during the centennial seminar to a reader's concern about male narrators is a reasonable perspective: "Willa Cather was an androgynous writer in the Virginia Woolf sense, so that she could project herself imaginatively into either the male or the female point of view."

As a writer, Cather presents Janus faces to her readers. Most prefer the forward-looking face Cather herself encouraged in earlier promotional material and interviews, that of the prairie girl turned novelist. A 1997 addition to several juvenile picture-book versions of this myth depicts young Willa exploring vast prairies on a horse, visiting immigrant families in "soddies," gathering wildflowers from a sea of grass, and planting seeds with her grandmother in a freshly plowed garden. The town of Red Cloud, the seat of Webster County, is strategic to this myth, although it is not depicted in the recent picture book. In 1884, after a year in the country, the Cathers moved into this town, where Willa spent her teenage years, developed close friendships with the Miner family and their hired-girl Annie Sadilek—who became, respectively, the Harlings and Ántonia Shimerda in *My Ántonia;* and met characters such as M. R. Bentley, the villainous Wick Cutter in the novel, and popular pianist Blind Boone, who was Samson d'Arnault in the novel. While in Red Cloud, Willa had her hair cut, cross-dressed, and took male parts in plays. She delivered an address on "Superstition *versus* Investigation" at the Red Cloud High School commencement in 1890 and in September left for Lincoln with the intention of studying medicine at the University of Nebraska. The fragments of this early biographical material have been gathered for scholars by Mildred R. Bennett, founder of the Willa Cather Pioneer Memorial in Red Cloud, in *The World of Willa Cather* (1951).

The other Janus face is highly sophisticated if somewhat backward-looking and owes its revelation to Bernice Slote, Virginia Faulkner, and William M. Curtin, who gathered Cather's newspaper and journal articles—including book, drama, music, and art exhibit reviews—from 1893 to 1902 into three large volumes, *The Kingdom of Art: Willa Cather's First Principles and Critical Statements, 1893–1896* (1966) and the two-volume *The World and the Parish: Willa Cather's Articles and Reviews, 1893–1902* (1970). From this material there emerged the portrait of an intellectual with incredibly eclectic reading and fine-art experiences, which included classics such as the Bible and the works of Virgil, Dante, and William Shakespeare; the music dramas of Richard Wagner; the works of Jean-Francois Millet and the Barbizon painters; performances by French tragedienne Sarah Bernhardt; and the fiction of Leo Tolstoy, Robert Louis Stevenson, and Kate Chopin. Such accomplishment, enhanced by a lengthy tour of Europe in 1902, explains why S. S. McClure, editor of the leading muckraking magazine in the country, *McClure's,* sought out Cather for his staff in 1906 and made her his managing editor two years later. Cather, who had been teaching and doing part-time editing in Pittsburgh, could now keep in touch with the artistic and intellectual life of New York on a daily basis and oversee a fiction department that published writers such as Thomas Hardy, Joseph Conrad, Arnold Bennett, Jack London, Sarah Orne Jewett, and Bret Harte. The exposure gave her mature fiction experimental dimensions and enabled her to develop subtexts through rich varieties of allusions. While *My Ántonia* (especially the "Lena Lingard" section) dramatizes how Cather transformed her prairie and Red Cloud experiences into major literature through intimacy with the arts and world culture, writing the two novels that preceded it, *O Pioneers!* (1913) and *The Song of the Lark* (1915), was strategic to the process of this achievement.

Cather's interest in landscape can be traced to her arrival in Nebraska, but in her early short fiction that landscape represents a challenge rather than an inspiration. From her perspective as a university student and later as a journalist in Lincoln, Red Cloud and Webster County in general became Siberia. The young men were rowdy, and social life was less than rustic—Cather was shocked during a New Year's Eve dance when sandwiches were served from a bushel basket. In her

stories from this period and into the years at *McClure's,* the prairie landscape and town are condemned as spirit-killing environments. In "On the Divide" (1896) the barren country, the heavy toil it demands, and the extremes of weather, especially the unbearable heat, drive men to insanity and suicide; in "The Sculptor's Funeral" (1905) the small town—Red Cloud barely disguised—is described as "a place of hatred and bitter waters." Woodress observes in *Willa Cather: A Literary Life* (1987), however, that these "tales of hardship, failure, deprivation . . . are not of a piece" with Cather's letters during this time, which describe Webster County as a beautiful green garden. Cather had not yet learned how to use the land positively in fiction and had adopted the environmental hostility of naturalist contemporaries such as Hamlin Garland, Frank Norris, and Stephen Crane. The process enabling her to rhapsodize over the Nebraska landscape was long and complex; it involved sojourns in France and the American Southwest, a great deal of maturing, and the advice of Jewett.

During her 1902 tour of Europe with Isabelle McClung, the Pittsburgh heiress with whom she shared a lifelong intimacy, Cather fell in love with France, especially with Provence. In travel notes she sent back to the *Nebraska State Journal* she is stirred during an afternoon spent at the Papal Palace in Avignon and by a sunset witnessed from its garden that transforms the distant Alps from white to lilac. She delights in white stucco villages nestled among rough arid hills, in wall peaches ripening in the hot sun, and in relics of the Roman past, such as the ruins at Arles. Not only is this landscape beautiful, but it has a past, a cultural dimension capable of romanticizing it. Ten years later, in 1912, at her brother Douglass's urging, Cather first visited the mesa country of the American Southwest. Using as her base Winslow, Arizona, where her brother shared a bungalow with another Santa Fe Railroad worker, Cather explored cliff dwellings in Walnut Canyon and visited Mexican communities. Not surprisingly, she compared this country to Provence. She wrote her friend Elizabeth Shepley Sergeant that the Albuquerque area resembled—in Sergeant's paraphrase—"the country between Marseilles and Nice but [was] more luminous. Even finer than the Rhone Valley. . . . She described Indian villages set around Spanish Mission churches built in Queen Elizabeth's time." Edith Lewis, who shared residences with Cather from the years at *McClure's* until her death and was usually her traveling companion, explains in *Willa Cather Living* (1953) how Cather was "deeply stirred" by the cliff dwellings, by contact with an "age-old but . . . intensely near and akin civilization."

Prior to her Southwestern adventure, Cather had published her first novel, *Alexander's Bridge* (1912), which she later disparaged as a conventional attempt to imitate Henry James and Edith Wharton. Cather's estimate is patently unfair; this novel, about a bridge-builder who compromises his great work as he does his marriage to a faithful wife, only partially resembles the novel of manners, and if the setting occasionally moves into the drawing room, the dramatic catastrophe is a spellbinding naturalistic scene of drowning workers struggling in the cold waters of the St. Lawrence River. However, Cather had recognized the validity of the advice Maine local colorist Jewett had given her four years earlier, that her true subject was the Nebraska material so much her own. In *Alexander's Bridge* Cather had not heeded Jewett's advice, although that advice seemed to have surfaced somewhat mysteriously in the Southwest, where she said she "recovered from the conventional point of view" to begin writing about Scandinavians and Bohemians who had been her neighbors back in 1883 on the prairie Divide. The novel she produced, *O Pioneers!* "had to do with a kind of country I loved."

*O Pioneers!* tells the story of Swedish immigrant Alexandra Bergson, who promises her dying father to dedicate herself to the family farm and keep her brothers in tow. As the product of Cather's experience of the Indian past in the Southwest, Alexandra is singled out to be sustained in her dedication by the "Genius of the Divide"—a "great, free spirit" that "breathes" over the prairies and resembles the Oversoul in Walt Whitman's poetry—as the "first . . . human face . . . set toward [this land] with love and yearning." Alexandra dominates the novel as Cather's first significant prairie heroine, surviving alienation from her older brothers and the killing of her beloved younger brother and her best friend by that friend's enraged husband—who discovers them at lovemaking—and contending with grief and the obligation to forgive the killer. What is most memorable about the novel, however, is the poetically rendered landscape, from the wintry opening suggestive of biblical chaos, to the unrolling of the dark earth toward the setting sun at Alexandra's reunion with her faithful friend Carl Linstrum. Cather's jubilation in the land, evident in letters, has successfully carried over into fiction, as does the impetus for that transference, the heart of Cather's next novel, *The Song of the Lark*.

While this work is at times ponderous and preachy, its heroine's discovery of her artistic power while bathing in a stream in an Arizona canyon is highly original and important for understanding Cather's own development as an artist. Drained by her duties as a church musician in Chicago that stifle her real career, Thea Kronborg—a singer whose story is

*Cather as a teenager, wearing her uncle's Confederate army cap (Nebraska State Historical Society)*

partially Cather's and partially that of Swedish-born, Minnesota-bred opera star Olive Fremstad—accepts an invitation to escape for a vacation in Arizona. Struggling to understand her art, Thea spends long days alone in a canyon of cliff-dwelling ruins. One day, standing upright in a pool and sponging water over her body, she associates the broken pottery left behind by the Indian women with her own throat and nostrils as receptacles for elusive life. These women, whose feet have worn a path to the stream, at once lengthen Thea's past and relate her art to the earth itself. Her world seems older and richer because of this experience, and she is able to unclutter her mind, to throw away the lumber. Thus, Cather shed the conventions of fiction and turned to Nebraska for her art. According to Sergeant, Cather was "suddenly in control of inner creative forces." Somehow, "the vast solitude of the Southwest, its bald magnificence, brilliant light and physical impact, too, had the effect of toning up [Cather's] spirit, and made available a path in which a new artistic method could evolve from familiar Nebraska subject matter."

The lengthening of the past that occurs during Kronborg's epiphany in the canyon filters the canyon—and, indeed, the entire landscape—through memory, a process strategic to understanding *My Ántonia,* Cather's Nebraska masterpiece. The story of this novel is almost autobiography, with narrator Jim Burden substituting for Cather in being uprooted from the Virginia mountains and deposited on the prairies, moving into a small town a year later, developing friendships with a Bohemian immigrant girl and the children of the leading merchant in the town, departing as a teenager for the university in Lincoln, and eventually taking up residence in New York. Although the concern in this work is Cather's process of transfiguring real landscape and people into fine art, other factors, such as Jim's failed marriage and inability to respond sexually to Ántonia, have intrigued readers disposed to view the work as sexual autobiography. In the central (third) section of the novel, as Jim is being introduced to Dante and Virgil and is mentally wandering back to "the places and people of [his] own infinitesimal past," which "stood out strengthened and simplified," he makes an intriguing confession: "They were so much alive in me that I scarcely stopped to wonder whether they were alive anywhere else, or how." This passage is Cather's definition of her artistry: she is recapturing in memory but in a memory burdened by significant exposure to and knowledge of literature, drama, opera, and painting. Jim views the prairie sunset as a picture framed by the window of his Lincoln study and heightened by aesthetic reference: "On the edge of the prairie . . . the sky was turquoise blue . . . with gold light throbbing in it. Higher up . . . the evening star hung like a lamp suspended by silver chains—like the lamp engraved upon the title-page of old Latin texts."

Such heightened vision cannot be sustained by Cather, however, and is undercut by the growing materialism and pettiness of prairie culture; it is as if the negatives condemned in "A Sculptor's Funeral" ultimately exhaust the burst of aesthetic energy that produced major fiction from the subject matter of Nebraska. The transfiguring light was brief, as is the light in the famous image in *My Ántonia* of the plough against the sun: "Magnified . . . by the horizontal light, [the plough] stood out . . . heroic in size," but as the sun dropped beneath the earth, "that forgotten plough . . . had sunk back to its own littleness." Cather virtually closes the book on Nebraska in *A Lost Lady* (1923) when Marian Forrester, an aging beauty—representing the prairie West—passes from a heroic pioneer to a shyster lawyer, while a rather effete intellectual, himself part of the social decline, evaluates the process. While this youthful aesthete, Niel Herbert, is frequently undercut as an unreliable idealizer of women, he nonetheless represents Cather's views about Nebraska culture. She couches his condemnation in exaggerated language satirizing his romantic attitudes and perhaps those of her own youth:

> The Old West had been settled by dreamers [like Captain Forrester, Marian's husband], great-hearted adventurers who were unpractical to the point of magnificence. . . . Now all the vast territory they had won was to be at the mercy of men like Ivy Peters [the shyster lawyer], who had never dared anything. . . . The space, the colour, the princely carelessness of the pioneer they would destroy and cut up into profitable bits.

Toward the conclusion of the novel, Niel is

> in a fever of impatience to be gone, and yet he felt that he was going away forever, and was making the final break with everything that had been dear to him in his boyhood. . . . He had seen the end of an era, the sunset of the pioneer. . . . It was already gone, that age; nothing could ever bring it back.

The subsequent prairie-set stories Cather wrote, "Neighbour Rosicky" (1928) and "The Best Years" (1945), focus on family relations and employ landscape as religious allegory rather than realistic setting; the lone novel, *Lucy Gayheart* (1935), a tragic love story involving a piano student and the men who fail her, could be set in any landscape from Maine to Oregon with ice and enough water to drown the heroine in a skating accident.

Cather's work now begins a shift outward culturally as it turns with deliberation from contemporary to past history and eventually to the Middle Ages. This movement is clearly evident in *One of Ours* (1922), which won a Pulitzer Prize, in which its doughboy hero, Claude Wheeler, is transported from Nebraska to France during World War I. Cather labored on this novel for five years between *My Ántonia* and *A Lost Lady,* obviously a soul-searching period for her. She returned to France in 1920 and stayed for five months to work on *One of Ours,* visiting the grave of her cousin, Lieutenant George P. Cather—upon whose life Claude Wheeler's story is loosely based—at Villers Tournelle near Cantigny, where he had been killed in 1918. Then, for about seven weeks she confined herself to the Left Bank of Paris to imbue herself in medieval culture. "And we did live in the Middle Ages, so far as it was possible," Lewis recalls. "We spent nearly all our time in the section between the Seine and the Luxembourg gardens, and on the Ile de Cite and the Ile-St. Louis." The two women escaped to the south of France during summer and fall and then "journeyed slowly back to

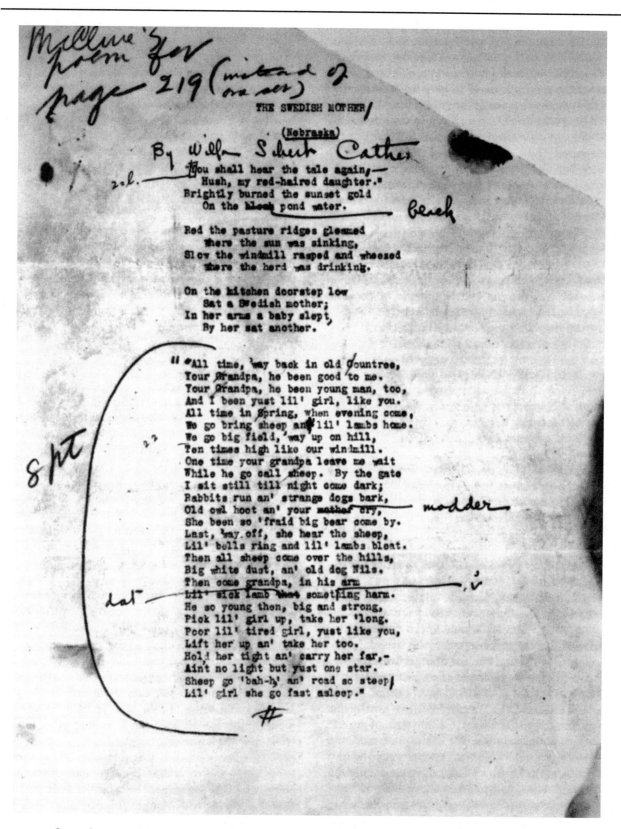

*Corrected typescript for a poem by Cather that was first published in the 11 September 1911 issue of* McClure's *magazine*
*(courtesy of The Lilly Library, Indiana University)*

Paris," for Cather "had to get the feeling of the whole of France to write about it."

During this period Cather published the most comprehensive statement of her philosophy of fiction, "The Novel Demeuble" (1922). She attacks the "property-man" who, under the pretense of realism, clutters the novel with "material objects and their vivid presentation." She distinguishes quantity from quality in fiction by relating quantity to the disposable and temporal and quality to art and the eternal. Selection becomes the artist's access to divinity: "Out of the teeming, gleaming stream of the present [art] must select the eternal." In addressing execution, Cather claims that the "high processes of art are all processes of simplification" and places artistic creation beyond language and in

> whatever is felt upon the page without being specifically named there. . . . It is the inexplicable presence of the thing not named, of the overtone divined by the ear but not heard by it . . . that gives high quality to the novel or the drama as well as to poetry itself.

Cather concludes with an extraordinary plea for an art of disembodiment, as far as that is possible, and for a room as bare "as that house into which the glory of Pentecost descended." The tone of this essay betrays the increasing religious direction of Cather's thought during the year, which she later used—in the "Prefatory Note" to Not Under Forty, a 1936 essay collection that reprints "The Novel Demeuble"—to date the breaking apart of the world. Two days after Christmas 1922, Cather, who grew up Baptist but was never devout, joined the Episcopal Church and was confirmed with her parents in Red Cloud by the bishop of Nebraska, George Beecher.

Claude Wheeler's story encapsulates this breaking in two, Cather's turning away from claustrophobic American materialism—represented in a cluttered rendering of the prairie West, the kind of Dreiserian realism Cather condemned—toward freedom and an age of faith (wartime and medieval France) in two related scenes. In the first scene Claude contemplates the equestrian statue of Kit Carson from the steps of the statehouse in Denver; he laments the passing of pioneer days and feels trapped beneath a sky "like a lid shut down over the world." In the second scene he wanders into St. Ouen, the old abbey church in Rouen, gazes up at one of the rose windows as he listens to a bell strike the hour, and experiences liberation: "The revelation of the glass and the bell had come almost simultaneously as if one produced the other; and both were superlatives toward which his mind had always been groping."

Almost everything is negative about the Nebraska of One of Ours. The landscape is unrelieved by lyricism, and family life becomes stifling. Claude's father, a business-type of farmer, and brothers resent and frustrate him at every turn. Education is third-rate and sacrificed to football; religious fundamentalism breeds hypocrisy; and marriage creates a prison within a prison. Claude marries a Prohibitionist who disapproves of sex and leaves him for missionary work in China. Conditions are such that it takes a war to rescue Claude. Cather's picture of France behind the trenches is exaggerated in the opposite direction. In a setting of flowery fields Claude develops a friendship with doughboy violinist David Gerhardt; this relationship becomes for him emotionally everything his marriage failed to be. Claude is killed in the war "believing his own country better than it is, and France better than any country can ever be."

The difficulty Cather experienced in writing One of Ours can be traced to the homoeroticism at the heart of the Claude-David relationship, although the true basis of the relationship remains latent and beneath the consciousness of the naive hero and to the war scenes of the novel. These scenes were attacked by several critics, including H. L. Mencken, and ridiculed by Ernest Hemingway, who accused Cather of lifting the final battle scene from D. W. Griffith's 1915 motion picture The Birth of a Nation. Such negative response was hardly deserved. Cather's scenes of trench warfare are strikingly similar to those in the World War I diary of British officer Edwin Campion Vaughan, which was discovered in the 1960s and published in 1981 as Some Desperate Glory. In The Professor's House (1925), a modernist variation on One of Ours, Cather avoided these difficulties. The war is over, and the doughboy hero, Tom Outland, is dead; his intimacy with the main protagonist, Professor Godfrey St. Peter, is given teacher-student, father-son dimensions and transfigured by memory.

Cather conceived this novel at Aix-les-Bains, Lewis believed, during their 1923 stay in France: "She did not work there, but it was perhaps in the peace and beauty of the Savoie countryside that the idea of The Professor's House took shape." Like One of Ours, this novel includes French settings, if only in memory, of the professor's student days in Paris and his home away from home with a French family in Versailles. Also, Cather continues the criticism of materialism, although it is generalized as the primary setting—a small, university city identified by some as Lincoln—and moves from Nebraska to the eastern shores of Lake Michigan. An experimental ingredient is the central Southwestern segment, "Tom Outland's Story," which is based on the Wetherill brothers' explorations of Mesa Verde. Cather, who returned to the Southwest repeatedly after her first visit, had spent a week at Mesa Verde with Lewis in 1915 that included a day at Cliff Palace ruins and a night stranded in Soda Canyon. Cather responded to this country somewhat as a New World substitute for France, particularly Provence; before the writing of this novel, as if by incremental repetition, her French and Southwestern experiences had formed an alternating pattern in her life and art, each adding to and influencing the other. Before his crisis Professor St. Peter associates Notre Dame in Paris with the "sculptured peaks and impossible mountain passes" of the American Southwest.

Cather revealed in a 1938 letter why she inserted "Tom Outland's Story" between the sections of the novel depicting the professor's family drama:

> I tried to make Professor St. Peter's house rather overcrowded and stuffy with . . . American proprieties, clothes, furs, petty ambitions, quivering jealousies— until one got rather stifled. Then I wanted to open the square window and let in the fresh air that blew off the Blue Mesa [Mesa Verde], and the fine disregard of trivialities which was in Tom Outland's face and in his behaviour.

She attributed the experiment, which amounts to interrupting a Jamesian novel with a cowboy adventure, to an exhibit she attended in Paris of Dutch paintings showing interiors, "drawing-rooms or kitchens," relieved by windows opening out on stretches of gray sea.

The "interiors" in *The Professor's House* depict an academic out of love with his wife, out of sympathy with his adult daughters, and out of sync with his university. His wife and daughters seem to have capitulated to gimmicks, careerism, social climbing, and bickering; and his university is becoming a business school. Professor St. Peter's means of survival had been his scholarly histories of Spanish conquests in the Americas, but now his work is done, and life around him is proving insupportable. Of the two people in his life who represent other values, one, Tom Outland, exists only in memory, and the other—the family seamstress, Augusta—is hardly taken seriously at first. This woman, a devout Catholic, is really the only religious person in the professor's world. He teases her about her church activities, but the teasing develops a serious edge; he is curious about her devotion to the Blessed Virgin and questions her about the Magnificat, Mary's canticle of acceptance of her role in the Incarnation. Augusta's presence seems to influence the professor's thinking, for quite early in the novel, in responding to a student, he condemns his own scientific century as inferior to the age of faith: science merely distracts people of this age "away from the real"—that is, "insoluble"— problems and demystifies life:

# O PIONEERS!

A stirring romance of the Western prairies, embodying a new idea and a new country. There are two heroines, — the splendid Swedish girl, Alexandra, who dares and achieves, and the beautiful Bohemian whose love story is the very story of Youth. It is only by a happy chance that a creature so warm and palpitating with life is ever enticed into the pages of a novel.

## By Willa Sibert Cather

*Dust jacket for Cather's 1913 novel about a woman's promise to her father to look after her brothers and the family farm after his death*

I don't think you help people by making their conduct of no importance—you impoverish them. As long as every man and woman who crowded into the cathedrals on Easter Sunday was a principle in a gorgeous drama with God, life was a rich thing. And that's what makes men happy, believing in the mystery and importance of their own individual lives.

"Tom Outland's Story" compounds the professor's problems while relieving readers from the stuffiness of his world. The mesa story celebrating a pre-Christian pueblo community becomes the record of a tribe defeated by its admirable qualities, and Tom's efforts to preserve that record are frustrated by greed and broken friendship. Reminded of these defeats in recalling Tom's telling the story, St. Peter simply wants to die. The religious theme in the first section intensifies in the third section in a near-death experience remarkably similar to sick-soul conversion as described in William James's *The Varieties of Religious Experience* (1902) and Leo Tolstoy's *My Confession* (1879–1882), large blocks of which James included in his text. Significantly, when the professor awakens to new life, Augusta is sitting near him reading a prayer book. She had dragged him from his gas-filled study after his stove failed. He appreciates having this woman with him and suddenly senses an obligation to humanity relative to her: "He even felt a sense of obligation toward her," and there was "a world full of Augustas." This sense alleviates the frustration the unregenerated man felt within his family, that "something" he had "let go" during his "temporary release from consciousness." Cather describes a grace experience, although grace remains "the thing not named," for the professor's world is secular. E. K. Brown and Leon Edel, writing in *Willa Cather: A Critical Biography* (1953), recognized that "by the problems it elaborates, and by the atmosphere in which they are enveloped, *The Professor's House* is a religious novel."

The direction of Cather's career becomes clear in *My Mortal Enemy* (1926), a brief first-person narrative pushing the principles of "The Novel Demeuble" to an extreme degree. *My Mortal Enemy* is Cather's first novel dominated by a religious theme and employing an explicitly religious resolution. Myra Driscoll Henshawe, who is never really fathomed by the impressionable young woman who tells her story, broke with her wealthy Irish Catholic uncle and her church to elope with a freethinker who infatuated her. She left her Illinois town to settle in New York, where her artistic and intellectual friends cushion her growing dissatisfaction with her marriage and the probable infidelity of her husband, Oswald. Years later, crippled, impoverished, and living in a flimsy apartment hotel in a California city, Myra turns against her husband, whom she now refers to as her mortal enemy. Myra's crucifixion involves her dependence on this enemy and recognition that because of him she had once rejected the charity now being offered through him. The challenge is compounded by Myra's awareness that the help being offered is not intended by Oswald for his dying wife but for someone like "the mother of the girl who ran away with [him]." This situation demands surrender of self on Myra's part; the grace to comply is offered her during a visit to a Pacific headland topped by a twisted cedar, a symbol of the cross, as the setting sun beats down on Myra like a burning-glass. "I'd love to see this place at dawn," she exclaims. "That is always such a forgiving time . . . it's as if all our sins were pardoned, as if the sky leaned over the earth and kissed it and gave it absolution." Although Myra returns to the headland to die, it is without the narrator, and so the reader never knows if she lives to see the dawn. She has, however, confessed her sins to a priest and taken Commun-

ion. In this novel Cather bares the stage for the descent of the Spirit and puts the mystery of grace beyond the narrator's vision and the reader's.

Cather now turned to nineteenth-century New Mexican history for the story of the two French missionary priests she fictionalized as the protagonists in *Death Comes for the Archbishop* (1927), undisputedly her masterpiece. The work combines her favorite settings; it is her one primarily Southwestern novel, but its protagonists gave her the opportunity to set several scenes in France. The result is both international and multicultural: the French priests, laden with memories of their native Auvergne, must contend with the Southwestern desert as they try to shepherd Hispanic, Pueblo, and Navajo peoples responding to the yoke of U.S. occupation after the Mexican War. As if to emphasize such universality, Cather begins in Rome with a group of bishops and cardinals discussing the far-flung affairs of a church reeling from insurrections generated by Italian unification.

In a 1927 letter to *The Commonweal* after the book was reviewed, Cather explained that the longer she stayed in the Southwest, "the more [she] felt that the story of the Catholic Church in that country was the most interesting of all its stories." Inspired by the old mission churches, "the utterly unconventional frescoes, the countless fanciful figures of the saints," she returned to the area as often as she could. Although "the story of the Church and the Spanish missionaries was always what most interested me," she wrote, it "was certainly the business of some Catholic writer, and not mine at all." However, she became fascinated by the life of Archbishop Lamy, the first bishop of New Mexico, whose statue stands outside the cathedral he built. Then she discovered Father Joseph Howlett's obscure 1908 diocesan biography of Joseph Machebeuf, Lamy's vicar and later the first bishop of Denver. Howlett's book was "as much about Lamy as about Father Machebeuf, since the two men were so closely associated from early youth." Howlett suggested an approach to the Southwest, since he peppered his book with Machebeuf's letters to his sister Anne, Sister Marie Philomene of the Visitation Convent in Riom, France. Through these letters Cather "found out what [she] wanted to know about how the country and the people of New Mexico seemed to those first missionary priests from France." Howlett's book helped her write about the Southwest from a French perspective, as she herself had viewed it in 1912, when, in letters to Sergeant, she compared the country around Albuquerque to southern France.

In the novel, which transforms Jean Baptiste Lamy into Bishop Jean Marie Latour and Joseph Priest Machebeuf into Father Joseph Vaillant, Cather dramatizes the worldview longed for by Professor St. Peter, one in which men and women participate in a cosmic drama of "glittering angels" and "shadows of evil." Since *Death Comes for the Archbishop* is a novel of evangelism, it presents a hurdle for nonbelieving readers unable to suspend their disbelief in the truth of the Christian message embodied in this work in a cathedral of native stone fashioned in the Romanesque style. Cather suggested her intention in a letter to her agent on 26 April 1926, when she was halfway through her novel: her subject, she says, concerns the French missionaries sent to New Mexico to bring order out of the chaos of Indian, Spanish, and Mexican superstitions. The many sources supplementing Howlett–historical, cultural, and biographical studies by Charles Lummis, Ralph Twitchell, Adolph Bandelier, Hubert Bancroft, Francisco Palou, J. B. Salpointe, and many others–were primarily Anglo, and she used them freely, at times even cavalierly. Cather "knew exactly what material she needed in order to write the story as she wanted to write it," Lewis writes, "and she seemed to draw it out of everything she encountered–from the people she talked with . . . ; from old books she found in the various libraries in Santa Fe . . . ; and from the country itself."

Cather seemed unaware of the controversial nature of her subject, although there are indications that she sensed its resistance to the mold she was using to shape it–as if the native stones in Lamy's cathedral were pressing against its Romanesque design. Sergeant refers to a crisis Cather once experienced during a visit to the pueblo of Santo Domingo, when she suddenly began to fear she was losing civilization: "Panic seized her–it said the West is consuming you, make tracks for home." In the novel, Latour experiences such a crisis twice–while saying mass at Acoma and during the night he spends with his Indian guide in Stone Lips cave. In the first instance, the Christian liturgy seems incapable of embracing the dark mystery of Indian life; in the second case, Latour recites the Paternoster, or the Lord's Prayer, to delay the lapse of control that later overtakes him and causes him to remember the cave "with horror." In her perceptive review of *Death Comes for the Archbishop* in the "Books" section of the *New York Herald Tribune* (11 September 1927), Rebecca West used this cave scene to compare Cather and D. H. Lawrence in their "daring" toward the unknown: "while he would have been through the wall after the snake . . . [and] the crack in the floor after the river," she stays outside with the bishop the whole time. West defines Cather's handling of darkness within the religious contexts of the story as an aesthetic antidote to the literature of annihilation being demanded by younger readers, a demand

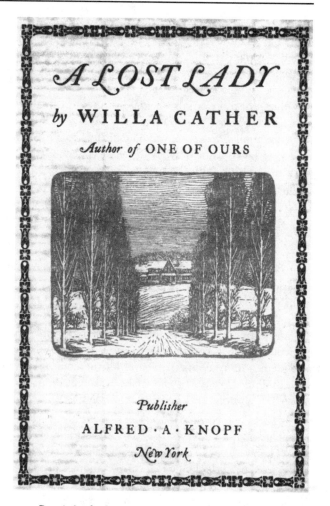

*Dust jacket for Cather's 1923 novel, about the social decline of a Western woman*

she labels as "pernicious" because it "deftly extracts all meaning out of life."

Having seen her most successful novel through publication, Cather planned to vacation in France in fall 1927, but both her elation and her travel plans ended when her father suffered a heart attack in August and died the following March. Before Christmas 1928 her mother suffered a paralytic stroke and then lingered in a sanatorium in Pasadena, California, near her son Douglass's home, until her death in the summer of 1931. The upheaval of this period was compounded for Cather when her apartment house in New York was demolished for a new building. With the Red Cloud house closed and little reason left for returning to Nebraska–she made her final visit during Christmas 1931–Cather became more dependent on her refuges in the Northeast. These places included Jaffrey, New Hampshire, where she had done much of her writing since 1917, and Grand Manan Island, New Brunswick, in the Bay of Fundy, in southeastern Canada, where she rented a cottage in 1922 and eventually built a house. In 1928 "Grand Manan seemed the only foothold left on earth," writes Lewis, as she explains how, on their way there by train in July, Cather got the idea for her next novel, *Shadows on the Rock* (1931). The two women spent an unplanned stopover of ten days in Quebec City after Lewis came down with the flu. When Cather "looked down . . . on the pointed roofs and Norman outlines of the town of Quebec, [she] was . . . overwhelmed by the flood of memory, recognition, surmise it called up; by the sense of its extraordinarily French character, isolated and kept intact through hundreds of years, as if by a miracle, on this great un-French continent." Not only had Cather discovered France in North America but also a French province culturally and religiously proximate to the Middle Ages. Cather now began to pore over Francis Parkman's Canadian histories and many other works; met with historian Abbe H. A. Scott, who was contributing to the "Makers of Canada" series; and became familiar with the countryside surrounding the city. In effect, she was repeating the process of writing *Death Comes for the Archbishop*.

The Quebec of *Shadows on the Rock* historically anticipates Latour's New Mexico by almost two centuries. The work, as Cather wrote in 1931 to Wilbur Cross, constructs "a kind of culture," "another age," "a kind of feeling about life and human fate." In her letter Cather envisions the rock of Quebec as a "stronghold" and "the curious endurance" of a particular worldview, one illustrated in her novel as starkly medieval and echoing the prescriptions set down by St. Augustine in the *City of God* (413–426/427). Augustine defines a shadow city on earth with citizens on pilgrimage to and in fellowship with the city of saints in heaven. Because Cather envisions Quebec as a prophetic image of the heavenly city, its citizens—heroic nursing and school sisters, missionary martyrs, ecclesiastical and government officials, woodsmen, and merchants—must act the part of the spiritual realities they, as mere shadows, represent. Cather uses history selectively: "An orderly little French household that went on trying to live decently . . . interests me more than Indian raids or the wild life in the forests," she told Cross. The cohesive center of the novel is the father-daughter relationship of widower Euclide Auclair, Count Frontenac's apothecary, and his twelve-year-old daughter, Cecile, intended by Cather to memorialize her own relationship with her father. Auclair has the recessive traits of Charles Cather, and Cecile, who is as dutiful as Cather might have wished she had been, wears "her brown hair shingled like a boy's."

The components of the novel work toward the splendor of the heavenly city, toward those realities manifest in the nuns' "well-ordered universe." God is the cause and center of this universe, having created the earth as the stage of his dramatic encounter with humanity, which Cather refers to as "a great purpose," making the sun "to light [this stage] by day, the moon . . . to light it by night,—and the stars . . . to beautify the vault of heaven like frescoes." It is all "lovingly arranged" and "congenial" and "safe." Quebec as altar and church are consistent themes. During the winter, "the whole rock ["of shivering spires"] looked like one great white church, above the frozen river"; in the June sunrise, "the rock of Kebec stood gleaming above the river like an altar with many candles, or like a holy city in an old legend, shriven, sinless, washed in gold." The contained and orderly picture resembles Giotto di Bondone's *The Last Judgment* (1305–1306) in the Arena Chapel of Padua, in which a seated Christ links the heavenly city above and the earthly domain below. Augustine writes that the shadow city on earth "gave birth to Christ himself in the flesh"; thus, Cather's opening description compares Quebec to "a theatric scene of the Nativity." A major episode in the second book is the Christmas celebration, when Cecile and Jacques, the waif child she fosters, set up the creche from France on terraces recalling the rocky ledges in the opening description of the novel. Creating and inhabiting so secure and comfortable a world as this one was therapeutic for Cather, "a sort of continuation, in a different key," writes Lewis, "of the Catholic theme which had absorbed her so for two years, and which still lingered in her thoughts after the completion of the *Archbishop*. . . ." It also gave Cather an excuse to return to France to visit Frontenac's old quarter of Paris and St. Malo, the Breton city from which many Quebec colonists had ventured to the New World. Coming on the coattails of *Death Comes for the Archbishop*, *Shadows on the Rock* enjoyed the greatest sales of any of Cather's novels.

After collecting reminiscences of family and Nebraska friends in *Obscure Destinies* (1932) and completing the somewhat frivolous love story of Lucy Gayheart, which she tired of writing, Cather began the closure of her career with two writing projects, only one of which she lived to complete. That work, *Sapphira and the Slave Girl* (1940), set in motion perhaps by the death of her parents, took her back to Virginia in 1938. Lewis describes the journey as "thrilling" and compares it to their journeys to New Mexico. Cather filtered her birthplace and the scenes of her childhood through her earliest memories and was intensely responsive to the landscape. "Every bud and leaf and flower seemed to speak to her with a peculiar poignancy," Lewis recalls, "every slope of the land, every fence and wall, rock and stream." Cather set her novel in 1856 in Back Creek Valley, near Winchester, an area then split into factions over the issue of slavery, and dramatized corresponding tensions within a slave-owning family, the Colberts. The matriarch and her husband were drawn from Cather's maternal great-grandparents, and their rebellious abolitionist daughter, from her maternal grandmother, Rachel Boak, after whom the character Rachel Blake was named. Although the mother and daughter are alienated when the latter helps one of her mother's slaves escape, the novel reflects the religious bent of Cather's fiction at this time by transforming into a story of forgiveness after one of Rachel's daughters dies in a diphtheria epidemic. In the epilogue, years after the Civil War has ended, Cather herself enters the novel to narrate in the first person the reunion of former slave girl Nancy and her mother. Cather explained in a letter that in the novel her end was her beginning, meaning that in old age she was evoking her earliest memories of Virginia.

The unfinished project would have completed Cather's long-impending break with the American continent. Lewis traces the genesis of this work to their 1935 visit to the Papal Palace at Avignon, the building that had stirred the youthful Cather during her 1902 European tour. As the two women wandered through the great white chambers, a guide began to sing in a voice that echoed under the arches "like a great bell sounding . . . from some remote past; its vibrations seemed laden . . . with the passions of another age–cruelties, splendours, lost and unimaginable to us in our time." Lewis "thought that Willa Cather wished to make her story like this song." The story, called "Hard Punishments" as its working title, was set in Avignon during the reign of Pope Benedict XIII (1334–1342) and concerned two young friends mutilated under medieval justice for petty crimes. A central scene Lewis remembered as "moving" involved one of the boys being comforted by a priest confessor. "Just what Cather intended to do with this relationship is not known," writes Woodress. Lewis carried out Cather's wishes and destroyed the unfinished work after Cather died.

A few finished stories left unpublished when Cather died in New York on 24 April 1947 were published the following year under the title *The Old Beauty and Others*. One of these stories, "The Best Years," is almost a religious allegory memorializing the Cather family when all the children lived together at home; the title story, drawing on Cather's visits to Aix-les-Bains and the Grande Chartreuse monastery, condemns the Jazz Age; the final story, "Before Break-

BY WILLA CATHER

Death comes for the Archbishop

· ALFRED A KNOPF ·                · NEW YORK ·

*Dust jacket for Cather's 1927 novel, about French Catholic missionaries in New Mexico after the Mexican War*

fast," set on Grand Manan, concerns an aging and alienated businessman and recalls *The Professor's House*. Cather's response to nature on the island gives this story a vitality the other two lack and manages to be almost optimistic. The midlife crisis of Henry Grenfell is relieved as he watches a young woman brave the icy Atlantic for a morning swim. Grenfell chuckles to himself that when the first "amphibious frog-toad found his water-hole dried up, and jumped out to . . . find another well, he started on a long hop." Cather seems to be hinting that humanity has a future after all, if only for the younger generation.

Surviving a long period of relative critical neglect by academics, Willa Cather's fiction has now assured her a place in the American canon as a major novelist unqualified by such tags as "female," "Western," or even "twentieth-century." Each of her novels responds to different technical challenges, and the elegant clarity of their style remains unsurpassed. Cather's themes, hardly confined to pioneering in the West, are as universal and perhaps even more varied than those of the greatest novelists.

**Letters and Interviews:**

*Willa Cather in Person: Interviews, Speeches, and Letters,* edited by L. Brent Bohlke (Lincoln & London: University of Nebraska Press, 1986).

**Bibliographies:**

Jo Anna Lathrop, *Willa Cather: A Checklist of Her Published Writings* (Lincoln: University of Nebraska Press, 1975);

Joan Crane, *Willa Cather: A Bibliography* (Lincoln: University of Nebraska Press, 1982);

Marilyn Arnold, *Willa Cather: A Reference Guide* (Boston: G. K. Hall, 1986).

**Biographies:**

Mildred R. Bennett, *The World of Willa Cather* (New York: Dodd, Mead, 1951; revised, with notes and index, Lincoln: University of Nebraska Press, 1970);

E. K. Brown and Leon Edel, *Willa Cather: A Critical Biography* (New York: Knopf, 1953);

Edith Lewis, *Willa Cather Living* (New York: Knopf, 1953; Lincoln: University of Nebraska Press, 2000);

Elizabeth Shepley Sergeant, *Willa Cather: A Memoir* (Philadelphia: Lippincott, 1953; Lincoln: University of Nebraska Press, 1963);

Sharon O'Brien, *Willa Cather: The Emerging Voice* (New York & Oxford: Oxford University Press, 1987);

James Woodress, *Willa Cather: A Literary Life* (Lincoln & London: University of Nebraska Press, 1987);

Hermione Lee, *Willa Cather: Double Lives* (New York: Pantheon, 1990).

**References:**

Joan Acocella, "Cather and the Academy," *New Yorker,* 72 (27 November 1995): 56–71;

Marilyn Arnold, *Willa Cather's Short Fiction* (Athens: Ohio University Press, 1984);

Edward A. Bloom and Lillian D. Bloom, *Willa Cather's Gift of Sympathy* (Carbondale: Southern Illinois University Press, 1962);

Harold Bloom, ed., *Modern Critical Views: Willa Cather* (New York: Chelsea House, 1985);

Deborah Carlin, *Cather, Canon, and the Politics of Reading* (Amherst: University of Massachusetts Press, 1992);

Leon Edel, "A Cave of One's Own," in his *Stuff of Sleep and Dreams: Experiments in Literary Psychology* (New York: Harper & Row, 1982), pp. 216–240;

Blanche H. Gelfant, "The Forgotten Reaping-Hook: Sex in *My Ántonia,*" *American Literature,* 43 (March 1971): 60–82;

Gelfant, "Movement and Melody: The Disembodiment of Lucy Gayheart," in her *Women Writing in America* (Hanover, N.H.: University Press of New England, 1984), pp. 117–143;

Philip Gerber, *Willa Cather,* revised edition (Boston: Twayne, 1995);

Richard Giannone, *Music in Willa Cather's Fiction* (Lincoln: University of Nebraska Press, 1966);

David Harrell, *From Mesa Verde to The Professor's House* (Albuquerque: University of New Mexico Press, 1992);

Granville Hicks, "The Case Against Willa Cather," *English Journal,* 22 (November 1933): 703–710;

Evelyn Helmick Hively, *Sacred Fire: Willa Cather's Novel Cycle* (Lanham, Md.: University Press of America, 1994);

Clinton Keeler, "Narrative without Accent: Willa Cather and Puvis de Chavannes," *American Quarterly,* 17 (Spring 1965): 119–126;

Sinclair Lewis, "The Greatest American Novelist," *Newsweek,* 11 (3 January 1938): 29;

John March, *A Reader's Companion to the Fiction of Willa Cather,* edited by Marilyn Arnold (Westport, Conn.: Greenwood Press, 1993);

Terence Martin, "The Drama of Memory in *My Ántonia,*" *PMLA,* 84 (March 1969): 304–311;

Jo Ann Middleton, *Willa Cather's Modernism: A Study of Style and Technique* (Rutherford, N.J.: Fairleigh Dickinson University Press, 1990);

John J. Murphy, "The Modernist Conversion of Willa Cather's Professor," in *The Calvinist Roots of the Modern Era,* edited by Aliki Barnstone and others (Hanover, N.H.: University Press of New England, 1997), pp. 53–72;

Murphy, *My Ántonia: The Road Home* (Boston: Twayne, 1989);

Murphy, ed., *Critical Essays on Willa Cather* (Boston: G. K. Hall, 1984);

Murphy, ed., *Willa Cather: Family, Community, and History (The Brigham Young University Symposium)* (Provo, Utah: Brigham Young University Press, 1990);

Margaret A. O'Connor, "A Guide to the Letters of Willa Cather," *Resources for American Literary Study,* 4 (Autumn 1974): 145–172;

John H. Randall III, *The Landscape and the Looking Glass: Willa Cather's Search for Values* (Boston: Houghton Mifflin, 1960);

Rene Rapin, *Willa Cather* (New York: McBride, 1930);

Phyllis Rose, "Modernism: The Case of Willa Cather," in *Modernism Reconsidered,* edited by Robert Kiely (Cambridge, Mass.: Harvard University Press, 1983), pp. 123–145;

Susan J. Rosowski, *The Voyage Perilous: Willa Cather's Romanticism* (Lincoln: University of Nebraska Press, 1986);

Rosowski, ed., *Approaches to Teaching My Ántonia* (New York: Modern Language Association, 1989);

Rosowski, ed., *Cather Studies 1* (Lincoln: University of Nebraska Press, 1990);

Rosowski, ed., *Cather Studies 2* (Lincoln: University of Nebraska Press, 1993);

Rosowski, ed., *Cather Studies 3* (Lincoln; University of Nebraska Press, 1996);

James Schroeter, ed., *Willa Cather and Her Critics* (Ithaca, N.Y.: Cornell University Press, 1967);

Jean Schwind, "The Benda Illustrations to *My Ántonia*: Cather's 'Silent' Supplement to Jim Burden's Narrative," *PMLA*, 100 (January 1985): 51–67;

Steven B. Shively, "'A Full, Perfect, and Sufficient Sacrifice': Eucharistic Imagery in Cather's *The Song of the Lark*," *Literature and Belief*, 14 (1994): 73–86;

Merrill Maguire Skaggs, *After the World Broke in Two: The Later Novels of Willa Cather* (Charlottesville: University Press of Virginia, 1990);

Bernice Slote and Virginia Faulkner, eds., *The Art of Willa Cather*, centennial seminar papers (Lincoln: University of Nebraska Press, 1974);

D. H. Stewart, "Cather's Mortal Comedy," *Queen's Quarterly*, 73 (Summer 1966): 244–259;

David Stouck and Janet Giltrow, "Willa Cather and a Grammar for Things 'Not Named,'" *Style*, 26 (Spring 1992): 90–113;

Stouck, "Willa Cather and the Indian Heritage," *Twentieth Century Literature*, 22 (December 1976): 433–443;

Stouck, *Willa Cather's Imagination* (Lincoln: University of Nebraska Press, 1975);

Erik Ingvar Thurin, *The Humanization of Willa Cather: Classicism in an American Classic* (Lund, Sweden: Lund University Press, 1990);

Lionel Trilling, "Willa Cather," *New Republic*, 90 (10 February 1937): 10–13;

Joseph Urgo, *Willa Cather and the Myth of American Migration* (Champaign: University of Illinois Press, 1995);

Dorothy Van Ghent, *Willa Cather* (Minneapolis: University of Minnesota Press, 1964);

Loretta Wasserman, *Willa Cather: A Study of the Short Fiction* (Boston: Twayne, 1991);

Rebecca West, "Miss Cather's Business as an Artist," essay review of *Death Comes for the Archbishop*, *New York Herald Tribune Books*, 52 (11 September 1927): 1, 5–6.

**Papers:**

Willa Cather materials are housed in various locations throughout the United States, including the Huntington, Morgan, and Newberry libraries; Columbia, Harvard, Indiana, Vermont, Virginia, and Yale universities; the Nebraska State Historical Society, Lincoln, and the Willa Cather Historical Center, Red Cloud, Nebraska. Perhaps the most comprehensive collection is in the Love Library at the University of Nebraska, Lincoln. Because of legal restrictions, all but a few public letters are uncollected and unpublished.

# Bernard DeVoto

*(11 January 1897 – 13 November 1955)*

Russell Burrows
*Weber State University*

See also the DeVoto entry in *DLB 9: American Novelists, 1910–1945.*

BOOKS: *The Crooked Mile* (New York: Minton, Balch, 1924);

*The Chariot of Fire* (New York: Macmillan, 1926);

*The House of Sun-Goes-Down* (New York: Macmillan, 1928);

*Mark Twain's America* (Boston: Little, Brown, 1932);

*We Accept with Pleasure* (Boston: Little, Brown, 1934);

*Forays and Rebuttals* (Boston: Little, Brown, 1936);

*Minority Report* (Boston: Little, Brown, 1940);

*Mark Twain at Work* (Cambridge, Mass.: Harvard University Press, 1942);

*The Year of Decision: 1846* (London: Eyre & Spottiswoode, 1942; Boston: Little, Brown, 1943);

*The Literary Fallacy* (Boston: Little, Brown, 1944);

*Mountain Time* (Boston: Little, Brown, 1947);

*Across the Wide Missouri* (New York: Houghton Mifflin, 1947; London: Eyre & Spottiswoode, 1948);

*The Hour* (Boston: Houghton Mifflin, 1951);

*The Course of Empire* (Boston: Houghton Mifflin, 1952); republished as *Westward the Course of Empire* (London: Eyre & Spottiswoode, 1953);

*The Easy Chair* (Boston: Houghton Mifflin, 1955).

OTHER: *The Writer's Handbook,* edited by DeVoto, W. F. Bryan, and Arthur Nethercot (New York: Macmillan, 1927);

*The Life and Adventures of James P. Beckwourth,* edited by DeVoto, Americana Deserta Series (New York: Knopf, 1931);

Samuel Langhorne Clemens (Mark Twain), *Letters from the Earth,* edited by DeVoto (New York: Harper, 1938);

Clemens, *The Adventures of Tom Sawyer,* edited by DeVoto (Cambridge, Mass.: Limited Editions Club at the University Press, 1939);

Clemens, *Mark Twain in Eruption: Hitherto Unpublished Pages about Men and Events,* edited by DeVoto (New York & London: Harper, 1940);

*Bernard DeVoto*

Clemens, *The Adventures of Huckleberry Finn (Tom Sawyer's Companion),* edited by DeVoto (New York: Limited Editions Club, 1942);

Clemens, *The Portable Mark Twain,* edited by DeVoto (New York: Viking, 1946);

Meriwether Lewis, *The Journals of Lewis and Clark,* edited by DeVoto (Boston: Houghton Mifflin, 1953; London: Eyre & Spottiswoode, 1954).

SELECTED PERIODICAL PUBLICATIONS–
UNCOLLECTED: "Utah," *American Mercury,* 7
(March 1926): 317–323;

"The Mountain Men," *American Mercury,* 9 (December
1926): 472–479;

"The Great Medicine Road," *American Mercury,* 11 (May
1927): 104–112;

"Footnote on the West," *Harper's,* 155 (November
1927): 713–722;

"Fossil Remnants of the Frontier: Notes on a Utah Boyhood," *Harper's,* 170 (April 1935): 590–600;

"Notes on the Red Parnassus," *Harper's,* 173 (July
1936): 221–224;

"Bernard DeVoto Answers a Polite Complaint," *Saturday Review of Literature,* 13 (February 1937): 8, 20.


In *Minority Report* (1940), a collection of his essays,
Bernard DeVoto admitted that he most enjoyed talking
with Robert Frost and Elmer Davis–eminent in the
field of literature and journalism, respectively–because
with them the obstreperous DeVoto at least had to
define his terms. Indeed, on those occasions when
DeVoto and Davis talked over a few bottles of beer,
they were apt to turn boastful and speak candidly. In
such instances Davis claimed that his "spread" was
wider because he had written a book about God,
whereas DeVoto had not. DeVoto countered that he
may as well have written a book on God because of the
thesis he had written on Immanuel Kant. What was
more, DeVoto had composed verse, whereas Davis had
not. Like bandits brandishing knives, the two would
then attack each other's bibliographies, and when the
sport became really rough, Davis would remind
DeVoto of his submissions to the *New Republic*–a
reminder that was akin to a boxer's hitting low.
DeVoto's admission to having works published in the
same magazine that he criticized for being a Marxist rag
was owning up to a lot.

Nonetheless, the competition did not end with
bibliography, for there was the matter of DeVoto's
pseudonym. Under the name of John August, DeVoto
had written–for certain women's magazines–fiction
that could be called "steamy-and-between-the-sheets."
DeVoto's reason for writing as August was a necessity
for money, so August was not above dashing off formulaic pulp. DeVoto craved that margin of time that
money can buy a man. On the other hand, when writing under his own name, DeVoto transformed himself
into a columnist and an historian of unsurpassed ability.
For twenty years he wrote "The Easy Chair," a regular
column in *Harper's.* At the apex of his career DeVoto's
writings won him both the Bancroft and Pulitzer prizes
in history in 1948 for *Across the Wide Missouri* (1947) and

the 1952 National Book Award in nonfiction for *The
Course of Empire* (1952).

These achievements make most people believe
that they have "arrived" in their careers. Yet, DeVoto
was peculiar in that despite his accolades he never
stopped apologizing for being from Utah–which on his
social map always remained well beyond the reach of
civilization. An Eastern gentlewoman once asked
DeVoto: "How did people live in Utah?" and the innocent question roused him so much that he worked up
his answer into the exposé "Utah" for the March 1926
issue of H. L. Mencken's *American Mercury.* By every
rhetorical device DeVoto could think of–both fair and
foul–he said repeatedly that life in Utah was, and probably always would be, "honestly rude."

Part of that roughness had simply to do with
Utah achieving statehood only one year before
DeVoto's birth. Bernard Augustine DeVoto was born
on 11 January 1897 to Florian Bernard, a teacher of
mathematics, and Rhoda Dye DeVoto in Ogden, Utah.
Florian and Rhoda came from different religious back-
grounds–he was raised Catholic, while she came from a
Mormon family. Although both parents were "backslid-
ers" from their respective churches, they sent their son
to the Mormon Sunday school and later to grammar
school at the Sisters of the Sacred Heart Academy.
Essentially a microcosm of the religious dissension in
Utah society at large, the division of faiths in young
Bernard's home affected him detrimentally, leading
DeVoto as an adult to view his provenance in a negative
way.

The exposure to two different religions was actually a parental attempt to guide their son toward conversion but had the unintended effect of producing an
agnostic. Even as a youngster, DeVoto settled religious
conflict by adhering to no faith. Beyond the perfunc-
tory duties he sometimes accepted as an altar boy, he
never took his Catholic baptism seriously at all. On the
other hand, although he experimented with Mormonism as an adolescent, he did nothing that would embar-
rass him in adulthood. DeVoto shares an experimental
incident in an essay for *Harper's,* "Fossil Remnants of
the Frontier: Notes on a Utah Boyhood" (April 1935).
When he was a student at Ogden High School, some
student leaders expressed their wish to have one of the
Mormon apostles as a commencement speaker. In
response the young DeVoto invoked the separation of
church and state by nominating a different person. He
sided with students who wanted Jesus Christ to address
the graduates, thus making his point. DeVoto's story
illustrates the kind of religious skirmish that has been
commonplace in Utah.

That such an iconoclast would break with Utah
was inevitable. In 1915, when DeVoto was a freshman

*DeVoto's wife, Avis, and their sons, Mark and Gordon, in 1940*

at the University of Utah in Salt Lake City, two English professors—one of whom had been DeVoto's teacher—were fired. Many suspected the firings were the result of the Mormon Church flexing its censorious muscles, and in protest fifteen other faculty members resigned. The university president, for his part, seemed curiously incapable of alleviating the escalating tensions, and word of what was going on eventually moved eastward, prompting an investigation by the American Association of University Professors (AAUP). The AAUP ended their inquiry by blacklisting the school, an action that forced the president's resignation. In support of the faculty, DeVoto himself withdrew from the university, which he had begun calling an "alleged institution." With resolve and self-confidence he applied to Harvard University, and after somehow raking together the tuition, DeVoto set off by train to Boston.

At Harvard, DeVoto affected the role of the wild man of the West. Even as he quaffed great draughts of Eastern culture, he found that he could turn his colorful Western antecedents to his advantage. That he had shouldered a rifle and had gone "plinking" for snakes and badgers in the foothills above Ogden commanded a fair amount of respect at Harvard. Bookishness was considered boring at the Ivy League school, whereas the big, active, outdoor life of the West riveted everyone's attention. In reality DeVoto had been a bookish kid back in Utah: he was a teacher's pet, had haunted his town's Carnegie Free Library, had clerked for a bookstore, and had even tried his hand at a column or two for *The Standard Evening Examiner*—all of which he did to convince himself and others that he was much more than the stereotypically illiterate, boorish Westerner.

DeVoto soon developed into an eastern Westerner, a paradox that is crucial to understanding his subsequent life and career. His perusal of the superb regional collections of the Widener Library at Harvard teased out the more colorful parts of his Western identity, intensifying the paradox. DeVoto's bibliomania quickly found its way into his writing, and in short order he made himself into a virtually unassailable authority on the West. Yet, because he wielded this authority from the distance of Cambridge, Massachusetts, interest in the West remained largely, and almost necessarily, academic.

The paradox of being both an academic and a novelist defines DeVoto to a great extent. His academic predilections arguably hurt his fiction long before they infused and enhanced his prizewinning history books. Specifically, DeVoto's immense erudition tended to stymie his attempts at authentic dialogue in fiction, since his characters spoke either in a lofty, learned way or aphoristically or in epigrams; many of the characters were simply too witty to be realistic. Quite a few years passed before DeVoto could advise others, as he did the historian Catherine Drinker Bowen. She quotes him in her essay in *Four Portraits and One Subject: Bernard DeVoto* (1963) as confiding that "As we grow older . . . our style becomes simpler, or it should. Age . . . reduces us to the ultimate simplicities." As a young man, however, he was fond of parading his education and upbringing–in all their depth and complexity–through his writing. In Frost's view DeVoto's strong, impressive prose style made him more like "an archer . . . than a pistol man." DeVoto's own considerable ego also swelled his fiction. Whatever the precise reasons were, he never wrote absolutely genuine dialogue, a flaw that regularly elicited complaints from critics.

The manuscript for his first novel was academically motivated, since he had to write it to fulfill an assignment at Harvard. Not one to slouch at studying, DeVoto thought that having a novel "in the works" would gain him some status in his composition courses. Yet, while his ambitious thinking may have helped him succeed in class, his manuscript "Cock Crow" was summarily rejected by Putnam in April 1921. "Cock Crow" was one of only two novel-length works not accepted for publication–although DeVoto later borrowed parts of it to put in his third and fourth published novels.

By the early 1920s DeVoto had served two years in the army during World War I, graduated Phi Beta Kappa from Harvard, and returned to Ogden to teach history at the junior high school and to nurse his dying mother. In 1922 he began a position as an assistant professor of English at Northwestern University in Evanston, Illinois, and on 30 June 1923 he married Helen Avis MacVicar, known as Avis, formerly his student.

They had two sons, Gordon King DeVoto and Mark Bernard DeVoto.

DeVoto's first published novel came out in 1924. *The Crooked Mile,* perhaps of all his fiction, brought him his finest critical moment; the reviews were positive, as the Chicago papers praised his work nearly without reservation. The novel, however, did not sell well–fiction about academics and their schoolyard capers seldom have much appeal with general readers. *The Crooked Mile* follows its protagonist, Gordon Abbey, through improbable success at Harvard and then into a precipitous depression upon his return home to the West. The oppressive family legacy of his father and grandfather, both of whom had turned their backs on the spirit of the pioneers by exploiting the land for quick profits, disturbs Abbey when he moves back to his hometown of Windsor. Abbey's poor understanding of this legacy complicates the action further and causes him to turn his frustrations inward. Eventually drawing on an inner strength derived from his years of learning, Abbey leaves a menial job laboring as part of a railroad gang, puts an end to his dalliance with a shallow woman, and at last finds the impetus that spurs him.

Significantly, in light of the studies in Western history that DeVoto wrote after *The Crooked Mile,* the author does not have Abbey reform himself nor Windsor on his own. DeVoto suggests that history comes to Abbey's aid–in the form of another central character, John Gale, a trained historian who mentors Abbey through the process of reformation. Abbey starts down the path of change by discovering all of the wrongs his forefathers have perpetrated against the land. DeVoto's academic tendencies are especially present in Gale. While the character of an activist historian may have been interesting to the author, critics have often singled out Gale's intrusive, didactic voice as the artistic flaw of *The Crooked Mile.*

*The Chariot of Fire,* DeVoto's second novel, appeared in 1926. First titled "The Burning Bush," then "The Great God Boggs," the book entails another "academic" effort by Devoto, because it draws on a specific historical event or movement. *The Chariot of Fire* takes place in the section of Upstate New York often called the "burnt-over district," referring to the millennial culture of religious fanaticism that once flourished there. DeVoto's interest in Upstate New York was unsurprising, since the western tier of the state had spawned the Mormonism that made his "gentile" adolescence in Utah so miserable. The writing of this story also gave him the chance to touch on a few religious splinters, groups of faith such as the Millerites, Campbellites, and Shakers. All of this history seemed promising material for a novel–as it certainly had to William Dean Howells, whose *The Leatherwood God* (1916) featured a simi-

*DeVoto in the 1940s*

of which found enthusiastic readers. While it, too, was based on the same set of notes as the three articles, *The House of Sun-Goes-Down* nonetheless received more criticism than the earlier novels.

After the publication of his third book, DeVoto found himself at a crossroads in his career. Having been in more or less continuous production as a novelist since his undergraduate days, he realized that he had made, at best, an ambiguous impression in the literary world. Not surprisingly, therefore, as DeVoto began to succeed with other kinds of writing—particularly with nonfiction books and essays—several years lapsed before he again attempted fiction. He devoted most of the next two decades, the 1930s and 1940s, to writing and editing magazine articles and essays for some of the major periodicals of the day, to scholarship on Samuel Langhorne Clemens (Mark Twain), and to a multivolume history of the American West.

By 1929 DeVoto had secured work as an instructor and tutor at Harvard and moved up in the mid 1930s to the level of lecturer. He fervently hoped to attain soon the position of professor at the university. At the same time, nevertheless, DeVoto harbored a swelling antipathy to the common deductive practices of scholars in the humanities, a flaw that probably attracted him to journalism. As a journalist DeVoto eschewed the deductive exercises, employing, rather, the inductive method of science. On assignment he commonly assembled, at first, a set of specific instances of a problem and then drew from this set some general conclusion. Such was his conviction in the soundness of his method that he was even willing to go about gathering his facts ad hoc if necessary. For DeVoto, any thesis or theoretical orientation set down in advance of evidence—or any argument introduced a priori of the facts—exemplified the worst sort of fallacy.

In 1935, while he was still lecturing at Harvard, he took over the "Easy Chair" column in *Harper's,* then the oldest continuing column in an American magazine, from Edward S. Martin. The "Easy Chair," however, was not immune from the effects of the Depression, since its subject matter was at odds increasingly with the times. In such a climate, DeVoto might just as well have renamed the column "The Uneasy Chair," which is the title Wallace Stegner selected for his 1974 biography of DeVoto. DeVoto wrote the "Easy Chair" pieces until his death in 1955. For poor pay he served up the requisite 2,650 words each month, enabling him to reach his largest, if not also his most appreciative, audience. As DeVoto often played consumer's advocate in the columns, his readership included a great many consumers of manufactured goods. His readers were also distressed by the "Big Brother" excesses of certain political and government groups: the House Un-American

lar messianic theme. DeVoto evidently set his mark by Howell's novel in an attempt to improve on *The Leatherwood God,* but the reviews for *The Chariot of Fire* ran from lukewarm to unpleasantly cool.

The magnetism of Harvard and New England had drawn DeVoto back to Cambridge by the time he was writing his third novel, *The House of Sun-Goes-Down* (1928). The change in location did not alter his fiction much, however, for he again turned to an event of the past—the Civil War. *The House of Sun-Goes-Down* reflects how much the West was still growing in importance for DeVoto through its story of a group of ruined Southerners escaping westward by train along the Platte River. This route constituted the first leg of the Oregon Trail, which he wrote about in his later scholarly books on history. The seeds for DeVoto's books on the history of the American West took the form of notes that he eventually turned into three essays—"The Mountain Men" (*American Mercury,* December 1926), "The Great Medicine Road" (*American Mercury,* May 1927), and "Footnote on the West" (*Harper's,* November 1927)—all

Activities Committee, the Reece Committee, the Federal Bureau of Investigation (FBI), the Veterans of Foreign Wars, Boston's Watch and Ward Society, and even the Daughters of the American Revolution. DeVoto used his column to criticize these groups for encroaching on the civil liberties of American citizens.

When Harvard failed to offer DeVoto a professorship, he took a job in New York City—a place he disliked almost as much as his hometown of Ogden—as an editor at the *Saturday Review of Literature*. One of the most influential journals of its day, the *Saturday Review of Literature* was founded in 1924 by a Yale professor, Henry Canby, who had also been the driving force behind the Book-of-the-Month Club. By the mid 1930s, however, the magazine had come to an impasse and badly needed a transfusion of funds and capital. The *Saturday Review of Literature* had been fighting, and losing, on two fronts: against both the Great Depression and the literary Marxists.

DeVoto could do little to help the magazine conquer the Depression; indeed, within sixteen months of accepting the job of editor, he himself was out of work. Yet, he did not leave the *Saturday Review of Literature* without attacking the ideological Left and its faith-promoting message of class struggle leading to the perfect society. DeVoto had learned about the "perfected" society from the Mormons, who practice communitarianism, and his independent studies had educated him on virtually every other form of American communism. He did not believe that communitarianism and communism differed much from each other, and he saw scarcely any distinctions among the various forms of communism themselves—at least too few to merit individual treatises on them. As he asserted in an "Easy Chair" column in *Harper's* titled "Notes on the Red Parnassus" (July 1936), Marxism was just one more utopian faith whose believers departed only slightly from "vegetarians, dew-walkers, numerologists, and swamis." In DeVoto's view these supposedly "true" believers held steadfast to their ideas only until something on the order of "wave-mechanics or Zoroastrianism" gave way "to the next fashion." DeVoto used his tenure at the *Saturday Review of Literature* to try to stem the spread of Marxist thinking among the readers of the weekly by injecting his articles with regular doses of reality, reason, common sense, and skeptical caution. His editorial stamp was the full-sized rendition of himself held up as, in his words, a "pluralist, a relativist, an empiricist." He held repeatedly "that behavior of the human race [could not] be accommodated to a syllogism."

In addition to publishing articles and essays in periodicals, DeVoto spent much of the 1930s and 1940s writing and editing scholarly works on Mark Twain. Sinclair Lewis once told DeVoto that, as the greatest critic in the country, he should not try to write novels. No doubt Lewis had in mind the project that kept DeVoto busy during his hiatus from fiction. *Mark Twain's America* (1932) is a work of exposition that shows its author coming demonstrably into his own as a literary critic. DeVoto's analytical approach in the book succeeds in part because of his unusually vigorous style. Indeed, he did not hesitate to hurl invective ad hominem at the critic Van Wyck Brooks in the dedication to the book, which includes the arresting line, "This Essay in the Correction of Ideas." DeVoto was not aiming at ideas, per se, however. He was eager to correct *The Ordeal of Mark Twain* (1920), which Brooks had written and which virtually established a school of thought on Twain that endured until DeVoto's study challenged Brooks's interpretation.

In *The Ordeal of Mark Twain* Brooks suggests that Twain did not realize his artistic potential. The scholar takes a psychoanalytical approach that begins, rather predictably, with the first influence on Twain as a child—his mother, Jane Clemens. Brooks saw Jane as "the embodiment of that old-fashioned, cast-iron Calvinism which had proved so favorable to the life of enterprising action." In Brooks's view, Twain had all too clearly allowed his mother and, later, his wife to coax him toward genteel conventions, just as he had let William Dean Howells and Richard Watson Gilder bowdlerize *The Adventures of Tom Sawyer* (1879) and *The Adventures of Huckleberry Finn* (1884). Even the innocent-sounding pen name "Mark Twain"—when tracked down in the lexicon of the river pilots—meant "safe water," and Brooks understood Twain as always steering for safe water.

Brooks's argument notwithstanding, DeVoto's reading of Twain has proven to be the more imperishable. Relying on common sense, he leveled his criticism at psychoanalysis. In his view the application of psychoanalytical thinking to Twain's life and art seemed "a form of metaphysical autobiography," permitting "its contriver to reconstruct facts in harmony with his prepossessions." In *Mark Twain's America*, DeVoto starts with the simple fact of Twain's huge readership—which arguably reached as far and as wide as Twain traveled. According to DeVoto, Twain combined the raw wit of the people of the Mississippi, of the Sierra Nevada, and of the San Francisco Bay; steeped this collective wit in his own southwestern humor; and then raised the end concoction to the level of art. In his book DeVoto urged Freudian critics to put away their dark theories and, if possible, to "laugh at" Twain's "humor without apology."

In checking the actual record of Twain's life, DeVoto also found that Brooks's reading was often in error. He confounded Brooks's premise about maternal

*DeVoto with students at Radcliffe College in
the summer of 1950*

example, Twain's papers disclosed a scoffing at religion that surpassed belief, intriguing the agnostic in DeVoto. The Mississippi-bred writer carried on his argument with the God of Christianity particularly in sketches–which DeVoto organized under titles such as "Papers of the Adam Family," the "Letter to the Earth," and the remaining "Great Dark" fragments. Eventually, DeVoto at his patient best–a rare side of him–steered Clara around to his side. Greater access to Twain's papers enabled him to produce more books on the author. He edited *Letters from the Earth* (1938), *The Adventures of Tom Sawyer* (1939), *Mark Twain in Eruption: Hitherto Unpublished Pages about Men and Events* (1940), *The Adventures of Huckleberry Finn (Tom Sawyer's Companion)* (1942), and *The Portable Mark Twain* (1946). DeVoto's second book on Twain, *Mark Twain at Work,* also came out in 1942.

This prodigious output should have made Clara grateful for DeVoto's active curatorship, but because the exchanges between them were abrasive and because his compensation had never been generous, DeVoto decided to resign as curator. He attempted to leave in December 1943 and then again in May 1944, staying each time at the urging of others and because of his own ambivalence. DeVoto remained in his post until October 1946, when Dixon Wecter–who had started work on *Samuel Clemens of Hannibal* (1952), his biography of Twain–became the third curator.

Two years after his first book on Twain was published, DeVoto returned to fiction writing. As if to usher in a new phase of composition, he wrote a novel that had nothing to do with the West. *We Accept with Pleasure* (1934) is grounded in autobiography, a feature that distinguishes the novel from DeVoto's previous three novels. Like DeVoto, the main character, Ted Grayson, starts his career as a junior professor at Northwestern. Central to the plot is Grayson's repudiation of Northwestern–an action that parallels the author's own experience–and the character's subsequent position at Harvard, which DeVoto had also hoped for when he was teaching at Northwestern. As for the other personages in the book, Libby Grayson is an accurate portrait of DeVoto's wife, Avis, and Julian Gale–whose ghost haunts the characters–resembles Kent Hagler, one of DeVoto's college pals; Hagler died mysteriously while leading a bohemian life on the West Bank in Paris. Even the incidentals of the narrative hark back to issues that were then much on DeVoto's mind, such as the executions of Nicola Sacco and Bartolomeo Vanzetti. *We Accept with Pleasure* was arguably DeVoto's most technically astute novel. Still, the events that unfold in the Ivy League setting of the story compelled few critics and readers, resulting in a mixed reception at best. The same self-conscious virtuosity in the author that had overpowered the

influence by demonstrating that Twain's childhood and youth had been normal–if not altogether nourishing. DeVoto believed that Twain's books, centered in the American vernacular, embodied a "greatness" that "American literature nowhere else" attained. In his own search for a work that was distinctively American, Ralph Waldo Emerson came up with *The Adventures of Huckleberry Finn,* a book that for Emerson verged on the quintessential American novel.

The critical success of *Mark Twain's America* enhanced DeVoto's reputation so much that he was invited to become the second curator of Mark Twain's papers–housed at Harvard's Widener Library–when Albert Bigelow Paine, the first curator, could no longer fulfill the role. DeVoto served for eight years, from 1938 to 1946. Paine had not always been helpful to DeVoto when the latter was researching and writing his book on Twain, even blocking access to manuscripts that DeVoto had requested. Yet, despite Paine's absence, the many tempting manuscripts that Twain had left behind continued to elude DeVoto. Twain's daughter, Mrs. Clara Gabrilowitsch, was overprotective of her father's reputation. Her consternation must have mounted as DeVoto began to delve into the files of the estate and found there the sort of writing closest to his own skeptical heart–an iconoclast's treasure trove. For

other stories apparently did so once more. Facing a barrage of less-than-positive criticism, DeVoto did not attempt a novel again for thirteen more years.

*Mountain Time* (1947) was his next and final novel. The protagonist, Cy Kinsman, is a brilliant internist searching for spiritual healing, a quest that leads him to resign from his position at an Eastern hospital and to retreat to obscurity in his Western homeland. Not until Kinsman passes through a kind of refiner's fire does he recapture the promise of his professional success and the love of a good woman. DeVoto had keen hopes for *Mountain Time,* but the reviews, as they trailed in, confirmed his nagging fears; critics found the novel overwrought, even mawkish, confirming that DeVoto had improved little in writing fiction. The poor reception of the novel marked a turning point for the writer, who had been able to absorb the lukewarm reviews of his previous books. DeVoto wrote no more fiction after *Mountain Time* and turned instead to journalism and to historical writing.

DeVoto's three histories of the American West represent the capstones of his career—works that he had been preparing himself for since he was a freshman at Harvard: *The Year of Decision: 1846* (1942), *Across the Wide Missouri,* and *The Course of Empire.* The first book begs the question of why 1846 is the "decisive" year in the history of the United States. DeVoto argues that the year marked the confluence of several expansive forces, which—seemingly all at once—pushed the territories from the open plains westward to the Pacific. The Mexican War brought about the Southwest, while the threat of war with England had virtually created the Northwest. At the same time, Mormon immigrants had effectively settled the "Great Basin," the least desirable land. A Mormon who was mustered out of the U.S. infantry march against the Mexicans also happened to come upon the find, in a California creek, that sparked the Gold Rush that lured more people westward. The anthropophagous ordeal of the Donner Party as well was woven into the fabric of these large events. DeVoto considered the historical "heft" of these episodes in U.S. history and concluded that within 1846 lay the keys to understanding not only why the country drifted into a civil war fewer than twenty years later but also why the North emerged the victor in that war.

DeVoto's way of writing about historical events, a style that recalled the narrative histories of Francis Parkman and George Bancroft, also commanded much attention. Parkman and Bancroft were famous for conveying history as a big, dramatic story. Yet, such an approach had actually become suspect in the "scientifically improved" historiography of the twentieth century. Yet, paying little heed to contemporary scholarship, DeVoto forthrightly announced in the

book that his was "a literary purpose: to realize the pre–Civil War, Far West frontier as personal experience." Moreover, his frustrated abilities as a novelist were not wasted, for many readers told of finding themselves somehow hooked by the feeling of a swarming pioneer movement; the several plotlines going forward simultaneously demanded a close reading. Despite these deviations from the norm, eminent historians praised the book, as did most reviewers in periodical publications. *Time* gave *The Year of Decision* four columns of positive copy; *The Atlantic Monthly* serialized the book in five parts; and the Book-of-the-Month Club made it one of its selections.

DeVoto used his narrative technique to even greater effect in *Across the Wide Missouri,* the historical study that won him the Pulitzer Prize. He succumbed to the project of writing this second history of the West largely because of a job composing captions for an oversize book of illustrations. Mae Reed Porter, the owner of more than one hundred watercolors of Western landscapes, painted by Alfred Jacob Miller in 1837, had asked DeVoto to oversee an edition of reproductions of Miller's watercolors. Both DeVoto and the publisher of the book, Houghton Mifflin, recognized the unparalleled historical importance of the paintings and pushed for more than a slickly produced coffee-table book. Thus, what began as a three-week caption job turned into three years of hard work for DeVoto and resulted in a major history of the fur trade.

The centerpiece of an historical trilogy, *Across the Wide Missouri* relays the experience of the American West to readers in a personal way. DeVoto prefaces his narrative by identifying the "Dramatis Personae": "The Company," which encompassed workers of the American Fur Company; "The Opposition," which included men who labored for the Rocky Mountain Fur Company; and both the individual trappers—of the Hudson's Bay Company, for example—and the fur trade entrepreneurs, such as Nathaniel Jarvis Wyeth. In addition, the book tells about the explorers Benjamin Louis Eulalie de Bonneville and Captain William Drummond Stewart who, separately, led expeditions to the West; Stewart once invited the painter Miller, whose watercolors inspired DeVoto to write *Across the Wide Missouri,* on one of the trips westward. For the author, all these people constituted lines of a narrative as compelling as any novel.

DeVoto intended to implement a narrative style in his next history, *The Course of Empire,* but because of the extensive scope of the project—the book covers almost three hundred years of westward expansion, from approximately the early sixteenth century to 1805—a narrative approach carried certain limitations. He soon discovered that the story of Meriwether Lewis

*Dust jacket for the collection of DeVoto's columns for*
Harper's *magazine (1955)*

and William Clark, for instance, could not be told without providing the historical context for their search for an opening to the Pacific Ocean. The instant DeVoto touched on any of Lewis and Clark's antecedents, he found himself contemplating Christopher Columbus and Cabeza de Vaca. He resolved to start with de Vaca, the sixteenth-century Spanish explorer who was the first European to write about his travels in what is now regarded as the Southwest. Ruefully joking that he might just as well have started with the Ice Age, DeVoto wrote more than four hundred pages of the manuscript before starting his discussion of Lewis and Clark. *The Course of Empire* turned into another three-year labor, earning DeVoto a National Book Award. He returned to the subject of Western exploration in his editing of *The Journals of Lewis and Clark* (1953), a book that complements *The Course of Empire*.

DeVoto died two years later on 13 November 1955. Away from his beloved Cambridge on the day he died, he was in New York to discuss the West on the television program *Adventure*. During an evening on the town with friends after his appearance, DeVoto suffered a massive heart attack. He was fifty-eight.

As his extensive body of work suggests, Bernard DeVoto was in search of an audience all his life, and his writings reveal him to be a dependable public thinker. He wrote twenty-four books and edited an additional thirty-one, and his periodical publications totaled an astounding 828 articles. Fond of boasting that he resembled a literary department store, he produced a broad range of nonfiction that an intelligent audience of lay historians and lay journalists devoured. Finally, DeVoto was arguably the last of that breed of "romantic" or "narrative" historians, who wrote about history as "personal experience" and thus made the events of the past more relevant and engaging to the general reader.

**Letters:**

*The Letters of Bernard DeVoto,* edited by Wallace Stegner (Garden City, N.Y.: Doubleday, 1975).

**Bibliography:**

Julius P. Barclay and Elaine Helmer Parnie, "A Bibliography of the Writings of Bernard DeVoto," in *Four Portraits and One Subject: Bernard DeVoto* (Boston: Houghton Mifflin, 1963), pp. 111–206.

**Biographies:**

Catherine Drinker Bowen, Edith R. Mirrielees, Arthur M. Schlesinger Jr., and Wallace Stegner, *Four Portraits and One Subject: Bernard DeVoto* (Boston: Houghton Mifflin, 1963);

Stegner, *The Uneasy Chair: A Biography of Bernard DeVoto* (Garden City, N.Y.: Doubleday, 1974).

**References:**

Van Wyck Brooks, *The Ordeal of Mark Twain* (New York: Dutton, 1920);

Tom Knudson, "The FBI Was Out to Get Free Thinking DeVoto," *High Country News* (8 August 1994);

Orlan Sawey, *Bernard DeVoto* (New York: Twayne, 1969);

Wallace Stegner and Richard W. Etulain, eds., *Conversations with Wallace Stegner on Western History and Literature* (Salt Lake City: University of Utah Press, 1983);

Lawrance Thompson, ed., *Selected Letters of Robert Frost* (New York: Holt, Rinehart & Winston, 1964), pp. 430–432;

Edmund Wilson, "Complaints: II. Bernard DeVoto," *New Republic,* 3 (February 1937): 404–406.

**Papers:**

A comprehensive collection of Bernard DeVoto's papers, dating from 1918 to 1955, is kept in Special Collections in the Cecil B. Green Library of Stanford University in Palo Alto, California. This collection was organized mostly by Wallace Stegner, author of *The Uneasy Chair,* a biography of DeVoto.

# David James Duncan

*(3 February 1952 –   )*

### Ron McFarland
*University of Idaho*

BOOKS: *The River Why* (San Francisco: Sierra Club
Books, 1983; London: Hutchinson, 1983);
*The Brothers K* (New York: Doubleday, 1992);
*River Teeth: Stories and Writings* (New York: Doubleday,
1995);
*My Story as Told by Water: Confessions, Druidic Rants, Reflections, Bird-Watchings, Fish-Stalkings, Visions, Songs and Prayers Refracting Light, from Living Rivers, in the Age of the Industrial Dark* (San Francisco: Sierra Club
Books, 2001).

SELECTED PERIODICAL PUBLICATIONS–
UNCOLLECTED: "Nonfiction-Fiction," *Orion,*
15 (Summer 1996): 55–57;
"Bird Watching as Blood Sport," *Harper's,* 295
(July 1997): 61–69;
"Four Henry Stories," *Orion,* 17 (Spring 1998): 24–33;
"Natives," *Orion,* 17 (Spring 1998): 18–26;
"The War for Norman's River," *Sierra,* 83 (May/June
1998): 44–55;
"Who Owns the West?–Four Possible Answers," *Sun,*
276 (December 1998): 10–17;
"The Raven in Logan's Body," *Orion,* 18 (Spring 1999):
36–45.

*David James Duncan (photograph by Douglas F. Frank;
from the dust jacket for* The Brothers K, *1992)*

David James Duncan's first novel is as outrageously overblown and as seriously comical as that of
Miguel de Cervantes, Laurence Sterne, and Charles
Dickens. While some reviewers agreed with Peter
Wild's assessment in *Western American Literature* (Fall
1983) that Duncan's first novel showed him to be "a
writer of radiant potential," others sided with David
Quammen's view in *The New York Times Book Review* (24
April 1983) that *The River Why* (1983) was limited in its
appeal and "fogbound in its pretentiousness." Nevertheless, the unusual novel of fly-fishing and spiritual
"questing" in western Oregon, which has the rare distinction of having been published initially by the Sierra
Club, was made a Book-of-the-Month Club selection.
Duncan's *The River Why* and Duncan's second novel,
*The Brothers K* (1992), which he has described as "a

nineteenth-century Russian baseball novel," each won a
Pacific Northwest Booksellers award. *The Brothers K* is
an epic reminiscent in some ways of Ken Kesey's *Sometimes a Great Notion* (1964); it was a New York Times
Notable Book in 1992 and won a Best Books Award
from the American Library Association. Although his
next book, *River Teeth: Stories and Writings* (1995),
received scant attention from reviewers, it led to an
unusual honor in which Duncan takes special pride: the
naming of a literary journal after the title essay from
that book. The journal *River Teeth* first appeared in the
fall of 1999. Editors Joe MacKall and Dan Lehman, at
Ashland University in Ohio, intend for the biennial
publication to combine "the best of creative nonfiction,
including narrative reportage, essays and memoir, with

*Duncan in 1987 (courtesy of the author)*

death of his older brother at the age of seventeen from a staph infection following several heart-valve surgeries; David was then thirteen. Although in another interview Duncan says his "distrust of church is as old as my memory," his brother's lingering death sparked a spiritual crisis of sorts that led him to investigate religion, particularly Eastern religions, in search of a "spiritual community" that would fit his definition as "any group of people united in the name of compassion."

He graduated in 1973 from Portland State University with a B.A. in English. Early on, Duncan decided he wanted to write novels, and he supported his writing with more than a dozen blue-collar jobs such as truck driver, bartender, and janitor. After an earlier marriage ended in divorce, he married sculptor Adrian Arleo on 10 September 1988.

Duncan's first book, *The River Why,* could be discounted as "another fishing novel," presumably a subgenre of slight interest to nonanglers, and a problem, because avid anglers are too busy fishing to read about their beloved sport; but as readers have recognized from the outset, the novel is much more specifically developed than that. In an article for *Aethlon* (Fall 1994), Blake Burleson connects *The River Why* with psychoanalyst Carl Gustav Jung's "individuation process," that is, the process by which the individual—the male in this case—acquires a unified sense of self. Burleson regards the novel as "a window into the male psyche" and a study in "the development of a masculine spirituality which rejects established religion while affirming the experience of the Divine." Burleson argues that Gus Orviston, the first-person narrator, follows the two critical phases of the individuation process: he breaks away from his parents both physically and psychologically, and, following a crisis in which "the shallowness of [his] life and its lack of spiritual foundation" is made manifest, he comes to terms with his spiritual self "not through the thinking mind, but through the unthinking body." Clearly, this enlightenment derives not from orthodox Christian dogma but from various Eastern religious sources, such as Buddhism and Taoism. Duncan's repudiation of conventional Christian modes, particularly of anything that smacks of fundamentalism, in favor of a less rational and reductive and a more intuitive and unitive vision, is the dominant theme in both of his novels and in some of his short fiction and nonfiction as well.

Like Norman Maclean's *A River Runs Through It, and Other Stories* (1976), from which Duncan quotes a passage as an epigraph to one chapter and with which *The River Why* might be profitably compared, Duncan's novel is also a celebration of—and perhaps something of an inquest into—the American family, particularly into the family in the northwestern United States. Echoing

critical essays that examine the emerging genre and that explore the impact of nonfiction narrative on the lives of its writers, subjects, and readers." Duncan's essay "River Teeth" is the lead piece in the inaugural issue. The naming of a literary journal after one of his essays is consistent with Duncan's faith in the reader: "The act of reading, to my mind, is more a gift from reader to author than the other way around."

Born on 3 February 1952 to Elwood Dean Duncan and Donna Jean Rowe Duncan in Portland, Oregon, David James Duncan grew up in the ever-dissolving suburbs of the city. His father, an avid sports fan and standout fast-pitch softball pitcher, worked for an electronics firm, and his mother worked for the billing department of Gresham Hospital. Duncan's siblings include two older brothers, one deceased; a younger sister; and a brother thirteen years his junior, whom he helped to raise after his parents divorced. Like various characters in his fiction, Duncan was raised as a Seventh Day Adventist. The event that Duncan describes in a 1992 interview as having "broke me open" was the

DAVID JAMES DUN-
CAN is the author of *The
River Why* and *The
Brothers K*. He lives (and
fishes) in western
Montana, where he is at
work on his next novel.

"Poignant, funny, and
artful, Duncan's 'river
teeth' are like elongated
American haiku, stretch-
ing their grainy syllables
from the home plate of
nostalgia to the outfield
fences of eternity."
—Tom Robbins

"The man, David James Duncan, is touched, touched by the spirit,
and he could be a prophet artist, but you can see that he chooses
to tell just story—for this is his mission on this go-around. Read
him, digest him. He is a friend."
—Victor Villasenor, author of *Rain of Gold*

"David James Duncan is in love with water, the rivers and streams
that have coursed through his life. Believe me, you will be swept
up by his rivers, carried downstream, and deposited in a new
place. In that new place, Duncan will build a fire and tell you a
bunch of stories. What else could you want?"
—Sherman Alexie, author of *Reservation Blues*

Please see back flap for critics' praise for the novels of David James Duncan.

US $20.00 / $26.95 CAN
ISBN 0-385-47727-9

52000

9 780385 477277

RIVER TEETH

DAVID JAMES DUNCAN

RIVER TEETH
*Stories and Writings*

DAVID JAMES DUNCAN
Author of *The River Why* and *The Brothers K*
Doubleday

*Dust jacket for Duncan's 1995 collection, which includes essays and short fiction*

Maclean, who described his novella as "my love poem to my family," Duncan has called his book "my love novel to rivers." The principal characters in the novels often bear symbolically significant or suggestive names. The family name Orviston, for example, echoes the maker of a quality line of fly-fishing tackle, Orvis, one of whose reels is the Wye–named after the "sylvan Wye," the river celebrated in William Wordsworth's "Lines Composed a Few Miles above Tintern Abbey" (1798). The father's full name is Henning Hale-Orviston, so Gus refers to him as H2O. Gus's paternal grandparents were English aristocrats, and the single-malt-scotch- drinking father, who sleeps in silk pajamas and drives a Rover in town and a Winnebago in the country, is a comically insufferable Anglophile, a fly-fishing purist, and a writer for such fishing magazines as *Sports Afield*. Gus's mother, a cowgirl bait-fisher known simply and democratically as "Ma," is her husband's antithesis in nearly every way. Gus, a child prodigy of angling, attempts to appease both parents by adapting his methods as necessary. Gus's younger brother, Bill Bob, deals with the problem by not fishing

at all. The novel satirizes everything from orthodox religiosity and conventional views of good parenting to the fishing obsession itself. Duncan's humor in *The River Why* might best be described as radically latitudinarian.

In the second of the five sections that compose the novel, Gus sets out on his own in Thoreauvian fashion to a cabin on a remote stream, so that he may fish at will and look into himself. The adventure turns into something of a quest, or a parody thereof, with Gus as the knight, wielding his fly rod (Rodney) and hooking the corpse of a drowned fisherman. Gus's confrontation with death helps him to come of age as he notes that in his father's fishing opus, the *Summa Piscatoria*–a teasing reference to the *Summa Theologica* of Thomas Aquinas–there are few references to death, even to that of fish, since H2O is a strict catch-and-release angler. In the third section Gus turns to the mountains in what becomes something of a vision quest as he struggles to deal with his solitude. His spirit animal turns out to be, in effect, his maiden fair: a fisher-girl named Eddy–after her father, Edwin; the name is also suggestive of a whirlpool. She is temporarily sup-

*Duncan (center) in 2000 with his sister, Keterine, and his brother Steve (courtesy of the author)*

planted with a more probable spirit animal in the form of a dog named Descartes. That the quest is spiritual is made clear by Gus's mentor, old Titus, who tells him, "Fishermen should be the easiest of men to convince to commence the search for the soul, because *fishing is nothing but the pursuit of the elusive.*"

When he returns to society and his family, Gus's first act is to follow a dying stream to its doomed source. He then returns to his cabin and renews his search for himself and for the meaning of life. He establishes close relationships with his odd neighbors–Ernest Hemingway enters the novel in the form of one of the children. Gus starts a business making flies and hand-crafted fly rods and briefly takes on a sidekick or disciple named Nick. When he hikes to the source of the Tamanawis, the river "why," near the cabin where he has been living, Gus finds some answers, not least of which is his need for a partner, and when he returns to his cabin he finds that Eddy has also returned. Gus discovers his "equilibrium" in love–and love, more than angling skill, helps him in his epic combat with a huge chinook salmon, a battle that he ends after several hours by intentionally breaking the line. The novel concludes in proper comic fashion with the birth of a daughter to H2O and Ma and with the marriage of Gus

and Eddy. The ending also hints at Duncan's next novel, as Gus burns his draft card and subsequently learns that he has a high number in the lottery, guaranteeing that he will not be sent to Vietnam.

Readers of *The River Why* may be divided among those who like the novel because of the fishing, those who dislike it because of the fishing, and those who like it despite the fishing. The same might be said of *The Brothers K* with respect to baseball. The long novel, more than seven hundred pages, covers a quarter of a century (1956 to 1980) in the history of the nation and of a family: the Chance family, a cleverly selected name that resonates with baseball legend and possesses overtones suggesting the gamble of life and, perhaps, the mystery of fate. The father, Hugh Chance, is an ace pitcher with major-league aspirations who, after an industrial accident, must be satisfied with a minor-league career as a pitching coach and relief artist. The decision nearly destroys his marriage to the fundamentalist Laura, a Seventh Day Adventist, whose piety divides the family, although it does not quite break it into pieces.

Duncan reverses the son's mythic, Oedipal rebellion against the father by making the mother the object of revolt in *The Brothers K*. The oldest son, Everett, rebels most fully, becoming a hippie radical at the University of Washington and eventually avoiding the draft by fleeing to Canada. Like his paternal grandmother, Everett becomes an atheist, but he grows increasingly hateful in his political and philosophical self-righteousness until he is saved by the love of a Russophile named Natasha. Peter, the intellectual of the family, becomes an avid student of Eastern religions, attends Harvard, and, like Duncan when he was twenty, sojourns in India. Irwin, the third son, remains loyal to his mother and to her faith but finds it inadequate for the harsh realities of Vietnam. Kincaid, the youngest of the four brothers, tells most of the story and mediates matters for the family as much as possible. The twin sisters, Bet and Freddy, are split in their loyalties—the former siding with her mother, the latter with her father. In effect, orthodox Christianity nearly destroys the family.

The epic novel took Duncan six and a half years to complete, and he was two years into it when he reread Fyodor Dostoevsky's *Brothers Karamazov* (1879–1880), an experience he credits with giving him some direction. The "K" in Duncan's title, however, refers to the box-score letter for a strikeout, a symbol that may be read two ways, of course: as a failure for the hitter, but as a success for the pitcher. While the familiar villains of the 1960s—everything from militarism to J. Edgar Hoover—are indicted and derided, so, too, are the radical rabble-rousers and the self-serving liberals of the day. While religious fanaticism is thoroughly debunked, so, too, is athletic fanaticism. As Morris Dickstein observes in "The Comeback Kids," an article for *The World & I* (October 1992), the novel "is built on a pattern of sin and redemption, exile and return." Unable to accept the officially sanctioned execution of a young Viet Cong prisoner, Irwin attacks his commanding officer and is placed in an asylum, where he is given electroshock therapy. The estranged family members unite in order to save Irwin, and even the Adventists join in to bring about what Duncan has described as the kind of "fiction that dances around the central miracle of our lives—which is that, despite everything, we're loved." Various readers have argued that the conciliatory, healing conclusion is forced, but, as Dickstein says in his article, Duncan appears intentionally to have risked the "soggy ending." In both parabolic and paradoxical ways, the conventional American family, orthodox Christianity, social activism, Eastern theosophy, and even baseball are repudiated—even denigrated—and, at the same time, celebrated. As Duncan observed in an interview with Christine Byl in *The Sun* (December 1998), "I think maybe on the eighth day God created paradox."

The eight short stories and thirteen essays that make up *River Teeth,* Duncan's next book, extend his love of paradox to the subject of literary genre as he carefully mingles the modes, italicizing the titles of the stories. This mingling is consistent with the stance he expressed in a 1998 interview: "We use the same tools to create, or recreate, both 'true' and imagined stories. In fact, all stories are imagined, because converting life into language is an imaginative process." The book opens with the title essay, in which Duncan reflects on his boyhood along Oregon streams, gathering the knots they called "river teeth," which he regards metaphorically as representing "hard, cross-grained whorls of memory, . . . time-defying knots of experience that remain in us after most of our autobiographies are gone." Much of the book is made up of such experiences in nature, many of them recalled from his childhood. The most memorable piece is almost certainly "The Mickey Mantle Koan," which reflects on his brother's death in 1965. Some of the stories, such as "Molting," which concerns a recently divorced father and his three-year-old son, seem hardly to be fiction at all, while some of the essays, such as "Red Coats," a memory of Duncan himself at age three walking with his mother in downtown Portland, seem more like fiction than nonfiction. The focal point of the book is a sixty-page story titled "The Garbage Man's Daughter," a striking piece narrated by a woman who looks back on her girlhood as a sort of latter-day Thomas Gradgrind, the no-nonsense, fact-abiding character from Dickens's *Hard Times* (1854); similar to Gradgrind, the woman in "The Garbage Man's Daughter" is disastrously committed to a "mission in life . . . to deal in facts." She relishes the power this mission gives her over her doting parents, but when she becomes aware of the Garbage Man, she finds herself "thrown into a state of wonder," and the lesson she eventually learns is similar to that of most of Duncan's characters: "only by experiencing ignorance can I be opened up to fresh knowledge." That lesson typifies those of most mystics in its antirational, paradoxical nature.

Duncan creates fascinating characters in his fiction, and his passionate and sometimes raucous humor has drawn the approbation of nearly all his reviewers; but he remains most of all a novelist of ideas. He has also explored environmental issues in a series of essays in *Orion,* a nature magazine, and other periodicals. The subtitle of "Bird Watching as Blood Sport," an essay that appeared in *Harper's* in 1997, suggests Duncan's thematic foundation, whether in fiction or what might be described as "politically committed" nonfiction: "the redemptive pain of loving the natural world." In that essay he writes, "In late winter, when I was ten, I made perhaps my first conscious connection between the mysteries of the inner life and those of the outer world."

Perhaps what is most remarkable about Duncan's fiction is how vulnerable it is to a range of accu-

romeo shows jamey the door  p. 18

Garbage grief for Romeo, garbage grief for Debbie, garbage grief for "this dying Earth," "my mortal love, Risa," "poor doomed little Lilly," and every other God-doomed God-damned cliché he could conjure and spew. ~~Jamey set out for the~~ ~~longer depths.~~ A flood of tears, flood of snot, flood of sounds he'd never made rose from his lungs and belly, and he worshipped at the altar of his own awful sounds. ~~He~~ gripped a corpse in his hands, imagined it the entire dog, picked that false entirety up in his arms, staggered to his truck, lay Romeo's head in his lap, began to stroke it, sobbed at the speed with which it was cooling, and drove, blubbering and stroking all the way, through the mist and birds and trees till he came to the beautiful grassy headland. ~~He~~ spewed and scattered rather than gathered in and protected the tk! Romeo died to show him Jamey

$T$his gets embarrassing. I'll fast forward:

Jamey had placed Romeo's body in the tuba case, lay the folding shovel on top of it, shut the case, staggered up the headland to a mawkishly poetic-looking old cedar tree, and begun digging a hole near the base of the tree.

Big mistake. Cedar trees have amazingly wide tough root systems. By the time the hole was two feet deep, Jamey was exhausted from hacking at roots and had raised bloody blisters on both palms. He'd planned to bury Romeo in his beloved tuba case, but the case was huge: the hole wasn't a third the size it needed to be. So Jamey decided to keep the tuba case. Yet another betrayal.

Angrily lifting Romeo's body out of the case, he lay it in the hole's bottom, curled it exactly the way Romeo used to curl himself for sleep, inspected the situation, found no fault with it at first, but then noticed that Romeo's eyes had opened. What's more, the cataracts that blurred his vision in life now prevented death from altering his gaze. Romeo seemed to be regarding Jamey just the way he always had.

Jamey reached down in the hole and closed the eyes.

They reopened.

He reached down and closed them again.

They reopened.

Jamey felt Romeo was doing it on purpose, because of the tuba case. He showed the dead dog his wrecked palms. "See?" he said. "This is how it's gotta

*Corrected typescript page for a novel in progress by Duncan (Collection of David James Duncan)*

sations that could undermine its credibility. Probably foremost among these is that it sometimes dwindles into farce, an accusation that he appears to have anticipated in *The Brothers K,* since he offers in it a brief defense of the "quirky little literary and theatrical genre" that has proven to be "surprisingly powerful." Duncan's fiction is also, by turns, programmatic—willfully loaded with socioeconomic and political propaganda—and burdened with rant: his characters tend to get carried away with their exuberant messages. Almost any close reading or interpretation of Duncan's fiction will also reveal that he allegorizes his characters and makes them representative types of, for example, the Intuitive Female or the Rationalist Male, the Religious Fanatic, the Jock, or the Hippie. Finally, as some reviewers have noted, Duncan tends toward the egregiously literary: of an encyclopedic mind, he steeps his pages in quotations that range from Porky Pig to Wallace Stevens, from Wordsworth to Izaak Walton, and from *The Mahabharata* to Yogi Berra. Such citations either enrich the text or distract from it, depending on the reader. Remarkably, Duncan not only gets away with all of these things—he glories in them.

The majority of the twenty-one essays that make up Duncan's most recent book, *My Story as Told by Water: Confessions, Druidic Rants, Reflections, Bird-Watchings, Fish-Stalkings, Visions, Songs and Prayers Refracting Light, from Living Rivers, in the Age of the Industrial Dark* (2001), were published first in such periodicals as *Harper's, Sierra,* and *Orion,* but many were revised extensively for inclusion in the book. In *My Story as Told by Water,* Duncan examines the politics of environment as well as topics of personal concern, blending anger with humor, lament with wit, and poetry with rhetoric. With his latest book he launches an assault on what he calls "capitalist fundamentalism," defined as the "perfect Techno-Industrial religion, its goal being a planet upon which we've nothing left to worship, worry about, read, eat, or love but dollar bills and Bibles."

In an essay titled "Beauty/Violence/Grief/Frenzy/Love: On the Contemplative Versus the Activist Life," Duncan explains that he turned to nonfiction at age forty "not out of a sense of calling, but out of a sense of betrayal, out of rage over natural systems violated, out of grief for a loved world raped, and out of a craving for justice." Although most of his activist rhetoric focuses

on Montana, his new home, he also considers other parts of the Northwest in these essays, touching on issues of environmental abuse particularly where rivers are involved—such as in Oregon, Washington, and Idaho. In his discussion of the environment Duncan is apt to turn strident: "the ongoing operation of the Snake River dams is one of the most overtly racist projects funded by our own, or any, modern government." The book is divided into three sections: "Wonder Versus Loss," which runs nearly ninety pages and, from a literary standpoint, probably has the strongest essays; "Activism," a section of almost 120 pages of potent political arguments; and, finally, "Fishing the Inside Passage," which delves into "the idiot joy of foraging fish" for approximately 60 pages. *My Story as Told by Water* was nominated in 2001 for a National Book Award in the nonfiction category.

As the inside dust jacket of his latest book notes, David James Duncan "lives with his family on a Montana trout stream." He continues to work on novels and freelance writing projects and to lecture—notably on "wilderness, the writing life, the nonmonastic contemplative life, the fly fishing life and nonreligious literature of faith."

## Interviews:

Clark Munsell, "An Interview with David Duncan," *World & I,* 7 (1992): 319–325;

Christine Byl, "Language of Devotion: A Conversation with David James Duncan," *Sun,* no. 276 (December 1998): 4–9;

W. Dale Brown, "David James Duncan: River Mud, Mysticism, and Corvette Stingrays," *Cimarron Review,* 130 (Winter 2000): 122–151.

## References:

Mark Browning, "A Visit to the River Why," in his *Haunted by Waters: Fly Fishing in North American Literature* (Athens: Ohio University Press, 1998), pp. 121–132;

Blake Burleson, "Fishing for Our Souls: David Duncan's *The River Why* as Masculine Individuation," *Aethlon,* 12 (Fall 1994): 41–54;

Lee Congdon, "Dostoevsky, or Tolstoy?" *World & I,* 17 (October 1992): 301–307;

Morris Dickstein, "The Comeback Kids," *World & I,* 17 (October 1992): 309–317.

# Frederick Schiller Faust
## (Max Brand)
### *(29 May 1892 – 12 May 1944)*

Paul Varner
*Oklahoma Christian University*

*Unless otherwise noted, all books were published under the pseudonym Max Brand.*

BOOKS: *The Untamed* (New York & London: Putnam, 1919); republished as *The Trail of the Panther* (London: Corgi, 1967);

*The Night Horseman* (New York & London: Putnam, 1920);

*The Ten-Foot Chain, or Can Love Survive the Shackles?* by Brand, Achmed Abdullah, E. K. Means, and P. P. Sheehan (New York: Reynolds, 1920);

*Trailin'* (New York & London: Putnam, 1920);

*Riders of the Silences,* as John Frederick (New York: Fly, 1920); republished as *Luck* (London: Hodder & Stoughton, 1926; Lincoln: University of Nebraska Press, 1997);

*Free Range Lanning,* as George Owen Baxter (New York: Chelsea House, 1921; London: Hodder & Stoughton, 1923); republished as *Way of the Lawless* (New York: Dodd, Mead, 1978);

*The Seventh Man* (New York & London: Putnam, 1921);

*The Long Chase* (New York: Street & Smith, 1922; London: Hodder & Stoughton, 1961);

*The Village Street and Other Poems,* as Frederick Faust (New York & London: Putnam, 1922);

*Donnegan,* as Baxter (New York: Chelsea House, 1923; London: Hodder & Stoughton, 1924); republished as *Gunman's Reckoning* (New York: G. K. Hall, 1976; London: Hale, 1977);

*Alcatraz* (New York & London: Putnam, 1923); republished as *Alcatraz the Wild Stallion* (New York: Pocket Books, 1961);

*The Long, Long Trail,* as Baxter (New York: Chelsea House, 1923; London: Hodder & Stoughton, 1924);

*Tiger* (London: Hodder & Stoughton, 1923);

*Bull Hunter* (New York: Dodd, Mead, 1924; London: Hale, 1981);

*Frederick Schiller Faust (Max Brand)*

*Bull Hunter's Romance,* as David Manning (New York: Chelsea House, 1924; London: Hutchinson, 1926);

*Clung* (London: Hodder & Stoughton, 1924); republished as *Ghost Rider* (New York: Pocket Books, 1971);

*Dan Barry's Daughter* (New York & London: Putnam, 1924);

*The Guide to Happiness* (London: Hodder & Stoughton, 1924); republished as *The Trap at Commanche Bend,* as Manning (New York: Chelsea House, 1927);

*Gun Gentlemen* (London: Hodder & Stoughton, 1924; New York: Chelsea House, 1927);

*The Range-Land Avenger,* as Baxter (New York: Chelsea House, 1924; London: Hodder & Stoughton, 1925);

*The Bronze Collar: A Romance of Spanish California,* as Frederick (London & New York: Putnam, 1925);

*The Brute* (New York: Chelsea House, 1925);

*King Charlie's Riders* (New York: Chelsea House, 1925); republished as *King Charlie* (London: Hodder & Stoughton, 1925; New York: Leisure, 1997);

*Beyond the Outpost* (London & New York: Putnam, 1925);

*Jerry Peyton's Notched Inheritance* (New York: Chelsea House, 1925); republished as *Gunmen's Feud* (New York: Dodd, Mead, 1982; London: Hale, 1984);

*Jim Curry's Test,* as Manning (New York: Chelsea House, 1925; London: Hutchinson, 1927); republished as *Gunfighter's Return* (London: Fawcett, 1954; New York: Dodd, Mead, 1979);

*The Shadow of Silvertip,* as Baxter (New York: Chelsea House, 1925; London: Hodder & Stoughton, 1926);

*Beyond the Outpost,* as Peter Henry Morland (New York & London: Putnam, 1925);

*The Black Signal* (New York: Chelsea House, 1925; London: Hale, 1989);

*His Third Master* (London: Hodder & Stoughton, 1925);

*Train's Trust,* as Baxter (New York: Burt Franklin, 1925; London: Hodder & Stoughton, 1927); republished as *Steve Train's Ordeal* (New York: Dodd, Mead, 1952; London: White Lion, 1974);

*Wooden Guns,* as Baxter (New York: Chelsea House, 1925; London: Hodder & Stoughton, 1927);

*Blackie and Red,* as Manning (New York: Chelsea House, 1926);

*Black Jack* (London: Hodder & Stoughton, 1926; New York: Dodd, Mead, 1970);

*The Border Bandit* (New York: Harper, 1926; London: Jenkins, 1950);

*Fate's Honeymoon* (London: Hodder & Stoughton, 1926);

*Fire Brain* (New York & London: Putnam, 1926);

*Harrigan!* (London: Hodder & Stoughton, 1926; New York: Dodd, Mead, 1971);

*Monsieur* (New York: Bobbs-Merrill, 1926);

*Ronicky Doone* (New York: Chelsea House, 1926);

*Ronicky Doone's Treasure,* as Manning (New York: Chelsea House, 1926);

*The Splendid Rascal,* as George Challis (Indianapolis: Bobbs-Merrill, 1926; London: Cassell, 1927);

*The Stranger at the Gate* (London: Hodder & Stoughton, 1926);

*The Whispering Outlaw,* as Baxter (New York: Chelsea House, 1926; London: Hodder & Stoughton, 1927);

*The White Wolf* (New York & London: Putnam, 1926);

*Bandit's Honor,* as Manning (New York: Chelsea House, 1927); republished as *Six-Gun Country* (New York: Dodd, Mead, 1980; London: Hale, 1981);

*The Blue Jay* (New York: Dodd, Mead, 1927; London: Hodder & Stoughton, 1927);

*The Outlaw Tamer* (New York: Chelsea House, 1927);

*The Mustang Herder* (New York: Chelsea House, 1927);

*The Garden of Eden* (London: Hodder & Stoughton, 1927; New York: Dodd, Mead, 1963);

*The Mountain Fugitive* (New York: Chelsea House, 1927);

*On the Trail of Four,* as Manning (New York: Chelsea House, 1927);

*Pleasant Jim* (New York: Dodd, Mead, 1927; London: Hodder & Stoughton, 1928);

*The Pride of Tyson* (London: Hodder & Stoughton, 1927);

*The Sword Lover,* as Frederick (New York: Henry Watterson, 1927);

*The Trail to San Triste,* as Baxter (New York: Chelsea House, 1927; London: Hodder & Stoughton, 1928);

*Western Tommy* (New York: Chelsea House, 1927); republished as *The Making of a Gunman* (New York: Dodd, Mead, 1983; London: Hale, 1984);

*Border Guns* (New York: Dodd, Mead, 1928; London: Hodder & Stoughton, 1954);

*Children of Night* (New York: L. Harper Allen, 1928);

*Pleasant Jim* (New York: Dodd, Mead, 1928; London: Hodder & Stoughton, 1928); republished as *Six-Gun Ambush* (New York: Popular Library, 1955);

*Señor Jingle Bells* (New York: Chelsea House, 1928); republished as *The Fastest Draw* (New York: Dodd, Mead, 1987);

*Lost Wolf,* as Morland (New York: Maisy-Masius, 1928; London: Melrose, 1929);

*Pillar Mountain* (New York: Dodd, Mead, 1928);

*The Gun Tamer* (New York: Dodd, Mead, 1929; London: Hodder & Stoughton, 1929);

*Mistral* (New York: Dodd, Mead, 1929; London: Hodder & Stoughton, 1930);

*Singing Guns* (Roslyn, N.Y.: Black's Readers Service, 1929; London: Hodder & Stoughton, 1938);

*Tiger Man,* as Baxter (New York: Macaulay, 1929);

Cover for the 1919 issue of the magazine in which Faust's
novel first appeared. It was published in book form
in 1920. The movie—which, ultimately, starred
Tom Mix rather than Fairbanks—was
released in 1921.

*Mystery Ranch* (New York: Dodd, Mead, 1930); republished as *Mystery Valley* (London: Hodder & Stoughton, 1930);

*Destry Rides Again,* as Faust (New York: Dodd, Mead, 1930; London: Hodder & Stoughton, 1931);

*The Rescue of Broken Arrow,* as Evan Evans (New York & London: Harper, 1930); republished as *The Revenge of Broken Arrow* (London: Jenkins, 1951);

*The Stingaree* (New York: Dodd, Mead, 1930; London: Hodder & Stoughton, 1969);

*Dionysus in Hades,* as Faust (Oxford: Blackwell, 1931);

*Smiling Charlie* (New York: Dodd, Mead, 1931; London: Hodder & Stoughton, 1931);

*The Killers* (New York: Macaulay, 1931); republished as *Three on the Trail* (New York: Dodd, Mead, 1984; London: Hale, 1987);

*The Happy Valley* (New York: Dodd, Mead, 1931; London: Hodder & Stoughton, 1932);

*Valley Vultures* (New York: Dodd, Mead, 1932; London: Hodder & Stoughton, 1932);

*Twenty Notches* (New York: Dodd, Mead, 1932; London: Hodder & Stoughton, 1932);

*The Jackson Trail* (New York: Dodd, Mead, 1932; London: Hodder & Stoughton, 1933);

*The Fighting Four* (Roslyn, N.Y.: Black's Readers Service, 1933; London: Hodder & Stoughton, 1948);

*Montana Rides!* as Evans (New York & London: Harper, 1933);

*The Longhorn Feud* (New York: Dodd, Mead, 1933; London: Hodder & Stoughton, 1933);

*The Outlaw* (New York: Dodd, Mead, 1933); republished as *Crooked Horn* (London: Hodder & Stoughton, 1934);

*The Return of the Rancher,* as Frank Austin (New York: Dodd, Mead, 1933);

*Silvertip* (Roslyn, N.Y.: Black's Readers Service, 1933; London: Hodder & Stoughton, 1942);

*Slow Joe* (New York: Dodd, Mead, 1933; London: Hodder & Stoughton, 1933);

*The Thunderer* (New York: Derrydale Press, 1933);

*Valley Thieves* (New York: Grosset & Dunlap, 1933; London: Hodder & Stoughton, 1949);

*Timbal Gulch Trail* (New York: Dodd, Mead, 1934; London: Hodder & Stoughton, 1934);

*Brothers on the Trail* (New York: Dodd, Mead, 1934; London: White Lion, 1972);

*Call of the Blood,* as Baxter (New York: Macaulay, 1934); republished as *War Party* (New York: Dodd, Mead, 1934); republished as *Red Hawk and the White Horse* (London: Hodder & Stoughton, 1934);

*The Sheriff Rides,* as Austin (New York: Dodd, Mead, 1934); republished as *Triggerman* (New York: Dell, 1952);

*The Rancher's Revenge* (New York: Dodd, Mead, 1934; London: Hodder & Stoughton, 1935);

*Montana Rides Again,* as Evans (New York: Harper, 1934);

*Red Devil of the Range* (New York: Macaulay, 1934); republished as *Horseback Hellion* (New York: Signet, 1950); republished as *The Man from Savage Creek* (New York: Dodd, Mead, 1977);

*Valley of Vanishing Men* (New York: Dodd, Mead, 1934; London: Hodder & Stoughton, 1949);

*The Bait and the Trap,* as Challis (New York: Harper, 1935);

*Cross over Nine,* as Walter C. Butler (New York: Macaulay, 1935);

*The Firebrand,* as Challis (New York: Harper, 1935);

*The Seven of Diamonds* (New York: Dodd, Mead, 1935; London: Hodder & Stoughton, 1935); republished as *Law of the Gun* (New York: Monarch, 1959);

*King of the Range,* as Austin (New York: Dodd, Mead, 1935);

*Hunted Riders* (New York: Dodd, Mead, 1935; London: Hodder & Stoughton, 1936);

*Brother of the Cheyennes* (New York: Macaulay, 1935); republished as *Rusty* (London: Hodder & Stoughton, 1937); republished as *Frontier Feud* (New York: Dodd, Mead, 1973);

*Rustlers of Beacon Creek* (New York: Dodd, Mead, 1935; London: Hodder & Stoughton, 1936);

*Happy Jack* (New York: Dodd, Mead, 1936; London: Hodder & Stoughton, 1936); republished as *Outlaw Rider* (New York: Monarch, 1960);

*The King Bird Rides* (New York: Dodd, Mead, 1936; London: Hodder & Stoughton, 1936);

*The Night Flower,* as Butler (New York: Macaulay, 1936; London: Stanley Paul, 1937);

*Secret Agent Number One,* as Frederick Frost (Philadelphia: Macrae-Smith, 1936);

*The Song of the Whip* (New York: Harper, 1936);

*South of the Rio Grande* (New York: Dodd, Mead, 1936; London: Hodder & Stoughton, 1937);

*The Bamboo Whistle,* as Frost (Philadelphia: Macrae-Smith, 1937);

*Six Golden Angels* (New York: Dodd, Mead, 1937; London: Hodder & Stoughton, 1938);

*Spy Meets Spy: Featuring Anthony Hamilton, America's Secret Agent Number One,* as Frost (Philadelphia: Smith, 1937; London: Harrap, 1937);

*The Streak* (New York: Dodd, Mead, 1937; London: Hodder & Stoughton, 1937);

*Trouble Trail* (New York: Dodd, Mead, 1937; London: Hodder & Stoughton, 1937); republished as *Desert Showdown* (New York: Popular Library, 1955);

*The Iron Trail* (New York: Dodd, Mead, 1938; republished as *Riding the Iron Trail* (London: Hodder & Stoughton, 1938);

*The Naked Blade,* as Challis (New York: Greystone, 1938; London: Cassell, 1939);

*Dead or Alive* (New York: Dodd, Mead, 1938; republished as *Lanky for Luck* (London: Hodder & Stoughton, 1939);

*Fightin' Fool* (New York: Dodd, Mead, 1939); republished as *A Fairly Slick Guy* (London: Hodder & Stoughton, 1940);

*Gunman's Gold* (New York: Dodd, Mead, 1939; London: Hodder & Stoughton, 1939);

*Marbleface* (New York: Dodd, Mead, 1939); republished as *Poker-Face* (London: Hodder & Stoughton, 1939);

*Calling Dr. Kildare* (New York: Dodd, Mead, 1940; Hornchurch, U.K.: I. Henry, 1978);

*The Dude* (New York: Dodd, Mead, 1940); republished as *Cleaned Out* (London: Hodder & Stoughton, 1940);

*Danger Trail* (New York: Dodd, Mead, 1940; London: Hodder & Stoughton, 1940);

*The Golden Knight,* as Challis (New York: Greystone, 1940);

*Riders of the Plains* (New York: Dodd, Mead, 1940; London: Hodder & Stoughton, 1941);

*The Secret of Dr. Kildare* (New York: Dodd, Mead, 1940; London: Hodder & Stoughton, 1940);

*Wine on the Desert and Other Stories* (New York: Dodd, Mead, 1940; London: Hodder & Stoughton, 1941);

*The Border Kid* (New York: Dodd, Mead, 1941; London: Hodder & Stoughton, 1941);

*Dr. Kildare Takes Charge* (New York: Dodd, Mead, 1941; London: Hodder & Stoughton, 1942);

*The Long Chance* (New York: Dodd, Mead, 1941); republished as *The Safety Killer* (London: Hodder & Stoughton, 1942);

*Vengeance Trail* (New York: Dodd, Mead, 1941); republished as *Striking Eagle* (London: Hodder & Stoughton, 1942);

*Young Dr. Kildare* (New York: Dodd, Mead, 1941; London: Hodder & Stoughton, 1941);

*Dr. Kildare's Crisis* (New York: Dodd, Mead, 1942; London: Hodder & Stoughton, 1943);

*Dr. Kildare's Trial* (New York: Dodd, Mead, 1942; London: Hodder & Stoughton, 1944);

*The Man from Mustang* (New York: Dodd, Mead, 1942; London: Hodder & Stoughton, 1943);

*Silvertip's Strike* (New York: Dodd, Mead, 1942; London: Hodder & Stoughton, 1944);

*Dr. Kildare's Search and Dr. Kildare's Hardest Case* (New York: Dodd, Mead, 1943; London: Hodder & Stoughton, 1945);

*Silvertip's Roundup* (New York: Dodd, Mead, 1943; London: Hodder & Stoughton, 1945);

*Silvertip's Trap* (New York: Dodd, Mead, 1943; London: Hodder & Stoughton, 1946);

*Silvertip's Chase* (New York: Blakiston, 1944; London: Hodder & Stoughton, 1946);

*Silvertip's Search* (New York: Dodd, Mead, 1945; London: Hodder & Stoughton, 1948);

*The Stolen Stallion* (New York: Dodd, Mead, 1945; London: Hodder & Stoughton, 1949);

*Mountain Riders* (New York: Dodd, Mead, 1946; London: Hodder & Stoughton, 1949);

*The False Rider* (New York: Dodd, Mead, 1947; London: Hodder & Stoughton, 1950);

*Flaming Irons* (New York: Dodd, Mead, 1948; London: Hodder & Stoughton, 1951);

Cover for a 1921 issue of a magazine that includes a serialized novel by Faust. The novel, which makes fun of marriage manuals, was published in book form with the same title in 1924 and republished in 1927, under Faust's pseudonym David Manning, as The Trap at Commanche Bend.

*Hired Guns* (New York: Dodd, Mead, 1948; London: Hodder & Stoughton, 1951);

*Gunman's Legacy* (New York: Harper, 1949); republished as *Sixgun Legacy* (London: Jenkins, 1950);

*The Bandit of the Black Hills* (New York: Dodd, Mead, 1949; London: Hodder & Stoughton, 1952);

*Seven Trails* (New York: Dodd, Mead, 1949; London: Hodder & Stoughton, 1952);

*Smugglers' Trail* (New York: Harper, 1949); republished as *Smoking Gun Trail* (New York: Paperback Library, 1951); republished as *Lone Hand* (New York: Bantam, 1951);

*Single Jack* (New York: Dodd, Mead, 1950; London: Hodder & Stoughton, 1953);

*Sawdust and Sixguns,* as Evans (New York: Harper, 1950; London: Jenkins, 1952); republished as *The Tenderfoot* (New York: Dodd, Mead, 1952; London: Hodder & Stoughton, 1955); republished as *Outlaw's Gold* (New York: Warner, 1976);

*The Galloping Broncos* (New York: Dodd, Mead, 1950; London: Hodder & Stoughton, 1953);

*The Hair-Trigger Kid* (New York: Dodd, Mead, 1951);

*Tragedy Trail* (New York: Dodd, Mead, 1951; London: Hodder & Stoughton, 1954);

*Smiling Desperado* (New York: Dodd, Mead, 1952; London: Hodder & Stoughton, 1955);

*Strange Courage,* as Evans (New York: Harper, 1952; London: Jenkins, 1953); republished as *Showdown* (New York: Paperback Library, 1967);

*Outlaw Valley* (New York: Harper, 1953; London: Hale, 1954);

*Outlaw's Code* (New York: Harper, 1953; London: Hale, 1955);

*The Gambler* (New York: Dodd, Mead, 1954; London: Hodder & Stoughton, 1956);

*The Invisible Outlaw* (New York: Dodd, Mead, 1954; London: Hodder & Stoughton, 1956);

*Speedy* (New York: Dodd, Mead, 1955; London: Hodder & Stoughton, 1957);

*Outlaw Breed* (New York: Dodd, Mead, 1955; London: Hodder & Stoughton, 1957);

*The Big Trail* (New York: Dodd, Mead, 1956; London: Hodder & Stoughton, 1958);

*Trail Partners* (New York: Dodd, Mead, 1956; London: Hodder & Stoughton, 1958);

*Blood on the Trail* (New York: Dodd, Mead, 1957; London: Western Book Club, 1959);

*Lucky Larribee* (New York: Dodd, Mead, 1957; London: Hodder & Stoughton, 1960);

*The Outlaw of Buffalo Flat* (New York: Dodd, Mead, 1958);

*The White Cheyenne* (New York: Dodd, Mead, 1960; London: Hodder & Stoughton, 1961);

*Tamer of the Wild* (New York: Dodd, Mead, 1962; London: Hodder & Stoughton, 1963);

*Mighty Lobo* (New York: Dodd, Mead, 1962; Hornchurch, U.K.: Henry, 1984);

*Cheyenne Gold* (New York: Dodd, Mead, 1963; London: Hodder & Stoughton, 1973);

*Golden Lightning* (New York: Dodd, Mead, 1964; London: Hodder & Stoughton, 1965);

*The Gentle Gunman* (New York: Dodd, Mead, 1964; London: Hodder & Stoughton, 1966);

*The Guns of Dorking Hollow* (New York: Dodd, Mead, 1965; London: Hodder & Stoughton, 1967);

*Phantom Spy* (New York: Dodd, Mead, 1965; London: White Lion, 1975);

*Torture Trail* (New York: Dodd, Mead, 1965);

*Ride the Wild Trail* (New York: Dodd, Mead, 1966; London: Hodder & Stoughton, 1967);

*Larramee's Ranch* (New York: Dodd, Mead, 1966; London: Hodder & Stoughton, 1967);

*Rippon Rides Double* (New York: Dodd, Mead, 1968; London: Hodder & Stoughton, 1968);

*Thunder Moon* (New York: Dodd, Mead, 1969; London: Hodder & Stoughton, 1970);

*Trouble Kid* (New York: Dodd, Mead, 1970; London: Hodder & Stoughton, 1971);

*Ambush at Torture Canyon* (New York: Dodd, Mead, 1971; London: Hodder & Stoughton, 1972);

*Drifter's Vengeance* (New York: Dodd, Mead, 1972; London: Hodder & Stoughton, 1974);

*The Luck of the Spindrift* (New York: Dodd, Mead, 1972; London & New York: White Lion, 1973);

*Big Game* (New York: Dodd, Mead, 1973; Hornchurch, U.K.: Henry, 1984);

*Dead Man's Treasure* (New York: Dodd, Mead, 1974; London: White Lion, 1975);

*The Last Showdown* (New York: Dodd, Mead, 1975; London: Hodder & Stoughton, 1976);

*Rawhide Justice* (New York: Dodd, Mead, 1975; London: Hale, 1977);

*Shotgun Law* (New York: Dodd, Mead, 1976; London: Hale, 1977);

*The Bells of San Filipo* (New York: Pocket Books, 1977);

*Rider of the High Hills* (New York: Dodd, Mead, 1977; London: Hale, 1978);

*The Reward* (New York: Pocket Books, 1977); republished as *Ronicky Doone's Reward* (Boston: G. K. Hall, 1995);

*Storm on the Range* (New York: Dodd, Mead, 1978; London: Hale, 1980);

*Galloping Danger* (New York: Dodd, Mead, 1979; London: Hale, 1980);

*The Man from the Wilderness* (New York: Dodd, Mead, 1980; London: Hale, 1982);

*Wild Freedom*, as Baxter (New York: Dodd, Mead, 1981; London: Hale, 1982);

*Thunder Moon's Challenge* (New York: Dodd, Mead, 1982);

*Thunder Moon Strikes* (New York: Dodd, Mead, 1982);

*Lawless Land* (New York: Dodd, Mead, 1983; London: Hale, 1988);

*Rogue Mustang* (New York: Dodd, Mead, 1984; London: Hale, 1986);

*Trouble in Timberline* (New York: Dodd, Mead, 1984; London: Hale, 1987);

*Mountain Guns* (New York: Dodd, Mead, 1985; London: Hale, 1987);

*The Gentle Desperado* (New York: Dodd, Mead, 1985; London: Hale, 1988)—comprises "The Gentle Desperado," "The Terrible Tenderfoot," and "Tiger, Tiger";

*One Man Posse* (New York: Dodd, Mead, 1987);

*The Nighthawk Trail* (New York: Dodd, Mead, 1988);

*Battle's End; The Three Crosses* (New York: Doherty, 1990);

*Coward of the Clan* (New York: Putnam, 1991);

*Fugitives' Fire* (New York: Putnam, 1991);

*The Red Bandanna/Carcajou's Trail* (New York: Tor, 1991);

*Outlaw Crew/The Best Bandit* (New York: Tor, 1991);

*Range Jester/Black Thunder* (New York: Tor, 1991);

*The Cross Brand* (London: Hale, 1993);

*The Collected Stories of Max Brand*, edited, with story prefaces, by Robert Easton and Jane Faust Easton (Lincoln: University of Nebraska Press, 1994);

*The Desert Pilot* (London: Hale, 1994);

*Dust Across the Range* (London: Hale, 1994);

*Valley of Jewels* (London: Hale, 1994);

*Sixteen in Nome* (Thorndike, Maine: Five Star Western, 1995);

*The Bells of San Carlos and Other Stories*, edited by Jon Tuska (Lincoln: University of Nebraska Press, 1996);

*The Black Rider and Other Stories*, edited by Tuska (Lincoln: University of Nebraska Press, 1996)—comprises *The Black Rider, The Dream of Macdonald, Partners*, and *The Power of Prayer;*

*Farewell, Thunder Moon* (Lincoln: University of Nebraska Press, 1996);

*The Ghost Wagon and Other Great Western Adventures*, edited by Tuska (Lincoln: University of Nebraska Press, 1996);

*The Lightning Warrior* (Thorndike, Maine: Five Star Western, 1996);

*The Legend of Thunder Moon*, edited, with an introduction, by Edgar L. Chapman (Lincoln: University of Nebraska Press, 1996);

*Red Wind and Thunder Moon* (Lincoln: University of Nebraska Press, 1996);

*Thunder Moon and the Sky People* (Lincoln: University of Nebraska Press, 1996);

*The Return of Free-Range Lanning* (New York: Leisure, 1997);

*The Sacking of El Dorado* (New York: Leisure, 1997);

*The Stone That Shines* (Unity, Maine: Five Star Western, 1997);

*The Abandoned Outlaw* (New York: Leisure, 1998);

*The Gauntlet: A Western Trio* (Unity, Maine: Five Star Western, 1998)—comprises *The Blackness of MacTee, The King of Rats*, and *The Gauntlet;*

*Chinook: A North-Western Story* (Unity, Maine: Five Star Western, 1998);

*In the Hills of Monterey* (Unity, Maine: Five Star Western, 1998);

*The Lost Valley: A Western Trio* (Unity, Maine: Five Star Western, 1998)—comprises *The Stage to Yellow Creek, The Whisperer*, and *The Lost Valley;*

*The One-Way Trail* (New York: Leisure, 1998);

*Table of contents in which works by Faust appear under the pseudonyms Max Brand, Dennis Lawton, and George Challis*

*Seven Faces* (Lincoln: University of Nebraska Press, 1998);

*Slumber Mountain* (New York: Leisure, 1998);

*The Quest for Lee Garrison* (New York: Leisure, 1999);

*Safety McTee* (New York: Leisure, 1999);

*Two Sixes* (New York: Leisure, 1999);

*The Survival of Juan Oro* (Unity, Maine: Five Star Western, 1999);

*Soft Metal* (New York: Leisure, 2000);

*The Rock of Kiever* (New York: Leisure, 2000);

*Tales of the Wild West* (New York: Leisure, 2000);

*Stolen Gold* (New York: Leisure, 2001).

**Editions:** *The Mountain Fugitive* (New York: Leisure, 1994);

*Riders of the Silences* (New York: Leisure, 1994);

*The Shadow of Silvertip* (New York: Leisure, 1994);

*The Whispering Outlaw* (New York: Leisure, 1994);

*The Return of the Rancher* (New York: Leisure, 1995);

*Speedy* (New York: Leisure, 1995);

*Timbal Gulch Trail* (New York: Leisure, 1995);

*Trouble in Timberline* (New York: Leisure, 1995);

*Bull Hunter* (New York: Leisure, 1996);

*Bull Hunter's Romance* (New York: Leisure, 1996);

*Donnegan* (New York: Leisure, 1996);

*Gun Gentlemen* (New York: Leisure, 1996);

*The Mustang Herder* (New York: Leisure, 1996);

*The Outlaw Tamer* (New York: Leisure, 1996);

*The Pride of Tyson* (New York: Leisure, 1996);

*The Desert Pilot; Valley of the Jewels* (New York: Leisure, 1997);

*Wooden Guns* (New York: Leisure, 1997).

Frederick Schiller Faust died in 1944, but a new Max Brand Western still appears on an average of once every four months, usually with the claim "First time in paperback." Evidently there is no slowing of the pace of new editions.

Faust began his life in humble circumstances and spent his early years as a manual laborer, but by the time he died he had become perhaps the most prolific fiction writer ever to live in the United States. Fittingly, this writer of violent, fast-paced Westerns died on the battlefield in World War II. Although he was born Frederick Faust, and although he eventually used at least seventeen pseudonyms, the world remembers him as Max Brand.

Faust was born on 29 May 1892 into a family of German-American-Irish origins. His family called him Schiller as a child. Gilbert Leander Faust, his father, the child of German immigrants, had grown up in Buffalo, New York. After serving in the Union army during the Civil War, the elder Faust led an unsettled life, moving from one job to another, and from one area of the country to another. He was a continual dreamer, always seeking overnight riches. At various times he was a lawyer in Illinois, a farmer in Iowa, and a land speculator in California. He married twice prior to marrying Shiller's mother, Louisa Uriel, whom he met in Iowa. He had two sons by prior marriages and two sons by Louisa. Altogether, the Faust household eventually consisted of four children: Karl Irving, Gilbert Goethe, Thomas Carlyle, and, the youngest, Frederick Schiller. Obviously, Faust came from a family with a strong literary heritage.

When Faust was born, his family was living in Seattle, Washington, where his father was once again trying to establish himself as a lawyer and businessman. Good times were followed by bad, however, and early in Faust's childhood his family was forced to move south to the Stockton, California, area of the San Joaquin Valley, where his mother had relatives. Faust grew up in humiliating poverty: the family's life was spent fleeing debt and creditors. When the parents could not afford to feed the children, they were sent off to relatives. Surely the memory of these early years influenced his obsession with the pursuit of wealth and the choice of an Italian villa for a home in later years.

For young Faust, the real turning point of his childhood was the death of his mother in 1900. From that point on, his father ceased to play a role in the family; he sent Schiller and his older brother Thomas to live with their mother's relatives on a wheat ranch in Collegeville, California, a few miles outside of Stockton. Faust was thirteen when he learned of his father's death.

His mother was the person who had developed his early but perpetual interest in reading. By the age of seven, no doubt to escape his miserable family life, Faust had turned to the fantasy world of books. Sir Thomas Malory's *Le Morte D'Arthur* (1485) was Faust's first favorite, but by age ten he was living a childhood absorbed in the escape world of fictional romance; besides Malory, his favorite authors were Johann Wolfgang von Goethe, Sir Walter Scott, and James Fenimore Cooper; he especially liked Greek and Roman mythology.

In 1907 Faust moved into Modesto to attend high school. The high school emphasized a rigorous classical curriculum on which he thrived. While there he lived for a time with the principal, also a relative, in a family surrounded by good books. During this period Faust began to develop a character that was governed by almost inhuman self-discipline as he absorbed himself in books, acquiring a first-rate education that enabled him to enter the University of California at Berkeley after graduation from high school.

But Faust was receiving an education outside the classroom as well. Modesto was a boisterous community filled with saloons and brothels. Together with his older brother and other friends, Faust developed a reputation as a street fighter. His skills became legendary in the small community. Thus, the tall, skinny boy was developing the two sides of his personality that persisted the rest of his life—the quiet, bookish scholar who loved classical literature and aspired to devote his life to poetry, and the reckless man of action who poured his soul into the production of hundreds of fast-action books and dreamed of a life of action for himself. This dichotomy of character manifested itself, as William A. Bloodworth Jr. and others have noted, in the contrasting personas of Max Brand and Frederick Faust.

Faust was already developing as a writer in high school. He published three items in the high school literary magazine during his senior year: a poetic monologue delivered by the emperor of an unnamed country in the distant past, a story of chivalry told by a dying Welsh knight, and a poem based on the Tristan and Isolde legend. At the University of California at Berkeley, which he entered in 1911, Faust continued to develop his writing talents. His love for great literature grounded him well in his major, English, and motivated him to seek the writing life as well. He wrote regularly for the college newspaper and the college literary magazine. During these years he produced poetry, essays, fiction, drama, and especially humorous, even satirical, writings. *The Occident,* an undergraduate literary magazine that many at the time considered on a par with the *Yale Literary Magazine,* published fifty-six of Faust's poems, and in September 1914 *The Occident* paid him a particularly high honor by publishing his "College Sonnets," a collection of twenty-one poems.

The years at Berkeley proved to have lifelong significance for Faust. He met men who were influential throughout his life, such as Sidney Coe Howard, who became a Pulitzer Prize–winning playwright and who wrote the screenplay for the movie *Gone with the Wind* (1939). Other friends included another screenwriter, Kenneth Perkins, and George Winthrop "Dixie" Fish,

*Faust in 1923 with his children, John and Jane*

who became a physician in New York and the inspiration for Faust's fictional Dr. Kildare.

Faust became a prominent student on campus both as a leader of the English Club and as a fighter and heavy drinker. He and his friends frequented the saloons of wharf areas in San Francisco, looking for action and excitement of any sort.

But the student who went on to become a famous writer never graduated from college. Just prior to graduation in 1915 the president met with Faust to seek an apology for the satiric literary attacks of this cocksure student. The interview did not go well, and a faculty committee met later to recommend that Faust not be granted a diploma; the reason given was excessive class absences. This failure to receive a diploma always hurt, and years later when the university offered to grant the diploma anyway, Faust refused it.

In the year following his university dismissal Faust joined the Canadian army but soon deserted when he discovered he would not be going into combat in Europe. During the year Faust resorted to heavy drinking and also took a short-term job in Hawaii as a journalist, but he also became serious about marriage with his college sweetheart, Dorothy Schillig.

As marriage became uppermost in his mind, he knew he had to get serious about a career, and thus he moved to New York to begin a career as a writer, although he really intended to seek a career as a poet, not as a writer of popular fiction. Nevertheless, he was willing to write anything in order to make a living.

Using some contacts from college days in a sense of desperation to develop an income, Faust was able to become acquainted with the mother of a classmate, Clemens Moffett. Mrs. Moffett was Samuel Langhorne Clemens's (Mark Twain's) sister, and she had contacts in the New York publishing world. Mrs. Moffett wrote a letter of introduction for Faust to Robert H. Davis, chief editor of Frank A. Munsey publications.

Davis was a major force in American publishing by 1916. Although usually associated with mass-marketed fiction, he had been an early promoter of Joseph Conrad. Also, he was William Sydney Porter's (O. Henry's) mentor as well as the publisher of such writers as Upton Sinclair and Edgar Rice Burroughs.

According to one perhaps apocryphal story, when the young Frederick Faust presented the letter to Davis, the editor scoffed, "You're supposed to be able to write? Well, let's see if you can." He gave the young man a plot sketch and pointed down the hall toward a room with a typewriter. Faust spent half a day at the typewriter and before five o'clock presented a perfectly publishable story to the editor. Davis was astonished and promptly paid him $78.00 for the story.

But this initial impression suffered from other early contacts with the editor. At one appointment Faust showed up drunk. He wrote on 29 January 1917 apologizing: "Hope I didn't talk absolutely like a fool. I incline toward that when the rum gets into my brain." Davis took his time replying to the apology, but when he did, he accepted gracefully:

February 14th, 1917
My dear Faust,
    Have yours of the 30th. Spoken like a man.
    Now I am going to be equally frank with you. I have one aversion—yes, that's it.
    I regard you as a man of tremendous potentialities. With a few short strides you can bridge the chasm between yourself and fame and take a high place among the writing men of this generation.

Throughout the next several years, Davis treated Faust almost as if he were an adopted son. He proffered advice freely about all phases of Faust's life as well as his stories, and he took an active role in promoting Faust's future marriage.

When Faust arrived in New York in 1916 to make his fortune, the two leaders in the pulp fiction market were the Street and Smith and the Munsey publications. Begun by Frank A. Munsey in 1896 with the introduction of *Argosy,* the Munsey pulps were magazines devoted to consumer fiction of about 128 pages printed on cheap pulpwood paper. They sold on newsstands for 10¢–25¢ per issue. Dozens of titles were mass-marketed mainly to either young or working-class male readers.

Davis recognized in the young writer a talent for composing stories quickly, an important qualification, and for adapting readily to the pulp style. Because of the targeted audience, the fiction of the pulps drew heavily on action, violence, and suspense with little subtlety of theme or characterization. Serial novels were a popular means of keeping readers hooked from one issue to the next. In order to develop name identification, Faust began writing under the pseudonym Max Brand. His first story under the new name was "The Sole Survivor," published in the 15 September 1917 *All-Story Weekly*. He chose the name in order to diminish the German connotation of his real name during the World War I days, and, perhaps more importantly, to save his own name under which to publish his serious literature.

Throughout his life Faust devoted much of his working routine to writing poetry, and he always maintained that his popular writing was beneath his dignity and merely made his livelihood. In fact, he did publish a poem ("The Secret") in the prestigious *Century Magazine* (February 1917) soon after coming to New York, and he worked with Henry Seidel Canby to make his long poem based on the Tristan and Isolde legend publishable. Canby, however, discouraged him from continuing with the project.

In 1917, as was the case throughout Faust's life, popular consumer fiction became his avenue to fame and fortune. His early stories were action stories of the swashbuckling variety or historical adventure stories. Davis quickly began selling the screen rights for his new young writer, and in 1917 and 1918 three motion pictures based on Max Brand stories appeared–*The Adopted Son* (1917), *Lawless Love* (1918), and *Kiss or Kill* (1918).

But a more important occurrence in 1917 was that Davis suggested Faust try his hand at writing Westerns. They were rapidly becoming the dominant genre of the pulps and of the best-selling novel lists. Clarence Mulford had begun in the pulps, publishing *Hopalong Cassidy* in *Argosy*, beginning in 1923; Zane Grey was having great success with his novels, particularly *The U.P. Trail* (1918), which was a runaway best-seller. So Faust began reading the serials by Grey that Davis sent him and in 1918 began submitting Western stories, or at least stories with Western settings. The first two Max Brand Western stories were "Above the Law," made into a movie titled *Lawless Love* the same year, and "Bad-Eye, His Life and Letters"; both stories appeared in *All-Story Weekly* on 19 October 1918.

"Bad-Eye, His Life and Letters" probably typifies the early Max Brand Western short story. It is a comedy of mistaken identity. The three main characters are Billy Masters, Jane Melrose, and "Bad-Eye" James Melrose. Bad-Eye is a loafer and a ne'er-do-well who has a strange source of income. Each month he gets a check in the mail, which he manages to spend quickly on drinks and gambling. Speculation is that a woman somewhere is supporting him. After he dies, a woman shows up in town inquiring about him. Obviously, she is his wife. In order to avoid hurting her feelings, Billy Masters, the proprietor of the saloon, delays telling her the truth about Melrose. Masters and the rest of the town take a liking to this woman who can ride like a man and carry herself as an independent woman of the West. When the truth comes out, the woman reacts with joy instead of grief, to the surprise of all. She turns out to be Melrose's cousin, and she has come looking for him on behalf of his abused wife. Now the wife can avoid a nasty divorce. Faust concludes the story with an uncharacteristic humorous touch:

> "Lady . . . if there ain't any more cause for me to talk about Bad-Eye, there's still something back in my mind that I want you to hear. . . . It's more or less of a real estate agent's talk," he said apologetically. He asks her to stay around for the good of the community. She needs a home.
>
> She sighed, "I wish I could, with all my heart . . . but it takes more money than I have. . . ."
>
> "H-m," said Masters, "but there are ways it can be done without money."
>
> "Without money?" she cried, astonished. "Do you mean to say that people around here will *give* away their homes to strangers?"
>
> "It wouldn't be charity," said Masters gravely, "It'd be a sort of partnership."
>
> Which is the reason that there are potted flowers, now, in the windows of the Masterses' place.

According to Bloodworth, Faust in these early stories uncharacteristically resembles Grey in style, especially in the way "he moved particularly close to Grey's popular evocation of western landscape." In "Bad-Eye, His Life and Letters" Jane, who is an Easterner visiting Nevada, observes the landscape from her hotel, seeing "the wild outlines of the mountains. They stepped back in four great ranges, the last imperious with purple. She smiled as she stared, for her heart wandered as freely as her eyes." As Bloodworth says, "The passage could have come from *Riders of the Purple Sage*."

Certainly, Grey exerted a significant influence on Faust. Jon Tuska has studied the influence in detail in *The Max Brand Companion* (1996), showing specific sources and analogues from Grey in Faust's

Faust and his wife, Dorothy, in 1929

early fiction. But the primary influence was of another type: "It consists rather in the fact that both Grey and Brand, in their finest Western fiction, eschewed realism in preference for psychodramas in the realm of the dream and the archetypes of the collective unconscious, even though they went about it in very different ways."

Grey explored the vast panoramas of the Western landscape as he personally experienced it. Faust "plunged instead into the no less vast cavity of the human soul—the expanse that is without measure."

Another early story that reveals both the future direction of Faust's Western fiction and the early immaturity is "A Sagebrush Cinderella," published 10 July 1920 in *All-Story Magazine*. The premise involves Jacqueline During, called Jac, a young girl who works for her father and is unappreciated and ignored by all the town. She has long been infatuated with Maurice Gordon, the town dandy and every girl's dream. A great dance is to be held in town, but Jac cannot go because she has nothing to wear; she could never compete with the other town girls; and

she has to work. Then a strange cowboy appears on the scene and sympathizes with Jac's plight. His name is Bill Carrigan, and he immediately rushes into town and buys a dress for Jac, helps her dress up like a visitor from back East, and then takes her to the dance. There Jac has a great time playing off all her newfound suitors against each other. Eventually, she finds Maurice Gordon wanting and at the end falls for her cowboy, Bill Carrigan. Obviously "A Sagebrush Cinderella" is a celebration of fairy tales and knight errantry with a Western twist. According to Tuska, Jac is a prototype for future Max Brand heroines: she "is a totally charming, fascinating character."

As Faust was beginning his career in the pulps, his relationship with Dorothy intensified, and he was determined to marry her. He returned to California to ask her to marry him only to find her engaged to a young lawyer. Dorothy's father had little confidence that Faust's freelance career in magazine writing held a stable future for his daughter and thus was supporting the lawyer's suit. Just in time, Robert Davis sold the rights for one of Faust's first movies, *A Thousand to One* (1920), based on the non-Western story "Fate's Honeymoon," published in a 14 July 1917 issue of *All-Story*. The income was quite a boost to both Faust's reputation as Brand and his financial appeal to Dorothy's father. The poor lawyer withdrew from the field, and Frederick Faust and Dorothy Schillig were married on 29 May 1917 in an Episcopal ceremony at the Schillig home.

In the month before the wedding, however, on 2 April 1917, President Woodrow Wilson asked for a declaration of war on Germany, so when Faust returned to New York with Dorothy, he was determined to enlist in the U.S. Army and try again to get into combat. However, he was even less successful than in the Canadian army because once he enlisted he was sent to Camp Humphreys, Virginia, the current Fort Belvoir, as an ordinary camp orderly. He spent the war performing basic camp chores—digging latrines, doing KP duty, and picking up cigarette butts. He did, however, learn to shoot, although he had a lifelong aversion to guns. At last he was ordered to Europe, but as he arrived in New York to ship out the armistice was announced.

Even during his army experience, however, miserable as he was, Faust never stopped writing. *The Untamed,* his first major novel, was written for the most part in this period and published in 1919. During this period Faust's national reputation as Brand and his financial success began to rise rapidly, primarily because of the personal management of Davis.

As Faust settled into New York with his new wife, financial success began to come quickly. According to Bloodworth, "In the 18 months that followed his wedding, Brand produced at least five book-length serials, seven novelettes, and five short stories, all of which were published in Munsey magazines before the end of 1918. All these works amounted to 600,000 published words. Even at Munsey's lowest rate, the dollars were flowing in."

The major career boost came in Davis's sale of motion picture rights to Faust's fiction. The early motion pictures were not Westerns, however. First there came *The Adopted Son,* a Metro Pictures production starring Francis X. Bushman and Beverly Bayne; then in 1918 came a movie titled *Lawless Love,* based on "Above the Law." This movie starred several major actors of the day—Jewel Carmen, Henry Woodward, and Edward Hearn. A month later, while Faust was digging latrines in Virginia, Universal released *Kiss or Kill,* starring Priscilla Dean. This movie proved to be his first big hit in Hollywood.

It was, however, with the publication of *The Untamed,* first as a serial in 1918 and then as a book

in 1919, that Faust's career as a major author began. Certainly, *The Untamed* is one of the most unusual of the Westerns usually considered classics—novels such as *Riders of the Purple Sage* (1912), *The Ox-Bow Incident* (1940), *Shane* (1949), or *Hondo* (1952). *The Untamed* is, as Bloodworth says, "to the classic western novel what a film like the mysterious *High Plains Drifter* is to *Stagecoach*."

The title of the novel refers to the central character, Whistling Dan Barry, an adult innocent of unknown origins with obvious associations to classical mythology. In fact, the title of the chapter that introduces him is "Pan of the Desert." The rancher Joe Cumberland found Whistling Dan as a child following a flock of wild geese and brought Whistling Dan into his family. The child has a mysterious ability to communicate with wild animals; as the story begins, he has a black stallion named Satan and a wolf-like dog named Black Bart as constant comrades. Only Whistling Dan can control these devilish animals. Another quality of Dan's is an eerie, unearthly faun-like whistling often heard in the woods in advance of his appearance. Further still, at times of special stress, his eyes emit a strange, eerie glow that forebodes some imminent action, usually violent in nature. Of course, the plot, while quite loosely constructed, revolves around Dan's movement from a state of innocence to a state of savage experience.

Jack Nachbar, in his introduction to the 1917 edition of *The Untamed,* considers this move away from innocence the element in the novel that elevates it into a major work of the American literary tradition: "A close reading of the novel shows it is both a highly unusual Western and an intriguing continuation of a major theme in so-called classic American literature." Nachbar then fits *The Untamed* into the framework of the tradition of classic American fiction by Samuel Langhorne Clemens (Mark Twain), James Fenimore Cooper, William Faulkner, Nathaniel Hawthorne, and Herman Melville. Nachbar especially notes the affinity of *The Untamed* to Hawthorne's *The Marble Faun* (1860) and Melville's *Billy Budd* (1924): "Both of these characters [Donatello and Billy Budd] are incapable of conscious sin and both of them kill as an act of blind instinct," much as Dan Barry does when he pursues Jim Silent because Silent has embarrassed him. Out of frustration Silent hits Barry across the face and causes him for the first time in his life to taste his own blood. Now for the first time the eerie yellow glow appears in Barry's eyes, and Whistling Dan Barry sets out on a trail of revenge in order to remove the taste of blood from his lips. Eventually, he achieves his goal.

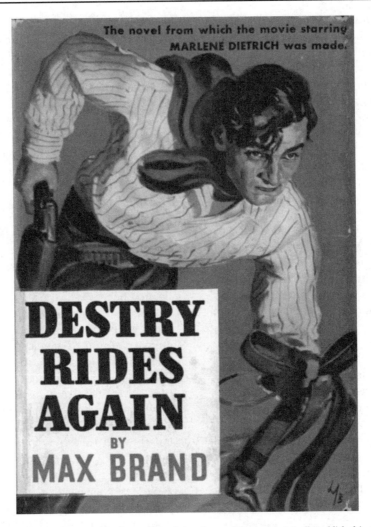

*Dust jacket for the 1940 edition of one of Faust's best-known Westerns, originally published in 1930, about a man who is framed twice by his best friend*

At first, all underestimate Barry's special talents. Jim Silent, the leader of an outlaw band, challenges this small-framed man, a man of delicate and perhaps effeminate appearance, to a shooting contest. To the amazement of all, Barry wins. But he does not just win; he humiliates Silent. When Barry shoots four coins tossed in the air before they hit the ground, Lee Haines exclaims, "it wasn't human." Both the coins and the gun that performed the impossible feat are treated as holy relics by all who are fortunate enough to own them. Barry does not seem human; he seems like a character out of myth, a "Pan of the Desert."

*The Untamed* was an immediate success and has remained one of the best-selling Brand novels. Robert Easton estimates that it has easily sold more than a million copies in hardback; twice it has been made into a motion picture—first with Tom Mix. But Faust, as usual, felt embarrassed. Writing to Dorothy, he said, "Daily I thank God in three languages that I write under a pen name."

Nevertheless, *The Untamed* was so successful that Faust was forced to write a sequel, *The Night Horseman* (1920), and then another sequel, *The Seventh Man* (1921), in which he killed off his hero. Even then his readers wanted more, so he published *Dan Barry's Daughter* (1924), which first appeared as six installments in serial form in *All-Star Weekly* (30 June 1923 – 4 August 1923). Despite his embarrassment, Faust doubled and even tripled his income from each book as it moved from serial to hardback book to, in the case of *The Night Horseman,* Hollywood movie.

As the first major Max Brand Western, *The Untamed* shows many characteristics of his later fiction. Perhaps the most significant difference between a classic Zane Grey Western, or even a Louis L'Amour Western, is that for Max Brand, Western landscape possesses little meaning. Grey's heroes derive their soul's sustenance from the land, and their author obliges his readers with page after page of landscape description. L'Amour claimed to have walked over every inch of the setting in his novels, so that if the hero hunkers down in a gully, the reader can be sure L'Amour had hunkered down in that same gully.

But *The Untamed,* like most other Brand Westerns, takes place in no specific geographic setting and in no particular time period, other than the time of "the Old West," whatever that might mean in a given novel. Faust seldom spends more than a short paragraph establishing a setting, and then the description is confined to vague references to mountain country or desert country.

Instead of centering his Westerns on geographic locale or time frame, Faust centers them on the larger-than-life myth of the West, a myth comparable to classical Greek or Roman myths, to biblical myths, or to medieval myths of King Arthur and his knights. *The Untamed* establishes the type that Faust works through more than six hundred Western stories and novels.

Nachbar has itemized the parallels in the novel to classical myth and the Arthurian legend, pointing out such references as the title of chapter 7, "The Mute Messenger," suggesting the soothsayers of Greek tragedy. Chapters 14 and 17 are named from Old Testament myths, "Delilah" and "Cain." Throughout the book the code of chivalry from Mallory is kept strictly. Certainly, the outlaws' respect for Kate Cumberland reflects the chivalric code, but also Lee Haines and Buck Daniels, both outlaws, become honorable as they try to protect and rescue Kate, an obvious damsel in distress.

Nachbar concludes, "Many Western heroes, because they are the saviors of the frontier community, are described as symbolic Christs. But Whistling Dan belongs to the ancient and medieval pagan world. Dan transcends human limitations and approaches divinity as the nature god Pan and not as Christian savior."

With the success of *The Untamed,* Faust began to see possibilities of great financial success; therefore, he established a writing pace almost unimaginable for any time period. He began producing so many stories for the pulps—Western adventures and suspense stories, mysteries, and other thrillers—that his publishers had to increase the number of pseudonyms under which his work appeared. Often several of his stories appeared in one issue of a magazine, but all under different names. For example, the 5 March 1932 *Western Story Magazine* show-

cased three stories by Faust on the cover but under three different names. The editors did not want to oversaturate the market for the Max Brand name; they also did not want to confuse their readers when a single issue of *Western Story* or *Argosy* might include two or three new stories alongside various parts of running serials.

Editors felt they had to develop the personas for the various names under which Faust wrote, too. Thus, fabricated biographies of the various pseudonyms appeared in the magazines throughout the years. Meanwhile, Faust carefully preserved his real name for his serious literature to which he was devoting nearly as much time as he was to his paying work. In 1924 he even attempted a blank-verse play, "Rimini," which was never performed nor published. Altogether, then, Frederick Faust wrote under seventeen pseudonyms: Frank Austin, George Owen Baxter, Lee Bolt, Max Brand, Walter C. Butler, George Challis, Peter Dawson, Martin Dexter, Evin Evan, Evan Evans, John Frederick, Frederick Frost, Dennis Lawton, David Manning, Peter Henry Morland, Hugh Owen, and Nicholas Silver.

In 1925 Faust and his family, which by then included two children—Jane, born in 1918, and John, born in 1919—moved to Europe to live out his dream. Eventually, he settled in a luxurious villa in Florence, Italy. From there he continued to produce a prodigious quantity of fiction, mostly Westerns. Yet, he never could cease self-deprecation. In a 1925 letter to an old college friend he remarked, "My serious occupation is teaching my family to play catch and jump rope, and in my spare moments I am doing ten thousand words a day, because Blackwell [of *Western Story Magazine*] recently refused a story. How that poor bum can continue to absorb this junk I cannot tell, but he still does it!"

One account from the daughter of a friend indicates the lavish lifestyle Faust led in Italy:

> He lives like a medieval prince in his Florentine villa. His swimming pool and tennis court are the envy of the petty aristocracy for miles around. He runs a pack of Newfoundlands and keeps the stars in sight with a telescope on his terrace. He has a weak heart which threatens momentarily to kill him; and against the advice of a battery of doctors he puts the heart in place by drinking deep, smoking like Vesuvius, playing tennis like a champion, driving an Isotta Fraschini a hundred kilometers an hour through the Rhone Valley, and keeping a work schedule that would murder a stevedore. . . . And the novels are stacked like cordwood in the offices of Brandt & Brandt. He writes them faster than they can be printed.

*Faust's home, Villa Negli Ulivi, in Florence, Italy*

In order to maintain his lifestyle, Faust had to publish even more prose and by 1932, as the pulp market was declining, he had to make up for sagging sales by demanding higher rates per word or demanding more work. More work was the usual solution. In order to work at the rate required he had to produce forty thousand words a day. Sometimes, despite a weak heart, he resorted to stimulants to maintain his stamina: "For the first time in eleven years," he wrote to his agent Carl Brandt in 1932, "I have found a dope that keeps my rotten heart from going crazy—digitaline and quinine, if you want to know the mystery—and now I can work at least twice as hard as I ever did before, and three or four times as hard in a pinch."

Faust was at the peak of his powers in the mid 1930s and was regularly producing best-selling Westerns. He produced many novels extolling sympathetically Native American life in conflict with the advancing white civilization, as in the Thunder Moon series or in *The White Cheyenne* (1960), published serially in six parts in *The Western Story Magazine* (12 December 1925 – 20 January 1926). Several series of novels found loyal readers demanding more and more sequels, as in the Silvertip series or the Montana Kid novels. But, with the Great Depression crippling the

U.S. economy in the 1930s, the great days of the pulps were coming to an end, and Faust was forced to seek other markets for his work. The slicks, such as *Esquire, Collier's, Cosmopolitan, Saturday Evening Post,* and *Harper's,* began carrying his stories, though not as many Westerns, and never to the extent that the pulps had carried Max Brand stories.

Then, when his efforts to move from pulps to slicks were beginning to pay off and when escape from his crushing debts was about to succeed, he accepted an offer from Metro-Goldwyn-Mayer (M-G-M) to move to Hollywood and work on a series of movies based on his Dr. Kildare character. With a bad heart and increasing recognition that his lifelong dream of developing a major reputation for his poetry was likely to be futile, perhaps he was growing weary. For whatever reason, he wrote few Westerns after 1937 and, instead, devoted his energies to motion pictures and to his Dr. Kildare novels. His Westerns are still on the top-selling booklists, but the Dr. Kildare novels are, perhaps, hopelessly dated.

The years in Hollywood, nevertheless, proved an adventure for Faust. Other M-G-M writers at the time were F. Scott Fitzgerald and Aldous Huxley, with whom he developed a deep friendship. While certainly a fresh experience for him, the Hollywood years were not good ones personally for Faust—he drank heavily and worried about his future with his bad heart. But professionally they provided him even greater national exposure than ever as his Dr. Kildare series became extremely popular and as his finest Western, *Destry Rides Again* (1930), was made into a popular motion picture in 1939 starring James Stewart and Marlene Dietrich. A later movie version stars Audie Murphy, and a Broadway musical version starring Andy Griffith has been staged.

The plot of *Destry Rides Again* is of Harry Destry's lifelong attempt to prove he is a peer to anyone in the town of Wham. The story is based on an Iago-like betrayal. Destry is framed by his best friend, Chester Bent, convicted by a jury of his peers, and sent to prison for robbery. As he leaves, he vows revenge on the jury that convicted him on the false charges. Through the years Bent invests his booty and becomes an important businessman in the town of Wham, all the while developing a close relationship with Charlie Dangerfield, the sweetheart Destry left behind. Destry returns from prison utterly broken. Bent takes him into his own house as his only friend. The townspeople begin to take advantage of him, and the former jury members even mock him. His girl renounces him as a coward and not a real man. But at last Destry comes alive in a blaze of gunfire as the town realizes the meekness was an act.

One after the other, each jury member either flees or faces the terrible wrath of Destry. But Bent grows desperate again as he becomes the victim of blackmail himself and once again commits a terrible crime–murder–and frames Destry. This time there is a witness, Willie, a world-weary boy disillusioned by the disgrace of his father and enraptured by his hero, Destry. With his dying breath, Willie reveals the villainy of Bent to the incredulous gunfighter. A showdown follows, and Destry achieves true revenge, renounces his guns, marries Charlie, and settles into a domestic life.

According to Richard W. Etulain, the genesis for *Destry Rides Again* came from a trip Faust made with his former editor and now close friend Davis. Perhaps several experiences from this trip worked into the novel. At one point Faust saw an incredible horse that could outrun any other horse. The town of Wham no doubt was reminiscent of Modesto, where Faust grew up. Biographer Robert Easton sees Willie, the hardscrabble youth, as particularly autobiographical, especially in the way Willie realizes his father's false bravado and runs off to declare his own independence.

*Destry Rides Again* is in all likelihood the best Max Brand novel, even though Christine Bold in *Selling the Wild West: Popular Western Fiction, 1800 to 1960* (1987) has stated a common opinion that the more pulp stories Faust wrote through the years the more rigid his formula became. Bloodworth, though, argues that *Destry Rides Again* violates the conventions of a standard *Western Story* serial by "providing explicit philosophical commentary and developing its protagonist through a form of defeat rather than victory." Furthermore, he continues, "Although Faust relied on a traditional form of adventure story–the revenge plot–he added distinctive touches to typical elements of pursuit and suspense."

The thematic climax of the novel occurs as Destry holds the dying Willie. Suddenly, what has been clear to the readers all along becomes clear to the gunfighter. He now realizes the villainy of his best friend and the relative innocence of the townspeople. Prior to this moment Destry had assumed a superiority over the townspeople–he was a man without a peer among them, especially among those on the jury. Now as he realizes he had been duped by Bent and that Charlie was in fact faithful, he faces the question of who exactly he is. This recognition scene approaches the tragic as he realizes how close he has come to committing a genuine crime. Unlike Othello, Harry Destry recognizes his weakness in time to avoid tragedy.

Thus, the novel is an extraordinary story of profound character change, unusual for typical Westerns but not unusual for Max Brand Westerns. Many of Faust's heroes have similar moments of recognition: Thunder Moon in *Thunder Moon and the Sky People* (1996), which was published as "Thunder Moon-Squawman" by George Owen Baxter in *The Western Story Magazine* (24 September 1927 – 22 October 1927), realizes his Indian heritage is ultimately superior to his white heritage as he rejects Charlotte Keene for Red Wing; Jeremy Saylor, the Whisperer of *The Whispering Outlaw* (1926), pays his penalty in one year of hard labor so that he can re-enter the world of civilization and marry Rose Percival.

With the coming of World War II, everything changed again for Faust, as it did for all of America. Still, after all the years of never having gotten over his thwarted efforts in World War I, he longed to prove himself in combat. His age, of course, ruled out military service, as did his heart condition. Nevertheless, with persistence he landed an assignment as a correspondent with the Eighty-eighth Infantry Division in Italy. As a correspondent he wrote about actual battlefield situations and experienced war himself. Even though he was assigned quarters with men from a socioeconomic level he had always avoided, he found the experience exhilarating. No doubt he also enjoyed the celebrity once his identity was discovered, for his comrades in arms were, of course, some of his most loyal readers. No longer did he just write about action; he became a man of action himself. He lived up to his dream. On 11 May 1944 Faust was wounded in the chest by shrapnel. He insisted to the medics that he was all right and that they should help those more seriously wounded than he was. Thus, he died a hero's death at the age of fifty-one.

Critics are divided over the merits of Faust's work. Many deride it as the perfect example of the depths to which formula Westerns could fall after their great beginning with the work of Owen Wister. Some think Faust degraded the Western, that he distorted the genre and, in fact, is the one writer primarily responsible for discrediting Westerns as serious literature. Faust would agree with that opinion, as he often considered his works mere "old melodramatic junk." Those who seek authenticity of detail will not find much in his incredible output.

That output comprises, according to Robert Easton, 196 novels of fifty thousand or more words apiece, 226 novelettes of from twenty thousand to fifty thousand words apiece, 162 stories of less than twenty thousand words, and 44 poems–a total of 628 separate titles. There has never been a time in which many of his novels have not been in print. Currently, the Golden West Literary Agency, in an arrangement with Leisure Books, is editing Faust's works—under the name Max Brand—and providing definitive editions. The project, though, is necessarily limited by the volume of works available.

Faust has defenders both in the popular market and among academic critics. His work has been subject to several book-length studies as well as many scholarly articles. He moved the Western away from a slavish dependency on the portrayal of an authentic West. Yet, when placed beside the works of those who claim authenticity, such as L'Amour, Faust's novels seem closer to the large realities of life. They develop the American Western myth to its fullest. Faust's heroes and heroines are larger than life, and they live on a landscape of mythological, not geographic, dimensions; these novels are where they ought to be, in the realm of myth. For that reason, Max Brand novels can appear in new covers endlessly to new readers in new generations.

**References:**

William A. Bloodworth Jr., *Max Brand* (Boston: Twayne, 1993);

Bloodworth, "Max Brand (Frederick Faust)" in *Fifty Western Writers: A Bio-Bibliographical Sourcebook,* edited by Fred Erisman and Richard W. Etulain (Westport, Conn.: Greenwood Press, 1982);

Bloodworth, "Max Brand's West," *Western American Literature,* 16 (1981): 177–179;

Christine Bold, *Selling the Wild West: Popular Western Fiction, 1800 to 1960* (Bloomington: University of Indiana Press, 1987);

Edgar L. Chapman, "The Image of the Indian in Max Brand's Pulp Western Novels," *The Heritage of the Great Plains* (Spring 1978): 16–45;

Robert Easton, *Max Brand: The Big Westerner* (Norman: University of Oklahoma Press, 1970);

Etulain, "Introduction," in *Max Brand: Destry Rides Again* (Boston: Gregg Press, 1979);

Cynthia S. Hamilton, "Frederick Faust," in *Western and Hard-Boiled Detective Fiction in America: From High Noon to Midnight* (New York: Macmillan, 1987), pp. 94–119;

Jack Nachbar, "Introduction," in Max Brand, *The Untamed* (Boston: Gregg Press, 1978);

Jon Tuska and Vicki Piekarski, eds., *The Max Brand Companion* (Westport, Conn.: Greenwood Press, 1996).

**Papers:**

Most of the papers of Frederick Schiller Faust (Max Brand) are in the Bancroft Library at the University of California at Berkeley. Other papers are kept by The American Heritage Center at the University of Wyoming.

# Judith Freeman

*(1 October 1946 –    )*

## B. W. Jorgensen
*Brigham Young University*

BOOKS: *Family Attractions: Stories* (New York: Viking, 1988);
*The Chinchilla Farm: A Novel* (New York: Norton, 1989);
*Set for Life* (New York: Norton, 1991);
*A Desert of Pure Feeling* (New York: Pantheon, 1996);
*Red Water* (New York: Pantheon, 2002).

OTHER: "How Does the Dance Begin?" in *The Stories that Shape Us: Contemporary Women Write about the West,* edited by Teresa Jordan and James R. Hepworth (New York: Norton, 1995), pp. 104–116;
"Wertheimer in the City," in *Absolute Disaster: Fiction from Los Angeles,* edited by Lee Montgomery (Los Angeles: Dove, 1996), pp. 171–194;
"Ofelia Rodriguez," in *Writers Harvest 2,* edited by Ethan Canin (New York: Harcourt Brace, 1996), pp. 245–276;
"Ursa Minor," in *Intimate Nature: The Bond between Women and Animals,* edited by Brenda Peterson, Linda Hogan, and Deena Metzger (New York: Fawcett Columbine, 1998), pp. 295–303.

SELECTED PERIODICAL PUBLICATIONS–
UNCOLLECTED: "India Journal," *Weber Studies,* 10 (Fall 1993): 59–70;
"The Tunnel Rock Diary," *Weber Studies,* 15 (Spring/Summer 1998): 91–94.

*Judith Freeman (courtesy of the author)*

"It came to me as an extraordinary gift," Judith Freeman said of her fiction in remarks before a reading on 30 May 1996, "and not one that I thought I would ever be given. Not one that I knew that I had, for a very long time." Freeman might best be described as a Mormon expatriate unwilling to forget her roots in the mountain West, both the rich and healing physical and emotional landscape and the "family attractions" of the Utah Mormon culture that nourished her, even though she early found that culture's "beliefs . . . quite confined to a particular view" that tended to level the rough complexity and amazing beauty of the world. In a letter of 6 November 1997, she acknowledges "a schism" in her psyche:

> I am a Mormon by birth: I am of that culture, but no longer a part of the religion. I miss being a part of the community of my youth. I have a fondness for Utah and for many people there. Yet, I am in the position of many writers and artists before me: it *is* hard to go home again. Everything has changed. Loved ones are gone. I'm not sure where I fit.

Chronologically, Freeman belongs to the same American literary generation as Anne Tyler, Richard Ford, Tobias Wolff, Raymond Carver, Frederick Busch, Josephine Humphreys, Marilynne Robinson, and many others born from the late 1930s through the late 1940s. Her literary career began a decade or so later than the careers of most of these writers, however, which puts her more in the company of somewhat younger writers emerging in the late 1980s and early 1990s—new writers of the American West such as Pam Houston, Allison Baker, Ron Carlson, Robert Bowsell, Antonya Nelson, and Melanie Rae Thon. Like these writers and many others, she writes in a predominantly realistic mode and often, though not exclusively, about contemporary domestic life—the love and trouble of wives and husbands, parents and children, sisters and brothers and friends; and about people who work mainly for and at their living, not the rich and famous nor the glamorous and powerful. Even her move into historical fiction in her most recent work is shared by some of her contemporaries. Yet, unlike most of those mentioned, Freeman is a native-born Westerner and born and raised a Mormon, and those differences are significant. Besides the writers she admires or acknowledges as influences, her most interesting literary affinities may be with earlier "lost-generation" or "expatriate" Utah Mormon writers of the 1940s, such as Maurine Whipple and Virginia Sorensen, or with Wallace Stegner, who grew up partly in Salt Lake City and often wrote out of a deep-grained love of both the physical and cultural landscape of Utah. Among living writers of the West and of Utah, Freeman seems most closely akin to another Mormon writer with a keen feeling for her native place and especially for the Great Salt Lake, Terry Tempest Williams. Both Williams and Freeman seek and celebrate that place of "refuge."

Judith Ann Freeman was born in Ogden, Utah, on 1 October 1946, the sixth of eight children of Roy and Alice Freeman, both descendants of Mormon pioneers and active members of the Church of Jesus Christ of Latter-day Saints who had met while serving church missions in Kentucky during the Great Depression. Freeman grew up attending Mormon religious services and Mormon children's and youth meetings. At Ogden High School she played Anne Frank in a drama production and, as she describes in her 6 November 1997 letter, "felt the power of literature to convey experience, how the experience of a Jewish girl hiding in an attic in Amsterdam could move a Mormon audience in Ogden, Utah."

Freeman's father sold shoes, drove freight, ran a clothing store, worked in the purchasing department at Hill Air Force Base, and commuted by rail to an office job at the Bingham Canyon mine of Kennecott Copper Corporation. He also "had the distinction of being the only Democrat in our [Mormon] ward—an uneducated man with an inquiring mind and sharp opinions," who loved music and who in the 1970s supported the Equal Rights Amendment when few Utah Mormons did. From him Freeman got her liberal political views, though in "How Does the Dance Begin?" (1995) she writes that his "peculiar brand of liberalism" was "more like renegade Western populism mixed with a class consciousness born of his own painful experiences, all combined with his deep religious beliefs."

Her father served for a time in the lay bishopric of the family's Mormon ward, and in her 6 November 1997 letter she recalls that when she was about twelve he told her she could no longer ride her horse in the nearby foothills on Sundays, because of objections from people in the ward: "He added that if it were up to him, he'd let me continue . . . but it wasn't up to him." Seeing that her father "didn't necessarily believe in what he was forcing me to do" gave Judith "permission to question . . . what I'd been taught" and "revealed my father to be very human, full of his own doubts, and at heart, my true ally." This incident was the beginning not only of skepticism and a desire to do things "not for appearance's sake but because they were right for me" but also, perhaps, of a fiction writer's "understanding why people do what they do, just how complex our interior lives really are, and how tender our affinities."

Other than church publications, doctrinal and historical, there were few books in the house; yet Freeman discovered, on her own, Gertrude Chandler Warner's *The Boxcar Children* (1942), Pearl S. Buck's *The Good Earth* (1931), Margaret Mitchell's *Gone with the Wind* (1936), and, most important, Admiral Richard E. Byrd's *Alone* (1938), in which, according to the typescript of the autobiographical "How Does the Dance Begin?," she found an "evocation of pure nature," the "spiritual feeling . . . that transcendental knowledge of the self can occur under the harshest conditions," and "a human voice, rather humble and self-effacing." She never intended to become a writer; answering a questionnaire in a church youth group, she wrote that she would "like to be either a secretary or a stewardess and then get married and be a mother."

Freeman married at seventeen, the day after high school graduation, according to "How Does the Dance Begin?," dreaming of "the Peace Corps, Africa, adventures"; and when she was eighteen, she bore a son with a deformed heart. Living in Springville, Utah, from 1965 to 1967 while her husband attended Brigham Young University, she worked in a bank. In remarks before the 30 May 1996 reading she recalled sitting at the drive-in window, writing poetry as she waited for customers. A year or so later, according to "How Does the Dance Begin?" she discovered the works of such writers as D. H. Lawrence, Thomas Hardy, James Joyce, Willa Cather, Sherwood Anderson, and Virginia Woolf in a class at Macalester College in St. Paul, Minnesota; from that experience, she

8.

If he wouldn't have pie, would he try the jello salad
or a little ham, the widow asked. Emilio protested that he
wasn't hungry.

It was stupid for people to think of food when they
should be mourning the dead. He couldn't understand this. Emilio
looked around the room filled with smiling people, some of whom
were busily eating from paper plates warped by the weight of the
food. He hadn't expected this. Why weren't they wailing and
bemoaning their loss?

He must have stayed an hour, not because he was enjoying
this picnic but because he couldn't figure out how to leave.
The Bishop, a sartorial figure, spoke of funeral arrangements to
the widow and life-insurance (his was the largest insurance company in the valley) ~~to a young ward member~~. People arrived
and left, ate and spoke of the deceased man's virtues, complimented
the donors of food and chucked children on their chins. Smiles,
smiles and more smiles. Even the widow's occasional tears ran
down a smiling face.

Emilio could have torn his hair out in frustration.
He wanted a howl to go up. This was not mourning as he knew it
in Mexico. How much better it was to have the dead present,
surrounded by black-dressed women who knew how to mark the passing of life with wails and cries, who rocked with their grief
and sent up a chorus of howls from the depths of their stomachs
so that neighbors passing the house would know from the pitch of
the moaning that the dead was receiving a rightful final song.
That was the way his father was treated at his death. His mother
had a sore throat and swollen face to show for it. But this was
an American house and these mourners fattened themselves on lemon
pie before they even buried their dead and the widow played hos-
tess and the Bishop wondered aloud whether the widow and her sons
might like to borrow his fancy car since the procession to the
cemetary was bound to be slow and his LeSabre had air conditioning!

It was an assault, a travesty, an affront to the dead
man and Emilio could take no more of it. Sweating and flushed,
he arose abruptly--too abruptly; his head became light and the room
assumed a reddish, and then yellow glow and he stumbled forward
a few steps.

Leon grabbed him by the arm. "You okay?"

"I just stood up too fast," Emilio said. "The blood
goes faster than I do these days." With great politeness he
said goodbye, nodding to each person in the room. Tears were in
his eyes when he touched the widow's hand.

Leon walked him out to his car and said, "Give Gloria
my love, would you?"

"Gloria," Emilio said softly as if intoning the conclusion
of the rosary. "Sometimes I think you didn't convert her good
enough."

Leon    laughed    and    laughed, sure that Emilio was
making some kind of joke. "How's that?" he said.

"She's still half a Catholic I think." And half a witch
he was going to add but he felt a tug of conscience, as if he was
betraying his wife, and so he stopped himself.

A yellow worm had lowered itself on a silvery thread
from the branches of the tree above Emilio's head and it twisted
and spun before his eyes  like a hypnotist's charm. Leon's

*Page from the first draft for Freeman's story "The Death of a Mormon Elder," included
in her 1988 collection* Family Attractions *(Collection of Judith Freeman)*

knew that she wanted to tell stories. In a summer creative writing class taught by the same teacher, Roger Blakely, she wrote her first short story, which "won first prize in the class. It was the story of a girl who falls in love in kindergarten with another little girl and waits for her in the coat closet in order to wrestle her to the floor and give her kisses among the galoshes."

In St. Paul, while her husband directed a newly coeducational dormitory at Macalester and she was "dorm mother" to students her own age or older, her son underwent surgery to repair his heart. But during this time the marriage fell apart, and Freeman shortly returned to Utah to raise her son with her parents' help and to work at a variety of jobs, including secretary, horse wrangler, and ski instructor. Though she attended church with her parents, she says in the letter of 6 November 1997 that she "had psychologically already left the church." Always "a somewhat rebellious daughter" who felt she could "argue everything, in Sunday school or seminary or around the dinner table at night," Freeman admits that she was never "presented 'belief' as a choice," and had thus never truly believed in the religion: "most simply stated I must have felt that Mormonism did not present me with a future I could embrace." She took a few more classes at Weber State College in Ogden (1969–1970) and moved to Sun Valley, Idaho, in 1970.

In 1972 or 1973 she met the television comedy writer Digby Wolfe, who became her partner and mentor for several years; in 1978 she moved to Los Angeles to live with Wolfe, and her son went to live with his father. In 1979 she took a writing class from Shelly Lowenkopf at the University of Southern California, and in the Beverly Hills house she shared with Wolfe she wrote, in 1980, the earliest draft of her first novel. After she and Wolfe parted a year or so later, they remained friends, and he still supported her work "through a kind of stipend," half of the rent from the house. The income enabled Freeman to sit down and write short stories for three years.

In "How Does the Dance Begin?" she says:

> I wanted to write about the world I knew, the world that had formed me—the West, Utah, Mormonism—the strange and exotic yet so terribly ordinary and very American experience I had gone through being raised the way I was. I wanted to tell family stories. These things, I felt, were mine, my landscape, both physical and emotional.

Freeman also enlarged her knowledge of contemporary fiction by writing book reviews for the *Los Angeles Times* and other papers. In a 31 May 1996 personal interview, she noted that she particularly admired Mary Gordon's *Final Payments* (1978) and "thought it was dealing with some of the same kinds of things:

early religious upbringing, . . . relationship with the father, a very strong, powerful figure; an emergence into a world of a person . . . brought up in a parochial secluded kind of way." In her attempts to learn the craft of narrative construction, Freeman took Gordon's book apart and "made a graph out of it." The first draft of her own novel, titled "Good Works," was not publishable, however; answering questions after a reading on 30 May 1996, she recalled, "even the woman I gave it to to type it . . . called me at page 76, and . . . said, 'Honey, I don't know how to tell you this, but I just don't think this is working.' . . . I didn't even get it past the typist!"

Freeman turned to short stories to experiment with different voices and situations: "I could try stories from memory, and I could completely make things up." But in three years of writing stories and sending them to magazines, not one was accepted, and her first book, *Family Attractions: Stories* (1988), appeared without any of its stories having been published previously. A writer friend read the stories, liked them, and sent them to a New York agent who also liked them well enough to circulate them. The third publisher to see the collection, Viking, bought the stories: Gerry Howard, an editor at Viking, thought they were "very unusual, very American."

Howard also asked if she was working on a novel. At the urging of her agent, Freeman went back to "Good Works" and discarded everything but the first chapter, which became the opening chapter of *The Chinchilla Farm: A Novel* (1989). Everything else was wrong, Freeman said at the 30 May 1996 reading, but she saved her protagonist-narrator. Freeman quickly wrote another seventy pages and soon sent the novel-in-progress to her agent. Getting a contract for both the stories and her novel gave her a sense that she had a future in writing. Her editor at Viking moved to W. W. Norton when the novel was in press, and Freeman chose to publish it with Norton. During this same period, 1985–1986, Freeman met and married Anthony Hernandez, a dedicated photographer. In the 6 November 1997 letter she explained that as a visual artist, Hernandez helped her "learn to 'see' in a different way and . . . helped me create fiction through a more intense observation of the world."

The eleven stories in *Family Attractions* display a variety of situations and voices—from the autobiographical "Going Out to Sea," a fictional version of the breakup of Freeman's first marriage that also anticipates her third novel, and "Clearfield," about single motherhood in northern Utah in the late 1960s, through a domestic comedy of remarriage in the title story, to bereavement and widowhood in "The Botanic Gardens," "What Is This Movie?" and "The Joan Crawford Letter." The settings range from Utah and Idaho to the Midwest, to the East and West Coasts, and to Mexico and Australia. Throughout, the stories are entangled in family relations, either centrally or peripherally, families made by marriage or remarriage, or sometimes—as later in her novels *The Chinchilla Farm* and *Set for Life* (1991)—cobbled together.

"Camp Rose" pays loving tribute to some of Freeman's own "family attractions." Unhurried, homely, and lyrical—and perhaps reminiscent of some of Alice Munro's stories, which Freeman admires—the story presents a series of moments in which Ann, Peter, and their aging parents, Ray and Ada, "find the center they've always wanted to occupy together, that moment of harmony." According to Freeman in the 31 May 1996 interview, her own favorite story in the volume is "Death of a Mormon Elder," inspired by a comic couple in one of Gabriel García Márquez's stories: "What if a couple like that were converted to Mormonism in Mexico, and somehow ended up in Utah running a church farm?" Acknowledging a "deity that unaccountably allowed for the death of good men in violent accidents [yet] was also supposed to be their protector," who "could even make the sons the instruments of their father's deaths," the story is in some ways a distinctly Mormon comic tale; yet at the same time it transcends its own Mormon ground. Healed of tick fever by a Mormon priesthood blessing from the sons of his dead friend Clayton Waterfall, Emilio Carranza feels that "There was magic in the world he didn't understand, but he felt he had been called into a circle to witness it" and that "*Mala suerte* [bad luck] did exist in the world, surely, but fortunately, so did *buena suerte* [good luck]."

The reviewer for *Publishers Weekly* (25 December 1987) found in *Family Attractions* "an able chronicle of the ordinary, bittersweet routine of family life" in "earthy, gentle prose." Elizabeth Shostak, reviewer for the *Wilson Library Bulletin* (May 1988), found that many of the stories center on "a woman, betrayed somehow by the ideal of marriage and motherhood, who is forced to find other meaning in life" and reveal "the depth of feeling possible in lives that have been offered cruelly few choices." Some critics saw the Mormonism in the book as undeveloped background, except in "Death of a Mormon Elder." Yet, Gregory L. Morris, writing for the *North American Review* (September 1988), saw Freeman as "particularly concerned with the effect of that belief—the large families, the larger *sense* of family: the Mormon community as family and the kinship of faith."

Freeman completed *The Chinchilla Farm* during the first year she and Hernandez lived in a small apartment in MacArthur Park; according to Freeman in the 6 November 1997 letter, much of that neighborhood came into the novel, especially a "feeling for the poor section of town and the struggles of people who live there, the place where Verna might realistically afford to live." A camping trip to Baja, California, with Hernandez's mother inspired the ending of the book.

*Dust jacket for Freeman's 1991 novel, about a man who receives a heart transplanted from his grandson*

*The Chinchilla Farm* is a novel of expatriation and self-discovery or self-creation, an odyssey across western America in three titled sections, from northern Utah to Los Angeles to Mexico. Its narrator-heroine, Verna Flake, strong-voiced and openhearted, a bruised American innocent defended largely by her own generosity of spirit, follows a trajectory that runs tangent to her creator's at some points: childhood in a large working-class Mormon family, a teenage Mormon marriage that falls apart, relocation to California and the making of a new marriage and home there on the rim of what Verna calls "a wide, fathomless ocean." But Verna's childless marriage lasts seventeen years before Leon Fields abandons her for a Miss Wyoming runner-up named Pinky, and Verna claims the pickup and horse trailer, loads a few worldly goods, and leaves. She gives another wanderer, Duluth Wing, a ride to Los Angeles, where he ends up sleeping in a park. Verna stays first with an old friend, Jolene, and Jolene's musicologist husband, Vincent—their marriage is also shaky—then gets her own apartment in MacArthur Park and finds work as a dentist's receptionist. When Verna's brother's Mexican widow, Inez, needs to escape an abusive third husband, Verna flees in the pickup to Baja California with Inez, Christobel (Inez's retarded daughter), and Duluth. Inez's husband tracks them down and in a violent climax, struggling with Christobel, falls into an open well and breaks his neck. Duluth stays for awhile in Mexico with Inez and Christobel and eventually moves to San Francisco. At the end, Verna has revisited Utah to be with her dying father, remains in affectionate contact with her mother, and has married Vincent and borne a daughter of her own, Silvia. Verna is Vincent's "muse," "a sanctifying woman," as he says; and "As for me and my outcome," Verna says, "–well, I am writing this book, aren't I?" It is New Year's Day, and out the window Verna watches "the little river" below her flow "out of the channel into the ocean" as her husband and daughter walk down toward the water, which "beyond them is coming in in fanciful rows, small, lacy waves. They just keep coming in, row after row of flowing ripples, these endless waves . . . and here we are, still on the rim."

Pagan Kennedy, reviewing The Chinchilla Farm for The Nation (11 December 1989), found Verna "a refreshing anomaly" in contemporary American fiction, as was "Freeman's depiction of America as, rather than a coast-to-coast shopping mall, a place of startling contrasts where local cultures flourish." This "local color" is "most vibrant in the Utah section," where Verna's childhood to her seems "dishwater" but to the reader seems "exotic" in its glimpses of the "mysteries of Mormonism" and of a "mythic" Great Salt Lake. Despite a "saccharine ending," Kennedy thought The Chinchilla Farm was "a tremendous coup for a first novel, for any novel." In a New York Review of Books essay, Diane Johnson said Verna Flake's story encompassed both faith and the loss of faith. The world Verna "finds outside Utah is bleak and derelict," but she "is unafraid of it"; in fact, the world Verna "leaves at the beginning is the one she finally affirms," though the tone of the novel, its "mournful note of gentle irony, seems to arise from her understanding . . . that American history is not on the side of 'qualities like friendliness . . . and forgiveness.'"

The Chinchilla Farm was also notably well received among the Mormon literary community, winning the prize for the novel in 1989 from the Association for Mormon Letters. It was hailed by Gary Topping in Dialogue: A Journal of Mormon Thought (Summer 1990) as exhibiting "the emergence of a major literary talent," though this review also questions the ending of the novel and notes some "gaffes" in Utah geography that "erode the story's realism." But from Freeman's father, the novel provoked a strong reprimand, as she relates in her essay "How Does the Dance Begin?" He called her from St. George, Utah, to upbraid her for writing about the Mormon religion, especially its Temple rituals, though Freeman believes his real concern was "the family stories I had

told," especially the circumstances of raising eight children on a meager income. The rift eventually healed. Freeman says that on his deathbed her father greeted her "with more love than I could have imagined. 'This is what I've been waiting for,' he said."

Freeman's second novel, Set for Life, takes place mainly in the Bear Lake Valley, which bridges northern Utah and southeastern Idaho, and the protagonist Phil Doucet's deceased wife was a Mormon from Bear Lake Valley who lapsed into "spiritualism and natural healing"; Phil "was never tempted to join her religion." Yet, in a sense, Set for Life might be as "Mormon" as any of Freeman's fictions, for its theme might be stated rather literally as turning "the heart of the fathers to the children, and the heart of the children to their fathers" (Malachi 4:6)–a central theme of Mormon culture, expressed mainly in genealogical research, family reunions, family history writing, and proxy Temple ordinances for kindred dead. Connecting the centrality of hearts in her work to her early and "defining" experience with her son, Freeman says in the 31 May 1996 interview, "it isn't maybe by accident that much later I would write a story about someone getting a new heart, someone needing a new heart. On the metaphorical level it works; but literally, hearts, heart surgery, is something that I've been thinking about, writing about for some time."

An unusual hero for a novel, Phil Doucet is a widowed retired carpenter saved from death by a heart transplanted from his beloved teenaged grandson, brain-dead after a car accident. With his new young heart Phil becomes the rescuer and caretaker of Louise, a refugee from an abusive neo-Nazi stepfather. "It's the old man who's truly innocent," Freeman says in the 6 November 1997 letter, and "the girl who has been corrupted early on by the viciousness of her upbringing, and when these two spheres, two very different notions of what constitutes a moral universe, collide, each will inevitably be altered." At the climax of the novel, when Louise's parents come to reclaim her, Phil risks his "borrowed heart" on Louise's behalf, taking from her stepfather a terrible blow to the chest, which probably breaks the sutures in his sternum. Phil's realization is the heart of the novel: "It seemed to him that he finally understood the power of love, how it would not be held back." Freeman combines this power with another great power in this novel, the natural world itself, the cosmos that comes into immense and sharp focus in a visionary ending:

Outside, the stars were emerging, a night full of stars, distant and beckoning in their brilliance, stars shining down on the marshes of Paris and the dead orchards of Ovid [Bear Lake valley towns], stars by the thousands, filling the heavens like the lights of dead souls who dwelt on a plane of peace, and his own soul was lulled by the sight.

*Dust jacket for Freeman's 1996 novel, about a writer who learns of her former lover's Nazi past when she encounters him on a cruise ship*

His heart was touched by those above, the feeling that the dead were never really far away, that their tranquillity surpassed human understanding, and yet, through careful listening, and feeling, and seeing, one's own soul could be transported to a place of refuge.

He felt himself being drawn upward, imperceptibly rising toward the pinpoints of light, ascending in universal feeling, the lost and the dead beckoning, and he seemed to lay an ear against the muscle of his own heart, feeling it open and close. His soul swooned into some new world, delivered of grief, purified, by the sight of pulsing stars, wave of light by wave of light, renewed in radiance.

Then the last sentence of the novel treads firmly on the ground: "With a fullness of heart, he began walking toward his car, the snow squeaking beneath his feet."

*Set for Life* won the Western Heritage Award for Best Novel from the Cowboy Hall of Fame. Reviews were generally favorable. A brief notice in *The New Yorker* (21 October 1991), though it finds "the shape of the story . . . unwieldy," calls Phil Doucet "truly heart-whole—unerring in his instinct for the right and good," and the book itself "a political novel in the best sense: it's about the moral

considerations at the root of political ideas, and about character as an embodiment of moral nature." Levi S. Peterson in *Dialogue* (Fall 1992) called Louise "a walking repository of American problems" in a world in which "the rural has become suburban."

Freeman wrote her third novel, *A Desert of Pure Feeling* (1996), during the three years she and Hernandez lived on a ranch on the Salmon River in central Idaho. Her father had died in 1991; her mother died a year and a half later; and her younger brother Jerry, to whom she had always felt closest, died of AIDS shortly before she finished the book. In remarks before a reading from the book on 30 May 1996, Freeman said that she was "contemplating what it means to face the death of those who are very close to you." She said in her acceptance speech, given by proxy, for the Mormon Letters Award that there was "a purity about working in such a pristine landscape" and believes "some of that purity came into this novel."

Freeman's writer-narrator in this novel, Lucy Patterson, has retreated to a literal desert, a motel on the outskirts of Las Vegas, a place originally settled by her own people, Mormon pioneers, but now "a meta-theme park arising amid a surreal expanse of windblown nothingness." Lucy tells at least three main stories from her own life: the early breakup of her teenage Mormon marriage in Minnesota after her husband's affair with a fellow graduate student and her own affair with the surgeon, Carlos Cabrera, who repaired her infant son's congenitally defective heart; her recent stint as a "guest writer" aboard a luxury liner on a five-day transatlantic crossing, during which she unexpectedly renewed her relationship with Carlos after more than two decades; and her present sojourn in Las Vegas, writing her versions of these stories but also becoming the rescuer and companion of a stripper, Joycelle, threatened by "slime-bag crooks" and, it turns out, gravely ill with AIDS-related Pneumocystis carinii pneumonia.

Lucy's son—unlike Freeman's, who did not remain active in the Mormon church—had disappeared eight years earlier, presumed killed in a terrorist bombing during his church mission in Guatemala; Lucy fruitlessly searched for him, then lived on a remote ranch in Idaho where she "felt my aloneness intensely" and her "failure at love most intensely"; thus, when a fellow writer asks her to replace him as guest writer on a cruise ship, Lucy accepts, hoping to remit her solitude and "breathe new life into my own troubled prose." The next-to-last night of the voyage, after Lucy reads from a story in which the protagonist finds her lost son in Guatemala, another passenger, Josef Himmelfarlo, threatens to expose Carlos's Hitler Youth past; and the last night, after Josef accuses Carlos of betraying Josef's brother to the death camps, Carlos falls or jumps overboard. So Lucy comes back to Las Vegas to recapitulate, to look at the stories of her life. At the end, she has left Las Vegas and taken Joycelle to live on her property in Idaho.

Most reviews did not attempt the patient unpacking that the complex structure of the novel invites. "Jumping between various time frames," wrote Ann H. Fisher in a review for *Library Journal* (1 June 1996), "the novel lurches somewhat breathlessly through revelations of the dark secrets of the past to a mildly happy, unexpected ending." *Publishers Weekly* (8 April 1996) noted "some awkward and dramatically flat exposition about the tricky nature of moral judgment," yet still found "Lucy's story . . . a moving, deliberate meditation on love," though its inclusion of "Nazis, Mormons, and Guatemalan terrorism" gave "a false, often melodramatic scope to what is, in the end, a very intimate novel." In the *New York Times Book Review* (26 May 1996) Susannah Hunnewell noted a "cast of characters worthy of Agatha Christie," yet with "too many plot lines" and "too many ambitious subjects." The

reviewer concluded, "You won't always feel out to sea—though you may wish you were."

Freeman describes *A Desert of Pure Feeling* as "a weighted book." And after its publication, reading the first of Italo Calvino's *Six Memos for the Next Millennium* (1988), on "Lightness," she expressed in the spring of 1996 a "wish to turn away from a kind of sadness and grief and weightiness that's really affected me heavily over the past few years and that's infused this particular story. I have a great wish . . . to bear things up once again, to create a new lightness."

In the 1990s Freeman became a frequent guest at writers' conferences and festivals, in Ucross, Wyoming; Park City, Utah; Sun Valley, Idaho; Reno, Nevada; and other Western and West Coast sites. From 1990 to 1996 she was a regular contributing critic to *The Los Angeles Times*. In 1991 she traveled to India with the photographer Tina Barney to collaborate on a book: "It was an amazing experience, living with a family for six weeks, traveling through Rajasthan," and Freeman later "finished a short story set in India." She and Barney intended to publish "India Journal" with Barney's photographs and Freeman's text; but the project was shelved when Freeman began working on her next novel. In 1997 Freeman taught a term as an adjunct professor of creative writing at the University of Southern California. In 1997–1998, supported by a Guggenheim Fellowship, she began research—especially into pioneer women's diaries—for a novel set in southern Utah in the nineteenth century, against the background of the Mountain Meadows massacre. Written in Idaho, *Red Water* (2002) relates the life story of John D. Lee as told by three of his nineteen wives. The women's voices, Freeman says, compose "a portrait of a complex and ambitious, generous and tortured man."

Judith Freeman would agree with Czech writer Milan Kudera's observation in *The Art of the Novel* (translated by Linda Asher; 1988) that "The world of one single truth, and the relative, ambiguous world of the novel are molded of entirely different substances." Freeman's autobiographical narrator in "Clearfield" comes to know a young Mormon returned missionary in whom she senses "a depth . . . that made me feel that if he was a believer, the church couldn't ever begin to contain all those feelings." In the 31 May 1996 interview Freeman said that art and literature "question" the "solace" and "structure" offered by the "single truth" of religion and "open it up, to give people different ways of thinking, to maybe make them less afraid of facing moral complexities or uncertainties." Through stories, she said, "we become more capable of not only understanding, but forgiveness."

# Frederick Dilley Glidden
## (Luke Short)
*(19 November 1908 – 18 August 1975)*

Dennis Cutchins
*Brigham Young University*

BOOKS: *The Feud at Single Shot* (New York: Farrar & Rinehart / London: Collins, 1936);

*Guns of the Double Diamond* (London: Collins, 1937); republished as *The Man on the Blue* (New York: Dell, 1954);

*Bull-Foot Ambush* (London: Collins, 1938); republished as *Marauder's Moon* (New York: Dell, 1954);

*Misery Lode* (London: Collins, 1938); republished as *King Colt* (New York: Dell, 1953);

*The Gold Rustlers* (London: Collins, 1939); republished as *Bold Rider* (New York: Dell, 1953);

*Weary Range* (London: Collins, 1939); republished as *The Branded Man* (New York: Dell, 1956);

*Raiders of the Rimrock* (New York: Doubleday, Doran / London: Collins, 1939);

*Six Guns of San Jon* (New York: Doubleday, Doran / London: Collins, 1939); republished as *Savage Range* (New York: Dell, 1948);

*Flood-Water* (London: Collins, 1939); republished as *Hard Money* (New York: Doubleday, Doran, 1940);

*Bounty Guns* (London: Collins, 1940; New York: Dell, 1953);

*Brand of Empire* (London: Collins, 1940; New York: Dell, 1954);

*Dead Freight for Piute* (New York: Doubleday, Doran, 1940); republished as *Western Freight* (London: Collins, 1941); republished as *Bull-Whip* (New York: Bantam, 1950);

*War on the Cimarron* (New York: Doubleday, Doran, 1940); republished as *Hurricane Range* (London: Collins, 1940);

*Gunman's Chance* (New York: Doubleday, Doran, 1941); republished as *Blood on the Moon* (London: Collins, 1943);

*Hardcase* (Garden City, N.Y.: Doubleday, Doran, 1942 / London: Collins, 1945);

*Ride the Man Down* (New York: Doubleday, Doran, 1942; London: Collins, 1943);

*Frederick Dilley Glidden (Luke Short)*

*Sunset Graze* (Garden City, N.Y.: Doubleday, Doran, 1942); republished as *The Rustlers* (New York: Bantam, 1949);

*Ramrod* (New York: Macmillan, 1943; London: Collins, 1945);

*Bought with a Gun* (London: Collins, 1943; New York: Dell, 1955);

*Gauntlet of Fire* (London: Collins, 1944); republished as *Raw Land* (New York: Dell, 1952);

*And the Wind Blows Free* (New York: Macmillan, 1945; London: Collins, 1946);

*Coroner Creek* (New York: Macmillan, 1946; London: Collins, 1947);

*Station West* (Boston: Houghton Mifflin / London: Collins, 1947);

*High Vermilion* (Boston: Houghton Mifflin / London: Collins, 1948); republished as *Hands Off!* (New York: Bantam, 1949);

*Fiddlefoot* (Boston: Houghton Mifflin / London: Collins, 1949);

*Ambush* (Boston: Houghton Mifflin, 1950; London: Collins, 1950);

*Vengeance Valley* (Boston: Houghton Mifflin, 1950; London: Collins, 1951);

*Trumpets West!* (New York: Dell, 1951);

*Play a Lone Hand* (Boston: Houghton Mifflin, 1951);

*Barren Land Murders* (New York: Fawcett, 1951; London: Muller, 1954); republished as *Barren Land Showdown* (New York: Fawcett, 1957);

*Saddle by Starlight* (Boston: Houghton Mifflin, 1952; London: Collins, 1953);

*Silver Rock* (Boston: Houghton Mifflin, 1953; London: Collins, 1954);

*Rimrock* (New York: Random House, 1955; London: Collins, 1956);

*The Whip* (New York: Bantam, 1957; London: Collins, 1958);

*Summer of the Smoke* (New York: Bantam, 1958; London: Hammond, 1959);

*First Claim* (New York: Bantam / London: Hammond, 1960);

*Desert Crossing* (New York: Bantam, 1961; London: Hammond, 1963);

*Last Hunt* (New York: Bantam, 1962; London: Hammond, 1963);

*The Some-Day Country* (New York: Bantam, 1964); republished as *Trigger Country* (London: Hammond, 1965);

*First Campaign* (New York: Bantam / London: Transworld, 1965);

*Paper Sheriff* (New York: Bantam / London: Transworld, 1966);

*Debt of Honor* (New York: Bantam, 1967);

*The Primrose Try* (New York: Bantam, 1967); republished as *A Man Could Get Killed* (New York: Jove, 1980);

*The Guns of Hanging Lake* (New York: Bantam, 1968);

*Donovan's Gun* (New York: Bantam, 1968; London: Corgi, 1969);

*The Deserters* (New York: Bantam, 1969);

*Three for the Money* (New York: Bantam, 1970);

*The Outrider* (New York: Bantam, 1971);

*Man from the Desert* (New York: Bantam, 1971);

*The Stalkers* (New York: Bantam, 1973);

*The Man with a Summer Name* (New York: Bantam, 1974);

*The Man from Two Rivers* (New York: Bantam, 1974);

*Trouble Country* (New York: Bantam, 1976).

**Collections:** *Luke Short's Best of the West,* introduction by H. N. Swanson (New York: Arbor House, 1983);

*The Marshal of Vengeance* (New York: Carroll & Graf, 1985).

PLAY PRODUCTION: *Retraction,* as Glidden, Columbia, University of Missouri Theater, 1930.

PRODUCED SCRIPT: "The Traveling Salesman," television, *Bristol Meyers Stage 7,* CBS, 1955.

OTHER: *Bad Men and Good: A Roundup of Western Stories,* foreword by Short (New York: Dodd, Mead, 1953);

*Cattle, Guns, and Men,* edited by Short (New York: Bantam, 1955);

"The Drummer," in *The Fall Roundup,* edited by Harry E. Maule (New York: Random House, 1955);

*Frontier: 150 Years of the West,* edited by Short (New York: Bantam, 1955; London: Transworld, 1957);

*Riders West: With Stories and Articles by Luke Short and Others* (New York: Dell, 1956);

*Colt's Law,* edited by Short (New York: Bantam, 1957);

*Rawhide and Bobwire,* edited by Short (New York: Bantam, 1958);

"The Hangman," in *Iron Men and Silver Spurs,* edited by Donald Hamilton (New York: Fawcett, 1967);

"Danger Hole," in *Western Writers of America Silver Anniversary Anthology,* edited by August Lenniger (New York: Ace, 1969).

SELECTED PERIODICAL PUBLICATIONS–UNCOLLECTED: "Six-Gun Lawyer," as Glidden, *Cowboy Stories* (August 1935);

"Blood of His Enemies," *Star Western* (October 1935);

"Gamblers Don't Quit," *Star Western* (October 1935);

"Caribou Copper," *Dynamic Adventures* (November 1935);

"Gambler's Glory," *Dime Adventure* (December 1935);

"Gun Boss of Hell's Wells," *Star Western* (December 1935);

"Border Rider," *Dime Adventure* (January 1936);

"Guns for a Peacemaker," *Star Western* (February 1936);

"Gun-Boss of Broken Men," *Dime Western* (April 1936);

"Son of a Gun-Curse," *Adventure* (April 1936);

"Tinhorn's Lost Gamble," *Star Western* (April 1936);

"Trigger Traitor," *Cowboy Stories* (April 1936);

"Long Rider Lawman," *Cowboy Stories* (June 1936);

"Booze-Head Heritage," *Top Notch* (July 1936);

"Boothill Ride," *10 Story Western* (August 1936);

"Dec Porter's Six-Gun Cure," *Ace-High Western* (September 1936);

"Trial by Fury," *Cowboy Stories* (September 1936);

"Boothill Brotherhood," *10 Story Western* (October 1936);

"Outlaws Make Good Neighbors," *Star Western* (October 1936);

"The Buzzard Basin Gun Stampede," *Star Western* (November 1936);

"Fighting Nesters of Sacaton," *Ace-High Western* (November 1936);

"Gunhawks Die Hard!" *Western Trails* (November 1936);

"Buckshot Freighter," *Star Western* (December 1936);

"Buckskin-Popper's Lost Ride," *Dime Western* (January 1937);

"Bandit Lawman," *Big-Book Western* (March 1937);

"Town-Tamer on the Dodge," *Dime Western* (April 1937);

"Pattern," *New York Daily News,* 4 April 1937;

"The Marshal of Vengeance," *Dime Western,* 18 (July 1937): 78–90;

"The Ivory Butt-plate," *Blue Book* (August 1937);

"Tough Enough," *Argosy* (4 September 1937);

"The Right Kind of Tough," *Blue Book* (October 1937);

"Lobo Quarantine," *Argosy* (4 June 1938);

"Light the War Fires," *Argosy* (24 September 1938);

"First Judgment," *Argosy* (22 October 1938);

"Test Pit," *Western Story* (7 January 1939);

"Brand of Justice," *Country Home* (February 1939);

"Indian Scare," *Argosy* (25 March 1939);

"Some Dogs Steal," *Argosy* (10 June 1939);

"Belabor Day," *Collier's* (9 September 1939);

"The Fence," *Adventure* (March 1940);

"Holy Show," *Sunday News* (August 1940);

"Smuggler's Bag," *Short Stories* (10 September 1940);

"Neutral Spirits," *Blue Book* (January 1941);

"The Strange Affair at Seven Troughs," *Blue Book* (June 1941);

"Brassguts," *Argosy* (26 July 1941);

"Bitter Frontier," *Argosy* (15 April 1942);

"Ernest Haycox: An Appreciation," in *The Call Number,* 25 (Fall 1963 – Spring 1964).

Luke Short, whose real name was Frederick Glidden, had a writing career that spanned almost forty years. He was enormously popular and prolific, the writer of fifty-one Western novels. During the 1930s, the years of the Great Depression, Glidden earned a good living with his writing. Although by the end of his career he had been eclipsed by writers such as Louis L'Amour (pen name of Louis Dearborn LaMoore), he had helped to define Western fiction, if for no other reason, by the sheer volume of his work. At the time of his death in 1975 more than thirty-five million copies of his novels had been sold. Contemporary Western novelists such as Larry McMurtry and Cormac McCarthy, though they may not acknowledge it, owe a debt to Glidden's vision of what a Western should be.

Frederick Dilley Glidden was born on 19 November 1908 in Kewanee, Illinois, the second son of Wallace Dilley Glidden and Fannie Mae Hurff Glidden. Their son Jonathan H. Glidden, two years older than Frederick, became a successful Western writer under the pen name Peter Dawson. Frederick and Jon's interest in the Old West is not difficult to trace. Kewanee, though hardly a frontier town in the early twentieth century, had been the setting of a good deal of Western American history. The transcontinental railroad had originated in Rockford, Illinois, a hundred miles to the north, and Hannibal, Missouri, the hometown of Mark Twain (Samuel Langhorne Clemens), lay only 150 miles to the south. A series of prehistoric Native American burial mounds exist a few miles from the Glidden home, and Wyatt Earp, the famous Western lawman, was born in 1848 in nearby Monmouth, Illinois. Born into such surroundings, the two brothers found themselves literally and figuratively drawn to the West.

Frederick's father, Wallace Glidden, died in 1921 when Frederick was only twelve years old. The effect his father's death had on Frederick is difficult to judge, but a direct result was that his mother, Fannie Mae, was forced to work to support the family. When Frederick was a boy, she taught English at Kewanee High School. She later became the dean of women at Knox College in Galesburg, Illinois. Frederick graduated from Kewanee High School in 1926 and entered the University of Illinois at Urbana. For reasons that are no longer clear, he transferred from the University of Illinois to the University of Missouri at Columbia in 1929, where he graduated with a degree in journalism in June 1930. After graduation, Glidden worked for a while at several Midwestern newspapers. He later reported, "I've read or heard that all newspapermen are disappointed writers, but in me you behold a writer who is a disappointed newspaperman. I've been fired from more newspapers than I like to remember, even if I could." Upon giving up the newspaper business, Glidden and a partner began a fur-trapping business in northern Alberta, Canada. The trapping business, with its hard and lonely work and brutal weather, was a failure, but it provided material for later writing, including his first stories, which were rejected by publishers, and at least one later novel, *Barren Land Murders* (1951; first published as *Spy of*

*Lon Chaney Jr. as Steve Murkill and Randolph Scott as Cole Arnim in the 1948 motion picture* Albuquerque. *The movie was based on Glidden's* Dead Freight for Piute, *published serially in 1939 and in book form in 1940 (Paramount Pictures).*

*the North* in *Adventure* magazine, 1940). After giving up the trapping venture, Glidden spent several years, during the depths of the Depression, moving from job to job. In 1933 he secured a position working as an archaeologist's assistant in and near Santa Fe, New Mexico. He eventually decided to try his hand at ranching and headed north to find work. On the way north, however, he stopped in Grand Junction, Colorado, to greet a family friend and met Florence Elder. They fell in love and were married in Grand Junction a few weeks later on 18 June 1934. The newlyweds returned to Pojoaque, New Mexico, where Glidden, prompted by the need to support his wife, decided to try his hand at writing stories for pulp magazines.

His first stories, set in the Northwest, were all rejected. A neighbor and friend suggested that Glidden contact Marguerite E. Harper, a New York literary agent. Harper, who had some experience with Western adventure stories, sold Glidden's "Six-Gun Lawyer" to the magazine *Cowboy Stories* in the spring of 1935. Glidden's thirty-two-year association with Harper, which lasted until her death in 1966, was profitable for both writer and agent and helped to shape Glidden's career. In August of 1935 he published his first novel, *The Feud at Single Shot* (first separate publication, 1936), in serial form in *Adventure* maga-

zine. Around this time he also adopted the pen name Luke Short, which he used for the rest of his life. Harper's suggestion, the pen name may have been based on the name of a late-nineteenth- century Dodge City saloon keeper, gunfighter, and gambler who lived from 1854 through 1893.

In 1935 Glidden convinced his older brother, Jonathan, to try his hand at writing Western stories. Jonathan at the time had a successful career as a salesman and was reluctant to start writing, but Frederick was persistent. Jonathan began writing in the evenings after work, and by the spring of 1936 he had produced a short story, "Gunsmoke Pledge," which Frederick felt was good enough to send to his agent, Harper. She sold the story to Street & Smith's *Complete Stories,* in which it appeared in May 1936. As she had done for Frederick, Harper suggested that Jonathan adopt a pen name. She chose Peter Dawson, and Jonathan's career as a Western writer was launched. Like his more famous brother, Jonathan also became successful, eventually publishing many novels and more than 120 short stories. Frederick Glidden was directly responsible for his brother's writing career as well as his choice of genre.

In the next four years Frederick Glidden quickly published thirteen more novels, as well as several short stories. He established a working routine that allowed him to generate more than two thousand words per day. Under the pressure of literally publishing or perishing, Glidden also adopted a formula that shaped most of his fiction for the rest of his life. This formula, familiar to readers of pulp Westerns, is a relatively simple one. It begins with a clearly established hero, who, though he may be somewhat wayward at first, is both competent as a Westerner (he can fight and use a gun) and honest at heart. The hero faces an equally clearly drawn villain, as well as the villain's henchmen, in a relatively specific geographical location. The novels begin in medias res, and Glidden wastes little time before pitting the hero against the villains. The conflicts are solved almost exclusively by violence, usually culminating when the hero confronts and kills the villain. Typically, in the course of the novel the hero is able to win the love of a good woman, who waits patiently for him to "do what a man has to do." Perhaps Glidden's best novel of the 1930s was *Dead Freight for Piute,* published serially from 18 November 1939 through 23 December 1939 (separate publication, 1940). Cole Armin comes to work for his uncle's freight-hauling business. Learning of his uncle's treacherous, bullying ways with the other haulers, however, Cole shifts his allegiance to the competition. While the action of the book is certainly one of its most important assets, the novel is both a tightly woven adventure story and a convincing mystery. Glidden's ability to create convincing vernacular dialogue sets this novel apart from the typical plot-driven adventure story. When Ted Wallace meets Cole, Wallace explodes, "Well I'm damned! . . .You've got more gall than the mules you drive!" The novel ends, in true Luke Short style, with Cole defeating his corrupt uncle and winning the heart of the beautiful Celia Wallace. Cole finally manages to confess his love for Celia in the final pages of the novel:

> "I had to say I was scared, because I was sinkin' you and Ted, Seely. I–I . . ." His voice died away.
> "You what, Cole?"
> "I loved you so much I couldn't drag you down with me, I reckon."
> "Oh, Cole," Celia said softly. "And I loved you so much that I didn't want to live if you weren't near me!"

Although predictable at times, *Dead Freight for Piute* has enough of an edge of humor and realism, particularly in the details of a turn-of-the-century mining town, to keep it from being melodramatic.

Perhaps the biggest influence on Glidden's early work was the writing of Ernest Haycox. After Haycox's death Glidden wrote "Ernest Haycox: An Appreciation," in which he credits Haycox for inspiring him to make the move from pulp magazines to slick magazines such as *Colliers* and *The Saturday Evening Post.* To the question "Why was his writing so special," Glidden responds that Haycox

transported readers to "a new and somehow fearsome country; in its harshness or darkness, there is a promise of cruelty. You have entered an unfriendly country with a man who has a grim past which he has conquered, and who is heading into an even grimmer future." (This generalized plot sums up Glidden's early novels and suggests his fascination with the Western ideal of a loner who must overcome, through violent action, the machinations of a faulty or cruel society. This pattern holds true even when Glidden shifts the setting of a novel away from the Old West, as in *Barren Land Murders.* That novel, set in the contemporary Northwest, concerns a communist spy ring and the attempts of an outdoorsman and the local police to shut it down. The novel ends as the hero single-handedly kills the leader of the spy ring, stops the bleeding of his own gunshot wound with a handful of flour (a favorite trick of Luke Short heroes), and returns to civilization to be vindicated by the authorities and rewarded with the love of a faithful woman.

By 1940 Glidden, having published fourteen novels, had finished his apprenticeship and was, notwithstanding his foray into contemporary settings, fast becoming the undisputed king of the action Westerns. In *Bought with a Gun* (1943) he helped to solidify that reputation. This novel, loaded with action, also clarified Glidden's definition of a hero. The protagonist, Sam Teacher, is a gunfighter who decides to go straight. He does not, however, lose his talent with a gun. When he confronts Santee, the villain of the novel, he taunts the bad guy by saying,

> "You want to stand up and shoot it out?" Santee didn't answer for a long moment, and Sam loaded both guns.
> "All right," Santee said, his voice strident. "You stand up first."
> "Not me, Santee," Sam said. "If I stand up first, you'll shoot. But if you stand up first, you know I won't shoot. I don't have to, Santee. I can kill you with an even break."
> "Go to hell!" Santee snarled.

Like all of Short's heroes, Sam is deadly, but he is honest to a fault and has a strong sense of fair play. The novel ends, predictably, with Sam finally being embraced figuratively by the legal authorities and literally by Celia Drury. The sheriff announces, "'I was wrong about you, and I admit it here and now.' He crossed over to Sam and put out his hand. 'I'd like to eat my crow in public. That amnesty still stands, Teacher, and we'll call the reward posters in. I can speak for the Governor in that. And I speak for myself when I say I would like to shake your hand.'" In a dialogue highly reminiscent of that found in *The Barren Land Murders* Sam admits his love for Celia:

> "I thought kind of that we should stay knowin' each other. Like, well–"
> "Sam, are you trying to tell me you love me?"

BLOOD ON THE MOON

By Luke Short

ILLUSTRATED BY BENTON CLARK

Plain sense made Jim yank his horse around and rowel it toward the bank.

*Illustration from the 15 March 1941 issue of* The Saturday Evening Post *for the first installment of Glidden's seven-part novel, in which gunslinger Jim Garry mends his ways (reprinted with permission of* The Saturday Evening Post, © 1942 [Renewed] BFL&MS, Inc.)

"Yes," Sam said, "Yes, I am."

"Then why don't you say so? I love you, Sam. I want to be near you all my life."

Glidden relied on formulas for his plots, and he chose formulas that enjoyed a special resonance in the minds of millions of Americans. His earlier efforts were beginning to pay off in a big way. In March 1941 *The Saturday Evening Post* began serializing *Blood on the Moon* (published separately in 1943; previously published in 1941 as *Gunman's Chance*). Centering once more on a gunslinger in the process of mending his ways, the novel is full of the kind of description and action that made Short so popular. His description of Joe Shotten, one of the villains in the novel, is both stereotypical and masterful:

He was a plain hard case, Jim thought. His hands were rope calloused, and he chewed tobacco with a patient violence. It bulged the left cheek of his concave face and seemed to draw his small eyes even closer together by widening his face. He stank of horse sweat, and its sweet, acrid smell, mixed with the even sweeter smell of the chew, clung to him like a sickening aura. A man of average height, he had narrow slanting shoulders that set his big head in bold and ugly dominance.

In a later scene, Riling, the villain, has an argument with Sweet, one of the small ranchers he has brought into a rough coalition against a larger rancher. The argument quickly escalates to violence:

Riling saw him move and remembered in a flash that his own gun belt was on the nail above Sweet's head. He grabbed the first thing he could reach, which was the ax. He swung it up with one hand and stepped to the stove. He saw Sweet's gun clearing leather and then he swung blindly with the ax, using both hands, bringing it down with a lashing sweep that caught Sweet full in the chest. . . . The head of the ax was entirely buried in the dead center of Sweet's chest, the helve angling up toward the door.

Though Short's novels are full of colorful descriptions of violent action, they include little sex. His heroes all seem to recognize that romance should only be attempted after the violent action is over. Since his novels typically end immediately after the violent action ceases, romance is always implied but is rarely illustrated. His heroes do, however, have romantic encounters. Glidden's cowboy protagonists often kiss the feebly protesting heroines, but their relationships rarely progress past that point in the course of the novel. Glidden's scenes of romance and his portrayal of women, though popular at the time, would probably be considered both dated and sexist by contemporary readers. Two scenes from *Blood on the Moon* illustrate this point. The hero, Jim Garry, first kisses Amy Lufton to teach her a lesson: "He stepped over to her and took her in his arms and kissed her roughly. She submitted without moving a hand in protest. Jim felt the sweet warmth of her lips, smelled her hair, and then he stepped away from her." In true Victorian style, the female lead, far from instigating or even encouraging Jim's romantic advances, simply submits to them. Women who do instigate romantic encounters in Glidden's novels are invariably portrayed as evil or tainted. Carol Lufton, Amy's older sister, for instance, seduces one of the ranch hands in order to help her in her plot to outwit her father.

> "Ted, you're in love with me aren't you?" . . . "You'd do anything in the world to save me from hurt, wouldn't you?" Carol went on brutally. "I know you would because you've done it today. It's in your eyes, in the way you talk. Isn't that true?"
>
> Ted nodded now, unable to speak.
>
> Carol moved her horse closer to him and reached out and laid a hand on his. "I thank you for that, Ted. I need your help terribly." She paused and she could feel the muscles in his hand iron-hard and trembling beneath her own.
>
> "I want you to forget this afternoon," Carol said, her voice hard. "I don't care what you think, but I don't want anyone ever to know. No one, Ted—*no one!* Do you love me enough to promise that?"
>
> "More," Ted said.

This scene is typical of Short's treatment of female characters; in his works, assertive women are usually dishonest and manipulative.

In April 1942 *The Saturday Evening Post* serialized *Ride the Man Down;* the book was also published separately in the same year. From this point on Glidden had no trouble finding a serial market for his work. Moreover, he already had his eye on Hollywood. In 1940 his Hollywood agent, H. N. Swanson, had sold Glidden's short story, "Hurry, Charlie, Hurry, There Are Indians in the Parlor" to RKO Pictures for $1,000. Glidden seemed drawn to Hollywood, where he spent parts of 1941, 1942, and 1943. His persistence in courting the studios paid off. In the course of his long career, Glidden saw nineteen of his novels produced as movies. He and his wife also had three children during the early 1940s–James, born 1940; Kate, born 1941; and Daniel, born 1942.

Glidden's poor eyesight kept him out of the armed services during World War II, but in 1943 and 1944 he worked for the Office of Strategic Services (OSS) in Washington, D.C. During his stint in Washington, Glidden's production as a writer sagged. At the insistence of his literary agent, Harper, however, he returned to his previous levels of production soon after his tour was over. In October 1944 the Gliddens returned to the Santa Fe area, and in 1945 he began a long and profitable relationship with the then-new paperback book industry. His Hollywood experience increased, too. In March 1946 he went to Hollywood again, this time as a consultant on the script for the movie adaptation of *Ramrod,* starring Joel McCrea.

*Ramrod* (1943) is a typical Luke Short novel and provides a good example of Glidden's plots, themes, and characters. The plot is both simple and tightly constructed. The novel begins as Dave Nash, a laconic cowboy, is forced to watch his good-hearted but braggart boss, Walt Shipley, run out of town by a local bully, Frank Ivey. The scene in the book illustrates Glidden's ideal of manhood:

> The silence ribboned on, until it was almost unbearable, and Dave knew swiftly that it would have to break soon.
>
> And then Walt Shipley said, in hot anger, "Listen Frank! You ain't God! You can't keep a man off a stage!"
>
> Dave felt a slow sick shame flood over him. It was over. Walt was not going, and those hot, angry words held a sentence he would never escape as long as he lived.

Walt Shipley is neither skillful enough with a gun nor brave enough to face Frank Ivey. He is forced to simply back down. He thus leaves in the middle of the night, abandoning both his ranch and his fiancée to Frank. Luke Short heroes must be appropriately violent when the occasion demands and must be willing to sacrifice anything rather than lose their honor. Confronted with a similar situation a few pages later, Dave reacts with the proper violence and is allowed to stay in the town. When a lesser villain, Red Cates, taunts him, Dave warns,

> "I'd go careful, Red."
>
> The bully responds, "Sounds like Shipley, doesn't he?"
>
> "No," Dave said gently. "He just talked."

"So do you."

Dave hit him. With his open palm he battered Cates across the mouth, and then stood there, watching the surprise and fury wash into Cates' face.

"I don't even like to talk," Dave murmured.

Dave then thoroughly beats Cates and leaves him moaning on the floor. After the fight, Frank Ivey, who has witnessed the whole thing, challenges Dave: "A man would never do that to me." Dave responds simply, "Or me." When Frank later tells him to leave town, Dave immediately accepts a job that will not only keep him around but will also put him into direct conflict with Frank and Red. The trajectory of the novel is clear within the first twenty pages; Dave will win the heroine's heart, defeat Frank and Red, and most likely be forced to kill them.

All the elements of a Luke Short novel are at work in this novel. The plot is swift moving, with clear, understandable conflicts. The characterizations in these scenes are neither subtle nor complex. The reader quickly recognizes the good men and the bad men. The realistic dialogue, however, helps keep the characters from being caricatures. The themes of honor, duty, and manliness are also apparent. Still, Glidden's novel is not simplistic. Several of the characters are more complex than either Walt, Frank, Dave, or Red, and each of them helps twist the plot in interesting ways. These characters, with a mixture of both good and bad traits, are perhaps the most interesting of Glidden's creations. They include Bill Schell, Dave's dangerous but fun-loving and shiftless friend, and Connie Dickason, Dave's boss and would-be lover. Early in the novel Bill lures Red Cates into a fight, against Dave's orders, and murders him. Dave is forced to bring Bill to town to answer to the authorities; Dave explains his reasoning to Connie: "Bill made a bargain, Connie. I told him my wishes, and when he hired on he did the same as give his word. If he's broken his word, he'll pay for it, like a man pays for everything he does." Readers are somewhat torn; like Dave, they mistrust Bill, but they like him at the same time. The readers' ambivalence about Bill is finally settled near the end of the novel as he willingly sacrifices himself to save Connie and Dave. Connie's fate is almost the opposite. At the beginning of the novel the reader, with Dave, trusts Connie. The course of the action, though, reveals that she is just as ruthless and manipulative as Frank Ivey. When her dishonest actions result in the death of the local sheriff, Connie refuses to acknowledge publicly her own guilt. She reasons, "I made a mistake, and I'm sorry for it. . . . But you can't look back." Dave finally rejects Connie in favor of Rose, a stereotypical prostitute with a heart of gold. Flawed characters such as Bill, Connie, and Rose fill Glidden's novels in secondary roles and help to make the stories both more interesting and more complex.

In August 1947 the Gliddens left New Mexico for the small town of Aspen, Colorado, where Glidden spent the rest of his life. The movie version of *Ramrod* was released in 1947 to critical and public acclaim, and in 1948 four of Glidden's novels were produced as successful Hollywood movies: *Albuquerque* (starring Randolph Scott and based on *Dead Freight for Piute*), *Blood on the Moon* (starring Robert Mitchum and based on *Gunman's Chance*), *Coroner Creek* (starring Randolph Scott), and *Station West* (starring Dick Powell). The year 1948 represents a peak in Glidden's career. Not only was his work popular in Hollywood, but there also was a great demand for his novels in the slick magazines. *The Saturday Evening Post* alone published nine of his novels in the 1940s. In 1946 Bantam Books began to republish Glidden's early novels, which had previously been serialized in America but had only been published in book form in England. In 1951 he established a similar relationship with Dell Books.

The 1950s, however, did not hold the same kind of success for Glidden, although Dell and Bantam worked steadily at republishing his earlier novels. These reprints were so popular that Dell even launched a new publication, *Luke Short's Western Magazine*. Although well produced, the magazine lasted only a year. Glidden's production as a writer, meanwhile, fell off sharply. As Robert L. Gale notes in *Luke Short* (1981), during the 1950s Glidden "published only six [novels], of which hardly half can be called excellent." Part of the reason for the sudden drop in Glidden's production is that he had turned his attentions elsewhere. He became involved in local politics as a member of the Aspen town council. In 1955 he dabbled in television scriptwriting with Lucille Ball and Desi Arnaz. That year he also helped found a doomed thorium mining corporation in Colorado and attempted to co-author an equally doomed book on mountain aviation. In addition to the other distractions of the 1950s, Glidden's older brother, Jon, died suddenly in 1957. All of this meant that Frederick Glidden did little Western writing during this period, although in 1958 he won a Maggie Award, Medallion of Merit, for *The Whip* (1957).

One of the most interesting novels of this period was *Silver Rock* (1953). Glidden's interest in and knowledge of mining played an important part in this book. Unlike most of Glidden's work, this novel is set in modern times. It concerns Tully Gibbs, a Korean War veteran and former prisoner of the North Koreans, who returns to the United States determined to strike it rich in mining. While in a North Korean prison camp he learns from Jimmy Russel, a wounded member of his bomber crew, about a rich mining claim that the Russel family had been unable to develop. Jimmy lives long enough to be rescued, and he and Tully are eventually shipped back to America. There Tully begins writing a

*Illustration for the concluding installment of Glidden's novel* Ride the Man Down *in the 16 May 1942 issue of* The Saturday Evening Post
*(reprinted with permission of* The Saturday Evening Post, © *1942 [Renewed] BFL&MS, Inc.)*

series of letters to Jimmy's father, Kevin, ostensibly for the dying Jimmy. Tully mentions his own name often in the letters in an effort to ingratiate himself to the old man. The novel begins as Tully arrives in the mining town of Azurite. His scheme seems to work, and by investing $10,000 of his own money he is able to keep the mine out of the hands of the evil Ben Hodes and begin developing it. In a departure from his usually violent plots, Glidden spends much of the novel describing the political and legal battle for the rich Russel holdings. The novel ends, however, as Tully and Hodes engage in a fistfight in the glare of a railroad locomotive headlight. Tully wins the fight and goes

immediately to Kevin Russel to admit his earlier dishonesty. Kevin, who has known about the scheme all along, frankly forgives Tully. "I'd suggest," Kevin advises Tully, "that you carry on from here, son." Sarah Moffit, the woman who has loved Tully for some time but been unwilling to accept his dishonesty, adds, "You heard the man. The same goes for me." Those words, "the same goes for me," neatly sum up the role of most of the women in Glidden's novels: they are prizes to be won, and they are only awarded after the heroes have proven themselves both victorious on the field of battle and honest in all their dealings.

If the 1950s were a tough time for Glidden, then 1960 was a low point in his life. In April his oldest son, James, accidentally drowned in the pool at Princeton University. Glidden later wrote, "It was the saddest part of life, that a father should see his son dead before him." In 1964 Glidden, now in his mid fifties and seeking an escape from the snow and winter tourism of Aspen, began to spend winters with his wife in Arizona. The couple soon bought a second home in Wickenburg, Arizona. Early in 1966 Glidden's longstanding literary agent and friend, Marguerite Harper, died. In May, Glidden hired H. N. Swanson, who had handled his movie-rights contracts for years, as his new literary agent. Glidden's eyesight, which had never been good, worsened through the 1960s, and much of what he published in these years was actually dictated to a secretary. Despite these setbacks, Glidden managed to re-create himself somewhat as a writer of Westerns. In an almost Faulknerian vein he created the fictional town of Primrose, Colorado, based loosely on his knowledge of Aspen, and he wrote several novels using the same setting and characters. The 1960s ended on a good note, as he was awarded the Levi Strauss Western Writers of America Award (Golden Saddleman Award) in 1969.

The first book of the Primrose series, *First Campaign* (1965), was also a solid return to Western action and featured the themes and ideals that had made Glidden so successful in the 1930s and 1940s. The folksy language, too, was Glidden at his best. In one early scene Cole Halsey tells his younger brother, "If you can't lick the teacher, you'd better study or quit school." The novel also reflects the political and social upheaval of the 1960s. Set in the late nineteenth century, the plot centers on the political campaign for governor of a new state. Bowie Sanson, a dishonest lawyer and campaign manager for Asa Forbes, connives, through political mudslinging and even murder, to get his candidate elected. Cole and Varney, the sons of the current governor, Harold Halsey, are caught in Bowie's political machinations and are forced to fight their way out. Glidden departs somewhat from the formula that had shaped his earlier plots. Though the novel does end in a gunfight, the events do not follow the pattern he established in earlier books. The erstwhile hero is killed, and the villain commits suicide. Despite these differences, *First Campaign* and the other Primrose novels were, for Glidden, a return to his Western roots.

Glidden continued to write in the 1970s, though cataracts and the subsequent operations to remove them all but blinded him. In 1974 he won the Western Heritage Wrangler Award, although he was too sick to attend the ceremonies. Later that year he was diagnosed with terminal throat cancer. He died 18 August 1975 at Aspen Valley Hospital, and his ashes were buried at Aspen Grove Cemetery, Aspen, Colorado. In February 1976 his fifty-first and last novel, *Trouble Country,* was published.

Though Frederick Dilley Glidden never wrote what a scholar might consider "serious" literature, he was, by most measures, a successful writer. He was, as Gale notes, "a craftsman proud to entertain." A few years after Glidden's death one of his friends quoted Glidden as saying that Western authors were "honorable entertainers who need apologize to no one." In the 1930s, in the midst of the Great Depression, Glidden literally wrote himself out of poverty. In the 1940s, years before it became popular for fiction writers to sell stories to Hollywood, Luke Short novels were "hot properties." Though he never really matched the success he experienced in the 1940s, Glidden seemed, for twenty years, to have his finger on an important pulse in America. His Western heroes showed readers what it was to be a man and exemplified the values of honesty, strength, and skill in a way that resonated for millions of readers. The amazing popularity of his work during the dark years of the 1930s and 1940s suggests that Glidden's message of strength and hope, of redemption through integrity, was one that Americans longed to hear.

**References:**

Richard W. Etulain, "Luke Short," *Twentieth-Century Western Writers,* edited by Geoff Sadler (Chicago: St. James Press, 1991), pp. 630–632;

Robert L. Gale, *Luke Short* (Boston: Twayne, 1981);

"Frederick Dilley Glidden," in *Encyclopedia of Frontier and Western Fiction,* edited by Jon Tuska and Vicki Pietarski (New York: McGraw-Hill, 1983), pp. 117–121;

H. N. Swanson, "Introduction," *Luke Short's Best of the West* (New York: Arbor House, 1983), pp. 9–15;

Jon Tuska, "Luke Short and the Western," in *A Variable Harvest: Essays and Reviews of Film and Literature* (Jefferson, N.C.: McFarland, 1990), pp. 630–632.

**Papers:**

Frederick Dilley Glidden's papers are housed at the Knight Library at the University of Oregon in Eugene, Oregon.

# Linda M. Hasselstrom

*(14 July 1943 –    )*

Rena Sanderson
*Boise State University*

BOOKS: *The Book Book: A Publishing Handbook for Beginners and Others* (Hermosa, S.Dak.: Lame Johnny Press, 1979);

*Caught by One Wing: Poems* (San Francisco: J. D. Holcomb, 1984);

*Roadkill* (Peoria, Ill.: Spoon River Poetry Press, 1987);

*Windbreak: A Woman Rancher on the Northern Plains* (Berkeley, Cal.: Barn Owl Books, 1987);

*Going Over East: Reflections of a Woman Rancher* (Golden, Colo.: Fulcrum Press, 1987; revised and enlarged, 2001);

*Land Circle: Writings Collected from the Land* (Golden, Colo.: Fulcrum Press, 1991);

*Dakota Bones: The Collected Poems of Linda Hasselstrom* (Granite Falls, Minn.: Spoon River Poetry Press, 1993);

*Roadside History of South Dakota* (Missoula, Mont.: Mountain Press, 1994);

*Feels Like Far: A Rancher's Life on the Great Plains* (New York: Lyons, 1999);

*Bitter Creek Junction* (Glendo, Wyo.: High Plains Press, 2000).

OTHER: *Next-Year Country: One Woman's View,* edited, with text, by Hasselstrom, photographs by Alma Phillips (Hermosa, S.Dak.: Lame Johnny Press, 1978);

James Clyman, *Journal of a Mountain Man,* edited by Hasselstrom (Missoula, Mont.: Mountain Press, 1984);

"Camping Ranches and Gear Junkies: New Scourge of the West," in *Discovered Country: Tourism and Survival in the American West,* edited by Scott Norris (Albuquerque: Stone Ladder Press, 1994), pp. 64–70;

"The Covenant of the Holy Monkey Wrench," in *American Nature Writing,* edited by John A. Murray (San Francisco: Sierra Club Books, 1994), pp. 28–35;

"Nighthawks," in *The Soul of Nature: Visions of a Living Earth,* edited by Michael Tobias and Georgianne

*Linda M. Hasselstrom with the cow pelvis that hangs in the backyard of her home in Cheyenne, Wyoming, to "remind me of my job" (courtesy of the author)*

Cowan (New York: Continuum Publishing, 1994), pp. 65–74;

"How I Became a Broken-In Writer," in *Imagining Home: Writing from the Midwest,* edited by Mark Vinz and Thom Tammaro (Minneapolis: University of Minnesota Press, 1995), pp. 145–162;

"The Song of the Turtle," in *American Nature Writing 1996,* selected by Murray (San Francisco: Sierra Club Books, 1996), pp. 72–84;

*Leaning into the Wind: Women Write from the Heart of the West,* edited by Hasselstrom, Gaydell Collier, and Nancy Curtis (Boston: Houghton Mifflin, 1997);

"The Cow as Totem," in *Writers on the Range: Western Writers Exploring the Changing Face of the American West,* edited by John A. Baden and Karl Hess Jr. (Niwot, Colo.: University Press of Colorado, 1998);

*Bison: Monarch of the Plains,* text by Hasselstrom, photographs by David Fitzgerald (Portland, Ore.: Graphic Arts Center, 1998);

*Woven on the Wind: Women Write about Friendship in the Sagebrush West,* edited by Hasselstrom, Collier, and Curtis (Boston: Houghton Mifflin, 2001).

SELECTED PERIODICAL PUBLICATIONS–
UNCOLLECTED: "Journal of a Woman Rancher," *Life* (July 1989): 89–94;

"The Price of Bullets," *Missouri Review,* 12 (1989): 7–16;

"Secrets of Today's Country Women," *South Dakota Magazine* (March/April 1992): 25–27;

"Buffalo Winter," *American Literary Review,* 5 (Fall 1994): 39–48;

"The Real Western Brand," *Rocky Mountain News* (26 March 1995): 12A, 20A;

"The Owl on the Fence," *Western American Literature,* 30 (Spring 1995): 29–36;

"The Second Half," *Northern Lights,* 11 (Winter 1996): 16–18;

"Between Grass and Sky: Antelope Hunt," *Northern Lights,* 11 (May 1996): 23–28;

"Looking for Life: Lightning," *North Dakota Quarterly,* 63 (Fall 1996): 20–25;

"On Writing Western," *Roundup Magazine,* 4 (December 1996): inside back cover;

"Going Back to Grass," *North Dakota Quarterly,* 64 (Winter 1997): 5–14;

"Rising from the Condos," *Chronicle of Community,* 2 (Spring 1998): 5–16;

"Living on This Land," *Green River Review,* 28 (Spring/Summer 1998): 65–76;

"Making Hay," *South Dakota Magazine,* 14 (July/August 1998): 70–76;

"Waddling Over the Dam," *South Dakota Magazine,* 14 (January/February 1999): 45–50;

"Badger's Business," *Weber Studies,* 16 (Winter 1999): 94–103.

For almost thirty years, Linda M. Hasselstrom has educated others about the practical, communal, historical, and spiritual dimensions of ranch life on the Plains of South Dakota. Going at this task with extraordinary energy, she has taken on a multiplicity of roles: first as teacher, editor, and publisher, and

later as poet, essayist, and historian. Hasselstrom's role as a woman rancher, however, has been the bedrock of her writing. Her favorite review, as she reveals in "On Writing Western" (December 1996), includes this line about herself: "She can deliver a calf and a poem on the same day–after mending a fence." Between 1979 and 2000, Hasselstrom published ten books of her own poetry and nonfiction, and her writings appeared in more than seventy magazines and in several anthologies. Insisting on the importance of local culture and local literature, she records the texture of living and working on a family-run cattle ranch and celebrates the values—industry, endurance, self-reliance, and neighborliness—associated with this disappearing way of life. To this list of virtues that are commonly attributed to rural life, however, Hasselstrom brings a twist of her own: an emphasis, somewhat unusual in the ranching community, on environmental awareness and ecologically sensitive stewardship. At the same time, she disdains those who want a prettified nature, the sort pictured on Sierra Club calendars. Through her careful, unsentimental depiction of ranching activities and of nature's destructive and restorative powers, she guides her reader to an understanding of natural cycles and their broader significance for human life. As a nature writer, Hasselstrom at her best evokes the philosophical richness of Henry David Thoreau. As a social observer, in the tradition of Tillie Olsen and Meridel Le Sueur, she speaks for unheard women and reclaims the experiences of women ranchers and their place in the history of the American West. The power of Hasselstrom's poetry and essays has been recognized, as a result, by several major awards.

Linda Michele Hasselstrom, pronounced "Hayzelstrom," was born 14 July 1943 in Houston, Texas, to Florence Mildred Bovard and Robert Paul Bovard. When she was still a small child, her parents divorced, and she moved in 1947 with her mother to South Dakota. There her mother married John Hasselstrom, whose family had ranched in the region between the Black Hills and the Badlands since the late nineteenth century. In 1952 John Hasselstrom adopted Linda as his daughter; embracing his family history and his way of life as her own, she has referred to him ever since as her father. At his ranch near Hermosa the nine-year-old Hasselstrom learned the ranching routine, acquired her first horse, grew enchanted with the grasslands—and began to write, keeping a journal and even attempting a novel.

This early affinity for writing continued to grow. After graduating from high school in Rapid City in 1961, Hasselstrom did summer internships with *The Rapid City Daily Journal.* As an English major at the

University of South Dakota in Vermillion between 1961 and 1965, she studied writing, published a chapbook of poems, edited the school newspaper, and won journalism awards. During a year of graduate work at the Vermillion campus from 1965 to 1966, she was employed as a reporter for *The Sioux City Journal*. In 1966 she married Daniel Lusk, a divorced man with three children, and moved with him to Columbia, Missouri, where she taught at Christian College, now Columbia College. In 1969 Hasselstrom graduated from the University of Missouri-Columbia with an M.A. in American literature.

Hasselstrom's contributions to the literature of the American West reflect three stages of development: between 1971 and 1985 she promoted regional literature and culture through teaching, editing, and publishing; before 1988 she wrote ranch-centered poetry and prose; and since the death of her second husband, George Randolph Snell, in 1988 and her displacement from the family ranch in 1992, she has written works centered in loss and recovery. During this last phase she has also resumed her work as a teacher and editor.

Hasselstrom's career as an editor and publisher began in earnest in 1971, when she and her first husband returned to South Dakota and began two publishing ventures, *Sunday Clothes: A Magazine of the Fine Arts* and Lame Johnny Press. In the next two years, between 1971 and 1973, while Hasselstrom worked on her parents' ranch for a year and then taught at Black Hills State College, she was also writing. In 1973 she and Lusk divorced, but she maintained amicable relationships with her three stepchildren. As she recalls later in *Land Circle: Writings Collected from the Land* (1991), she withdrew to the ranch after her divorce, "not trusting anyone or anything–but the land." She remembers that the land healed her and that she then "began to write seriously and well for the first time." At the same time, however, Hasselstrom continued to operate the magazine and the publishing house, both of which were considerable accomplishments. Although *Sunday Clothes* went broke three times, she considered the magazine an important instrument for promoting regional art, and she managed to publish it quarterly for an eleven-year period, from 1971 to 1982, featuring approximately three hundred artists and writers. In addition, during the period 1971 to 1985, as the owner-director of Lame Johnny Press, Hasselstrom edited and produced twenty-three books related to the Great Plains, including a few books that she herself wrote or compiled.

The books about the Great Plains published by Lame Johnny Press treat themes that continue to be central to Hasselstrom's later writing. For example,

Cover for Hasselstrom's 1987 journal of life on her parents' ranch

her fascination with local social history appears in *Next-Year Country: One Woman's View* (1978), a collection of photographs taken in the early 1900s by a rural Nebraska wife and mother named Alma Phillips. As Hasselstrom explains in her preface, the photos, which depict the daily lives of Alma's farm family, preserve a way of life that has nearly vanished; but just as importantly, they also show that an ordinary farm wife could know and accept the difficulties of her work and still find in its depths "the time and inspiration" for artistic creativity. The intersection of place, physical hardship, and creativity is a repeated theme in Hasselstrom's later writings, as is the need to establish the too-often-ignored significance of women in the history of the American West.

With the exception of ranch work, almost all of Hasselstrom's activity is driven by a powerful didactic impulse aimed at preserving Plains life from outside encroachment or control. For example, in 1979, the year she was named South Dakota Press Woman of

Achievement, she wrote and published through Lame Johnny Press a detailed guide to self-publication, *The Book Book: A Publishing Handbook for Beginners and Others* (1979). Written in the spirit of Western self-reliance, *The Book Book* seeks to promote the independence of writers from established publishers. Like her other school-related activities, such as conducting writing workshops and conferences and judging writing contests, she designed this guide to self-publishing, according to its preface, "with schools in mind."

Hasselstrom's attachment to the land led her, by the late 1970s, to a growing involvement in South Dakota's environmental movement, whose first order of business was public education. In 1979 she joined the Black Hills Energy Coalition, an organization that sponsored a ballot initiative banning nuclear power generation, uranium mines, and waste repositories. Although that initiative failed, she was an important spokesperson later in a successful drive against a nuclear-waste dump. Hasselstrom was also both president and board member of the Technical Information Project, which Kathleen Danker identifies in her 1996 essay on Hasselstrom in *American Nature Writers* as "a research group organized to provide data concerning environmental issues."

An important turning point in Hasselstrom's life came in 1979, when she married George Randolph Snell, with whom she shared a great appetite for life and a mutual love of the landscape. She and George lived at the Hasselstrom ranch, first in a cramped addition to her parents' home and later in a house they built for themselves. The couple never had any children of their own, but George's son by a previous marriage, Michael, regularly visited in the summer. During their nine years together, George strongly supported his wife's creative work.

Having spent her early professional years helping others give birth to literary creations, Hasselstrom decided in the early 1980s to concentrate on her own writing. Encouraged by the publication of her first poetry collection, *Caught by One Wing: Poems* (1984), and by the support of a National Endowment for the Arts fellowship for poetry, she discontinued her publishing ventures and began to divide her time between ranching and writing. Three years later, Spoon River Poetry Press published her second book of poems, *Roadkill* (1987), and in 1990 reprinted *Caught by One Wing*. The early poems established Hasselstrom as a writer for whom ranch life on the Great Plains served as a microcosm of life in general. Informed by her intimacy with that life, her poetry provides compelling pictures of the natural order, in all its contradictions, and of humanity's place in that order. As Geraldine Sanford notes in an article for *The South Dakota Review*

(Autumn 1992), the land has taught Hasselstrom "to accept oppositions as part of the natural condition, to be integrated, through a variety of resolutions, into the totality of her philosophy."

In her poetry Hasselstrom shows both sides of the exchange between humans and the land they work—that is, the destructive as well as the nurturing presence of humans and, in the words of Leo Marx, their "machine in the garden." In the poem from which the first collection, *Caught by One Wing,* takes its title, the "I" of the piece—the rancher—feels responsible for a meadowlark becoming fatally "caught by one wing" on the fence wire; and in "Roadkills and the I Ching," because of some traveler's car, "In the ditch / a deer's dead eyes / give back the night's confusion." Several other poems, such as "Blackbirds," examine the complexities of responsible stewardship. Hasselstrom shows the rancher—who is more dependent on machinery than most—in the precarious situation of having to negotiate between the dictates of efficiency and loyalty to the land; the rancher's survival will not allow sentimentality.

Ranch work is hard and dangerous. In "Rancher Roulette"—a lighthearted poem that Garrison Keillor read on his radio program, "A Prairie Home Companion," on 22 April 1996—Hasselstrom reminds the reader that "It's no trick to get killed ranching." She then lists in the same poem various means of accidental death, from horses and tractors to winter weather and lightning. In a more serious vein, the poem "Spring" suggests that ranching also imposes difficult ethical choices, demanding at times an unblinking practicality:

> It's spring;
> time to kill the kittens.
> Their mewing blends with the meadowlark song.
> I tried drowning them once;
> it was slow, painful.
> Now I bash each with a wrench,
> once, hard.

Pain, loss, violence, bloodshed, and death are as much a part of her reality as joy, hope, birth, and renewal. Traditionally in literature a much romanticized season of new life and hope, spring is also a season of death and pain for the rancher: "A calf born dead yesterday / was found by coyotes in the night: / only the head and one front foot remain. / . . . A blue jay is eating baby robins." Spring teaches the rancher the ironic contradictions at the heart of reality. Like Walt Whitman, Hasselstrom reconciles those contradictions through her vision of a cyclical, regenerative nature in which death and life are interconnected. Thus, ranching life is demanding yet rich in philosophical and aesthetic consolations. The poem "Mulch," for example, which is always well received at Hasselstrom's public readings, humorously asserts the regenerative momentum of life. The speaker in "Mulch" makes a garden compost out of old love letters and bills and memories—the costs and disappointments of the past: "Nothing is wasted." Loss and pain, like death, give meaning to life.

In "Bone," a poem dedicated to Georgia O'Keeffe, "a polished jawbone, teeth white / against the grass" represents, with stark beauty, the essence of life. Throughout Hasselstrom's writings, bones, whether of animals or of humans, symbolize at once individual mortality and the continuation of life. In "Memorial Day" the speaker—who is weeding her ancestors' graves—recognizes an affinity between her own bones and those of the dead generations who earlier worked the same land. In many of Hasselstrom's poems, the sense of rootedness through place and work bridges the present and the past, the living and the dead. In "Planting Peas," the speaker remembers her grandmother's hands performing the same gardening task and experiences her grandmother's continued presence in the earth. Many other pieces in *Caught by One Wing* and in *Roadkill* recount the lives of earlier settlers and homesteaders and express the poet's kinship with them.

Hasselstrom's next book, *Windbreak: A Woman Rancher on the Northern Plains* (1987), is an autobiography in journal form that records the author's life working with her husband George on her parents' ranch. Much as Le Sueur and Olsen represent in their writings the underrepresented working class, Hasselstrom's journal provides information on the unfamiliar, endangered way of life of family ranchers, including women ranchers, and insists on preserving their rightful place in the national memory. In keeping with this instructive purpose, she includes a biographical preface, an introduction providing information on the Hasselstrom ranch—including its history, operation, and location—a map of the ranch, and a glossary of ranching terms. During a question-and-answer session at the Prairie Winds Writers' Conference, Hasselstrom called *Windbreak* her favorite work.

Like Thoreau in *Walden* (1862) Hasselstrom in *Windbreak* asserts the value of staying in one place: "We're never bored; seeing the same scenery over and over only seems to make us notice more. . . ." She shares Thoreau's belief in firsthand, personal observation, and *Windbreak* chronicles her and her family's intimate knowledge of their corner of South Dakota. Like *Walden,* Hasselstrom's *Windbreak* may be read on two levels: literally, as a localized field

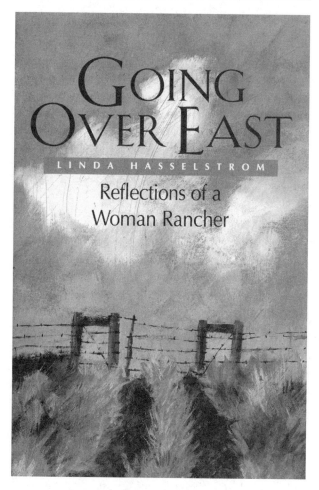

Dust jacket for Hasselstrom's 1987 guide to the history and geography of her home state

study, and symbolically, as a philosophical exploration. The title of Hasselstrom's book refers to its central symbol: A windbreak—"a little hill that breaks the wind can save a herd of cattle in a blizzard"—is a natural symbol for the good that is inherent in ranching. A windbreak is "a promise in fall, a lifesaver and a place of warmth in winter, a sign of hope in spring, and a place of loveliness in the dry heat of summer."

At the same time, although Hasselstrom alludes to Thoreau's example in this and other writings, she has also insisted on the differences between Thoreau's situation and her own. As a participant in a symposium about nature writing that was moderated by John A. Murray, Hasselstrom observed that "Thoreau was creating an experiment and a book at Walden Pond, but others were doing jobs that inspired their writing." Pointing to the examples of Wendell Berry, Sue Hubbell, Gretel Ehrlich, Loren Eisley, Aldo Leopold, and John Wesley Powell, she aligned herself with writers for whom "the work was foremost, and the writing a side effect." Indeed, *Windbreak* emphasizes the grueling work and hardships of cattle ranching. Nancy Mairs, in *The New York Times Book Review,* praised Hasselstrom's willingness to record "the minutiae of daily life rather than sacrifice them to heroic moments." In fact, though, the minutiae of daily life are full of heroic moments, and the daily drudgery accentuates the preciousness of rest, beauty, and epiphanies.

Drawing indirectly on the journals that Hasselstrom has kept since she was nine, *Windbreak* continues the tradition of journal writing as practiced by Hasselstrom's grandfather, father, and mother. The journal form ideally suits *Windbreak.* As a journal it captures the concrete details of a life in which each day, beyond the repetitive routine of work, is filled with the drama and surprises that changes in the seasons, weather, landscape, animals, community, and economics supply. With the exception of entries about a brief vacation away from the ranch, each entry specifies the date and temperature of that day—thereby stressing the distinctive nature of each day and experience. *Windbreak* is, however, also carefully organized by seasons—with sixteen poems strategically placed, one at the beginning of each season and one at the end of each month—to reflect, as in Thoreau's classic, the cyclical coherence of an entire year.

The book opens with the autumn season, described largely in terms of almost idyllic garden imagery. The days are long, filled with harvesting, canning, animal watching, writing, and preparing for winter. Hasselstrom enjoys her ritualistic fall chores and the company of visitors, including Leslie Marmon Silko. Nevertheless, the beginning of *Windbreak* also hints at ever present danger. The first entry describes a fire, set by railroad sparks, that demolishes fifteen thousand dry acres. Although the incident illustrates the ranchers' helpless exposure to the careless use of machinery, the community's response to the crisis demonstrates the power of "neighboring" and of human ingenuity and strength. In addition, the crisis confirms each person's usefulness—as do the many regular hardships and chores that are part of the rancher's year.

Early September brings hail that destroys the flowers and a windstorm that knocks down the fence. Extremes of winter threaten the survival of cattle and humans alike, testing the physical limits of both. Personal work injuries are common—Hasselstrom gets trampled by a horse—and George's exhaustion and breathing problems are ominous signs of his deteriorating health. Every day holds unexpected complications. Spring, the season of calving, brings birth complications and close-up views of death. Because Hasselstrom and her husband can afford the veterinarian only in serious emergencies, they handle the normal and difficult births and must also deal with the many fatalities. They then brand, dehorn, castrate, and medicate the surviving calves. Despite the difficulty—or perhaps because of it—the author's involvement in such life-and-death struggles makes her feel that her work "really means something." With summer arrive thunderstorms, wind, drought, grasshoppers, and the threat of fire from lightning or from a carelessly dropped cigarette. On returning from a short trip, the couple finds that a hailstorm has destroyed their garden and much of their summer pasture. Yet, throughout the year, there are treasured special moments: Hasselstrom enjoys "looking at the tracks in the snow—mouse, coyote, rabbit—noticing the pure line of a single blade of grass against a snowdrift"; she treasures her ritual of watching every sunset; she observes the "prairie punk" of "a dozen brilliant orange butterflies perched on a cluster of purple coneflowers."

As she asserts in *Windbreak,*

It is up to the rancher to figure out a way, every year, in every emergency, to survive. It's less like a battle than a marriage. The problems perhaps serve to enhance our feeling of accomplishment when we succeed, and the more complex or dangerous the situation, the greater the exhilaration when we live through it.

Hasselstrom's work thus generally fits into the tradition of literature and myths of the American West, a tradition suggesting—as Diane Dufva Quantic reminds us in *The Nature of the Place: A Study of Great Plains Fiction* (1995)—that the settling of the frontier could be accomplished only by "dragon-slayers, superhuman in strength and in intelligence and willing to sacrifice themselves to the demands of the land."

When Hasselstrom first submitted *Windbreak* for publication, her Eastern readers found the realities of ranch life unbelievable. In "How I Became a Broken-In Writer" she recounts that one agent in New York found the descriptions of ranch life "so relentlessly hard and tied to the routine of the daily chores involved in the struggle for survival that it would be difficult to sustain a reader's interest." The book was rejected by twenty-four publishers before it finally appeared in print and was praised by reviewers for the very qualities that agents and publishers had found objectionable. In his review of *Windbreak,* Quentin Howard credited its "vivid description of hard work and survival" for making the "virtually unknown" world of ranch work accessible, thus fill-

January 20, 1999
February 9, 1999

"Make a hand!" My father'd holler when my friends came down to visit.
All the arty folks I knew came sometime to see what ranch life was all about.
"Make a hand!" He didn't care if they were men or women when we needed
help. "This job's beyond an old man and a crippled girl," he'd say.
"Make a hand and drive those yearlings up the chute so we
can truck 'em to the sale and get some cash. Your mother wants
linoleum but I'm thinking my old truck is about to crash.
The gender issue didn't surface until we got around to branding
and even then he didn't call it that. "Make a hand," he'd yell and startle
some romantic poet who had never had a callus on his finger
unless it was from midnight communication with the muse,
some romantic poet whose occupation and vacation was sitting by a dandle
sighing while he scribbled at his masterpiece, a villanelle on spring and
resignation, on assignations, and on love. "Make a hand!"
That skinny poet vaulted fence plank faster than he thought he could
to grab a calf's bobbed tail – frozen off the night his mother birthed him,
March and forty-two below. The poet grabbed the calf's stubbed nub
and shoved him up the chute so I could catch him in the headgate,
lay him flat and make hair sizzle when the hot irons hit his ribs.
Before that calf could realize his potential he lost them both,
his gender symbols banded tight to turn him bloodlessly
into a steer while he lurched behind his mama
through the greening April grass. Before that calf or poet
could blink or think of grumbling, one of them was branded,
ear tagged, received a fusillade of shots inoculating him against
anything we'd heard of and went bucking out the chute
while the other headed back for another leggy critter,
jeans just oozing with authentic green manure.

"Make a hand!" It's been six years or better since we closed that narrow casket
where he finally got to rest. We tamped the yellow gumbo down
that summer, filled and tamped some more come spring.
I planted wild blue flax, brought some plugs of redtop
from the pasture, big and little bluestem. Found a sego lily
like the ones he brought my mother every spring.
With the rains, the gumweed flourished, creeping jenny,
thistles, until I yanked them out barehanded because --
I could hear him say it – I wasn't wearing gloves.

"Make a hand!" I hear him shout when I quit work and wander out
to see if the mail has come yet. "Make a hand!" he'll beller
when I sit down to read a bit of that new mystery

*Page from the first draft of Hasselstrom's poem "Make a Hand," published in her 2000 collection* Bitter Creek Junction *(Collection of Linda M. Hasselstrom)*

ing "a long-standing gap in the written history" of the American West and in "the story of women" in the West. *Windbreak* indeed established Hasselstrom as a writer. Its success brought the author many letters from readers—she has answered almost seven hundred personally—along with new opportunities for academic speaking engagements on writing and the environment. The book even received what is proverbially the highest form of praise: large portions of the book were plagiarized by a Harlequin romance writer; Hasselstrom eventually got an out-of-court cash settlement.

Opportunities for publications multiplied. A second book of nonfiction, *Going Over East: Reflections of a Woman Rancher* (1987), won the first American Writing Award by Fulcrum Publishing. As in *Windbreak,* the setting of *Going Over East* is the Hasselstrom ranch, and the local and personal are once again of political and universal significance, but this collection of essays presents much more fully developed environmental discussions and social criticism.

The organization of *Going Over East*—structurally perhaps Hasselstrom's tightest work—reflects the eleven-mile journey that she, her husband George, and her stepson Mike take in their pickup truck as they are "going over east" from their house to the summer pasture. Each gate through which they pass corresponds to one of the twelve essays that make up the bulk of the book; a final chapter offers tentative conclusions about the issues raised.

Particular landmarks and natural phenomena encountered on the trip—vegetation, animals, and deserted homesteads and missile sites—trigger the telling of stories and histories that illustrate both harmonious and intrusive forms of human interaction with the land. The author's main concern throughout is good stewardship of the land. Insisting that people must respond with intelligence to a region where "Mother Nature has a talent for nasty surprises," Hasselstrom believes that ranchers can live in harmony with the land. She advocates the concept of bioregionalism, the idea that each biological region of a country should concentrate on its own strengths and produce only whatever the natural resources of the region support—such as wind generators that utilize the prairie winds. The grasslands of western South Dakota, she claims, are ideally suited for livestock grazing, and cattle ranching is thus a commonsense activity, mutually beneficial to both humans and the land.

Hasselstrom fears, however, that the future of ranching is in danger. Rampant monoculture may erase any regional distinctiveness and authenticity, and more populous areas will see the land as "empty,

unused, and thus a fit place for garbage or fun." The low population, lack of industry, and eagerness for employment in the region have led some to propose that the region take what no other place wants—uranium mines and mills, disposal sites for all sorts of toxic waste, strip mining operations, and ammunition plants. In addition, both the family ranch and the environment are endangered by lack of appropriate government support, by corporate ranching methods, and by misinformed environmentalists.

Then there are personal uncertainties. Although Hasselstrom values as her legacy "the knowledge and love of the land" gained from working it, she worries that her father's "penny-pinching philosophy" may not be enough to get her through periods of shrinking profit margins. She also worries about the physical toll that the hard labor will take on their aging bodies generally and on George's poor health in particular. Finally, Hasselstrom wonders whether she "will have to choose between this land and a husband who is talking of getting a job in town, getting away from the endless isolation of winter, the silence, the wind, the cattle." The revised edition of the book that appeared in 2001 includes an epilogue, "The Final Gate," that offers the rest of the story up to September 2000.

The reception of *Going Over East* was quite positive. In her review of the book, Kate Arneson stressed that Hasselstrom's position—that the "center of the universe *is* South Dakota"—should not be misunderstood as "narrow provincialism" but should be recognized as a reminder that universal truths are to be gained from the situation in South Dakota. Hasselstrom's message, according to Arneson, is that loss of contact with nature will produce not technological nirvana but the loss of an important part of humanity. Reviewers also praised the book for its structure, its fully developed discussions, and its balance of the didactic and the aesthetic.

At precisely the point when her career was blossoming, her husband George died. George had suffered from recurrences of Hodgkin's disease; in the end, a tumor caused by radiation treatment led to his death on 7 September 1988. At the time, Hasselstrom was working on her second collection of essays and poems, a book that was essentially finished. In response to George's death, however, she added a section devoted to him, partly derived from a journal she kept during his last ten days at the hospital. In addition, she included poems that, as she told Murray in an interview, "seemed to add something I could not say in essays." The resulting work richly combines different tones and genres—from the polemical to the personal, perhaps reflecting a transi-

Hasselstrom,                                                                              24

discover that events in a collection of essays did not happen as the writer says they

did. Therefore, I find it necessary to note that

The events in the essays that follow actually happened, and they happened to

me, with certain exceptions I'll explain shortly. I consider the most important part of

my job to be telling the truth about grasslands ranching as I see it. I understand that

even as I write about receiving a turtle as a birthday gift, the reader may be making

judgments about ranching based on what I write. Readers who trust my veracity, who

have confidence in my judgment as shown in my writing, may be more willing to

listen to my viewpoints, to vote, or to take other significant action to preserve

ranching on the plains. How could I expect a reader to trust my opinion if I lie about

facts?

I have not always aspired to be a nature writer, or a spokesperson for ranching.

Early in my writing days, I intended to become a Great American Novelist. One of

these essays, "Song of the Turtle" and "Running with the Antelope," began with a

real experience which I fictionalized for its first publication. As I turned to essay

writing, my views on what constitutes allowable license changed. So I have removed

the fictional elements from the essays. The events in "Song of the Turtle" occurred

later in my life than the essay indicates, and I have changed the name of the man

involved. In "Running with the Antelope," the events are likewise true, though one

male character is a composite of two real men, and the names of both male characters

have been changed. If I were writing these experiences for the first time today, I

would not alter the timing of the events, or use composite characters. I would have

tried to stop the hunt, but once the

*Corrected typescript page for an untitled essay by Hasselstrom, for a collection to be published
in 2002 by the University of Nevada Press (Collection of Linda M. Hasselstrom)*

tional stage in the author's life and career. The book was published as *Land Circle: Writings Collected from the Land,* a title that reiterates her belief in the circularity of life even after her faith in the natural order has been tested by changing circumstances and by losses.

The author herself, in an unpublished interview from the Prairie Winds Writers' Conference, called *Land Circle* "the most serious, the most extended, the most complex book" she had published. The volume consists of thirty-six poems and thirty-three essays arranged in alternating order, with each poem typically complementing and accentuating the essay it introduces. As Dianne Ganz Scheper notes in an article that appeared in *Belles Lettres: A Review of Books by Women* (Spring 1995), the material in *Land Circle* is divided into three parts "inscribing three dimensions of place: communal, familial, and political."

The poems and essays in "Part I: Where Neighbor Is a Verb" stress the distinctive characteristics and the interdependence of people who live close to the land. In the poem "Chant for the Rain," ranchers use the first-person singular when speaking of their land during drought: "'I'm dry clear to the bone,' / ranchers say. 'Dry clear to the bone.'" And in the essay "Finding Buffalo Berries," the locals are equated with the tart buffalo berries: "we tend to be a little prickly if we've been here long." Sentimental myths of the Wild West are satirized in the poem "The Wild and Woolly West." What is needed in the real West, as she suggests in the essay "The Cowboy and the Ride," is a "knowledge of survival and a clear-eyed practicality that is missing from all sides of land-use debates today." Finally, Part I also celebrates the rewards of physical work and the concept of "neighboring"–mutual assistance in times of trouble.

"Part II: George: In Beauty Walk," the most personal section, centers on George's death and the author's widowhood, with some exploration of related issues such as aging, health care, and the funeral industry. In the essay "George R. Snell, 1946–1988" she offers a moving character sketch and description of her husband's dying, while in "Vultures" she analyzes the modern denial of death. One "can't have nature without manure, blood, pain, unfair deaths, fleas," Hasselstrom reminds us, but "most folks . . . don't like *real* nature."

In "Part III: A Woman's Covenant," Hasselstrom voices her sometimes controversial position on ecological issues and her fierce commitment to protect her region and the values it represents. Her essay "Confessions of a Born-Again Pagan" supports the view of Lynn White and Berry: Christian misreadings of God's directive to "subdue" the earth–

from Gen. 1:28–have encouraged a doctrine of domination and exploitation of the planet and of humans. As an alternative to such a doctrine, she embraces those principles of ecofeminism and of paganism that emphasize respect for all life and advocate a nurturing, rather than an intrusive, human interaction with the land and with others. Only those who are "still in touch with the land" can "save the nation and world from the ecological crisis we've created by our greed and exploitation." In the essay "Land Circle: Lessons," Hasselstrom tells what the land has taught her concerning individual and collective responsibility for life. She defends selective logging, water conservation, firearms for women's self-protection, and, most of all, thoughtful ranching "that will support itself without damaging the land beyond its own inherent power to recover." In "The Cow versus the Animal Rights Activist," she argues that properly managed family cattle operations in suitable regions are land-friendly. The final poem shows, in a lighthearted tone, how the rancher identifies with her beloved cow–even, or especially, by cooking and eating its heart:

> Often I dip pan juices,
> pour them lovingly over the meat.
> When I open the oven,
> the heart throbs
> in its own golden fat.
> . . . . . . . . . . . . . . .
> My friends have begun to notice my placid air,
> which they mistake for serenity.
> Yesterday a man remarked on my large brown eyes,
> my long eyelashes,
> my easy walk.

The poem reflects Hasselstrom's suggestion, expressed in the essay "The Cow as Totem," that cows might serve as "totems" since "they represent certain excellent qualities" and symbolize "a benign way of living on the earth," and that eating the heart of a vanquished animal is a sign of respect.

Hasselstrom's views have attracted criticism from both sides, from ranchers and environmentalists alike. As Paul Higbee explains in his article in *South Dakota Magazine* (September/October 1992), locals object that Hasselstrom's environmental activism has cost towns in the southern Black Hills jobs–particularly in relation to a proposed nuclear-waste storage near the town of Edgemont. Environmentalists, convinced that livestock grazing is destructive to Western lands, also question her claims of land-friendly ranching. In addition, Hasselstrom has been criticized for her reservations about organized religion and for her interest in supposedly pagan concepts, which she developed more fully in her essay "The Covenant of the Holy Monkey Wrench."

Nevertheless, *Land Circle*, like Hasselstrom's other works, enjoyed an enthusiastic reception. John Murray, in introducing his interview with Hasselstrom, calls her "narrative counterpoint of poetry and prose" a "daring approach" and, listing other prose writers who have failed at poetry, praises her for having "succeeded brilliantly." In a review of *Land Circle* for *Western American Literature* (Winter 1993), William Kittredge commends her "tone of quiet, well-earned authority." As another sign of the success of the book, two of its essays appeared in condensed form in *The Reader's Digest* (April 1992 and April 1995). *Land Circle* also gained its author several awards. In 1991 *Nebraska Territory* awarded her the Elkhorn Prize for Poetry—a trophy belt buckle; in 1992 Mountains and Plains Booksellers named *Land Circle* one of the year's best books, and the same year *Rapid City Journal* chose Hasselstrom as one of the ten West River Notables.

The early 1990s brought, however, not only successes but also disappointments. In 1992, after her father had suffered a series of strokes, and after her relationship with him had deteriorated, he demanded that she choose between ranching and writing. Though she had spent almost forty years on the ranch, she chose writing and moved to Cheyenne, Wyoming. Shortly thereafter, on 7 August 1992, her father died. Five months later, at a time when she most needed support, her longtime friend Margaret Brazell also died. Her father had left everything to his widow, who was ill and needed to be placed in a nursing home. It took Hasselstrom two years to settle her father's estate. In the end she managed to buy the ranch but had to sell all the cattle and lease out the land to a neighbor, whose hired hand moved into her parents' house. No longer directly involved in ranch work, she kept her residence in the city.

These changes obviously cast into question her identity as a writer who had successfully combined the roles of wife, daughter, and working rancher. Although Hasselstrom has expressed ambivalence about her new situation, she has also acknowledged that it provides her with new subject matter and more time for her writing. Indeed, since her departure from the ranch, she has published a large number of significant works. One in particular, *Dakota Bones: The Collected Poems of Linda Hasselstrom* (1993), is dedicated "to my father, John Hasselstrom." *Dakota Bones* was published one year after her father's death and offered thirty new poems in addition to those of the first two poetry volumes.

The following year she published a major research and writing project, *Roadside History of South Dakota* (1994), which she had begun in 1991 and which reflects her unwavering commitment to the region, its history, and its people. As the title indicates, this 467-page book records the state's history along highways, or, in the author's words, "the pathways devised by humans who change the land and its culture." *Roadside History of South Dakota* divides the state into four geographic regions—eastern South Dakota; the Missouri River and its Great Lakes; western South Dakota; and the Black Hills and the Badlands. It has been praised for its lively mixture of geography, topography, and information on various persons and events from the state's past, along with many photos, illustrations, and maps. Although the nature of this project encouraged the use of an impersonal, official rhetoric, Hasselstrom becomes quite personal when she addresses her own bias "as a custodian of the land" and asks the reader to suspend judgment on "historical acts now thought unseemly," such as the shooting of Indians and the rape of women.

Just as *Roadside History of South Dakota* asks readers to accept the wrongs of the past in South Dakota, so do Hasselstrom's various writings since George's death in 1988 express more explicitly her own need to accept the "wrongs"—the unexpected injuries, changes, disappointments, and losses—in her private history. Although she continues to write essays on environmental topics, such as "Camping Ranches and Gear Junkies: New Scourge of the West" (1994), an essay on tourism, she has also perfected the personal essay and produced masterpieces in that form. Typically in these essays, the author introduces some conflict in the present and then dramatizes an encounter with a particular Great Plains animal. Hasselstrom—the observant naturalist—provides detailed descriptions of the animal and its habits, while Hasselstrom the poet transforms the animal into an emblem of psychological, philosophical, or spiritual significance. Several such essays have appeared in magazines and anthologies, including "Nighthawks," "Buffalo Winter"—listed as one of the best one hundred essays in *Best American Essays 1995*—"The Owl on the Fence," and "The Song of the Turtle." Like *Land Circle*, these essays illustrate Hasselstrom's turn to nature for consolation and healing. As John Murray observes in his interview with Hasselstrom, such nature writing fits into a growing tradition of recovery narratives written by contemporary Western women—narratives such as *The Solace of Open Spaces* (1985) by Ehrlich and *Refuge: An Unnatural History of Family and Place* (1992) by

*Hasselstrom with her West Highland white terrier, Duggan (courtesy of the author)*

Terry Tempest Williams. Hasselstrom suggests in the same interview

> women who don't feel that they're getting enough religious nourishment, mental nourishment, from the cultural structures we have—our churches, our families, our society—turn to nature and find it there.

Committed to raising public awareness about prairie women's unique situation and strengths, Hasselstrom has written individual pieces on that topic, such as "Secrets of Today's Country Women" (1992), and she has encouraged prairie women to speak. With two other ranch women, Gaydell Collier and Nancy Curtis, she edited *Leaning into the Wind: Women Write from the Heart of the West* (1997), a collection of stories and poems by ordinary contemporary Western women who have worked the land. A second anthology in the series, *Woven on the Wind: Women Write about Friendship in the Sagebrush West,* followed in 2001, and Hasselstrom and her co-editors have been collecting manuscripts for a third book. The publication of these anthologies by a major press indicates Hasselstrom's success in attracting national attention to the place and people of her beloved region. In 1996 she turned the ranch home that she

and George built into a retreat—Windbreak House—where aspiring women writers may find their voices. She thus extended the significance of the ranch as a sanctuary of creativity and at the same time committed herself even further to mentoring and teaching others.

Although Hasselstrom finds herself wintering in Cheyenne, she commutes to the ranch to teach in the summer and she describes herself in a biographical typescript as "rooted in southwestern South Dakota." *Feels Like Far: A Rancher's Life on the Great Plains* (1999), her most comprehensive autobiography to date, bears testimony to that rootedness. Interweaving old and new writings, she offers in this book a moving account of a life devoted to ranching, from her earliest experiences as a child on the ranch through her displacement from the ranch and subsequent invention of a new life.

Meanwhile, Linda M. Hassselstrom's accomplishments continue to gain recognition. In 1996 the South Dakota Newspaper Association honored her with the Distinguished Achievement Award, and in 1997 the South Dakota Council of Teachers of English named her Author of the Year. In 1999 the Independent Publishers Association named *Bison:*

*Monarch of the Plains* the Best Environmental and Nature Book. In 2000 the National Cowboy and Western Heritage Museum in Oklahoma City, Oklahoma, declared *Bitter Creek Junction* the Best Poetry Book; that same year the book also won the Fine Arts Award of the Wyoming Historical Society. Finally in 2001, Hasselstrom was given a "Failure is Impossible" Award on Women's Equality Day in Rapid City, South Dakota.

**Interviews:**

Robin Kacel, "An Interview with Linda Hasselstrom," *Writing!* (September 1988): 11–13;

John Murray, "Of Ranching and Writing: A Talk with Linda Hasselstrom," *The Bloomsbury Review*, 12 (July/August 1992): 1, 20;

**References:**

Gaydell Collier, "Linda Hasselstrom," *Roundup Magazine* 3 (February 1996): 39;

Kathleen Danker, "Linda Hasselstrom," in *American Nature Writers*, volume 1 (New York: Scribners, 1996), pp. 337–348;

Paul Higbee, "At Home on the Range," *South Dakota Magazine* (September/October 1992): 23–26;

John R. Knott, "Reimagining Windbreak House," *Michigan Quarterly Review*, 40 (Winter 2001): 74–90;

Leo Marx, *The Machine in the Garden: Technology and the Pastoral Ideal in America* (New York: Oxford University Press, 1964);

John A. Murray, "The Rise of Nature Writing: America's Next Great Genre?" [Nature-Writing Symposium] *Manoa*, 4 (Fall 1992): 73–96;

Diane Dufva Quantic, *The Nature of the Place: A Study of Great Plains Fiction* (Lincoln: University of Nebraska Press, 1995);

Geraldine Sanford, "The Dichotomy Pulse: The Beating Heart of Hasselstrom Country," *South Dakota Review*, 30 (Autumn 1992): 130–155;

Dianne Ganz Scheper, "Our Erotic Center," *Belles Lettres: A Review of Books by Women*, 10 (Spring 1995): 32–34;

Laurel Speer, "Jump into These," *Small Press Review*, 20 (February 1988): 3;

Jed Stavick, "A Vegetarian Critical Response to *Dakota Bones:* Becoming a Wrangler of Moral Dilemmas with Linda Hasselstrom," *South Dakota Review*, 33 (Summer 1995): 120–129;

Kathlene Sutton, "Botany and Beef," *South Dakota Magazine* (November/December 2001): 77–80.

**Papers:**

There are collections of Linda M. Hasselstrom's papers at The American Heritage Center at the University of Wyoming–including correspondence, photographs, and financial records relative to *Sunday Clothes: A Magazine of the Fine Arts* and to Lame Johnny Press; it also houses books published by Lame Johnny Press. Other materials related to Hasselstrom's writing include audiotapes, copies of her publications, and some early drafts. The archives at the I. D. Weeks Library, University of South Dakota, has papers relative to Lame Johnny Press, including publishing files and copies of its book publications.

# Elmer Kelton
*(29 April 1926 – )*

## Mark Busby
*Center for the Study of the Southwest,
Southwest Texas State University, San Marcos*

BOOKS: *Hot Iron* (New York: Ballantine, 1955);

*Buffalo Wagons* (New York: Ballantine, 1956; London: Landsborough, 1960);

*Barbed Wire* (New York: Ballantine, 1957; London: Four Square Books, 1961);

*Shadow of a Star* (New York: Ballantine, 1959; London: Four Square Books, 1961);

*The Texas Rifles* (New York: Ballantine, 1960; London: Four Square Books, 1960);

*Donovan* (New York: Ballantine, 1961; London: New English Library, 1962);

*Bitter Trail* (New York: Ballantine, 1962);

*Horsehead Crossing* (New York: Ballantine, 1963);

*Massacre at Goliad* (New York: Ballantine, 1965; London: New English Library, 1967);

*Llano River* (New York: Ballantine, 1966; London: Panther, 1968);

*After the Bugles* (New York: Ballantine, 1967; Bath, Eng.: Chivers, 1987);

*Captain's Rangers* (New York: Ballantine, 1969; London: Arrow, 1971);

*Hanging Judge* (New York: Ballantine, 1969);

*Shotgun Settlement,* as Alex Hawk (New York: Paperback Library, 1969);

*The Day the Cowboys Quit* (New York: Doubleday, 1971);

*Bowie's Mine* (New York: Ballantine, 1971);

*Wagontongue* (New York: Ballantine, 1972);

*Looking Back West; Selections from the Pioneer News-Observer* (San Angelo, Tex.: Talley Press, 1972);

*The Time it Never Rained* (New York: Doubleday, 1973);

*Manhunters* (New York: Ballantine, 1974);

*Joe Pepper,* as Lee McElroy (New York: Doubleday, 1975);

*Long Way to Texas,* as Lee McElroy (Garden City, N.Y.: Doubleday, 1976);

*The Good Old Boys* (New York: Doubleday, 1978; London: Vintage, 1995);

*The Wolf and the Buffalo* (New York: Doubleday, 1980);

*Eyes of the Hawk,* as Lee McElroy (New York: Doubleday, 1981; Bath, Eng.: Chivers, 1987);

*Elmer Kelton (photograph by Jim Bean Professional Photography; courtesy of the author)*

*The Western and the Literary Ghetto* (Austin: University of Texas, 1983);

*Stand Proud* (New York: Doubleday, 1984; Bath, Eng.: Chivers, 1988);

*Dark Thicket* (New York: Doubleday, 1985);

*The Big Brand* (New York: Bantam, 1986);

*There's Always Another Chance, and Other Stories,* edited by Lawrence Clayton (San Angelo, Tex.: Fort Concho Museum Press, 1986);

*The Man Who Rode Midnight* (New York: Doubleday, 1987);

*Living and Writing in West Texas* (Abilene, Tex.: Hardin-Simmons University Press, 1988);

*Sons of Texas,* 6 volumes, as Tom Early (New York: Berkley, 1989–1990);

*Fiction Writers Are Liars and Thieves* (Denton: University of North Texas Press, 1990);

*Honor at Daybreak: A Novel of One Town's Battle for Justice* (New York: Doubleday, 1991);

*Slaughter* (New York: Doubleday, 1992; Bath, Eng.: Chivers, 1995);

*Elmer Kelton Country: The Short Nonfiction of a Texas Novelist* (Fort Worth: Texas Christian University Press, 1993);

*The Far Canyon* (New York: Doubleday, 1994);

*My Kind of Heroes: Selected Speeches* (Austin, Tex.: State House Press, 1995);

*The Pumpkin Rollers* (New York: Forge, 1996; Thorndike, Me.: Thorndike, 1996);

*Cloudy in the West* (New York: Forge, 1997);

*The Smiling Country* (New York: Forge, 1998);

*The Buckskin Line* (New York: Forge, 1999);

*Badger Boy* (New York: Forge, 2001);

*Way of the Coyote* (New York: Forge, 2001).

**Editions:** *The Time it Never Rained,* Chisholm Trail Series, no. 2, afterword by Tom Pilkington (Fort Worth: Texas Christian University Press, 1984);

*The Good Old Boys,* Texas Tradition Series, no. 1, afterword by Don Graham (Fort Worth: Texas Christian University Press, 1985);

*The Day the Cowboys Quit,* Texas Tradition Series, no. 7, afterword by James W. Lee (Fort Worth: Texas Christian University Press, 1986);

*The Wolf and the Buffalo,* Texas Tradition Series, no. 5, afterword by Lawrence Clayton (Fort Worth: Texas Christian University Press, 1986);

*Stand Proud,* Texas Tradition Series, no. 13, afterword by Terence A. Dalrymple (Fort Worth: Texas Christian University Press, 1990);

*The Man Who Rode Midnight,* Texas Tradition Series, no. 14, afterword by Kenneth W. Davis (Fort Worth: Texas Christian University Press, 1990);

*Manhunters: A Novel,* Texas Tradition Series, no. 22, afterword by Bill Crider (Fort Worth: Texas Christian University Press, 1994);

*Wagontongue: A Novel; With the Short Story, "Man on the Wagontongue,"* Texas Tradition Series, no. 14, afterword by Judy Alter (Fort Worth: Texas Christian University Press, 1996);

*Dark Thicket: A Novel,* Texas Tradition Series, no. 26, afterword by Laurie Champion (Fort Worth: Texas Christian University Press, 1999).

OTHER: Jerry Lackey, *Papa Didn't Spare the Rod,* illustrated by Kelton (San Antonio: Naylor, 1968);

*The Art of Howard Terpning,* text by Kelton (New York: Bantam, 1992);

Frank C. McCarthy, *The Art of Frank McCarthy,* text by Kelton (New York: Morrow, 1992);

*The Art of James Bama,* text by Kelton (Trumbull, Conn.: Greenwich Workshop, 1993);

*The Indian in Frontier News,* edited by Kelton (San Angelo, Tex.: Talley Press, 1993);

*Texas Cattle Barons: Their Families, Land, and Legacy,* text by Kelton, photographs by Kathleen Jo Ryan (Berkeley, Cal.: Ten Speed Press, 1999).

Before Elmer Kelton's *The Good Old Boys* (1978) was made into a television movie for Turner Network Television in 1995 by Tommy Lee Jones, Kelton had a loyal following among Texans and readers of Westerns, but he had not gained wide national recognition. Jones had been intrigued by Kelton's novel, and the famed actor, a San Saba, Texas, native, wrote the screenplay, directed, and starred in the movie, along with Sissy Spacek, Sam Shepard, and Wilford Brimley. Kelton finally came to national attention after a long and productive career. He is now recognized as a writer who has long written what might appear to be "formula Westerns"; but closer analysis reveals that much of Kelton's work demonstrates the human qualities that characterize good literature.

Kelton was born at Horse Camp on 29 April 1926, on the Five Wells Ranch in Andrews County, Texas, and grew up on the McElroy Ranch near Crane. There he learned much about the cattle business, although he realized early that the cowboy life would not be his life. At Crane High School he studied journalism with Paul Patterson, a Texas poet and folklorist. After graduation in 1942, Kelton set out to become a writer.

Kelton's studies at the University of Texas at Austin were interrupted by World War II. While serving in Austria, Kelton met Anna Lipp; they were married on 3 July 1947; the couple eventually had three children: Gary, Stephen, and Kathryn. After the war Kelton returned to the University of Texas, where he finished his bachelor's degree in journalism in 1948. Western novelist J. Frank Dobie had resigned by the time Kelton took advanced courses in English, so Kelton studied with folklorist Mody Boatwright. After graduation, Kelton became an agricultural reporter for the *San Angelo Standard-Times,* and in 1963 he became editor of the *Sheep and Goat Raisers* magazine. In 1968 he joined *The Livestock Weekly* in San Angelo, where he was associate editor until his retirement in 1990.

Traveling the state while writing about the livestock business, Kelton also collected the kernels of stories and eventually became a prolific writer of more

*Kelton and his future wife, Anna Lipp, in Ebensee, Austria, in 1946 (courtesy of the author)*

judged as third Best Western Mini-Series of All Time—*Lonesome Dove* and James A. Michener's *Centennial* (1974) were first- and second-place winners.

Throughout Kelton's long career, he has written several different types of books—formula Westerns, historical novels, and serious novels about the West. Within these categories, Kelton has traditionally written, as Lawrence Clayton observes in his 1986 biography of Kelton, about three general subjects: "early Texas history, lawman-outlaw conflicts, and the range cattle industry." More recently, with *The Pumpkin Rollers* (1996) and *Cloudy in the West* (1997), Kelton has turned to youthful characters in the West for his fiction.

Kelton has also often commented on his own works. In *My Kind of Heroes: Selected Speeches* (1995) Kelton points to one of the continuing elements of his work—the value of writing about history in such a way as to preserve the historical record and to provide fictional insight:

> Some time back, I was talking to a group of students at Angelo State University. One asked me why most of my novels are set in history. The past is gone, she said. History is about dead people. Why should history mean anything to us, living today?

> I told her that our everyday lives are rooted in history. We are all products of what has gone before. We live where we live because of things that have happened in our past and to those who preceded us. The way we live, the things we believe in, are all rooted in the times, the beliefs, the many, many generations before them. History is a part of the present and the future.

Seeking a vision for the future, he also notes how he sees his work as a force for positive change:

> I write Western novels. None of them are going to bring world peace or end old racial hatreds. Most people who read them do so for entertainment, not to be preached to. But I can use these novels to express my own feelings about prejudice and I try to do so without beating the reader over the head with them.

> If even a few readers are encouraged to take a more liberal look at their neighbors, and recognize that they have a worth even if their skin is of a different color and their speech a different pattern, I feel that they have gotten something more than just entertainment.

> For a few people, at least, the world becomes a little better.

These comments emphasize some of Kelton's continuing themes. Judy Alter in her study of Kelton's work, *Elmer Kelton and West Texas: A Literary Relationship*

than forty books. His first published story, "There's Always Another Chance," appeared in *Ranch Romances* in 1948. Since then, he has received the Western Heritage Award from the Cowboy Hall of Fame, the Levi Strauss Golden Saddleman Award from the Western Writers of America for his distinguished body of work, and the Western Literature Association Distinguished Achievement Award. He has also been inducted into the Texas Institute of Letters. He has six times won the Western Writers' Spur Award for the best Western novel of the year: for *Buffalo Wagons* (1956), *The Day the Cowboys Quit* (1971), *The Time It Never Rained* (1973), *Eyes of the Hawk* (1981), *Slaughter* (1992) and *The Far Canyon* (1994). In 1996 the Western Writers of America selected Kelton as the Best Western Writer of All Time. In that survey *The Time It Never Rained* tied with Larry McMurtry's *Lonesome Dove* (1985) for third place in the Best Western Novel of All Time category—A. B. Guthrie's *The Big Sky* (1947) and Jack Schaefer's *Shane* (1949) took the top two spots. *The Good Old Boys* was also

(1989), identifies several recognizable thematic and stylistic qualities:

> . . . there is the elusive subject of voice, an area that in Kelton's narratives is best characterized by a wry humor, characteristic of West Texas and of the author himself; there is the theme of racial concerns . . . ; there is change, a deep knowledge that society and the world around us is constantly changing and that man must ultimately adjust to that change if he is to prevail; there is the land itself, and the life it forces upon men and women . . . there is the problem of women . . . of sex and violence . . . and finally there is characterization.

In an interview with Patrick Bennett for Bennett's book *Talking with Texas Writers* (1980), Kelton identified "change and the resistance to it" as perhaps the major theme of his work; he also said, "Maybe that's the theme of a lot of my stories: that you can't stop change. A new group of people trying to do something different, and the opposition that is natural. It's just a natural basis for fiction."

Many of his early works published by Ballantine Books and the Paperback Library, several under the pseudonyms of Lee McElroy and Alex Hawk, are admittedly formulaic, written for popular consumption. But Kelton also wrote a series of novels based on Texas history; in fact, his work throughout his career is marked by his careful use of historical material as a backdrop for his fiction. *The Texas Rifles* (1960), *Bitter Trail* (1962), *After the Bugles* (1967), *Captain's Rangers* (1969), *Bowie's Mine* (1971), *Long Way to Texas* (1976), *Eyes of the Hawk* (1981), and *Dark Thicket* (1985) all deal with early Texas history. Several of these novels follow the lives of a fictional Texas family, the Buckalews, through various events in Texas history, from the Alamo, Goliad, and Indian depredations, to the Battle of Glorieta Pass, the Civil War, and the coming of the railroad.

With *The Buckskin Line* in 1999 Kelton returned to fiction based on Texas history with a series of novels about a young red-haired Texan named Rusty Shannon, who is kidnapped by the Comanche after they kill his family, and who then joins the Texas Rangers and finds himself on the trail of the Comanche. In *Badger Boy* (2001), as the Civil War ends, an older Rusty Shannon returns to his farm on the Colorado River to try to find his lost love and again finds himself engaged with the Comanche, who have kidnapped a white boy they call Badger Boy. In *Way of the Coyote* (2001), Kelton's thirty-seventh novel, Shannon and Andy Pickard, the Badger Boy, find themselves in conflict with former Confederates in post–Civil War Texas and become involved in another kidnapping, this time the son of Rusty's old love, Geneva Monahan.

*Kelton as a livestock journalist in the early 1950s*
*(courtesy of the author)*

Among the historical novels, besides this recent series, two of the more interesting are *Wagontongue* (1972) and *Manhunters* (1974), both of which deal with racial issues. *Wagontongue* concerns the Jim Crow practice on ranches in the nineteenth century that required black cowboys to sit on the tongue of the chuck wagon to take their meals in a kind of back-of-the-bus segregation. *Manhunters* is based on the story of Gregorio Cortez, a young Texas Mexican who killed a South Texas sheriff after a misunderstanding and whose heroic escape became the subject of legend and folklore as well as the subject of Americo Paredes's now-classic study *With His Pistol in His Hand* (1958). With his usual balance, Kelton presents the circumstances of the misunderstanding of cultures with grace and the recognition that misunderstanding knows no cultural bounds.

Kelton honed his craft in these novels, but he also felt that he could write serious novels. Indeed, his reputation now rests more on a series of novels that broke free from the limitations of formulaic writing. Asked once about the difference between his novels and Louis L'Amour's, Kelton replied that L'Amour's heroes are seven feet tall and invincible, while his are five feet eight inches tall and nervous. This presentation of recognizable men and women in understandable human situations is what lifts Kelton's work above the ordinary. Among these significant works are *The Day the Cowboys Quit, The Time It Never Rained, The Good Old Boys* and its sequel *The Smiling Country* (1998), *The Wolf and the Buffalo* (1980), *Stand Proud* (1984), and *The Man Who Rode Midnight* (1987). These important works fall into three major types: nineteenth-century works that reflect important frontier themes about the clash between civilization and wilderness, late nineteenth- and early-twentieth-century stories examining the end of the frontier, and twentieth- and twenty-first-century novels that focus on the ways frontier legacies have continued.

Frontier mythology refers to a cluster of images, values, and archetypes that grew out of the confrontation between the uncivilized and the civilized worlds, what Frederick Jackson Turner called the "meeting point between savagery and civilization." Texas mythology draws from frontier mythology, particularly the emphasis on Texas as a land of freedom and opportunity, where individuals can demonstrate those values that the Texas-Anglo myth reveres, such as courage, determination, ingenuity, and loyalty. But as Kelton and other Texans know, the frontier history and geography of Texas produce deep feelings of ambivalence. On the one hand, the vastness of its area seems to negate borders; on the other hand, the location of Texas on the edge of Southern and Western cultures and along the long Rio Grande border with Mexico reinforces an awareness of borders. As William T. Pilkington points out in *My Blood's Country: Studies in Southwestern Literature* (1973), Texas is a land of borders: "Men have always been fascinated by rims and borders, ends and beginnings, areas of transition where the known and the unknown merge. In the Southwest one feels something of this fascination, because one of the central, never-changing facts about the region, I believe, is that it is a borderland." Both borders and the frontier suggest a line where differing cultures, attitudes, and factions meet. In fact, one of the major features of Texas fiction is ambivalence–the act of being torn in several directions at once. Early settlers who both conquered nature and felt simultaneously at one with it began the feelings of ambivalence that Larry McMurtry admitted in his essay "Take My Saddle From the Wall: A Valediction," published in *In a Narrow Grave: Essays on Texas* (1968), and still cut him "as deep as the bone." The ambivalence of being drawn at the same time toward such opposing forces as civilization/wilderness, rural/urban, individual/community,

past/present, aggression/passivity, and many others is central to the Southwestern legend.

Three other important elements of the Southwestern frontier myth were identified by Larry Goodwyn in a 1971 essay titled "The Frontier Myth and Southwestern Literature." Goodwyn concludes that the "frontier legend is pastoral," with a strong emphasis on a primitivistic belief in the inherent power of living close to the land. Furthermore, he writes, "the legend is inherently masculine: women are not so much without 'courage' as missing altogether; cowgirls did not ride up the Chisholm Trail." Finally, Goodwyn finds that the frontier myth "is primitively racialist: it provided no mystique of triumph for Mexicans, Negroes, or Indians." Kelton's best novels reflect these important elements, tracing them from the days of the frontier to the present.

*The Day the Cowboys Quit* dramatizes the changing face of the open range in the nineteenth century, much as does Dobie's *A Vaquero of the Brush Country* (1929). Similarly, the open range is limited not so much by civilization or the capitalism of corporate ranching as by human greed. The novel turns on the conflict between large and small ranchers, with the major sympathy on the side of the small rancher. But again Kelton presents a balanced, not a one-sided, picture of the history of the West, for Hugh Hitchcock is genuinely torn between the arguments on both sides, especially by the admirable life that Charley Waide leads as a large rancher and by the outlaw life of Law McGinty. Similarly, the picture Kelton paints of the cold killer Lafey Dodge is balanced, especially in the episode during which Dodge catches Hitchcock defenseless while he tries to erect a fence around the grave of McGinty. Working against type, Kelton does not have Dodge kill the unarmed Hitchcock but instead has him get down and help Hitchcock complete the fence around the grave of the man Dodge had killed.

*The Wolf and the Buffalo* treats both black and Indian peoples sympathetically, and again uses Texas history for the backdrop. In this case Kelton deals with the assignment of black soldiers to Fort Concho and San Angelo after the Civil War. The central character, Gideon Ledbetter, and his friend Jimbo leave slave quarters and head west, where they eventually confront Gray Horse, Gideon's Comanche counterpart. This novel is another one about the end of the West, and Kelton demonstrates the irony of the black soldiers' fighting to diminish their counterparts. Toward the end of the novel, Gideon realizes the similarity between the positions of the blacks and the Indians when he tells Captain Hollander: "'When it's all over the Indian'll still be red, and I'll still be black–but the land'll be white.'"

The real history of the ninth and tenth cavalry regiments of buffalo soldiers lies behind the novel, as does the story of Mackenzie's slaughter of more than one thousand Indian horses in Palo Duro Canyon, the signal of the end of Indian power on the Texas plains. Treatment of horses becomes a powerful symbol of sympathetic connection with the natural world and one suggestion of the theme of primitivism. But this novel does not romanticize the Texas landscape. One of the most powerful scenes concerns the outfit's survival without water for eighty-six hours in a hot West Texas summer, an experience that takes the life of Sergeant Esau Nettles, whose strength of character inspires Gideon.

*Stand Proud* examines the power of primitivism and provides a broad look at the end of the open range through the eyes of the main character, Frank Claymore, who, like Charlie Flagg in *The Time It Never Rained* (1973), is an individualist. The novel uses flashbacks stemming from the aging Claymore's trial for the death of his former friend, George Valentine, and surveys the end of the open range; the growth of settlements in West Texas; Indian warfare and the connection between Claymore and his friend Red Shield; and such traditional frontier elements as buffalo hunters, gamblers, outlaws, and rangers.

The main theme of the novel is ambivalence about the end of the open range. Claymore continues to stand proud in his memory of carving out settlement from the wilderness, and he recalls the pastoral beauty of the land:

Frank . . . studied his long valley. He saw it in memory as he had seen it the first day . . . vast, beautiful, its thick grass winter cured, grazed by buffalo, so many that he would never have believed they could be annihilated in a few brief years. To the north he saw cattle now where the buffalo had been. . . . They were fewer than the buffalo had been, but they kept the grass grazed short. In places the ground had turned chronically bare. Wind whipped away the loose soil, leaving scars that stirred his conscience each time he looked upon them. To the south lay the farms that crept steadily in his direction. . . . This was a defacement, in his sight, an invasion by unworthy men who thoughtlessly fenced and plowed and plundered, who did not realize the enormity of what they had done because they did not share his memory of the valley.

But his pride in that accomplishment is lessened by his refusal to acknowledge that he is responsible for creating the world that now diminishes him.

In *Stand Proud* Kelton uses the position of women in the West as an important subtheme. Claymore loses his childhood sweetheart, Rachal, when Valentine tells her that Claymore has been impressed into the Rang-

*Dust jacket for Kelton's 1971 novel about the conflict between large and small ranchers*

ers, leaving her to have his child out of wedlock. She marries Valentine instead, and Claymore settles for Letty Zachary, one of Kelton's powerful Western women. Shortly after she sees Claymore, Letty swears he will one day be her husband, and after her father dies, she uses her business sense to force Claymore to marry her:

"Let's see . . . you now own a quarter of the ranch, and Homer owns a quarter. Marry me and you would own three quarters. Don't marry me and you own none."

He pushed angrily to his feet. "That's blackmail."

"It's business." She smiled, but the smile had a sharp edge. "Each of us wants something. All each of us has to do is agree to an honest trade."

Claymore marries her under duress, still longing for his first love, Rachal, and lamenting his lost son, Billy, who grows up as a Valentine and a bitter killer.

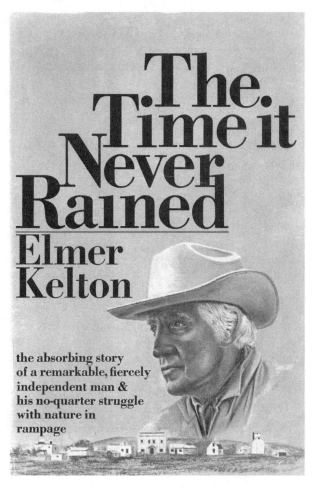

*Dust jacket for Kelton's 1973 novel, set in West Texas during the seven-year drought of the 1950s*

Eventually, Claymore realizes that his dream of Rachal has been false and his treatment of Letty insensitive. At the end of the novel, he tries to make amends, telling Letty he is sorry for the lost years. She forgives him, and they move into the future as a stronger family.

*The Good Old Boys* (1978) focuses upon the powerful schism between the older agrarian world of cowboys and the rapidly approaching industrialism of the twentieth century. The title could easily have been "The Good Old Cowboys," for it focuses upon the aging of perennial innocents, as change made the cowboy archaic. Hewey Calloway and Snort Yarnell are symbolic of the footloose cowboy, following the freedom of the frontier and eschewing the civilizing influence that women have traditionally represented in the Western.

The novel turns upon a series of oppositions symbolized in different ways—freedom/restriction, home/not home, drifter/settler, pastoralism/industrialism, and wilderness/civilization. The women, especially Walter Calloway's wife, Eve, and the schoolteacher, Spring

Renfro, represent the demands of home, civilization, family, and being settled. The pastoral/industrial opposition is represented most directly in the contrast between Hewey's two nephews—Tommy, the inheritor of cowboy skills and likes, and Cotton, who will enter the new industrial century with a fascination for machines.

While the indictment of the evils of capitalism is achieved in the novel through Fat Gervin, especially in the broad humor of the scene in which Hewey leads a dog to urinate on Fat's leg, ultimately the novel reveals ambivalence about the split between family and freedom. Accepting responsibility is a settling force, and Hewey demonstrates not only that he can rise to the occasion when he needs to but also that his attraction to the settled life represented by Spring Renfro is genuine. He is ultimately torn between his desire to live the free life of the good old cowboy and the sweet seduction of family life. At the end, he rides off into the sunrise: "The sun broke over the prairie in a sudden red blaze. The family all pulled together, arms around each other, Spring standing to one side, still alone. They watched as Hewey seemed to ride into the fire, sitting straight-shouldered and proud on Biscuit's back. And finally he was gone, melted into the relentless glow of a new day." What the good old boy will become if he continues the fiddle-footed life is symbolized by Boy Rasmussen, who has become so disconnected and homeless that he wanders the country until he dies alone—symbolically, by a fence. The novel suggests that if Hewey is ever to settle down, it will be with Spring Renfro, whose name suggests a new life, for she too recognizes the ambivalence that Hewey feels, knowing as she does, the powerful pull of the open life.

Kelton's themes are some of the powerful themes of Western movies, from *Stagecoach* (1939) to *Shane* (1953) to *The Misfits* (1961), to *Lonely are the Brave* (1962), and to *Ride the High Country* (1962). Most Westerns are laden with the *ubi sunt* (Where are they now?) theme, all dripping with nostalgia for a lost way of life. But Kelton dispels thematic sentimentality by making this novel comic, from the broad humor of a dog scene to the largely comical way of looking at life through Hewey's eyes. In 1997 Kelton completed *The Smiling Country,* a sequel to *The Good Old Boys.*

What will happen next is actually explored in *The Smiling Country* (1998), a sequel to *The Good Old Boys.* The sequel is set in 1910, four years after the earlier novel. Hewey Callaway is still a fiddle-footed cowboy, trying to avoid responsibility and stave off aging. But the world is changing, as more automobiles, trucks, telephones, and fences intrude upon his world. His youthful nephew, Tommy, son of his brother Walter and his wife, Eve, runs away from home to find his favorite uncle working first on the J Bar and then on the Circle W ranch near Alpine, the smiling country of the title.

Fat Gervin, the mean-spirited banker from before, is back as well, and up to some of his old tricks. He sells Hewey's boss, Morgan Jenkins, some rangy horses and one outlaw stud that throws and injures Hewey badly. Aging cowboys are a sorry sight, Hewey decides, when he has to return to Upton City to accept the help of friends and ponder the changes in his world.

There he finds that Spring Renfro, the schoolteacher who let him ride off into the sunrise at the end of the earlier novel rather than try to tie him down, is still there, but she has a new suitor. These then are the elements that Kelton weaves together into this novel, which, like his previous ones, dramatizes the reality rather than the myth of cowboy lfie. At one point, Hewey considers shooting the outlaw horse but then recalls that he

> had not fired his pistol in a long time. The barrel might be rusted enough to blow up in his hand. He was not even sure he had any cartridges in his war bag. He felt about guns much the same way he felt about posthold diggers, they were simply a working tool that he took no pleasure in.

Working hard from sunup to sundown with unpredictable animals—a life one cowboy described as a long period of boredom punctuated by moments of sheer terror—is the cowboy life in Kelton's world.

Kelton has often said that of all his books *The Time It Never Rained* was his favorite, because "it was the most personal one I've ever done." *The Time It Never Rained* is set during the calamitous seven-year drought of the 1950s, which was especially devastating to West Texas, where rainfall was usually scarce. The main character, Charlie Flagg, owns a medium-sized ranch near Rio Seco, south of San Angelo. Charlie tries every possible method to survive but gets deeper in debt. He sells his cattle and buys mohair goats, all the while refusing to accept any form of government assistance. Like many other Texas figures, he maintains his love of the land: "It was a comforting sight, this country. It was an ageless land where the past was still a living thing and old voices still whispered, where the freshness of the pioneer time had not yet all faded, where a few old dreams were not yet dark with tarnish." Charlie continues and endures because "he felt a deep and binding obligation to the land itself. It mattered little who held the title; the land was a sacred thing."

The most ambivalent scene in the book is the final one, in which a drought-breaking downpour soaks Charlie and his vulnerable, newly shorn goats. Although this rain brings an end to the seven-year-drought, it also brings death to the goats—Charlie's last hope to stave off his creditors this season.

Charlie is one of the most memorable, fully rendered characters in recent Texan and American fiction. As Pilkington notes,

> Charlie . . . embodies what we believe were the best qualities of the legendary Texas rancher: strength of will, independence, self-sufficiency. His primary commitment is to the land, harsh and unyielding as it is. His sense of right does not waver. He opposes equally . . . bureaucratic regulation and the evil of untrammeled power that too often crushes the powerless. Part of the appeal of Charlie is that he is an anachronism, one of the last survivors of a dying breed. He springs from an older, better time.

Like other West Texans, Charlie believes in frontier self-reliance. He believes that a "man had to make his try, and when that didn't work he had to try something else. Try and keep trying. Endure, and try again."

Another of the significant themes in the novel concerns the racial chasm separating the Texas-Anglo and the Mexican. Flagg is sometimes surprised to find that even he is not immune to myths. When Anita Flores, the daughter of Charlie's ranch foreman, is almost raped by Danny Ortiz, Charlie vows retribution. Anita's father persuades Charlie not to go to the sheriff because "he will say she is just a Mexican girl out with a Mexican boy, and that's the way it is with Mexicans." When Anita's father asks, "But what if she was some other girl, some Spanish girl you don't know? What would you think?" Charlie suddenly understands that he, too, is guilty of racial narrow-mindedness. Although Kelton portrays Charlie Flagg as sympathetic, he also notes,

> Charlie never tried to analyze or rationalize his feelings toward Mexican people; he would never have thought of apologizing to anyone for them. He did not dislike Mexicans; on the contrary he liked most of the ones he personally knew and respected them. Yet he tended to distrust the strangers among them. It was an inherited attitude going back through generations of forbears whose names he did not even know. It was deeply grounded in history, in wars won and lost, in the Texas Revolution and the bitter decades of border strife that followed, when each side feared and hated the other with equal blindness and ferocity.

42

Alpine, Texas

May 21 1910

Dear Walter & Eve

I take pencil in hand to tell you I have not seen Tommy.
I have just come into a little extra mony and am sendin it
to you to put against your dett on the farm, like I have
done before. Dont worry, I dont need it.  If Tommy shows
up I will let you no.

                    Yours very truly.

                    Hewey Calloway

P. S. If you see Miss Spring Renfro

He could not think how to end the last sentence and tried to
erase it, but it would not all come off the paper.  He addressed
an envelope to Walter and Eve Calloway, Upton City, Texas, and
tucked the letter into it with fifty dollars in paper money.
Licking the envelope and sealing it, he handed it to the
bald-headed bartender along with a quarter.  "I don't have a
penny stamp, but I'd be obliged if you'd put one on this and see
that it gets to the postoffice.  Keep the change."

    "You're a generous man, Hewey Calloway.  It'll be the
starvin' of you someday.  You ready for another drink?"

    "Ready and rarin'."

    He had had several already, but not enough to make him
overlook the risk of falling over the edge, splurging the wages
Old Man Jenkins had paid him and the bet he had won from Snort,
He was sending most of it to Walter and Eve.

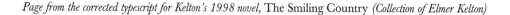

*Page from the corrected typescript for Kelton's 1998 novel,* The Smiling Country *(Collection of Elmer Kelton)*

Though Charlie is aware of his "inherited attitude," he is also slowly becoming aware of a new, changing set of beliefs. This change is apparent through the story of Manuel Flores and Kathy Mauldin, whose growing attraction troubles Charlie. Manuel hopes to become a veterinarian, not a manual laborer. Ultimately, Flagg comes to accept the changes, but he pointedly recalls a friend for whom "the old principles that he anchored to, they've come a-loose; nobody's payin' attention to them anymore. He's an old gray headed man livin' in a young man's world, and all his benchmarks are gone."

*The Time It Never Rained* is arguably Kelton's best novel and one of the major achievements of contemporary Texas writing. And, as Pilkington notes, "much of the book's power derives from Kelton's sympathetic understanding and portrayal of Charlie Flagg's intense feelings for his plot of West Texas earth."

*The Man Who Rode Midnight* (1987), set in the 1980s, is, as Kelton observes in his introduction to the Texas Christian University reprint, a natural "follow up" to *The Time It Never Rained,* primarily because it, too, focuses on the economic and human changes that the altered face of ranching took after the middle of the twentieth century. Farming and ranching changed radically as the twentieth century wore on, not only as the result of drought but primarily because of economic and technological changes. The title character is seventy-eight-year-old Wes Hendrix, who at some time in the past rode the legendary bucking bronc Midnight. In the 1980s that feat is just another detail from a murky past that grows less important with each ranch sold and each ranching son and daughter leaving to find life in the city.

In fact, Wes's son, Truman, has long since moved to the city and begun plans to build a recreational lake and develop the old family property, recalling Larry McMurtry's *Horseman, Pass By* (1961) and Preston Jones's *The Oldest Living Graduate* (1974). But Kelton demonstrates that elements of the old world continue to resonate in a contemporary world, particularly in the relationship between Wes and his grandson Jim Ed ("Tater"). Jim Ed sheds many of his city ways as he grows to understand the value of hard work and good fellowship that he finds in the rural world of Big River. The bond between Jim Ed and his grandfather is sealed through their building a fence together, but just as they complete it a passing airplane overhead frightens Ol' Snort, a whitetail buck Wes has long admired. After Snort breaks his legs trying to leap the barbed wire fence, Wes, in a scene reminiscent of Homer Bannon's killing of his longhorns in *Horseman, Pass By,* puts Snort out of his misery and acknowledges that he had been trying to keep the old wildness inside his fence.

Six-time winner of the Spur Award

ELMER KELTON

"One of the best of a new breed of Western writers who have driven the genre into new territory." —*The New York Times*

BADGER BOY

*Dust jacket for Kelton's 2001 novel about a Texas ranger who returns a white youth to the Comanche family who raised him*

Through working with his grandfather and his growing relationship with Glory B., daughter and granddaughter of Wes's neighbors, Jim Ed becomes more attuned to the rural life. But he also brings to bear his college study of accounting on the ranching business.

Kelton's primitivistic focus on the value of open landscape appears in his emphasis on the value of the area called Liveoak Camp and in his attack on the negative results of the oil industry on the countryside. Glory B. says that she carries an image of it in her head and draws "comfort" from it when she needs it. Later the place becomes the redemptive device to lift Wes after he has lost his own farm to his grasping, materialistic son. And the Liveoak Camp holds promise for the future, as it will become Jim Ed's and Glory B.'s in their seemingly inevitable union. As Glory B. comments, "Times change. People come and people go, but those old hills stay the same. However mixed up or troubled I may get, I can look at them and recover my perspective. They're timeless."

The reverential treatment of Liveoak Camp is countered when he visits it late in the novel by the description of the damage the oil industry has wreaked on Wes's hometown, only to find "abandoned oilwell locations . . . like scars on the grassland, their pads sterile of vegetation because of the deep caliche and the oil spillage. Concrete foundations stood like tombstones to mark the death of dreams. Rusted pipe and twisted piles of heavy cable lay scattered like the relics of a lost war." Kelton is aware that change is inevitable, but he opts for evolutionary change that adapts the values of the old to the circumstances of the new without jettisoning all of the old simply because it is old.

The changing face of the frontier Southwest is indeed a primary theme of Kelton's work, as it is with many of the writers with whom he has been compared, such as Larry McMurtry and Benjamin Capps. Kelton's strengths lie in his vivid characterization arising from his long experience in West Texas, in growing up there and working among the men and women who toiled on the farms and ranches there over his forty-year career as a full-time livestock journalist. Elmer Kelton's life and works reflect a remarkable combination of hard work, endurance, and attention to detail, which combine to make him one of the important writers of the U.S. West and Southwest.

**Interview:**

Patrick Bennett, *Talking with Texas Writers* (College Station: Texas A & M University Press, 1980).

**References:**

Judy Alter, *Elmer Kelton and West Texas: A Literary Relationship* (Denton: University of North Texas Press, 1989);

Lawrence Clayton, *Elmer Kelton* (Boise, Idaho: Boise State University Press, 1986);

Clayton, "Epic Qualities in Kelton's *The Wolf and the Buffalo,*" *Re: Artes Liberales,* 8, no. 2 (1981): 5–13;

Clayton, "Kelton's Charlie Flagg as Modern Western Hero," *Re: Artes Liberales,* 14, no. 1 (1987): 13–20;

Kenneth Davis, "Elmer Kelton," *Updating the Literary West* (Fort Worth: Texas Christian University Press, 1997): 580–584;

Anne Dingus, "The Good Old Boy," *Texas Monthly* (23 December 1995): 80+;

Fred Erisman, "Elmer Kelton's 'Other' West," *Western American Literature,* 28 (Winter 1994): 291–299;

Dorys C. Grover, "Bowie's Mine: Legend into Fiction," *Re: Artes Liberales,* 7, no. 2 (Spring 1981): 9–17.

**Papers:**

Most of Elmer Kelton's papers are in the Southwest Collection at Texas Tech University, Lubbock.

# Herbert Krause

*(25 May 1905 – 22 September 1976)*

Arthur R. Huseboe
*Augustana College*

BOOKS: *Wind Without Rain* (Indianapolis: Bobbs-Merrill, 1939; London, 1939);
*Neighbor Boy* (Iowa City, Iowa: Midland House, 1939);
*The Thresher* (Indianapolis: Bobbs-Merrill, 1946);
*The Oxcart Trail* (Indianapolis: Bobbs-Merrill, 1954);
*Poems and Essays of Herbert Krause,* edited by Arthur R. Huseboe (Sioux Falls, S.Dak.: Center for Western Studies, 1990).

PLAY PRODUCTIONS: *Bondsmen to the Hills,* Cape Girardeau, Mo., Midwestern Folk Drama Tournament, 4 April 1936;
*Crazy Horse: A Drama of the Plains Indians and the Black Hills,* Sioux Falls, S.Dak., Center for Western Studies, 20 June 1994.

PRODUCED SCRIPT: *The Big Four,* television, 8 September 1960.

OTHER: "Horning in the Fall," in *Eve's Stepchildren,* edited by Lealon N. Jones (Caldwell, Idaho: Caxton, 1942), pp. 150–161;
"The Oak Tree," *Prairie Prose,* 1 (Winter 1943): 3–7;
"Herbert Krause," in *Minnesota Writers: A Collection of Autobiographical Stories by Minnesota Prose Writers,* edited by Carmen Nelson Richards (Minneapolis: T. S. Denison, 1961), pp. 19–27;
*Fiction 151–1: Short Stories,* edited with an afterword by Krause (Manila, Phillipines: MDB Publishing, 1968);
"The McCown's Longspur," in *Life Histories of North American Cardinals, Grosbeaks, Buntings, Towhees, Finches, Sparrows, and Allies: Order Passeriformes, Family Fringillidae,* edited by Arthur Cleveland Bent (Washington, D.C.: Smithsonian, 1968), pp. 1564–1597;
*Prelude to Glory: A Newspaper Accounting of Custer's 1874 Expedition,* edited by Krause and Gary D. Olson (Sioux Falls, S.Dak.: Brevet, 1974).

*Herbert Krause*

SELECTED PERIODICAL PUBLICATIONS–UNCOLLECTED: "Clear Light of Children's Joys Shines on in Memory," *Chicago Sun Book Week,* 2 December 1945, p. 57;
"Nesting of a Pair of Canada Warblers," *Living Bird,* 4 (1965): 5–11.

Herbert Krause made his most important contributions in his three novels about the American West and in his founding of a center for the study of the northern plains. In his first novel, *Wind Without Rain* (1939), he sets out in rich detail the cost in human suffering of the settling of one part of the frontier, the hill country of western Minnesota, where an intractable soil and a rigid religion can crush or warp the spirits of the sensitive—as happens with the central character of the novel, Franz Vildvogel. Recounting a young man's painful upbringing in a hostile environment, Krause's second novel, *The Thresher* (1946), is set in that highly significant era of transition in the economic and social history of American agriculture when farmers, accustomed to labor-intensive, horse-powered equipment, began changing to high-speed, steam- and gasoline-powered machinery. The third of Krause's novels, *The Oxcart Trail* (1954), is less successful in its plot and character development. The historical novel takes place in frontier Saint Paul, Minnesota, and on the trail north to the Red River, through the battleground of the Dakota Sioux and the Chippewa Indians. Despite its flaws, *The Oxcart Trail* sold well in a time of poor sales for fiction, and many reviewers and readers admired its meticulous re-creation of a particular place and time in American history. James Gray, in his review of the book for *The New York Herald Tribune* (4 April 1954), believed that Krause had created a "new design" for historical novels, in which the characters' behavior dramatizes certain details of history. After the publication of his third novel, Krause completed no more fiction. As a professor of English at Augustana College in Sioux Falls, South Dakota, he devoted himself increasingly to the study of ornithology and environmental concerns and in 1970 founded the Center for Western Studies to facilitate research and writing about the history and cultures of the northern plains. In a talk to South Dakota English teachers in 1955, Krause shared a belief that pervades both his early and late works: that writing history and literature of significance can take place only

> when after scrutiny and study we try to understand all aspects of our region, not as something apart from or separate from America but as an integral part of it; not as an area famous for its quaintness or its landscape or its provincialism but as part of the cultural pattern of America—a part of the whole fabric.

Herbert Arthur Krause was born on 25 May 1905 in Friberg Township, Otter Tail County, Minnesota, in the heart of the wooded rolling hills that he later called Pockerbrush. Both his parents, Arthur Adolph and Bertha Peters Krause, hailed from the neighboring township of Elizabeth. Arthur and Bertha were the children of German immigrants who had come earlier to western Minnesota and had started small farms there, and both were members of the Immanuel Lutheran

Church congregation in rural Friberg. The eldest of six children—four boys and two girls—born to the couple, Krause was the first to leave home for an education.

Krause was a precocious child, fascinated at a young age by the sounds and rhymes of words, as he recalled later; as a five-year-old boy he tried to find the words to describe a snowstorm in which the sun shone through the falling snow. By the age of ten he was writing in notebooks, a practice he continued in a dilatory fashion all of his life. Krause read enthusiastically as a child, although the gray, one-room schoolhouse—in District 115—that he attended for eight years had but one bookshelf, about four feet long, with books that he read repeatedly. At the age of twelve he determined to write a book—"Probably," he told Ethel Reid Winser in 1939, "because I had been reading Carpenter's *Geographical Readers* and *Robinson Crusoe* and was fascinated by the way words made pictures. But I'd also read *Snowbound*—and couldn't get over the music of the rhyme." He received little encouragement at home to fulfill his ambition to become a writer or a teacher, although his own teachers and his pastor recognized the youth's potential and emboldened him to continue his education. Many years later, in January 1933, the Reverend William D. Kanning, who had been Krause's pastor at Immanuel, wrote to remind the young man of that ambition: "In a few months, God willing, you will have realized your hope which ten years ago you indeed had, but hardly dared to utter to anyone except me. I sincerely hope that you will be fortunate enough to land a teaching position and I know you will be successful."

In 1921 Krause graduated from his school in District 115. Five years passed before he enrolled in school again, during which time he labored on the family farm and in his father's blacksmith shop. In 1925 he found his first opportunity to earn money toward his education when the Otter Tail Power Company began to construct a dam nearby. Working as the driver of a pair of horses and as a scraper, he earned $6.50 a day, enough to resume his education in the fall of 1926 as a boarding student at Park Region Lutheran Academy and College in Fergus Falls, Minnesota. The death of his father in the spring of 1927, however, threw Krause into a dilemma that recurred for much of his life: ahead of him lay a succession of opportunities for an education that would enable him to teach—ultimately—at the college level, but as the eldest son in the family he also felt an obligation to provide for its livelihood. For Krause to excel in both these roles—as a student and as his family's breadwinner—was not possible, and so he wrote in his diary on 15 March 1928:

My desire, my paramount dream, burns within me like a white-hot fire, searing me, burning my brain, threatening to consume my heart, to incinerate my whole being.

And what can I do? What, oh, what? Nothing. I can only try to wrest from a cold and heartless universe a semblance of things to be, of dreams come true.

At Park Region, an institution operated by the Norwegian Lutheran Synod, Krause studied hard, trying his hand at verse—which included a bitter poem about a boy in rebellion against his father—and writing essays and reviews for the school paper. Despite the encouraging environment at the academy, Krause decided in the summer of 1929 to take his pastor's advice and enter one of the Lutheran Church–Missouri Synod colleges in order to prepare either for a teaching career in a parochial school or for a career in the ministry. Scholarship help from both District 115 and the synod made Krause's decision possible, since his family was still in serious financial straits. Yet, his decision brought about failure: at Concordia Teachers College in River Forest, Illinois, Krause was hazed mercilessly, and upon transferring to the Concordia Theological Seminary in Springfield, Illinois, he discovered that his German and Latin were inadequate for the rigors of the preseminary program. The ill treatment he had undergone from "his Germans" at the college and his poor preparation for the seminary left Krause embittered and affected him permanently. Years later, when he moved to Sioux Falls, South Dakota, to join the faculty of Augustana College—also founded by Norwegian Lutherans—Krause still considered himself to be a Missouri Synod Lutheran but only "nominally," as he wrote on his faculty data sheet.

Krause returned to Park Region, eager to continue his efforts to write and to be published, and by the end of his sophomore year he began to see results: a poem appeared in *The Lutheran Herald* and another in *Parchment,* a literary journal at the University of Kansas. In the summer of 1931 he completed a set of six poems—all of which appeared in his master's thesis four years later at the University of Iowa.

In 1931 Krause entered another Norwegian Lutheran institution, St. Olaf College in Northfield, Minnesota. The college attracted him in part because the novelist O. E. Rölvaag was on its faculty. Yet, while Krause was never able to study under Rölvaag, and indeed, likely did not meet the eminent author because he died in the fall of Krause's first year at St. Olaf, Krause *did* meet the chairman of the English department, Professor George Weida Spohn, who—like Krause—was a poet of German extraction. Mentored by Spohn over the next months and years, Krause soon considered Spohn and his wife, "Mud-

die," a second family. "You are my god-father, Pop," Krause wrote to Spohn from Iowa in July 1936. "I wouldn't be the same if I lost you, any more than I remained unchanged after my father went away." With Spohn's encouragement, Krause began to write the story that became his first novel, *Wind Without Rain,* and completed a powerful one-act play, *Bondsmen to the Hills* (1934), which Rölvaag's daughter, Ella Valborg, directed at St. Olaf. Telling the tragic story of a promising young boy, *Bondsmen to the Hills* won first prize in performance and second prize in playwriting at the Midwest Folk Drama Tournament in Cape Girardeau, Missouri, on 4 April 1936.

Following his graduation, magna cum laude in English, from St. Olaf College in 1933, Krause sought—unsuccessfully—a position as a teacher in high school. Such jobs were scarce, and, as Krause learned, one of his teachers at St. Olaf, Professor Engebret Tufte, had given him an unfavorable recommendation; these two factors caused Krause to be rejected by all the high schools at which he had applied for positions. Reviewing his options that summer, he wrote to his mother in Friberg, "Oh, no, I haven't forgotten Pockerbrush or the fact that I want to put it 'on the map.'" Throughout the school year, from 1933 to 1934, he worked as both a janitor and an assistant librarian at St. Olaf and found the time to write poetry, drama, and—in outline form—the first sixty-nine pages of *Wind Without Rain,* which Krause had begun as an undergraduate. He also applied successfully to the University of Iowa for admission to its graduate program, where it was possible to substitute a novel, play, or body of poetry for a thesis or dissertation in partial fulfillment of a degree.

At the University of Iowa, Krause's star continued its ascent. Excelling in his course work, he was befriended by faculty members, such as Norman Foerster, Wilbur Schramm, and Paul Engle, and other students such as Wallace Stegner and Charles Foster—all of whom contributed to his growth as a novelist in later years. In June 1935 Krause completed his M.A. degree with a collection of verse called "Pockerbrush," about "a country of tangled underbrush in a region of western Minnesota." Awarded a scholarship to attend the Bread Loaf School of English in Middlebury, Vermont, he spent six weeks that summer studying and writing intensively—an experience that affected his career profoundly. Not only did he become acquainted that summer with the poet Robert Frost, who inspired the young writer for years afterward, but Krause's work also began to receive notice because of his attendance in the famed writing program.

Krause's participation in the Bread Loaf School confirmed that his writing had merit. He was motivated to continue his studies at Iowa and to work more on his

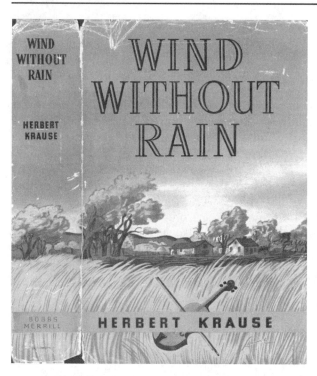

*Dust jacket for Krause's first novel, published in 1939,
about the hardships endured by settlers in the
western Minnesota hill country*

novel, which he planned to submit as his dissertation now that he was engaged in doctoral studies. The strongest encouragement yet came in the fall of 1935 when one of Krause's poems, published in the periodical *American Prefaces* by his teacher Schramm, drew the attention of Maria Leiper, an associate editor at Simon and Schuster. "'Hillside Burial' sticks in my mind," she wrote on 30 December 1935. "Is there any chance that you're at work on a novel? If so, and your commitments permit, we'd like very much to hear from you." This inquiry led Krause to explore other options for publication, and as the novel grew over the next two years, he had reason to hope that what had begun as a dissertation would be accepted by a major publisher.

Krause and Frost also kept in touch beyond that summer at Bread Loaf. Krause promptly became an admirer of the older poet's work, and Frost in turn took a special interest in the young "Pockerbrusher." In February 1937, eighteen months after his first acquaintance with Frost, Krause was pleased to learn from H. G. Owen, dean of the School of English at Bread Loaf, that the poet had inquired after him there. Still deeply engaged in his doctoral studies at the University of Iowa and often troubled by doubts about his future, Krause promptly wrote to Frost that he was "hacking away at the academic underbrush," and that he was not satisfied with the verses that had composed his master's thesis. Yet, he added in the letter that one of his plays

had just won a prize and reported optimistically, "Just now I'm swinging at a novel which Simon & Schuster have been kind enough to ask about." Frost's response was immediate and inspirational. He wrote, "You are one of my great hopes," continuing,

> When I ask myself where better can you be at your age than in college, I have no answer. Certainly not knocking round in the world of cold misunderstanding. . . .
>
> There is too much idle doubt. Let the chatter go on. We'll give up beaten when we know. So in religion, so in everything.

In 1939 the two men renewed their acquaintance and met again in 1942 as lecturers at a summer session of writers at the University of Iowa. At Iowa that summer Frost inscribed the last four lines of his verse "The Strong Are Saying Nothing," one of Krause's favorite lyrics, in his friend's copy of *A Further Range: Book Six* (1936).

By the late 1930s Krause's lifelong goals of becoming a teacher and a published writer came rapidly within his grasp. On 26 October 1937 Jessica Mannon of the Bobbs-Merrill Company cabled an enthusiastic offer to publish his first novel, and an interview with the president of Augustana College during the Christmas holidays led to a job as chairman of the English department and head of the new creative-writing program there. Krause accepted both offers. To Mannon he wrote on 2 November 1937 that he had decided to call the novel *Wind Without Rain,* "being based partly on a Pockerbrush saying and partly on the biblical line, 'As clouds and wind without rain.'" To Augustana president Clemens Granskou he wrote on 21 January 1938 an eager letter of acceptance, including remarks–by his professor and writer friends at the University of Iowa–that young writers at Augustana should be taught to appreciate their heritage in fiction, poetry, and drama. Finally, to his best friend, John Danielson, Krause ecstatically wrote on 29 January 1938 that after all these years of struggle and poverty, "bitten by the acid of tears and worn thin as a shingle by empty pockets and a flat belly, now the Divine Maker has dropped this bushel of luck, pressed down and running over, into my hands. I can scarcely believe it." In September 1938 Krause began his first semester of teaching at Augustana, a small Lutheran college in eastern South Dakota, near the Minnesota-Iowa border. He continued there as a writer in residence, producing more novels and poetry, for the next thirty-eight years.

*Wind Without Rain,* the novel that Krause had been preparing since his first year at St. Olaf College, appeared in February 1939–just twenty-four months after he had admitted to dissatisfaction with his career in the letter to Frost. Published to widespread critical applause, the book achieved national recognition as one of the best first novels of 1939. Stegner, whom Krause had met at the University of Iowa and who had remained a friend, reviewed the novel for *The Saturday Review of Literature* (11 February 1939) at the suggestion of another Iowa associate, Schramm. In "A Strong Novel of the Minnesota Land," Stegner called *Wind Without Rain* "neither a very soothing nor a very easy book to read," and "the cross-grained, cinder-textured stuff of reality," with a hero whose "love of music and beauty are checked and thwarted by the labor of rocky acres, the rigors of a rocky religion, and the domination of a father hewn from granite." Stegner closed with the promise that Krause "should shoot even bigger game before he's through."

Other critics were remarkably alike in their applause for the book—especially in the New York newspapers, which Krause respected for their influence. A Bobbs-Merrill advertisement quoted Charles A. Wagner of *The New York Daily Mirror* as writing that Krause was "someone with poetry, earth piety and a horizon-clear pulse. Bravo!" while Lewis Gannett of *The New York Herald Tribune* (15 February 1939) called *Wind Without Rain* "the first exciting first novel of 1939." Writing in *The New York Times* (12 February 1939), Margaret Wallace described the setting of the book, Pockerbrush, as less a place than a "peculiarly joyless and tortured realm of the mind," and yet Krause's style is his own—"febrile, poetic, with something of the incantatory quality which first surprised us in the work of Thomas Wolfe. . . ." More than one hundred reviews in all appeared, several of them suggesting *Wind Without Rain* for the Pulitzer Prize. The comments that Krause's dissertation adviser, Edwin Ford Piper, submitted to Bobbs-Merrill particularly pleased the writer: "Here are sharply-etched vital characters, real people, genuine turns of folk-speech. The best of first novels. Herbert Krause has made a lasting contribution to American fiction." Piper, however, died a few months after the publication of *Wind Without Rain,* and Krause's new adviser was not supportive; as a consequence the writer never received his Ph.D. degree. Yet, the warm reception of his novel and his new position at Augustana were, for the time being, all that he required.

The few negative reviews found the gloomy atmosphere of the novel unrealistic and the figures of speech excessive. Clifton Fadiman of *The New Yorker* (11 February 1939) sneered at the poetry: "By the time Mr. Krause tackles his second novel he will have forgotten to be proud of the bits of fine writing that stud his prose like cheap jewelry." Krause was distressed: Fadiman was a highly respected literary man, and the poetry that he scorned was the part of the novel that Krause most cherished. Consequently, when Krause was awarded the $1,000 Friends of American Writers Award in Chicago on 16 March 1939, he was amazed to hear Fadiman, the featured speaker, refer to him as one of the most talented of young American novelists.

To the many readers who wondered if the novel was not, in fact, the story of his own life, Krause's reply was consistent: "The book is not autobiographical at all," he told his mentor, Spohn, in an interview on the St. Olaf radio station, WCAL (11 February 1939):

> My father, beyond exploding into German when his temper flared, was as unlike Vildvogel as he could be. And if you had heard my mother descending verbally upon my father for tracking mud on her newly scrubbed floor, you'd realize how unlike Minna she is. And certainly, I'm not Franz. I don't believe I'm particularly repressed, as Franz was. I know little about the technical side of music and I can't play the fiddle. Neither have I ever walked with crutches—as Jeppy did—at least up to this moment I haven't.

Nevertheless, many elements of the Vildvogel family are strikingly autobiographical. One can find clear indications among Krause's notes in his papers at the Center for Western Studies that the inspiration for Franz was a man named Drager, who—like Krause—was from the Friberg area. Julius A. Friedrich, Krause's pastor in Iowa City, reminded the writer in a letter that much of what Krause had told him of his early life in Friberg was reproduced in the first fifty-three pages of *Wind Without Rain.* Robert Whitehand, one of Krause's student friends at Iowa, moreover, recalled their many conversations about the origins of the book: "You told me often of the grudge you had against those people up there around Fergus, and I know you waited and waited for a chance to put it all on paper." Although Krause replied that his own struggles since graduation from the University of Iowa had led him to understand how the "relentless acres" had warped his Pockerbrush people, the great emotional power of *Wind Without Rain* clearly owes much to the psychological turbulence that the youthful Krause suffered among the hills north of Fergus Falls, Minnesota.

The sales of *Wind Without Rain* were not remarkable, considering that Bobbs-Merrill had placed the novel at the head of their spring fiction list and that by mid March it was listed as a best-seller by both *The New York Herald Tribune* and *The Chicago Daily News.* By August the Bobbs-Merrill royalty report showed total sales of 8,839 copies in the United States, 155 in Canada, 2 in France, and 5 in China.

For the next eight years Krause published no more novels. He brought out a collection of verse in the fall of 1939—*Neighbor Boy,* which sold 629 copies—and published two short stories, "Horning in the Fall" and "The Oak Tree," in a collection and a periodical, respectively; both stories hark back to the Pockerbrush people in *Wind Without Rain.* A novel about the threshers in western Minnesota had been in Krause's mind, however, almost as long as the story of the Vildvogels. In October 1939 Krause reported to a Bobbs-Merrill editor, Lawrence Chambers, that he had been out scouting for material for a new novel.

By the summer of 1940, however, Krause had almost made up his mind not to complete the novel—much to the dismay of Spohn, who did not agree with Krause that it was a bad time to publish. Among the writer's many concerns—including his mother's financial situation and his own fear of being drafted—was Adolf Hitler's militaristic course in Europe and the fostering of anti-German sentiment in the United States. Engle, a teacher whom Krause knew from his University of Iowa days, tried to dissuade Krause from giving up on the thresher novel and to convince him that he was not in danger of conscription. Krause's letter to Chambers, written from Friberg in late 1940, summed up his dilemma: he had thought he could dispel his doubts about the project, but these are days "when one's skin tightens with a kind of shame at the blood that runs in the veins—blood tainted even after nearly three generations of dilution with American ways." Krause recalled the anti-German hysteria of World War I, when—as a young teenager—he wondered if Germanness were a disease, "like insanity or brain fever." He still loved his Pockerbrush neighbors, but writing about them was difficult

while the Nazis devastated country after country. It sounds horsy but Nazi goose-steps and "Heil Hitlers" got mixed up with the threshing and the shindandies. Johnny Black (whose name was Schwartz), the strutting, swashing buckling [sic] but I think lovable main character, took on strange and rather terrifying resemblances to the arrogant and ruthless mechanized men, crowding the Norwegians into the fiords and smashing the mild pale-eyed Dutch into the ground.

And worse, Krause concluded, for some of those neighbors, irked by taxes and government interference, "Nazi-ism—the sort of pre-chewed and half-digested propaganda of Nazi-ism, which for them goes for truth—would be not too unfavorably regarded."

By the fall of 1943 Krause was determined to proceed after all with his thresher book, and in March 1944 a one-year fellowship in regional writing at the University of Minnesota gave him the incentive to organize a first draft out of the mass of notes he had by then accumulated. On 25 September 1944 he revealed in a letter to Chambers that he was ready to write, and by 8 November he had completed thirty typed pages. On 11 August 1945 he returned the contract for the novel, *The Thresher*, to Chambers and added that he had in mind two more novels—one about the oxcart trail and the other about a strong-willed Pockerbrush woman named Emma-August.

By June 1946 the completed novel—all 240,000 words of it—was in Chambers's hands.

When *The Thresher* appeared in January 1947, its success differed from that of *Wind Without Rain* in that many more copies of the second novel were printed; yet *The Thresher* won no national prizes. Arranging for book club distributions, Bobbs-Merrill vigorously promoted *The Thresher*. It appeared in bookstores on 6 January and was featured for distribution in the Family Book Club, the Literary Guild—including the Young People's Division—the Home Book Club, the Book League of America, and an Armed Forces edition. In February 1947 *The Thresher* was ranked fourth on the nationwide best-seller list of *The Retail Bookseller* and appeared on *The New York Times* and *The New York Herald Tribune* best-seller lists in both February and March. By the end of 1947, according to Bobbs-Merrill figures, there were 350,000 copies in circulation—excluding an *Omnibook Magazine* abridgment, for which Krause was paid $2,000. The sales of the novel appeared so substantial that for a time Krause contemplated leaving teaching altogether to devote himself to writing fiction, but he brought himself back to reality with the thought, expressed to Chambers—now the president of Bobbs-Merrill—on 21 July 1947, that after five years of digging and "eighteen months of agony" only 15,000 copies of the regular issue had been sold.

Critics and reviewers wrote favorably about the story of Johnny Black, a Pockerbrush thresherman whose use of steam-powered threshing machines fosters a powerful ambition to dominate his farming community. His attempt at such domination leads him to sacrifice himself, his best friend, Snoose Marchen, and Marchen's wife, Lilice. Many readers also liked how Krause developed the background of the story, recording in detail an almost-forgotten chapter in the economic and cultural history of the West—namely, the transition from horse-powered to steam-powered and, finally, to gasoline-powered threshing. Moreover, whereas *Wind Without Rain* took place in the narrow valleys of western Minnesota hill country, *The Thresher* extends into the Red River valley and the rich wheat fields beyond.

In an article dated 8 February 1947 Nancy Groberg Chaikin of *The Saturday Review of Literature* admired the "strong, poetic writing which fondles its metaphors almost sensually." James Gray of the *Chicago News* titled his review "Herbert Krause Takes Mantle of O. E. Rölvaag—His *The Thresher* Is Story of Man Against Destiny" (6 January 1947). The *Washington Post* review stated on 26 January 1947, "Certainly not since Hamlin Garland's Middle Border stories or perhaps *Giants in the Earth* have we had so powerful a novel of the soil." The "Briefly Noted" section of *The New Yorker* (18 January 1947), however, offered the sort of parochial complaint that Eastern critics typically level against Western writers:

THE OXCART TRAIL
~~The~~ Village

I

The cabin boy, new this trip, was calling, "St. Paul Landing round the bend. Baggage. St. Paul Landing—"

Shawnie held the locket tightly for a moment, all his young manhood bare in his eyes and struggling against the thrust of grief that tighetened in his throat.

"St. Paul Landing."

Here in the seclusion of the tiny cabin this past moment while the NORTHERN GAL plowed north, he had let pain and sweetness betray his nearly twenty years, knowing even then that with sweetness would come fear and the tensing of muscle against the onslaught of remembering. Somewhere he'd read something about a fool and his deception—

He shook his head. The locket tightened in his grip. His eyes clouded. After this moment, a space between yesterday's uncertainty and tomorrow's promise, he would let no man betray him into tenderness. No man, or woman either, he decided grimly.

"Baggage. Baggage." He heard the boy calling as if from far away. His luggage was ready, except for the carpet-bag unfastened on the bunk.

From overhead came the shuffle of feet on the hurricane deck. Outside the small window there was the slaplike sh-tat, sh-tat, sh-tat of the paddle wheels, underfoot the throb of the steamboat's engine, all about him the high-pitched excitement of passengers about to land. The locket lay open on his palm. Slowly his thumb began to press against the cover. Then, moved by a notion more boy than man, he swiftly put a finger on the face in the locket, as if at his touch, time would reverse its spiky wheels and roll yesterday back uphill into today; and laughter, frozen in color and form, would shatter the icy glass and flow like

*Page from the corrected typescript for Krause's 1954 novel*
*(Herbert Krause Papers, The Center for Western Studies, Augustana College)*

"It is hard to believe that anybody wants to know as much about threshing as he is bent on telling."

In the intervening years between *The Thresher* and *The Oxcart Trail,* his third book, Krause did not stop teaching at Augustana in favor of writing novels full-time, as he had once envisioned doing. Rather, he reduced his course load by half, a move that enabled him to continue planning and researching for several projected novels–among them the book about Emma-August, a narrative about the Selkirk Settlement in Canada, and another work about a young Korean War veteran who returns to Pockerbrush with a Japanese bride; although Krause completed writing this last novel, his dissatisfaction with its ending compelled him in the end to destroy the manuscript. He was so intent on completing these narratives that are set in the Middle West, that in the spring of 1947 he turned down an offer from Stegner to teach at Stanford University.

By February 1948, as Krause informed Chambers, he had turned out ten thousand words on *The Oxcart Trail.* The writer reported to Feike Feikema, also known as Frederick Manfred, in the fall of 1948 that research for the book was getting "in the way of the narrative and the development of the idea and theme." Four years later, in the spring of 1952, Krause sent the first twenty-eight pages to Chambers, and by the following January, Bobbs-Merrill set a publication date of 30 March 1953. Yet, because delays kept occurring, *The Oxcart Trail* did not appear until February 1954–in the midst of a "generally poor" hardbound fiction market, as Chambers characterized it in a letter to Krause on 16 December 1953.

The plot of *The Oxcart Trail* divides itself into two parts. The first is centered in old St. Paul, when Minnesota was a territory, and life in the Mississippi River frontier town was a turmoil of the comings and goings of traders, immigrants, and other types of transients. The central figure in the novel, Shawnie Dark, is a young fugitive who killed a lawman in the East while aiding in the Underground Railroad. The fear of pursuit that troubles Shawnie pales in comparison with the bone-deep anxiety that dominates Franz in *Wind Without Rain* or the lust for vengeance that drives Johnny in *The Thresher.* The action of the first half of the story–the politics, tavern life, church doings, and missionary activity–prepares Shawnie for the second part, "The Trail." The perilous journey of an oxcart caravan north to the Red River country will finally unite the young adventurer with Debbie Wells, the feminist school-teacher-turned-missionary who also risks the passage through the battleground of the Chippewa and Sioux Indians.

The reviews of *The Oxcart Trail* were fewer and more mixed than those for Krause's previous novels. Some critics suggested that Krause should have published the novel as two separate stories. John T. Flanagan in *Minnesota History* (Autumn 1954) called the two parts of the book "badly fused," and Victor Hass in *The New York Times* (11 April 1954) pointed out that Krause took 287 pages "to get to the subject promised by the title." In Krause's opinion Gray wrote the best review, for he recognized the novelist's epic intent: "The important thing about *The Oxcart Trail* is that it offers a new design for the historical novel. Mr Krause's plan makes room for a vast amount of historical research, each detail of which has been dramatized in the behavior of a character."

Although his editors at Bobbs-Merrill had been cautioning Krause that fiction sales in general had declined since the astonishing success of *The Thresher,* he nonetheless grew increasingly depressed as the months passed with no improvement in the sales of the book. Bobbs-Merrill printed ten thousand copies–five thousand of which were a special Minnesota edition–and thus no more than had been published of *Wind Without Rain.* In his correspondence to some people, Krause attributed the poor sales of *The Oxcart Trail* to the sudden popularity of television; to others he complained about an atmosphere of indifference toward his work. His supporters at Bobbs-Merrill tried to reassure him and to encourage him to dive into his next project, whether it be the manuscript "Emma-August" or the novel about the war bride. Yet, Krause completed no fiction after *The Oxcart Trail,* and his creative efforts turned in new directions.

After the mediocre reception of his third book, Krause returned to an interest that had begun in childhood, the study of birds, which developed into a passion that consumed Krause for the next twenty years. He made many field trips during this period, published copiously in ornithological journals and books, served as president of the South Dakota Ornithological Union, and in 1956 was awarded a grant from the American Association for the Advancement of Science to complete a bibliography of South Dakota birds, dating from 1794 to 1954. In 1960 he completed the script for a twenty-five-minute color film for the University of Minnesota on the need for wildlife preservation and control and on the work of the game biologist. Titled *The Big Four,* the film dramatizes through conversations among a boy, his grandfather, and a game biologist the principles that govern wildlife population behavior. Krause's love for his home state of Minnesota and his deserved fame as a native son led to a commission for a poem in honor of Statehood Day. "Giant from the Wooded Earth," 121 lines of free verse, was Kraus's poetic offering. The poem was read by the actor Walter Abel in Memorial Stadium at the University of Minnesota on 11 May 1958.

In addition, the extensive research that Krause had executed in preparation for *The Oxcart Trail* eventually resulted in the two major works that capped his writing career: an epic stage pageant about the Lakota Sioux

Indian leader Crazy Horse and a co-edited book of dispatches written by the newspaper correspondents who traveled with Lieutenant Colonel George Armstrong Custer into the Black Hills of South Dakota in the summer of 1874. In *Crazy Horse: A Drama of the Plains Indians and the Black Hills* (performed in 1994) Krause covers the life of the Sioux leader, who was born sometime in the 1840s and died in September 1877. Living during the most turbulent years in the history of his people, Crazy Horse led his victorious Sioux warriors against the U.S. military in a series of battles that climaxed at the Little Big Horn on 25 June 1876. Unperformed during Krause's lifetime, the play was produced before an audience of three hundred in an abbreviated form by a largely Indian cast in Sioux Falls on 20 June 1994. The other important work at the end of Krause's career was the collecting and editing of dispatches, by six different newspaper correspondents, that instigated the subsequent rush of gold seekers into the Black Hills and ultimately led to the end of Indian resistance to white settlement on the northern plains. In *Prelude to Glory: A Newspaper Accounting of Custer's 1874 Expedition* (1974), Krause wrote of the Custer expedition that it might have encouraged Custer's political ambitions and that certainly his own dispatches and statements favored the "extinguishment of the Indian title to the Black Hills." *Prelude to Glory* was widely and favorably critiqued when it appeared; Carl R. Baldwin of the *St. Louis Post-Dispatch* (25 August 1974) called the book "a masterpiece of sorts, in the words of the reporters, scientists and military men who participated in the 'scientific foray' into the sacred land of the Sioux and Cheyenne."

Herbert Krause's work on *Prelude to Glory* was closely related to the creation of the Center for Western Studies at Augustana College, which he had founded in part to increase the publication of important books about the northern plains. Throughout his teaching career at the college, beginning with his first interview with President Granskou, Krause set his mind on encouraging his students to tell the stories of the people who settled the West and of the Native Americans whom they met there. Thus, in 1970, approximately thirty-one years after Krause started teaching at the college, he established the center with the support of several colleagues and the Board of Regents at Augustana. Upon his death of a stroke on 22 September 1976, Krause—who had never married—bequeathed his modest estate and his thirty-thousand-volume library to the center. A place devoted to interpreting and preserving the history and cultures of the northern prairie plains, the Center for Western Studies signified a project that in Krause's final years was as vital to him as his career as a writer of the American West.

**Bibliography:**

*The Herbert Krause Collection Bibliography,* 2 volumes, compiled by Raymond Veryl Dunmire (Sioux Falls, S.Dak.: Augustana College, 1975).

**Biography:**

Arthur R. Huseboe, *Herbert Krause,* Western Writers Series, no. 66 (Boise, Idaho: Boise State University Press, 1985).

**References:**

Carl R. Baldwin, "What Custer Was After," *St. Louis Post-Dispatch,* 25 August 1974, p. 4B;

Nancy Groberg Chaikin, "A Man's Drive for Power," *Saturday Review of Literature* (8 February 1947): 12;

James Gray, "Liquor, Love and Brawling on the Long Road Westward," *New York Herald Tribune Book Review* (4 April 1954): 5;

Walter Havighurst, "Driving Force on the Prairie," *New York Herald Tribune Weekly Book Review* (12 January 1947): 4;

Arthur R. Huseboe, "Rölvaag and Krause, Two Novelists of the Northwest Prairie Frontier," in *A Literary History of the American West,* edited by Thomas J. Lyon (Fort Worth: Texas Christian University Press, 1987), pp. 716–738;

Judith M. Janssen, "Black Frost in Summer: Central Themes in the Novels of Herbert Krause," *South Dakota Review,* 5 (Spring 1967): 55–65;

Roy W. Meyer, *The Middle Western Farm Novel in the Twentieth Century* (Lincoln: University of Nebraska Press, 1965);

Kristoffer F. Paulson, "Ole Rölvaag, Herbert Krause, and the Frontier Thesis of Frederick Jackson Turner," in *Where the West Begins,* edited by Huseboe and William Geyer (Sioux Falls, S.Dak.: Center for Western Studies, 1978), pp. 2–33;

Robert C. Steensma, "'Our Comings and Our Goings': Herbert Krause's *Wind Without Rain,*" in *Where the West Begins,* edited by Huseboe and Geyer (Sioux Falls, S.Dak.: Center for Western Studies, 1978), pp. 13–22;

Wallace Stegner, "A Strong Novel of the Minnesota Land," *Saturday Review of Literature* (11 February 1939): 5;

Margaret Wallace, "*Wind Without Rain* and Other Recent Works of Fiction," *New York Times Book Review* (12 February 1939): 6.

**Papers:**

Herbert Krause's papers and personal library are housed at the Center for Western Studies at Augustana College in Sioux Falls, South Dakota.

# Clinton F. Larson

*(22 September 1919 – 10 July 1994)*

David L. Evans
*Brigham Young University*

BOOKS: *Button, Button: A Play in Three Acts* (Provo, Utah: C. F. Larson, 1961);

*Coriantumr and Moroni: Two Plays by Clinton F. Larson* (Provo, Utah: Brigham Young University Press, 1961);

*The Tower of Winds* (Provo, Utah, 1961);

*The Mantle of the Prophet and Other Plays* (Salt Lake City: Deseret, 1966);

*The Lord of Experience: Poems by Clinton F. Larson* (Provo, Utah: Brigham Young University Press, 1967; enlarged, Salt Lake City: Promised Land Publications, 1968);

*The Prophet: Poetry, Drama, and Grand Opera Libretto* (Provo, Utah: Eugene H. Chapman, 1971);

*Counterpoint; A Book of Poems* (Provo, Utah: Brigham Young University Press, 1973);

*The Western World: An Anthology* (Provo, Utah: Brigham Young University Press, 1975);

*Centennial Portraits: Brigham Young University Centennial, 1975–76* (Provo, Utah: Brigham Young University Press, 1976);

*The Works of Clinton F. Larson,* 13 volumes, compiled and edited by Wayne Taylor and Miriam Pierce (Provo, Utah: Brigham Young University, 1985);

*Romaunt of the Rose: A Tapestry of Poems* (Provo, Utah, 1986);

*Egyptian Poems* (Provo, Utah: Brigham Young University Studies, 1987);

*Selected Poems of Clinton F. Larson,* edited, with an introduction, by David L. Evans (Provo, Utah: Brigham Young University Press, 1988);

*Civil War Poems* (Provo, Utah: Brigham Young University Studies, 1989);

*Sunwind,* edited, with an introduction, by David L. Evans (Orem, Utah: Geneva Steel Corporation, 1990);

*Conversions of God: A Poem* (N.p., 1964?).

PLAY PRODUCTIONS: *The Mantle of the Prophet,* 1960;

*Clinton F. Larson (from the dust jacket for* The Mantle of the Prophet and Other Plays, *1966)*

*Button, Button,* Helsinki, Finnish National Theater, 1961;

*Snow White and the Mirror,* Pasadena, California, Pasadena Playhouse, 1966.

OTHER: *La poésie contemporaine aux Etats-Unis,* preface by Larson, edited by André Maurois (Paris: Editions de la Revue Moderne, 1962);

*Illustrated Stories from the Book of Mormon,* edited, with narrative, by Larson, illustrated by Raymond H. Jacobs (Salt Lake City: Promised Land, 1967–1971);

*Modern Poetry of Western America: An Anthology,* edited by Larson and William Stafford (Provo, Utah: Brigham Young University Press, 1975).

Clinton F. Larson is one of the most challenging poets of the Intermountain West and probably of all of Western America. The reader who casually approaches Larson's poetry is doomed from the start to miss most of the linguistic innuendos, subtlety of emotion, and depth of ideas that characterize his best works and stand out in his more incidental writings. His verse is thus especially rewarding to readers who put forth the required mental, emotional, and spiritual effort.

Through his writings Larson always sought a careful balance between religious insight and scientific descriptions of pragmatic experience. At the same time, considered by many readers as the premier "Mormon" poet, Larson experimented significantly by combining the religious elements in his work with the precise language of science. Many members of the Church of Jesus Christ of Latter-day Saints find Larson's work a poetic inspiration to their faith, and for readers outside the church his poems arguably serve as guideposts in their struggle to confront the complexities of modern life—especially the struggle for harmony between faith, science, and art.

Although Larson was a prolific writer, he has not been much studied or publicized by critics; little critical evaluation or even explication of his work is available. Karl Keller discusses Larson's *The Lord of Experience: Poems by Clinton F. Larson* (1967) in his article "A Pilgrimage of Awe" for *Dialogue* (Spring 1968). In 1977 Thomas D. Schwartz wrote a Master's thesis, "The Erosion of Belief in the Poetry of Clinton F. Larson," at Brigham Young University and followed his thesis with an article in *Dialogue* (Autumn 1978), "Sacrament of Terror: Violence in the Poetry of Clinton F. Larson." When Larson published *Centennial Portraits: Brigham Young University Centennial, 1975–76* in 1976, Marden J. Clark, a colleague, wrote the introduction to the book. David L. Evans wrote two introductions about Larson and his work in books that Evans edited—*Selected Poems of Clinton F. Larson* (1988) and *Sunwind* (1990).

Larson was the son of Clinton and Lillian Foster Larson. Clinton was a teacher who had gone to Europe with the American Expeditionary Force during the Great War and had distinguished himself in athletics by winning the high-jump championship at the Allied Games in France with a record-setting jump. This accomplishment remained a point of pride for the younger Larson throughout his life, although he was frustrated by his inability to excel,

like his father, in sports. After Clinton returned home from the war, he taught school in Duchesne, Utah—at that time an extremely small rural community. Because Lillian was about to have a child, the couple decided that she should move temporarily to American Fork—a slightly larger rural community close to Salt Lake City and thus not as far as Duchesne from medical help—to live with her mother, Emily Foster. Clinton Foster Larson was born in American Fork on 22 September 1919.

When the baby was about a year old, Clinton took a teaching position in Salt Lake City, and the family settled in a brick bungalow on Hawthorne Avenue. Larson's education—from grade school through graduate level studies—took place completely in Salt Lake City. He attended Hawthorne Elementary School, Irving Junior High School, South High School, and the University of Utah. Entering the university just before his seventeenth birthday in 1936, he registered at first for courses in premedicine but soon changed his major to English; Brewster Ghiselin, the preeminent poet and onetime student of D. H. Lawrence, encouraged Larson to switch. Tongue in cheek, Larson thus often referred to himself as a "literary grandson of Lawrence."

Like most young men in his church, Larson took time out from his education to do missionary work. He traveled to England for his mission in 1938 and was transferred in 1940, shortly after the outbreak of World War II, to Maine, where he completed the last few months of his mission. While away from Utah he exchanged letters with Naomi Barlow, a young woman he had met prior to his mission, at the wedding of his grandmother, Emily, to Naomi's uncle, Rob Sweeten. Larson and Naomi married on 24 June 1942 after he graduated from the University of Utah. Determined to join the U.S. military effort in World War II, he enlisted in the U.S. Army Air Force the next day.

Nine months later Larson went on active duty, and for three years his army career took him from one post to another within the United States. Although he and Naomi occasionally lived together, they were more often apart at this time. In December 1944, however, they were able to return to Salt Lake City together for the birth of their first daughter, Sue. In the summer of 1945 Larson was scheduled to be sent to Asia for the invasion of Japan, but the war ended before he left. In December 1945 he was honorably discharged, and he returned to the University of Utah to begin studying toward a Master's degree in English.

After receiving his M.A. in 1947, he immediately accepted a position in the English Department of Brigham Young University (BYU), in Provo, Utah, and during his first year of teaching Naomi gave birth to their second daughter, Diane. In 1956 Larson was awarded his Ph.D. from the University of Denver. In 1963 he was promoted to the rank of full professor at BYU and in 1974 was named Poet in Residence—positions that he held until his retirement in 1985. Although Larson dedicated a great amount of time and effort to his teaching, he wrote on a daily basis and even built a special writing room above his garage. Because he liked to pace around the room while he worked, he had not only a desk at which to sit for correcting manuscripts but also a higher surface—outfitted with a typewriter and plenty of pens—at which he could stand while writing. He re-created this arrangement in his office at BYU, retaining a desk for teaching duties but positioning a high counter along one wall for his creative work.

Although Larson primarily considered himself a poet and is known to his readers chiefly through his verse, he was also an active playwright. His dramatic works actually reflect a fusion of both his poetic and playwriting talents, as he was one of the most stubborn advocates of poetic drama in an age that had turned away from the form. Although Larson did not publish his first book of poems until 1964, by which time he had completed several plays and seen some of them produced locally and even abroad, he was continually busy composing verse. He talked occasionally about his plays, but every few days he made the rounds to his colleagues' offices to read in a sonorous chant his latest lyrical work. Thus, while the 1960s represent his richest poetic period, when he composed many of his finest works, they also signify a decade of intense playwriting for him.

The completion and local production of his first major play, *The Mantle of the Prophet,* in 1960 launched Larson's playwriting career. This poetic drama recounts the dilemma that the Latter-day Saints faced after the death of their founding prophet, Joseph Smith Jr., when church members had to decide whether his mantle would fall upon his son, upon one of Smith's counselors in the presidency of the church, or upon Brigham Young, the head of the Council of the Twelve Apostles in the church. In a lyrical way, Larson captures the personal feelings and societal frustrations of church members as they seek a successor for their slain leader. The drama reaches its emotional and spiritual climax in the miraculous transfer of the prophetic mantle to the capable shoulders of Brigham Young.

Larson kept busy during 1960 and for most of 1961 as founding president of the National Federa-

tion of State Poetry Societies. In addition, he spent a great deal of time on the scene of international culture, collaborating with André Maurois in preparing a preface, in French, for *La poésie contemporaine aux Etats-Unis* (1962)—an anthology that, incidentally, included one of Larson's early poems, "Crematorium." Larson also kept himself sufficiently busy by writing the prose play *Button, Button,* whose world premiere took place at the Finnish National Theater in late 1961. The "button" of the title refers to the mechanism for releasing atomic-headed missiles upon the world.

Also in 1961 BYU Press published its first book, *Coriantumr and Moroni: Two Plays by Clinton F. Larson,* works that Larson based on characters in the Book of Mormon. He also enjoyed writing in several genres for children. One of his own favorite projects was his *Illustrated Stories from the Book of Mormon* (1967–1971), designed to make the Latter-day scripture attractive to the young. Later in 1963 he finished *The Redeemer,* a dramatic representation of Christ as a powerfully masculine figure. In Larson's view, Western culture portrays Christ so meekly and humbly that he comes across as a passive figure, conversing and preaching rather than doing. Through his play, however, Larson interprets Christ vividly and memorably. While Christ conveys his ideas in *The Redeemer* through powerful, dramatic rhetoric, he also makes his presence known through quick, forceful actions. As a result the play elicited mixed response from the audience at the first performance; some were simply shocked by Larson's shouting, emotional Christ.

*Conversions of God: A Poem,* Larson's first published work of poetry—which initially appeared in *Proceedings of Utah Academy of Sciences, Arts and Letters* in 1964—typified both the predominant subjects and favorite techniques of the poet's early lyrics. The subject of the verse collection is the religious disparity between the Being that a culture worships and the diminishing presence of that God in daily life. Repeatedly, Larson's technique is to take a set of actions embodying a series of thoughts—about which most readers feel that nothing new can be said because of certain prevailing stereotypes—and then surprise the reader with a pattern of new attitudes and images based on a thoughtful approach to the beliefs in question.

Larson develops *Conversions of God* in six parts, with no attention to chronological succession. The opening section, titled "West End Clinic, or God the Scientist," concerns how people in modern times regard the scientist, particularly the physician, as a god. The poem constitutes a monologue delivered

*Dust jacket for Larson's volume of religious dramas. The title work concerns the crisis in Mormon leadership after the assassination of the church's founder, Joseph Smith.*

by the chemical-oriented doctor—"I see the image of me at large in heaven, / Zit! it is I, glory, the synopticon, the oracle!"—and counterpointed with occasional antiphonies from a lady who needs the ministrations of the God-Doctor to solve any and all moral and pragmatic dilemmas, such as pregnancy or escape from reality. Intoning "holy, holy– / Hysterectimus, eclectimus," she continues, "And the chyme will sing, / Abba, abba, the pill hath virtue." Thinking of her as an emblem of the entire world, the doctor assures her, "Peace I leave with you,"

> My peace I give unto you,
> Not as heaven giveth,
> Give I unto you.
> And she said, Abba, father,
> All things are possible unto thee.

The pun on "chyme"—a favorite practice of Larson's—is particularly apt in this interchange, juxtaposing the aesthetic suggestion of bells in traditional rituals with the harshly unaesthetic overtones of semidigested food passing from the stomach to the intestines. The God-Scientist may promise perfection and peace, but one is always able to see into the underlying realities of physical processes:

> Elevatio hostiae!
> Take this now in daily ritual,
> Replenished when you come and come again.
> Withdraw into the sepulchres of gold,
> Shining in your prosthetic sheath of skin.

In the second part of *Conversions of God,* "The Gull, or God as Philosopher," God concentrates his being on trying to understand and explain everything in his universe in organized, rational terms. He is forced to say, "I pace the empty station, / I gaze at the bracketing hours / That package departed trains," and concludes, "from my red claws / I drag the luggage of my sterling viscera."

In the third section, "Angkor Thom, or God the Brahmin," Larson uses the fixed, unchanging temple in the jungle to focus on the fixed, static, unchanging nature inherent in a doctrine such as nirvana, or in a spiritual life that holds up a lack of change and development as its ideal. "The spirit lofts from the flesh, / Lost in the analogues or braziers . . . / But the continent gods hover, wraiths of scent / In the dusk of sandalwood."

The next part, "The Chain, or God the Catholic," opens with vignettes of Thomas Aquinas and the Virgin. When, Larson suggests, God is reduced by the tenuous philosophy of Aquinas to mystical terms that defy visual or tactile reality, the "lamb of grace" turns to someone concrete, such as the Virgin Mary—"the niche of blue prayer." To provide his own concrete imagery, Aquinas "posits his endless chain / And the Index near the ground of God." Yet, when God is everywhere and nowhere present, the chain is unanchored and "Into the high valleys the grey wind comes / Like the creeds of believers."

"Gothic Ulm," the fifth section, can be summed up in one short passage: "the inestimable animal world repines / And dies / In fear of the god that made boredom immortal." God himself speaks in the last part of this section and admits, "I, honest among Calvinists, barely remember my identity / As the sign of rain." In "The Chieftain, or God the Father," the final section of the poem, Larson presents for the believer in modern times—using modern terms—his own idea of the nature of God. The section begins with a prose paragraph, titled "Epigraph sub rosa," in which Larson employs a technique that becomes more common and more complex in his late lyrics. He transforms the language of the physicist into the language of poetry, and—after presenting a scientific concept or group of concepts—he expands on his idea in language that is common to science, religion, and traditional poetry. Larson uses a modified definition of gravitation based on his reading of discussions about the search for a unified field—a search he hoped someday to enlarge by including both science and the arts in a unified field. He concludes the "epigraph" by defining "magnetism" as "the false light, specious and temporal: negation, heresy, and hate" and identifying gravity as "the light and firmament of love."

In concluding *Conversions of God,* Larson introduces what is probably the most important and most frequently used symbol of all his poetry—light. He thinks of Christ primarily as "the Light of the world," and his use of light imagery signals an invitation—even an expectation—to his readers to search passages in his verse for a religious suggestion or statement. In "The Chieftain, or God the Father" he brings in the image of light to prefigure the ensuing light imagery of the section. Addressing Yahweh, the speaker says, "You are the resurrection whose craft is power, / Whose reason is love," immediately crying out, "But the binding of light! The rose of conception / Impends like the blue power of stars in your vision." "I watch the sands of Asia shine," the speaker continues, "In the prism of morning." A ghostly moonlight scene makes him realize that "I have seen the frieze of sunlight in the dust of fields." Finally, feeling at ease with the world, he is able to say, "The hidden peace began / In the glare of the average sun." The speaker's sense of peace at the end of *Conversions of God* allows him to feel the blending of the past with the present and eternity, "Light golden in chivalric halls. / Where are the thousand years / That have brought me here?" Larson ends the poem by associating its light imagery with the divine afflatus, or inspiration: "Glory and the fall of centuries / Come like the willows' wind."

Larson's primary purpose in *The Conversions of God* is undoubtedly to look closely at some of the major anthropomorphic interpretations of deity. He wants to show how concepts of godhood grow out of cultures and then help shape the later development of those cultures. Instead of tracing these cultures in a chronological or geographical order, he moves from the most simpleminded and egregious of cultures to one that he is on the verge of embracing. Yet, Larson is careful not to make his long poem a parochial work. *Conversions of God* may have didactic overtones, but it does not promote Mormon theology. Rather, the poem ridicules the modern tendency of some scientists to think of themselves as God's rivals, particularly in terms of his power over the elements. The poem does not reject science, neither as a source of much wisdom nor as a study whose language can be used in poetry.

By 1967, when *The Lord of Experience* came out, Larson had done his most extensive and best work by focusing on themes such as religion and science. While *The Conversions of God* revealed his understanding of religion, Larson did not write didactically about religion, nor did he develop patently orthodox religious themes. In Larson's hands each religious poem discloses an unexpected turn of some sort, as illustrated keenly in "Advent," the opening lyric of *The Lord of Experience*. The persona of the poem, a member of a priestly class, anticipates the coming of a "gentle God" and lists the delicacies prepared in honor of the arrival:

> The table is set for the gentle God:
> The roasted fowl entice the savoring tongue:
> The marmalade and sweetmeats brim
> The centerpiece, a horn:
> The fruit is full, plucked in prime,
> Oranges, apples, pears
> Like noon-shade autumn leaves.
> The supper will please the gentle God
> Who surely comes,
> Who comes like the breath on a veil.

Yet, confused by the sounds of "temblor," "hurricane," "rages," and "vengeful steel on stone," the persona asks, "Who rends the imminent door?" and adds, "Our guest is a gentle God, a Lamb."

Through its suggestion of paradox, "Advent" harks back to William Butler Yeats's "The Second Coming" (1920) and recalls William Blake's "The Lamb" from *Songs of Innocence* (1789) and "The Tyger" from *Songs of Experience* (1794); Blake balances the Lamb's tame nature with the Tyger's wildness, while Larson contrasts the thunderous arrival of God with his gentle demeanor. The main theme of "Advent"—that in one's efforts to stress the meekness, the gentleness, and other "feminine" qualities of Christ, his "masculine" side is ignored or even denied—also underlies Ezra Pound's "Ballad of the Goodly Fere" (1909). Larson's lyric, however, is distinguished in its language, specific tone, and skillful use of dramatic monologue. Although "Advent" reflects the influence of Yeats, Blake, and Pound, Larson does not copy or mimic these poets. He reminds modern believers that while Christ is known as the Lamb, he also plays Christ the Tiger, the Avenger, the Harrower of Hell; Christ, Larson implies, was not acting out of character when he angrily threw the money-changers out of the temple.

Another religious poem in *The Lord of Experience,* "The Song of Light," has been central to Larson's entire poetic career. The poem is based on a traditional metaphor that he had employed previously and continued to use for years afterward in his verse: Christ as "the Light of the World." In "The Song of Light" Larson investigates a large number of variations on the theme of light as symbolic of Christ and his transcendent spiritual power. As readers who are new to Larson's poetry soon gather, any reference to light evokes almost automatically a religious significance.

A pivotal book, *The Lord of Experience* encompasses certain thematic patterns that characterize Larson's later works. Some of these themes retained paramount importance in his writings, while some declined in significance for him. Those that grew less important are poems that are based on his missionary experiences in England and other poems recounting his personal experiences. Three well-executed poems in the volume that retell mission experiences are "Affair in Evesham," "The English Rains," and "An English Graveyard." Perhaps the most vivid lyrics about his personal experiences are "Fighter Pilot" and one based on his father's athletic prowess, which always made Larson feel a certain inadequacy. In "An Old Athlete Speaks of His Son" the father/athlete recognizes that his poet/son may not be able to leap physically but in his art "leaps where cirri drift, / Blazing, golden, wind-swept, swift." Although the themes that prove crucial in Larson's later books are scattered throughout *The Lord of Experience,* only one poem with a Civil War subject is included—"The Defender of Cemetery Hill."

The theme of shared or universal experience, which constantly concerned Larson, is also well represented in *The Lord of Experience.* The representations include typical family occurrences, neighborhood relationships, and the universal events of birth, love, and death. While such subjects are prone to stereotypical interpretations, Larson considers each of them from an unexpected viewpoint, writing with fresh diction and metaphors. "In Memoriam: June 10, 1963" is particularly poignant, for the verse honors the accidental death of one of Larson's closest friends, H. Darrel Taylor. Another of these universal-event poems, "To a Dying Girl," ranks among his most often anthologized and quoted poems.

> How quickly must she go?
> She calls dark swans from mirrors everywhere:
> From halls and porticos, from pools of air.
> How quickly must she know?
> They wander through the fathoms of her eye,
> Waning southerly until their cry
> Is gone where she must go.

Verses such as "To a Dying Girl," written upon the death of people close to the poet, frequently correspond to another of Larson's most pervasive and distinctive themes: the darker side of life. A few titles from the collection illustrate this dark side well: "The Pyromaniac," "Crematorium," "Before the Casket," "Mortuary," "Graveside," and "Polio"—as well as a poem innocently titled "The Visit." The visit that Larson writes about in this lyric is an excursion into the past; the imagery in "The Visit" focuses on armor, weapons, and scenes of violence. The lyric reaches a climax when the visitor sits among "the toys / Of the departed young," trying to hear "the voice of light in the window," but the spiritual cannot be heard above the voice "that drones in the marrow of dolls strewn and unsewn." The visitor finds not the God of Light but the "Statuary God" and is left at the end to ask, "What pogrom lights my eyes across the vistas of broken tombs?"

"Homestead in Idaho," probably Larson's best-known poem from *The Lord of Experience,* also portrays the darker side of life. Developed in considerable detail in order to present the facts of the harshness of life that faced settlers of the difficult, undeveloped lands of the West–and also to present convincingly the people who faced such difficulties–"Homestead" is Larson's longest and most complete narrative. In brief, the story relates how Solomon, a homesteader, builds a place for his family in the Idaho Panhandle, far from any neighbors. His wife, Geneva, feels confident that they can succeed on their farm, but first they need some money. She convinces him that he should work in town that winter, while she remains on the homestead with their daughters.

He leaves, works throughout the winter, and then returns. No friendly smoke greets him as he approaches the cabin–only snow on the roof and an open door. Inside he finds the bodies of his wife and children and gradually figures out what happened. Bitten by a rattlesnake, his wife had tried cutting her fang-wounds open, but the cut was too deep and she failed to stop the bleeding with a tourniquet. Foreseeing the impending painful death of their daughters from starvation and exposure, Geneva managed to get the family's gun and used it to spare the children. She then crawled into the bed and with her blood wrote a message to Solomon on the sheet: "Rattlesnake bit. Babies would star–."

Larson's technique for presenting the story is simple yet skillful, for he writes the lyric as a monologue within a monologue: the townsman of the small Oregon community in which Solomon settles after the catastrophe tells of his conversation with Solomon, and Solomon in effect tells his own tale in appropriately plain yet poignantly lyrical words. One of Larson's least complex poems, "Homestead in Idaho" is also one of his most gripping and is often featured as one example of an American poem in British school textbooks.

In 1965 Larson returned to "Mormon" themes by writing *The Prophet,* a play about Smith, the founder of Mormonism, that was set in the period before Smith attained martyrdom. In 1966 he pro-

duced a "children's" musical drama, *Snow White and the Mirror.* The play seems aimed at the mature child, since the Wicked Queen and her coconspirators, for example, plot their mischief while singing and dancing to "cha-cha-cha" rhythms. At the same time that he helped produce *Snow White and the Mirror,* Larson also oversaw the printing of five of his plays by the Deseret Book Company in one volume, *The Mantle of the Prophet and Other Plays* (1966). Although his energies turned increasingly to lyrical poetry, Larson was not finished with the writing of plays. In 1969 he revised *The Prophet* as the libretto for an opera, with music by Douglas Isaacson, and in 1970 he produced another play, *Before the Sepulchre;* both of these works were collected and published later as *The Prophet: Poetry, Drama, and Grand Opera Libretto* (1971).

When Brigham Young University celebrated its centennial in 1975, Larson contributed to the festivities by writing seventy-five poems that described nearly as many of his colleagues, whom he selected as subjects to represent all disciplines of study and other areas of campus activity. He was careful to include, for example, colleagues who did only research rather than taught courses–as well as custodians and secretaries. Larson subtly and carefully crafted each poem to have its own appropriate style and method of development. Although the subjects are limited and dated, for lovers of poetry the lyricism and variety of *Centennial Portraits* are worth scanning and even reading closely.

Larson's next major book, *The Western World: An Anthology,* appeared in 1975. A collection of mostly lyrical poems, *The Western World* variously continued the themes and methods of *The Lord of Experience*–expanding some and almost completely omitting others. For example, no poems about Larson's mission period and scarcely any poems about his personal experiences appear in this volume; moreover, poems on strictly religious themes play an insignificant role. Nonetheless, Larson did include a few verses about local people and family. One of these, "Jesse," stands out for its simplicity of development, coupled with a depth of feeling and a startling twist at the end. The lyric recounts an incident from Larson's youth when he and a friend, Jesse, would spend days enjoying the outdoors near their homes in American Fork. They typically left from Jesse's house, where his father kept a loaded shotgun with the safety off, leaning it against a wall by the door for spur-of-the-moment exits to go hunting. Out in nature, the two boys would ride along the edge of the nearby lake and feel close to spiritual realities. In the poem Jesse articulates their feelings when he says, "I know the prince that stands beyond the air." Later, in England, the speaker–who is ultimately Larson himself–hears the news of his friend's fate. Returning home after a spiritual interlude in the outdoors, Jesse accidentally dislodged the gun by the door and was killed by the ensuing shot. Larson concludes the poem, "I felt the slow gait of the horses / Near the lake, where the lights of evening ease / And whisper into evening beyond the gloss of day."

*The Western World* also consists of, in large measure, poems that convey universally shared, everyday experiences–as these titles suggest: "Flirt," "Bachelor," "Soft Sell," "Hard Sell," "Executive," and "The Five O'Clock News Has Spoiled My Dinner." There is one Civil War poem, "The Turning Point: General Stonewall Jackson at Chancellorsville." As in his earlier work, several poems about the dark side of life appear in *The Western World:* "Sepulchre," "Hitler's Meat Hooks," "Rollover on Interstate 15," and "The Samaritan Butcher," which tells of a butcher in Samaria, Idaho–hence the title. The butcher is helping a friend dig a well, using a horse to move the gravel that they are digging out. When the horse moves too close and falls inside the well onto the friend, the Samaritan butcher has to take an ax and chop the horse into small enough pieces "from strewn fetlock, spine, and viscera / To save that friend."

One group of verses that quite differs from Larson's earlier writings has poems that depict aspects of life in nature. The titles of the poems disclose what appeals to Larson about nature. He is attracted to a "Spring Morning," "Shells," a "Lakeshore," a "Tornado," a "Well-Fed Chipmunk," and the "Grand Teton." *The Western World* also incorporates a brief cycle of short poems in which Larson attempts on a small scale what he does later on a large scale, with more complicated techniques, in his longer poems. He tries to blend science, art, and religion together–as in the short poem "Arcturus." He describes at first a marina at midnight on a cloudy night, where a sudden "shaft of midnight" provides a glimpse of Arcturus through deep-stacked clouds: "Ancient star, you are pure as a silvering / Beam as your light shivers in the western / Air." He sees "the milfoil galaxies / Shimmer across its surface as retortion / For sin as I say, / Resurrection, / The world's dying is the shiver of eternal spring." While light that flashes across galaxies, as in "Arcturus," remains for Larson a symbol of Christ and of the spiritual, light also symbolizes–as "Arcturus" shows–the struggle of science to understand the nature of energy and also to construct a model of the universe.

Larson believed that some of the themes in his later poetry were important enough to collect and

*Dust jacket for Larson's 1976 collection of poems about his university colleagues, including professors, secretaries, and custodians*

publish in small chapbook editions. His early love for France continued to grow through the years and finally led him to publish his translations of sonnets by Jean de la Ceppède from the French and Larson's own poems on French topics in *Romaunt of the Rose* (first published in *Brigham Young University Studies,* 1983). Larson also delved increasingly into comparative mythology, pursuing several Egyptian mythic elements and discovering parallels in Greek, Hebraic, Christian, and Oriental mythic images and character types. His fascination led to *Egyptian Poems* (1987). By 1989 Larson's interest in the Civil War had also intensified, resulting in the publication of *Civil War Poems* that same year; many of the lyrics in the volume consist of dramatic monologues delivered by generals after important battles.

In the late 1980s and early 1990s most of Larson's late poems appeared in two edited collections, *Selected Poems of Clinton F. Larson* and *Sunwind. Sunwind* in particular bears an interesting inception. Once, when Larson was traveling on an airliner, he struck up a conversation with the man seated next to him. Larson explained why he had become a poet, then began reciting some of his poems. His seating companion, an executive at the Geneva Steel Corporation, which was located a few miles from Provo, showed such great interest that he convinced other company executives that Geneva Steel should contribute to local culture by publishing a book of Larson's poetry—and providing a copy to all company employees as well as making the book available to the general reader. Like most books of verse, *Sunwind* was not a universal success but was still well received by a large number of readers.

Many of the new poems found in both *Selected Poems of Clinton F. Larson* and *Sunwind* show continued interest in the experiences of all people as well as in phases of modern life. These include "Sleeping in Church," "Everybody's Getting Old," "Television Evangelist," "Gallery on the Eighteenth Green," "Rocket Sled," "Nuclear Winter," and "Pac Man: An Enormity." Some poems concern old subjects in a new light because of scientific or technological advances. The poem "Parable," for instance, converts the time-honored image of sunset colors into "The wick of God whose energy is hydrogen / Fuming at twenty million degrees / In that cause of light, the sun." Larson then addresses the "Savior" to "teach me warmth / And gravity through the gentle epithet / In the sentimental glow of twilight, / . . . Easement of the infinite fire."

In his late works Larson attempted to bind together the scientific, the religious, and the poetic in a unifying vision, experimenting with form, diction, and technique in highly ambitious, original, and far-reaching ways. These poems often begin with a humorous, even flippant title, such as "Quirky Quarks," found in *Selected Poems of Clinton F. Larson.* The poem begins "from Uhuru," an allusion to the efforts to comprehend infinite structures through the infinitesimal by using space probes, such as X rays and electrical impulses so weak as to be almost imperceptible. "From Uhuru" immediately precedes an asterisk, a lowercase "o," and a capital "O," which together represent developing stars, solar systems, and galaxies.

"Adonoi at the Creation," from *Selected Poems of Clinton F. Larson,* especially captures Larson's efforts to find a unified field linking science, religion, and poetic art. Essentially an ongoing monologue in the mind of Adonoi the Creator, moments after he has set creative forces in motion, the lyric invites a comparison with the biblical account of the first day. The Book of Genesis summarizes the first creative deed with no concern at all for methodology: "And God said, Let there be light. And there was light." Larson implies that God utters this terse statement of cause and effect, a statement that describes how the first day began, from a stance that is wholly outside the act of beginning itself and thus free of time. In striving to understand the event from his position inside time and space as part of an expanding universe governed by relativistic principles, Larson portrays Adonoi as looking into the future physicist's mind. For Larson, the language of the physicist provides a useful, albeit unexpected—and, for some readers, aesthetically unacceptable—set of metaphors and patterns of diction that unites the scientific vision with the poetic pronouncement of a creation myth.

In blending the two visions, Larson begins with what on the surface constitutes the most unpoetic type of language: exponentially rendered measurements of time, space, and temperature, as hypothesized by the scientists to describe the developing sequence of the post-creative events. "Singularly and vastly hot at $10^{-43}$ second at trillions / Of degrees centigrade, burgeoning at $10^{32}$K, . . . / . . . the universe . . . / At this point is but a mote of $10^{-28}$ centimeter in a pylon / Of force irradiating into an inflationary epoch like nylon / In strands and tides to $10^{-24}$ cm." Soon the universe becomes "about the size of an elation / Of egg." At an age of $10^5$ or 100,000— years, matter has cooled to 3000°K, the point at which quasars begin to form. Central to all of these developments and images is the person of the speaker, Adonoi, who approves of the scientist's terminology: "Why banter further about how it is said?" Whether one views the universe as developing from a mythological egg or "an elation / Of egg," the result is the image of a fetal universe. Larson's poem insists on a recognition of the ultimate "doer," someone who acts. Adonoi serves all at once as creator, viewer, and narrator.

Adonoi's determination—similar to that of a modern scientist—to focus on a Unified Field results in the development of the real from the imaginary, particularly with respect to unity: "I $= $ i x $i^3$, that is I AM." The idea of a creation of "something" from "nothing," a mystery that potentially yet insurmountably challenges even the deepest faith, is thus transferred into the realm of fairly basic mathematics— and, at the same time, placed in the center of an aesthetic context.

The relation between scientific and spiritual implications pivots in the poem around Adonoi's pun "My Word!" Whatever man's efforts to understand the methodology of creation, Adonoi willingly accepts such efforts as being valid in a descriptive sense; yet, the search for reality grows pointless unless the doer, along with the method, is found–as well as the moral imperatives that such knowledge entails. Fortunately, the entire created universe as one now knows it continues to exist "on the tip of the tongue / As the Word"–the creative Word of God, the descriptive word of the scientist, and the perceptive word of the poet. When all these are brought together, Larson hints, a complete appreciation for man's place in the universe becomes possible.

Clinton F. Larson died on 10 July 1994. He had great skill as a prosodist and used many traditional forms, especially blank verse, sonnets, and quatrains. He experimented with meters and sound patterns of all types. He sometimes described his writing process as "playing" with words, but writing was never "child's play" for Larson. Throughout his career Larson remained an experimenter in poetic language and techniques; he responded thoughtfully and with a depth of feeling to human experiences of all kinds. Larson's constant and unflagging effort to bring together all the seeming oppositions in life perhaps best characterizes him as a writer, as seen in the lyric, "Unified Field," which–the poet told Evans in many conversations–was Larson's personal favorite.

An endless line cast to a curve in the pearling dark
Allows the universal light.

.  .  .  .  .  .  .  .  .

There, beyond, is the mind's fine tether
That we cannot drop abroad in a meadow where a lark
Rises to warble and trill. We cast our linear wishing
Along the imperial curve, but straighten it to fit
Lines of the parallax whose points are the nearby sun
Of our envisioning. If the two become one, swishing
Infinitesimally then drawn into the infinite heat,
The circling Alpha and Omega, the decimal One.

Larson in effect believed that two views of the same truths actually existed: science and religion, expository analysis and poetry, the pragmatic and the transcendent, the ancient and the ultramodern, the ordinary and the exotic, the complicated and the simple, and the objective observation and the subjective aspiration. He worked tirelessly to combine in his poetry all these opposites and more into a harmonized vision of physical and spiritual forces.

**Interview:**
Edward Geary, "A Conversation with Clinton F. Larson," *Dialogue,* 4 (Autumn 1969): 74–80.

**References:**
Marden J. Clark, "Introduction" in *Centennial Portraits: Brigham Young University Centennial, 1975–76* (Provo, Utah: Brigham Young University Press, ca. 1976), pp. xi–xviii;

David L. Evans, "Introduction" in his *Selected Poems of Clinton F. Larson* (Provo, Utah: Brigham Young University Press, ca. 1988), pp. xi–xv;

Evans, "Introduction" in *Sunwind,* edited by Evans (Orem, Utah: Geneva Steel Corporation, ca. 1990), pp. xiii–xviii;

Karl Keller, "A Pilgrimage of Awe," *Dialogue,* 3 (Spring 1968): 111–118;

Thomas D. Schwartz, "The Erosion of Belief in the Poetry of Clinton F. Larson," M.A. thesis, Brigham Young University, 1977, pp. 53–75;

Schwartz, "Sacrament of Terror: Violence in the Poetry of Clinton F. Larson," *Dialogue,* 9 (Autumn 1978): 39–48.

**Papers:**
Clinton F. Larson's papers are housed at the Harold B. Lee Library at Brigham Young University in Provo, Utah.

# Ursula K. Le Guin

*(21 October 1929 – )*

Zina Petersen
*Brigham Young University*

See also the Le Guin entries in *DLB 8: Twentieth-Century Amerian Science-Fiction Writers* and *DLB 52: American Writers for Children Since 1960: Fiction.*

BOOKS: *Rocannon's World* (New York: Ace, 1966; London: Tandem, 1972; revised edition, New York: Harper & Row, 1977);

*Planet of Exile* (New York: Ace, 1966; London: Tandem, 1972);

*City of Illusions* (New York: Ace, 1967; London: Gollancz, 1971);

*A Wizard of Earthsea* (Berkeley: Parnassus Press, 1968; London: Gollancz, 1971);

*The Left Hand of Darkness* (New York: Ace, 1969; London: Macdonald, 1969);

*The Lathe of Heaven* (New York: Scribners, 1971; London: Gollancz, 1972);

*The Tombs of Atuan* (New York: Atheneum, 1971; London: Gollancz, 1972);

*The Word for World Is Forest* (New York: Berkley, 1972; London: Gollancz, 1977);

*The Farthest Shore* (New York: Atheneum, 1972; London: Gollancz, 1973);

*From Elfland to Poughkeepsie* (Portland, Ore.: Pendragon, 1973);

*The Dispossessed: An Ambiguous Utopia* (New York: Harper & Row, 1974; London: Gollancz, 1974);

*Dreams Must Explain Themselves,* compiled by Andrew Porter (New York: Algol Press, 1975);

*Le Guin's Three Short Science Fiction Stories* (Tokyo: Sansyusya, 1975);

*Wild Angels of the Open Hills* (Santa Barbara: Capra Press, 1975);

*The Wind's Twelve Quarters: Short Stories* (New York: Harper & Row, 1975; London: Gollancz, 1976);

*Nebula Award Stories Eleven* (London: Gollancz, 1976; New York: Harper & Row, 1977);

*Very Far Away from Anywhere Else* (New York: Atheneum, 1976); republished as *A Very Long Way from Anywhere Else* (London: Gollancz, 1976);

*Orsinian Tales* (New York: Harper & Row, 1976; London: Gollancz, 1977);

*Ursula K. Le Guin (photograph © Marion Wood Kolisch; from the dust jacket for* Searoad: Chronicles of Klatsand, *1991)*

*The Language of the Night: Essays on Fantasy and Science Fiction,* edited by Susan Wood (New York: Putnam, 1979; London: Women's Press, 1989);

*Leese Webster* (New York: Atheneum, 1979; London: Gollancz, 1981);

*Malafrena* (New York: Berkley, 1979; London: Gollancz, 1980);

*Tillai and Tylissos,* by Le Guin and Theodora Kroeber (St. Helena, Berkeley & Portland: Red Bull, 1979);

*The Beginning Place* (New York: Harper & Row, 1980); republished as *Threshold* (London: Gollancz, 1980);

*Hard Words and Other Poems* (New York: Harper & Row, 1981);

*The Adventure of Cobbler's Rune* (New Castle, Va.: Cheap Street, 1982);

*The Compass Rose: Short Stories* (Portland & San Francisco: Pendragon Press/Underwood-Miller, 1982; London: Gollancz, 1983);

*The Eye of the Heron* (London: Gollancz, 1982; New York: Harper & Row, 1983);

*In the Red Zone* (Northridge, Cal.: Lord John Press, 1983);

*Solomon Leviathan's Nine Hundred and Thirty-First Trip around the World* (New Castle, Va.: Cheap Street, 1984);

*The Visionary: The Life Story of Flicker of the Serpentine of Telina-na,* by LeGuin; with *Wonders Hidden: Audubon's Early Years,* by Scott Russell Sanders (Santa Barbara: Capra Press, 1984);

*King Dog: A Screenplay,* by Le Guin; with *Dostoevsky: A Screenplay,* by Raymond Carver and Tess Gallagher (Santa Barbara: Capra Press, 1985);

*Always Coming Home* (New York: Harper & Row, 1985; London: Gollancz, 1986);

*Buffalo Gals and Other Animal Presences* (Santa Barbara: Capra Press, 1987; London: Gollancz, 1990);

*Catwings* (New York: Orchard Books, 1988);

*A Visit from Dr. Katz* (New York: Atheneum, 1988; London: Collins, 1988);

*Wild Oats and Fireweed: New Poems* (New York: Perennial Library, 1988);

*Catwings Return* (New York: Orchard Books, 1989);

*Dancing at the Edge of the World: Thoughts on Words, Women, Places* (New York: Grove, 1989; London: Gollancz, 1989);

*Fire and Stone* (New York: Atheneum, 1989);

*Tehanu: The Last Book of Earthsea* (New York: Atheneum, 1990; London: Gollancz, 1990);

*No Boats* (Seattle & Portland: Ygor & Buntho Make Books, 1991);

*Searoad: Chronicles of Klatsand* (New York: HarperCollins, 1991; London: Gollancz, 1992);

*A Ride on the Red Mare's Back* (New York: Orchard Books, 1992);

*Fish Soup* (New York: Atheneum, 1992);

*The Ones Who Walk Away from Omelas* (Mankato, Minn.: Creative Education, 1993);

*Earthsea Revisioned* (Cambridge, Mass.: Children's Literature New England / Cambridge, U.K.: Green Bay Publications, 1993);

*A Fisherman of the Inland Sea: Science Fiction Stories* (New York: HarperPrism, 1994);

*Going Out with Peacocks and Other Poems* (New York: HarperPerennial, 1994);

*Wonderful Alexander and the Catwings* (New York: Orchard Books, 1994);

*Four Ways to Forgiveness* (New York: HarperPrism, 1995);

*Unlocking the Air and Other Stories* (New York: HarperCollins, 1996);

*Steering the Craft: Exercises and Discussions on Story Writing for the Lone Navigator or the Mutinous Crew* (Portland, Ore.: Eighth Mountain Press, 1998);

*Jane on Her Own: A Catwings Tale* (New York: Orchard Books, 1999);

*Sixty Odd: New Poems* (Boston: Shambhala, 1999);

*Tom Mouse and Mrs. Howe* (New York: DK, 1999);

*The Telling* (New York: Harcourt, 2000);

*Tales from Earthsea* (New York: Harcourt, 2001);

*The Other Wind* (New York: Harcourt, 2001);

*The Birthday of the World and Other Stories* (New York: HarperCollins, 2002).

**Collections:** *Three Hainish Novels*—comprises *Rocannon's World, Planet of Exile,* and *City of Illusions* (Garden City, N.Y.: Doubleday, 1967);

*Five Complete Novels*—comprises *Rocannon's World, Planet of Exile, City of Illusions, The Left Hand of Darkness,* and *The Word for World Is Forest* (New York: Avenel Books, 1985).

OTHER: *Wild Angels of the Open Hills,* words by Le Guin; musical score by Joseph Schwantner (New York: C. F. Peters, 1978);

*Interfaces: An Anthology of Speculative Fiction,* edited by Le Guin and Virginia Kidd (New York: Ace, 1980);

*Edges: Thirteen New Tales from the Borderlands of the Imagination,* edited by Le Guin and Kidd (New York: Pocket Books, 1980);

*Lairs of Soundings,* words by Le Guin, musical score by Dan Locklair (Westbury, N.Y.: Pro Art, 1982);

*Lockerbones/Airbones,* words by Le Guin, musical score by Elinor Armer (Berkeley, Cal.: Fallen Leaf Press, 1985);

*Tao Song,* words by Le Guin, musical score by David York (Portland, Ore.: York, 1987);

*Way of the Water's Going: Images of the Northern California Coastal Range,* text by Le Guin, photographs by Ernest Waugh and Alan Nicholson (New York: Harper & Row, 1989);

*Blue Moon over Thurman Street,* text by Le Guin and Roger Dorband, introduction by Le Guin, photographs by Dorband (Portland: NewSage Press, 1993);

*The Norton Book of Science Fiction: North American Science Fiction, 1960–1990,* edited by Le Guin and Brian Attebery, introduction by Le Guin (New York: Norton, 1993);

"Unchosen Love," in *Killing Me Softly,* edited by Dozois (New York: HarperPrism, 1995);

Cover for the 1987 paperback edition of Le Guin's complex
1985 work about the Kesh, a people of the distant future
who live in what is now California

*Uses of Music in Uttermost Parts,* words by Le Guin, musical score by Armer (Port Washington, N.Y.: Koch International Classics, 1995);

"The Matter of Seggri," in *The Year's Best Science Fiction, Twelfth Annual Collection,* edited by Gardner Dozois (New York: St. Martin's Press, 1995); also included in *Flying Cups and Saucers,* edited by Debbie Notkin and the Secret Feminist Cabal (Cambridge, Mass.: Edgewood Press, 1998) pp. 351–382;

Mark Twain, *The Diaries of Adam and Eve,* introduction by Le Guin (New York: Oxford University Press, 1996);

*The Twins, The Dream: Two Voices (Las Gemalas, El Sueño: Dos Voces),* translated by Le Guin and Dianna Bellissi, introduction by Le Guin (Houston, Tex.: Arte Publico Press, 1996);

"Coming of Age in Karhide," *Year's Best SF,* edited by David G. Hartwell (New York: HarperPrism, 1996);

"Solitude," *Nebula Awards 31,* edited by Pamela Sargent (New York: Harcourt Brace, 1997), pp. 29–58;

*Tao te Ching: A Book about the Way and the Power of the Way,* translated into English by Le Guin and J. P. Seaton (Boston: Shambhala, 1997);

"Dragonfly," in *Legends,* edited by Robert Silverberg (New York: Tor, 1998), pp. 273–320;

"Old Music and the Slave Women," in *Far Horizons,* edited by Silverberg (New York: Avon Eos, 1999), pp. 7–52.

SELECTED PERIODICAL PUBLICATIONS– UNCOLLECTED: "The Lost Children," *Thirteenth Moon* (January 1996): 9–10;

"Mountain Ways," *Asimov's SF* (August 1996): 14–39;

"Which Side Am I On, Anyway?" *Frontiers* (September/ December 1996);

"All Happy Families," *Michigan Quarterly* (Winter 1997);

"Six Great SF Movies That Could Be Made without Audible Explosions in the Vacuum of Space," *Fantasy and Science Fiction* (July 1998): 115–116;

"The Island of the Immortals," *Amazing* (Fall 1998): 32–37.

Best known for her works of speculative fiction, Ursula K. Le Guin made her name as the foremost early feminist voice in fantasy and science fiction. She is also notable as one of few to break the imposing barrier of respectable academic disdain for what she has called the "ghetto" genres of fantasy, science fiction, and children's literature. In fact, Le Guin's work is collected more frequently into literature anthologies than that of any other science-fiction author, in the 1980s surpassing that of Arthur C. Clarke and Ray Bradbury. She is readily accepted by the establishment as a "serious" literary writer rather than regarded as a mere genre writer. She finds these distinctions problematic, with good reason: no writing exists without some kind of genre, serious or not; and she herself has produced works of serious and unserious literature in all the genres she explores. Le Guin believes beauty and imagination, not market, should drive artistic activity. Science-fiction, fantasy, and children's books are wide open to beautiful and imaginative experimentation, especially since the postmodern breakdown of canonical and generic distinctions typified in the allegedly mainstream but strange works of Jorge Luis Borges, Toni Morrison, Gloria Naylor, and Isabel Allende. Le Guin writes fantasy, science fiction, young-adult fiction, mainstream fiction, nonfiction, short story and novella collections, poetry, screenplays, translations, children's picture books, dances, and whatever else presents itself at the moment as a vehicle for her discoveries. She is not restricted by convention or expectation but writes, as fellow ghetto author Orson Scott Card notes, "what she believes in and cares about . . . and lets us sort ourselves into communities as we respond."

A self-described "California kid," Ursula Kroeber was born 21 October 1929, the fourth child and only daughter of Theodora Kracaw Kroeber and Alfred L. Kroeber. Alfred Kroeber taught anthropology at the University of California at Berkeley, and Theodora Kroeber, who had a master's degree in psychology, compiled and popularized Native American stories; she also wrote the biography of Ishi, the last living Yahi Indian, whom the Kroebers had befriended before his death in 1916. The Kroebers provided for a richly imaginative future for their four children, and Ursula set about immediately to fulfill it with a fiercely creative childhood. The Berkeley area was home during her school years, and the family spent their summers on their forty-acre Napa Valley ranch. Now residents of Portland, Oregon, Le Guin and her husband, historian Charles Le Guin, remain devoted to the West Coast and the environmental issues that concern it.

Ursula grew up happy and well loved, with her parents erring if at all on the side of affection and patience, teaching all their children by example the value of listening carefully to others. Their home was a gathering place for people of many different cultures, and storytelling and story collecting were her parents' professions, what she saw grown-ups doing. She never had to make a conscious decision to be a writer and share stories, because she never expected *not* to be a story sharer. At age fourteen she discovered her father's copy of the *Tao te Ching* (A.D. 220), which she found wonderful. The Chinese scripture became a centrally important guide in her own thinking, and its tenets and gentle philosophies figure prominently in her writing; in 1997 she published her own version, *Tao te Ching: A Book about the Way and the Power of the Way,* with notes on Taoist thought and on her treatment of the work.

Ursula Kroeber received the best available education, graduating from Radcliffe in 1951 and going on to graduate school. In her last year of college she had an unexpected pregnancy, a situation far more socially difficult then than now. Her parents' help in her decision to terminate it and their obtaining for her a then-illegal abortion were painful and shaping events for her. After her secure and trusting earlier life, encountering the irresponsible cowardice of a lover and the stark finality of abortion were disillusionments that ultimately contributed to the complexity of her feminism and to her ongoing support for individual rights, as well as to motifs of betrayal, loss, and consequence in her work.

For graduate school she attended Columbia University, receiving her M.A. degree in 1952 and winning her first Fulbright fellowship for study in Europe. On her way to England in 1953, aboard the *Queen Mary,* she met history student Charles Le Guin. They were married 22 December 1953 in Paris, and Ursula gave up her Ph.D. work in order to live her life and write her words. Her daughters, Elisabeth and Caroline, were born in 1957 and 1959; her son, Theodore, was born in 1964. In the 1960s, as both her children and her reputation as a writer grew, she was able to devote more time to writing. By the mid 1970s she had become one of the most highly respected writers in the field of science fiction and had earned several prestigious awards.

Le Guin is urgently committed to the freedom of the individual. Concern with individuals is a central motif in her writing, although such a claim should be made with caution; generalizing or labeling themes makes it easy to lose the power of the explorations of freedom to be found in the individual works. Finding freedom is never simple in a Le Guin story, and it is never easy. Freedom is not mere lack of restraint, but mindfulness—a realization of the fundamental interconnectedness of choice and consequence. The fictitious worlds she creates may present a limitless range of choices, but no choice is without results. To be human is to recognize this fact; to ignore it is to be less than human. Thus, in a Le Guin story, any sentient, self-aware being is a person, a human, no matter what its extraterrestrial or fantastical physiology, and the monsters are the unaware. The science fiction Le Guin writes is thus social science fiction, and her other fiction is also colored by her understanding of anthropology and sociology, using such elements as journeys of discovery, tradition and ritual, archetype, cultural clash, societies in flux, gender dynamics, and the interplay of individuals within communities.

Many of Le Guin's stories take place in one of four major world settings: the communities of the Ekumen, a confederation stemming from the explorative history of the planet Hain; Earthsea, her fantasy archipelago world where magic is a function of balance; Orsinia, an imaginary Eastern European country with political history in common with the countries of Le Guin's own ancestry; and western North America, particularly the endangered and environmentally delicate Northwest coastal regions where Le Guin has lived most of her life.

Though Le Guin's first published story was set in the imaginary Europe of Orsinia, her earliest novels—*Rocannon's World* (1966), *Planet of Exile* (1966), and *City of Illusions* (1967)—are set in the Hainish universe and deal with alien cultures from Terran viewpoints. The Hainish universe is also the setting for her two novels that

BUFFALO GALS
And Other Animal Presences

URSULA K. LE GUIN

*Dust jacket for a 1987 collection of Le Guin's short stories*

won the unprecedented double honor of receiving both the Hugo and the Nebula awards–*The Left Hand of Darkness* (1969) and *The Dispossessed: An Ambiguous Utopia* (1974). Twelve other short stories and novellas have Hain as a background setting, as does her 2000 novel *The Telling.*

Le Guin began her foray into young adult and children's literature at the invitation of publisher Herman Schein. She responded to his request with *A Wizard of Earthsea* (1968), which, beginning with the Boston Globe Horn Book Award, won immediate and repeated accolades. The Earthsea books tell the story of Ged, a young man with an obvious gift for magic, and of his adventures and training in becoming a wizard. *A Wizard of Earthsea* deals with his apprenticeship and his need to encounter and own his shadow in order to have the balance he needs to be not just a wizard but a human. Le Guin's initial trilogy of Earthsea books has been compared to J. R. R. Tolkien's *Lord of the Rings* (1954–1955), a comparison she finds flattering, and C. S. Lewis's *Chronicles of Narnia* (collected in 1965), a comparison that

makes her nervous. A self-described "congenital non-Christian," Le Guin would rather let allegory alone; Lewis's blatantly religious works are not to her taste as much as are Tolkien's open-ended mythologies.

Le Guin's Hainish novel *The Left Hand of Darkness,* which won the Nebula award in 1969 and the Hugo in 1970, began for Le Guin as a thought experiment about a culture that had never fought a war. Intriguingly, the possibility of such a society then led backward in its logic not to highly evolved idealism, or to primitivism or timidity, but to the absence of fixed sexual identity. In the course of the book the hermaphroditic character Estraven helps the Terran Genly Ai to confront his personal resistance to the natives' different reproductive strategy, as well as Ai's own inability to reconcile his inadequate ideas of purely human love with his gender-determined notions of love.

Throughout the next few years Le Guin published *The Tombs of Atuan* (1971), which is the second Earthsea novel; *The Lathe of Heaven* (1971), a science fiction thriller; and *The Farthest Shore* (1972), the third and then presumably the last of the Earthsea "trilogy." *The Tombs of Atuan* continues the wizard Ged's story, but tells it slant, from the point of view of a young woman, Tenar, who has been stripped of her identity and assigned to be "the Eaten One," a puppet high priestess for the gods of a decadent religion. Ged restores Tenar's name and self to her, and together they escape the suffocating sterility of the tombs. Le Guin took a break from Earthsea and published *The Lathe of Heaven* in 1971; it was made into a PBS movie in 1978. An Earth-based science-fiction novel about the conflict between a man with a knack for dreaming reality into existence and the mad scientist who wants to use his patient's power for world control, the book features the moral importance of acceptance and noneffort and is among Le Guin's most Taoist works. Returning to Ged and Tenar's universe, her next publication was *The Farthest Shore.* This last offering of the initial Earthsea trilogy deals with the frightening possibility of the absolute rejection of death. In this work, Ged must journey to the Otherworld and restore the order and balance of life and death. In going to stop the passageway that allows death to be temporary rather than final, Ged takes a traveling companion, Prince Arren, who is destined to become the first high king of Earthsea. *The Tombs of Atuan* and *The Farthest Shore* won many awards between them, including Newbery Honors, for *The Tombs of Atuan,* the Lewis Carroll Shelf Award, the American Library Association honor citation, and the National Book Award for *The Farthest Shore.*

Le Guin's 1974 Hainish novel, *The Dispossessed,* won both Hugo and Nebula awards for 1975. This novel is Le Guin's extended experiment with anarchism, the idea of a community of individuals committed to freedom at its most radical and thus at its most necessarily ethical. The plot involves a gifted physicist, Shevek, who discovers principles that will solve the space/time problems prohibiting interstellar communications. An anarchist idealist, he hopes to share his ideas with the largest community possible and travels from his home world to a neighboring planet in order to do so. Shevek's position as an envoy of an ethically higher cause serves as the background against which the disadvantages of the various social systems of the book are highlighted. The novel is told as a circle, alternating chapters of Shevek's present adventure and his history to the point of his journey, the final chapters catching up to a conclusion of Shevek's return to his home.

Le Guin's next publication was the short story collection *Orsinian Tales* (1976). The word *Orsinia* is from the same root as *Ursula* (bear); the stories are in effect tales of Le Guin's own archetypal background, a primordial history of imaginary ancestry and autobiography. Jungian universalism is appropriate for wizards and space travelers, but cultural particulars are a focus in this work, and Le Guin tries to capture the personality types of an ethnicity. The stories take place in different times from 1150 to 1962, arranged achronologically. Their order in the book seems at first to be haphazard, but as Elizabeth Cummins points out, the "skewed" ordering urges the reader to see connections other than merely sequential ones. With this device, Le Guin balances perception of time as moment with time as duration. Thus, she situates each of her characters inside *chronos,* or clock time, as well as *kairos,* or mythological time, the once-upon-a-time of fairy tales and dreams. The collection concludes with an intrusive narrator's statement, the only one in the book: "I do not know if it happens now, even in imaginary countries." This statement reinforces the real/unreal mixture in the tales, highlighting without solving the problems of the relationship of personal mythology to personal history.

Around this time Le Guin also produced her longest Orsinian work, the novel *Malafrena* (1979), and a young adult novel, *The Beginning Place* (1980), which ties a fantastic otherworld to present-day California. Set in the early 1800s, *Malafrena* is a political coming-of-age story for a young aristocrat. Itale Sorde, a university student full of revolutionary catchphrases and hope for the people, sets out to participate in the social transformations of the turn of the nineteenth century. His adventures take him to other countries, to prison, into battle, and ultimately home again, aware that his entire life will be journeys of discovery. Contrasted to his traveling is the subtler growing up of his sister, whose viewpoint is shown in alternating chapters, a structure

similar to that of *The Dispossessed.* Laura has no opportunity to venture out (or grow) as Itale does, but she represents the usually invisible female function of stability that makes possible the questing of men. Although half-set in a dreamworld, her next book, *The Beginning Place,* is the story of two young people's efforts to escape the oppressions of their dreary and damaging home lives in an ugly, overdeveloped, undernourished American suburb. In this coming-of-age story, the protagonists discover and explore a mysterious wooded area near their homes and find that the woods are an intersection to another world, where they must face and overcome the challenges they had hoped to escape.

Keeping the California setting but little else, Le Guin's next major effort, *Always Coming Home* (1985), is perhaps her most thoroughly Western work. Set in the extreme distant future country of Napa Valley and featuring the Kesh, Le Guin's imaginary "new" "ancient" inhabitants, this work is an archaeological dig in mixed media. It includes a novel; intricate anthropological details of the characters' cultures, including artwork, recipes, a lexicon, and poems in the invented language of her characters; the commentary of Pandora, the anthropologist guide who has opened up the whole problematic project; and a tape of music of the Kesh, composed and set with Le Guin's Kesh lyrics, by Todd Barton. As are many of Le Guin's anthropological works, *Always Coming Home* is more thought driven than plot driven, and thus the ethnography of the work is as central as its characters. The distant future California of its setting has been fractured, and the world of today does not exist. Le Guin's introductory "first note" begins, "The people in this book might be going to have lived a long, long time from now in Northern California." She makes complication but no deception in the six-word verb, of tense (future) or aspect (perfect and past-perfect) or mood (subjunctive). As with the past of Orsinia, she does not know that the future of this California will be factual—merely that she is telling the truth. *Always Coming Home* is a complicated experience in imaginary cultures. The complexity of the book is a testament to Le Guin's confidence in the world she made.

The Native American slant continues in Le Guin's 1984 short story "Buffalo Gals Won't You Come Out Tonight"—the title story of *Buffalo Gals and Other Animal Presences* (1987)—as the spirits of Native American animal people interact with a receptive human person. Le Guin describes human traits as well as features of animals as she develops the characters, skirting in and out of animistic generalizations and personal detail. In the story, a plane crash in the desert has left the only survivor, a little girl, blinded in one eye. She is found and rescued by the trickster Coyote, who takes the child back with her to the dwellings of the Old People, the animals of the desert, who help the little girl survive. Bluejay, irascible bird and man in a bright blue shirt, replaces the little girl's lost eye with one he has made of pine pitch; after Coyote blesses the new eye with a thorough cleansing, the girl can see the spiritual truths of the world as well as the physical phenomena. When Horse agrees to carry her to a settlement of the New People (*homo sapiens* humans), the child sees both the town and a horrifying void in the fabric of spiritual reality. She cannot bear the thought of leaving the more real people of the desert to go back to human life and returns to live with Coyote, whom she loves despite the relative chaos and riskiness of Coyote's life. Coyote's risks catch up to her, and on an outing close to the human town she eats poisoned bait and dies. The devastated child gets some small comfort from Grandmother Spider, who assures her that Coyote "gets killed all the time" and promises the girl that she can keep her new eye, her new vision, as she goes back to live with her own people, and that the natural world will never be too far away.

In 1990 Le Guin revisited Ged and Tenar, publishing a fourth Earthsea novel, the prematurely titled *Tehanu: The Last Book of Earthsea,* which won the Nebula award. Ged, having lost all his power of wizardry in the efforts of *The Farthest Shore,* in *Tehanu* has become an ordinary man. As an ordinary man, however, he is free to love an ordinary woman. He rediscovers one in Tenar, now a widow with her children grown, who has taken in a badly abused and disfigured little girl, Therru. A hero in her own right, although no one but her true kindred, the dragon Kalessin, sees beyond her scars, Therru travels with Tenar to help sick friends, tend house, run the farm that by law belongs to Tenar's useless son, and heal the psychic wounds of Ged, who is demoralized and ashamed of his new powerlessness. Tenar and Ged have both lost the privileges and powers of their youth, but Tenar's wry acceptance of her loss helps to mellow Ged's bitterness, and the two of them choose to live in calm now that the days of their youthful adventuring are over.

During the 1990s Le Guin published mainly collections, including *Searoad: Chronicles of Klatsand* (1991), a critically well-received collection of interpenetrating stories from the points of view and time of various inhabitants of a tiny Oregon coastal village, including their concerns about the community and the land that sustains it; *A Fisherman of the Inland Sea: Science Fiction Stories* (1994), a collection of science-fiction short stories; *Unlocking the Air and Other Stories* (1996), which gathers many of the stories Le Guin published in mainstream magazines and journals and includes Orsinian as well as Western American settings; and the Hainish *Four Ways to Forgive-*

*ness* (1995). The four novellas in *Four Ways to Forgiveness* feature interrelated characters and events, but each is told from a different character's point of view. The stories take place on a pair of planets, Werel and Yeowe, which have a history of slavery and ownership based on race; every person is either an "owner" or an "asset." In addition to their racial segregation, the cultures of slaves and bosses have differing religious systems, which Le Guin gets absolutely right according to anthropological principles. The owner classes worship abundance and material security associated with matriarchal religions; their object of worship is the goddess Tual, who represents, as do all fertility or sexuality goddesses, success and luxury through profusion. The asset and warrior classes of Werel and Yeowe follow the masculinist teachings of the "Arkamye," a book of scripture similar in its idealization of endurance, sacrifice, and strife to the Judeo-Christian Bible. Neither religion is psychologically healthy, and each system serves to confirm established beliefs about reality and thus to maintain the hegemonic status quo. As its title suggests, this book is painful but deeply compassionate, presenting, as it must, both the reasons forgiveness is necessary and the soulful creativity and resilience of the individual characters who do forgive.

The turn of the millennium was a busy time for Le Guin: she completed fifth and sixth books in the Earthsea universe and one more in the Hainish. *Tales from Earthsea* (2001) is a collection of novellas exploring various times and places in the history of Earthsea, including a love story of a wizard who sacrifices his magical gift for love; the story of the founding of the school for wizards on Roke Island; and the story of Irian, a woman who dares breach the male-only law of the magical school in Earthsea and reveals her own powers to be those of the ancient dragons. This last story, "Dragonfly," serves as a bridge to the latest Earthsea novel, *The Other Wind* (2001), which takes the reader back to Ged, Tenar, and Therru, who now goes openly by her true name, Tehanu. *The Other Wind* begins well after Ged has lost his powers and is no longer Archmage of Earthsea. While his wife Tenar and daughter Tehanu are away at the King's court on Havnor, Ged is visited by a relatively minor wizard named Alder, who is having troubling dreams about the land of death. In the dreams the dead can reach out to him, speak to him, and even touch him, none of which Ged experienced when he traveled to that realm. Knowing that the trouble in the world is far greater than a village wizard's nightmares, Ged sends Alder to Lebannen, and from there the implications of Alder's dreams unfold. The ancient history of Earthsea notes that dragons and humans were once a single race and that an ideological division between them resulted in

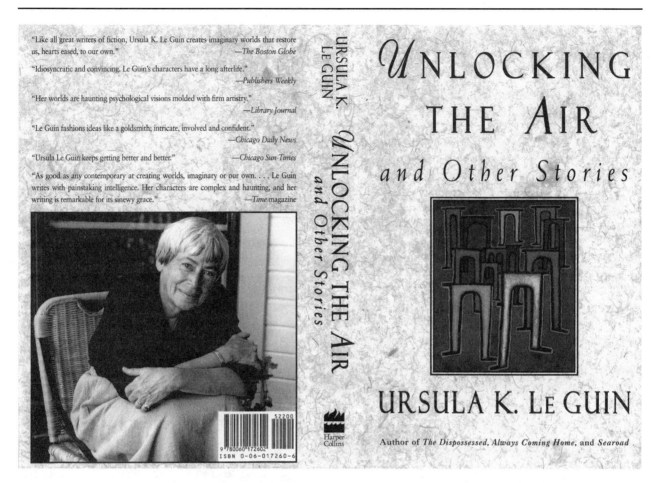

*Dust jacket for a 1996 collection of Le Guin's stories that includes pieces set in western North America
and in her imaginary Eastern European country, Orsinia*

the split: dragons chose freedom, air, and fire; "humans" chose power, earth, and water. To heal the world requires the healing of this primordial split, and the reunion of all the elements of the world will cure the ills of both dead and living.

In addition to science fiction and fantasy, Le Guin writes a considerable amount in other arenas as well. She has published two books of essays, *The Language of the Night: Essays on Fantasy and Science Fiction* (1979) and *Dancing at the Edge of the World: Thoughts on Words, Women, Places* (1989), and an instructional book for creative writing, *Steering the Craft: Exercises and Discussions on Story Writing for the Lone Navigator or the Mutinous Crew* (1998). An area that she speaks strongly about, however, is the respect due, and not forthcoming, to authors of books for children. Writing books for children is simple, she says, "just as simple as bringing them up." Brian Attebery is among a growing cadre of critics who see Le Guin's children's literature as some of her most artistically adept and satisfying. To tell a story for a child is to speak to an audience far more attuned to the sounds of language than most adults, who usually listen for plot.

Le Guin has written the text for five picture books, with various illustrators, and a four-part series, Catwings, about a family of five flying cats. The Catwings books– *Catwings* (1988), *Catwings Return* (1989), *Wonderful Alexander and the Catwings* (1994), and *Jane on Her Own* (1999)–are gently told stories about individuality and freedom. Cats with wings are a genetic rarity, and their mother, a wingless alley cat, knows it. She sends her litter out into the world, away from her protection but also away from the dangers of the city, and into their adventures. This cat is a good mother, recognizing her responsibility to release her children because of their specialness, allowing them to live free from captivity or experimentation.

Those who read Le Guin for her sharp social commentary or her sweeping imagination are sometimes brought up short on discovering her rather wicked sense of humor. In the laboratory of thought that is science fiction, imagined hypotheses are distilled and posed for the experiment of story to answer: What if X? Sometimes the answer is terrifying, but sometimes it is hilarious. As Le Guin points out in her Introduction to the *Norton Book of Science Fiction: North American Science Fiction, 1960–1990* (1993), language, particularly metaphor, contributes significantly to the experimental design of science fiction; much of her parody in the area participates in a literalization of the figurative, playing with cliché and reality. In "Schroedinger's Cat," collected in *Buffalo Gals and Other Animal Presences,* Le Guin pushes both metaphor and thought-experiment into a convoluted relationship with reality until—as in the famous physics thought-experiment from which it takes its name and plot—neither the reader nor the characters have any way of knowing what the state of reality is. Her story "Intracom" in *The Compass Rose: Short Stories* (1982) is not only a devastating parody of *Star Trek* but also a satire by extension of the masculine tradition of referring to ship-as-body and vessel-as-female, again by making the figure of speech literal. Another technique Le Guin uses in her humor is deadpan scientific style and jargon in "articles" about scientific impossibilities, as in her stories "Some Approaches to the Problem of the Shortage of Time," and "The Author of the Acacia Seeds and Other Extracts from *The Journal of the Association of Therolinguistics,*" both in *The Compass Rose,* and "Ascent of the North Face" in *A Fisherman of the Inland Sea* (1994).

Even though her gifts for whole-world vision, for characterization, and for seeing implication in choices are remarkable in her prose fiction, Le Guin's word craft, the tools and materials of raw language, are at their most exposed and challenging, their purest and starkest, in her poetry. She is not a chatty or casual poet nor a balladist; her poetry is seldom lyrical narrative, and even her rhymed and metered poems can sting as they dance. Charlotte Spivack says of her early collection of poems, *Wild Angels of the Open Hills* (1975), "The sparse surface is deepened by mythic roots rather than elaborated by figures of speech." The fineness of her detail has only increased in the poetry she has written since. Le Guin now has ten collections of verse, including her 1998 version/translation of the *Tao te Ching* and a collaboration of poems and translations done with Argentinian poet Diana Bellessi, *The Twins, The Dream: Two Voices (Las Gemalas, El Sueño: Dos Voces)* (1996). The other collections are *Tillai and Tylissos* (1979), which she wrote with and for her ailing mother; *Hard Words and Other Poems* (1981); *In the Red Zone* (1983); *Wild Oats and Fireweed* (1988); *No Boats* (1991); *Blue Moon over Thurman Street* (1993), poems that complement and accompany black and white photos by Roger Dorband; *Going Out with Peacocks* (1994); and her latest book of poetry, the critically acclaimed volume *Sixty Odd: New Poems* (1999).

Ursula K. Le Guin was probably the first woman author to reject, practically and critically, the reduction of science fiction to the macho Caucasian techno-novels of the 1940s and 1950s, the single plot of which she has summarized as "Dick White and his raygun defeat the Mongloobian hordes." She was also the first fantasy author to do for a non-Christian religious philosophy—Taoism—what C. S. Lewis had done for Christian philosophy: she gave it a mythologically satisfying setting in a successful story for young people. She defies critics who seem hopeful and pleased to announce that she has "grown" away from science fiction, fantasy, or children's literature whenever she writes in another vein; such hopes are usually dashed as she grows right back into it, with yet another superior work in a supposedly inferior genre. Le Guin remains an activist for feminism, tolerance, environmental intelligence, and freedom for all the earth's creatures.

**Interviews:**

"Ursula K. Le Guin: In a World of Her Own," *Mother Jones* (January 1984): 23–27, 38–53;

Larry McCafferry and Sinda Gregory, "An Interview with Ursula K. Le Guin," *The Missouri Review,* 7, no. 2 (1984): 64–85;

Nicholas O'Connell, "Ursula K. Le Guin," in his *At the Field's End: Interviews with Twenty Pacific Northwest Writers* (Seattle: Madrona, 1987), pp. 19–38;

"Gender: The Enduring Paradox," Video (WETA and the Smithsonian Institution, Producers, 1991);

Jonathan White, *Talking on the Water: Conversations about Nature and Creativity* (Los Angeles: Sierra Club Books, 1994);

Eric M. Heideman, "An Interview with Ursula Le Guin," in *Tales of the Unanticipated: A Magazine of the Minnesota Science Fiction Society,* 18 (1997/1998): 32–36.

**Bibliographies:**

Elizabeth Cummins Cogell, *Ursula K. Le Guin: Primary and Secondary Bibliography* (Boston: G. K. Hall, 1983);

David Bratman, *Ursula K. Le Guin: A Primary Bibliography* (Oakland, Cal.: Potlatch 4, 1995).

**References:**

Brian Attebery, "Growing Up with Ursula K. Le Guin: Ursula K. Le Guin and Children's Literature," unpublished paper given at Hollins College, July 1998;

James Bittner, *Approaches to the Fiction of Ursula K. Le Guin* (Ann Arbor: University of Michigan Research Press, 1984; Essex: Bowker, 1984);

Harold Bloom, *Modern Critical Interpretations: Ursula K. Le Guin's The Left Hand of Darkness* (New York: Chelsea House, 1987);

Bloom, ed., *Modern Critical Views: Ursula K. Le Guin* (New York: Chelsea House, 1986);

Barbara J. Bucknall, *Ursula K. Le Guin* (New York: Ungar, 1981);

Orson Scott Card, ed., *Future on Fire* (New York: Tor Books, 1991);

Elizabeth Cummins, *Understanding Ursula K. Le Guin* (Columbia: University of South Carolina Press, 1990);

Joe DeBolt, *Ursula K. Le Guin: Voyager to Inner Lands and to Outer Space* (Port Washington, N.Y.: Kennikat Press, 1979);

Peter Fitting, "The Turn from Utopia in Recent Feminist Fiction," in *Feminism, Utopia, and Narrative*, edited by Libby Falk Jones and Sarah Webster Goodwin (Knoxville: University of Tennessee Press, 1990), pp. 141–158;

Len Hatfield, "From Master to Brother: Shifting the Balance of Authority in Ursula K. Le Guin's *The Farthest Shore* and *Tehanu*," *Children's Literature*, 21 (1993): 43–65;

Margarete Keulen, *Radical Imagination: Feminist Conceptions of the Future in Ursula K. Le Guin, Marge Piercy and Sally Miller Gearhart* (New York: Peter Lang, 1991);

Mario Klarer, "Gender and the 'Simultaneity Principle': Ursula Le Guin's *The Dispossessed*," *Mosaic*, 25 (Spring 1992): 107–121;

Perry Nodelman, response to 1993 article on Ursula K. Le Guin by Len Hatfield, *Children's Literature*, 23 (1995): 179–201;

Joseph Olander and Martin Greenburg, eds., *Ursula K. Le Guin* (New York: Taplinger, 1979);

Suzanne Elizabeth Reid, *Presenting Ursula K. Le Guin* (New York: Twayne, 1997);

Bernard Selinger, *Le Guin and Identity in Contemporary Fiction* (Ann Arbor: University of Michigan Press, 1988);

George Edgar Slusser, *The Farthest Shores of Ursula K. Le Guin,* Popular Writers of Today: The Milford Series (San Bernardino, Cal.: Borgo, 1976);

Judith A. Spector, "The Functions of Sexuality in the Science Fiction of Russ, Piercy, and Le Guin," in *Erotic Universe: Sexuality and Fantastic Literature*, edited by Donald Palumbo (New York: Greenwood Press, 1986), pp. 197–207;

Charlotte Spivack, *Ursula K. Le Guin* (Boston: Twayne, 1984);

Darko Suvin, ed., "The Science Fiction of Ursula K. Le Guin," *Science-Fiction Studies*, 2 (1975);

Ann Welton, "Earthsea Revisited: Tehanu and Feminism (Ursula Le Guin has never shrunk from addressing large issues)," *Voice of Youth Advocates,* 14 (April 1991): 14–16–also, Margaret Miles's discussion: 301–302;

Carl B. Yoke, ed., Special Ursula K. Le Guin issue, *Extrapolation,* 21 (Fall 1980).

**Papers:**

The University of Oregon Library in Eugene houses Ursula K. Le Guin's manuscripts.

# Barry Lopez

*(6 January 1945 –    )*

David Stevenson
*Western Illinois University*

BOOKS: *Desert Notes: Reflections in the Eye of a Raven* (Kansas City, Kans.: Sheed, Andrews & McMeel, 1976);

*Giving Birth to Thunder, Sleeping with His Daughter: Coyote Builds North America* (Kansas City, Kans.: Sheed, Andrews & McMeel, 1977);

*Of Wolves and Men* (New York: Scribners, 1978);

*River Notes: The Dance of Herons* (Kansas City, Kans.: Andrews & McMeel, 1979);

*Desert Reservation* (Port Townsend, Wash.: Copper Canyon Press, 1980);

*Winter Count* (New York: Scribners, 1981);

*Arctic Dreams: Imagination and Desire in a Northern Landscape* (New York: Scribners, 1986);

*Crossing Open Ground* (New York: Scribners, 1988);

*Crow and Weasel* (San Francisco: North Point Press, 1990);

*The Rediscovery of North America* (Lexington: University Press of Kentucky, 1990);

*Children in the Woods* (Eugene, Ore.: Lone Goose Press, 1992);

*Field Notes: The Grace Note of the Canyon Wren* (New York: Knopf, 1994);

*Looking in a Deeper Lair* (Eugene, Ore.: Lone Goose Press, 1996);

*Apologia* (Eugene, Ore.: Lone Goose Press, 1997);

*Lessons from the Wolverine* (Athens: University of Georgia Press, 1997);

*About This Life: Journeys on the Threshold of Memory* (New York: Knopf, 1998);

*The Letters of Heaven* (Eugene, Ore.: Knight Library Press, 1999);

*Light Action in the Caribbean: Stories* (New York: Knopf, 2000).

RECORDINGS: *Barry Lopez* (Kansas City, Mo.: New Letters, 1978);

*Of Wolves and Men* (New York: Encyclopedia Americana/CBS New Audio Resource Library, 1978);

*Barry Lopez Reads Winter Count, Trying the Land, Searching for Ancestors, and a Short Manifesto* (Columbia, Mo.: American Audio Prose Library, 1987);

*Stone Horse* (New York: Academy of American Poets, 1989);

*Light Action in the Caribbean* (New York: HighBridge, 2000);

*Crossing Open Ground* (St. Paul, Minn.: HighBridge, 2000);

*Field Notes* (St. Paul, Minn.: HighBridge, 2000);

*About This Life* (New York: Phoenix, 2001).

OTHER: *Coyote Love: Native American Folktales,* adapted by Lopez (Portland, Maine: Coyote Love Press, 1989);

*Galápagos,* photographs by Nathan Farb, introduction by Lopez, text by Michael H. Jackson (New York: Rizzoli, 1989);

*The Sagebrush Ocean: A Natural History of the Great Basin,* text and photographs by Stephen Trimble, foreword by Lopez (Reno: University of Nevada Press, 1989);

Tiana Bighorse, *Bighorse the Warrior,* edited by Noel Bennett, foreword by Lopez (Tucson: University of Arizona Press, 1990);

*Natural Light: American Photographers Collection,* Joseph Holmes, foreword by Lopez (Berkeley, Cal.: Nature, 1990);

*Helping Nature Heal: An Introduction to Environmental Restoration,* edited by Richard Nielsen, foreword by Lopez (Berkeley: Ten Speed Press, 1991);

*Heart of the Land: Essays on Last Great Places,* edited by Joseph Barbato and Lisa Weinerman, foreword by Lopez (New York: Pantheon, 1995);

"Waiting on Wisdom," in *Testimony: Writers of the West Speak on Behalf of Utah Wilderness,* compiled by Trimble and Terry Tempest Williams (Salt Lake City: West Wind Lithos, 1995);

*Tales from the Rain Forest: Myths and Legends from the Amazonian Indians of Brazil,* retold by Mercedes Dorson

*Barry Lopez (photograph by Maslon; Michael/Corbis; from the dust jacket for*
About This Life: Journeys on the Threshold of Memory, *1998)*

and Jeane Wilmot, foreword by Lopez (Hopewell, N.J.: Ecco Press, 1997).

SELECTED PERIODICAL PUBLICATIONS—
UNCOLLECTED: "Renegotiating the Contracts," *Parabola*, 8 (Spring 1983); corrected and reprinted in *This Incompareable Lande: A Book of American Nature Writing*, edited by Thomas J. Lyon (Boston: Houghton Mifflin, 1989);

"California Desert: A Worldly Wilderness," *National Geographic*, 171 (January 1987): 42–77;

"Landscapes Open and Closed," *Harper's*, 275 (July 1987): 51–58;

"A Chinese Garland," *North American Review*, 273 (September 1988): 41–42;

"Our Frail Planet in Cold, Clear View," *Harper's* (May 1989): 43–49;

"Discovering the Americas, Again," *New York Times*, 12 October 1990, p. A17;

"Benjamin Claire, North Dakota Tradesman, Writes to the President of the United States," *North American Review*, 277 (September/October 1992): 16–20;

"The Interior of North Dakota," *Paris Review*, 34 (Winter 1992): 134–144;

"Thomas Lowdermilk's Generosity," *American Short Fiction*, 12 (Winter 1993): 36–46;

"Reuben Mendoza Vega, Suzuki Professor of Early Caribbean History, University of Gainesville, Offers a History of the United States Based on Personal Experience," *Manoa,* 6 (Summer 1994): 43–49;

"Offshore: A Journey to the Weddell Sea," *Orion,* 13 (Winter 1994): 48–69;

"Caring for the Woods," *Audubon,* 97 (March/April 1995): 58–60, 62–63;

"Looking in the Deeper Lair," *Northern Lights,* 11 (Summer 1995): 28–29;

"A Literature of Place," *Portland,* 16 (Summer 1997): 22–25;

"The Language of Animals," *Wild Earth,* 8 (Summer 1998): inside front cover, 2–6;

"The Naturalist," *Orion,* 20 (Fall 2001): 38–43.

The linearly minded critic might wish to encompass the arc of Barry Lopez's oeuvre chronologically, in which case one would begin with *Desert Notes: Reflections in the Eye of a Raven,* which appeared in 1976, and continue through to his most recent work, *Light Action in the Caribbean: Stories* (2000). Others might attempt to fix him by genre: the frontispiece of his latest book lists his previous work as nonfiction, fiction, and essays. It does not mention that all these pieces seem to cross the boundaries of genre and also include the collection of American Indian myths *Giving Birth to Thunder, Sleeping with His Daughter: Coyote Builds North America* (1977) and the illustrated young-adult works *Crow and Weasel* (1990) and *Lessons from the Wolverine* (1997). Within the context of the human relationship to landscape that pervades Lopez's body of work two more subtle themes emerge–the sense of mystery that he illuminates without damaging or dissecting, and the description of his methodology as a writer: sometimes firsthand observer, sometimes participant, and always meticulous researcher. In the end this method is not merely a writing strategy but also an ethical framework through which he seeks to redefine the relationship of humankind with the natural world.

Lopez grew up in Southern California and made his home in the Pacific Northwest. His writing frequently, but not exclusively, describes landscapes of the American West from the Mojave Desert to Alaska. The landscapes of his work are not merely background for his writing but integral, "a central issue." He told interviewer Nicholas O'Connell in 1985 that "Eventually what American literature is going to offer among the world's literatures . . . is an illumination of this issue of man and landscape. . . ." His work is a fierce and lyrical effort in bringing about this illumination.

Barry Holstun Lopez was born 6 January 1945 in Port Chester, New York, to John Edward Brennan and Mary Holstun Brennan. He spent many of his most formative childhood years in what was then the rural San Fernando Valley of Southern California before returning to live in New York in 1956, the year he was legally adopted by Adrian Lopez, his mother's second husband. Although originally intending to become an aeronautical engineer, he graduated cum laude with an A.B. degree in communication arts from the University of Notre Dame in 1966. He married Sandra Jean Landers on 10 June 1967 (the couple divorced in 1999). He received a Master of Arts in teaching in 1968. His first nonacademic writing experiences grew from the simple desire to describe what he saw "when he went outside." He mentions in passing that in regard to this desire, Herman Melville's *Moby-Dick* (1851), a book he read three times before going to college, served as a model. Although Lopez's inspiration is first and foremost in and of the natural world, he lists (with little elaboration) William Faulkner, Thomas Hardy, Willa Cather, Gerard Manley Hopkins, and Ernest Hemingway as literary influences, particularly on his sense of story and sensitivity to language. During his undergraduate years Lopez traveled to nearly every state by car and spent two summers working on a ranch in Wyoming. Upon leaving Notre Dome and northern Indiana in 1968, he had a vague notion to teach at a prep school but instead enrolled at the University of Oregon in the Master of Fine Arts (MFA) writing program, attending courses there in 1969 and 1970. He became a full-time writer in 1970 and has been a contributing editor to *The North American Review* since 1977, *Harper's* since 1984, and *The Georgia Review* since 2001. His writing began to receive national acclaim when *Of Wolves and Men* (1978) inspired *The Los Angeles Times* to rank him among "the cadre of wilderness writers like John McPhee and Edward Abbey." The book earned for him the John Burroughs Medal, the first of many national awards, and his reputation was further solidified when *Arctic Dreams: Imagination and Desire in a Northern Landscape* (1986) received the National Book Award in 1986. Lopez is also the recipient of a Literature Award from the American Academy of Arts and Letters, a Lannan Foundation Award, a Pushcart Prize for fiction and one for nonfiction, and a PEN Syndicated Fiction Award; he has also been a Guggenheim Fellow. In 2002 he received the Orion Society's John Hay Award for significant contributions to the literatue of nature. Lopez has lived in the rain forest of western Oregon on the banks of the

McKenzie River "in relatively undisturbed country" since 1970.

*Desert Notes,* Lopez's first book, comprises twelve short fictional pieces unified generally by their subject, the desert. The word *notes* in the title accurately describes these writings, which average less than five pages each and seem to defy conventional generic designations. In form these chapters rarely take on the familiar characteristics of the traditional short story; instead, they vary from what seems to be traditional nonfiction, to ethnography, to myth, to the prose-poem.

Lopez begins the book with an epigraph from Charles Darwin and precedes the introduction with a line from Thomas Merton; thereby, he claims as his literary heritage both the naturalist and the spiritual traditions. Lopez begins the introduction with the line "The land does not give easily." He is writing about a particular landscape, the desert, but he is also reflecting on expectations of the landscape and the process of learning how to see it, how simply to be in it. He writes of the necessary abandonment of "systems of roads, road signs, and stop lights." "By a series of strippings such as this," he says, "one enters the desert."

Both the introduction and the second story, "Desert Notes," employ a first-person narrator who directly invites the reader into a desert landscape. This narrative landscape does not easily reveal its secrets. Patience and a determined attentiveness are advised repeatedly: "When you have done these things you will know a little more than you did before." The search for knowledge of self is, for Lopez, inseparable from the understanding of place.

In "The Hot Spring" the quest is narrated in the third person: an unnamed man drives 278 miles into the desert, where ritually and symbolically he removes his clothes to enter a hot spring. At the end of the story, in fewer than three pages, ". . . he had come to life again." "Twilight" traces the genealogy of ownership of a Navajo storm-pattern rug. "The School" narrates the history of a long-abandoned desert schoolhouse through the eyes of an aging woman who had once been a student there. The narrator of "The Blue Mound People" describes a mysterious existence and disappearance of a small band of desert dwellers who lacked the powers of speech and were "bound up in an unusual relationship with the desert." Indeed, this whole collection is a meditation on humankind's unusual relationship with the desert. *Desert Notes* ends with "Directions," in which a first-person narrator, as in the first two chapters, instructs the reader on how to see such a place. The story is full of warnings, most particularly about the

Dust jacket for Lopez's 1977 retelling of Native American folk tales about the hero-trickster, Coyote

reliability of maps. According to Lopez, one can only trust the maps one makes for oneself.

In 1977 Lopez published *Giving Birth to Thunder, Sleeping with His Daughter,* a work written at the University of Oregon seven years earlier under the direction of Barre Toelken, a folklorist; Toelken provided the foreword for the published book. Lopez "retells" sixty-eight tales of Coyote from the oral tradition of forty-two American Indian tribes. According to Toelken, the most important element of style in these stories is their "feeling for place—both geographic and sacred."

Lopez believes that attempts to define Coyote's character, such as Stith Thompson's description of Coyote in *Tales of the North American Indians* (1966) as "trickster demigod, a beneficent being, bringing culture and light to his people, and a creature of greed, lust and stupidity," have "kept us at a distance from the stories themselves." Lopez believes that the purpose of these stories was always more than a way to pass time: the stories "detailed tribal origins; they emphasized a worldview thought to be the correct one; and they dramatized the value of proper behavior. To participate in these stories by listening to them was to renew one's sense of tribal identity."

In his retellings, Lopez attempts to amend the record of previous translations written for non–Native American audiences. He restores to the record Coyote's erotic adventures, "invariably expurgated from popular collections in the past"; he is also keenly aware of a "restructuring" of the tales by folklorists to give the stories what he calls a "that's why the beaver has a flat tail!" effect. In other words, it is a non–Native American notion that stories should have a purpose or a moral, something beyond simple enjoyment or tribal identity. Another misconception that Lopez addresses is the hero/trickster dichotomy. Lopez's sense is that the dichotomy is artificial, constructed to make one aspect essential at the expense of the other. Lopez tries to show the fullness of the coyote–emphasizing universality, mutability, and mystery.

*Giving Birth to Thunder, Sleeping with His Daughter* exemplifies Lopez's respect for Native American worldviews, including the deep ties of culture to nature and the dynamic balance between the two. In addition, the influence of a Native American worldview, as well as narrative strategies, becomes increasingly evident throughout Lopez's work.

*Of Wolves and Men* was Lopez's first sustained book-length work on a single topic and won him the wide audience that accompanies best-seller status and the prestige of the Burroughs Medal. *Of Wolves and Men* might best be described as comprehensive, both in its treatment of subject and in its dazzling range of research and writing strategies. Lopez combines traditional European-American scholarship–historical, literary, and scientific–with many interviews, particularly with indigenous peoples such as the Nunamiut of the Brooks Range in Alaska, and with days of firsthand observations of both wolves in the wild and "domesticated" animals. Above all else, Lopez positions himself with great care among the many competing and sometimes contradictory views of the wolf that he has uncovered for his readers. "The truth is we know little about the wolf. What we know a good deal more about is what we imagine the wolf to be."

This treatment, then, of what the wolf is imagined to be is divided into four sections. The first section reviews the traditional scientific view of wolves. Lopez is particularly interested in showing the reader the limitations of this view, exposing it as simplistic. In the second section Lopez builds on his sense of the scientific record as incomplete and begins his exami-

nation of the views of indigenous peoples, particularly the Nunamiut. He concludes that the scientific community does not know much about animals because scientists often approach animals solely in terms of their own ethnocentric needs and experiences. The indigenous hunting cultures, who understand hunting as a sacred activity, see the world in a way similar to how a wolf might see it.

In the third section, Lopez describes the centuries-old project to destroy the wolf. Lopez believes this history of the near annihilation of an entire species has been both cruel and irresponsible. He believes this human behavior toward the wolf is a kind of moral failure, that people "simply do not understand our place in the universe and have not the courage to admit it."

In the fourth and final section of the book, Lopez considers a complete cultural archaeology of the wolf, in effect unifying the thematic focuses of the previous three sections. He explains that "enlightened observation (science), fanciful anthropomorphism (indigenous peoples' view), and agricultural necessity (rationale for annihilation)" are all conventions that have arisen from humankind's "struggle to come to grips with the nature of the universe." In his 1985 interview with Nicholas O'Connell included in *At the Field's End: Interviews with Twenty Pacific Northwest Writers* (1987), Lopez says, "The relationship between human beings and that part of the landscape called *Canis lupus* is what the wolf book is about." *Of Wolves and Men* was published to enthusiastic critical reviews.

*River Notes: The Dance of Herons* (1979) follows the model set forth in *Desert Notes:* it comprises twelve stories of varied voice and form, focusing on the natural world as embodied in the river. In the introduction, Lopez places his first-person narrator once again in a scene of observation and reflection– on this occasion on the shoreline where a river enters the ocean. The concepts of patience and ritual familiar to the reader of the earlier work are evident, but with marked shifts. The communing with animals is more pronounced: the narrator hears "the sound of fish dreaming," and he himself dreams he is a salmon; birds of many species land on him, weighing him down; sparrows observe him. In the final line there is a vision of "sun-drenched bears stretching in an open field like young men." The suggestion is that this narrator has successfully dissolved the distance between the human and animal worlds, a consideration that occupies Lopez throughout his writing, particularly in *Of Wolves and Men.*

Despite the continued insistence that "It is impossible to speak with certainty about very much,"

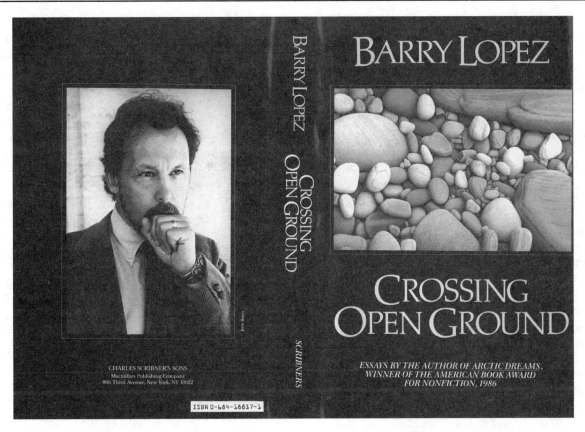

*Dust jacket for Lopez's 1988 collection. It includes his essay on the art of storytelling, "Landscape and Narrative."*

Lopez is much more precise in his articulation of what has become one of his most pervasive themes— a sorrow, shared by the natural world, for what the earth has lost. In the longest of these stories, "The Log Jam," six moments in the lives of people who interact with the river are marked by the addition their actions make to a logjam. These people, best described as ordinary, are unknown to each other and share with other of Lopez's narrators and characters a barely, if at all, understood need for ritual that connects their lives intimately to the natural world. Olin Sanders's son throws the bloodstained stump upon which his father dies in a logging accident into the river. Rebecca Grayson, quietly suffering in a marriage marked for both parties by an unarticulated loss, dumps a bowl full of flower blossoms collected over twenty years into the river. Gene Thompson is a boy so finely attuned to the sounds of nature that he can hear the air moving through termite tunnels in a 447-year-old fir moments before it weakens and crashes to the ground; its crown ends up at the logjam as a home for osprey.

*Winter Count* (1981), Lopez's third collection of short fiction, takes its title from the Native American concept of marking time between summers by a sin-gle memorable event. The sequence of these events, Lopez says in an epigraph, "recorded pictographically on a buffalo robe or spoken aloud, was called a winter count." Lopez further adds that more than one winter count may be occurring simultaneously and that each varies according to the personality of its "keeper." Thus, Lopez continues his critique of modern science and its quest to quantify and explain the natural world. The natural world as revealed in Lopez's work is illuminated, but its mystery remains intact. Characters in these nine stories are searching for connection with landscape, history, and other peoples. By profession there are curators, book restorers, and historians seeking to preserve, restore, and ultimately understand the natural world and their place in it.

In the story "Winter Count 1973; Geese, They Flew Over in a Storm," an aging scholar of Native American studies reads from a paper titled "Winter Counts from the Dakota, the Crow and the Blackfeet: Personal Histories." Thus, the concept of winter count is reiterated many times: in the book title, the definition, the epigraph, the title of the story, the title of the paper read in the story, the "actual" winter counts as fictionally recorded in the character's paper, and the character's personal winter counts that mark his own life. In the scholar's closing remarks, he urges, "As professional historians, we have too often subordinated one system to another and forgotten all together the individual view, the poetic view, which is as close to the truth as the consensus. Or it can be as distant." The scholar is nearly overcome by a sense of loss, both of native cultures and of his own life, which is nearly over. His final thought is "Everything is held together with stories."

*Arctic Dreams* won the National Book Award for Lopez in 1986, earning him a place "among those same individuals, who ventured to the northern limits of the earth and made of their journey a lasting record of its fierceness and beauty," in the words of Michiko Kakutani in *The New York Times* (12 February 1986). Lopez's longest and most ambitious book, *Arctic Dreams* is a work of natural history, much in the same vein as *Of Wolves and Men*. Like the earlier book, *Arctic Dreams* combines a wealth of research with firsthand experience, the result of fifteen trips to the arctic over a five-year period. Though the arctic is not strictly speaking a Western landscape, it is clearly a frontier landscape, possessing the characteristics to which Lopez is drawn: open space that is at the same time isolated and circumscribed, on the periphery of the human. Within these landscapes Lopez is concerned with the fate of indigenous peoples, cultures, and animal life in the face of an encroaching different way of life and a technological world.

The book is structured into nine chapters, which move through the terrain conceptually, rather than chronologically or geographically. In addition, there are epigraphs, acknowledgments, an author's note, a preface, and a prologue preceding the chapters; following the chapters are notes, maps, appendices—"Geographic Place Names," "Scientific Names for Animals and Plants," and a chart showing a time line of "Human Culture and Civilization."

In the prologue Lopez explicitly identifies the three themes that his narrative will address: the effect of the arctic landscape on the imagination, the way in which utilitarian values shape consideration of the landscape, and the way an unknown landscape shapes the conception of wealth. Lopez's hope is to acquire an intimacy with "a place where the common elements of life are understood differently," thus acquiring the possibility of imagining afresh both past and future.

The first chapter, "Arktikós," named after the ancient Greek term for the region—country of the great bear—describes the country generally in terms of "the annual movement of the sun across the arctic sky," pointing out that solar radiation is the defining factor in any ecosystem. This introduction touches on flora, fauna, and human history—both of indigenous peoples and of visitors from the south—and is interspersed with personal anecdotes.

The next three chapters, "Banks Island: *Ovibos moschatus*," "Tôrnârsuuk: *Ursus maritimus*" and "Lancaster Sound: *Monodon monoceros*" link species of wildlife—musk ox, polar bear, and narwhal respectively—with a particular geographical location and a personal visit by the author to observe the animals firsthand. These observations figure heavily into the fifth chapter, "Migration: The Corridors of Breath," in which Lopez observes that "A fundamental difference between our culture and Eskimo culture . . . is that we have irrevocably separated ourselves from the world that animals occupy." This separation in turn has led to considering animals "impersonally," a view that allows rationalizing a utilitarian disregard for environment.

In chapter 6, "Ice and Light," Lopez examines physical features of the landscape, such as icebergs, polynas (water that remains permanently unfrozen), and the aurora borealis. The range of Lopez's scholarship is evident; in a remarkable associative passage he considers Frederic Church's nineteenth-century painting "The Icebergs," a massive canvas in which Church tried to capture icebergs as the embodiment of light in nature. From this consideration Lopez moves to the comparison of icebergs to cathedrals and their common characteristic as repositories for light; he ends ultimately with the question of whether intelligence is reason or love. The reader sees how Lopez moves gracefully from landscape topography to the philosophical and spiritual inquiry of the most daunting human questions.

In the seventh chapter, "The Country of the Mind," Lopez applies Frederic Jackson Turner's "Frontier Hypothesis" to the arctic region. Lopez is particularly concerned with Jackson's idea that landscapes in which history unfolds are not only real but also, in his words, "projections, artifacts of human perception."

The last two chapters chronicle a thousand-year history of European exploration of the arctic, from Irish monks seeking the "Isles of the Blessed" as early as the sixth century, to contemporary miners and oil-field workers. Few, if any, of these visitors felt a sense of reciprocity that Lopez deems necessary in order for human relationship to the landscape to be sustainable. Lopez thinks that the land must be approached with an attitude of obligation; only then can dignity emerge.

*Dust jacket for Lopez's 2000 collection of short fiction*

Early in the book Lopez describes walks along the Ilignorak Ridge and his repeated visits to the ground-nesting birds that lived there. He "developed the habit of bowing to them out of regard for what was wonderful and mysterious in their lives." Lopez repeats this gesture in the closing lines of the book, this time bowing to the great unknown North in an attitude of appreciation for all that he had seen.

*Crossing Open Ground* (1988) collects fourteen essays written between 1978 and 1986. The essay "The Stone Horse," which opens the collection, was selected by Robert Atwan and Gay Talese for *The Best American Essays of 1987* (1988) and is typical of Lopez's work. In *Crossing Open Ground* Lopez describes a hike to an archaeological site, a stone intaglio of a horse as old as four hundred years, in a remote location in the Mojave Desert of California. In a short sixteen pages he tells of not only his actual journey but also of the natural and human history of this desert, moving to the observation that history is "inscribed everywhere in the face of the land."

The single most self-reflexive essay in which Lopez explicitly discusses storytelling is "Landscape and Narrative," first published in 1984. The title might function as a subtitle for his entire body of works. Its first sentence begins, as his works typically do, by fixing the self in a particular landscape at a particular time:

> One summer evening in a remote village in the Brooks Range of Alaska, I sat among a group of men listening to hunting stories about the trapping and pursuit of animals.

In addition to establishing temporal and geographical context, the central action of this sentence is "listening," establishing once again that for Lopez the appropriate relationship of humanity to the exterior world is one of observation. The stories of the particular evening described happen to concern the wolverine, a seldom observed, largely unknown North American mammal. Lopez's response to these stories is a sense of renewal of purpose in his life. The stories work symbiotically with the landscape, which "seemed alive because of the stories"; likewise, the view of the Brooks Range, after hearing the stories, inspired "exhilaration, and a deeper confirmation of the stories." In the rest of the essay he sets out to discover just what evoked this response.

For storytelling to engender such a response, Lopez claims two things are necessary: "the context must be intimate and the story is told for its own sake, not forced to serve merely as the vehicle for an idea." For Lopez, that intimacy with his subject is the result of a disciplined and varied process requiring both a physical and an intellectual engagement. Intimacy is reached through the humility of the storyteller and through the sharing of idiomatic expression and details of physical setting.

Lopez's personal humility is demonstrated throughout his work, and the best examples are found perhaps in his admiration of indigenous peoples and his profound respect for animal life. Both of these elements are present in "The Passing Wisdom of Birds," the essay that closes *Crossing Open Ground*. In this essay Lopez chronicles the historical moment that Hernán Cortes, in a vengeful and violent siege, destroyed the city of Tenochtitlán–Mexico City–and, in a move designed "to humiliate and frighten the Mexican people," set fire to their aviaries. The moment symbolizes for Lopez

> a fundamental lapse of wisdom in the European conquest of America, an underlying trouble in which political conquest, personal greed, revenge, and national pride outweigh what is innocent, beautiful, serene, and defenseless–the birds.

In this scenario not merely the birds themselves function as the locus of innocence and beauty, but also the people who held them in reverence and who coexisted peacefully with them in what, in his firsthand account, *The Discovery and Conquest of Mexico, 1517–1521,* Bernal Diaz described as an Eden-like garden. While his admiration and sympathy are clearly with Montezuma and his people, Lopez humbly understands that by virtue of birth and education his cultural ancestors are the European invaders. Here, and elsewhere, Lopez finds himself implicated in the process of debasement of the natural world, a notion echoed in his observation about the landscape photographer Robert Adams, of whom he writes, "He does not hold himself apart from what he indicts." Despite Adams's self-indictment, indeed because of it, Lopez continually makes a plea for a new relationship with the natural world, "one that is not condescending, manipulative, and purely utilitarian."

Both *The Rediscovery of North America* (1990) and *Apologia* (1997) are short essays in the style of those in *Crossing Open Ground,* which were published as essays before they found their way into book form. *The Rediscovery of North America,* first presented at the University of Kentucky as the inaugural Thomas D. Clark Lecture in 1990, reads like Lopez's manifesto,

both a summing-up and a clarification. Although a short book, it is a distillation of the whole, an adherence to Henry David Thoreau's dictum to "keep your accounts on your thumbnail." Lopez argues that the history of the European conquest of North America was, from the outset, motivated by a ruthless quest for material wealth, a quest that has shaped attitudes toward the land and resources, a quest that ultimately has dire consequences for the natural world and all of humanity. Lopez further argues that change is possible.

In one sense, Lopez seems to be a simple naturalist, an emissary to the outback, the careful observer who reports back to his readers both his marvelous and his sad perceptions. But over and over again one senses in his works a more complicated strategy, in which the self-conscious narrator comments on his own technique, on the purpose of writing, on the potential power of writing to effect positive change. When Lopez asks the rhetorical question, how does one come to know the land? his answer also appears to provide an answer to the question, how does one become a writer?

In *The Rediscovery of North America* Lopez states that one must learn to look on the land not as "its possessor but as a companion." One must cultivate intimacy with the land as one would with a human being, by taking up residence in a place. The next step is to read history. Lopez's sense of history begins by acknowledging "ourselves as recent arrivals" and continues to local history, then to anthropological and archeological literature "of those we moved out of our way." Only at this point should one "come forward" to complete the record of observation. His goal is that this record would enable one to see beyond the "human span of three score and ten." In other words, one should strive for an understanding of the land in which man is not the measure of all things, but rather in which all things are the measure of all things.

*Apologia* tells of a cross-country drive from Oregon to Indiana during which Lopez stops along the way to offer gestures of respect to animals that have been killed alongside the road by automobiles. Illustrated with woodcut prints by California artist Robin Eschner, this essay addresses the need for respect and awareness and asks people to reconceptualize their relationship with the natural world.

*Lessons from the Wolverine,* which first appeared in *Field Notes: The Grace Note of the Canyon Wren* (1994), and *Crow and Weasel* are short fictional works illustrated by Tom Pohrt and published in book form. Designed for young adult readers, as well as for adults, these stories are fables written in the tradition

2

they will challenge themselves to know all there is to know

about ~~mountain lions~~ *the ice bear*. It never works. More seasoned field

biologists, not ~~so~~ *as* driven by ~~a~~ *the* need to prove themselves, ~~to~~

~~their colleagues and superiors,~~ are content to ~~apprentice~~ *concentrate*

~~themselves so~~ *on* smaller arenas of knowledge. ~~or, in the case~~ *Instead of* ~~the~~ *speaking*

*definitively* ~~of wilderness at the coyote,~~ *coyote, armadillo or widgeon,*

~~of the best ones, they pursue thoughts that carry them beyond~~

*they tend to say* "this ~~animal~~ *one animal, that one time, did this in*

~~the borders of their work.~~ *that place."*

*One naturalist's*

The great ~~little~~ change in the frame of mind ~~of a naturalist~~

*It seems to me*

over the past fifty years has been the growing awareness that

*most*

to get anywhere deep with a species, you ~~immerse~~ *must* immerse yourself in *its*

*I believe. You must learn its*

ecology. If you wish to understand the bear, you need to know

*exactly*

a great deal about where the bear lives, and *when* what the bear's

*in that particular geography,* *real*

relationships are with everyone else living there, *and* with all

*its*

components of that *place,* including ~~the~~ weathers.

*II*

Since the time of Gilbert White, at least, we have known

~~formal~~ *civilized* *the and write about the*

of the existence of a cohort of humans who study natural world

~~and write about it.~~ ~~What Darwin added -- as Heisenberg would~~

~~later in physics -- is the notion that we, ourselves, are involved~~

~~in unsettling ways in the very processes that we are trying to~~

*the treatment was in*

~~describe. Culture adds a~~ *from* *general was respectful,*

*and write about it from personal experience.* *AND tended toward*

~~and write about it.~~ Darwin brought ~~a~~ unprecedented depth to *fascination now crueler.*

*Fifty years later*

this kind of work. ~~because~~ He accentuated the need for scienfic

*studies* *he*

rigor in the naturalist's ~~pursuits,~~ but, also ~~because he~~ suggested

*here.*

~~there were~~ implications, ~~There were~~ entanglemensts. People,

*he said* *of change*

too, were biological, and subject to the same laws as the finch.

① *It is a frame of mind, ~~an All approach to nature~~*

*that characterizes the approach to nature of many hunting*

*and gathering peoples to this day.*

*The real matter—that the prose*

*was often simply a reminder not*

*to ignore or overlook creation.*

*Corrected typescript page from the first draft of Lopez's article "The Naturalist," which appeared in the*
*Autumn 2001 issue of* Orion Magazine *(Collection of Barry Lopez)*

of American Indian stories, with a straightforward style and no sense of irony. Both stories feature young protagonists journeying into the Far North and experiencing the sacredness of the land and an understanding of the animals that live there.

*Field Notes: The Grace Note of the Canyon Wren* is another collection of short fiction, much in the vein of *Winter Count,* in which the stories have a far greater topographical range than those in *Desert Notes* and *River Notes.* Most of these stories feature characters who step outside the daily world and into the natural world to learn something about themselves and the world that could not be acquired in any other way. In "The Entreaty of the Wiidema" an anthropologist travels with an indigenous Australian tribe unknown to the civilized world. He is stunned by the degree of their intimacy with the places through which they travel. The strictest tenet of these people is their insistence on listening as a means of approaching the world. In the end the scientist is concerned that his scholarly report will not be able adequately to "reciprocate" or repay what he has learned from these people and is searching for a language that "offers hope."

In "The Runner" a lawyer contemplates his estranged relationship with his sister, who has abandoned the trappings of civilization to live fully in the Grand Canyon. In the end he realizes that his judgments of her had been wrong and that the intimacy she had acquired with her surroundings has a value generally unrecognized by the world he inhabits.

In *About This Life: Journeys on the Threshold of Memory* (1998) Lopez has collected seventeen essays and has arranged them into four thematic groupings covering travels, home, memory, and youth. In the last section, the focus on recollections of his own childhood, his writing takes a more specifically autobiographical turn than in his previous works. Throughout *About This Life* Lopez insists on seeing the big picture through a precise consideration of the miniature; he insists that no single version of "the truth" about the physical world is likely to represent the whole truth. He works against stereotypes, particularly in essays such as "The American Geographies" and "Learning to See," which warn against homogenizing the landscape in images favored by popular and corporate culture. He warns that single images tell an oversimplified story by leaving out context, in effect turning nature into a sanitized, safe "mother" earth.

In "Replacing Memory" he literally returns to one of the houses of his childhood in southern California and describes watching a column of ants in a crack on a concrete path. He becomes conscious of

having watched ants in the same crack forty years earlier: "These were their progeny, still gathering food here. The mystery of their life, which had once transfixed me, seemed in no way to have diminished." This fascination with mysteries, particularly his contentedness to allow them to remain mysterious, is a recurring response to the world he encounters.

*Light Action in the Caribbean* (2000) is a collection of short fiction. The stories in it, like those of *Field Notes,* extend the scope of Lopez's work both culturally and geographically. In "Mornings in Quarain" a son negotiates with a man who may be able to return his murdered mother's papers to him. Set in the Middle East during Ramadan, this story explores in a typically evenhanded manner an instance of personal intersection between Muslim and Christian worldviews. In the story that closes the collection, "The Mappist," the narrator uncovers an obscure writer and mappist, Corlis Benefideo, who had devoted his life to knowing and to recording the intimacies of place. Near the end of the story, the mappist states: "What I oppose is blind devotion to progress, and the venality of material weatlth. If we're going to exchange the priceless for the common, I want to know exactly what the terms are." Finally Benefideo asks the narrator: ". . . the real question, now, is what will *you* do?" This is the question Lopez seems to ask both of himself and his readers.

Scott Slovic, in his chapter on Lopez in *Seeking Awareness in American Nature Writing* (1992), observes that American writing about nature from its inception has been not merely descriptive but prescriptive. Clearly this observation can be applied to Lopez, who reminds his readers both implicitly and explicitly that by learning how to see the world, they might, if they pay attention, learn how to live in it. Slovic argues that Lopez's concerns are primarily epistemological, citing Lopez's questioning of Edward O. Wilson in their conversation recorded in *Writing Natural History: Dialogues with Authors* (1989): "what do we know? how do we know? how do we organize this knowledge?" These questions, like Thoreau's famous last lines in "Ktaadn"(1848), "Who are we? Where are we?" are always being addressed in Lopez's work. Lopez's written body of work represents not only what he has learned but also serves as an example of how the material might be organized. He often takes great care in telling the reader how the story was learned and constructed.

If anything can be learned from Lopez about the task ahead–establishing "a new relationship with the natural world," it is that only through cultivating intimacy, humility, and reverence that such a relationship might be earned. Barry Lopez's writing serves its readers both as an example of how to live and as a beacon of hope that such a new relationship to the natural world is yet possible.

**Interviews:**

Trish Todd, "Barry Lopez Recalls His Arctic Dreams," *Publishers Weekly,* 288 (11 October 1985): 35–36;

Jim Anton, "An Interview with Barry Lopez," *Western American Literature,* 21 (Spring 1986): 3–17;

Nicholas O'Connell, "Barry Lopez," *At the Field's End: Interviews with Twenty Pacific Northwest Writers* (Seattle: Madrona, 1987), pp. 3–18;

Kay Bonetti, "An Interview with Barry Lopez," in *Missouri Review,* 11, no. 3 (1988): 59–77;

Edward Lueders, *Writing Natural History: Dialogues with Authors* (Salt Lake City: University of Utah Press, 1989), pp. 7–36;

Ray Gonzalez, "Landscapes of the Interior, the Literature of Hope: An Interview with Barry Lopez," *Bloomsbury Review,* 10 (January/February 1990): 5+;

Alice Evans, "Leaning into the Light: An Interview with Barry Lopez," *Poets and Writers,* 22 (March/April 1994): 62–79;

Douglas Marx, "Barry Lopez: 'I Am a Writer Who Travels,'" *Publishers Weekly,* 241 (26 September 1994): 41–42;

John A. Murray, "About This Life: A Conversation with Barry Lopez," *Bloomsbury Review,* 18 (September/October 1998): 8+;

David Sumner, "Nature, Writing, American Literature, and the Idea of Community–A Conversation with Barry Lopez," *Weber Studies,* 18 (Spring 2001): 2–26.

**References:**

Dan Griggs, *Barry Lopez,* video recording (Los Angeles: The Lannan Foundation, 1992);

Michiko Kakutani, review of *Arctic Dreams, New York Times Book Review,* 12 (February 1986);

Sherman Paul, "Making the Turn: Rereading Barry Lopez," in *For Love of the World: Essays on Nature Writers* (Iowa City: University of Iowa Press, 1992), pp. 67–107;

Daniel W. Ross, "Barry Lopez's *Arctic Dreams:* Looking into a New *Heart of Darkness,*" *CEA Critic,* 54 (Fall 1991): 78–86;

William H. Rueckert, "Barry Lopez and the Search for a Dignified and Honorable Relation with Nature," *North Dakota Quarterly,* 59 (Spring 1991): 137–164;

Scott Slovic, *Seeking Awareness in American Nature Writing: Henry Thoreau, Annie Dillard, Edward Abbey, Wendell Berry, Barry Lopez* (Salt Lake City: University of Utah Press, 1992), pp. 137–166;

Peter Wild, *Barry Lopez,* Western Writers Series, no. 64 (Boise, Idaho: Boise State University, 1984).

# Cormac McCarthy

*(20 July 1933 –     )*

Marty Priola
*Cormac McCarthy Society*

See also the McCarthy entries in *DLB 6: American Novelists Since World War II, Second Series* and *DLB 143: American Novelists Since World War II, Third Series*.

BOOKS: *The Orchard Keeper* (New York: Random House, 1965; London: Deutsch, 1966);

*Outer Dark* (New York: Random House, 1968; London: Deutsch, 1970);

*Child of God* (New York: Random House, 1974; London: Chatto & Windus, 1975);

*Suttree* (New York: Random House, 1979; London: Chatto & Windus, 1980);

*Blood Meridian, or The Evening Redness in the West* (New York: Random House, 1985; London: Picador, 1990);

*All the Pretty Horses* (New York: Knopf, 1992; London: Picador, 1993);

*The Stonemason: A Play in Five Acts* (Hopewell, N.J.: Ecco Press, 1994; London: Picador, 1997);

*The Crossing* (New York: Knopf, 1994; London: Picador, 1994);

*The Gardener's Son: A Screenplay* (Hopewell, N.J.: Ecco Press, 1996);

*Cities of the Plain* (New York: Knopf, 1998; London: Picador, 1998).

**Collection:** *The Border Trilogy: All the Pretty Horses, The Crossing, Cities of the Plain* (New York: Knopf, 1999).

PRODUCED SCRIPT: *The Gardener's Son,* television, *Visions,* PBS, 1976.

SELECTED PERIODICAL PUBLICATIONS–
UNCOLLECTED: "Wake for Susan," as C. J. McCarthy Jr., *The Phoenix* [Literary supplement to the *Orange and White,* University of Tennessee student newspaper] (1959): 3–6;

"A Drowning Incident," as C. J. McCarthy Jr., *The Phoenix* [Literary supplement to the *Orange and White,* University of Tennessee student newspaper] (1960): 3–4.

*Cormac McCarthy (photograph © Marion Ettlinger)*

Cormac McCarthy has been hailed as one of the finest writers of the twentieth century. His work has been compared to that of Herman Melville, William Faulkner, Mark Twain, and William Shakespeare. McCarthy was awarded both the National Book Award and the National Book Critics Circle Award for *All the Pretty Horses* (1992), the first book of his *Border Trilogy* (1999). His narratives have been lauded for their stark depiction of nature as well as for their sheer stylistic beauty, which entwines the lushness and fecundity of Faulkner's prose with the trenchant austerity of Ernest Hemingway's. Although McCarthy's writing has been universally recognized for its more evocative passages—which in their subtlety rise to the level of poetry—his brutal and exacting depictions of violence and the seamier side of life in the South and in the West have drawn both praise and revulsion from readers and critics.

Charles Joseph McCarthy Jr. was born in Providence, Rhode Island, on 20 July 1933 to Charles Joseph McCarthy and Gladys Christine McGail McCarthy. The eldest of three brothers in a family of six children, McCarthy early in life began to be addressed as "Cormac," the Gaelic equivalent of "son of Charles"; some sources suggest that McCarthy's parents initiated a legal name change. In 1937 the family moved to Knoxville, Tennessee, where his father began a long tenure as a lawyer for the Tennessee Valley Authority (TVA): McCarthy's father served on the TVA legal staff from 1934 to 1967—including a term as chief counsel from 1958 to 1967. In 1967 McCarthy's parents moved from Knoxville to Washington, D.C., where Charles McCarthy served as the principal attorney in a law firm until retirement.

The McCarthys raised their children in the Roman Catholic tradition. Cormac attended Catholic High School in Knoxville, then matriculated at the University of Tennessee in 1951, majoring in liberal arts. In 1953, by which time he had been out of college for a year, McCarthy entered the U.S. Air Force for four years of service—including two in Alaska, where he also hosted a radio show. Beginning in 1957, McCarthy resumed his studies at the University of Tennessee and—under the name C. J. McCarthy Jr.—published two stories, "Wake For Susan" and "A Drowning Incident," in the student literary magazine, *The Phoenix*. McCarthy won the Ingram-Merrill Award for creative writing for two consecutive years, in 1959 and 1960, while still an undergraduate at Tennessee. McCarthy married Lee Holleman, also a student at the University of Tennessee, on 3 January 1961, and they had a son, Cullen. The marriage was brief, ending in divorce sometime in the early 1960s. Records providing the exact date of the divorce have yet to be brought to light, and Lee McCarthy's 1991 book of poetry, *Desire's Door,* mentions their marriage only in passing.

Before the publication of McCarthy's first novel, *The Orchard Keeper* (1965), he received a travel fellowship from the American Academy of Arts and Letters. The fellowship enabled McCarthy to visit Ireland, the home of his ancestors—King Cormac McCarthy had built Blarney Castle—and he sailed from the United States on the liner *Sylvania* in 1965. On the trip he met Anne DeLisle, then working as an entertainer on the liner, and the two wed in England in 1966. The same year that he married Anne, McCarthy received a two-year grant from The Rockefeller Foundation. He and Anne toured southern England, France, Switzerland, Italy, and Spain, ending up on the island of Ibiza. Home to so many creative people at that time in the 1960s, Ibiza resembled an artists' colony. Fittingly, then, while living on Ibiza, McCarthy completed revisions for his second book, *Outer Dark* (1968).

During McCarthy's travels in Europe, *The Orchard Keeper* had been published to critical acclaim in the United States and won the author the William Faulkner Award for first-novel achievement. In *The Orchard Keeper* the characters' illusions about each other are shattered when they discover that what they had previously believed is not the truth. The three protagonists are Arthur Ownby, Marion Sylder, and the young John Wesley Rattner. Ownby, the eldest of the three, works as a tender of an orchard; he has also been caring for a corpse, whose identity is unknown to him, that mysteriously appeared in his rain-filled spray-pit tank made of concrete and set in the ground for mixing insecticide. Ownby never contacts the authorities about the body and watches over the makeshift crypt for several years. In *The Orchard Keeper* McCarthy also shows Ownby trying to pass on his knowledge of the mountains and the forests to Rattner, whose father was murdered—as the novel gradually reveals—by the bootlegger Sylder, who disposed of the body in Ownby's spray-pit, an in-ground tank that was once used for mixing insecticide. Rattner's father was a petty criminal; the son, who is ignorant of this history, regards his father as a hero. Sylder also becomes a hero to Rattner when he defends the latter in a conflict with the sheriff, Rattner's nemesis. Sylder, however, is unaware that the man he murdered and dumped in Ownby's spray-pit was Rattner's father. Tangled in these ironies, Ownby, Sylder, and Rattner play out their tragic fates. McCarthy's descriptions of nature and accurate rendering of local dialect are distinguishing features of the novel. Notable, too, is the beginning of a trend that continues through much of McCarthy's fiction: the author's practice of never revealing his characters' thoughts to the reader.

*The Orchard Keeper* has often been read as a conflict between old mores and newer ones. In an essay in *Perspectives on Cormac McCarthy* (1993) David Paul Ragan says:

> McCarthy depicts a world in which traditional embodiments of value—religion, community relationships, agrarian connections with the earth—have deteriorated as a result of the increasing pressures of urban culture, commercial interests and governmental intrusions upon the lives of the essentially rural characters in the novel.

# The Orchard Keeper

## a novel by CORMAC McCARTHY

### A RANDOM HOUSE BOOK

*Dust jacket for McCarthy's first novel (1965), set in Tennessee, about the relationship of a young man's admiration for a bootlegger who—unbeknownst to either of them—has killed the young man's father*

Ragan identifies deterioration as a theme persisting throughout McCarthy's novels that are set in the Appalachian Mountains. The theme is not limited, however, to the Southern works; McCarthy treats it more expansively in *The Border Trilogy*, with emphasis on the cowboy's and rancher's vanishing ways of life.

By contrast, while John M. Grammer views McCarthy in general as a writer of antipastoral literature, he says of *The Orchard Keeper* in an essay for *Perspectives on Cormac McCarthy* that the novel is "a more or less straightforward, elegiac celebration of a vanishing pastoral realm." According to Grammer, the novel treats the pastoral in such a positive way that *The Orchard Keeper* becomes a touchstone for the "later and bleaker examinations of the pastoral impulse" that arise in McCarthy's subsequent fiction. For Grammer, then, McCarthy's first novel represents an archetypal pastoral ideal against which the author's later works are in continual revolt.

Edwin T. Arnold, also in an article for *Perspectives on Cormac McCarthy*, holds another view of the novelist, one that may be applied as well to *The Orchard Keeper*. Arnold suggests that McCarthy's works are unified by their revelation of "a profound belief in the need for moral order, a conviction which is essentially religious." For Arnold, the apparent chaos of McCarthy's world manifests the deeper truths of a higher cosmological order. For Vereen M. Bell, on the other hand, metaphysical speculation carries little weight. In *The Achievement of Cormac McCarthy* (1988) Bell argues that *The Orchard Keeper* exemplifies "the irrelevance of the human in the impersonal scheme of things." Bell's seminal reading of McCarthy as a purveyor of an essentially amoral and nihilistic world has been quite influential; her perspective often serves as a point of departure for criticism of McCarthy's work.

In 1967, after traveling and writing in Europe for two years, Cormac McCarthy—along with his wife Anne—returned to the United States. A year later, in 1968, Random House published *Outer Dark*, and—like *The Orchard Keeper*—McCarthy's second novel received favorable reviews. One critic, Guy Davenport, noted in his article for *The New York Times Book Review* (24 September 1968) that McCarthy does not "waste a single word on his characters' thoughts"; rather, McCarthy describes his characters' actions and, as if simply recording speech, takes down what the characters say with complete objectivity. Walter Sullivan, writing in the *Sewanee Review* (October 1970), said bluntly that there is "no way to overstate the power, the absolute literary virtuosity, with which McCarthy draws his scenes." Sullivan added that McCarthy seems to look for "those devices and people and situations" that engage one because of the very strangeness of them. Sullivan's comments indeed prove true in *Outer Dark*, a book that tells an almost archetypal story with such particularity that its "strangeness" shocks its readers anew.

*Outer Dark* relates the tale of Culla and Rinthy Holme and explores the consequences of the incestuous relationship between them. After Rinthy's baby is born, her brother, Culla, takes the child from her. He abandons the baby in the woods, telling Rinthy that it died after birth. Rinthy, who does not believe her brother, sets out in search of her baby. Culla, too, wanders, and three murderous men pursue both him and his sister. Although the influence of Faulkner and Flannery O'Connor is palpable in *Outer Dark*, McCarthy's novel remains inescapably original. As Grammer notes, Bell has indicated in her work on McCarthy that the character of Rinthy recalls Lena Grove in Faulkner's *Light in August* (1932): "But Rinthy is a dark and hopeless version of Lena, just as *Outer Dark*—the very title suggests it—is a dark and hopeless version of *Light in August*." Yet, there persists a moral center to *Outer Dark*. "In McCarthy's highly moralistic world," Arnold asserts, "sins must be named and owned before they can be forgiven." For Arnold, neither good nor evil—nor the agents of them—is distinguished easily in McCarthy's fiction; the "state of the soul," rather, is what McCarthy examines and narrates.

In 1969 the John Simon Guggenheim Memorial Foundation awarded McCarthy a fellowship for creative writing. At this time, McCarthy and his wife, Anne, moved near Louisville, Tennessee, where they lived in a barn that McCarthy had renovated completely on his own. His next book for Random House, *Child of God* (1974), was inspired by actual events in Sevier County. Unlike McCarthy's previous two novels, *Child of God* garnered mixed reviews. A few critics, such as Doris Grumbach—in a review of the book for *The New Republic*—praised *Child of God* for bringing about "a reading experience so impressive, so 'new,'" as to leave one's enthusiasm for the book almost indescribable. Reviewer Richard Brickner, on the other hand, did not agree. For Brickner, whose assessment appears in *The New York Times Book Review* (13 January 1974), *Child of God* had no "human momentum or point"; he derided its "carefully cold, sour diction" and noted a "hostility" in the book that is directed "toward the reader." *Child of God* relates the story of Lester Ballard, a murderous necrophiliac, and his gradual alienation from society and descent into madness; Lester Ballard inhabits the macabre world of the caves of rural Appalachia—caves that he "peoples" with corpses. *Child of God* is a spare and compelling read but a challenging one nonetheless, since McCarthy portrays Lester with sympathy uncommon for such a deranged character. Also challenging for the reader is the method of storytelling: in the aftermath of Lester's crimes, some of the narration is voiced by various unidentified townspeople.

Yet, *Child of God* is not merely a horror novel, not just a tale of a grotesque come to life in a gothic and nightmarish Appalachia. As Arnold points out, McCarthy devotes more than one-third of the book to "setting up the *reasons* for Lester's otherwise unimaginable actions, creating a world in which such actions have a cause." McCarthy does so without irony, giving us a sympathetic portrait of a man who, once he loses everything else, then loses his mind. McCarthy suggests, too, that the community is partly to blame for the fate of Lester Ballard. Arnold notes such blame by citing McCarthy's direct address to the reader at the point in the book when Ballard almost drowns in a flooded creek:

He could not swim, but how would you drown him? His wrath seemed to buoy him up. Some halt in the way of things seems to work here. See him. You could say that he's sustained by his fellow men, like you. Has peopled the shore with them calling to him. A race that gives suck to the maimed and the crazed, that wants their wrong blood in its history and will have it. But they want this man's life.

As Arnold observes, Lester is "created by those around him, a necessary figure of the community, the scapegoat that embodies their weird alienation and stoked violence but also their terrible sadness. . . ."

In *Child of God* McCarthy explores further the themes of loneliness, alienation, and violence that he had previously examined in both *Outer Dark* and *The Orchard Keeper*. *Child of God,* however, presents a view bleaker and harsher than his first two novels disclosed—and thus a view more difficult for the reader to assimilate. Although the book is more accessible in terms of the plot, it forces the reader to wrestle with feelings and emotions regarding Lester Ballard and his crimes. The ambiguity of McCarthy's portrayal of Ballard is prototypical of several of McCarthy's later characters, and the difficulty of dealing with a character as horrific as Lester Ballard is amplified later in McCarthy's first Western.

In 1974 McCarthy took a respite from novel writing and spent a year working on a screenplay for a Public Broadcast Service television movie, *The Gardener's Son*, which had its premiere in 1976. In the preface to the Ecco Press edition (1996) of the screenplay, the director of the movie, Richard Pearce, alerts readers that its source material is "based on nothing more than a few paragraphs in the footnotes to a 1928 biography of a famous industrialist of the pre-Civil War South." *The Gardener's Son* takes its plot from events that occurred in the mill town of Graniteville, South Carolina, in 1876. McCarthy's drama concerns two families: the Greggs, who founded The Graniteville Manufacturing Company, and the McEvoys, an Irish Catholic family who previously owned a farm somewhere else. The McEvoy family has come to Graniteville looking for work. At the beginning of the screenplay, Dr. Perceval—family physician to the Greggs—has arrived in Graniteville to check on the condition of William Gregg, the founder of the mill, and finds that Gregg is near death. Gregg's wife requests that Perceval also examine seventeen-year-old Robert McEvoy, who has broken his leg. The doctor, and more importantly Mrs. Gregg, convince McEvoy to have his leg amputated.

As McEvoy heals, he watches a new generation come to prominence in the Gregg family. William Gregg has died, and his son Jason takes over management of the mill. Jason is a cruel master, and the young McEvoy is out-

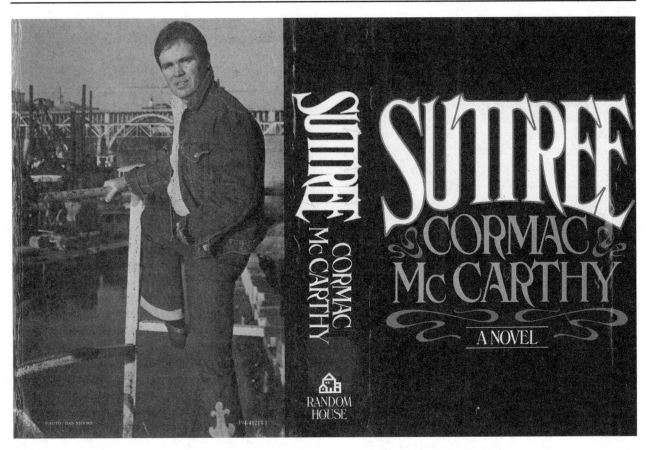

*Dust jacket for McCarthy's 1979 novel, a dark comedy set in Knoxville, Tennessee*

raged; quitting his job at the mill, McEvoy decides to leave Graniteville. Two years later, McEvoy returns to Graniteville and murders Gregg, a crime for which he is put on trial. The suspicion is that McEvoy murdered Gregg because Gregg had attempted to seduce McEvoy's younger sister, Martha. Martha, however, denies that she ever told her brother about the event. Throughout the play, McEvoy himself never articulates his reasons for killing Gregg, and by the end of the play, McEvoy has been hanged for his crime.

Although it ranks as a minor work in the McCarthy canon, *The Gardener's Son* is regarded as the writer's first historical work and thus a precursor to the violent, bloody, and gruesome *Blood Meridian, or The Evening Redness in the West* (1985). Dianne C. Luce's article, "Cormac McCarthy's First Screenplay: *The Gardener's Son*," which appears in *Perspectives on Cormac McCarthy,* is the definitive treatment of the work; as Luce observes, "*The Gardener's Son* is as impressive an achievement as a first screenplay as *The Orchard Keeper* is as a first novel." Luce also comments in the article on how *The Gardener's Son* "attempts a history of the inarticulate," much as *Outer Dark, Child of God,* and—later—*Blood Meridian* do.

According to Luce, the last scene in the screenplay suggests that "a true vision of the past or of our own inarticulate brothers is a potential avenue of redemption for the human family."

Screened at film festivals in Berlin and Edinburgh, *The Gardener's Son* was nominated for two Emmy Awards in the United States. McCarthy's personal life, however, was suffering. In 1976 DeLisle and McCarthy separated—they did not have any children—and McCarthy moved soon after the separation to El Paso, Texas, where he currently lives. The two were divorced some time later.

In 1979 McCarthy published his fourth novel, *Suttree,* a book that had occupied his writing life on and off for almost twenty years. Critics such as William C. Spencer—in an essay for *Perspectives on Cormac McCarthy*—assert that *Suttree* is McCarthy's finest novel, notwithstanding his later forays into Western writing. Luce calls it "McCarthy's 'big' book." *Suttree* nonetheless drew a few negative reviews as well. *The Memphis Press-Scimitar* ran a review of the book, whose content is summed up in the title of the review: "'A Masterpiece of Filth': Portrait of Knoxville Forgets to be Fair." This angry assessment occasioned an impassioned defense of McCarthy's book from novelist and historian Shelby Foote and from Walter Sullivan, who hailed McCarthy as "certainly the most talented novelist of his generation" in his article for *The Sewanee Review* (April 1979).

An ambitious book by any measure, *Suttree* is a dark comedy set along the Tennessee River in the seamy underbelly of 1950s Knoxville. Difficult to summarize, the novel is, nonetheless, meticulously arranged. Its hero, Cornelius Suttree, has abandoned his family's prosperous way of life for a simpler existence as a fisherman—but that life does not prove to be as simple as he had imagined. He meets "hermits, drunks, thieves, bullies, prostitutes, transvestites, blind men, grifters, preachers, gravediggers, mussel harvesters, parasites, innkeepers, and a witch"—to name just a few of the people who become Suttree's associates and companions in the course of the novel. With more than a hundred named characters, many of whom have more than one name, *Suttree* is a difficult and daunting read. Reminiscent of James Joyce's *Ulysses* in the portrayal of a specific place and time now lost, the dark humor of McCarthy's *Suttree* is unequaled by any of McCarthy's other work.

A lynchpin of sorts, *Suttree* culminates the Southern phase of McCarthy's writing. Thomas D. Young Jr. points out two crucial facts that make the novel "anomalous" among McCarthy's works. First, *Suttree* is an urban novel and, as such, unlike any of McCarthy's other books up to this point in his career. Second, Suttree himself differs from most of McCarthy's main characters: "In taking Cornelius Suttree as its protagonist, the book provides a texture of experience that is considerably more intricate and layered than elsewhere in McCarthy's work." Young continues to argue that despite these departures, the thematic nature of the book does not deviate radically from that of McCarthy's other work.

In 1981, two years after *Suttree* was published, McCarthy received a "genius grant"—a MacArthur Fellowship from the John D. and Catherine T. MacArthur Foundation. McCarthy used his fellowship funds to support himself while writing his fifth novel, an apocalyptic Western set in Texas and Mexico during the 1840s. McCarthy researched thoroughly and extensively for the novel, attaining a feel for the setting of the book by visiting all the locales mentioned in it and even going so far as to learn Spanish. The resulting work, *Blood Meridian, or The Evening Redness in the West,* published in 1985, drew little critical attention at the time of its appearance, although the novel is now regarded as perhaps McCarthy's finest. In his article for *The New Republic* (6 May 1985), Terence Moran deemed the novel "boring," advising McCarthy to "go home, and

take another, closer, look," because the author would "find the real devil soon enough there." Caryn James, writing for *The New York Times Book Review* (28 April 1985), did not agree. She called *Blood Meridian* McCarthy's "most important," because it casts "into perspective the Faulknerian language and unprovoked violence running through the previous works." Through *Blood Meridian,* James asserts, McCarthy prevails on the reader to "witness evil not in order to understand it, but to affirm its inexplicable reality."

As the fifth book in a line of novels by McCarthy that—in Young's view—make up "a sort of interior account of the pioneering of America," *Blood Meridian* takes the topic of the country's western expansion to its "eschatalogical conclusions." The nameless teenage protagonist, "the kid," leaves his home in Tennessee for the West. There he becomes involved with the notorious Glanton Gang, which has contracted with the government to obtain scalps in the Indian wars that are taking place along the frontier. A nightmare of Manifest Destiny, *Blood Meridian* gruesomely details scalpings, beheadings, and other atrocities as the fate of the gang—led by the inscrutable and Ahab-like Judge Holden—is played out in the bleakness of the landscape. Most of the Glanton Gang is killed in a massacre at the Yuma Ferry; the novel ends with the kid dying, years later, at the hands of the judge.

Whereas *Suttree* is dense and tangled, like the flora and fauna of Appalachia, *Blood Meridian* is stark and bleak; none of the detail of the former book, however, is missing in the latter. As always in McCarthy's novels, nature in *Blood Meridian* has a prominent, palpable presence—so much so, that a reader may wonder whether the natural world of the novel actually bears ill will toward its characters. A passage in which the Glanton Gang crosses a gypsum lake demonstrates this seeming malevolence of the landscape:

> On the day that followed they crossed a lake of gypsum so fine the ponies left no track upon it. The riders wore masks of bone-black smeared about their eyes and some had blacked the eyes of their horses. The sun reflected off the pan burned the undersides of their faces and shadow of horse and rider alike were painted upon the fine white powder in purest indigo. Far out on the desert to the north dustspouts rose wobbling and augured the earth and some said they'd heard of pilgrims borne aloft like dervishes in those mindless coils to be dropped broken and bleeding upon the desert again and there perhaps to watch the thing that had destroyed them lurch onward like some drunken djinn and resolve itself once more into the elements from which it sprang.

Bell notes in *The Achievement of Cormac McCarthy* that the nonhuman world of *Blood Meridian,* as presented throughout the novel in terms of the forces and features of nature, competes "for a standing equivalent to the human." At times in *Blood Meridian,* however, McCarthy portrays nature as breathtakingly beautiful, and Bell says of such descriptive passages that they are altogether "incongruous against the backdrop of gore and human depravity." While scenes of carnage and violence pervade *Blood Meridian,* making it a strong contender for the most violent Western ever written, the character of Judge Holden is given to philosophical and metaphysical speculation, as well as musings, regarding the nature of war. The uncompromising and unflinching focus upon violence in the book, exuberantly rendered, is nonetheless the feature that makes *Blood Meridian* distinctive, as shown in this shocking episode that comes early in the novel:

> By and by they came to a bush that was hung with dead babies.
>
> They stopped side by side, reeling in the heat. These small victims, seven, eight of them, had holes punched in their underjaws and were hung so by their throats from the broken stobs of a mesquite to stare eyeless at the naked sky. Bald and pale, and bloated, larval to some unreckonable being.

Although McCarthy frequently writes long, elaborate, Byzantine descriptions of violence and atrocity, in the passage above he adopts a matter-of-fact, understated language. In *Blood Meridian,* according to Bell, language itself has a presence, "and whatever it is that this presence may be said to be is precisely what the judge and his cerebral violence have declared war upon." For the judge, as Bell asserts, "War is God."

Critical opinion about *Blood Meridian* has been sharply divided. Bell and other critics see it as a postmodernist masterpiece, a celebration of brutality and violence. Arnold, on the other hand, refuses to accept such a bleak and nihilistic reading of the novel. He maintains that the kid's quest in *Blood Meridian* is in fact a moral one. He also argues that the presence of Tobin, a character who is supposedly a former priest, presents McCarthy's point of view—an argument that departs from that of most critics, who understand the powerful voice of Judge Holden as McCarthy's own. In a scene from the book, Tobin in stark and staccato dialogue urgently implores the kid to kill the judge, who symbolizes absolute evil in Tobin's mind:

> You'll get no second chance lad. Do it. He is naked. He is unarmed. God's blood, do you think you'll best him any other way? Do it, lad. Do it for the love of God. Do it or I swear your life is forfeit.

The kid will not do so, despite the fact that he has the opportunity; the judge is literally in his sights. As the end of *Blood Meridian* proves, the kid's refusal to kill the judge at Tobin's urging seals the young man's fate. Although it stands as perhaps the most commented upon of all of McCarthy's novels, *Blood Meridian* is finally elemental, irreducible. Defying easy categorization and qualification, the novel ultimately reflects the pinnacle of McCarthy's distinguished career.

McCarthy's reputation among critics began to improve following the publication of *Blood Meridian,* which is dedicated to Albert Erskine, McCarthy's editor at Random House. Erskine's retirement brought about a change of publishers for McCarthy. After *Blood Meridian,* McCarthy began receiving editorial advisement from Gary Fisketjon of Alfred A. Knopf, and at Knopf the author began to receive wider exposure for his work. For example, McCarthy finally agreed to an interview with *The New York Times Magazine* in 1992, the same year that Knopf published *All the Pretty Horses.* The first volume of *The Border Trilogy, All the Pretty Horses* instantly became—unlike McCarthy's earlier books—a publishing sensation and a *New York Times* best-seller. Herbert Mitgang of *The New York Times* (27 May 1992) called the book "a major achievement." *All the Pretty Horses* captures, in Mitgang's words, an "unforgettable journey: part literary, part adventure, part romance, part dream." McCarthy's first book for Knopf sold more than 190,000 copies in hardcover within the first six months of its publication, finally giving McCarthy the broad readership he had been wanting.

*All the Pretty Horses* is a picaresque novel, detailing the adventures of young John Grady Cole. Cole is another of McCarthy's adolescent protagonists, although he may be the only one deserving of the term "hero." On realizing that he will not inherit the family ranch, Cole strikes out for Mexico in 1949 with his friend Lacey Rawlins. En route the boys pick up the younger Jimmy Blevins. Impulsive and rash, Blevins ultimately leads them into trouble. In Mexico, Cole meets Alejandra, and the two fall in love. The couple's youth and the opposition of Alejandra's family keep the lovers from marrying, and Cole eventually returns to the United States alone after killing a man, going to prison, and witnessing Blevins's death. In one of the many dream sequences that permeate not only *All the Pretty Horses* but also the entire *Border Trilogy,* it becomes clear that Cole has an uncommon affinity for horses:

> That night he dreamt of horses in a field on a high plain where the spring rains had brought up the grass and the wildflowers out of the ground and the flowers ran all blue and yellow far as the eye could see and in the dream he was among the horses running and in the

*Dust jacket for McCarthy's extremely violent 1985 novel, about a young man who joins a gang of cutthroats on the Western frontier*

dream he himself could run with the horses and they coursed the young mares and fillies over the plain where their rich bay and their rich chestnut colors shone in the sun and the young colts ran with their dams and trampled down the flowers in a haze of pollen that hung in the sun like powdered gold. . . .

In *All the Pretty Horses* McCarthy adopts a kinder tone than in any of his previous novels. The work takes on an elegiac beauty and simplicity, qualities that were sometimes missing from his earlier books. The story of John Grady Cole is told with sympathy that never lapses into sentimentality. Although some of his experiences in Mexico are brutal, John Grady Cole survives them without becoming violent or depraved as had many of McCarthy's earlier characters.

Response to *All the Pretty Horses* among the McCarthy faithful was mixed. Some believed that McCarthy had abandoned his dark vision for the idyllic and more traditional Western romance, but it seems apparent that McCarthy knew differently. Commenting on that aspect of *All the Pretty Horses,* Richard B. Woodward quotes McCarthy from his 1992 interview with the author:

"'You haven't come to the end yet,' says McCarthy, when asked about the low body count. 'This may be nothing but a snare and a delusion to draw you in, thinking that all will be well.'"

Criticism of McCarthy's works increased markedly in 1992 and 1993. Arnold and Luce edited a special issue of *The Southern Quarterly* devoted to McCarthy's writing; the issue was published, coincidentally, just as *All the Pretty Horses* was gaining momentum and popularity. Many of the essays that first appeared in this special issue were later republished in *Perspectives on Cormac McCarthy*. In 1993 Bellarmine College in Kentucky hosted the first international conference on Cormac McCarthy, from which selected papers were later published in a compilation titled *Sacred Violence: A Reader's Companion to Cormac McCarthy* (1995). Also in 1993, John Emil Sepich's crucial *Notes on Blood Meridian* was published to mark the occasion of the Bellarmine conference. Sepich's book, essentially a work of historical research, demonstrates that much of the story of *Blood Meridian* is factual rather than fictional; Sepich's discovery has led other scholars to undertake similar work with other McCarthy novels. Perhaps the chief contribution to McCarthy scholarship from *Notes on Blood Meridian* is the identification of Samuel Lawrence Chamberlain's *My Confession: Recollections of a Rogue* (1956) as one of McCarthy's primary sources for *Blood Meridian* and as the principal source for McCarthy's depiction of the mercurial Judge Holden.

As critical response to McCarthy's work grew steadily, McCarthy remained committed to his writing. In 1994 Ecco Press published a play, *The Stonemason,* which McCarthy had written in the mid 1970s. *The Stonemason* is a tragedy that explores the fortunes of three generations of an African American family in Kentucky. Papaw, the scion of the Telfair family, is a stonemason. A devoutly religious man, Papaw believes that the Bible has the answers to all the questions of life. Papaw's grandson, Ben Telfair, narrates the play by means of a curious device that places him behind a podium with a double on the stage: while Ben on the stage acts, Ben at the podium comments upon the action the audience is watching. Ben is taken with his grandfather's simple life, a life devoted to the craft of stonemasonry and to God; Ben abandons his extensive education to follow his grandfather's vocation. Ben's father, who Ben believes is worthless, kills himself midway through the play. Ben also has a nephew, Soldier—the son of Ben's sister—who has a severe drug problem. Soldier runs away from the family; later, when Soldier calls Ben and asks for help, Ben gives him money—only to find Soldier dead in a hotel room the next morning, the victim of an overdose. So that the family will not learn the facts of his nephew's death, Ben removes all proofs of identification from Soldier, but he later tells the police he knows who the boy is.

The play has been harshly criticized as one that cannot be produced, primarily because of the demands it places on the set designers. As Peter Josyph noted, speaking of the staging of the play as written:

> . . . the stage-right of *The Stonemason* is one of the most oppressed in theatrical history, for it has to accomodate: 1) Ben's basement study, 2) a country farmhouse *with a real stone wall,* 3) a neighbor, Mrs. Raymond's house, 4) Carlotta's bedroom, 5) a parkbench and a streetlamp, 6) a backyard with picnic tables, chairs, lanterns and bunting, 7) Papaw's bedroom, 8) Big Ben's and Mama's bedroom and bathroom, 9) the family cemetery—with a stone farmhouse in the background!

Critics have also faulted *The Stonemason* for its depiction of African Americans. Arnold in his contribution to *Myth, Legend, Dust: Critical Responses to Cormac McCarthy* (2000), details the problems associated with

the first attempted production of the play at the Arena Stage in Washington, D.C. Although the McCarter Theatre at Princeton University held a workshop production of the play in 1999, *The Stonemason* has yet to be formally produced for the stage by a theater company. A performance of monologues from the play took place on 12 October 2001 at the Arts Alliance Center in Clear Lake, Texas.

Shortly after the publication of *The Stonemason,* Knopf published *The Crossing* (1994), the second volume of McCarthy's *Border Trilogy. The Crossing,* which had a first printing of two hundred thousand copies, sold briskly—thus justifying a second printing of twenty-five thousand copies before the end of the first month after publication. Although *The Crossing* is a picaresque novel, it is darker than the first volume of the trilogy, *All the Pretty Horses,* and its protagonist, Billy Parham, is not a wunderkind—unlike Cole in *All the Pretty Horses.* Parham's story also takes place slightly earlier than Cole's, beginning in the years just before World War II and ending just before the close of the war, whereas the narrative of *All The Pretty Horses* starts well after World War II, in 1949.

Like Cole, Billy Parham is sixteen when the story of *The Crossing* begins. He and his father attempt to trap a wolf that has been killing cattle. Billy successfully traps the wolf and, deciding to return it to its home in Mexico, sets off alone. After a series of adventures, Billy returns to find that his parents have been murdered and their horses stolen. He and his younger brother, Boyd, who has been deeply traumatized by the death of their parents, embark for Mexico to recover the stolen horses. There, Boyd falls in love with a young woman and becomes a hero of the people after being gravely wounded in a fight for their horses. Boyd and his young girlfriend leave without telling Billy, and Billy begins the search for his brother. Billy eventually returns to the United States without his brother and tries to enlist in the military, but he is rejected because of a heart defect. Finally, after working for a time at odd jobs, Billy returns to Mexico, where—instead of finding Boyd—he finds his brother's bones. Somewhat quixotically, he returns them to the United States and buries his brother.

*The Crossing* is a book concerned with the nature of storytelling and the nature of stories themselves. Although sometimes criticized for McCarthy's use of nested tales, these stories—which are told to Billy as he travels—lend the book a poignancy and depth that recalls McCarthy's earlier work. As Luce remarks in her essay "The Road and the Matrix: The World as Tale in *The Crossing*" (*Perspectives on Cormac McCarthy*), "Stripped of these tales, the road narrative of Billy's life is a greatly diminished thing." Throughout his journey, Billy meets older people—sage-like elders who give him advice and suggest to him how he might avoid his tragedy or deal with it once it has occurred. Billy appears, however, not to listen to the tales he is told.

*The Crossing* was a critical success. Robert Hass's front-page review of the novel in *The New York Times Book Review* (12 June 1994) was particularly effusive, as the first paragraph of his critique makes evident:

> How does a writer like Cormac McCarthy—if there is any writer like Cormac McCarthy—follow up on the immense critical and popular success of his novel *All the Pretty Horses,* which won a National Book Award for 1992 and accumulated extraordinary praise? Mr. McCarthy got compared to William Faulkner—he has often been compared to Faulkner—Mark Twain, Herman Melville and Shakespeare. The answer provided by *The Crossing,* the second novel in his projected Border Trilogy, is that he writes an even better book.

Hass, who also called *The Crossing* "a miracle in prose, an American original," suggests that McCarthy is a master stylist writing at the height of his powers.

Much of the critical work about *The Crossing* has been devoted to its nested tales, which provide the reader with hints about McCarthy's elusive worldview. Attempts to explain the nested tales—to unify them—have not always met with success. A few critics also view the tales as ponderous and unnecessary to the simple tale of Billy Parham. Luce is correct, however, when she says in *Perspectives on Cormac McCarthy* that "*The Crossing* is indeed a matrix of intersecting stories, partial or complete, often competing, with varying relationships to truth, and cutting across and interwoven with the apparently simple linearity of the road narrative of Billy's life." The stories are crucial, in other words, to the meaning of the book. According to Luce, *The Crossing* suggests that "the human capability for narrative . . . is our primary means of accessing and perhaps communicating the thing itself: the world which is a tale." *The Crossing,* then, is a multifaceted book, one that is much deeper and more profound than it might first appear—rendering it no mere picaresque novel.

In the spring of 1998, McCarthy married again, this time to thirty-three-year-old Jennifer Winkley, a graduate of the University of Texas at El Paso, who majored in English and American literature. In the summer of that same year, the third volume of *The Border Trilogy, Cities of the Plain,* was published. *Cities of the Plain,* which McCarthy had conceived originally as a screenplay sometime in the late 1970s, received mixed reviews that were generally positive. The book, like both its predecessors in *The Border Trilogy,* was a

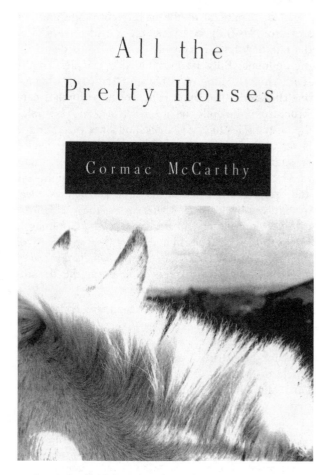

*Dust jacket for McCarthy's 1992 novel, about the misadventures of three young Americans in Mexico in 1949*

*New York Times* best-seller. McCarthy casts Cole from *All the Pretty Horses* and Billy from *The Crossing* as the main characters in *Cities of the Plain.* The novel opens with the two men working on a ranch and describes in haunting and elegiac language the ways of ranch life—which all the characters know will end, because the government is preparing to take the land for a military base.

Cole meets and falls in love with Magdalena, an epileptic Mexican prostitute, and his romance leads to tragedy. Her pimp, Eduardo, who would rather see her die than watch her run away with Cole, kills her. Naturally, Cole must avenge her death, which he does; he kills Eduardo in a knife fight but is himself mortally wounded. Billy, who had warned Cole of the danger inherent in Cole's plan to take Magdalena away and marry her, had nonetheless tried to help Cole achieve his objective. Deeply troubled by the death of his young friend, who had in many ways replaced his long-dead brother, Boyd, Billy leaves the ranch and wanders for years on end.

The epilogue to the novel represents another story told to Billy and takes place a few years after the tale of John Grady Cole ends with his death. In the epilogue, Billy Parham meets a traveler on the road who tells him an elaborate tale of two dreams, one enclosed in the other. The dream-within-a-dream structure of the epilogue in *Cities of the Plain* resembles the nested tales of *The Crossing,* and since the epilogue is set under an interstate highway overpass, it also resonates with McCarthy's 1979 novel, *Suttree,* a narrative set largely in an urban landscape of highways and bridges. Thus, McCarthy ends *The Border Trilogy* by harking back to his earlier work—the philosophical speculation lying at the heart of *The Crossing* is foregrounded once again in *Cities of the Plain.* Many of the events and dream sequences in *The Border Trilogy* are illuminated by the reflection upon the dreams and stories that fill the epilogue.

Most reviewers found the bizarre epilogue in the book confusing, even distressing. However, one scholar views the epilogue as a staggering achievement for McCarthy. As Stacey Peebles writes in an article on McCarthy for *Southwestern American Literature* (Fall 1999), the conclusion of the epilogue shows that

> The borders between childhood and old age, dream and reality, the teller and the tale have dissolved. Cormac McCarthy's parable is this very paradox. . . . By the end of *Cities of the Plain,* we have become the story, staring back through the glass at the person we once were.

Peebles also explores the influence of the literature of the fantastic upon McCarthy's writing. She concludes that McCarthy, in borrowing from writers such as Jorge Luis Borges and Julio Cortázar, creates a work that, in the end, is distinctively his own.

Although *Cities of the Plain* was not ecstatically reviewed upon its publication, it did receive some thoughtful commentary from critics. Sara Mosle, writing in *The New York Times Book Review* (17 May 1998), said that McCarthy is "perhaps the greatest writer since Melville on the subject of work." Illuminating a crucial aspect of McCarthy's writing, she elaborated in the following way:

> His interest in the preservation of lost trades accounts for a lot of his arcane language and links his recent novels with much of his previous writing. He even improves on Melville, for while the encyclopedic descriptions of whales in *Moby-Dick* often remain undigested, McCarthy's intricate recording of how to set a steel trap, say, forms the very fabric of his fiction.

Mosle also noted the recurrence of a pervading theme in all of McCarthy's work, one that in particular infuses *The Border Trilogy:* a concern with the moment just before a culture vanishes. The theme of—in Mosle's words—"That brief moment between a culture's existence and extinction" prevails throughout McCarthy's works, from *The Orchard Keeper* onward.

Finally, critics did not fail to note the intertextuality of the trilogy. As Michiko Kakutani remarked in her review of *Cities of the Plain,* also in *The New York Times* (22 May 1998), a familiarity with the three books that make up *The Border Trilogy* means that one becomes intimate with McCarthy's "use of theme and variation." The "repetition and recapitulation of incidents" do not result from a seeming lack of imagination in McCarthy: "Rather, they are meant to underscore his conviction that certain experiences are mythic in nature, that they are enacted over and over throughout history." For Kakutani, *The Border Trilogy* is best understood not as three single novels but as a unified work—one that takes on deeper meaning and resonance upon the reexamination of each of its parts.

The same is true of Cormac McCarthy's work as a whole. As Michael Dirda, writing a review of *Cities of the Plain* in *The Washington Post Book World* (24 May 1998), observed, "Cormac McCarthy has created an imaginative oeuvre greater and deeper than any single book. Such writers wrestle with the gods themselves." McCarthy's wrestling with the gods began in obscurity with the publication of his first novel, *The Orchard Keeper.* Using the themes of loss, alienation, and the vanishing of cultures, McCarthy's demanding and difficult books were published without fanfare or wide acclaim. Although he received awards and grants for his writing, and despite the fact that he had developed a cult-like following, McCarthy was practically unknown until his sixth novel, *All the Pretty Horses,* captured the imagination of the world of letters. Since then, McCarthy's work has been moving toward the position it should rightly hold in the American canon, not only in Western writing but also in the broader category of American literature. For McCarthy, the work is what matters—rather than the fame that he tries almost constantly to avoid. His prose style, although sure to have its detractors, is wholly original, as is his dark and uncompromising view of humanity.

**Interview:**

Richard B. Woodward, "Cormac McCarthy's Venomous Fiction," *New York Times Magazine* (19 April 1992): 28–31+.

**Bibliography:**

Dianne C. Luce, "Cormac McCarthy: A Bibliography," in *Perspectives on Cormac McCarthy,* edited by Luce and Edwin T. Arnold (Jackson: University Press of Mississippi, 1993), pp. 195–210.

**References:**

Edwin T. Arnold and Dianne C. Luce, eds., *A Cormac McCarthy Companion: The Border Trilogy* (Jackson: University Press of Mississippi, 2001);

Arnold and Luce, eds. *Perspectives on Cormac McCarthy* (Jackson: University Press of Mississippi, 1993; revised, 1999);

Vereen M. Bell, *The Achievement of Cormac McCarthy* (Baton Rouge: Louisiana State University Press, 1988);

Mark Busby and Dick Heaberlin, eds., *Southwestern American Literature,* special McCarthy issue, 25 (Fall 1999);

Wade Hall and Rick Wallach, eds., *Sacred Violence: A Reader's Companion to Cormac McCarthy: Selected Essays from the First McCarthy Conference, Bellarmine College, Louisville, Kentucky, October 15–17, 1993* (El Paso: Texas Western Press of the University of Texas at El Paso, 1995);

David Holloway, ed., *Proceedings of the First European Conference on Cormac McCarthy, The John F. Kennedy Institute of the Free University of Berlin, June 1988* (Miami: The Cormac McCarthy Society, 1999);

Robert L. Jarrett, *Cormac McCarthy,* Twayne's U.S. Authors Series No. 679 (New York: Twayne, 1997);

John Emil Sepich, *Notes on Blood Meridian* (Louisville, Ky.: Bellarmine College Press, 1993);

*Southern Quarterly,* special McCarthy issue, 30 (Summer 1992);

Wallach, ed., *Myth, Legend, Dust: Critical Responses to Cormac McCarthy* (Manchester and New York: Manchester University Press, 2000).

**Papers:**

While Cormac McCarthy has not housed all of his papers in a library, a few McCarthy-related items are to be found in the Southwestern Writers Collection at Southwest Texas State University. The McCarthy holdings consist of all of McCarthy's published works, as well as copies of the screenplays—both unpublished—"Whales and Men" and "Cities of the Plain" and of his play, *The Stonemason.* Also included are items related to the publication of *Perspectives on Cormac McCarthy,* and several screenplay treatments of the Western novels, notably Ted Tally's screenplay of *All the Pretty Horses* and Steve Tesich's treatment of *Blood Meridian.* Finally, the collection consists of items given by McCarthy, Bill and Sally Whitliff, John Emil Sepich, Edwin T. Arnold, and Dianne C. Luce.

# Ron McFarland

*(22 September 1942 –    )*

Keith Browning
*Lewis-Clark State College*

BOOKS: *Certain Women* (Lewiston, Idaho: Confluence, 1977);

*Composting at Forty* (Lewiston, Idaho: Confluence, 1984);

*The Villanelle: Evolution of a Poetic Form* (Moscow: University of Idaho Press, 1988);

*David Wagoner,* Boise State University Western Writers Series, no. 88 (Boise, Idaho: Boise State University Press, 1989);

*The Haunting Familiarity of Things* (Canton, Conn.: Singular Speech, 1993);

*Norman Maclean,* Boise State University Western Writers Series, no. 107 (Boise, Idaho: Boise State University Press, 1993);

*Tess Gallagher,* Boise State University Western Writers Series, no. 120 (Boise, Idaho: Boise State University Press, 1995);

*The World of David Wagoner* (Moscow: University of Idaho Press, 1997);

*Ballgloves and Other Baseball Poems* (Cincinnati, Ohio: Polo Grounds Press, 2000);

*The Mad Waitress Poems* (Fairbanks, Ala.: Permafrost, 2000);

*Stranger in Town: New and Selected Poems* (Lewiston, Idaho: Confluence, 2000);

*Understanding James Welch,* Understanding Contemporary American Literature Series (Columbia: University of South Carolina Press, 2000);

*Catching First Light: 30 Stories and Essays from Idaho* (Pocatello: Idaho State University Press, 2001);

*The Hemingway Poems of Ron McFarland* (San Antonio, Tex.: Pecan Grove, 2001).

OTHER: *American Controversy: Readings & Rhetoric,* edited by McFarland and Paul K. Dempsey (Glenview, Ill.: Scott, Foresman, 1968);

*Eight Idaho Poets,* edited by McFarland (Moscow: University of Idaho Press, 1979);

*James Welch,* edited by McFarland, The Confluence American Authors Series (Lewiston, Idaho: Confluence, 1986);

*Ron McFarland (courtesy of the author)*

*Idaho's Poetry: A Centennial Anthology,* edited by McFarland and William Studebaker (Moscow: University of Idaho Press, 1988);

*Norman Maclean,* edited by McFarland and Hugh Nichols, The Confluence American Authors Series, no. 2 (Lewiston, Idaho: Confluence, 1988);

*Deep Down Things: Poems of the Inland Pacific Northwest,* edited by McFarland, Franz Schneider, and Kornel Skovajsa (Pullman: Washington State University Press, 1990).

SELECTED PERIODICAL PUBLICATION–
UNCOLLECTED: "Not to Worry," 17 poems, *Audit/ Poetry,* 9 (Spring 1978).

Soon after Ron McFarland began teaching at the University of Idaho in 1970, he not only produced the scholarship expected of a young professor intent on gaining tenure but sent out, as well, poetry and fiction to a variety of periodicals. Not surprisingly, in addition to courses and seminars in seventeenth-century and modern British poetry, contemporary Northwest writers, and Ernest Hemingway, McFarland has taught classes in creative writing for many years at the university. McFarland also played a role in the literary renaissance that has evolved in recent years in Idaho. Many Idaho-born writers and educators have joined forces with writers and educators who grew up outside the state but now consider Idaho their home, developing and modernizing a community of writers that is also nationally renowned. This community includes such authors as Kim Barnes, Mary Blew, Claire Davis, Gary Gildner, and Robert Wrigley as well as Kent Anderson, Rick Ardinger, Robert Olmstead, and William Studebaker. McFarland in particular stirred up interest in contemporary Northwest writers by inviting them to the University of Idaho campus for readings of their works and by becoming well acquainted with an older generation of Northwest writers–including Richard Hugo, William Stafford, David Wagoner, and James Welch.

Born 22 September 1942 in Bellaire, Ohio, to Earl A. and Maxine Stullenburger McFarland, Ronald Earl McFarland had an enviable childhood and young adulthood unblighted by the kinds of family dysfunctions that members of other generations have had to bear. An Eagle Scout and a high school band cornet player, McFarland–the firstborn of four–learned out of necessity how to work and to get by on his own money. While the McFarlands were never in any great financial difficulty, they were not well-to-do. Of his parents, Earl McFarland seems to have had a more significant impact on his son's life; many of McFarland's poems feature his father. In World War II, Earl McFarland was an army officer attached to a communications unit in Hollywood that made military movies. Earl McFarland talked wryly about fighting the "Battle of Hollywood" and being in the same unit as cowboy star Gene Autry. After the war the family moved to Cocoa, Florida, where McFarland attended grade school and high school, had a paper route, and worked as a box boy in a grocery store and as a part-time evening library staff member.

McFarland received an associate degree in 1962 from Brevard Junior College in Cocoa. In 1963 he received a B.A. in English from Florida State University. A teaching assistantship in the English department there helped him to complete his M.A. in 1965. On 29 January 1966 McFarland married Elsie Watson; the couple eventually had three children–Kimberly, Jennifer, and Jonathan. McFarland taught as an instructor at Sam Houston State College, now Sam Houston State University, in Huntsville, Texas, for two years before starting graduate school at the University of Illinois, Urbana, from which he received a Ph.D. in English in 1970. The completion of his doctorate led McFarland, in the fall of that year, to a position as an assistant professor in the English Department at the University of Idaho.

McFarland is a "middle-American" writer who has lived long enough in the Northwest to have a sense of how the region differs from other areas in the United States. Some of McFarland's poems could be illustrated by Norman Rockwell, especially if the all-American illustrator could have resisted coloring his work with sentiment. *Certain Women* (1977), McFarland's first collection of poems, introduces a preoccupation that flits in and out of the poet's works to date–the "riddle" of the presence of females on this earth, as mentioned in the truncated sonnet "Five Women at the Garden Lounge":

> As if beneath the table your rung-entangled legs
> will solve the riddle of your presence,
> my eyes unscramble wood and flesh
> and reassemble.
> My ears collect and classify each syllable,
> dissect the sounds that tumble from your lips,
> and help my eyes to handle what they see
> amid the jumble
> of cigarette packs, gin-and-tonic
> and the rubble of wet napkins which
> my fingers clutch for the softness
> they resemble.

In these lines an interior trail of slant and near rhyme leads to the key word at the end, "resemble"–there is no semblance of softness about these women. "Certain Women," as the initial poem in the chapbook suggests, takes masculinity a step further. "Women like that," the poet speculates, "cannot stand tenderness. / Not of their flesh, / your soft caress / wears like a cold stare." Beyond this brief examination of the masculine side of femininity, McFarland pursues his riddle relentlessly: he considers subjects from many angles, poetic forms, and points of view. Yet, for the most part, he keeps his style light, whimsical, and witty.

Several of the poems in *Certain Women* consider women as mythic or legendary figures. In "Moon Women," Hecate, Selene, Diana, and Luna appear reincarnated according to the moods of a single second-person subject. In "Circe," Ulysses' crew—or a single member thereof—understands such reincarnation: "She changed us into what we had become." "The Phasian Bird" and "The Lentil Queen" both update and localize their subject matters. "The Phasian Bird" may or may not belong in this collection. Readers are lured into the land of Colchis and the Phasian River from which Jason has departed with the king's daughter:

> he sailed her away to civilization
> and lived to regret it.
> . . . . . . . . . . . . . . . .
> At night she was strange
> and at dawn she longed
> for the Phasian bird that carried the sun
> in its wings.
>
> Jason began to stray from his throne,
> to stay out hunting days at a time
> returning with the smell of the kill
> and something else,
> a new silence.
> . . . . . . . . . . . .
> The pheasant folds and drops.
> Eager teeth clutch the still colors,
> hold an old silence.

Moving swiftly from antiquity to a field in Idaho or Ohio, the above lines call forth a few questions. Who is the "certain woman" in this poem? Is she Jason's beloved, Medea? Is she the markswoman or the retrieving dog? Or is the certain woman actually a composite of these three—pheasant, markswoman, and dog combined as one? McFarland suggests that it does not matter. For example, in "The Lentil Queen," the Lentil Queen may or may not be Persephone, but she is surely a twentieth-century teenager from the Idaho panhandle:

> Heir apparent to the peas,
> you ease the hard red wheat
> beneath your combine
> green as a crown jewel,
> jasmine cigarettes censing the cab.
>
> What does your wheat whisper
> under a cold half moon?
> "Remember Ceres beautiful as you.
> We feel her presence in our roots,
> feel her pain in your sickle. Beware."
> . . . . . . . . . . . . . . . . . . . . . . . . . . .
> You bend the brim of your leather hat.
> "I have a beauty. I fear nothing.

> Tomorrow I disk the wheat stubble
> relentless. What does it mean?
> I flourish. I am the lentil queen."

Two short lyric-narratives in *Certain Women*, "Japanese Novel" and "At the Nursing Home," read like "sudden fiction"—a short story of a paragraph or less—and show an early bent for mixing genres. "Japanese Novel" resembles a haiku closely enough to sound authentic:

> An old story told with ancient delicacy
> like a nearly transparent teacup.
> When you look into it from the top
> the oolong magnifies a figure
> at the bottom:
> Mrs. Ota
> committing suicide with quiet
> powders.
> Where did she get them?
> Her daughter telephones the lover
> announcing the death as softly as she can,
> so he may be guilty
> without remorse.

"At the Nursing Home" features an old woman awaiting death and with just a single story to tell: how she canned vegetables one fall in central Idaho while her sister was there. Telling the story, she peels the apples, snaps the beans, and slices the carrots: "Again that legend. John, her husband, / loved his applesauce. / Only one jar failed to seal."

In the spring of 1978, *Audit/Poetry*—the literary journal of State University of New York at Buffalo—published a double chapbook featuring seventeen of McFarland's poems. In 1979 he edited an anthology of poetry called *Eight Idaho Poets* and began a one-year stint as poetry editor at *The Slackwater Review*, serving as general editor from 1981 to 1982. *The Slackwater Review* was the literary journal of Confluence Press, the publisher of several chapbooks and monographs by McFarland, and was located at Lewis-Clark State College in Lewiston, Idaho, since 1976. In the fall of 1983, the Idaho Commission on the Arts—led by distinguished Northwest writer William Stafford—announced that McFarland would become the first "Idaho State Writer in Residence." Confluence and the poet immediately began planning a new book of verse.

The book, *Composting at Forty,* came out in the spring of 1984. Suggesting a whimsical combination of the serious, the comic, and the satirical, *Composting at Forty* encompassed new poems as well as poems selected from two prior chapbooks and the anthology *Eight Idaho Poets.* The cover of the book and the illustrations in its five sections originate from seventeenth-century "emblemes" by George Wither, a metaphysical poet, consisting of a graphic woodcut and moral couplet; the moral couplet that accompanies the emblem on the cover reads, "*A* Fortune *is ordained for thee, / According as thy* Labours *be*."

The emblems in the collection employed an agricultural metaphor, and the title poem, "Composting at Forty"–from section three–seemed appropriately agricultural when the book was published. Today, however, from a distance of nearly two decades, the poem "Composting at Forty" hints at an interesting tension between the form and the content of the book as a whole. The poet muses on the early morning arrival of the city garbage crew in a "great green gorging truck" that has come to "cram the rinds of my oranges, / succulent honeydew, exotic coffee grounds, / into your maw." "No more," he declares. "Now I'm plowing it all back in, / reinvesting it along with rotten apples, / maple leaves, grass clippings, cigarettes / and other bad old habits in this bank of dirt." Then he tells the reader:

> I am cultivating a new reverence
> for the undevoured, for all the small
> unsavory things on the earth,
> for all the half-cooked peas,
> burnt beans, stale crusts of bread, eggshells.
> By God
> they shall be nobly put to use
> through the intercession of the acids,
> friction, heat, weight of the soil,
> rain and melting snow dissolving
> their weak identities
> for a new, rich, dark and fertile earth.

The above lines in actuality reflect little whimsy, giving an idea of the tonal range of the collection–from very dark, indeed, to gray. Even the little Lentil Queen–from the poem of the same title and republished in *Composting at Forty*–seems less sure of herself.

The emblematic motto for the first section of the book states, "*He that delights to* Plant *and* Set, / *Makes* After-ages *in his* Debt." The opening poem in this first section, "Poet in Residence," is a sufficiently gray self-portrait:

> Who is your modern poetry man
> is rather what is your modern poetry man
> is the fellow with the dark mad hair
> and fluffy mustache
> leaning over there against the wall
> looking tweedy and seedy all at once
> and wondering about his book and tenure
> and the look of a brown-eyed coed
> and where the next poem is coming from.

In the lyric titled "Some of You," McFarland delivers a fantasy lecture to a group of students, some of whom "should not even be" there, being just "green kids from Kansas"; some of whom "don't even know what love and beauty are"; and for some of whom "there is no excuse unless you can find it somewhere in this enormous text." The poems "At Sixty" and "Have Fun" merit comment, since the first is as impersonal as the second is personal. "At Sixty" could be a portrait of almost any World War II draftee for whom the war represented the best years of his life–a life that has now become a "curiosity" and an hour-by-hour existence full of frustration:

> Slim fingers slip away from your clasp.
> The war confuses itself with films
> about the war or books about the war.
> Three memories from Morotai reserved
> for such occasions: the heat, mosquitoes,
> no Japs. It must be hard,
> someone says, living these days
> on a fixed income.

"Have Fun" describes an evening coincidental to the literary history of Montana and Idaho:

> We aren't having fun.  These women,
> they are all grey and they keep on
> getting greyer whenever you touch them.
>
> The waitresses, especially the young blondes,
> turn greyest of all, and quickest.
> . . . . . . . . . . . . . . . . . . . . . . . .
>
> Tomorrow we'll fish the Clearwater,
> and the water will be grey. We'll drink
> coffee, rub our heads, swear off
> these funny drunks. We'll talk
> about anything but women, Italy,
> Glenn Miller, food, and poetry.
> You will drive to Montana alone,
> tell everyone there that you had fun.

In this poem McFarland as Idahoan poet pays tribute to the late Montanan poet, Richard Hugo, who wrote about his home state in–among other lyrics–"Degrees of Grey in Phillipsburg."

The second section of *Composting at Forty* carries the motto, "*Behold, you may, the* Picture *here, / Of what keeps* Man *and* Childe *in feare*." This part of the book includes a few poems from *Certain Women*, continuing the poet's scrutiny of the opposite sex. In a poem titled "Other Women," McFarland describes other women as the "rarely beautiful" yet interesting and, sometimes, mysterious figures at the peripheries of male imaginings: "These priceless women are / just barely tangible / quick touches, kisses that / don't quite happen, some-

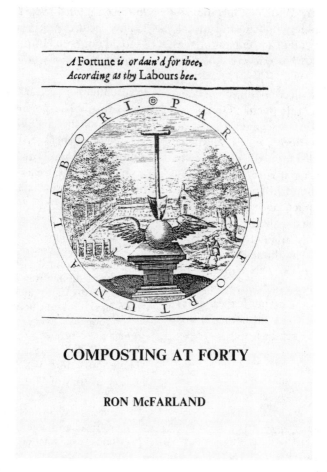

*A* Fortune *is* or dain'd for thee, *According as thy* Labours *bee.*

**COMPOSTING AT FORTY**

**RON McFARLAND**

Cover, with emblem and couplet from the seventeenth-century metaphysical poet George Wither, for McFarland's 1984 collection of verse

times, / words, barely beautiful." "Portrait of an Independent Woman" ponders the reality of being a female bachelor. "The Hanford Wives" is a memorable Northwest satire based on a popular Hollywood movie and a "city that does not exist" but has been a Northwest problem for decades, the Hanford nuclear plant:

Here in Richland, Kennewick, Pasco,
suburbs of a city that does not exist,
we study our lives
in brief verses,
we, the Hanford wives.
. . . . . . . . . . . . . . . . .

Dust can storm in here
from any direction, blotting the sun.
North of us something
more unstable than ourselves
happens in a language
even the sun would not understand.
Bees keep my husband occupied
when he's not occupied with the reactor.
The children love it.

Three poems in this section about women merit consideration because of their interesting "degrees" of darkness. The genesis of "Not To Worry" is a news report of a missing girl:

By the way, that seven-year-old girl
was found this evening
unmolested in her strawberry
red sweater,
                her sky-blue eyes
still unexperienced.

The poem also reveals that the girl was not in the empty lot full of chest-high thistles and empty ovens. The weird, effete stamp collector who had brought her a popsicle that day had been visiting his mother in Nebraska when the girl was missing. Although the news item reported that her parents were divorced, they were not; they were merely busy planning a vacation to the Grand Canyon.

She was next door
all the time, eating cookies

with a wonderful old Lutheran lady
who collects salt and pepper shakers,
plays the piano and keeps
tropical fish.
           The old lady has no warts
on her fingers,
but she speaks with a slight Latvian accent.
She says her name is Madame Rasputin
and she is waiting for a visit
from Madame Blatvatsky and the Czar.

McFarland casts into question whether the nice old lady is a lunatic or simply an eccentric with an academic's sense of humor. Either way, there is an element of mockery pointing to what might just as easily have been the truth. There is no ambiguity in "Asotin Girl Still Lost"–rather, a chillingly probable conclusion to a twelve-year-old girl's night at a country fair and carnival:

What happened later, when the gears of The Whip
stiffened?
           I think, Christine, you heard the moon
ring out eternity,
and your bicycle sliced its choppy trail,
                              its river-silky light
                              its doubtful path,
like a hand over a mouth.

How would Rockwell have painted the poem "An American Grandma Foresees Her Death?" Would he have depicted a horde of loving relatives gathered for Easter Sunday or only grandma's dim old eyes able to see Jesus with a beatific smile, holding out his hands? McFarland knows that "fictive" subjects wink most when widows and grandmas wince:

When was it death
began to whisper at your crocheted edges?

Suddenly you cannot turn the pages.
Grinning physicians mock your dreams.
Your teeth rattle
like someone else's teeth,
and if you turn the page, what then?
You reserved your life for love,
learning to hate nothing.
Now what do you have to greet this confusion?
Central Florida's finest collection
of salt and pepper shakers.

The new poems in *Composting at Forty* do wax whimsical here and there. "Remains of Icarus Uncovered" begins, "Last week we found the bones of Icarus / a few miles west of Pine Bluff, Arkansas." "The Sagebrush Rebellion" takes popular catchwords out of Western politics and puts them in a more natural, even surreal, setting. The poem shows

the sagebrush from Wyoming to Oregon and Washington actually rebelling. Ultimately, the "rarest" stuff to sprout from this veritable McFarland compost heap are the poems that derive from a writer who has lived in the intermountain West long enough to be able to lend it the benefit of a broader Eastern experience in spite of his academic leanings. "Goodbye Washtucna" is a good example. A farming community in eastern Washington, Washtucna is typical of those places where there is not much for young people to do, and ways to get into trouble are in short supply as well:

Tumbleweed blusters across the road
as if intent on some gray mission
among green shoots of wheat.
. . . . . . . . . . . . . . . . . . . . . .
The schoolbus crushes them,
leaves their spindly bones along the way,
but most of them carry on.

The farmers send their children
to Washtucna to learn things, play
football, or just grow up
in some clandestine way and go,
not causing trouble. After school
they stop for soft drinks and a game of pool,
and everything's great
except the eightball's gone,
but most of them carry on.

McFarland's next book-length collection of verse was *The Haunting Familiarity of Things* (1993). Deborah Clifford Gessaman remarks in her review of the book for *Western American Literature* (February 1995) that "Narrative poems flow like stories, without sections or chapter titles." She suggests that McFarland's narrative poems reflect

a serendipitous technique that leads readers into individual seeing. McFarland examines ways of knowing at all ages and stages of life; ways of believing that guide lives. He provides tension and movement by forging "eastern" intellectualism for "western" recovery from our "stingy sensibilities" grown that way by passively "waiting daily for something to happen. / It never does." Thus he elevates, enlivens, and enlarges small happenings through ways of seeing that raise the ordinary nearer the extraordinary.

On the back cover of *The Haunting Familiarity of Things,* poet Pattiann Rogers observes, "The transformation of the ordinary into the rare has always been one crucial responsibility of the poet. McFarland's poems give honor to the ordinary things of his life." Rogers's assessment is undoubtedly true, yet from the stand-

Burning the Bad Nuns          Peruvian          5-4-91
This afternoon I burned the four nuns
You may have heard about a few months ago,
the ones caught smuggling cocaine in their
old habits, having been expelled from the order.

Burning with the dry raspberry canes
Dry raspberry canes gave flare to the fire,
but mostly I burned them the old Spanish way,
in the slow green sizzle of apple branches
pruned from the trees to improve the fruit.

Smoking my two-dollar cigar, I gave
hardly a second thought to their Third world
souls gone graceless or to their once proud
families in disgrace, the taken dead from
living in squalor. Cholera,
Feeling religious for the first time in years,
I righteously raked their gray ashes
believing they would nurture my garden.
Then I sprayed them till they turned black.

Lords, what heat those gloomy ladies gave!
Later I found my eyebrows singed from
moving too close, wanting to save
no stick, no, not one clipping from the
conflagration.

Cool now, I recall how then my face
burned, how my resilient anger fed
on their shame, and how the sweat
rushed down my cheeks almost like tears.

Streaked my glasses and poured down
my cheeks
almost like tears.

*First and third drafts for a poem that appears in McFarland's 1993 collection,* The Haunting Familiarity of Things
(Collection of Ron McFarland)

point of *Certain Women* and *Composting at Forty,* one can go even further. Specifically, *The Haunting Familiarity of Things* includes two touchstone poems; the other lyrics in the book are, in effect, permutations or combinations of the two touchstone poems and other poems from McFarland's first two books of verse.

"Home from Vacation" describes a disruption of one's sense of what is known–the familiar–and what is not known–the formal. The lyric suggests a need to structure or formalize what is unknown and uncertain; in such a way, the formal is antithetical to the familiar. One takes the familiar for granted and relaxes with it, while the formal prohibits such familiarity:

Nothing seems quite right.
The neighbors wave as if we were strangers
or worse,
          long lost relatives.
. . . . . . . . . . . . . . . . . . .

          The quiet relief
of our own front door feels odd.
. . . . . . . . . . . . . . . . . . .

We bewilder ourselves.
Who left these coffee grounds to mold all month?
Who forgot to throw away
                    that half loaf
of hard gray furry bread?
                    Is this really the last
chance to renew *Time?*
                    Who were these people? Who
had these grotesque artifacts?
. . . . . . . . . . . . . . . . . . .
Should we call to have the paper
aim us back into time and place?
                    Everything seems
hauntingly familiar.

Through these lines McFarland shows how the ambiguity of the familiar and the formal can open doors to imaginative speculation and creativity. Poetry, McFarland

```
              Burning the Bad Nuns


     This afternoon I burned the four Peruvian nuns
     you may have heard about a few months ago,
     the ones caught smuggling drugs in their
     old habits, having been expelled from the order.

     Dry raspberry canes gave flare to my fire,
     but mostly I burned them the old Spanish way,
     in the slow green sizzle of apple branches
     pruned from the trees to improve the fruit.

     Smoking my two-dollar cigar, I gave
     hardly a second thought to their Third World
     souls gone graceless or to their once proud
     families in disgrace, their sisters living in squalor,
     the father dead from cholera.

     Feeling religious for the first time in years.
     I righteously raked their gray ashes,
     believing they would nurture my garden.
     Then I sprayed them till they turned black.

     Lord, what heat those gloomy ladies gave!
     Later I found my eyebrows singed from
     moving too close, wanting to save no stick,
     no, not one clipping from that conflagration.

     Cool now, I recall how then my face
     burned, how my resilient rage rekindled
     in their  shame, and how the merciless sweat
     streaked my glasses and poured down my cheeks
     almost like tears
```

8-28-91

hints, thrives on such ambiguity. "Home from Vacation" is also a verse that, much like an overcoat, gathers several other poems from the collection into its folds—such as "A Disturbing Sense of Reality" and "Ghost Mall." Another lyric, "Burning the Bad Nuns," tells what happens when the warping of the familiar and the formal becomes self-referential, leading to speculation in the dark side of one's own psyche: "This afternoon I burned the four Peruvian nuns / you may have heard about a few months ago, / the ones caught smuggling drugs in their / old habits, having been expelled from the order." Poems such as this one and others are not unrelated to the darker pieces in the previous collection.

"Out Here" is the "cover" poem for all those readers who are basically concerned with Western, intermountain ways of living and thinking:

In New York, L.A., Chicago, even Seattle
passions run riot in ways we cannot
feel with our stingy sensibilities.
People keep on living there as if
they were going to die

in the next minute,
so of course they do.
A friend who works for the *Wall Street Journal*
says it's the only honest way to live.

Out here we live as if
we're going to live forever.

"Spring Comes to the Clearwater" is typical of McFarland's lyrics that concern the ways of western life: "Outside Kooskia, Idaho / where the mill closed last week, / April stirs in the roots of grass / as if everyone / had work." "Town Marshall" explains why a small intermountain Western town "doesn't need a good cop."

The Western as opposed to Eastern ways of life, rural as opposed to urban—these themes come together in McFarland's poems about small towns, the proverbial "little guy," and middle-American values. The eccentric wit, academic training, and intellectual restlessness that are characteristic of McFarland make these poems especially interesting. *Stranger in Town: New and*

*Selected Poems* (2000), his most recent book-length collection, includes approximately fifty new poems, proving that McFarland's restlessness has not diminished. *Stranger in Town* discloses different slants on the old themes and interests of McFarland's previous poetry volumes as well as a new focus—as his title poem, "A Stranger in Town," shows:

> Being a stranger in town you head
> straight for the wrong restaurant,
> where the crab sandwich is something
> fishy, the coffee is instant but cold,
> and the pie was stamped out by machine
> two months ago, then flash-frozen
> in a faraway city, spirited here,
> and microwaved for you, personally.

The waitress "feels sorry for herself" and "even sorrier for you," so she relates her life story. "Stranger in Town" shows the second-person speaker "Stumbling into the night," finding a bad bar and a worse bartender, recently divorced. As the lyric conveys, this is not the first time the stumbling has occurred:

> You have done all this before.
> Your wife says you always do it.
> Best not to spend the night here, but
> skedaddle now before High Noon
> catches up with you about midnight.
> You've seen that movie before.
> Being a stranger in town you can
> hardly wait to get out by sundown,
> but it's always already too late.

Through this poem and others like "Wheatspill," "At the Museum of Lost Toys," "Taking Fire," and "The Apology," one is faced with experiences of psychic dislocations, as opposed to mere warps or disruptions—lost in parallel mental universes from which one cannot, or is quite unlikely to, escape. The formal has displaced the familiar in the direction of nightmare. Ultimately, these poems present "virtual realities," and most of the other lyrics in the collection are written in different modes as well. McFarland is neither a Western nor an Eastern writer, tied one way or another to the land or a particular location. A McFarland lyric creates its own world—one that is almost always fascinating.

From a literary or cultural standpoint, what does the fictive world in McFarland's verse signify? McFarland's muse has always been as restless as his intellect and is indebted to his academic background. His middle-American nurturing and his many years living in the intermountain Northwest have been equally important, resulting in a poetic canon that has escaped the extremes of "postmodernist" polemics and experimentation—as well as the "modernist" fondness for opacity.

McFarland depicts a quirky world, one that is always accessible yet rarely lacks depth.

Creative writers, particularly poets, tend to focus their professional energy on one genre. Likewise, scholars typically publish in or around their major field of disciplinary expertise. McFarland, however, has not confined his interests, time, or efforts to one type of writing. He treads both paths of scholarly and creative writing, having contributed significantly in each discipline. Indeed, he has written widely on such Northwest writers as Wagoner, Welch, Norman Maclean, and Tess Gallagher, and on the poetry of seventeenth-century England, yet he is also a published poet of eminent standing in Western American literature. McFarland has served twice as Director of Creative Writing at the University of Idaho.

When Confluence published *Stranger in Town*, McFarland had four other books under consideration or already accepted at other presses. These were all published by 2001. *The Mad Waitress Poems* (2000) divides its attention between two familiar McFarland themes: small-town, middle-American life and the riddle of hardheaded females, which the poet initiated in *Certain Women* (1978). In this curious volume one is confronted with rural middle-America in its bleak cafés, where scrambled eggs can be ice-cold and waitresses never smile, as in "The Homestead Café." One must sympathize with these waitresses, however, upon meeting the maddest one of them all who "begins going crazy before sunrise / shaking herself from bed like a box of cornflakes / or a tablecloth." *The Mad Waitress* won the Permafrost Chapbook Contest in spring 2000. *Ballgloves and Other Baseball Poems* (2000), a chapbook of eight lyrics, is full of nostalgia for the days when the game was less commercial and more like an art form that fit the American psyche like a good outfielder's glove might fit an aficionado's youthful hand. Another well-wrought chapbook, *The Hemingway Poems of Ron McFarland* (2001), could be written only by a poet who is also a competent Hemingway scholar. It won the Summer 2000 National Chapbook Competition.

*Catching First Light: 30 Stories and Essays from Idaho* (2001) is McFarland's first book of prose. Diverse in themes and narrative viewpoints, the book consists of twenty short stories and ten essays. While nine of the stories and essays concern hunting or fishing in some way, all of the essays are set in the first person, as in a memoir. The title essay humorously recalls a duck-hunting trip. Its narrator admits that—unlike his companions—he has never relished rising with the sun, even if the chances of successful hunting or fishing are improved by "catching first light." The stories, on the other hand, are told from the perspectives of both first-person and third-person narrarors. In addition, three of the stories present a woman's viewpoint.

Virtually all of the characters in the stories live in small towns in Idaho. As readers move through the narratives, they might find themselves at an out-of-control college faculty party, as in "The Hullaballoo, or A Kind of Good Time Was Had by Almost Everyone," or inside the head of a whiny redneck, as in "A Three-Bar Town." One story featured in *Catching First Light,* "Different Words for Snow," won the Dr. O. Marvin Lewis Prize from Weber Studies in 1999; a comedy, the story is about a fish-and-game officer who lives near Grangeville and speaks ungrammatically.

The experience of moving in a linear way through *Catching First Light* involves an emotional oscillation that recalls the blending of wit and pathos in McFarland's poetry. Almost always, an element of whimsey is at play in his work—though not without a hint of sadness at the edges. He shares John Keats's perspective as expressed in "Ode on Melancholy" (1819): "joy, whose hand is ever at his lips / Bidding adieu."

A University of Idaho research bulletin, *Idaho Research* (Winter 1996), discusses the kind of intellectual restlessness that McFarland himself terms "eclecticism":

> Generally, his research and scholarly writing follow the directions of his teaching. For example, when he was in hot pursuit of tenure and promotion in the early 1970s, he was teaching 400- and 500-level courses on 17th century British poets. Accordingly his scholarship dealt with such writers as Thomas Traherne, Ben Johnson, and John Donne. But eclectics rarely become committed to a single group of writers or to a specific critical agenda. Thus, when he came across poems by Edward, Lord Herbert of Cherbury, about a "green-sickness beauty," he took time to investigate the disease known as chlorosis, studied Renaissance medical work on the subject, and wrote an article on several poems dealing with it. Teaching Ovid's *Metamorphoses* in English 111 classes led him to write essays on the myth of Apollo and Daphne and of Daedalus and Icarus in Renaissance poetry.

Through his writing, as the article goes on to point out, Ron McFarland deals with whatever interests him—and his interests are catholic, to say the least. What is remarkable is the amount of material—scholarly and creative—he has published and, no doubt, will continue to publish.

**References:**

*Contemporary Authors New Revision,* 32 (1991): 293–294;

Deborah Clifford Gessaman, "Manic Eclecticism: English Professor Revels in Diverse Studies," *Idaho Research* (Winter 1996): 15–18;

Gessaman, "Review Essay," *Western American Literature,* 29 (February 1995): 381.

# Larry McMurtry

*(3 June 1936 – )*

Mark Busby
*Center for the Study of the Southwest*
*Southwest Texas State University, San Marcos*

See also the McMurtry entries in *DLB 2: American Novelists Since World War II* and *DLB 143: American Novelists Since World War II, Third Series.*

BOOKS: *Horseman, Pass By* (New York: Harper, 1961); republished as *Hud* (New York: Popular Library, 1963; London: Sphere, 1971);

*Leaving Cheyenne* (New York: Harper & Row, 1963; London: Sphere, 1972);

*The Last Picture Show* (New York: Dial, 1966; London: Sphere, 1972);

*In a Narrow Grave* (Austin: Encino Press, 1968);

*Moving On* (New York: Simon & Schuster, 1970; London: Weidenfeld & Nicolson, 1971);

*All My Friends Are Going To Be Strangers* (New York: Simon & Schuster, 1972; London: Secker & Warburg, 1973);

*It's Always We Rambled: An Essay on Rodeo* (New York: Frank Hallman, 1974);

*Terms of Endearment* (New York: Simon & Schuster, 1975; London: W. H. Allen, 1977);

*Somebody's Darling* (New York: Simon & Schuster, 1978);

*Cadillac Jack* (New York: Simon & Schuster, 1982; London: W. H. Allen, 1986);

*The Desert Rose* (New York: Simon & Schuster, 1983; London: W. H. Allen, 1985);

*Lonesome Dove* (New York: Simon & Schuster, 1985; London: Pan, 1986);

*Film Flam: Essays on Hollywood* (New York: Simon & Schuster, 1987);

*Texasville* (New York: Simon & Schuster, 1987; London: Sidgwick & Jackson, 1987);

*Anything for Billy* (New York: Simon & Schuster, 1988; London: Collins, 1989);

*Some Can Whistle* (New York: Simon & Schuster, 1989; London: Century, 1990);

*Buffalo Girls* (New York: Simon & Schuster, 1990; London: Century, 1990);

*The Evening Star* (New York: Simon & Schuster, 1992; London: Orion, 1992);

*Larry McMurtry (photograph by Diana Lynn Ossana)*

*Streets of Laredo* (New York: Simon & Schuster, 1993; London: Orion, 1993);

*Pretty Boy Floyd,* by McMurtry and Diana Lynn Ossana (New York: Simon & Schuster, 1994; London: Orion, 1996);

*The Late Child* (New York: Simon & Schuster, 1995; London: Orion, 1996);

*Dead Man's Walk* (New York: Simon & Schuster, 1995; London: Orion, 1995);

*Comanche Moon* (New York: Simon & Schuster, 1997; London: Orion, 1997);

*Zeke and Ned,* by McMurtry and Ossana (New York: Simon & Schuster, 1997; London: Orion, 1997);

*Crazy Horse* (New York: Lipper / Viking, 1999; London: Weidenfeld & Nicolson, 1999);

*Duane's Depressed* (New York: Simon & Schuster, 1999; London: Orion, 1999);

*Walter Benjamin at the Dairy Queen: Reflections at Sixty and Beyond* (New York: Simon & Schuster, 1999);

*Boone's Lick* (New York: Simon & Schuster, 2000);

*Roads: Driving America's Great Highways* (New York: Simon & Schuster, 2000; London: Orion, 2000);

*Paradise* (New York: Simon & Schuster, 2001);

*Sacagawea's Nickname: Essays on the American West* (New York: New York Review of Books, 2001).

PRODUCED SCRIPTS: *The Last Picture Show,* motion picture, by McMurtry and Peter Bogdanovich, Columbia, 1971;

*Montana,* television, HBO, 19 February 1990;

*Memphis,* television, by McMurtry and Cybill Shepherd, TNT, 27 January 1992;

*Falling from Grace,* motion picture, Columbia, 1992;

*Larry McMurtry's Streets of Laredo,* television, by McMurtry and Diana Lynn Ossana, CBS, 12 November 1995;

*Larry McMurtry's Dead Man's Walk,* television, by McMurtry and Ossana, ABC, 12 May 1996;

*The Evening Star,* motion picture, Paramount Pictures and Rysher Entertainment, 1996.

OTHER: *Still Wild: Short Fiction of the American West, 1950 to the Present,* edited by McMurtry (New York: Simon & Schuster, 2000).

SELECTED PERIODICAL PUBLICATION—
UNCOLLECTED: "Ever a Bridegroom: Reflection of the Failure of Texas Literature," *Texas Observer* (23 October 1981): 1, 8–19.

Larry McMurtry's work is marked by his imaginative connections with the American West. Drawn to place, McMurtry demonstrates in his work the mythic pattern of escape and return to his "blood's country," his homeland. After garnering initial celebrity by writing about the passing of the Southwest known to the cowboy, McMurtry soon scorned the work his critics praised and praised the work his critics scorned—urban novels cut off from the old Southwest. In the 1980s McMurtry returned to the settings and themes he had rejected, and the critical fame he previously had enjoyed came back as well. In fact, McMurtry's novels and his life both demonstrate that traveling is an axiomatic part of both. Throughout much of his life, McMurtry has found his home territory an awkward, uneasy place. Growing up in Texas created productive tension between his love for the land that nourished him and an equally strong aversion to the narrow-minded elements of his heritage.

McMurtry's productivity suggests that he is a compulsive writer, and he has admitted that he gets a headache if he does not complete his self-imposed task of writing at least 5 double-spaced pages every day—more than 1,800 manuscript pages a year. McMurtry may have produced a phenomenal amount of work because he is the offspring of a Texas ranching family that extolled hard work and physical production.

Larry Jeff McMurtry was born 3 June 1936 in Wichita Falls, Texas, to William Jefferson McMurtry Jr. and Hazel Ruth McIver McMurtry and grew up in Archer County, Texas, in a family that had ranched in Texas for three generations. There he learned about Southwesterners' violence, intolerance, hypocrisy, and puritanical attitudes, as well as their strength of character, endurance, emphasis on hard work, courage, and particularly what became the most important tools in his workshop—the powers of storytelling and humor. He also discovered one of the chief themes of his work, what he calls the tragic theme of the twentieth- and twenty-first-century Southwest—the end of a way of life signaled by the move off the land. Climbing on the barn at night, young McMurtry looked out across the Texas prairie and sent his imagination with the night trains to Los Angeles and the eighteen-wheelers pointed toward Fort Worth.

McMurtry's grandparents, originally from Boston County, Missouri, moved to Archer County from Denton County, Texas, in 1889. They bought a half-section of Archer County land near a spring, reared twelve children, and watched the last cattle drives. Larry McMurtry was admittedly out of place among the hardworking but anti-intellectual west Texans who lived along the area called Idiot Ridge. He was "insufficiently mean" in a world where meanness meant survival, where violence against animals in the form of bronco-busting, calf throwing, cattle dehorning, and castrating were all part of daily life. He was a "bookish boy" in a "bookless" part of the state.

McMurtry's parents lived on his grandfather's ranch near Windthorst, eighteen miles from Archer City, when he was born, but his mother desired to live in town. A confirmed bridge player, she wanted her family to be nearer civilization, and by the time she had convinced her wiry, taciturn husband to move the family to a small white frame house in Archer City, Larry was six. Living in the small town and visiting the ranch led to his consciousness that he was living on the cusp of change.

McMurtry's parents made the passage from country to town in 1942, and McMurtry's three siblings were born after the family moved. His high-school yearbook entry suggests a rather normal life. He was a four-year letterman in band, three-year letterman in basketball, one-year letterman in baseball, 4-H Club member for four years, editorial writer on the *Cat's Claw* staff, member of the cast of the junior- and senior-class plays, winner of fourth place in the district mile race, and winner of second place in editorial writing.

Archer City was a small town ruled by religious fundamentalism and sexual strictures. Football reigned, as it still does in west Texas. The time spent with his friends and acquaintances in Archer City was as important for McMurtry as was the time spent with his family. Classmate Ceil Slack Cleveland is usually acknowledged as the model for Jacy Farrow in *The Last Picture Show* (1966) while Bobby Stubbs provided the outline for Sonny in the first novel and later for Duane in *Texasville* (1987). Before Stubbs's death in the early 1990s McMurtry inscribed books to him, always suggesting that Stubbs was the model for one character or another. Ceil Slack lived only two blocks away from Larry, and they competed for the various school awards. Ceil's mother, a poet and painter, encouraged Larry's friendship, and he dedicated *Anything for Billy* (1988) to her and his first agent. In 1997 Cleveland published a book about her life, *Whatever Happened to Jacy Farrow?* (1997).

In 1954 after graduating with honors from Archer City High School, McMurtry enrolled briefly at Rice University in Houston, where encountering the library became a transforming experience for the boy who had grown up in a bookless town. Still, he did not stay at Rice, saying his "chief nightmare was a freshman math course (the calculi, trig., analytics) which I failed completely." He transferred to North Texas State College (now the University of North Texas), where he studied literature.

McMurtry also published in an unauthorized literary magazine, the *Coexistence Review,* and the student magazine, the *Avesta.* During his last two years at North Texas State College, McMurtry said he wrote and burned fifty-two "very bad" short stories. Next, he turned to his cowboy past and wrote a story about the destruction of a cattle herd and another about a cattleman's funeral. He then decided to connect the two stories and extend them into a novel. McMurtry sent the manuscript to the *Texas Quarterly,* which was publishing book supplements, and Frank Wardlaw read it and sent it on to a friend at Harper Brothers in New York, who decided to publish it.

On 15 July 1959 McMurtry married Jo Ballard Scott—with whom he had a son, James Lawrence McMurtry, named for Henry James and D. H. Lawrence; the couple divorced in 1966. McMurtry received an M.A. degree from Rice University in 1960, writing his master's thesis on "Ben Jonson's Feud with

the Poetasters: 1599–1601." McMurtry then accepted a Wallace Stegner creative-writing scholarship at Stanford University as one of a group of remarkable new writers, including Wendell Berry, Australian novelist Chris Koch, Tillie Olsen, Ernest Gaines, Robert Stone, and Ken Kesey. McMurtry was still a shy young man and did not get to know many people in this group well, but he was close to Koch, author of *The Year of Living Dangerously* (1978), and he connected with Kesey—the big, boisterous red-haired wrestler from Oregon—primarily because of their mutual Western backgrounds. McMurtry later dedicated *In a Narrow Grave* (1968) to Kesey, calling him "the last wagon-master."

In 1961 McMurtry returned to Texas and taught at Texas Christian University in Fort Worth during the 1961–1962 academic year. He began teaching at Rice in 1963 and remained there for most of the 1960s, except for 1964–1965, when he was awarded a Guggenheim Fellowship for creative writing. At Rice University, McMurtry taught literature and creative writing. One of his students was Gregory Curtis, later editor of *Texas Monthly,* who recalled that McMurtry's teaching style could best be called "polite discouragement." Ambling into class in boots and jeans, McMurtry exhibited little interest in students' work. Still, McMurtry inspired his students by example, told them about his own work, and demonstrated that he read constantly and eclectically by passing out long reading lists. At the same time McMurtry worked at a shop called The Bookman and established a lifelong passion for book collecting.

Escape and return—looking-to-leave and longing-to-return—characterize much of McMurtry's life and writing. McMurtry referred to this pattern in his first essay collection, *In a Narrow Grave,* published in 1968, recalling a poem by Constantine Cavafy based on a scene in William Shakespeare's *Antony and Cleopatra* (written 1606–1607), in which Hercules abandons Mark Antony, and the guards hear a strange music to mark the god's passing. As he listened to the wind blowing along the Llano Estacado, McMurtry found "the music of departure . . . faint, the god almost out of hearing," and he speculated on the god then abandoning Texas: "Sometimes I see him as Old Man Goodnight, or as Teddy Blue, or as my Uncle Johnny, . . . but the one thing that is sure is that he was a horseman, and a god of the country."

Throughout his career McMurtry has examined the disappearance of the cowboy god and the frontier that was his range. His books have focused on the golden days of cowboys and trail driving and on the transitional time between the early rural life and the new urban one, looking for values to replace the old ones that have disappeared. In his work McMurtry approaches these subjects with a "contradiction of attractions" that produces an "ambivalence as deep as the bone."

His early works both dramatize and reflect the uncertainty that is central to his oeuvre. For many years while critics awarded his works high praise, McMurtry disparaged them as juvenile, sentimental, overedited, and poorly realized. And yet, as William T. Pilkington notes in *Taking Stock*, they marked a radical change in Texas letters:

> Despite their nostalgia and sentimentality, despite the fact that their creator would apparently disown them if he could, they continue, as we . . . confront a world far removed even from the one sketched in the novels, to speak to readers in a strong and passionate voice.

These early Thalia novels–*Horseman, Pass By* (1961), *Leaving Cheyenne* (1963), and *The Last Picture Show* (1966)–take as their central theme the end of the frontier way of life on the sere landscape of west Texas. They examine a world bereft of the comforting values of an earlier time, a world where ideal and reality often clash. The novels present these significant collisions and confrontations through believable characters who speak a recognizable language and deal with people who, for the most part, laugh and love, and who feel pain and alienation. Thomas Landess in his 1969 biography of McMurtry notes that McMurtry's novels are concerned with the "effect of the passing years on the hopes and dreams of the young." They weave together the two main strands of McMurtry's attitudes toward his home, his blood's country, what Dave Hickey calls "elegy and exorcism," with both strands often intertwined in uneasy tension. These same concerns are presented directly in McMurtry's nonfiction collection, *In a Narrow Grave*, in his own voice–or at least that of the persona he presents to the public.

McMurtry took the title *Horseman, Pass By* from William Butler Yeats's poem "Under Ben Bulben." Yeats's epigraph provides the elegiac tone for the novel and suggests the comparison between Yeats's mythic horseman and the death of the cowboy god that Homer Bannon represents. Indeed, the novel ends with Lonnie in the churchyard after Homer's funeral "thinking of the horseman that had passed." The novel pays homage to the end of the rural life and the passing cowboy god McMurtry later detailed in *In a Narrow Grave*, but the novel both looks back at the old and forward to the new, and makes escape and ambivalence important themes.

In *Horseman, Pass By,* the central conflict is between Hud and his stepfather, Homer Bannon, who represents the old way of life. As Homer is replaced by Hud, raw amorality signals a new course. Lonnie, the youth-

*Dust jacket for McMurtry's 1966 novel, about life in a small Texas town in the 1950s*

ful narrator whose awareness grows from this conflict, tries to decide which–if either–character's values to adopt. On the surface McMurtry seems to have him side with Homer and lament the passing of the old, for in many ways Homer is a courageous, heroic figure. Yet, the novel reveals an implicit ambivalence toward the old that becomes explicit in McMurtry's later works. Homer's stubbornness and his insensitivity to Hud's youthful desires bring about the old man's downfall.

McMurtry's uncertainty toward the possibility of fulfillment in Southwestern rural life is more subtly presented in *Leaving Cheyenne*, published in 1962. In this book Molly tries to choose between two recognizable Southwestern figures: Johnny, the unfettered, forever-free cowboy, and Gid, the acquisitive, settled rancher. The two impulses cannot be reconciled, nor can Molly choose. Rather, she marries a third man, Eddie, a brutal oil-field worker. Throughout, she tries having both Johnny and Gid, as each tries unsuccessfully to possess her. As they age, their world, the West of the cowboy, the blood's country passes on.

McMurtry's third novel, *The Last Picture Show,* published in 1966 and based on Archer City, also treats blunted initiation, loneliness, and lack of fulfillment not as a nostalgic lament but as biting satire of the small-mindedness of small-town Texas life. Duane and Sonny try to combat the boredom in Thalia through sex, sports, and movies; but living close to the earth in McMurtry's world does not create enlightened beings. The most admirable character, Sam the Lion, owner of the pool hall and a former ranger, dies long before the end of the novel.

Satire gives way to a bitter, goodbye-to-all-that attitude in McMurtry's first collection of essays, published in 1968. Written during Lyndon Johnson's presidency, when being Texan was not chic among intellectuals, *In a Narrow Grave* strikes out at many things Southwestern, including small towns where "many Texans . . . live and die in woeful ignorance." This antagonism to the rural marks the shift to the second category of McMurtry novels—the urban novels set in Texas.

In 1969 McMurtry left Texas and moved to Waterford, Virginia, forty miles northwest of Washington, and for most of the 1970s he lived there with his son, James. Later he moved into the District of Columbia and lived above Booked Up, his rare-book store in Georgetown. He taught briefly at George Washington and American Universities.

McMurtry's next three novels mark his transition from examining the effect of change on the frontier values of small towns in Texas to considering the difficult adaptation of the new, urban West to the loss of those values. Don Graham calls the Houston trilogy "the end of the 'Old Texas,' and the beginning of a 'New (e)rotic Texas." Despite McMurtry's avowed belief that Texas writers should mine urban territory, these three novels do not abandon the rural Southwest. In fact, McMurtry continues his contradiction of attractions for the old and new Texas, since each Houston novel includes elements of the old Texas: *Moving On* (1970) shifts between an urban plot that concentrates on the marriage of Patsy and Jim Carpenter and the rodeo world of Sonny Shanks; *All My Friends Are Going To Be Strangers* (1972) moves from Danny Deck's Houston to his Uncle L's Hacienda of the Bitter Waters; and *Terms of Endearment* (1975) introduces the rural by means of Vernon Dalhart, who embodies the old ways.

Still, Houston is the setting, and the main characters are urban. The Houston trilogy illustrates how McMurtry stretched his subject matter and style and attempted to put into practice the carefully examined conclusions that he had articulated in his nonfiction.

These novels are also connected by their varying emphases on literary and artistic creation as a sufficient substitute for the physical production of the rural cowboy world.

*Moving On* (1970) concentrates on Patsy Carpenter—slim, dark-haired twenty-five-year-old wife of Jim Carpenter—a wealthy, drifting young Dallasite. The novel concerns three types of characters and settings—rural, rodeo types; urban sophisticates; and Hollywood characters who use the world of illusion to bridge the two worlds. The major rodeo character is Sonny Shanks, world-champion cowboy, who seduces women in his white hearse adorned with painted longhorns. The major rural character not related to rodeo is Roger Wagonner, Jim's rancher uncle, who leaves the Carpenters his Panhandle ranch when he dies.

Danny Deck in *All My Friends Are Going To Be Strangers* (1972) is McMurtry's most clearly identified alter ego. A young, rural-Texas writer who achieves early success, Deck wanders from Texas to California and back, searching for satisfaction in life, love, and family but finding little that sustains him. At the end of the novel he drowns his manuscript in the Rio Grande. In this portrait of the artist as a young "frontier genius," McMurtry makes Danny a young Texas writer with a biography similar to his own and brings to the forefront his own ambivalence about literary and artistic production as an option to being a cowboy and trail driving.

For the central consciousness of his next novel, McMurtry moved far from his own voice and turned to a middle-aged New England widow relocated to Houston. Throughout the Houston trilogy, McMurtry examines various sides of the dualities that have intrigued him throughout his career, such as rural/urban, old/new, male/female, isolation/community, art/life, marriage/divorce-separation-widowing, home/not-home, and upper/lower. With *Terms of Endearment* (1975), he moves on from the isolated young male writer struggling in a symbolic borderland immerses himself in an imaginative re-creation of an aging, urban society woman, and examines the terms that endear one to another. Of all the characters in these novels, only Aurora Greenway in *Terms of Endearment* appears to escape the suffering that the others endure. However, her power is belied by an inner tumult that surfaces alarmingly and leads her to find order where she can. Her daughter, Emma, another wanderer, dies young from cancer after following her graduate-student, then college-professor, husband Flap from Houston to Kearney, Nebraska, leaving her young lover Danny Deck to wander on his own.

Although the next series of novels is often called "the Trash Trilogy," the name is only partly fitting. Unlike some of McMurtry's work, *Somebody's Darling* (1978), *Cadillac Jack* (1982), and *The Desert Rose* (1983)

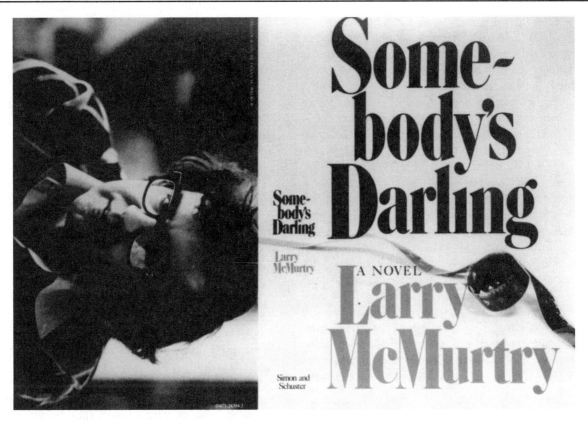

*Dust jacket for the 1978 novel that constitutes the first volume in McMurtry's "Trash Trilogy," a series that continued with*
Cadillac Jack *(1982) and* The Desert Rose *(1983)*

have no interconnected characteristics. In fact, *Some-body's Darling* makes a reasonable quartet with McMurtry's three previous novels, since two of its main characters appear in earlier novels. McMurtry, however, does not regard *Somebody's Darling* as part of the Houston novels. Nor are these works necessarily "trash," but, of all McMurtry's novels, these three have been more generally maligned by critics. Therefore, to call them trash makes a ready grouping, and, in the long look at McMurtry's fiction, they rank low on the list of achievements. But the term also mirrors the subject matter of the three novels—the tawdry, uncentered worlds of Hollywood and Las Vegas, and the trash and garbage through which Cadillac Jack McGriff sifts. While many critics flayed these three books, all three include commendable elements, and each one also received some favorable reviews. These three novels move far afield from the Texas settings of McMurtry's previous work and demonstrate his shifting attitude about his home.

McMurtry became friends with Peter Bogdanovich and Cybill Shepherd during the filming of *The Last Picture Show* in 1971, for which McMurtry wrote the screenplay. In Bogdanovich's *Daisy Miller* (1974) Shep-

herd played the title role, and McMurtry's son James played the younger brother.

In 1981 McMurtry created another disturbance on the Texas literary scene with a speech titled "Ever a Bridegroom: Reflection of the Failure," delivered at the Fort Worth Art Museum. He again found the Texas literary scene insufficient and provoked almost everyone in Texas. The novels set principally outside Texas echo McMurtry's attitude at the time that the "country—or western, or Cowboy—myth had finally been worked through." Calling it "Country and western literature," McMurtry concluded in the speech that the myth of the West was dead: "The death of the cowboy and the ending of the rural way of life had been lamented sufficiently, and there was really no more that needed to be said about it." He also began traveling around the country and maintained apartments in California for his movie-writing connections and in Arizona after developing a close friendship with the Native American writer Leslie Marmon Silko. But McMurtry's health suffered; he developed what was then called "Valley Fever," an enervating condition.

What makes the trash trilogy significant to his canon is that the novels show how McMurtry investigated his continuing techniques and themes while exorcising his ambivalence toward writing about the Southwest. More significantly, the novels reveal a writer's dark night of the soul, for with *Somebody's Darling* McMurtry lost his excitement for writing, a circumstance that endured through *Cadillac Jack*. With *The Desert Rose* McMurtry regained some of his lost enthusiasm. He continued to work sporadically on a trail drive novel that had started as a screenplay. He soon finished *Lonesome Dove,* the novel he had been tinkering with for years, and it was published in 1985. He was attending a writers' conference in Uvalde, Texas, when he learned that he had won the Pulitzer Prize.

*Lonesome Dove* dramatizes one Texas Ranger's promise to take his friend and partner's body back to Texas for burial. Similarly, McMurtry returned to Texas and the old Southwest as the subject and setting for his fiction. The two main characters—former Texas Rangers Augustus "Gus" McCrae and Woodrow Call—embody negative and positive traits of the fabled, vanishing Southwesterner and counter the simple, one-dimensional characters McMurtry often attacked in books written by what he called "symbolic frontiersmen" (*In a Narrow Grave*).

*Lonesome Dove*—begun as a movie treatment titled *Streets of Laredo* for John Wayne, James Stewart, and Henry Fonda—is in many ways the culmination of McMurtry's work. As the son and grandson of Texas cattle people, as one who touched the garment of the passing cowboy god, as a voracious reader and moviegoer who knew both the literature and the movies that had promoted the frontier myth, McMurtry was primed to retell the story in an ambivalent novel that portrays the paradoxical tale of those now mythic figures—the Texas Rangers and trail drivers/Indian fighters—who pushed the civilization westward, the same civilization that then destroyed their way of life. *Lonesome Dove* is the novel his critics had clamored for him to write since he first appeared on the literary scene in the 1960s, and the subject of the novel is the kind he had solidly attacked for fifteen years. The novel is packed with unforgettable and credible characters and exhilarating adventures; developed with details that ring with truth—Hawkens and Henrys, half-breeds and hackamores, riatas and remudas; told with language that is supple and clear; presented with wit, generosity, and discernment; and undergirded with themes, images, allusions, and structural devices that lift it far beyond the scrub literature McMurtry had attacked.

Despite some critics' belief that McMurtry contradicted himself by denouncing novels about the past and then writing a novel about the past, McMurtry did not simply offer up a nostalgic formula Western. Rather, as he had done throughout his career, he persisted in his antimythic ways. The major characters—McCrae, Call, the miscreant Jake Spoon, the scout Deets, the slow but steady Pea-Eye, the yearning initiate Newt, and the competent but cowlike Dish—form a synthesis embodying the best, the worst, and the diverse traits of the mythic passing Southwesterner and contravening those "symbolic frontiersmen" whom McMurtry had often thrashed. McMurtry's heroic figures Gus and Call embody both mythic traits and positive ones that are not part of the traditional myth by being witty, talkative, sexually aware, and communal rather than individualistic. They also reveal laziness; incapacity to effect enduring, mutual heterosexual love; unscrupulous behavior (the cattle and horses they drive north are stolen); and folly for undertaking the long drive without clear reason. For many readers, these flaws do not destroy the myth; instead, the humanity of the characters makes them more fully realized than the "country and western" formula fiction could ever achieve.

Ultimately, *Lonesome Dove* interweaves myth and antimyth; it does not simply attack the myth, nor does it offer a formula novel with larger-than-life heroes without human traits. Rather, it uses the basics of the old—the trail-drive structure; archetypal Texas Rangers; stock obstacles (river crossings, thunderstorms, sandstorms, hailstorms, windstorms, lightning storms, grasshopper storms, stampedes, Indian attacks, quicksand bogs, drought, rustlers, snakes, and a bear); a captivity narrative; love stories (love acknowledged—Gus/Clara; love denied—Call/Newt); and a search for the father.

*Lonesome Dove* elevated McMurtry into the lofty realm of serious American novelists who make the best-seller list. It made the onetime bad boy of Texas letters the preeminent Texas writer and signaled that Larry McMurtry had come home.

Since 1987 McMurtry has published eight single-authored novels, alternative between contemporary sequels and frontier novels until *Streets of Laredo* in 1993 merged the two braids with a sequel set in the late nineteenth century. The contemporary sequels underscore McMurtry's concern for the inconsequential nature of a modern world filled with material possessions and mass entertainment that render paltry sustenance. McMurtry portrays a world in sharp contrast to the heroic universe of Augustus McCrae and Woodrow Call, a contemporary world marked by steady shrinkage and loss; defective and destroyed families; diseased and disturbed minds; and a cosmos fraught with sadness, suffering, and trifling sex allayed only occasionally by moments of humor and compassion. The relationship between past and present, both the mythic past and a character's personal past, becomes part of the central concern in each novel.

*Texasville,* published in 1987, is a sequel to *The Last Picture Show,* whose biting satire about small-town Texas was winningly original. Even though McMurtry peopled the first novel with tag-named caricatures, there were also the full-blown, believable characters such as Sam the Lion, the owner of the pool hall, whose compassion gave the book strength. What makes *Texasville* initially interesting is McMurtry's premise that his readers might want to know what happened in the past twenty years to those characters he created in *The Last Picture Show.* Those characters are memorable to many—from those who have read McMurtry all along to those who met Sonny, Duane, and Jacy in Bogdanovich's 1972 movie starring Timothy Bottoms, Jeff Bridges, and Shepherd. *Texasville,* dedicated to Shepherd, is also noteworthy because, as the first of several sequels, it indicates continuity and change in McMurtry's career.

While Sonny was the dominant character in *The Last Picture Show,* Duane is the focus of *Texasville.* He became a millionaire during the oil boom, but the novel takes place in 1986, the year of the 150th anniversary of Texas independence, and, as Thalia is going under with the oil bust, its inhabitants demonstrate the trauma of going from boom to bust in such a short period. Duane exhibits the excesses of the boom: he lives in a large, expensive house, complete with hot tub and gadgets of the rich. When he gets depressed, he shoots at the two-story, log-style doghouse behind his house. Thalia's frontier legacy is debased into a doghouse and a silly festival planned to celebrate the history of the county, with plans to build a replica of the first settlement, called Texasville, and to stage a pageant that recalls major historical events, including Texas independence. The title *Texasville,* in fact, points to McMurtry's continuing criticism of his home state, reducing the state to village status and suggesting McMurtry's denigration of his materialistic, grasping, home state.

In *Some Can Whistle* (1989) McMurtry returns to his most consistent alter ego, Danny Deck, the struggling writer in *All My Friends Are Going To Be Strangers.* The earlier novel examined the problems faced by a young writer cleft by the demands of living in the world and the need for solitude and isolation necessary for success in the writing life. In *Some Can Whistle,* a fifty-one-year-old Deck, last seen drowning his novel in the Rio Grande, returns, an overweight multimillionaire who made his millions as a scriptwriter for a top-grossing sitcom, *Al and Sal,* about the foibles of an ordinary family. Danny has led an isolated life lacking in family contact. He considers writing a novel again and ponders its first line, his solitude broken by what is actually the first line of McMurtry's novel, "Mister Deck, are you my stinkin' Daddy?" This scene includes the primary conflicts of the novel: communica-

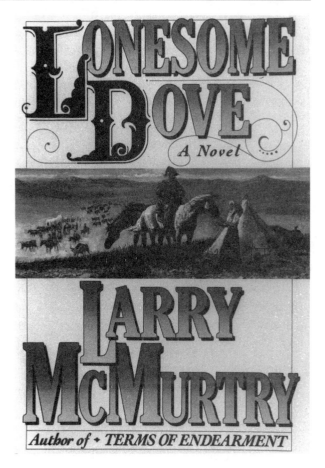

Dust jacket for McMurtry's 1985 novel, about the trail-drive adventures of the former Texas Rangers Augustus McCrae and Woodrow Call

tion-connection-community instead of silence-disconnection-isolation. Danny has become adept at avoiding personal communication. With his former girlfriends, mostly aging actresses he has known over the years, he communicates by answering machines, a fitting symbol of disconnectedness. *Some Can Whistle* explores the frontier legacy of individualism and reveals it as limiting and isolating.

If Danny Deck, a writer withdrawn from life, is McMurtry's masculine alter ego, then perhaps Aurora Greenway is his feminine counterpart. She reappears in *The Evening Star* (1992). While Danny spends his life pursuing art and entertainment and finds himself alienated from life and family, Aurora, despite her artistic sensibility, never achieves the artistic goal she thought she was meant to produce. But she lives her life as fully as she can in a world where chance, misfortune, class distinctions, aging, and the vicissitudes of daily life beset her constantly.

The title *The Evening Star* refers to an earlier McMurtry practice of using elegiac titles. The star of the evening in this novel is Aurora Greenway, goddess of dawn and River Oaks in the earlier novel and aging seductress in the sequel. Her suitor from *Terms of Endearment*, General Hector Scott, has moved in with Aurora and her maid Rosie. Even though a septuagenarian, Aurora remains the self-absorbed character she was before, manipulating suitors and contemplating seductions. Her major seduction occurs when she directs her energies toward Jerry Bruckner, a lay psychoanalyst more than thirty years her junior. Like *Lonesome Dove*, *The Evening Star* is about aging and death, but, in contrast to the final acts of Gus and Call, not much of outward consequences happens to anyone in this novel. Aurora drives to her favorite eatery, the Pig Stand, for pie.

In 1995 McMurtry returned to one of his favorite novels, and most critics' least favorite, *The Desert Rose*, and wrote a sequel, *The Late Child*. In the first novel, Harmony—an aging, beautiful Las Vegas showgirl—serenely suffers as her equally beautiful daughter, Pepper, replaces her on the stage. Both characters have been roundly criticized for being shallow and insignificant. The sequel begins with a universally recognized significant event, the death of a child. Harmony learns that Pepper has died in New York City of AIDS. Harmony's life belies her name, for this knowledge tests her ability to endure. With the help of her two sisters, Harmony learns to grieve by searching for a new life and by focusing her attention on her young son, Eddie—the late child of the title.

These five contemporary sequels—*Texasville, Some Can Whistle, The Evening Star, The Late Child,* and *Duane's Depressed*—continue McMurtry's critique of twentieth-century American life. Returning to the characters, themes, and settings of previous novels renews his criticism of materialism, classicism, individualism, and religious hypocrisy. These novels also present aging characters who, although they suffer from the problems of modern life, increasingly find something of value. The possibility is less clearly realized in *Texasville,* but in *Some Can Whistle, The Evening Star,* and *Duane's Depressed* the main characters' real and projected futures reveal moments of transcendence that validate their lives.

Early in 1999 McMurtry, Texas's preeminent novelist for almost forty years, announced he had published his twenty-third and final novel, *Duane's Depressed,* which wrapped up the Thalia trilogy that began with *The Last Picture Show* (1966) and continued with *Texasville* (1987). Barely had the loud, sad sigh escaped from Texas readers when *Crazy Horse,* a biography of the famous Sioux warrior, appeared. Hard on the hooves of those two books came *Walter Benjamin at the Dairy Queen: Reflections at Sixty and Beyond,* a memoir on cowboying, writing, storytelling, reading and book collecting, aging, and fatherhood, reminding us once again why McMurtry's shadow looms large over the Texas literary landscape.

*Walter Benjamin at the Dairy Queen: Reflections at Sixty and Beyond* suggests why McMurtry began a memory project, something like Aurora Greenway's in *The Evening Star.* McMurtry says that after his 1991 heart bypass operation he felt as though he had become someone separate from his previous life: "I was one person up until the morning of December 2, 1991, at which date I had quadruple-bypass surgery at the Johns Hopkins hospital in Baltimore. When I woke up from the operation, after about twelve hours in deep anesthesia, I began—although I didn't realize it immediately—my life as a different person—my life as someone else."

The reborn Larry McMurtry wrote *Duane's Depressed,* and, while it clearly looks back at the two earlier Thalia novels, it rounds them off and revises them in interesting ways. Duane Moore, erstwhile love of Jacy Farrow in the first novel, successful then failing oilman in the second, is sixty-two years old and dissatisfied as the third novel begins. Duane decides to trail a singular life and dispossess himself of extraneous things, particularly his pickup truck, and to move out of his giant house filled with kids and grandkids to a cabin six miles outside of Thalia. Duane is a "rebel without a car," as Don Graham noted in the *Texas Observer,* or at least without a pickup, and in conscious emulation of Henry David Thoreau tries to simplify his life by refusing motorized transportation.

The ragged lives of his family and friends intrude. His son, Dickie, is leaving drug rehab for the third time while his other son, Jack, roams the country trapping wild pigs and studying survivalist tracts. His daughters, Nellie and Julie, deposit their children with Duane and his wife, Karla, as they wander off to Cancun and other destinations. Now in her nineties and almost blind, Ruth Popper, wife of the football coach in the first novel and aging jogger in the second, still works for Duane's oil company. She teams up with Bobby Lee, one of Duane's employees anxious about having lost a testicle, to question Duane's state of mind.

Duane seeks and finds a shaman, or at least a psychiatrist, Honor Carmichael, to help him understand his mental state. Her prescription is literary; she directs Duane to Marcel Proust's three-thousand-page *Remembrance of Things Past* as a way to evaluate a long history of memory. Just as Duane seems about to reach some personal understanding, the world crashes in on him, short-circuiting his quest, but this novel about depression is not depressing, for it traces the possibilities of remaking the self despite lifelong habits that are materialistic and mindnumbing.

For example, after a lifetime of driving pickups and throwing beer cans along roadsides, Duane begins tending to litter's desecration of the natural world when he becomes a dedicated walker. He creates a magnificent garden in his backyard, growing organic vegetables that he gives away to anyone willing to pick them and respect the new Eden he has cultivated.

As the final novel in the trilogy, *Duane's Depressed* is something of a novel of attrition as McMurtry finishes off many of the characters who had become like old friends to McMurtry's readers. Fairly early in the novel, we learn that Jacy Farrow has been dead for five years, lost with her bush pilot lover that she met on a trip to the Arctic circle to make a beer advertisement. Before the novel ends, Sonny Crawford loses his feet (another intertextual reference to the numerous characters throughout McMurtry's career who lost body parts) and then dies quietly in the Quik-Sack store he runs; Karla dies a violent death in a car wreck. McMurtry has long been drawn to the theme of transitions, and this novel quietly but fully remembers the previous novels in the trilogy.

*Duane's Depressed,* then, dwells on the past, but it also represents new directions for a writer who has lived a life mostly critical of his home country. The harsh satire of *The Last Picture Show,* which attacked the boredom and small-mindedness of small-town Texas and gave way to an almost condescending paternalism in *Texasville,* comes round to Duane Moore's redemptive vision in *Duane's Depressed,* an unschooled product of a materialistic culture and aesthetically challenged landscape. McMurtry says that it was as if his old life slipped away from him. This new and perhaps final novel blazes a trail along the byways of a new life.

Although some of its farce is tiresome, *Duane's Depressed* is one of McMurtry's most satisfying novels with a contemporary setting. Rather than standing outside or above the subject of his novel, McMurtry moves into the story. Duane's experiences are not the stuff of irony and satire here; instead they are the genuine concerns of an aging man who is led to reflect upon the process.

For the characters in his twentieth-century novels, much of the past with which they grapple is influenced by the mythic past. In between his forays into contemporary life, McMurtry returned to the old frontier.

Since the writing of *Lonesome Dove,* McMurtry has alternated between novels with contemporary settings that resuscitate characters from previous works and novels about historical Western characters. Both types demonstrate one of his predominant themes–the end of a way of life–a subject McMurtry examines with a complex ambivalence. With *Streets of Laredo* McMurtry merged two types by writing a sequel and

by using nineteenth-century historical figures Judge Roy Bean and Charles Goodnight as fictional characters. *Dead Man's Walk* (1995) and *Comanche Moon* (1997) introduce a new pattern: both are prequels to *Lonesome Dove.*

The novels with nineteenth-century settings that focus on historical characters explode much of the myth of the frontier and the legendary figures who carried the stories. Although McMurtry returns to the frontier, his themes remain similar, regardless of setting, and probe the universality of human fear and desire. Additionally, the first two books return to McMurtry's enduring ambivalence about the role of the writer. Both books display nineteenth-century novelistic conventions. *Anything for Billy,* published in 1988, is narrated by a dime novelist and becomes something of a dime novel in the process; *Buffalo Girls* (1990) evokes the epistolary novel, with Calamity Jane as the primary writer.

McMurtry was surprised by the strong response to the romantic elements in *Lonesome Dove.* While he had set out to debunk the myth, he discovered instead that many readers filtered out the antimythic material and understood only the powerful romance of the Western legends. With *Anything for Billy* McMurtry leaves little room for readers to find anything heroic about his imaginative re-creation of Billy the Kid. McMurtry calls his youthful killer Billy Bone, partly to indicate that his is a fictional creation and partly to refer to Billy's literary forebears, Herman Melville's Billy Budd and Ken Kesey's Billy Bibbit. Like his literary forebears, Billy Bone is an innocent, and he becomes the victim of his own legend, one that McMurtry makes clear had little basis in reality. In an interview with Mervyn Rothstein for *The New York Times* (1 November 1988) shortly after the novel was published, McMurtry said that he was a critic of the Western myth because the frontier West was "a very crude environment and an uncertain way of life [and not] something heroic. . . ."

Ugly and unappealing, suffering from migraines and myopia, frightened of lightning and shadows in the night that remind him of the "Death Dog," a poor shot and poorer horseman, and a failed cowboy, Billy Bone is not a heroic figure. In fact, McMurtry's unremitting emphasis on Billy's shortcomings makes it difficult to understand why anyone likes Billy at all. Still, the narrator, Ben Sippy, says, "There was a time when I would have done anything for Billy."

Although the ostensible focus of the novel is on the title character, this novel is also another that examines the writer and the writing process with an ambivalence similar to that of *All My Friends Are Going To Be Strangers.* Ben, a dime novelist from Philadelphia,

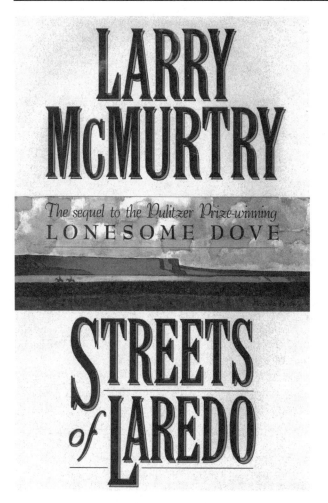

*Dust jacket for McMurtry's 1993 novel, in which characters from* Lonesome Dove *reunite to track down a killer*

escapes his marriage, family, and tedious life on Chestnut Street to discover the West he has learned of in dime novels and then begins to write. Reading these novels, he becomes so enthralled by the world they present that he develops a fever, "a kind of mental malaria," treated only by more reading. His initials, "B.S.," his street name, "Chestnut," and his real name symbolize the insipid work he begins producing.

By revisiting a notable historical episode, McMurtry probes several themes that have engaged him before. Of primary importance is the frontier myth, which the dime novels and movies have fabricated and sustained over the years. But he also questions subjective history, as he does in his next novel about the nineteenth century, *Buffalo Girls,* published in 1990. Although populated by legendary characters Calamity Jane and Buffalo Bill Cody, *Buffalo Girls* portrays them not as larger-than-life heroes but as lonely sufferers—dislocated, lacking community, sexually frustrated, and fearing loss and death. *Buffalo Girls*

both laments the loss of the frontier and attacks the nostalgia associated with the loss, emphasizing that the frontier is a metaphor for the human condition, since loss permeates human consciousness and literature. The title recalls the song "Buffalo Girls," who are beckoned to "come out tonight and dance by the light of the moon." But, like the buffalo, which the novel stresses have almost completely vanished, these Buffalo Girls and the life they represent are also about to disappear.

McMurtry writes much of the novel in epistolary form, as Calamity Jane writes to her daughter, Jane, proclaiming, "I am the Wild West, Janey, no show about it, I was one of the people that kept it wild. . . ." In her letters, Calamity Jane functions as Ben Sippy did—as a firsthand reporter on the reality of the mythic West. For example, she writes that she "shed no tears for Custer when he fell" because she had seen "him quirt soldiers for the least little thing." Like Sippy, she questions the historians, writing her daughter: "You will read of all this in the histories, Janey, do not let them tell you Custer was a hero, he was cold and careless, listened to no one." But Calamity Jane is hardly the rough-and-tumble figure of legend. Rather, she is a sad and lonely woman. Before the novel is over, she questions her sexuality, acknowledges her loneliness, and, in a nod to *Who's Afraid of Virginia Woolf* (1962), confesses her own mythmaking.

When *Streets of Laredo* appeared in August 1993, the long-awaited sequel to *Lonesome Dove* hit the best-seller list and marked a significant point in McMurtry's career—the first time McMurtry had written a sequel to a novel set in the nineteenth century. In it Captain Call returns and sets out to hunt down a notorious killer and bandit named Joey Garza by gathering a band that includes Pea-Eye. Don Graham, in *The Austin Chronicle* (August 1993), finds that reading "the new novel is sort of like looking through old annuals of Lonesome Dove High" and wryly notes that it gives readers Call and Lorena redux but "not Blue dux." Indeed, many of the old characters return, but the vision and tone in the sequel are quite different from the original.

One of the primary themes of the book concerns the pull of loyalty. Over and over again, characters point to the demands of fidelity. For a writer whose career has been marked by divided loyalty about his profession and his home country, this novel makes wavering allegiances central to both theme and structure. The novel ends with McMurtry's familiar return pattern, as Lorena, Pea-Eye, Call, and Maria's children return to Pea-Eye's home along the Quitaque, and the pregnant Lorena expands her family to include Call, Theresa, and Rafael. In the final scene, Lorena, distraught after learning of Clara's death, sends Pea-Eye to sleep in the horse barn. But she relents, comes to the barn, and summons her husband, who "followed his wife back to their house." Marriage, family, stability, and home–these are the forces for facing the newly arriving century.

*Dead Man's Walk* (1995), the first prequel to *Lonesome Dove,* is set in the days of the independent Republic of Texas, when Gus McCrae and Woodrow Call are in their early twenties. McMurtry seems intent on making up for any misreadings of *Lonesome Dove,* ensuring that readers recognize that these two neophyte Texas Rangers are just simple young men fumbling through life. As in other novels with historical backdrops, McMurtry manipulates the historical record, in this case the 1842 expedition of Texans to capture for Texas what is now New Mexico. This expedition is one of those failures that has no tragic overtones, unlike the Mier foray to Mexico, with its now famous story of Texans who drew from a jar of beans to determine who would be executed. In reality Bigfoot Wallace went on the expedition to Mexico and lived to tell the tale. In McMurtry's retelling, Bigfoot joins the expedition to Santa Fe, where McMurtry transplants the story of the beans; in his version Bigfoot draws a black bean and is executed.

If McMurtry draws from well-known history for the basic plot, he looks to his own imagination for the climax of the story–one of the most bizarre scenes in Western American literature. After surviving the *malpais,* the rangers end up in a leper colony near El Paso. Among the residents is an English aristocrat, Lady Carey, ravaged by leprosy but a sophisticated woman with a beautiful soprano voice. She and her black companion accompany the rangers when they leave El Paso for central Texas, but an Indian band surrounds them. When all seems lost, Lady Carey disrobes, mounts her horse sidesaddle, wraps her pet snake around her neck, sings her favorite aria, and rides untouched through the stunned renegade band. Thus, the heroes, inept and inane, feckless and foolish, are saved in one of the strangest deus ex machina scenes in McMurtry's oeuvre.

In the middle prequel, *Comanche Moon,* published in 1997, McMurtry broke new ground, for he wrote a novel that was at once a prequel and a sequel. The novel is a prequel to *Lonesome Dove* and traces roughly the years from 1855 to 1865; it is also a sequel chronologically to *Dead Man's Walk,* which covers the early 1840s. Gus and Call in this novel are much like the Gus and Call of *Lonesome Dove* and *Comanche Moon,* an everything-you-wanted-to-know-about-everything book that explains much about the characters, including

how Call got together with the whore Maggie Tilton, who became Newt's mother; Blue Duck's parentage and relationship with the Comanches; how Gus and Call became captains; how and when they discovered the town of Lonesome Dove; and much more.

Like *Lonesome Dove,* this new novel introduces some highly original, compelling characters. In this case new characters are Texas Ranger Captain Irish Scull and his wife Inez. Scull rides a gigantic horse so admired by the Comanche as "The Buffalo Horse" that Kicking Wolf and Three Birds steal it and take it to Mexico as an offering for Ahumando, one of the most vicious villains in all of McMurtry's novels. Although McMurtry has developed a loyal readership for the Lonesome Dove saga, *Comanche Moon* will be, says McMurtry, the final book in the series.

McMurtry's life changed following the publication of *Lonesome Dove,* when Archer City, his hometown, after years of being unfavorably characterized by McMurtry, embraced him and welcomed him home. After excoriating his home town in *The Last Picture Show* and portraying it as small-minded and "bookless" in *In a Narrow Grave,* McMurtry and his family have in the 1990s transformed the small county seat into a literary oasis amid dry, mostly flat cattle and oil country. McMurtry has renovated the Archer City golf course clubhouse for his residence and has bought many of the downtown buildings to house a rare-book operation that is one of the largest in the Southwest.

Even though he moved back to his hometown, life has often called him away. In 1989 he succeeded Susan Sontag as president of the American Center of PEN, and he threw himself into the activities of the group. Normally a shy person, he was called upon to speak out against censorship, especially in support of Salman Rushdie after he was condemned to death for writing *The Satanic Verses* (1988). The stress of the PEN position, along with a lifetime of poor eating and exercise habits, took a toll. When the PEN position ended in 1991, McMurtry began working on *The Evening Star* and completing renovations on the house in Archer City. After a day of moving boxes of books into the house, he slept fitfully and drove himself to his doctor in Wichita Falls, who confirmed that McMurtry was having a heart attack. The doctor insisted that McMurtry needed an operation immediately, but McMurtry elected to finish the novel before undergoing quadruple heart bypass surgery that many feared (and others hoped) would slow his writing career. The welcome publication of *Streets of Laredo* in 1993 indicated that he had returned to form, though perhaps with a darker vision.

*McMurtry's bookstore in his hometown of Archer City, Texas. It bears the same name as one he founded in Georgetown, D.C., in the 1970s (photograph by Marla Sweeney).*

The dark vision of *Streets of Laredo,* published almost two years after his surgery, caused some of his friends to worry about him. The dust jacket photograph revealed a thinner, grayer man. Indeed, he had suffered the usual postoperative depression, and it had taken him some time to recover. Ultimately, he wrote himself out of depression. When he finished the novel, he told friends and family that he was saddened on completing it because it had given his life a focus. But he accepted his doctor's restrictions and began exercising regularly on a treadmill. He also received support from his companion, Diana Ossana, whom he met in Tucson in the mid 1980s. Their first collaborative book was *Pretty Boy Floyd* (1994), begun originally as a screenplay, and the second was *Zeke and Ned* (1997).

McMurtry describes their working style as fully collaborative:

> I write five pages early. Diana makes them ten, a little later. My narrative is spare, she expands it. It is a full collaboration, meaning the division of labor is as

equal as equal can be. We work on it together, and we work on it separately, as well. We researched it together.

To help readers, the authors attached an introductory "Collaborators' Note" to *Pretty Boy Floyd* that tells that the work began as a screenplay for Warner Brothers in 1993, but the screenplay is an "austere form" that "welcomes no longeurs," the undefined but seemingly extra details provided in a big, baggy novel.

An additional publisher's note identifies Ossana as an Italian American from St. Louis who attended Eastern New Mexico University and who met McMurtry in a Mr. Catfish restaurant in Tucson in the mid 1980s. McMurtry spent time in Tucson in the 1970s when he and Silko became close friends. In the early 1990s McMurtry opened another bookstore in Tucson and expanded it into an antique store as well, so by the mid 1990s he was alternating between Archer City and Tucson. Ossana was managing a law office when they met, and it was she who encouraged McMurtry to diet and exercise after his heart bypass operation in 1992. Perhaps collaborative writing allows McMurtry to break free from the isolation writing alone demands. Throughout his career, McMurtry has complained about the isolation of writing, noting that he grew up among cowboys who often worked communally. His most famous work, *Lonesome Dove,* celebrates the trail drive community and the bonding of Gus McCrea and Woodrow Call.

Whatever the impulse, the result was a collaborative novel based on the life and times of a celebrated Oklahoma outlaw and following the broad outline of Charles Arthur Floyd's rise from an obscure Salisaw, Oklahoma, farm boyhood to Public Enemy No. 1 on J. Edgar Hoover's most wanted list in 1934. Floyd is presented as a basically nice kid, a young family man who loves his wife and child, longs for nice clothes and new cars, but is caught in the economic depths of the Depression. Circumstances turn him into a successful bank robber. Late in his career Floyd tells a reporter: "I was just a green country kid that got caught on a job that I didn't know much about, but I guess that was the job that put its mark on me and I could never shake it off. I tried, though."

On the surface *Pretty Boy Floyd* has some McMurtry traits—a realistic plot filled with readable dialogue and memorable supporting characters; a chronological organization structured by random, cross-country journeys; a concern for the events that lead an innocent young man astray; an interest in human sexuality; a critique of the emphasis on materialism in the modern world and on the power of the media. Ultimately the novel fails to connect with deep themes about the loss of frontier values that have characterized McMurtry's best works.

In 1997 McMurtry and Ossana produced *Zeke and Ned,* again focusing on historical figures. In this case they chose two Cherokees, who are less well-known on the national stage than Floyd. Still, Ned Christie and Zeke Proctor were real people who lived in Indian Territory in the late 1800s and whose lives provide the broad outline for the novel. In McMurtry and Ossana's novel, the two men are living apparently normal lives in the Going Snake District of the Cherokee Nation Indian Territory in the 1870s. Zeke's trial in Cherokee court after an accidental killing ends with a violent shoot-out that draws the attention of white marshals and begins the series of events that lead to the destruction of Zeke's family and to Ned Christie's becoming the most notorious outlaw in the Cherokee nation.

This second collaboration also has some recognizable McMurtry traits, but like the first collaboration, it does not connect with the deep themes about the loss of frontier values found in McMurtry's best

work. In fact, while in his earlier frontier works, McMurtry is strongly antimythic, deconstructing the various myths of the West, the two collaborative books with Ossana uphold rather than attack the myths of the West. In *Zeke and Ned,* McMurtry and Ossana even appear to engage in mythologizing by elevating two rather obscure Indians into large, heroic figures. Ned Christie in *Zeke and Ned* is strong, honest, handsome, and wise; he is also a crack shot. Ned is a tragic figure, driven to build a solitary fortress for his family because of misguided and largely stupid white men who act mainly out of silly or materialistic motives. Zeke, older, more down-to-earth and more human than Ned, suffers from human foibles; still he is stronger and more positively presented than any of the whites.

Through collaboration, McMurtry seems to have addressed one difficulty of his craft—the isolation of the novelist. McMurtry describes collaboration as "different, an interesting kind of change," and the collaborations have extended beyond writing novels. Ossana was the cowriter of the teleplay *Larry McMurtry's Dead Man's Walk* (1996) following McMurtry's interest in movies that permeates his career. Movies have shaped his imagination, and the more he began to work with the industry, the more his fiction reflected his knowledge of the industry. Still, he has had a mixed relationship with moviemaking. On one hand, he has enjoyed successful movie and television adaptations such as Martin Ritt's *Hud* (1963), Bogdanovich's *The Last Picture Show* (1972), James Brooks's Academy Award–winning *Terms of Endearment* (1983), and the acclaimed *Lonesome Dove* (1989) television miniseries. In both *In a Narrow Grave* and again in *Film Flam: Essays on Hollywood* (1987), however, McMurtry has distanced himself from movies, although he has worked on them steadily.

Late in 1998 McMurtry, Texas's preeminent novelist for almost forty years, announced that he would write one more novel, his twenty-second, and *Duane's Depressed* was barely in the bookstores before another book, *Crazy Horse,* a biography of the famous Sioux warrior appeared, short-circuiting any hand-wringing and sense of ending that might have attended McMurtry's announcement. Before the year was out, a second nonfiction book, *Walter Benjamin at the Dairy Queen,* was published, followed quickly by a similar memoir, *Roads,* and then another, *Paradise.* These books indicated that as McMurtry approached the age when many retire, he was working hard to reconsider his life and work.

McMurtry's biography of Crazy Horse indicates another new direction, for, although he has published nonfiction, it was his first monograph. In it he combines his considerable skill as a storyteller with a life of reading to make sense of Crazy Horse, a man about whom reams have been written but still little is known. McMurtry sketches the outlines of the life of the famous Sioux warrior from his birth near the Belle Fourche River in South Dakota around 1840, through his adolescence and first vision quest when he took his father's name and had visions that led him to fight with a rock behind his ear. McMurtry also describes Crazy Horse's doomed love for Black Buffalo Woman, his fateful meeting with General George Armstrong Custer at the Little Big Horn in 1876, and finally his death at Fort Robinson, Nebraska, on September 6, 1877, stabbed by an army private while Little Big Man held his arms. McMurtry makes clear that many of the details about the famed Oglala leader are obscure, but the legend speaks both to history and contemporary times: "Crazy Horse's legend grew in the main from a broken people's need to remember and believe in unbroken heroes, those who remained true to the precepts of their fathers and to the ways of the culture and the traditions which bred them." McMurtry's biography kicked off the Penguin Lives series and pointed to a new path along the writing route of a man who once said he was driven to write daily.

McMurtry initially made his presence felt in nonfiction with his first collection, *In a Narrow Grave*. Since then McMurtry's fiction has often focused on the moment when an old order gives way to a new, especially the old rural Southwest's uneasy transition to the new urban order. In *Walter Benjamin at the Dairy Queen* transitions are important too, with McMurtry himself the major transitional figure. The title image refers to the moment McMurtry recalls beginning these reflections. Drinking a lime Dr. Pepper at the Dairy Queen on Highway 79 just south of Archer City, McMurtry was reading the work of European literary critic Walter Benjamin on the importance of the storyteller. The volume focuses on four major elements. The first chapter, "Place—and the Memories of Place," moves from his initial reading of Benjamin's "The Storyteller" to an examination of his hometown, Archer City, and his family's connection to the region. Listening to talk at the Dairy Queen in 1980, the year of Archer City's centennial, he realized that DQs function as community centers and observed that few storytellers came in for Dilly Bars. He was struck by Benjamin's distinction between the communal act of storytelling and the isolating craft of novel writing, to which McMurtry had devoted much of his life.

The second chapter, "Reading," concerns how McMurtry spent his time when he wasn't writing. Long lamenting that he grew up in a "bookless town in a bookless part of the state," McMurtry became attached to the power of books after a cousin left the six-year-old Larry a box of nineteen children's books. He traces his reading to the Archer City drugstore racks and then to his education by Alan McKillop at Rice, whom McMurtry calls a "great reader" who taught him that "literature, whether one wrote it, taught it, or just read it, could be a lifelong occupation . . ." (101).

In the third chapter, "Book Scouting," McMurtry recalls his life as a book scout and collector. He remembers his visit in 1954 to his first real bookstore, Barber's in Fort Worth, and recollects the bookstores of his life—Brown's in Houston and Harper's in Dallas. Chapter Four, "The End of the Cowboy—The End of Fiction," applies McMurtry's favorite theme of the dying craft to his own life and work. McMurtry examines his father's devotion to ranching as an essentially tragic enterprise, since it depended on the wrong animal, the imported cow, instead of the natural grazing creature of the plains, the buffalo. He then compares his own work of writing largely about the ranching West, often attempting to demythologize it (unsuccessfully, he notes), with his father's. Fathers and sons return throughout the book, which is dedicated to Austin singer-songwriter James McMurtry, Larry's son, to James's wife, Elena, and to their son, Curtis, Larry's grandson.

Perhaps McMurtry's subtitle points to the overarching idea in the book—*Reflections at Sixty and Beyond*. The book ponders the labyrinth of memory and the lassoes of retrospection. The book is Larry's looking back, his consideration of a life spent herding words toward coherence and books toward clean, well-lighted places where human communities may reflect upon their significance.

The title of the first companion memoir, *Roads: Driving America's Great Highways* (2000) points to the fact that most of McMurtry's novels are structured by journeys of some type, often leading nowhere in particular except to the act of traveling itself. Even his epic *Lonesome Dove* with its apparently purposeful goal of getting the cattle up the trail to Montana splinters into the varied reasons all the individual drovers are headed north. So it is not unusual to find that McMurtry's latest nonfiction effort, with the straightforward title of *Roads*, takes the journey as its subject and organizational center. The book traces a series of random drives along the interstates over a several month period. McMurtry would fly into an airport, rent a car, and head out along the interstate. He rarely seems interested in a particular landmark and often notes that he has decided not to stop at something as he zooms by.

But as he drives along, the main impression he leaves is that he is not really interested in either the places that he passes or the roads on which he travels. Readers looking for the usual travel book information about places will be disappointed unless they like to hear curmudgeonly complaining about too many trucks, too much urban sprawl, too much construction, too much lightning-speed change. The trips themselves are desultory, occasionally aborted, and usually unsatisfying.

The places often zip by without arresting McMurtry's attention, except when a particular place is connected to one of book collector McMurtry's favorite writers: William Faulkner's Mississippi; James Agee's Knoxville; Teddy Blue's Montana; Ernest Hemingway's Michigan, Idaho, and Key West. It seems clear that this is not really a book about taking trips along specific roads but another Proustian journey along the trails in Texas's most famous novelist's varied past as he traces the places that have been central to his life and work: Washington, D.C., Hollywood, and Archer County, Texas, especially Archer County.

This book, therefore, should be read as a companion piece to McMurtry's last memoir, *Walter Benjamin at the Dairy Queen*. There McMurtry explained how after heart bypass surgery in 1991, he felt as though he had become someone separate from his previous life and has since been trying to find again the person he used to be. Driving along familiar roads, he says in this new book, is part of that process.

The next memoir, *Paradise* (2001), begins on board the *Aranui*, a freighter out of Tahiti. Watching deckhands handle tight cables, McMurtry confesses that he is leery of taut lines, having at fifteen seen an oil field worker decapitated when a line snapped. This memory serves as a metaphor for this tight little book. On one hand, this is a travel book about visiting the South Sea islands of Gauguin and Melville, the fertile paradise of the title. But it is also tautly tied to that little arid postage stamp of soil that is the homeland of McMurtry's heart, Archer County, Texas, where he was born and raised and where his parents lived out their difficult marriage. Memory connects us irrevocably to people and places in ways that both sustain and limit. For a writer like McMurtry, that tension is the heart and soul of his work. Charting the twains of heaven and hell, ecstasy and agony, is the cartography of the writer and the terrain of *Paradise*.

Such varieties of tension pull the peripatetic writer throughout the book. On the one hand, he rails against the creeping capitalism that is now rampant everywhere, so that the unloading of Coca-Cola cases indicates the entry of the serpent into the Garden. On

*McMurtry outside his Archer City bookstore in 2000 (photograph by Marla Sweeney)*

the other, his need to connect to home because his mother's death looms on the horizon leads him to complain about the cost of phone cards, the scarcity of phone booths, or the locals hogging the phones that are available.

Like *Roads,* this is a curmudgeonly travel book. While the traveling writer becomes the observer of his little band of travelers and clearly likes some of them, many of them strike him as obnoxious, boring, or lacking in respect for his need for privacy. They find him odd for refusing to drink the wine and for being unmarried at sixty-four. The gap between the South Seas islands that captivated Captain Cook, Melville, Gauguin, Henry Adams, Robert Louis Stevenson, Thor Heyerdahl, and Jacques Brel and the current stop for the tourist boat produces another tension for McMurtry. But soon, when he has the chance to walk forty minutes to see the second largest tiki in the Marquesas, and again to the consternation of his boat mates, McMurtry chooses to stay on board and read Melville's *Typee*. Later he eschews a "Polynesian fete" for Joan Didion's *White Album,* "not exactly a cheerful book, but it easily beats Polynesian night" (122).

For those who have followed McMurtry throughout his career, this book is less interesting as a travel book than as another entry into the McMurtry memory project brought on after the unease produced by his heart bypass surgery. That life is bound by two main elements—his growing up on the ranch near Archer City, the son of Hazel and Jeff

McMurtry and son and grandson of ranchers, and his becoming a man of books as reader, collector-dealer, and writer.

Over his long career McMurtry has become the best known Texas novelist. His next collection of essays, *Sacagawea's Nickname: Essays on the American West,* along with his other recent nonfiction books and earlier essay collections, demonstrates that had McMurtry chosen to write essays rather than fiction, he would no doubt have created a national reputation as literary essayist, a Southwestern Edmund Wilson. Over the years, McMurtry has reviewed hundreds of books for varied publications. More recently he began writing review-essays for the *New York Review of Books; Sacagawea's Nickname: Essays on the American West* collects those essays into a coherent arrangement. Most of the essays are less reviews than McMurtry's musing on issues inspired by the books that are the ostensible subject of the review.

The twelve essays primarily take off from books about the American West. McMurtry deals with such topics as the life of John Wesley Powell, the one-armed explorer of the Colorado River, Buffalo Bill, Annie Oakley, and Zane Grey, purveyors of the Western myth; the dispossession of the Five Civilized Tribes; Zuni Pueblo and the varied, grasping anthropologists who converged on it; historians Angie Debo and Patricia Limerick. The last two essays examine the Lewis and Clark's expedition on the Missouri River.

The last essay, "Old Misery," demonstrates just how central the Missouri River is to McMurtry's last novel, *Boone's Lick* (2000), and how much the voracious reader McMurtry researches as he writes. In "Old Misery," McMurtry muses on the Missouri in a long piece that ultimately praises *The Journals of Lewis and Clark* as "the first American epic," but the river is his real subject.

McMurtry has often mentioned his fondness for travel books, and in these reviews he makes it clear just how much he has absorbed over the years.

The title essay demonstrates why the essayist has spent much of his life working in fiction. *The Journals of Lewis and Clark* lead him to reflect on the relationship between explorer Captain William Clark, who finally began to refer to his Snake Indian guide as "Janey" instead of the "squaw." The human dimensions of the relationship that is only suggested in the journals and letters is the imaginative region of the fiction writer.

What we get in the essays that we do not get in the novels is the persona of Larry McMurtry. Irascible, opinionated, erudite, pragmatic, wryly humorous, keen observer, and clear writer—these traits typify the essayist revealed here. These same traits lie behind the best novels, submerged beneath the narrative strategy of the fictionist, but it is a pleasure to see them laid bare in these crisp essays.

When he turned to nonfiction, McMurtry declared that he was done with fiction, but he could not do it; he could not stay away from the work that had driven him for so many years. Tracing the story of Crazy Horse pointed him perhaps down the path of the novel that marked his return to fiction, *Boone's Lick,* for Crazy Horse appears as an unnamed Indian who playacts having a lame horse and leads Colonel William Judd Fetterman and eighty cavalrymen into a trap on December 21, 1866. This event entered history as the "Fetterman Massacre," and it becomes the linchpin of this novel, where McMurtry returns to his fictional examination of the nineteenth-century American West.

While there are echoes of McMurtry's masterpiece, *Lonesome Dove* (1985), this new novel is more reminiscent of *Anything for Billy* (1989) and *Buffalo Girls* (1991), effectively told stories but less ambitious books. Like many of McMurtry's other works set in the nineteenth century, *Boone's Lick* assembles a cast of effectively drawn, often eccentric, fictional characters who eventually set out on a journey in the historical West, where they meet up with McMurtry's versions of historical characters like Colonels Fetterman and Carrington and Wild Bill Hickok, who makes a cameo appearance in the first part before disappearing.

The primary fictional characters are members of the Cecil family of Boone's Lick, Missouri (the home of Kit Carson, who does not appear here). Fifteen-year-old Shay, whose voice clearly recalls another Missouri youth, Huckleberry Finn, tells their story. Shay's mother, Mary Margaret, gets tired of waiting for her wayward husband, Dick, to return from another of many freight-hauling trips to the West during their fifteen-year marriage, so she gathers her clan, which includes Shay's siblings, G. T., Neva, and baby Marcy; Shay's uncle, Seth; his Grandpa Crackenthorpe; and Mary Margaret's wayward half sister, Rose. They set out by riverboat and wagon to travel from Boone's Lick to Fort Kearny in Wyoming territory to search for Dick.

Along the way they add to their entourage when they meet a barefooted priest named Father Villy and an Indian named Charlie Seven Days, who recalls other admirable McMurtry fictional Indians such as No Ears from *Buffalo Girls* and Famous Shoes from *Streets of Laredo.* To balance such villainous Indians as Blue Duck from *Lonesome Dove,* McMurtry has created full and sympathetic Indian characters who grapple with both personal difficulties and the reality of the large events at the end of the frontier—positive affirmations of Indian culture within McMurtry's typically elegiac view of the passing West. Charlie is similar to these characters, but he is never fully fleshed out in this novel of attrition, where many of the interesting secondary characters like Charlie die, wander off, or just disappear without explanation before novel's end.

The most forceful character is clearly Mary Margaret. Over the years McMurtry has been recognized for his ability to create interesting women characters like Aurora Greenway in *Terms of Endearment,* and Mary Margaret Cecil fits the category of spunky, determined women. But this is more Shay's story, and much of the appeal of this novel comes from the ease with which McMurtry writes from the point of view of a teenage boy. Shay, like young Sam Clemens on the Mississippi, is learning to read the Missouri River.

It is a supple move for McMurtry to shift from concentrating on an aging Duane Moore in *Duane's Depressed* to the youthful experiences of Shay Cecil. In fact, Shay's initiatory experiences carry the weight of this story more than Mary Margaret's journey to find her husband, which functions mainly as the reason to get them going on the journey west rather than being the primary story. Shay and the other travelers leave the relative calm of Missouri for the fearful crossings of raging streams, the sudden appearance of grizzly bears, and the sheer terror of Indian attacks (including the physical mutilation of victims). Shay's awareness of the random violence of the West is punctuated by his recognition of the awesome beauty of the vast territory. Additionally, he begins to realize that the buffalo and beaver are disappearing and that Indian cultures and the openness of the West are being diminished as civilization advances, a steady stream of pioneers journeying along the "Holy Road."

*Boone's Lick,* then, is another of McMurtry's ambivalent stories of the American West as it tells a story of both the beauty and terror of the westering experience. It is the first of a new McMurtry series, and so it signals that Larry McMurtry, who began his literary career with a novel, *Horseman, Pass By,* in 1961, will probably write fiction until the end.

Through all of his work Larry McMurtry's Texas background looms large. Growing up on a ranch and learning the ranch work ethic, in which every day began early and ended late, McMurtry approaches his work with an intensity and tenaciousness that drive him to produce. He is concerned about production and works steadily without wasting time. In the process he has become the best-known Texas writer of the twentieth century. Fictional Thalia and Hardtop County have become as recognizable to many readers as Faulkner's Jefferson and Yoknapatawpha County.

## Interviews:

Patrick Bennett, "Larry McMurtry: Thalia, Houston, and Hollywood," *Talking with Texas Writers* (College Station: Texas A & M University Press, 1980): 15–36;

Mervyn Rothstein, "A Texan Who Likes to Deflate the Legends of the Golden West," *New York Times* (1 November 1988): C 17+;

"A Novelist of Characters and Place," *Humanities Interview,* 7, no. 2 (Summer 1989): 1–6.

## Bibliographies:

Charles D. Peavy, "A Larry McMurtry Bibliography," *Western American Literature,* 8 (Fall 1968): 235–248;

Dwight Huber, "Larry McMurtry: A Selected Bibliography," in *Larry McMurtry: Unredeemed Dreams,* edited by Dorey Schmidt (Edinburg, Tex.: Pan American University Press, 1978);

Charles Williams, "Bibliography," *Taking Stock: A Larry McMurtry Casebook,* edited by Clay Reynolds (Dallas: Southern Methodist University Press, 1989).

## References:

Kerry Ahearn, "Larry McMurtry," *Fifty Western Writers: A Bio-Bibliographical Sourcebook,* edited by Fred Erisman and Richard Etulain (Westport, Conn.: Greenwood Press, 1982), pp. 280–290;

Ahearn, "More D'Urban: The Texas Novels of Larry McMurtry," *Texas Quarterly,* 19 (Autumn 1976): 109–129; reprinted in *Critical Essays on the Western American Novel,* edited by William T. Pilkington (Boston: G. K. Hall, 1980), pp. 223–242;

Mark Busby, "Damn the Saddle on the Wall: Anti-Myth in Larry McMurtry's *Horseman, Pass By,*" *New Mexico Humanities Review,* 3 (Summer 1980): 5–10;

Busby, "Larry McMurtry," *Twentieth-Century Western Writers,* edited by James Vincent (Detroit: Gale, 1982), pp. 534–536;

Busby, *Larry McMurtry and the West: An Ambivalent Relationship* (Denton, Tex.: University of North Texas Press, 1995);

Craig Edward Clifford, *In the Deep Heart's Core: Reflections on Life, Letters, and Texas* (College Station: Texas A & M University Press, 1985);

Don Graham, "Is Dallas Burning? Notes on Recent Texas Fiction," *Southwestern American Literature,* 4 (1974): 68–73;

Graham, "*Lonesome Dove:* Butch and Sundance Go on a Cattledrive," *Southwestern American Literature,* 12, no. 1 (1986): 7–12;

Dave Hickey, "McMurtry's Elegant Essays," *Texas Observer* (7 February 1969): 14–16;

Roger Jones, *Larry McMurtry and the Victorian Novel* (College Station: Texas A & M University Press, 1994);

Thomas Landess, *Larry McMurtry* (Austin: Steck-Vaughn, 1969);

Lera Patrick Tyler Lich, *Larry McMurtry's Texas: Evolution of the Myth* (Austin: Eakin, 1987);

Raymond L. Neinstein, *The Ghost Country* (Berkeley, Cal.: Creative Arts, 1976);

Jane Nelson, "Larry McMurtry," *A Literary History of the American West,* edited by J. Golden Taylor (Fort Worth: Texas Christian University Press, 1987), pp. 612–621;

Charles Peavy, *Larry McMurtry* (Boston: Twayne/G. K. Hall, 1978);

Pilkington, *My Blood's Country: Studies in Southwestern Literature* (Fort Worth: Texas Christian University Press, 1973), pp. 163–182;

Pilkington, "The Recent Southwestern Novel," *Southwestern American Literature,* 1 (January 1971): 12–15;

Jan Reid, "Return of the Native Son," *Texas Monthly,* 21, no. 2 (February 1993): 202, 228–231;

Clay Reynolds, ed., *Taking Stock: A Larry McMurtry Casebook* (Dallas: Southern Methodist University Press, 1989);

R. C. Reynolds, "Back Trailing to Glory: *Lonesome Dove* and the Novels of Larry McMurtry," *Texas Review,* 8 (1987): 22–29;

Reynolds, "Come Home Larry, All Is Forgiven: A Native Son's Search for Identity," *Cross Timbers Review,* 11 (May 1985): 65;

Dorey Schmidt, ed., *Larry McMurtry: Unredeemed Dreams* (Edinburgh, Tex.: Pan American University Press, 1978);

Ernestine Sewell, "McMurtry's Cowboy-God in *Lonesome Dove,*" *Western American Literature,* 21 (1986): 219–225;

C. L. Sonnichsen, *From Hopalong to Hud: Thoughts on Western Fiction* (College Station: Texas A & M University Press, 1978), pp. 7–8, 125–126, 157–160, 164, 167, 173–176;

Janis P. Stout, "Cadillac Larry Rides Again: McMurtry and the Song of the Open Road," *Western American Literature,* 24, no. 3 (November 1989): 243–251;

Stout, "Journeying as a Metaphor for Cultural Loss in the Novels of Larry McMurtry," *Western American Literature,* 11 (1976): 37–50.

**Papers:**

The University of Houston has the typescripts of Larry McMurtry's *The Last Picture Show, Leaving Cheyenne,* and shorter published works; the manuscripts of two unpublished novels and an unpublished screenplay; and other miscellaneous manuscript materials. Rice University has transcripts of late works. Southwest Texas State University has the screenplay "Streets of Laredo," which became *Lonesome Dove.* The University of North Texas has copies of student papers. The Ransom Center at the University of Texas has the typescript of the manuscript for *Horseman, Pass By.*

# N. Scott Momaday

*(27 February 1934 – )*

Suzanne Evertsen Lundquist
*Brigham Young University*

See also the Momaday entries in *DLB 143: American Novelists Since World War II, Third Series* and *DLB 175: Native American Writers of the United States.*

BOOKS: *The Journey of Tai-me* (Santa Barbara: Privately printed, 1967);

*House Made of Dawn* (New York: Harper & Row, 1968; London: Gollancz, 1969);

*The Way to Rainy Mountain* (Albuquerque: University of New Mexico Press, 1969);

*Colorado: Summer, Fall, Winter, Spring,* text by Momaday, photographs by David Muench (New York: Rand McNally, 1973);

*Angle of Geese and Other Poems* (Boston: Godine, 1974);

*The Colors of Night* (San Francisco: Arion, 1976);

*The Gourd Dancer* (New York & London: Harper & Row, 1976);

*The Names: A Memoir* (New York: Harper & Row, 1976);

*The Ancient Child* (New York: Doubleday, 1989);

*In the Presence of the Sun: A Gathering of Shields* (Santa Fe: Rydal, 1992);

*In the Presence of the Sun: Stories and Poems, 1961–1991* (New York: St. Martin's Press, 1992);

*Circle of Wonder: A Native American Christmas Story* (Santa Fe: Clear Light Publishing, 1993);

*The Man Made of Words: Essays, Stories, Passages* (New York: St. Martin's Press, 1997);

*In the Bear's House* (New York: St. Martin's Press, 1999).

PLAY PRODUCTIONS: *The Indolent Boys,* Syracuse, N. Y., Syracuse Stage, 8 February 1994;

*Children of the Sun,* Tucson, Ariz., Kennedy Center, 4 March 1997.

PRODUCED SCRIPT: *House Made of Dawn,* motion picture, by Momaday and Richardson Morse, Firebird Production, 1987.

OTHER: *The Complete Poems of Frederick Goddard Tuckerman,* edited by Momaday (New York: Oxford University Press, 1965);

*N. Scott Momaday*

"The Man Made of Words," in *Indian Voices: The First Convocation of American Indian Scholars,* edited by Rupert Costo (San Francisco: Indian Historian Press, 1970), pp. 49–84; reprinted in *Literature of the American Indians: Views and Interpretations,* edited by Abraham Chapman (New York: Meridian, 1975), pp. 96–111; revised for *Religion and the Humanizing of Man,* edited by James M. Robinson (Los Angeles: Riverside Press, 1973), pp. 191–203;

S. Carl Hirsh, *Famous American Indians of the Planes,* foreword by Momaday (Chicago: Rand McNally, 1973);

"I Am Alive," in *The World of the American Indian,* edited by Jules B. Billard (Washington, D.C.: National Geographic Society, 1975), pp. 11–26;

"Native American Attitudes toward the Environment," in *Seeing with a Native Eye: Essays on Native American Religion,* edited by Walter H. Capps (New York: Harper, 1976), pp. 79–85;

"N. Scott Momaday: Kiowa Poet and Novelist," in *This Song Remembers: Self-Portraits of Native Americans in the Arts,* edited by Jane B. Katz (Boston: Houghton Mifflin, 1980), pp. 195–201;

*With Eagle Glance: American Indian Photographic Images 1868–1931,* from the collection of Warren Adelson and Ira Spanierman, foreword by Momaday (New York: National Museum of the American Indian, 1980);

"Landscape with Words in the Foreground," in *Old Southwest/New Southwest: Essays on a Region and Its Literature,* edited by Judy Nolte Lesink (Tucson: Tucson Public Library, 1987), pp. 1–5;

Michael J. Caduto and Joseph Bruchac, eds., *Keepers of the Earth: Native American Stories and Environmental Activities for Children,* foreword by Momaday (Golden, Colo.: Fulcrum, 1988);

Skeet McAuley, *Sign Language: Contemporary Southwest Native American Photographs,* introduction by Momaday (New York: Aperture, 1989);

Marcia Keegan, *Enduring Culture: A Century of Photography of the Southwest Indians,* foreword by Momaday (Santa Fe: Clear Light Publishing, 1990);

Thomas A. Drain, *A Sense of Mission: Historic Churches of the Southwest,* foreword by Momaday (San Francisco: Chronicle, 1994);

Trudy Griffin-Pierce, *Earth Is My Mother, Sky Is My Father: Space, Time, and Astronomy in Navajo Sandpainting,* foreword by Momaday (Albuquerque: University of New Mexico Press, 1995).

SELECTED PERIODICAL PUBLICATIONS–
UNCOLLECTED: "The Heretical Cricket," *Southern Review,* 3 (1967): 43–50;

"Ancient Vision," *Revue Française d'Etudes Americaines,* 13 (1988): 369–376;

"Only an Appearance," *Native American Literatures,* 1 (1989): 1–8.

In 1969, the same year that N. Scott Momaday began his tenure as associate professor of English and Comparative Literature at the University of California at Berkeley, he won the Pulitzer Prize for fiction for *House Made of Dawn* (1968), published his autobiograph-ical work *The Way to Rainy Mountain,* and was initiated into the Kiowa Gourd Dance Society. This confluence of events is remarkable. The critical recognition of Momaday's novel, for example, stimulated public interest in Native American literary history as well as in contemporary Native American writers in general. Furthermore, *The Way to Rainy Mountain,* over time, came to rival *House Made of Dawn* in literary circles throughout the world. That Momaday can reside successfully in both Native American and Euro-American traditions brings crucial attention to previously unfamiliar "assimilation" patterns in American history. The status of Momaday's work, however, results not only from his prowess as a writer but also from his capacity as mythmaker.

Momaday was born on 27 February 1934 in the Kiowa and Comanche Indian Hospital in Lawton, Oklahoma. He is the only child of Alfred Mommedaty (of Kiowa heritage) and Natachee Scott (of European and Cherokee ancestry). The name Novarro Scotte Mommedaty appears on Momaday's birth certificate; and in his book *The Names,* Momaday records that a document issued by the U.S. Department of the Interior considered him to be "of 7/8 degree Indian blood." Six months after his birth, at Devil's Tower, Wyoming, the storyteller Pohd-lohk, who was Momaday's step-grandfather, gave him the Kiowa name *Tsoai-talee,* which refers to the "rock tree boy" who turned into a bear in Kiowa mythology. This myth of the bear child is so much a part of Momaday's identity that it recurs throughout his works–especially in *The Ancient Child* (1989) and *In the Bear's House* (1999). Momaday's second Indian name is *Tsotohah,* meaning "Red Bluff." In *The Names: A Memoir* (1976), Momaday says that Pohd-lohk "believed that a man's life proceeds from his name, in the way that a river proceeds from its source." If this belief is true, Momaday's names assure that his destiny originates from the intermarriage of many Old World and New World bloodlines. Momaday also imagines throughout his creative works that his names participate in the sacred; indeed, *Mammedaty* means "walking above."

Momaday's understanding of complex cultural contexts comes naturally out of his own experience. Both parents were educators, and Momaday traveled with them as they pursued various teaching opportunities within the Native cultures that inform Momaday's vision. The Momadays taught among the Navajo for ten years, first at Shiprock, New Mexico, and then in Tuba City and Chinle, Arizona. In 1946 the family moved to the Jemez Pueblo in New Mexico, where Momaday's parents were the only two teachers at the day school. Both parents taught in Jemez for twenty-five years. In an interview with Camille Adkins,

Momaday explains that his father was both a teacher and a painter. He would "take" the young pueblo children and "make artists of them. . . . His students had shows internationally." Of his mother, Momaday says, "She is a remarkable woman. She was a teacher most of her life, and she says she loved every moment of her twenty-five years at Jemez working with children. She's been completely satisfied with her work and her life." Momaday acquired his love of literature and writing from his mother; his love of teaching and painting from his father; and his love of life from the bounty of experiences he had as his parents' son.

During his youth, Momaday was educated in New Mexico at the Franciscan Mission School in Jemez, the Indian School in Santa Fe, and in Bernnalillo. He also attended the Augustus Military Academy in Fort Defiance, Virginia. He received his undergraduate university education—from 1952 to 1958—at the University of New Mexico (UNM) in Albuquerque, where he studied political science, English, and speech. Momaday interrupted his stint at UNM in 1956–1957 to study law at the University of Virginia; while there, Momaday met and fell under the influence of William Faulkner. In 1958, on graduating from UNM, Momaday accepted a teaching position on the Jicarilla Apache reservation in Dulce, New Mexico. He married Gaye Mangold on 5 September 1959; they have three daughters, Cael, Jill, and Brit. On 21 July 1978 Momaday was married a second time, to Regina Heitzer, whom he met when he was a visiting professor at the University of Regensburg in Germany; they have one daughter, Lore.

In 1959 Ivor Winters selected Momaday for a Wallace Stegner Creative Writing Fellowship to attend Stanford University. Under Winters's guidance, Momaday pursued both a career in writing and a Ph.D. in American literature. Although Momaday had fully intended to resume his teaching career after his one-year fellowship, Winters convinced Momaday that he should not refuse a scholarship to complete his Ph.D. at a renowned institution. Winters clearly saw Momaday's talents and even predicted his future acclaim. Under Winters's influence Momaday wrote and published his dissertation, an edition of the works of nineteenth-century American poet Frederick Goddard Tuckerman (1965). Winters also critiqued several drafts of *House Made of Dawn,* but he died in 1968, a year prior to Momaday's receiving a Pulitzer Prize.

Baine Kerr suggests in a 1978 article for the *Southwest Review* that *House Made of Dawn* is Momaday's attempt to "transliterate Indian culture, myth, and sensibility into an alien art form, without loss. He may in fact be seeking to make the modern Anglo novel a vehicle for a sacred text." Paula Gunn Allen proposes that

*Momaday's mother, Natachee Scott*

"As the mythic structure of *Moby Dick* is the Bible, so the mythic structure of *House Made of Dawn* is Beautyway and Night Chant." *House Made of Dawn* is not merely a reenactment of Navajo cosmology. As Allen further explains, the departures from the Navajo mythic vision are a witness for "the nature of continuity," which is "to bring those structures and symbols which retain their essential meaning forward into a changed context in such a way that the metaphysical point remains true, in spite of apparently changed circumstances." The Navajo "structures and symbols which retain their essential meaning" are twofold in *House Made of Dawn.* Certain behaviors cause individuals and peoples to experience disharmony, and ritual procedures available to estranged humans and cultures can reestablish harmony and beauty.

*House Made of Dawn* is about Abel, a young Pueblo Indian and World War II veteran who had "been long ago at the center, had known where he was, had lost his way, had wandered to the end of the earth," and is, for most of the novel, "reeling on the edge of the void." Being "at the center" means living and moving in an appropriate relationship to language, landscape, lineage, and time. Chronologically and spatially, the novel moves through four sections—a symbol for wholeness—

from Abel's failed arrival home on 20 July to his Pueblo community in Walatowa through 2 August 1945; to his brutalizing stay in Los Angeles, memorialized on 26–27 January 1952; to his recuperative return home on 20 February 1952; and finally, at the end of the novel, to his successful assumption on 27 February 1952 in Walatowa of his inherited role as a dawn runner.

The story of Abel's life is told from multiple perspectives and memories that are, at first read, difficult to navigate. Such difficulties prompted critic Roger Dickinson-Brown in a 1978 article for the *Southern Review* to call the novel a "batch of often dazzling fragments" and "a memorable failure" because of the "incoherence of large parts" of the text. Indeed, psychological, historical, and cultural fragmentation are amply represented in a mosaic of images and memories with few familiar chronological standards. Part of Dickinson-Brown's discomfort might have come from his lack of education in Kiowa, Pueblo, or Navajo myth and ritual. The title of *House Made of Dawn* is taken from the Navajo "Night Chant," one of the sixty-two healing rituals held sacred by the Navajo. In fact, "Night Chant" came into the possession of the Navajo through the adventures of the Stricken Twins—one blind and the other lame—who are orphaned and seek not only healing but also familial ties and true community. Part of the search taken on by these twins is a search for father, for they are fathered by Talking God, whose identity becomes revealed only because of the twins' long-suffering efforts. These twins, finally, seek *hózhó*—defined by Gary Witherspoon as a term that "expresses such concepts as beauty, perfection, harmony, goodness, normality, success, well-being, blessedness, order and ideal." In "Night Chant," the wish to "walk in beauty" is an expression of this ideal.

According to Paul Zolbrod in his article "When Artifacts Speak, What Can They Tell Us?" collected in *Recovering the Word: Essays on Native American Literature* (1987), Navajo sacred stories often tell "of errant and persecuted heroes and heroines thrust into alien situations where they are pushed, abused, or injured, sometimes fatally." Moving toward the center or toward recreation with the ability to "walk in beauty" is the goal of healing rituals. "Ultimately," says Zolbrod, "protagonists are saved or restored by the gods and eventually return to their kinship groups with valuable information about how others might be cured of the same afflictions." The problem with Abel is complicated; he is of mixed or unknown kinship. As the chapter "Longhair" explains, Abel "did not know who his father was. His father was a Navajo, they said, or a Sia, or an Isleta, an outsider." If Abel lived in a matriarchal society, such facts would not matter. But he lives in a patriarchal cul-

ture organized "according to family and clan," and Abel is of mixed blood. His grandfather, Francisco, is "the man of the family"; but even when Abel is a boy, Francisco is "old and going lame." Furthermore, Abel loses both his mother and his brother in his youth. What he inherits, then, must come from his grandfather, his own character, and what wisdom he can glean from living within conflicting multicultural environments.

Each of the four sections of the novel is told from a particular Native American perspective. The four chapters move in a cycle from the perspective of the "Longhair," Abel and his grandfather Francisco, Pueblo Indians; to the views of "The Priest of the Sun," Reverend H. B. B. Tosamah, an urban Kiowa Indian; to the viewpoint of "The Night Chanter," Benally, a relocated Navajo; and back to reawakened perspectives of the dying Francisco and his grandson, Abel–"The Dawn Runner." Indeed, as Bernard A. Hirsch suggests in his article "Self-Hatred and Spiritual Corruption in *House Made of Dawn*" (Winter 1983), these perspectives are entirely necessary. For example, the "strong responses Abel generates" in various male characters–the albino, Martinez, Tosamah, and Benally–"indicate their perception of something unyielding and incorruptible in him, something which throws into stark relief the humiliating spiritual compromises they have felt compelled to make."

Despite this strength, Abel is not an exemplary Native American; He is, according to his acts, a dysfunctional person–a drunk, a womanizer, and a murderer. His dysfunction, however, comes from what is now called posttraumatic stress disorder, a psychological inability to connect with one's environment caused by repeated exposure to violence (in Abel's case, during the war) and loss (in his case, of family members). Primary symptoms of this disorder are the incapacity for self-expression or reflection as well as a vulnerability that resembles the posture of a victim. In other words, Abel attracts the actions and attitudes he fears most–violence, pity, and contempt. Indeed, as the narrator says,

> Had he been able to say it, anything of his own language–even the commonplace formula of greeting "Where are you going"–which had no being beyond sound, no visible substance, would once again have shown him whole to himself; but he was dumb. Not dumb–silence was the older and better part of custom still–but inarticulate.

In "The Native Voice in American Literature" Momaday explains the "unconditional belief in the efficacy of language" that resides "at the heart of the American Indian oral tradition." He maintains that

Words are intrinsically powerful. . . . By means of words can one bring about physical change in the universe. By means of words can one quiet the raging weather, bring forth the harvest, ward off evil, rid the body of sickness and pain, subdue an enemy, capture the heart of a lover, live in the proper way, and venture beyond death. Indeed, there is nothing more powerful. When one ventures to speak, when he utters a prayer or tells a story, he is dealing with forces that are supernatural and irresistible. He assumes great risks and responsibilities.

Abel's inarticulateness, then, is a malady of enormous consequence.

Hirsch says that Abel is "someone both to fear and reverence, for he reminds" other Native characters "of who and what they are—of what they find most contemptible in themselves and most holy." Abel, with all the biblical echoes his name implies, is a scapegoat for the inadequacies of his fellows. Furthermore, only through the female characters are readers able to grasp his hidden potential for holiness. Despite his estranged status, Abel, through memory and susceptibility, is *able* to grasp the holiness offered by Tosamah (Kiowa theologian) and Benally (Navajo) as well as his grandfather (Pueblo). In other words, in multicultural contexts, as Abel heals, he is free to integrate and make new what sacred truths he encounters from whatever resource, including Christianity.

Tosamah teaches his congregation the implications of the sacred included in the "medicine" of "the word" and the power of his grandmother's oral narratives. He discourses on the theory of the word included in the Gospel of John as compared to Native conceptions of the word. He also retells the "Kiowa Way to Rainy Mountain" to his congregation. His underlying theory comes through examples of the Kiowa sacred Tai-me story, which "has existed for hundreds of years by word of mouth" and "represents the oldest and best idea that man has of himself. It represents a very rich literature, which because it was never written down, was always but one generation from extinction. But for the same reason it was cherished and revered." On the other hand, claims Tosamah, nothing is so "commonplace" as words and literatures to the white man: "On every side of him there are words by the millions, an unending succession of pamphlets and papers, letters and books, bills, and bulletins. . . ." The white man's "regard for language—for the Word itself—as an instrument of creation has diminished nearly to the point of no return," preaches Tosamah. Benally shares Navajo ritual songs with Abel. Within such ritual is the willed restoration of one's body—a body that exists within the house of dawn, male and female clouds, rain, pollen, insects, and deities. Crippled Abel is in need of such

*Momaday as a child*

reorientation and restoration: restore my feet, legs, body, mind and voice for me, is the compelling injunction of such chants. The desire to live and walk in beauty "as it used to be long ago" is the goal of Navajo ritual. From his grandfather, Abel inherits the ritual of becoming a man, "the larger motion and meaning of the great organic calendar itself," and how to heal a child or purify the world for a new dawn. A dawn runner, for example, is an initiated male who continually chases away evil, chaos, darkness, and ugliness, as he moves toward constant re-creation at the center.

In a 1986 interview published in *Conversations with N. Scott Momaday* (1997) Louis Owens questioned Momaday about the problems such assimilative processes pose: "You . . . who . . . [identify yourself] as Kiowa, write a novel set in Jemez Pueblo, and . . . weave different cultures together. Could all of this be achieving a kind of synthesis in the American imagination of what an Indian is, so that it obscures the diversity of American Indian cultures?" Momaday's answer to Owens's question is "Maybe all writing is a working toward a similar synthesis. I'm not concerned to define or delineate American Indian experience, except to myself and for my own purposes. But I am very concerned to understand as much as I can about myth-making."

The fact remains that in a postcolonial Native America, individuals often live in and learn from multiple cultural contexts. Some critics feel the day of the consummate traditionalist is no longer feasible. Momaday himself is at once a university professor, a mixed-blood Indian living outside the boundaries of his primary tribe's native lands and customs, and a nomad—one who finds home in various settings. His mythic vision includes Judeo-Christian and Western myths as well. Abel's particular journey exposes such mythic, postmodern, postcolonial processes for the heterogeneous complexities they impose on individuals. In other words, such issues are central to Abel's disorientation. Indeed, many Pueblo ceremonies are Christian and Native conglomerates. Two versions of Indian Christianity exist in *House Made of Dawn,* the Catholicism of the Jemez Pueblo and the peyote cult of the Native American church. Indeed, layers of Christianity contribute to the mosaic of values prevalent in the Pueblo. Father Olguin, the primary Christian representative in the novel, is constantly rereading his predecessor's (Fray Nicolas's) journal, which exposes changes in attitudes toward Indian ceremonialism. In fact, Father Olguin defends Abel at his trial, trying to be a bridge for understanding between Indian and white conceptions of death/murder. When Francisco dies, Abel prepares Francisco's body in the Pueblo manner and then informs Father Olguin. With so many systems of value, Abel must, as a matter of survival, redefine the center.

Abel's struggle to make a center for himself, however, leads to brutality and further estrangement, or *hócho*. In truth, the Navajo emergence narrative underscores several causes of disharmony: offending other sentient or insentient beings, willing harm or injury onto others through witchcraft, misusing reproductive capacities, seeking power over others, and wanting more than one needs. Throughout the novel, Abel either participates in or is the object of such offenses. Before the war, he takes the life of an eagle during a ritual sponsored by the ancient Tanoan Eagle Watchers Society. After the war, he cohabits with a pregnant woman, Angela Grace Martin St. John, who has come on retreat to the Pueblo. When Abel is inordinately beaten by an albino during the feast of Santiago, he later kills the albino, who symbolizes an enemy to the sacred, an aberrant mutation of whiteness. For taking the life of the albino, Abel is sent to prison for six years and then relocated to Los Angeles, where he fails, miserably, to adapt to the American Dream. In Los Angeles, Abel cohabits, in a rather sexually brutal manner, with Millie, a kind but errant social worker with tragic familial relations of her own.

Susan Scarberry-Garcia in *Landmarks of Healing: A Study of House Made of Dawn* (1990) discusses the strong commonalities between Navajo cosmology and *House Made of Dawn.* Of particular importance is her insistence that Abel's final gestures not only help his dying grandfather gain passage into another world but also give his own suffering meaning. "Abel offers his broken body in the run, the gift of his life, to his people. Physical pain is partially transcended and no longer matters, but the survival of the Pueblo through cooperative behavior does," claims Scarberry-Garcia. Abel's running toward the dawn with the words of the "Night Chant" coming to voice "confers dignity on him, for Abel was beginning 'to see according to holiness,'" Scarberry-Garcia continues. However, *House Made of Dawn* is still an exploration of a particularly male journey, and, as Zolbrod insists, the Navajo creation story "relates how [cosmic] order is to be established and maintained, especially in male-female relationships." In fact, says Zolbrod, "the basic theme of the Navajo creation story is that solidarity must be maintained between male and female if there is to be harmony in the world." Such a vision is lacking in Momaday's novel. The women, while at times sympathetically presented, are still only useful in the part they play to advance Abel's transformation. Momaday recognizes, however partially, such gender imbalances in his first novel by addressing them more fully in his second novel, *The Ancient Child,* published in 1989. Even in this novel, however, Set's wife and unborn child appear to take second place to the narrative of masculine transformation and ascendency.

*The Way to Rainy Mountain,* published in 1969, is undoubtedly Momaday's greatest contribution to world literature. In "Tribal Identity and the Imagination" (1988), an interview by Matthias Schubnell published in *Approaches to Teaching Momaday's The Way to Rainy Mountain,* Momaday says that he was in his thirties when he suddenly realized that

> my father had grown up speaking a language that I didn't grow up speaking, that my forebears on his side had made a migration from Canada along with . . . Athapaskan peoples I knew nothing about, and so I determined to find out something about these things, and in the process I acquired an identity: it is an Indian identity, as far as I am concerned.

Winters, Momaday's mentor at Stanford, strengthened the author's resolve to uncover his roots. He told Momaday that "unless we understand the history which produced us, we are determined by that history; we may be determined in any event, but the understanding gives us a chance." And furthermore, says Momaday, "If I don't understand my Kiowa background, I forsake a lot of my human potential. By understanding it as far as I can I fulfill my capacity for being alive as a human being." In other words, Moma-

*Momaday, circa 1968 (photograph by Gilbert's of Goleta; from the dust jacket for* House Made of Dawn*)*

day has identity by descent (through bloodlines) as well as identity by consent (through agency and the power of the imagination).

Although Momaday, with his father's help, gathered and translated many of the fragments of Kiowa identity from Kiowa storytellers and printed the results in a privately published work, *The Journey of Tai-me* (1967), not until Momaday worked on *The Way to Rainy Mountain* did he fully realize the import of his reclamation project. *The Way to Rainy Mountain* is the story of the journey of the Kiowa people from their mythological emergence into the world to Rainy Mountain in Oklahoma and their decline as a people. Momaday retraced this journey both intellectually and physically. His comments on his interaction with his Kiowa heritage accompany the mythical and historical narrative. Momaday, therefore, is able to validate the present and living qual-

ity of Kiowa identity. The metaphor of a *way* is multifaceted—it includes temporal/eternal (diachronic/synchronic) and spatial (geographical/cosmic) coordinates; a recombining of sacred and secular elements; an awareness of the profound interaction between myth and reality; and an understanding of the cultural (ancestral) demands for balance and continuity in the context of radical change. Combining all these elements is accomplished through a method of storytelling that transcends generic boundaries. The goal of Momaday's journey is a physical, spiritual, and psychological place—Rainy Mountain. Lawana Trout, in "*The Way to Rainy Mountain:* Arrow of History, Spiral of Myth," collected in *Approaches to Teaching Momaday's The Way to Rainy Mountain* (1988), says, "To the outsider, Rainy Mountain may lack sacred stature–'a large lumpy hill,' as one Oklahoma student described it—but for the Kiowas,

*Se-pya-dalda* remains the sacred center of their tribal history." For Momaday, Rainy Mountain symbolizes the starting and finishing point of his quest as well as the custodian of his grandmother's grave. Although his journey is particular to his Kiowa heritage, the movement he encounters is paradigmatic.

In the prologue to *The Way to Rainy Mountain* he writes that

> In one sense . . . the way to Rainy Mountian is preeminently the history of an idea, man's idea of himself, and it has old and essential being in language. The verbal tradition by which it has been preserved has suffered a deterioration in time. What remains is fragmentary: mythology, legend, lore, and hearsay–and of course the idea itself, as crucial and complete as it ever was. That is the miracle.

Momaday writes that the journey is also an "evocation of three things in particular: a landscape that is incomparable, a time that is gone forever, and the human spirit, which endures." Such assertions thrust this text into several orders of reality. When Trout held the book up in front of her Native American literature class, she reports, "a young Kiowa exclaimed, 'That book is not true. He was never around our people that much.'" Several issues of ultimate concern for Native peoples are addressed here: authenticity, sovereignty, and intellectual property. Who, in other words, has a right to gather, reconstruct, and disperse tribal myth, lore, and history?

Any recombination of materials constitutes a re-creation and determines the image, worth, and standing of tribal peoples in the minds of the public, especially when the outcome is an auto-ethnography–a masterpiece of creative nonfiction. Momaday does not claim to speak for his people or to assume the role of holy man with regard to the transmission of this sacred history. Schubnell, in "Tribal Identity and the Imagination," collected in *Approaches to Teaching Momaday's The Way to Rainy Mountain* (1988), explains Momaday's ethnographic endeavors:

> As Momaday focused his attention on retrieving the remnants of Kiowa oral tradition, he realized how much American Indian oral poetry and mythology had already deteriorated and that speedy research was imperative to salvage what was still within reach. Deprived of his grandparents as living sources of Kiowa tradition, Momaday collected stories from tribal elders.

Momaday did, however, rely heavily on his father's fragile recollections of Kiowa traditions as well as on his father's ability to gain access to tribal elders, whose stories he then translated for his son. Momaday also researched folklore archives, anthropological records, and various histories for fragments of information relative to his project. The genius of this project, then, is in the power of his imagination to give *The Way to Rainy Mountain* form from diverse fragments. Indeed, in Momaday's famous essay, "The Man Made of Words" (1970), he says that his primary assumption is "that we are what we imagine. Our very existence consists in our imagination of ourselves. Our best destiny is to imagine, at last, completely, who and what and that we are. The greatest tragedy that can befall us is to go unimagined." In fact, Momaday's theory of imagination creates an invaluable philosophy with regard to the relationship between ethnographic and creative processes.

On a chronological level, *The Way to Rainy Mountain* records the rise and fall of the Kiowa tribe–"The Setting Out," "The Going On," and "The Closing In"– enveloped by a prologue, introduction, and epilogue, all framed by two poems: "Headwaters" and "Rainy Mountain Cemetery." In many respects, the work records the passing of an old Kiowa order and the emergence of a people into appalling times. In "The Man Made of Words" Momaday recounts the final moments of writing *The Way to Rainy Mountain;* he thought he was finished but realized "a whole, penultimate piece was missing." He then records one of the "earliest entries" in the Kiowa's calendar–the "explosion of Leonid meteors in 1833." He calls this memory "living" in both verbal tradition and the person of Ko-sahn, an old "venerable" woman who personally witnessed portions of the short-lived "golden age" of the Kiowa tribe, including the celebration of the Sun Dance. Prior to the falling of the stars, the Kiowa "suffered a massacre at the hands of another tribe, and Tai-me, the sacred sun dance doll and most powerful medicine of the tribe, had been stolen. At no time in the history of their migration from the north, and in the evolution of their plains culture, had the Kiowas been more vulnerable to despair," he notes.

When the stars fell, the people "ran out into the false day and were terrified." The Kiowa, however, gave that false day a symbolic meaning. Momaday records, "With the coming of natural dawn there began a new and darker age for the Kiowa people, and the last culture to evolve upon this continent began to decline." The Kiowa "superimposed" their "imagination" upon the "historical event" and "invested" it with meaning. "They accounted for themselves with reference to that awful Memory. They appropriated it, re-created it, fashioned it into an image of themselves; they imagined it. And by means of that act of the imagination could they bear what happened to them thereafter." He claims, "No defeat, no humiliation, no suffering was beyond their power to endure, for none of it was meaningless." This kind of myth-making activity, therefore, does not represent some kind of invented (fantastic) truth, but the power of the imagination to recollect varied events and interpret them in a process that insures cultural continuity in the face of discontinuity.

William Dilthey wrote (1976) that to "communicate experience," one is inevitably self-referential. Interpretation "is only made possible by plumbing the depths of subjective experience." Dilthey's ideas are fundamental to understanding the processes Momaday engaged in when writing *The Way to Rainy Mountain*. Edward M. Bruner clarifies Dilthey's statement: "The critical distinction . . . is between reality (what is really out there . . . ), experience (how that reality presents itself to consciousness), and expressions (how individual experience is . . . articulated)." *The Way to Rainy Mountain,* then, is an anthropology of personal and cultural experience–an autoethnography raised to an art form, as in the following example of the process.

In 1963 Momaday's grandmother Aho invited him to come to Oklahoma with his father, Al, to view the Tai-me bundle. This event was later transformed in *The Way to Rainy Mountain* into three paragraphs–each constructed from a different epistemological orientation: the mythos (historical), logos (anthropological), and ethos (philosophical) of the event. Such a reconstruction of the event is vertical or synchronic in nature. The mythos, for example, is the sacred narrative (Kiowa scripture) describing how Tai-me came to the Kiowa during a period of famine. A man, so the story goes, heard the cry of hunger from his children and walked four days in search of food. On the fourth day he heard a voice say, "'Why are you following me?' 'What do you want?'" When the man explains the plight of his family, Tai-me volunteers to go with the Kiowa and give them whatever they want. "From that day Tai-me has belonged to the Kiowas," the tale concludes. The logos paragraph is taken from anthropologist James Mooney's *Calendar History of the Kiowa Indians* (1889). This paragraph explains that "The great central figure of the kado, or Sun Dance, ceremony is taime." Mooney describes the size, shape, color, and symbolic design of the figure. He also notes that "It is preserved in a rawhide box in charge of the hereditary keeper, and is never under any circumstances exposed to view except at the annual Sun Dance, when it is fastened to a short upright stick planted within the medicine lodge, near the western side. It was last exposed in 1888."

The ethos portion (Momaday's personal commentary on his experience with Tai-me) challenges Mooney's assertions of exclusivity. Momaday says,

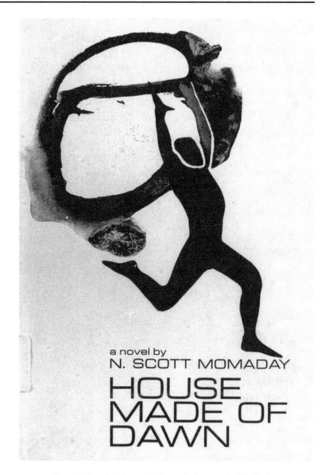

*Dust jacket for Momaday's novel about a Pueblo Indian war veteran's difficult return home*

Once I went with my father and grandmother to see the Tai-me bundle. It was suspended by means of a strip of ticking from the fork of a small ceremonial tree. I made an offering of bright red cloth, and my grandmother prayed aloud. It seemed a long time that we were there. I had never come into the presence of Tai-me before–nor have I since. There was a great holiness all about in the room, as if an old person had died there or a child had been born.

When Momaday locates his witness within the parameters of the moment of death and birth, he gives his experience both a personal and an ontological value. Momaday, then, in Bruner's words, acknowledges that "the anthropology of experience sees people as active agents in the historical process who construct their own world." Furthermore, Momaday confirms Bruner's assertion that "Culture is alive, context sensitive, and emergent." In addition, to note Victor Turner's evaluation of such anthropological undertakings, "Experience always seeks its 'best,' i.e. most aesthetic expression in performance–the vital dance with what it conceives to be its semiogenetic, meaning-begetting past." Thus, *The*

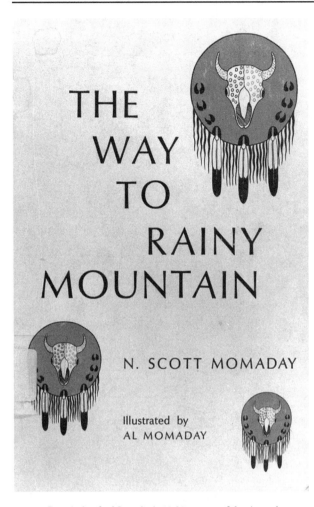

*Dust jacket for Momaday's 1969 account of the rise and fall of the Kiowa*

*Way to Rainy Mountain* is a work of autoethnography or creative nonfiction—aesthetic expression.

Each of the twenty-four triads in *The Way to Rainy Mountain* could yield similar discussions. The mythos portions of "The Setting Out," for example, record the story of the sacred family—father sun, earth mother, and their son (who becomes twins as a result of his father's aggression and mother's death). The twins' exploits bring about the bipolar or contingent nature of the mortal world as well as the possibility for healing those violent separations consequent to mortality. Many of the tales are exemplary or cautionary in intent. Grandmother spider guides the orphaned twins in their sojourn. Typical of myths everywhere, the mythos sections in *The Way to Rainy Mountain* record the genesis of many behaviors and practices among the Kiowa. In "The Going On" section, Momaday's ancestors assume mythos status. And in the "The Closing In" portion, the first paragraphs also recount the tragic errors of par-

ticular Kiowa people—mistakes that contributed to their decline.

*Colorado: Summer, Fall, Winter, Spring* (1973), Momaday's paintings and sketches together with photographs by David Muench, *Angle of Geese and Other Poems* (1974), and *The Gourd Dancer* (1976) precede *The Names: A Memoir* (1976), Momaday's second autobiographical work. *Colorado* explores the visual and verbal meaning of place through various seasonal transformations—ageless transformations that put the human tenure on the land into the perspective of geologic time. Momaday's nature writings approach a mystical plane where physical and spiritual landscapes commune. As with many of Momaday's works, *The Gourd Dancer* is an ensemble of the entire poetic works from *Angle of Geese* accompanied by two dozen additional poems.

Since its publication, *The Names* has gained almost as much status as *The Way to Rainy Mountain*. A five-generation genealogical chart and an italicized philosophical revision of the philosopher René Descartes's dictum "I think, therefore I am"—"*My name is Tsoai-talee. I am, therefore, Tsoai-talee; therefore I am*"—precede the prologue. Family photographs accompany the four sections, each of which concludes with a testament regarding transcendent qualities open to consciousness or speaks of transitions from one state of being to another—the passage rites of a young artist. Book 1 names the landscapes and people—primarily the grandmothers and grandfathers—from whose existence Momaday takes his being and definition. It concludes, "I am. It is when I am most conscious of being that wonder comes upon my blood, and I want to live forever, and it is no matter that I must die."

Book 2 records Momaday's early travels between Oklahoma and the area in and around the Navajo reservations in New Mexico and Arizona—Rainy Mountain, Shiprock, Monument Valley, Tuba City, Chinle, Gallup—the names of places whose imprint weaves through Momaday's memories like elemental fibers. He celebrates the power of memory and imagination, as well as the energy humans gain from living in the presence of incomprehensible landscapes. He says, for example, that "Memory begins to qualify the imagination, to give it another formation, one that is peculiar to the self. I remember isolated, yet fragmented and confused images—and images, shifting, enlarging, is the word, rather than moments or events—which are mine alone and which are especially vivid to me." Such memories are "storylike," "mythic," and "never evolved but evolving ever." He reassembles and reevaluates events. For example, Momaday assumes that he was brought by his father into the presence of his Kiowa great-grandmother:

She reaches out for me and I place my hands in hers. *Eh neh neh neh neh.* She begins to weep very softly in a high, thin, hollow voice. Her hands are little and soft, so soft that they seem not to consist in flesh and bone, but in the softest fiber, cotton or fine wool. Her voice is so delicate, so surely expressive of her deep feelings. Long afterwards I think: That was a wonderful and beautiful thing that happened in my life. There, on that warm and distant afternoon, an old woman and a child, holding hands across the generations. There is great good in such a remembrance; I cannot imagine that it might have been lost upon me.

The entire work is a testimony to Momaday's underlying belief, along with Henry James, that one should be someone upon whom nothing is lost. The human imagination can, however, receive only a portion of what is available. In the concluding paragraph of this section Momaday says of his child's mind: "He knew at once that this moment, the blink of an eye, held more beauty and wonder than he could know. He had not enough life to deal with it. He could only suffer the least part of it; he could only open his eyes and see what he could see of the world." Of such finitude he writes, "I have a moment, and it is too big for me, and I cannot hold it in my little hands. And you, God, you give me the night and the world. It is a good joke, and, God, we laugh. But I have seen how you draw the sky with light."

In books 3 and 4 of *The Names* Momaday relates his experiences in Hobbs, New Mexico, and at the Jemez Pueblo. He uses a stream-of-consciousness technique to record his memories of growing up as an Indian. Book 4 includes a short story that was later published separately and illustrated by Momaday as the children's book *Circle of Wonder: A Native American Christmas Story* (1993). Momaday says that this story, dedicated to his granddaughter, Skye, "centers upon a world that is so dear to me as to be engraved on my memory forever." It is a story of Tolo, a deaf boy, and the experience he has with his dead grandfather on a Christmas Eve on the Jemez Pueblo. "The stars were close by, all the creatures of the earth were close by, all the living and the dead," explains Momaday. In his preface to *Circle of Wonder,* Momaday says of his first Christmas in Jemez, "In all the years of my life, I have not gone farther into the universe. I have not known better the essence of peace and the sense of eternity. I have come no closer to the understanding of the most holy." This "essence of peace" is defined in the story: "The boy, the bird, and the beasts made a circle of wonder and good will around the real gift of the fire, and beyond them were other, wider circles, made of the meadows, the mountains, and the starry sky, all the fires and processions, all the voices and silences of all the world." This story gives voice to the possibility of

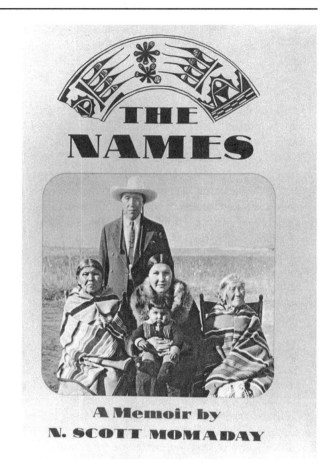

*Dust jacket for Momaday's 1976 autobiography*

the reconciliation of all life forms in the particular healing of the loneliness of a deaf boy.

Book 4 of *The Names* describes the end of Momaday's childhood. While climbing down from the top of a mesa, he reports, he had a near-death experience. When he returned to consciousness on the valley floor, he realized that he had "been within an eyelash of eternity" and that he had also come to "the end of an age. I should never again see the world as I saw it on the other side of that moment, in the bright reflection of time lost. There are such reflections, and for some of them I have names," he concludes. This breach between time and eternity, life and death, also marks the epilogue. In the epilogue Momaday, through the power of his imagination, comes into the presence of the dead—*Mammedaty, Aho, Pohd-loch, Keahdinekeah, Kau-au-ointy,* and *Kosahn.* In the Arbor at Rainy Mountain, Momaday contends that "we told stories, the old people and I."

Momaday's second novel, *The Ancient Child* (1989), has not received the critical acclaim of his other works, perhaps because of the complex nature of the abundant conjectures in the work. Locke Setman (Set), the male protagonist in the novel, is disillusioned and near a breakdown. "At forty he was in the first rank of American artists, and he was in danger of losing his soul." Set has prostituted his art to commercial demands despite his belief that he paints "to astonish God." What sustains God, Set insists, "is the satisfaction, far deeper than we can know, of having created a few incomparables—landscapes, waters, birds and beasts." Set also asserts that "there is only one story, after all, and it is about the pursuit of man by God, and it is about a man who ventures out to the edge of the world, and it is about his holy quest, and it is about his faithful or unfaithful wife, and it is about the hunting of a great beast." Set must delineate this story. His pursuit is fundamentally tied to the philosopher Friedrich Nietzsche's Great Thought: Eternal Recurrence. Momaday's notion of recurrence, however, describes humans as potential Centaurs—a radical kind of kinship that bespeaks the god in man or man in beast of Native American mythology.

In this novel the shape-shifting between planes of reality is brought about through the guidance of a shaman, Grey Koi-ehm-toya, a woman of Kiowa and Navajo ancestry. Grey must, however, also go through a transformation from being an irresponsible tomboy—who lives in her wild sexual fantasies of Billy the Kid—to being a shaman, wife, and mother. These are roles proffered through her relationship and eventual marriage to Set, a marriage promising the continuance of the sacred circle. The notion of sexual ignorance plagues both Set and Grey. Set is susceptible to sophisticated groupies who exchange sexual favors for some attempt at intimacy with an artist. Although Set's primary partner, Lola Bourne, is empathetic and sincere in her regard for Set, she lacks the spiritual capacity to function as midwife to his potential. She does not have the mythic vision that Grey has access to. Lola does, however, recognize Set's imminent transformation as expressed in his painting *Night Window Man*. The painting described in the text resembles Momaday's 1988 *Self Portrait with Leaves,* a painting inspired by Emil Nolde's *Sternenwandler*. Set and Lola's intimacy fails on another level: Set does not know himself and, therefore, cannot offer true human intimacy. Grey's obsession with Billy the Kid consumes her creative energy: she writes a chapbook to Billy in which she sorts out her fascination with the meaning of his life as a symbol of the American West. She finally concludes,

I have heard that certain organisms—sharks, for example—are virtually mindless, that they are creatures of pure instinct. So it was with this man, I believe. If a rational thought, or a whole emotion had ever grown up inside of him, he should have suffered a great dislocation of himself in his mind and soul. Such was my impression; he should have been like a plate of glass that is shattered upon a stone. But at the same time I had the sense that his instincts were nearly infallible. Nothing would ever take him by surprise—and no one, except perhaps himself. Only one principle motivated him, that of survival—his own mean and exclusive survival. For him there was no morality in the universe but that, neither choice nor question. And for that reason he was among the deadliest creatures on the face of the earth.

Grey's renunciation of her addiction to the legend of Billy accompanied by her acceptance of her role as medicine woman—which she inherits from her great-grandmother Kope'mah—thrusts her into identity as Set's spiritual midwife.

Camille Dumoulie in "Eternal Recurrence: Nietzsche's 'Great Thought,'" collected in *Companion to Literary Myths, Heroes and Archetypes* (1996), claims that Nietzsche rediscovered the idea of Eternal Recurrence as a "desire to strike back at the cult of the historical fact and the dreams of the determinists, which represented the last manifestations of metaphysics, while it was also a weapon against nihilism." The names given to Momaday's central character signify this response. In his essay "Navajo Place-Names," published in *The Man Made of Words: Essays, Stories, Passages* (1997), Momaday contends, "That which bears a name bears being as well. *I have a name; therefore I am.* And, of course, there is a wonderful particularity in names." Locke Setman's names support these contentions. They refer to the tensions between John Locke's theory that the human mind is, at birth, a blank page upon which ideas are written through experience and Momaday's tribal notions of racial memory.

Actually, *Set* is the Kiowa word for bear; therefore, Locke Setman's name also suggests that he is the mythic reincarnation or this generation's bear man—a calling Set inherits from Catlin Setmaunt, Set's natural father. Set's father, in the beginning of the text, exists outside Set's memory. In fact, both of Set's parents are beyond memory. He was orphaned at a young age. And yet, the narrator says of Set's mother: "She was his immediate and most personal antecedent, that matter of which he was made, the spirit which drove his blood. He could imagine her, Catherine Locke Setman, in a way no one else could." And Set believed his father, then thirty years dead, was "*his* genesis. He wanted to see his father there in the shadows of the still creek, the child he once was, himself in the child and in the man. But he could not. There was only something like a photograph, old and faded, a shadow within a shadow." Yet, these shadows—of ancestry and myth—lay in Set's unconscious waiting to be born. Set's identity and, therefore, his destiny, unfold through others—Grey and Grey's Navajo mother and Kiowa great-grandmother. Indeed, each book begins with and continues the Kiowa story of

Tsoai–the original boy who transformed into a bear and chased his seven sisters into the sky to become the stars of the Big Dipper. Set's contemporary experiences follow Tsoai's ordeal within the particularities of a postmodern world. In both Navajo and Kiowa mythology, the bear is closely associated with the great power of healing rituals–both re-creative and, therefore, also potentially destructive.

Locke Setman's nickname is Loki, a name implying that events are inseparable from the geographical locations in which they take place–that one can only be at home when morally invested in the stories of particular places. In an artistic metaphor of place, Set explains,

> You have to be always aware of the boundaries of the plane, and you have to make use of them; they define your limits, and they enable you to determine scale, proportion, juxtaposition, depth, design, symmetry correctly. You see, you can make something, a line, a form, an image. But you have to proceed from what is already there–defined space, a plane. You can make something out of something, but you cannot make something out of nothing.

Momaday's version of eternal recurrence is firmly grounded in coexistent landscapes–the physical (ancestral and geographic), psychological (maturational), and spiritual (mythical) landscapes of the Native American West–Bote, Lukachukai, and the area around the rock tree, or Devil's Tower. In *Bloodlines* (1993), Janet Campbell Hale, a Coeur d'Alene Indian, explains this Native American insistence that retention of ethnic identity is attached to land. Most Americans are marginally conscious of their ethnic origins, Hale claims. However, "if Irish or Italian culture dies in America it really isn't that big a deal. They still exist in Italy and Ireland. Not so with us. There is no other place. North America *is* our old country." Therefore, *tribal homeland* takes on an ontological density unfamiliar to those who speak of the Wild West, the American Frontier, or other such allusions to untamed or conquerable space.

In *The Ancient Child,* art moves from creative product to creative process. Indeed, the four major books of the novel–"PLANES," "LINES," "SHAPES," and "SHADOWS"–are all terms indicative of those images emerging from or framed by creative expression. These terms also identify the mystery that exists beyond Western cognition. This enigma is not the cruel survival instincts of Billy the Kid; rather, it is an acknowledgment of the human potential to live in good relationship to God, community, the land, and one's potential. This human potential is still experienced as arising from the unconscious–not as some kind of determinism but as infinite possibility for beauty and well-being.

"Shadows" ends ambiguously, with the possibility of Set becoming bear man. Whether his transformation

*Dust jacket for Momaday's 1997 collection, which includes the title essay*

is creative or destructive is not revealed. Nor are readers led to expect Set's return. However, in his marriage to Grey, Set has attained "explicit knowledge, that they were married. In ceremony in tradition out of time, in a sacred manner, in beauty they were married forever." Set's love for Grey is "a source of endless wonder to him. The greatest thing about it was that it had no definition; it was boundless." Set prays to be "worthy" of Grey. He prays that she be "well." He prays for Grey "that today you will have all you need to sustain you in your body and in your mind and in your heart. I pray," says Set, "that today you will know peace and joy, that you will have good thoughts of yourself and of me and of our child." Set also prays that Grey will give to the world, as a freewill offering, all the good she has to give. This prayer reflects that harmony that should exist between male and female if there is to be harmony in the world. Futurity, therefore, is expressed in the promise of the new life of their child. *The Ancient Child* is not a rejection of the Western culture. Whether Grey relates to Set as the inferior gender becomes doubtful if Grey's midwifery can be accepted as an equally important role to that of Set's transformation into bear man. Both Grey and Set are also greatly enhanced by their experiences with the arts. *The Ancient Child* is both a conversation with Western and American ideologies and an invitation to consider what Native America has to offer those who have been transplanted into her soil.

*In the Presence of the Sun: Stories and Poems, 1961–1991* (1992) is an expansion of *In the Presence of the Sun: A Gathering of Shields* (1992). The expansion is a selected accumulation of the poetry of thirty years plus Momaday's collected musings on "The Strange and True Story of My Life with Billy the Kid," "A Gathering of Shields," and twenty-seven new poems. However, this edition of Momaday's poetic and selected short prose works is punctuated with sixty illustrations by Momaday–etching, watercolor, ink, and graphite and wash compositions dating from 1976 through 1992. This combination of word and image is central to his understanding of the creative process–"the bonding of voice and image, the translation of sound into symbol, the word made visible: imaging, imagining, incising, writing," writes Momaday in "Sacred Images."

In his preface to *In the Presence of the Sun,* Momaday suggests, "The poet says, Here, let me show you something. That is, let me help you to see something as you have not seen it before. And so says the painter." Furthermore, he claims that

> Poetry is a very old and elemental expression, as venerable as song and prayer. In various times and languages we have tried to elevate it to our current notions of formality and eloquence. And we have succeeded, for language, by its nature, allows us to do so. But poetry remains elemental. In poetry we address ourselves really, without pretension or deceit, without the intervention of interest. At its best, poetry is an act of disinterested generosity. The poet gives his words to the world in the appropriate expression of his spirit.

Examples of the "appropriate" expressions of Momaday's spirit are his frequently anthologized poems, such as "Earth and I Gave You Turquoise," "Angle of Geese," "The Gourd Dancer," and "Carriers of the Dream Wheel." "Carriers of the Dream Wheel" is a celebration–like much of Momaday's poetry–of those people whose voices

> spin the names of the earth and sky,
> The aboriginal names.
> They are old men, or men
> Who are old in their voices,
> And they carry the wheel among the camps,
> Saying: Come, come,
> Let us tell the old stories,
> Let us sing the sacred songs.

"A Gathering of Shields" is a collection of sixteen images of plains shields accompanied by brief narrative accounts of each shield's maker. These sixteen shields carry additional power because they are four collections of four shields. The shields invite perceptive listeners and viewers to fast before experiencing the shields so that they might also become healthy, worthy, and "pure in spirit." Traditionally, these shields were round, often made of hides, and adorned with artwork that Momaday claims is reminiscent of "Archaic Greek vase painting." Shields often served as armor–or protection from enemies. Each shield "bears a remarkable relationship to the individual to whom it belongs," he says. Each shield is also like a mask that "bespeaks sacred mystery" and ushers the viewer into the sacred power of the possessor. Every shield, he explains, is a story, a charm, a spell, and a prayer.

Many of Momaday's works are founded on Kiowa and Navajo mythology. His play *Children of the Sun* (1997), for example, is a dramatic re-creation of the stories of the half-boys of Kiowa mythology also written about in *The Way to Rainy Mountain.* The boys' mother, named Aila in the play, is wife of the Sun. The boys, therefore, are part god and part human; they provide the Kiowa with an understanding of their kinship with the Sun. And their exploits create exemplary models of appropriate or inappropriate behavior. Many of Momaday's themes are clearly established in his collection *The Man Made of Words,* also published in 1997. In this work Momaday explores his conceptions of language, land, and storytelling. Momaday says that "Our stories explain us, justify us, sustain us, humble us, and forgive us. And sometimes they injure and destroy us." He also says that "In order to be perceived in its true character, the landscape of the American West must be seen in terms of its sacred dimension. *Sacred* and *sacrifice* are related. Something is made sacred by means of sacrifice; that which is sacred is earned." Finally, he says that "We Americans must come again to a moral comprehension of the earth and air. We must live according to the principle of a land ethic. The alternative is that we shall not live at all." Momaday's 1999 collection of paintings, poetry, and prose, *In the Bear's House,* engenders a delightful dialogue between Urset (the primordial Bear, a representation of wilderness) and Yahweh about the nature of creation, language, storytelling, evolution, thought, and time. Clearly reminiscent of Platonic dialogues, *In the Bear's House* demonstrates the conversation possible between Old World and New World mythic, philosophic, and literary traditions. Certainly, this work represents the scope of Momaday's mythic vision.

After the first recognition of Momaday's literary talents in 1959–his winning of the Wallace Stegner Creative Writing Fellowship at Stanford University–in

1962 he was recognized by the Academy of American Poets award for his poem "The Bear," a tribute to Faulkner's short story by the same name. Four years later Momaday received a Guggenheim Fellowship to study Emily Dickinson and the Transcendentalists at Amherst College in Massachusetts. His novel *House Made of Dawn* won the Pulitzer Prize for fiction in 1969. During the ten years following the Pulitzer Prize, Momaday was honored by the National Institute of Arts and Letters, received a Gold Plate Award from the American Academy of Achievement, and was also awarded the highest literary award Italy bestows, the *Premio Letteraio Internationale Mondelio* (1979). In 1992, thirty years after his literary career began, Momaday was given the Returning the Gift Lifetime Achievement Award, an award that acknowledges contributions beyond literary productivity.

Perhaps Momaday's involvement in sacred matters precludes proper critical evaluation of his works. Arnold Krupat notes in *The Turn to the Native: Studies in Criticism and Culture* (1996) that Matthias Schubnell's 1985 overview of Momaday's work, *N. Scott Momaday: The Cultural and Literary Background,* "is more hagiography than critical study." And Kathleen M. Donovan, in her *Feminist Readings of Native American Literature: Coming to Voice* (1998), suggests that Momaday has "such a looming presence that the very process of undertaking a feminist deconstruction of his representation of women in his novels feels like a transgression of the first order." Donovan admits that Momaday is "a brilliant, lyrical writer whom, on one level [she wants] to admire uncritically for the elegant artistry of his use of language." Yet on another level, Donovan claims, Momaday's representation of female characters is "paradoxical and disturbing." Underlying these assessments, nonetheless, is a respect for Momaday and his artistic expressions. Momaday's continued struggle to arrive at new mythic visions in a world plagued with ethnic factionalism and violence against the earth and her creatures, however, continually draws favorable attention. Many critics recognize that Momaday's imaginative new vision of sacred matters breaks new ground. Michael W. Raymond suggests that "By advocating compatibility in cultural pluralism and the authenticity of individual identity within that pluralism, Momaday emphasizes the potential for the individual to find a sense of place in contemporary life." As Momaday's works mature, so does his understanding of the ongoing relationship between myth and ritual. Perhaps this growing understanding in the midst of the postmodern challenge to sacred

*Painting of a bear by Momaday; from his 1999 collection,*
In the Bear's House

narrative constitutes Momaday's continual appeal to readers.

During the First Convocation of American Indian Scholars in 1970, Rupurt Costo asked Momaday's advice on how to preserve a Native worldview in the face of many negative alternatives offered by Western culture. He answered,

> For a long time, . . . the traditional values in the Indian world have not been valued in the terms of the modern dominant society. We've always, I think, thought of acculturation as a kind of one-way process in which the Indian ceases to be an Indian and becomes a white man. That's been an objective, whether we want to admit it or not, in historical diplomacy. I think, for the first time, that it is not a one-way process at all. Acculturation means a two-way, a reciprocal kind of thing in which there is a realization of one world that is composed of both elements, or many for that matter. I think many young people are aware of this. I think certain others are completely lost, because there are so many alternatives on the horizon. But I think more and more we ought to educate the white man. We ought to reconstruct the institutions within the dominant society, so that the Indian values are available to the dominant society.

Perhaps *House Made of Dawn* was awarded the Pulitzer Prize for just this reason: Indian values were made available to the dominant society through Momaday's artistic and myth-making talent.

**Interviews:**

Robert W. Reising, "The Voice and the Vision: A Visit with N. Scott Momaday," *Pembroke Magazine,* 19 (1987): 120–124;

Charles L. Woodward, *Ancestral Voice: Conversations with N. Scott Momaday* (Lincoln: University of Nebraska Press, 1989);

Matthias Schubnell, ed., *Conversations with N. Scott Momaday* (Jackson: University of Mississippi Press, 1997).

**Biographies:**

Martha Scott Trimble, *N. Scott Momaday* (Boise, Idaho: Boise State College, 1973);

Matthias Schubnell, *N. Scott Momaday: The Cultural and Literary Background* (Norman: University of Oklahoma Press, 1985).

**References:**

Camille Adkins, "Interview with N. Scott Momaday," in *Conversations with N. Scott Momaday,* edited by Matthias Schubnell (Jackson: University Press of Mississippi, 1997), pp. 216–245;

Paula Gunn Allen, "Bringing Home the Fact: Tradition and Continuity in the Imagination," in *Recovering the Word: Essays on Native American Literature,* edited by Brian Swann and Arnold Krupat (Berkeley: University of California Press, 1987), pp. 563–569;

Edward M. Bruner, "Experience and Its Expressions," *The Anthropology of Experience,* edited by Victor W. Turner and Bruner (Chicago: University of Illinois Press, 1986), pp. 3–33;

Rupert Costo, "Discussion: The Man Made of Words," in *Conversations with N. Scott Momaday,* edited by Schubnell (Jackson: University Press of Mississippi, 1997), pp. 3–19;

Roger Dickinson-Brown, "The Art and Importance of N. Scott Momaday," *Southern Review,* 14 (1978): 30–45;

Kathleen M. Donovan, *Feminist Readings of Native American Literature: Coming to Voice* (Tucson: University of Arizona Press, 1998);

Camille Dumoulie, "Eternal Recurrence: Nietzsche's 'Great Thought,'" in *Companion to Literary Myths, Heroes and Archetypes,* edited by Pierre Brunel (London & New York: Routledge, 1996), pp. 420–424;

Janet Campbell Hale, *Bloodlines* (New York: Harper Perennial, 1993);

Bernard A. Hirsch, "Self-Hatred and Spiritual Corruption in *House Made of Dawn,*" *Western American Literature,* 17 (Winter 1983): 307–320;

Baine Kerr, "The Novel as Sacred Text: N. Scott Momaday's Myth-Making Ethic," *Southwest Review,* 63 (1978): 172–179;

Arnold Krupat, *The Turn to the Native: Studies in Criticism and Culture* (Lincoln: University of Nebraska Press, 1996);

Louis Owens, "N. Scott Momaday," in *Conversations with N. Scott Momaday,* edited by Schubnell (Jackson: University Press of Mississippi, 1997), pp. 178–192;

Michael W. Raymond, "Tai-me, Christ, and the Machine: Affirmation through Mythic Pluralism in *House Made of Dawn,*" in *Studies in American Fiction,* 11, no. 1 (Spring 1983): 61–71;

Susan Scarberry-Garcia, *Landmarks of Healing: A Study of House Made of Dawn* (Albuquerque: University of New Mexico Press, 1990);

Scarberry-Garcia, "N(avarre) Scott Momaday," in *Handbook of Native American Literature,* edited by Andrew Wiget (New York: Garland, 1996), pp. 463–469;

Schubnell, "An Interview with N. Scott Momaday," in *Conversations with N. Scott Momaday,* edited by Schubnell (Jackson: University Press of Mississippi, 1997), pp. 67–87;

Schubnell, *N. Scott Momaday: The Cultural and Literary Background* (Norman: University of Oklahoma Press, 1985);

Schubnell, "Tribal Identity and the Imagination," in *Approaches to Teaching Momaday's The Way to Rainy Mountain,* edited by Kenneth M. Roemer (New York: Modern Language Association, 1988), pp. 24–32;

Lawana Trout, "*The Way to Rainy Mountain:* Arrow of History, Spiral of Myth," in *Approaches to Teaching Momaday's The Way to Rainy Mountain* (New York: Modern Language Association, 1988), pp. 32–41;

Ivor Winters, *Forms of Discovery* (Chicago: Alan Swallow, 1967);

Gary Witherspoon, *Language and Art in the Navajo Universe* (Ann Arbor: University of Michigan Press, 1977);

Paul Zolbrod, "When Artifacts Speak, What Can They Tell Us?" in *Recovering the Word: Essays on Native American Literature,* edited by Brian Swann and Krupat (Berkeley: University of California Press, 1987), pp. 13–41.

# John G. Neihardt

*(8 January 1881 – 4 November 1973)*

Dennis R. Hoilman
*Ball State University*

See also the Neihardt entries in *DLB 9: American Novelists, 1910–1945* and *DLB 54: American Poets, 1880–1945, Third Series.*

BOOKS: *The Divine Enchantment: A Mystical Poem* (New York: White, 1900);

*The Wind God's Wooing* (Bancroft, Nebr.: Blade, 1904);

*A Bundle of Myrrh* (New York: Outing, 1907);

*The Lonesome Trail* (New York & London: John Lane, 1907);

*Man-Song* (New York: Kennerley, 1909);

*The River and I* (New York & London: Putnam, 1910);

*The Dawn-Builder* (New York: Kennerley, 1911);

*The Stranger at the Gate* (New York: Kennerley, 1912);

*Life's Lure* (New York: Kennerley, 1914);

*The Song of Hugh Glass* (New York: Macmillan, 1915);

*The Quest* (New York: Macmillan, 1916);

*The Song of Three Friends* (New York: Macmillan, 1919);

*The Splendid Wayfaring: The Story of the Exploits and Adventures of Jedediah Smith and His Comrades, the Ashley-Henry Men* (New York: Macmillan, 1920);

*Two Mothers* (New York: Macmillan, 1921);

*Laureate Address of John G. Neihardt* (Chicago: Bookfellows, 1921);

*The Song of the Indian Wars* (New York: Macmillan, 1925);

*Poetic Values: Their Reality and Our Need of Them* (New York: Macmillan, 1925);

*Collected Poems of John G. Neihardt*, 2 volumes (New York: Macmillan, 1926); volume 1 republished as *Lyric and Dramatic Poems* (Lincoln: University of Nebraska Press, 1965);

*Indian Tales and Others* (New York: Macmillan, 1926);

*The Song of the Messiah* (New York: Macmillan, 1935);

*The Song of Three Friends and The Song of Hugh Glass* (New York: Macmillan, 1935);

*The Song of Jed Smith* (New York: Macmillan, 1941);

*When the Tree Flowered: An Authentic Tale of the Old Sioux World* (New York: Macmillan, 1951); republished as *Eagle Voice; An Authentic Tale of the Sioux Indians* (London: Melrose, 1953; Lincoln: University of Nebraska Press, 1991);

*John G. Neihardt (by permission of Hilda N. Petri, Trustee of the John G. Neihardt Trust)*

*All Is But a Beginning: Youth Remembered, 1881–1901* (New York: Harcourt Brace Jovanovich, 1972);

*Luminous Sanity: Literary Criticism Written by John G. Neihardt*, edited by John Thomas Richards (Cape Girardeau, Mo.: Concordia, 1973);

*Patterns and Coincidences: A Sequel to All Is But a Beginning* (Columbia: University of Missouri Press, 1978);

*The Ancient Memory and Other Stories*, edited by Hilda Neihardt Petri (Lincoln: University of Nebraska Press, 1991);

*The End of the Dream and Other Stories*, edited by Petri (Lincoln: University of Nebraska Press, 1991).

**Editions and Collections:** *A Cycle of the West: The Song of Three Friends, The Song of Hugh Glass, The Song of Jed Smith, The Song of the Indian Wars, The Song of the Messiah* (New York: Macmillan, 1949);

*The Mountain Men* (Lincoln: University of Nebraska Press, 1971)–comprises *The Song of Three Friends, The Song of Hugh Glass,* and *The Song of Jed Smith;*

*The Twilight of the Sioux* (Lincoln: University of Nebraska Press, 1971)–comprises *The Song of the Indian Wars* and *The Song of the Messiah.*

RECORDINGS: *The Wonder of It All,* read by Neihardt, Roto Records, RC-1044, 1970;

*Flaming Rainbow: Reflections and Recollections of an Epic Poet,* read by Neihardt, United Artists Records, UA-LA-157-L3, 1973;

*John G. Neihardt Reads from His Cycle of the West and Selected Poems,* Caedmon, CDL5 1665, 1981.

OTHER: *The Poet's Pack,* edited by Neihardt (Chicago: Bookfellows, 1921);

Nicholas Black Elk, *Black Elk Speaks: Being the Life Story of a Holy Man of the Oglala Sioux,* edited by Neihardt (New York: Morrow, 1932; London: Barrie & Jenkins, 1972).

Throughout his seventy-five-year career as a writer, John G. Neihardt's aspiration was to be the epic poet of the American West; he is remembered chiefly, however, for his work as an editor. His ambition was to fulfill what he became convinced at an early age was his destiny, poetic greatness; but the autobiography he edited, *Black Elk Speaks: Being the Life Story of a Holy Man of the Oglala Sioux* (1932), has far eclipsed Neihardt's epics. It has been described as a masterpiece "of the literature on Indians, the standard by which other efforts to tell the Indian story are judged" by Vine Deloria Jr. in his introduction to *A Sender of Words: Essays in Memory of John G. Neihardt* (1984) and has been called "the first American Bible" by Frederick Manfred in his essay in the same volume. Peter Iverson, in another essay from *A Sender of Words,* has credited Neihardt and the Commissioner of Indian Affairs John Collier with being the two people in the twentieth century "most influential in shaping a new conception of the American Indian."

If it were not for *Black Elk Speaks,* Neihardt's original poetry would undoubtedly receive much more attention than it does. In fact, Neihardt seems one of those rare persons destined from birth to be a poet; at least, his parents must have thought so. Born on 8 January 1881 in a rented two-room shack near Sharpsburg, Illinois, to Nicholas Nathan Neihardt and Alice Culler Neihardt, he was christened John Greenleaf Neihardt after the poet John Greenleaf Whittier–the middle name was later changed to

Gneisenau. Nicholas deserted his family after moving them to Kansas City, Missouri, where he had found work as a cable-car conductor; John was ten at the time his father left.

Neihardt's mother was the major influence on his early years; she took him and his two older sisters to live with her parents in a sod house on the upper Solomon River in western Kansas, where Neihardt grew up on the edge of poverty, but happily, and where he acquired that love of open spaces and wide horizons that made him decide at an early age to live always and only in the West and as much as possible in the country. Neihardt wrote in his introduction to *A Cycle of the West: The Song of Three Friends, The Song of Hugh Glass, The Song of Jed Smith, The Song of the Indian Wars, The Song of the Messiah* (1949) that his

maternal grandparents were covered-wagon people. . . . The buffalo had vanished from that country only a few years before, and the signs of them were everywhere. I have helped, as a little boy could, in "picking cow-chips" for winter fuel. If I write of hot-winds and grasshoppers, of prairie fires and blizzards, of dawns and noons and sunsets and nights, of brooding heat and thunderstorms in vast lands, I knew them early. They were the vital facts of my world, along with the talk of the old-timers who knew such fascinating things to talk about.

When he was eleven, Neihardt had the dream that was to provide the guiding vision of his life, an experience that he later regarded as similar to the dream visions that young Sioux boys sought by fasting. This dream left him convinced that his mission in life was to be a poet, as he wrote in his early lyric "The Ghostly Brother." This sense of mission was with Neihardt all his life; he referred to it not only as "The Ghostly Brother" but also as "Otherness," or simply as "It." This force impelled him to write only poetry, never prose.

In 1891 Neihardt's mother moved the family to Wayne, Nebraska, where John finished elementary school and was able to earn an advanced science degree at Nebraska Normal College in just two years. While in college Neihardt read the classics, fell under their spell, and began writing poetry. By the age of seventeen he had completed a long epic derived from his study of Hindu mysticism. In 1900, when he was nineteen, at a cost to himself of $200, he was able to publish *The Divine Enchantment: A Mystical Poem.* The poem–which describes the vision of Devanaguy, the mother of Krishna, in which the "meek souls" see that "all is one"–suggests themes that occupied Neihardt throughout his career, especially in Black Elk's vision and in *The Song of the Messiah.* In spite of some favorable reviews, the poem was not successful, and in later years Neihardt destroyed all the copies he could find, referring to it as "the case of posterity against John G.

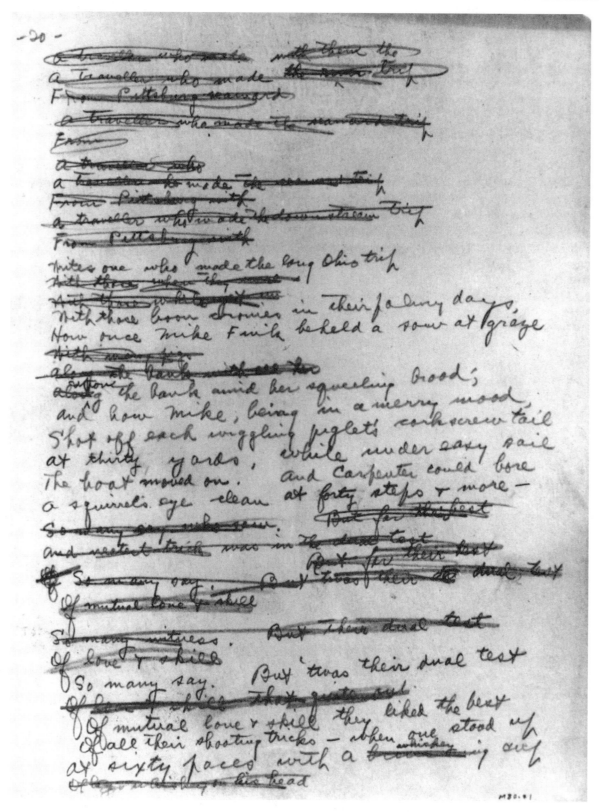

*Page from the first draft of the manuscript for* The Song of Three Friends *(1919), part of Neihardt's epic poem,* A Cycle of the West, *which was published in five volumes between 1915 and 1941 (Joint Collection, University of Missouri, Western Historical Manuscript Collection—Columbia State Historical Society of Missouri Manuscripts)*

Neihardt." Also in 1900, Neihardt and his mother moved to Bancroft, Nebraska, where he edited the newspaper for several years and served as assistant to an agent on the Omaha Indian reservation, where he came to know Indians and sympathize with their poverty and helplessness in the face of unscrupulous white men who took advantage of them.

In 1908 he undertook the great adventure of traveling with two friends in a handmade canoe two thousand miles down the Missouri River, "the path of conquerors" as he called it, from its headwaters at Fort Benton, Montana, to Sioux City, Iowa. His fascination with the Missouri River had begun in Kansas City when he was six years old. As he later recalled in the introduction to *A Cycle of the West,* it was his "first wee glimpse into the infinite":

> I was a very little boy when my father introduced me to the Missouri River at Kansas City. It was flood time. The impression was tremendous, and a steadily growing desire to know what had happened on such a river led me directly to my heroes. Twenty years later, when I had come to know them well, I built a boat, . . . descended the Missouri in low water and against head winds, dreamed back the stories men had lived along the river, bend by bend. This experience is set forth in *The River and I.*

He published a series of articles about the river trip adventures in *Outing Magazine* (1908), and they were collected in book form in *The River and I* (1910).

*The River and I* records Neihardt's effort, successful as it turned out, to experience the epic story of Meriwether Lewis and William Clark and the fur trappers who followed them up the river in heroic adventures that, he thought, rivaled those found in the works of Homer and Virgil. Neihardt's life's work, as he now envisioned it, became the creation of a poetic epic chronicling the history of the American West that would be worthy of his classical predecessors, Homer, Virgil, and John Milton.

Also much influenced by the British Romantic poets, Neihardt had already been writing and publishing lyric poetry, mostly love poetry, that treated the subject with immature enthusiasm and, for its time, frank sensuality, but with little sense of reality. *A Bundle of Myrrh,* a collection of these poems, was published in 1907. It attracted the attention of Mona Martinsen, who had just returned to New York from studying sculpture in Paris with Auguste Rodin when she came across Neihardt's book. She wrote to Neihardt; love blossomed in a long-distance correspondence; and before the year was out she arrived in Omaha, where he met her train with the marriage license in his pocket. They were married the next day, and the marriage lasted until her death in 1958. They had four children: Enid, Sigurd, Hilda, and Alice.

*Man-Song* (1909), love lyrics inspired by Neihardt's marriage, shows a surer control of his craft than the poems in *A Bundle of Myrrh,* but *The Stranger at the Gate* (1912), a collection of poems inspired by the birth of his first child, has little to recommend it to readers today. Although critics at the time were kind to Neihardt's early lyric poetry, recent critics have found it of value only to those who are interested in tracing Neihardt's growing mastery of the technical aspects of his poetic craft. Blair Whitney, in *John G. Neihardt* (1976), wonders "how an intelligent, sensitive poet, a man who loved truth and honored purity of line, a man who liked to work with his hands and lived a vigorous outdoor life, could write such awful, silly, insipid poetry."

During this early period Neihardt also experimented with poetic drama. Between 1909 and 1912 he wrote plays on allegorical themes, such as the love of nature and the evils of greed, and on classical subjects such as Alcibiades and Agrippina. His first two novels, *The Dawn-Builder* (1911) and *Life's Lure* (1914), also date from this period. But his most successful writing at this time was his short stories, many of which, unlike his lyric poems, poetic dramas, and novels, can still be read with enjoyment. One group of stories dealing with Indians derives from Neihardt's contact with the Omahas. Among these stories is the notable "The Singer of the Ache," the story of a young Omaha who receives a vision of eternal beauty that drives him to become a singer and a poet, and alienates him from his tribe and from his wife and children. Out of this young man's suffering and his dedication to his vision, a true poet is born, and in their time of need people find his songs in their hearts and are comforted. Another excellent story is "The Last Thunder Song," which anticipates the concluding section of *Black Elk Speaks.* Along with "The Heart of a Woman" and "Vylin," it deals with the theme of the inability of different cultures to understand each other. Other stories, such as "The Alien" and "The Scars," deal with fur trappers and anticipate themes that Neihardt returns to in his masterpiece, *A Cycle of the West.* "The Look in the Face" deals with betrayal in the wilderness, thus anticipating *The Song of Hugh Glass* (1915), and several of the stories deal with the supernatural, a theme that had interested Neihardt since his childhood dream.

After 1912 Neihardt's major efforts were devoted to the project that was to occupy him, with only a few interruptions, for the next twenty-nine years. *A Cycle of the West* is his epic of Western American history from 1822, when General William H. Ashley and Major Andrew Henry led their band of trappers to the upper Missouri, to 1890, when the Battle of Wounded Knee put an end to the Indian wars on the Plains. In his introduction to *A Cycle of the West,* Neihardt writes that the poem is designed to celebrate the great mood of courage that was developed west of the Missouri River in the nineteenth century. . . . The period with which the cycle deals was one of discovery, exploration, and settlement—a genuine epic period, differing in no essential from the other great epic periods that marked the advance of the Indo-European peoples out of Asia and across Europe.

Neihardt continues his explanation of why he regards *A Cycle of the West* as an epic, referring to the intense individualism, the rootlessness of society, the needs and greed of a powerful people, and the mood and meaning of the material, but disclaiming pretensions of writing "synthetic *Iliads* and *Odysseys*." The cycle, he says in the introduction, describes "the richly human saga-stuff of a country that I knew and loved, and of a time in the very fringe of which I was a boy."

*A Cycle of the West* is divided into five parts, each published separately. Neihardt says, also in the introduction, that "more than five thousand days were devoted to the work," and Lucille Aly, on the basis of "discussions and interviews with Neihardt and his family," says in her critical biography titled *John G. Neihardt* that he wrote only in the morning, that he "waited for his 'Otherness' to operate," and that he was satisfied with three lines a day, although sometimes he was able to produce as many as eight or ten. Neihardt points out in the introduction to *A Cycle of the West* that in addition to the chronological and geographical progression through the five parts, "those [readers] who feel as I have felt while the tales were growing may note a spiritual progression also—from the level of indomitable physical prowess to that of spiritual triumph in apparent worldly defeat."

The meter that Neihardt chose for *A Cycle of the West* is sometimes referred to by critics as "blank verse" and sometimes as "heroic couplets." As he explained in his introduction to the *Cycle,* Neihardt himself objected to the term "heroic couplet," even though the lines rhyme in pairs. He preferred to think of the meter as rhymed blank verse because the meaning was not confined to the couplets but often ran over the boundaries of the rhyme. The second of the five parts chronologically, *The Song of Hugh Glass* was the first published and was followed by the first in chronological order, *The Song of Three Friends* (1919).

The three friends celebrated in the first song are Will Carpenter, Mike Fink, and Frank Talbeau. Fink and Carpenter fight over an Indian girl, who chooses Carpenter over Fink, and Talbeau tries to mediate between them and to restore the friendship. In a demonstration of skill and trust, Fink and Carpenter agree to shoot a cup of whiskey off each other's head, tossing a coin to determine who shoots first. The coin favors Fink, but he misses the cup—accidentally, he claims—and drills Carpenter through the head, killing him. Later Fink con-

fesses that he meant to kill Carpenter, and Talbeau steals Fink's gun and water flask, forcing Fink out into the desert, with Talbeau in constant pursuit. Finally, Talbeau has a change of mind and forgives Fink. But forgiveness comes too late; Fink is dead and Talbeau finds his corpse a feast for a flock of crows. Talbeau,

> halting at the place
> Where late the flock had been, . . . strove to break
> A grip of horror. . . .
> The thing remained! It hadn't any eyes—
> The pilfered sockets bore a pleading stare!
> A long, hoarse wail of anguish and despair
> Aroused the echoes. Answering, arose
> Once more the jeering chorus of the crows.

Talbeau realizes that he has proved to be no better than Fink, no more willing to forgive and leave vengeance to a higher power than was Fink himself.

Second in chronological order in the cycle, *The Song of Hugh Glass* takes place in 1823.

> It happened then that Major Henry went
> With eighty trappers up the dwindling Grand,
> Bound through the weird, unfriending barren-land
> For where the Big Horn meets the Yellowstone;
> And old Hugh Glass went with them.

Hugh conceives a fatherly feeling toward young Jamie, for whom he risks his own life in a fight with the Indians. Later Hugh is sent ahead to scout a campsite for the main body of trappers. When the trappers arrive at the site, they find Hugh horribly mauled by a bear, unconscious but incredibly still clinging to life. Two men, Jamie and Jules, are left behind to wait with Hugh until he dies, while the other men, fearing an imminent Indian attack, move on. After four days, Hugh still clings to life and Jules tricks Jamie into thinking that Indians are near. Jules takes Hugh's gun, hunting knife, flint, blanket—everything of value that Hugh has—and he and Jamie abandon Hugh to die alone. But Hugh does not die; instead, he regains consciousness and, crippled by his wounds but driven by the desire for vengeance, he begins a hundred-mile crawl to the nearest human habitation. When Hugh finally catches up with Henry's men, he spares Jules but declares his intention to take his revenge on Jamie, his friend. Jamie, tortured by the wrong he has done, has left Henry's camp and returned to the spot where he and Jules abandoned Hugh, intending to bury the body as a means of trying to make amends for his betrayal. But Jamie finds no body there, and when he returns, he learns that Hugh has survived. Ready to die to escape the pangs of a guilty conscience, Jamie sets out to meet Hugh, carrying Hugh's stolen gun, which explodes in his face and blinds him. He is taken in by the Piegans; awaiting death, he longs for a

*Neihardt and Black Elk at the Pine Ridge Reservation on 14 September 1945 (Collection of Hilda Neihardt)*

priest to whom he can confess. Meanwhile, during his search for Jamie, Hugh has come to question himself:

> So long of love bereft,
> So long sustained and driven by his hate,
> A touch of ruth now made him desolate.
> No longer eager to avenge the wrong,
> With not enough of pity to be strong
> And just enough of love to choke and sting,
> A gray old hulk amid the surge of Spring
> He floundered on a lee-shore of the heart.

By the time that Hugh finds Jamie at the Piegan village, Hugh has passed beyond this floundering ambivalence and now thinks that

> to forgive and to forget were sweet:
> 'Tis for its nurse that Vengeance whets the tooth!
> And oh the golden time of Jamie's youth,
> That it should darken for a graybeard's whim!
> So Hugh had brooded, till there came on him
> The pity of a slow rain after drought.

Hugh has moved beyond vengeance to a higher level of spiritual awareness. At first he conceals his identity from the blinded boy and takes Jamie's confession as if he were a priest. Then, as the poem ends, Hugh reveals himself

and forgives Jamie. Neihardt does not reveal whether or not Jamie survives, for Neihardt is concerned with the spiritual growth of his two characters rather than with their physical survival.

*The Song of Hugh Glass* is one of Neihardt's most complex and satisfying works. Despite what the bare outlines of the plot suggest, it is not a simple story of man's indomitable will to survive or a conventional sermon on the necessity of forgiveness. It is full of ironies and strengthened by its reticence and understatement, uncommon qualities in Neihardt's poetry. Crucial to an adequate understanding of the poem is the recognition that Hugh has, in a sense, been the author of his own abandonment. On that day when Hugh saved Jamie's life, Jamie had stood his ground against the Indians when all the other trappers fled. After rescuing Jamie, Hugh takes

> the lad upon his knee: "My Son,
> Brave men are not ashamed to fear," said Hugh,
> "And I've a mind to make a man of you;
> So here's your first acquaintance with the law!"
> Whereat he spanked the lad with vigorous paw
> And, having done so, limped away to bed;
> For, wounded in the hip, the old man bled.

This "acquaintance with the law" is precisely the practical wisdom that Jules had urged when convincing Jamie to abandon Hugh rather than to risk their lives by remaining with him until he died. But, as Jamie realizes as he confesses,

> The Devil traffics in the fear of death,
> And may God pity anyone who buys
> What I have bought with treachery and lies—
> This rat-like gnawing in my breast!

Ultimately, both men have grown into the realization that unselfish love, not self-love, vengeance, or mere survival, gives life meaning and gives a man a reason to struggle to survive.

The third segment of *A Cycle of the West* in terms of chronology is *The Song of Jed Smith* (1941). With it, Neihardt completes that segment of the cycle that deals with the history of the fur trappers. Neihardt had already done extensive research on Jedediah Strong Smith, whom he regarded as the most interesting and most fully heroic of all the Western trappers and explorers, for a biography of Smith that Neihardt, at the request of his publisher, had produced for the school trade. The biography, *The Splendid Wayfaring; The Story of the Exploits and Adventures of Jedediah Smith and His Comrades, the Ashley-Henry men* (1920), is full of the sights and sounds and facts of the Old West, from its beginning in Cincinnati in 1822 to Smith's death at the hands of the Comanches along the Cimarron River in 1831. The book still deserves to be read on its own merits and not just as background to the stories of the mountain men in *A Cycle of the West*.

In *The Song of Jed Smith* Neihardt departs from the omniscient point of view of the first two songs and uses a framework device to provide three different perspectives on his hero, those of three of Jed's friends—Art Black, Bob Evans, and Squire—who are reminiscing around their campfire in 1838, some seven years after "A parcel of Comanches got his hair / Away down yonder on the Cimarrone." Because of his faith, his endurance, his courage, and his integrity, Jed Smith is Neihardt's ideal man; he combines an unshakable spirituality with the practicality necessary to survive in a world fraught with dangers. The reminiscences of the three friends are chiefly focused on Smith's journeys across the unmapped West in 1826 and 1827, journeys which took him through South Pass to the Great Salt Lake and on to California and Oregon. Perhaps because Jed Smith's story lacks the potential for internal conflict and tragedy that Neihardt exploits so successfully in the other four songs, *The Song of Jed Smith* is regarded as the least successful segment of *A Cycle of the West*.

*The Song of the Indian Wars* (1925) deals with the period from the end of the Civil War to the murder of Crazy Horse in 1877, and *The Song of the Messiah* (1935) deals with the Ghost Dance religion and the massacre at Wounded Knee Creek in 1890. Neihardt presents the story of the Sioux wars from both sides, striving for the impersonal quality of the great epics, but his sympathies are ultimately with the losers. The earlier volume covers the Fetterman massacre, the Wagon Box Fight, the fight at Beecher's Island, the massacre of Crazy Horse's village, and the Custer battle, as well as the death of Crazy Horse. *The Song of the Messiah*, which Neihardt regarded as his best work, takes up ten years after the death of Crazy Horse and deals with the journey of four Sioux to visit Wovoka, the "Piute Messiah," whose vision inspired the Ghost Dance; the spread of the Ghost Dance among the Sioux; the death of Sitting Bull; and the flight and massacre of Big Foot's people at Wounded Knee.

*A Cycle of the West* thus divides into two distinct parts, the first made up of the three songs dealing with the heroic achievements of the mountain men, and the second made up of two songs dealing with the heroic resistance and tragic defeat of the Indians. Neihardt's purposes were, as he once wrote, "to preserve a great heroic race-mood which might otherwise be lost" and, as previously noted, to demonstrate "spiritual triumph in apparent worldly defeat." Four of the songs end in obvious worldly defeat—the deaths of Mike Fink, Jed Smith, Crazy Horse, and Big Foot. The ending of *The Song of Hugh Glass* is left open, but Jamie himself clearly anticipates dying as he makes his confession to Hugh. *The Song of Three Friends* ends in the spiritual defeat of Talbeau as

well as Fink's physical death, but at the end of the following four songs, Neihardt is successful in achieving his aim of conveying a sense of spiritual triumph and in presenting an interpretation of American history from 1822 to 1890 that finds grounds for hope beyond conventional notions of material progress.

As preparation for *The Song of the Messiah*, Neihardt had sought to interview some of the old-timers among the Sioux who had lived through the "Messiah craze," as he called it in the introduction to *Black Elk Speaks*, perhaps "some old medicine man who had been active in the Messiah Movement and who might somehow be induced to talk to me about the deeper spiritual significance of the matter." In 1930 Neihardt found sixty-seven-year-old Nicholas Black Elk, an Oglala Sioux holy man who had been at both the Custer fight and the Wounded Knee massacre, and who was a second cousin to Crazy Horse. Neihardt considered Black Elk to be "the most significant single influence upon his [Neihardt's] life and thought."

Inclined to mysticism himself, Neihardt recognized in Black Elk a spirituality that transcended anything he had previously encountered and, after he had known "the great old man for some years," Neihardt wrote in the introduction to *Black Elk Speaks*, he came to believe that Black Elk "certainly had supernormal powers." After conversations with Black Elk at the Pine Ridge Reservation in South Dakota in 1930, Neihardt returned to Pine Ridge in May 1931 with his two daughters to record Black Elk's life story, which, Neihardt had come to see, had to be preserved not only for the Sioux people themselves but for all people. Black Elk told his story in Lakota; Black Elk's son Ben translated it; and Neihardt's daughter Enid wrote it down in shorthand in four spiral notebooks as Ben translated it to her, then typed a manuscript version of the notes, from which Neihardt worked as he was writing *Black Elk Speaks*.

Neihardt took no casual attitude toward the material he was getting from Black Elk; rather, he treated it with the utmost respect and employed the most scholarly methods possible under the circumstances. In a preface, revised in 1971 for the Pocket Books edition of the book, Neihardt summarized his role in bringing Black Elk's story to publication:

> It was my function to translate the old man's story, not only in the factual sense—for it was not the facts that mattered most—but rather to re-create in English the mood and manner of the old man's narrative. This was often a grueling and difficult task, requiring much patient effort and careful questioning of the interpreter.
>
> Always I felt it a sacred obligation to be true to the old man's meaning and manner of expression. I am convinced there were times when we had more than the ordinary means of communication.

When *Black Elk Speaks* was published in 1932, it received highly favorable reviews, but the publication did little to improve Neihardt's precarious financial situation. The general public, Neihardt said in the introduction to the Pocket Books edition, "gave it a very modest reception. In less than two years the publisher 'remaindered' the edition at forty-five cents a copy and the book was forgotten." Neihardt, in this instance, was about thirty years ahead of his time; fortunately, he lived to see the book receive the attention it deserves.

Somehow, a copy of *Black Elk Speaks* made its way to Zurich, Switzerland, where it came to the attention of the eminent psychologist Carl Jung, whose comments recommended it to anthropologists and psychologists. Next, the book was republished by the University of Nebraska Press in 1961, at which time the ascription on the title page was changed from "as told to John G. Neihardt" to "as told through John G. Neihardt." In 1971 Neihardt appeared on Dick Cavett's television talk show; in doing so, he created broad interest in Black Elk and made himself an overnight celebrity. The book became a best-seller on the wave of interest in native cultures and alternative lifestyles that swept the 1960s and 1970s.

If it was these fortunate circumstances that brought *Black Elk Speaks* its great success, its continuing appeal can be attributed to its spirituality, its message of universal brotherhood—not just among human beings but among all living things—and its tragic and elegiac tone. Black Elk told his story to Neihardt because he wanted to preserve the great vision that he had when he was nine years old, a vision of such power and significance that he came to feel it was given to him to use to save his people, a mission that he was not strong enough to fulfill. Neihardt recognized in this vision something of the same guiding purpose he himself had found in the dream of the Ghostly Brother that had given him his sense of poetic mission when he was eleven.

Neihardt's respect for Black Elk's words was not, however, completely literal. Some of the most often quoted passages in the book are those that Neihardt added either to provide historical detail or by way of introduction (the three introductory paragraphs) and conclusion (the three final paragraphs)—articulating what Black Elk would have said but did not. In a 1971 interview Neihardt said that

*Black Elk Speaks* is a work of art with two collaborators, the chief one being Black Elk. My function was both creative and editorial. . . . I think he knew I was the tool—no, the medium—he needed for what he wanted to get said. And my attitude toward what he said to me is one of religious obligation. . . . At times considerable editing was necessary, but it was always worth the editing. The beginning and the ending are mine; they are what he would have said if he had been able. At times I changed a word, a sentence, sometimes created a para-

graph. And the translation—or rather the *transformation*—of what was given me was expressed so that it could be understood by the white world.

Since Neihardt's death, scholarship on *Black Elk Speaks* has been devoted to the nature of Neihardt's "transformation" of Black Elk's message and to the effects on Black Elk's own interpretation of traditional Lakota beliefs of two facts Neihardt never mentions—Black Elk's conversion to Christianity in 1904 and his twenty-seven years as an active Catholic prior to his interviews with Neihardt in 1931. The tendency has been to minimize the effects of Black Elk's Christianity, but to find, as does Clyde Holler in *Black Elk's Religion: The Sun Dance and Lakota Catholicism* (1995), the most thorough study of the subject, that

the book's essential religious and social perspective—its message—is Neihardt's and not Black Elk's. . . . If *Black Elk Speaks* did not interpret, if it did not reflect Neihardt's understanding of Black Elk, it would not be a work of art. Defenders of Neihardt who insist on his faithfulness to Black Elk's message simply reveal the shortcomings of their understanding of literature.

Along with *Black Elk Speaks,* Neihardt produced a second book on the Sioux people, *When the Tree Flowered: An Authentic Tale of the Old Sioux World* (1951). Often considered to be on a par with *A Cycle of the West* and *Black Elk Speaks,* though not so well known as either, it has been said to rank with the best novels of its time. Eagle Voice, an old Sioux warrior, is modeled in part on Black Elk but mostly on Eagle Elk, an Oglala who died in 1945 at the age of ninety. The novel consists of the story of his life as he tells it to a young white man to whom he feels a strong bond: "You shall be my grandson, Wasichu [white man] though you are; for it is no man's fault how he is born, and your heart is as much Lakota as mine," a statement suggesting a parallel to the relationship between Neihardt and Black Elk. Eagle Voice experiences many of the same battles that Black Elk told about, but the freer form of the novel allows Neihardt to elaborate to good effect. However, the novel never loses its feel of authenticity and truth.

Neihardt expressed his views on literature in the *Laureate Address of John G. Neihardt* (1921), a lecture that he delivered—and later published—when he was made Poet Laureate of Nebraska by an act of the state legislature, in the reviews that he published as literary editor of the *St. Louis Post-Dispatch,* and in *Poetic Values: Their Reality and Our Need of Them* (1925). Art, Neihardt says in *Poetic Values,* offers relative stability in a world of ceaseless change,

for even in change there are principles that endure, and there is an essential humanness that, at least for our brief planetary life, is constant. We cannot live

*Neihardt in 1931 with his daughter Hilda; Nicholas Black Elk, the Oglala Sioux holy man whose autobiography Neihardt edited in 1932; and Chase-in-the-Morning at the Pine Ridge Reservation in South Dakota, preparing for a hoop-and-spear game (by permission of Hilda N. Petri, Trustee of the John G. Neihardt Trust)*

humanly without an abiding sense of such constancies; and it is by virtue of what we have called the creative dream that these may be vividly realized.

In his ordinary state of consciousness, the poet, like other men, experiences nothing but the "usual factual regard of things familiar." However, suddenly the poet will experience an altered state of consciousness in which

areas of hitherto hidden meaning are illumined as in a dream; relations normally concealed are suspected or revealed as in a vision. It is in this swift and ecstatic widening of conscious regard that the substance of the poem is conceived.

Neihardt seems to be foreseeing his own career when he explains, in the same work, that the poet may

conceive in a flash of the wider regard [that is, expanded consciousness] a poem that only the labor of years can translate in terms of sense. And when this has happened to him, significantly enough, he will feel gloriously safe in the cosmos, and his petty self, with its innumerable hurts and fears and desires, will be lost in

an overwhelming sense of love for all things and all men—so long as the revealing moment remains vivid.

In his own childhood dream he experienced a "great Voice," which drove him on, impelled him beyond the usual state of consciousness—the "regard" to which most people are confined all their lives—and into another less personal, more spiritual level of consciousness, into "the creative dream, the loss of self in a wider regard of the object." From his childhood on, Neihardt never lost his "wider regard," never relinquished his dedication to creating poetry.

In his major works, Neihardt attempts to create in his reader that same "wider regard," the same, or at least a closely similar, "creative dream" that impels him as a poet to create. He strives to re-create in his reader that sense of what it is to be a poet, to achieve a state of consciousness in which the reader's self would disappear, merged through the poetry into the wider consciousness into which the poet's self has also merged. Neihardt connects his reader to the past through his use of the epic tradition and through a host of classical allusions, thus widening the reader's regard—consciousness—with respect to time. More important, however, he also attempts to expand the reader's consciousness in a spiritual sense through raising the reader to a higher level of truth, the level that Hugh Glass achieves when he forgives Jamie, the level that Sitanka achieves when he struggles to utter the word "brother" to the soldier who is clubbing him to death.

Neihardt, however, objects to being placed among the "Art for Art's sake" school of poets; he protests in *Poetic Values* that he had never "fallen into the belief that even the greatest poetry is important in itself. Life is everything, and both art and science are merely strategic methods by which men may live more fully." But science is the tool of practical, sense-bound men who base their schemes on "brutal values." Art provides a vision of a more "humanly habitable world" in which the "sense-bound mass" of men are "shepherded by men of the wider awareness," a "genius society" such as once existed briefly in ancient Athens. What is needed, Neihardt believes, to achieve such a society is an education that, through attention to art, would develop that "wider field of consciousness by which alone it is possible to be human, to identify oneself with the race, and to be moved to throw oneself away in the furthering of as much of the great process as one can perceive."

In the final chapter of his autobiographical work titled *All Is But a Beginning* (1972), Neihardt lists four good things about human existence. First is love, "love given rather than love received. With neither, there is nothing; with either, even sorrow and suffering may become beautiful and dear." The theme of love runs throughout his life's work, from his early love lyrics through *A Cycle of the West* to Eagle Voice's love for Tashina in *When the Tree Flowered.* The second good thing about life is

> The satisfaction of the instinct of workmanship, . . . for that instinct is the noblest thing in man after love, from which indeed it springs. Just to do your best at any cost, and afterward to experience something of the Seventh Day glory when you look upon your work and see that it is good.

What Neihardt describes is, of course, the satisfaction he himself gets from writing. The third good thing, which can occur spontaneously, but can also sometimes be achieved through fasting and prayer, is the experience of "expanded awareness in moments of spiritual insight." And the fourth is "deep sleep," not mere slumber, but "ocean-deep and dreamless" sleep that restores the spirit as well as the body. And, Neihardt concludes, each of these four goods involves "the loss of the sense of self in some pattern larger than self" for "life, as commonly conceived, is part of some vaster pattern."

As he approached the end of his long life, John G. Neihardt wrote that he had a slogan that he wanted to leave for his young friends to help them through times of great stress, a slogan that he had learned from an old Sioux friend who in turn had it from an eagle in his spirit vision—"Hold fast, hold fast; there is more!" Aside from *Black Elk Speaks,* which has proved to have a universal appeal, Neihardt's works have always had a limited audience, and despite generally favorable reviews, have failed to find a significant audience outside the West, the region with which most of his work is concerned. Within that region, his reputation has not dimmed; in the years since his death on 4 November 1973, it has in fact "held fast."

**Bibliography:**

Richard W. Etulain, *A Bibliographical Guide to the Study of Western American Literature* (Lincoln: University of Nebraska Press, 1982).

**References:**

Lucille F. Aly, *John G. Neihardt,* Boise State University Western Writers Series, 25 (Boise, Idaho: Boise State University, 1976);

Aly, "John G. Neihardt and the American Epic," *Western American Literature,* 13 (February 1979): 309–325;

Aly, "Poetry and History in Neihardt's *Cycle of the West,*" *Western American Literature,* 16 (Spring 1981): 3–18;

W. E. Black, "Ethic and Metaphysic: A Study of John G. Neihardt," *Western American Literature,* 2 (Fall 1967): 205–212;

Vine Deloria Jr., ed., *A Sender of Words: Essays in Memory of John G. Neihardt* (Salt Lake City: Howe, 1984);

Raymond J. DeMallie, *The Sixth Grandfather: Black Elk's Teachings Given to John G. Neihardt* (Lincoln: University of Nebraska Press, 1984);

Clyde Holler, *Black Elk's Religion: The Sun Dance and Lakota Catholicism* (Syracuse, N.Y.: Syracuse University Press, 1995);

Julius T. House, *John G. Neihardt: Man and Poet* (Wayne, Nebr.: Jones, 1920);

Sally McKluskey, "*Black Elk Speaks* and So Does John Neihardt," *Western American Literature,* 6 (Winter 1972): 231–242;

Julian Rice, *Black Elk's Story: Distinguishing Its Lakota Purpose* (Albuquerque: University of New Mexico Press, 1991);

Blair Whitney, *John G. Neihardt* (Boston: Twayne, 1976);

David Young, "Crazy Horse on the Trojan Plain: A Comment on the Classicism of John G. Neihardt," *Classical and Modern Literature,* 5 (Fall 1982): 45–53.

**Papers:**

The papers of John G. Neihardt are located in the Western Historical Manuscripts Collection at the University of Missouri Library, Columbia, Missouri. These papers include letters, manuscripts, and other related materials.

# Leslie Norris

*(21 May 1921 –    )*

Eugene England
*Utah Valley State College*

See also the Norris entry in *DLB 27: Poets of Great Britain and Ireland, 1945–1960.*

BOOKS: *Tongue of Beauty* (London: Favil, 1943);
*Poems* (London: Falcon, 1946);
*Finding Gold* (London: Chatto & Windus / Hogarth Press, 1967);
*The Loud Winter* (Cardiff, Wales: Triskel, 1967);
*Ransoms* (London: Chatto & Windus, 1970);
*His Last Autumn* (Rushden, Northamptonshire: Sceptre, 1972);
*Glyn Jones,* Writers of Wales Series, edited by Meic Stephens and R. Brinley Jones (Cardiff: University of Wales Press, 1973; revised, 1997);
*Mountains, Polecats, Pheasants and Other Elegies* (London: Chatto & Windus / Hogarth Press, 1974);
*At the Publishers'* (Berkhamstead, Hertfordshire: Priapus, 1976);
*Sliding: Short Stories* (New York: Scribners, 1976 / London: Dent, 1978); enlarged as *Sliding: Fourteen Short Stories and Eight Poems* (London: Harlow / Longman, 1981);
*Islands Off Maine* (Cranberry Isles, Me.: Tidal, 1977);
*Ravenna Bridge* (Knotting, Bedfordshire: Sceptre, 1977);
*Merlin and the Snake's Egg: Poems* (New York: Viking, 1978);
*Hyperion* (Knotting, Bedfordshire: Sceptre, 1979);
*Water Voices* (London: Chatto & Windus / Hogarth Press, 1980);
*Walking the White Fields: Poems 1967–1980* (Boston: Little, Brown, 1980);
*A Tree Sequence* (Seattle: Sea Pen, 1984);
*Selected Poems* (Bridgend, Wales: Poetry Wales, 1986);
*The Hawk's Eye* (Rexburg, Idaho: Honeybrook, 1988);
*Sequences* (Layton, Utah: Peregrine Smith Books, 1988); enlarged as *A Sea in the Desert* (Bridgend, Wales: Seren, 1989);
*Norris's Ark* (Portsmouth, N.H.: Tidal, 1988);
*The Girl from Cardigan: Sixteen Stories* (Salt Lake City: Gibbs M. Smith, 1988; enlarged edition, Bridgend, Wales: Seren, 1988);
*Collected Poems* (Bridgend, Wales: Seren, 1996);

*Leslie Norris ( from the dust jacket for* The Girl from Cardigan: Sixteen Stories, *1988)*

*Collected Stories* (Bridgend, Wales: Seren, 1996);
*Holy Places* (Aurora, N.Y.: Wells College Press, 1998);
*Albert and the Angels* (New York: Farrar, Straus & Giroux, 2000);
*Winter Wreaths* (Provo, Utah: Tryst, 2000).

RECORDINGS: *Poetry Reading,* read by Norris, British Council, Recorded Sound Department, 1965;

229

*Poets of Wales: Dannie Abse, Leslie Norris,* Norris's work read by Norris, Argo Gramophone PLP1155, 1971.

OTHER: *Vernon Watkins, 1906–1967,* edited by Norris (London: Faber & Faber, 1970);

"The Poetry of Edward Thomas," in *Triskel One,* edited by Sam Adams and Gwilym Rees Hughes (Llandybie, Wales: Davies, 1971), pp. 164–178;

"Seeing Eternity: Vernon Watkins and the Poet's Task," in *Triskel Two,* edited by Adams and Hughes (Llandybie, Wales: Davies, 1973), pp. 88–110;

*Andrew Young: Remembrance and Homage,* compiled, with an introduction, by Norris (Cranberry Isles, Me.: Tidal, 1978);

*The Mabinogion,* translated by Lady Charlotte Guest, edited by Norris (London: Folio Society, 1980);

Dylan Thomas, *Dylan Thomas: The Collected Stories,* foreword by Norris (London: Dent, 1983);

Rainer Maria Rilke, *The Sonnets to Orpheus,* translated into English by Norris and Alan F. Keele (Columbia, S.C.: Camden House, 1989);

Rilke, *The Duino Elegies,* translated by Norris and Keele (Columbia, S.C.: Camden House, 1993).

SELECTED PERIODICAL PUBLICATIONS–
UNCOLLECTED: "The Poetry of Vernon Watkins," *Poetry Wales,* 2 (Winter 1966): 3–10;

"A Land Without a Name," *Poetry Wales,* 13 (Spring 1978): 89–101;

"A Profound Simplicity: The Poetry of Andrew Young," *New Criterion,* 4 (1985): 41–44.

Only late in life, after a lengthy and unusual preparation, did Leslie Norris become an outstanding American Western writer and a master of the long poem. Since the publication of his first book of poetry, *Tongue of Beauty,* in 1943, Norris has continually reinvented himself and transformed his art–crossing countries, cultures, and genres throughout his long life and career. As a writer of short lyrics in the 1950s and early 1960s, he contributed to the Anglo-Welsh literary renaissance–led by his friends Dylan Thomas, Glyn Jones, Vernon Watkins, and Meic Stephens. From the mid 1960s to the late 1970s Norris gained renown as a much anthologized English poet and a gentle but perceptive critic, a friend of Ted Hughes and Ted Walker, and a respected writer of short stories published in *The Atlantic Monthly* and *The New Yorker.* After appointments as Visiting Poet at various institutions in the United States, Norris settled down in Utah in 1983. Soon afterward, he began to write long odes as well as third-person autobiographical lyrics–many set in the Western landscape. Norris is cur-

rently shaping these recent poems into a book-length, autobiographical poem, to be called "Selves."

Leslie Norris was born on 21 May 1921 in Merthyr Tydfil, Wales, son of George William Norris, an electrician in one of the valley's many collieries, and Mary Jane Jones Norris, whose family came from west Wales. His father was disabled by a mine accident when Norris was six and later worked as a milkman until his death in 1942. George Norris loved music and books and "debates" in the home concerning matters of the day and was "a superb raconteur" and reciter of humorous verse. Norris's maternal grandfather, Dan Jones, wrote verse in Welsh and was a deacon at Bethel Welsh Baptist Chapel. The Jones family farm, Y Wern, on the mountain above industrial Merthyr, was a childhood center of wild beauty and storytelling that was crucial to Norris's artistic identity.

Merthyr Tydfil–also referred to as Merthyr–was an ancient seat of Welsh culture and home of bards. In the nineteenth century it became, with the development of the coal and iron of the Taff Valley, the first real city of Wales. Attracting workers from Spain and Ireland, Merthyr Tydfil became home to the largest ironworks in Europe. Then, by the time Norris was born, when the big works were shutting down, the city slid into a period of depression and out-migration–with unemployment rising to more than 60 percent–until World War II.

From ages five to ten, Norris attended Georgetown Primary School, where he was taught by Brinley Phillips. As Norris reveals in his personal notes, for two hours each day Phillips "read with great sensitivity to words" from the distinguished Welsh and English classics and "educated our senses" by such devices as taking the whole class out on a stormy day and having them put their arms around the trees, ears to the bark, to hear the "protesting" inner fibers of the tossing limbs. Norris began to write verse then, but not until later did he "know" he would be a poet. In 1931 he began attending the Cyfarthfa Castle Grammar School, housed in a mansion that originally belonged to the owner of the largest steelworks in town. Norris was tutored at the grammar school by Sam Adams, whom he remembers as "a fine teacher of literature," and began to write much more poetry. He studied those who would influence him, such as Daniel Defoe, Gerard Manley Hopkins–and especially Dylan Thomas. Norris read Thomas's work in *Best Poems of 1934* (1934), seeing "for the first time . . . what poetry could really do." When Norris was thirteen he had a "revelatory experience" while touching the surface of a stone wall near Merthyr; as described in the poem, "A Grain of Sand" (*Collected Poems,* 1996), the experience hinted at poetry as his calling and gave him a sense of what his subject matter should be: "He will sing the earth, / its textures and tiered strata. . . . He names the solid properties of house, tree, petal, friend." As Norris claims in his personal notes, this moment was "something much stronger than insight, in which I said, 'This is what you have to do is be aware of elements and the way in which they are combined and make the world.' This has been my calling and my purpose."

Often, walking home from school, Norris visited the W. H. Smith bookshop, where the staff allowed him to read what he wanted and even pushed new poetry books his way–including Edward Thomas's *The Trumpet and Other Poems* (1940), which had a lifelong influence on him. Norris was also a first-rate football player and a good boxer. He often bicycled and camped with a small group of friends in Brecon Beacons National Park, just outside Merthyr. He frequently examines, in his poems and stories, the ambiguous joy of growing up on the border between two worlds–between a cultured yet economically depressed, industrially wasted town and the "inhospitable" yet beautiful wilderness surrounding it.

Norris published his first poem in 1938 but, despite the encouragement of Phillips, could not afford a university education and took a job as a clerk in the town hall. He was drafted in May 1940 into the Royal Air Force and trained as a mechanic at Blackpool and Little Rissington; he was "invalided out" in June 1941, however, after a prolonged bout with an injury sustained in a crash during flight training. Crippled enough that he could not even take part in soccer except as a referee, Norris worked for the duration of the war in the town hall in Merthyr. At this time he began to study the emerging Anglo-Welsh writers, especially Glyn Jones–who became a profound influence and, later, perhaps his closest friend–and some of the new Anglo-Welsh journals also started to publish Norris's poems. Then, in 1943 he bought a copy of a London monthly featuring some of Dylan Thomas's poems. Seeing a letter to the editor about the nature of writing, he wrote a brash rebuttal to the author of the letter, Peter Baker–an even younger man, who had started Favil Press and who, in his response to Norris, asked to publish some of Norris's poetry.

As a result, Norris's first book of verse, *Tongue of Beauty,* became the ninth in Baker's series of pamphlets called "Resurgam Younger Poets." *Tongue of Beauty* was favorably reviewed in successive weeks in *The Times Literary Supplement* in February 1944; but the periodical failed to review Norris's second collection, *Poems* (1946), although it encompassed the poems from *Tongue of Beauty* as well as new lyrics. The verses in *Tongue of Beauty* reveal intense religious feelings in many ways: through a connected series of ten sonnets; a

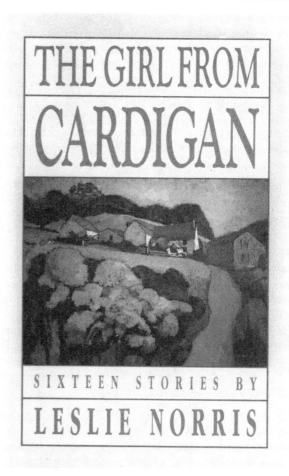

*Dust jacket for Norris's second collection of short fiction*

yearning for literary connection–to the poet's Welsh roots in particular; and through the clear influence of Dylan Thomas, evidenced not only by the speaker's emotional self-dramatizing but also in his rhetorical power and rhythmic command. However, since the poems are comparatively immature, Norris did not include them in his later collections.

On 30 July 1948 Norris married Catherine (Kitty) Morgan, from the nearby town of Dowlais. Within a few weeks they moved to Coventry, England, to attend the Teacher Training College. Thereafter, the Norrises returned to Wales in the 1970s and 1980s only to spend parts of the summer in their cottage in Saron in West Wales country. After completing college, the couple found teaching jobs in Yeovil, Somerset: Leslie taught in a high school, while Kitty taught young children. In 1952 Norris took a position at a junior school in Bath, while his wife studied English at the City of Bath College. After three years, good reports on Norris's work led to a position as principal of a school in Chichester, Sussex. He bought a home in nearby Aldingbourne, where the Norrises lived until 1973–returning to it in the summers between 1973 and 1995, when it was finally sold. By 1955 the Norrises were essentially teachers of pedagogy: Leslie served as head teacher until 1958, then as a lecturer to teachers in training at Bognor Regis College of Education–later renamed West Sussex Institute of High Education; Kitty was also a trainer of teachers and, after 1966, taught with Leslie at West Sussex Institute.

Although Norris for twenty years shied away from the literary career that beckoned in the mid 1940s, he did continue to write–his poetry was published occasionally in Anglo-Welsh journals and in such avant-garde English periodicals as *Outpost Magazine* and *Priapus*. He innovatively incorporated poetry into his teaching. Norris took his large classes on field trips and–like his mentor, Phillips–teaching his students to observe the natural world closely, to do research in libraries and museums, and to write up their findings in reports. Yet, Norris had his classes do the reports as poetry. He then had the students broadcast these reports to the whole school on Fridays and preserve the poems in collections he still treasures; as he has remarked, "For children of that age poetry is much easier to write than prose." While teaching full-time, Norris completed an M.Phil. thesis on Vernon Watkins at Southampton University in 1958. By this time he had become close friends with Walker and Andrew Young, poets who were living near Chichester. Norris began reading his poems on British Broadcasting Corporation (BBC) television–where he became a friend of John Ormond, who filmed Norris at his cottage in Saron for BBC television–and then by invitation read at more venues in southern England and London. In the 1960s Norris's verse began appearing regularly in *Poetry Wales,* edited by Stephens, and in 1966 he met Jones, who became an influential mentor and friend.

In 1967 ten of Norris's poems about Merthyr Tydfil were published by Stephens as *The Loud Winter* in a "Triskel Poets" pamphlet. In the meantime, Norris had made contacts in the London literary world. He became acquainted with Cecil Day-Lewis–an editor at Chatto and Windus–who published Norris's first four major books of poetry as part of the distinguished "Phoenix Living Poets" series. The first, *Finding Gold* (1967), consists of all the poems from *The Loud Winter*–including the popular "Ballad of Billy Rose," which, after Norris had read it on the BBC, schools had started to include in their curricula; "Ballad of Billy Rose" has been anthologized in more than eighty books. *Finding Gold* gathered together Norris's finest recent lyrics, ending with the excellent title poem that revealed the characteristic voice of a mature poet:

> From his house each day the child moves to school
> Through a deliberate ceremony. He is obsessed
> By a chosen maze, marking his ritual
> With clear jumps over long stones full
> Of inescapable bad luck. . . .
> His frail, unswerving rule
> Is to impose order on a chaotic world.

On this day, however, the child's disciplined ritual is broken when it takes him directly to the spot where gamblers, surprised by police, have run off–leaving their spilled coins. The boy quickly gathers them up and all day in school, "full of pennies / To his round eyes," contemplates a new world where "one step from broken practice the spread gold lies." Much of Norris's verse of the next ten years features sharp details of youthful experience, which the poet makes universal; he often deconstructs past visions, moving the reader's experience, along with Norris's, across some border–to find "gold."

In the first critical essay on Norris, published in *Priapus* (Winter 1967–1968), Walker gave *Loud Winter* and *Finding Gold* positive reviews, praising in particular the poet's awareness that "his life, since his boyhood in a poor area of Wales, has been 'A blunt invasion of the better streets.'" The quoted line of verse comes from a piece highlighting a childhood skirmish that Norris and his friends had with a boy from another neighborhood, Thompson, who had "Come up in his torn jersey from even poorer / Streets to state his value." After exchanging "the conventional words" with the outsider, the speaker in the poem–actually Norris as a youth–strikes the outsider, and "yellow blood" runs from the boy's "agonized head" as, without tears, the outsider "stupidly" tells the others he has a boil in his ear. An older Norris ponders in the lyric that if, as adults, he and Thompson were to meet, the two of them would smile in mutual realization that, as boys, both their lives had been invasions, "Our values / Challenged always, / Our triumphs accidents."

Walker noted that many of Norris's best poems were elegies for his lost friends–some of them killed in World War II, others in accidents–and for the poet's lost youth in Merthyr, a city of slag heaps surrounded by the natural beauty of the Brecon mountains. In his review Walker also expressed a remarkably prophetic hope about Norris's work. He considered Norris "on the brink of writing poetry of even greater importance, perhaps a long poem in which he will gather together all that is of significance from the past and present." Walker believed that all Norris needed was time.

The end of the 1960s marked a pivotal period for Norris–a second awakening of artistic creativity that led to a crescendo of publication and prizes and to an even more dramatic border crossing into a new genre and a new country. Peter Davison began to publish Norris's poems in *The Atlantic Monthly,* and verses by Norris appeared in *The New Yorker*. An American agent that Norris met at a party asked him for some fiction; soon afterward, Norris wrote his first short prose work, "Plus Fours," and it was sold to *The Atlantic Monthly*. Other short stories were sold to *The New Yorker,* and Norris quickly crossed genres to become a fiction writer-in-demand, being granted first-refusal contracts by both *The Atlantic Monthly* and *The New Yorker* and receiving solicitations from publishers for a novel. Norris was widely and favorably reviewed. In 1970 the Poetry Society awarded Norris the Alice Hunt Barlett Prize, and in 1978 he won the Cholmondeley Prize, also for poetry. That same year Norris received the David Higham Prize for Fiction for *Sliding: Short Stories* (1976). In addition, Norris appeared regularly on BBC radio and television to read his poetry, especially his verses for children—which he collected for publication in *Merlin and the Snake's Egg: Poems* (1978).

The most immense border crossings for Norris, however, came in 1973, when he accepted an invitation from the University of Washington to be Visiting Professor and Poet, and then in 1974, when Norris officially left his position as head teacher at West Sussex Institute and began devoting himself to writing full-time. These professional decisions eventually enabled him to redefine his career. For Norris, to leave a secure job at age fifty-three was a courageous choice, but he did have many resources—including income not only from his poetry and fiction but also from readings, broadcasting, and, increasingly, from foundation awards and visiting appointments. In 1974 the British Arts Council Bursary awarded Norris a grant; in 1977 he was Resident Poet at Eton College in England; in 1980 and 1981 he returned to the University of Washington, then headed to East Carolina University in 1982 at the invitation of Peter Makuck, a poet and the editor of *Tar River Poetry;* and in 1983 Brigham Young University (BYU) invited Norris to be Visiting Poet. The appointment worked out so well at BYU that Norris returned in 1984 and 1985. The university then gave Norris a permanent position as P. A. Christiansen Professor of Poetry and asked him to head the creative writing section of the English department. Since 1989 he has held the post of Humanities Professor of Creative Writing at BYU continuing both to teach popular courses in Romantic poetry and creative writing and to mentor young poets. Norris also devotes a generous amount of time to speaking about poetry and to reading his work, often in schools and colleges throughout Utah.

Meanwhile, Norris has been honored in the three nations he calls home—Wales, England, and the United States—and has been productive in several genres. Norris is one of a handful of literary figures to be elected a fellow of both the Royal Society of Literature (1974) and the Welsh Academy (1990). In 1981 he received the Katherine Mansfield Award, which is given every three years for the best short story in English. In his chapter on Norris in *DLB 27: Poets of Great Britain and Ireland, 1945–1960,* published in 1984, Thomas Emery gave insightful praise about Norris; in 1986 a special issue of *Poetry Wales* was devoted to Norris; and in 1991 a laudatory study by James A. Davies of Norris's life and work was published by the University of Wales as part of its "Writers of Wales" series. Also in 1991, BYU bestowed the Karl G. Maeser Distinguished Scholar Award—its highest faculty honor—to Norris, and in 1994 a collection of essays and poetry, *An Open World,* was published in his honor. Norris's range of skills includes editing and translating: he has edited collections of criticism, a volume of Dylan Thomas's short stories (1983), and a 1980 translation of the great Welsh epic, the *Mabinogion* (first collected, 1838–1849); and he translated two works by Rainer Maria Rilke, *The Sonnets to Orpheus* and *The Duino Elegies* in 1989 and 1993, respectively. Norris's diverse body of work reached a high point of recognition in 1996, when Poetry Wales Press—now Seren Books—published handsome volumes of both the *Collected Poems* and the *Collected Stories*.

Besides redefining his career, Norris's professional decisions have also influenced his writing, as he crossed from Anglo-Welsh master of the short lyric and short story in the 1960s and 1970s to—since the 1980s—master of the American long ode and book-length poem. Consequently, critics have struggled to come to terms with Norris. Walker, despite his high praise and prophetic hopes for the writer in the late 1960s, has indicated his displeasure with some of the directions Norris's work has taken since the 1990s. Some reviewers have complained that Norris's poems and stories are not socially or politically angry or activist—his work does not focus, for example, on the pain of an economically depressed Wales in the years between the two world wars. On the other hand, others detect in Norris's work a sharp analytical edge beneath his English reasonableness and sweet temper. Some, such as James Dickey in his assessment of *Walking the White Field,* praised the distinctively authentic "convincingness of tone" in Norris's poems. Others, such as Elizabeth Tallent in *The New York Times* (22 May 1988) view his stories as "so distinct and fully realized they have the resonances of novels"; in Tallent's words, Norris's fiction leaves "the unexpectedly sweet aftertaste of a writer experienced in affection." Still others are unanimous in their assessments of the poet. In *DLB 27,* Emery called Norris's poems and stories "some of the

*Cover for the 1996 omnibus volume that includes poems from Norris's earlier collections:* Finding Gold *(1967),* Ransoms *(1970), and* A Sea in the Desert *(1989)*

best in the English language." David Wagoner claims that Norris is "obviously one of the best living British poets," and Peter Davison once described Norris as the finest contemporary British poet.

Perhaps Norris's ephemeral popularity and, thus, his virtual neglect by critics have been caused by his being, almost always, a little out of fashion—unable to be pegged comfortably anywhere. His work seems characteristic of the ingenious prosody and exquisite singing so prevalent in Welsh literature, and yet he has adapted to the modern American convention of deceptively conversational free verse. Norris is a hardworking craftsman, rather than a mere bardic declaimer, who is willing to take on huge ontological and epistemological questions, especially in his work of the last decade. He makes the reader ponder his poetic identity: is he a Romantic nature poet, a profoundly religious thinker, or a generous but incisive modern skeptic—or, perhaps, all three?

With respect to both genres and nations, Norris has crossed borders incessantly, bluntly invading new streets, where many critics have encountered—at least at first—difficulty following the poet. The high regard for Norris's work in the United States has perplexed some in Wales and England, but many Americans, especially those who wrote about him in *An Open World* and were discovering him for the first time, wonder why Norris is not known more widely. Indeed, Norris's most recent crossing has been the hardest to follow: he has shifted direction to the huge and abrupt Western American landscape of his current home, Utah, and has established himself as one of the finest Western writers. Norris has combined such a landscape with that of his Welsh childhood, mastering a new genre while facing the ultimate borders of identity and death. For example, since the early 1990s Norris has been engaged in a distinctive, personal, and poetic project, tentatively called "Selves," a book-length work that expressly attempts to defeat time and death by gathering into a mystical present the fragments of his scattered life.

The Welsh critic and scholar Meic Stephens, who is also Norris's friend, wrote in 1986 in *The Oxford Companion to the Literature of Wales* that the poet's "American experience has made him more diffuse and urbane"; for Stephens, Norris's "emotional centre is less visible and his emphasis more descriptive, but his contact with Wales has by no means diminished." Although the Norrises sold their cottage and the poet's ancient landholding in Saron in the 1980s—an experience that Norris recounts in his story "The Holm Oak"—he confided in a 1988 interview in *The New York Times* that he would always be a Welshman. He admitted in the same interview that years of permanent residence in the United States meant that American themes had started to appear in his poetry: "I'm very slow to absorb scenes and places. I take a long time doing it, but it seems to be surfacing all right."

One lyric that shows Norris's absorption of American scenes and places is "A Sea in the Desert" (published in *The New Criterion* [April 1988]), a verse that could be called Norris's most "American" lyric at the time; the long poem appeared in a collection of the same name in 1989. In "A Sea in the Desert," the speaker considers himself at home in Utah—like Norris—yet haunted by the world of water from his past:

> A man is moon to his own sea—
> he draws it after him,
> like a dog it follows him
> the days of his life.

Particularly in terms of form and content, "A Sea in the Desert" marks a dramatic stage in Norris's development. It is his longest completely unified poem, full of highly developed skills in diction and rhythm, with precise natural details and a convincing tone of voice. In a fresh departure from Norris's previous verse, "A Sea in the Desert" completely lacks the excessively clever, somewhat mannered literary devices that had marred a few earlier works. Instead, a new spirituality imbues "A Sea in the Desert"–unsentimental yet full of feeling, even evoking ideas of conversion and baptism.

In late 1988 Norris finished "Decoys," his second long poem and most complex and morally weighty lyric up to this point. "Decoys" came about almost entirely because of Norris's American experience and a new creative vision. He dedicated "Decoys" to his friend the Welshman John Davies, who had also been Visiting Poet at BYU. During his appointment Davies had heard about some obsessive decoy-makers in Utah and told Norris about these men; as in the words of Norris's poem, they retreat to their "cold sheds" and "basements under harsh lights" after work each night and use their humming electric tools to "set the false birds free" from the wood, as "in a dream." "Decoys" especially shows how Norris delights readers with detailed observation and verbal skill:

> With the flat of their palms
> they measure the neck's right curve
> and set with an eye
> an angle to the beak.

The compression of energy in these lines, which describe where the man's eye and the bird's eye are conjoined, resembles the tightening of a spring that explodes with each reading. Furthermore, after detailing how such decoys are made and then comparing them to the real birds–who "would find your decoys faulty"–Norris connects the birds to death and human complicity, eventually adopting an elegiac tone as he invokes the memory of another group of men: the professional birdcallers who reside in Norfolk, England, in villages that border salt marshes. The birdcallers have a vivid and precise awareness of the natural world–an awareness that the wild creatures, whom the hunters entice with calls, in effect make possible. Norris likens the birdcallers to poets; both types share the same burdens and gifts: "Nothing changes in their country but they know it; / The angle of a gate, a dropped branch, shifts of the wind." "Decoys" suggests that callers and poets alike express grief by creating anew–by naming what they have lost in a world of incessant change and death:

> they blow through cupped hands
> for a meeting of birds and animals.
> Call again and again, the note rising,

> an elegy for vulnerable creatures, . . .
> for pied shelduck, for skeins of geese,
> brent goose, snow goose, pinkfoot, Canada, . . .
> all humble on land, on their pliable webs.

Finally, the speaker directly addresses the reader, whom Norris has merged into all the personages of the verse–the decoy-makers, birdcallers, poets, and hunters. The speaker's unlikely moral command and penetrating new vision of natural religion–justifying such a command–hasten an end to the poem. In the closing lines of the lyric, Norris invokes William Wordsworth by depicting the edifying powers of the natural world, for like Wordsworth, Norris hints that nature bestows the ability to perceive and to articulate:

> Let the men put away rapacious lead, let them be still.
> The birds have given them the wide, cold sky.
> They have given them voices.

Wordsworth also informs "Borders," a long poem that Norris wrote in 1990 and which *The New Criterion* published in November of that year. The influence of Wordsworth on Norris surfaces in the form and epistemology of "Borders," including the reliance of the lyric on "spots of time." "Borders," like "Decoys," is an elegiac irregular ode, in that it has iambic lines of varied length. The poem was composed in remembrance of John Ormond, an eminent Welsh journalist and director and producer of documentaries for BBC Wales, who was also Norris's friend. While the structure of "Borders" recalls that of the great Romantic odes, the natural scene upon which the speaker meditates in "Borders" is located in the American West, namely the Wasatch Range of the Rocky Mountains. Shortly after the start of the poem, the speaker's meditation swiftly recedes in time to the mystical past of Norris's Welsh boyhood. Norris describes crossing a certain bridge every Saturday, a bridge that separated his town from the Breconshire wilderness; in traversing the bridge weekly as a boy, Norris "lived a moment in adventurous limbo," in which he "felt an unseen line / divide me, send my strong half forward, keep my other timidly at home." The lyric then shifts ahead in time to the universal present, at which point Norris confesses–with openness and brevity–what is ultimately the narrative of his life: the fact that he has "always lived that way, / crossed borders resolutely / while looking over my shoulder."

As if in homage to his Romantic models, Norris also incorporates "spots of time" or specifics in "Borders": three anecdotes about borders and death that transcend time, bringing the lyric back to Ormond and the speaker and locating them at the ultimate border. The first anecdote or spot of time tells of an experience

LESLIE NORRIS
*Collected Stories*

*Cover for the companion volume—also published in*
*1996—to Norris's* Collected Poems

distinctive only to the western United States. Stopping to buy jewelry from Indians, the speaker finds himself at a specific spot—the boundary marker where four states meet; he places one foot in Utah and the other in Arizona, with "palms flat / in the dust of Colorado and New Mexico." Through an imitative falling line of verse, the speaker applies the specific spot to his general self: "Restless as dust, scattered." The second spot of time is about Ormond, whom Norris explicitly contrasts in the beginning with his own scattered self, because Ormond "moved out as I did, but returned, / followed his eyes and crossed the borders / into his own country. . . . The world grew small / for him, to one country, a city, a house."

By this time in the lyric Ormand has departed, and Norris raises the emotional and spiritual stakes with two accounts of dying women and their awareness of beings from beyond the final border. One is Ormond's mother, who "in the evening called into her

room / someone unseen. 'Who would have thought it,' / she said, very clearly, and crossed the border / for which all others are a preparation." The other woman is the mother of Norris's colleague at BYU—this colleague is also a poet:

And Sally Taylor, her mother dying in the next room,
heard women's voices, young and laughing,
come in to fetch the old lady.

The sure and simple tone of such passages is common in Norris's work, but in the foregoing lines he uses it for an entirely different topic—death. Not unlike Emily Dickinson and her rather innocent methods, Norris transports the reader to the precise edge or threshold of an impenetrable entrance. In her most lauded verses, while Dickinson did not pretend to know what is found beyond the threshold of death, she reflected with artistic precision on the variables of nature: Dickinson liked to call nature a "haunted house," for example, and art "a house that tries to be haunted." Dickinson created, as a result, a vision of what might lie beyond death that is worthy of hope. Thus, Norris—albeit admitting in all honesty that one cannot follow or know what comes after death—rendered his own uncommon hope in "Borders" by returning to a motif that commonly occurs in Romantic odes: the natural scene, where the warmth and vitality of spring is melting the final, fatal snows:

For all the boundaries I have crossed, flown over,
knowingly, unknowingly, I have no answers;
but sit in the afternoon sun, under mountains
where stale snow clings in shadowy patches,
remember my friend, how he had sung,
hope he is still singing.

"Borders" denotes a remarkable turn in Norris's remarkable career. While the poem reflects the rich verbal and epistemological strengths of his Welsh bardic and English Romantic mentors, as well as the sharply honed technical and observational skills of his earlier work, it also depicts how Norris uses the large, raw Western landscape and the spiritual energy and directness of Mormon culture to bear on quite new personal hopes and perspectives. In an interview in 1993, Norris recognized that the long poems of the 1980s signified preparation, and "Borders" was the crucial final step. The idea for "Borders" resulted from both Norris's painful need to keep his friend Ormond alive and the poet's realization that by dying, his friend had now crossed borders that Norris had not. However, the writing of "Borders" helped Norris to learn that he, too, had traversed boundaries through previous and imagined selves. As he writes in his personal notes, "Each of us experiences something important, cleansing, necessary to our development, and we leave the person there though utterly changed. I still hold within me those younger people."

Shortly after "Borders" was published, Norris conceived of and began a new work, responding at last to expectations—expressed by Walker in his article on Norris—for a long poem gathering together "all that is of significance from the past and present." As mentioned earlier, Norris has tentatively titled the long poem "Selves." With more than twenty "segments" of "Selves" completed, Norris has published excerpts in periodicals as diverse as *Poetry Wales* and *The Atlantic Monthly* and has also started to work out a long-term scheme. Told from a mostly third-person point of view, "Selves" describes the past and present "other" selves of Norris's life—content that marks a departure for the poet and yet, paradoxically, is crucial to his trademark vulnerability; Norris introduces previously veiled or unrecognizable personae into the work as a whole and is able to talk about them—a composite of himself, actually—with a sense of both distance and intimacy. Some of the lyrics in "Selves" are in first person, which—Norris once believed—robbed the work in its entirety of a sense of connectedness, but he now views such lyrics as possible segments of a unifying commentary.

Norris is in search of a title more fitting than "Selves"—one evocative of, as he says in his notes, "the Odysseus theme that underlies the poem." One segment of the long poem, called "Ithaca" and published in *Poetry Wales* (October 1992), explicitly recalls the story of Odysseus as well as Norris's "Borders," which is ultimately seminal to "Selves." The speaker in "Ithaca" tells of "Journeying in Ithaca / in his old age," encountering the statue of Odysseus; as he views the statue, he "thinks of the men, / wherever their fortune, / who turn their faces / to the fires of home." The speaker is no such man, however—as Norris made clear in "Borders" that Ormond was—and although the speaker's dissimilarity causes him regret, he nonetheless "records with his Leica / the face of the demi-god." Norris suggests that the life that Ormond and Odysseus enjoyed is impossible for the speaker, a paradoxical revelation conveyed through an image that is stunning for its perception, beauty, and haunting effect:

> White sunlight lifts the mist.
> The sea begins to juggle
> its silver platters.
>
> In that blinding dazzle
> he sees with clarity
> Ithaca vanishing.

"Ithaca" hints, rather, that Norris has become a different kind of Odysseus. As Norris has expressed in his personal notes, "Our compass turns to many different poles. Some of them are entirely fortuitous, and for us, ours is a continually onward voyage, blown by winds of chance. Ithaca, for us, is wherever we drop our bones . . . , astonished to find ourselves where we are."

The defeat of time—an attempt to use art for temporal crossings—marks another theme of "Selves," which Norris projects as "very long," a "sturdy" book, united through its voice and continuing images. As mentioned previously, Norris recalls in "A Grain of Sand"—a lyric that appeared first in *Tar River Poetry* (1992) and later in *Collected Poems*—the "revelatory experience" that he had as a thirteen-year-old, which gave him a sharpened awareness of time, space, and, consequently, a sense of his calling as a poet; since it examines a self from another time, "A Grain of Sand" is included in "Selves." For Norris, in "A Grain of Sand," the world as a whole and the entire time of its lengthy creation—symbolically unified in the "four elements" of the ancient world—are linked to himself. All the world and its long creation essentially signify his vocation—his "life's work"—as a poet: "Earth, air, fire, water; / a little of each, / to comfort life / and define death." The speaker of "A Grain of Sand" then describes that

> He is moving away,
> his feet slow on the hot ground.
>
> He knows where he walks.

As he invokes the self of his boyhood—the adolescent of the "revelatory experience"—Norris appears to know with increased assurance where he walks; he seems at home within himself. In the mid 1980s, in writing the long sequences of "Stone Trees Water" and "The Hawk's Eye," Norris returned to the form and, to some extent, to the content of the ten religious sonnets from *Tongue of Beauty,* his first book of verse. He progressed then to his first long ode, "A Sea in the Desert," which—in Norris's view—explores a vital phase in religious understanding, making it central to the ode: the powerful symbol of water in all its spiritual significance, which played a more implicit role in his early verse.

With "Decoys" and "Borders" Norris carries on his development of religious understanding, focusing more intently on the ideas of moral passion and spiritual openness that many people have found key to their religious quests. Yet, a sense of certainty in crossing to something new or previously hidden in the self has also proven key to such a search, as the writing of "Selves" thus far suggests about Norris. In his personal notes he refers to a new clarity in himself—that he is writing much less and thinking more, as he prepares and revises, and that he no longer feels the temptation to flaunt his technical skill. Norris is conscious of himself changing. He is in the process of moving to a new, even risky, openness about his own and others' mystical experiences–experiences that some might deem sentimental: "I have been a private person, and a tough person. And one doesn't drop one's guard easily, but I don't have to keep it up anymore." These words, along with Norris's recent poetry, disclose how he continues to move out of bounds, reinventing himself and transforming his art.

**Interviews:**

John Ormond, Interview with Norris, *Leslie Norris,* television, BBC Wales, 1970;

Bruce Jorgensen, "A Sense of the Actual: A Conversation with Leslie Norris," *Literature and Belief,* 3 (1983): 41–53;

Stan Sanvel Rubin and Brce Bennett, "'A Sound Like a Clear Gong': An Interview with Leslie Norris," *Tar River Poetry* (Fall 1993);

Meic Stephens, "At the Edge of Things," in *An Open World,* edited by Eugene England and Peter Makuck (Columbia, S.C.: Camden House, 1994), pp. 1–9;

Kendall Wilcox, Interview with Norris, *Crossing Borders: The Life and Works of Leslie Norris,* television, Public Broadcasting System, 26 March 2001.

**References:**

Sam Adams, "The Poetry of Leslie Norris," *Poetry Wales,* 7 (1971): 14–27;

Tony Curtis, *How to Study Modern Poetry* (London: Macmillan, 1990), pp. 123–129;

John Davies, "Approximate Rivers Move: The Sound of Water in Norris's Poetry," *Poetry Wales,* 28 (October 1992);

Peter Davison, "Stony Wales and the Soft South," *Tar River Poetry* (Fall 1993);

Thomas Emery, "Leslie Norris," in *Poets of Great Britain and Ireland,* edited by Vincent B. Sherry Jr. (Detroit: Gale, 1984), pp. 264–269;

Eugene England, "Crossing Borders: Norris's Recent Long Poems," *Literature and Belief,* 13 (1993);

England and Peter Makuck, eds., *An Open World: Essays on Leslie Norris* (Columbia, S.C.: Camden House, 1994);

Mike Jenkins, "The Inner Exile: the Merthyr Poems of Leslie Norris," *Poetry Wales,* 21 (1986): 76–82;

Randal Jenkins, "The Poetry of Leslie Norris–An Interim Assessment," *Anglo-Welsh Review,* 20 (1971–1972): 26–36;

Glyn Jones, "Leslie Norris," in *Contemporary Poets,* edited by James Vinson, second edition (London: St. James Press, 1975), pp. 1122–1123;

Jones and John Rowlands, "Leslie Norris," in *Profiles* (Llandysul, Wales: Gomer, 1980), pp. 329–331;

Robert Minhinnick, "Leslie Norris–Insistent Elegist," *Poetry Wales,* 21 (1986): 83–86;

Mercer Simpson, "Leslie Norris: Reluctant Exile, Discovered Alien," *Poetry Wales,* 21 (1986): 87–94;

David Smith, "Confronting the Minotaur: Politics and Poetry in Twentieth-Century Wales," *Poetry Wales,* 15 (1979): 4–23;

Meic Stephens, "Leslie Norris," in *The Oxford Companion to the Literature of Wales,* compiled and edited by Stephens (Oxford: Oxford University Press, 1986): 432;

Sue Ellen Thompson, "The Paradox of Winter," *New Review* (Fall 1993);

Ted Walker, "On the Poetry of Leslie Norris," *Priapus,* 11/12 (1967–1968).

**Papers:**

The main collection of Leslie Norris's papers is in the process of being established at Brigham Young University in Provo, Utah. However, a few items are scattered in various libraries, such as the National Library of Wales and the libraries of Leeds University, the University of Durham, and the University of Exeter; in the archives of publishers such as Chatto & Windus; and in periodicals such as *Planet* and *Poetry Wales.*

# Simon J. Ortiz

*(27 May 1941 – )*

## Dennis R. Hoilman
*Ball State University*

See also the Ortiz entries in *DLB 120: American Poets Since World War II, Third Series,* and *DLB 175: Native American Writers of the United States.*

BOOKS: *Naked in the Wind* (Pembroke, N.C.: Quetzal-Vihio, 1971);

*Going for the Rain* (New York: Harper & Row, 1976);

*A Good Journey* (Berkeley, Cal.: Turtle Island, 1977);

*Song, Poetry, and Language* (Tsaile, Ariz.: Navajo Community College Press, 1977);

*The Howbah Indians* (Tucson: Blue Moon, 1978);

*The People Shall Continue* (San Francisco: Children's Book Press, 1978; revised, 1988);

*Song, Poetry and Language: Expression and Perception* (Tsaile, Ariz.: Navajo Community College Press, 1978);

*Fight Back: For the Sake of the People, For the Sake of the Land* (Albuquerque: University of New Mexico Press, 1980);

*A Poem Is a Journey* (Bourbonais, Ill.: Pteranadon, 1981);

*From Sand Creek: Rising in This Heart Which Is Our America* (New York: Thunder's Mouth, 1981);

*Blue and Red* (Acoma, N.Mex.: Pueblo of Acoma, 1982);

*The Importance of Childhood* (Acoma, N.Mex.: Pueblo of Acoma, 1982);

*Fightin': New and Collected Stories* (New York: Thunder's Mouth, 1983);

*Woven Stone,* Sun Tracks, volume 21 (Tucson: University of Arizona Press, 1992);

*After and Before the Lightning,* Sun Tracks, volume 28 (Tucson: University of Arizona Press, 1994).

**Edition:** *A Good Journey,* Sun Tracks, volume 12 (Tucson: University of Arizona Press, 1984).

**Collection:** *Men on the Moon: Collected Short Stories,* Sun Tracks, volume 37 (Tucson: University of Arizona Press, 1999).

PRODUCED SCRIPT: *Surviving Columbus: The Story of the Pueblo People,* video, PBS Home Video, 1992.

OTHER: "The San Francisco Indians," "Kaiser and the War," "A Story of Rios and Juan Jesús," "The

*Simon J. Ortiz, 1978 (photograph by LaVerne H. Clark)*

Killing of a State Cop," and "The End of Old Horse," in *The Man to Send Rain Clouds: Contemporary Stories by American Indians,* edited by Kenneth Rosen (New York: Vintage, 1974), pp. 9–13, 47–60, 79–81, 101–108, 145–148;

*Carriers of the Dream Wheel: Contemporary Native American Poetry,* edited by Duane Niatum, contributions by Ortiz (New York: Harper & Row, 1975), pp. 141–159;

*The Remembered Earth: An Anthology of Contemporary Native American Literature,* edited by Geary Hobson, contributions by Ortiz (Albuquerque: Red Earth Press, 1979), pp. 257–297;

*A Ceremony of Brotherhood,* edited by Ortiz and Rudolfo Anaya (Albuquerque: Academia, 1981);

*Earth Power Coming: Short Fiction in Native American Literature,* edited by Ortiz (Tsaile, Ariz.: Navajo Community College Press, 1983);

"Always the Stories: A Brief History and Thoughts on
My Writing," in *Coyote Was Here: Essays on Contemporary Native American Literary and Political Mobilization,* edited by Bo Schöler, *Dolphin,* 9 (Århus, Denmark: Seklos, 1984), pp. 57–69;

"The Language We Know," in *I Tell You Now: Autobiographical Essays by Native American Writers,* edited by Brian Swann and Arnold Krupat (Lincoln: University of Nebraska Press, 1987): 187–194;

*Harper's Anthology of 20th Century Native American Poetry,* edited by Niatum, contributions by Ortiz (New York: Harper & Row, 1988), pp. 139–151;

"What We See: A Perspective on Chaco Canyon and Pueblo Ancestry," in *Chaco Canyon: A Center and Its World,* edited by Mary Peck (Santa Fe: Museum of New Mexico Press, 1994);

*Speaking for the Generations: Native Writers on Writing,* edited by Ortiz (Tucson: University of Tucson Press, 1998).

SELECTED PERIODICAL PUBLICATIONS–
UNCOLLECTED: "Towards a National Indian Literature: Cultural Authenticity in Nationalism," *MELUS,* 8 (Summer 1981): 7–12;

"The Creative Process ['That's the Place Indians Talk About']," *Wicazo Sa Review: A Journal of Indian Studies,* 1 (Spring 1985): 45–49;

"Our Image of Ourselves," *Akwe:kon Journal,* 10 (Spring 1993): 38–39;

"Believing the Story," *Winds of Change,* 10 (Autumn 1995): 114–119;

"Meeting Our Elders," *Winds of Change,* 10 (Autumn 1995): 117, 119.

Simon J. Ortiz stands out among major Native American writers such as N. Scott Momaday, Leslie Marmon Silko, Gerald Vizenor, James Welch, Paula Gunn Allen, and Louise Erdrich in that, unlike these writers, he was not raised in a bi- or multicultural home with English as his first language. Rather, Ortiz grew up in a traditional Native American home–speaking, understanding, perceiving, and feeling in the Acoma language. As he says in *Woven Stone* (1992), "if there is anything that has sustained me through my years of writing it is that fact."

Ortiz is best known for his several books of poetry, chiefly on such Native American ideas as the importance of identification with a sacred place, the sense of the poet as the equivalent of the traditional storyteller, and the struggle for cultural survival. The theme of the journey recurs frequently in his verse, as the titles of his early collections of poetry indicate: *Going for the Rain* (1976), *A Good Journey* (1977), and *A Poem Is a Journey* (1981).

Simon Joseph Ortiz was born in Albuquerque, New Mexico, on 27 May 1941 and raised in McCartys–the "Deetseyamah" of several of his poems. The village of McCartys is located approximately fifty miles west of Albuquerque on the Acoma Indian Reservation. Ortiz's family belongs to the *Dyaamih hanoh*–Eagle clan or, literally, Eagle people–a tightly knit clan that fosters close family and kin relationships as well as a communal outlook and sense of responsibility. Ortiz's parents, Joe L. Ortiz and Mamie Toribio Ortiz, attended St. Catherine's Indian School in Santa Fe and spoke English quite fluently, but the Acoma language–*Aacqumeh dzehni*–was spoken in the home. Ortiz, whose father worked as a laborer for the Santa Fe Railroad, was brought up in frugal, difficult circumstances. Ortiz's father and other relatives abused alcohol, a habit that–as Ortiz describes in *Woven Stone*–"caused family tension, arguments, distrust, fear, pain, all of the trauma of alcoholism." Ortiz continues, "Alcoholism I had known all my life. As a child I was traumatically afraid of the behavior of my father and others under the influence of alcohol. I just didn't understand it, yet I knew its fearsome, destructive impact first hand." Ortiz, whose own life and career also suffered because of alcoholism, later referred to his family as "dysfunctional," and alcoholism constitutes another theme that runs throughout his writing.

Ortiz attended the McCartys Day School, operated by the Bureau of Indian Affairs. At McCartys, as he later said, the policy was to "brainwash" the children and turn them into white people. He especially liked reading because of his interest in stories. He had been hearing them all his life–some were traditional stories of mythic heroes, while others evolved from current gossip about the Aacqumeh (Acoma) community in which he lived. All of these stories, however, interested the young Ortiz greatly, because–although unbeknownst to him at the time–they tied him into the communal body of his people and his heritage. As Ortiz elaborates in *Woven Stone,*

> Consequently, when I learned to read and write, I
> believe I felt those stories continued somehow in the
> new language and use of the new language and they
> would never be lost, forgotten, and finally gone. They
> would always continue.

He says that his poetry attempts to "instill that sense of continuity" and to connect directly to its primary source in the oral tradition as he knew it in childhood.

Except for an interruption during the fifth grade–when the family moved temporarily to Skull Valley, Arizona–Ortiz was able to remain in McCartys Day School through the sixth grade; McCartys provided him with a strong connection to his people. While in school in Skull Valley, he began to write poetry and song lyrics influenced by country and western singers, such as Jimmy Rodgers and Hank Williams. His first poem—written for Mother's Day—was also published in the school newspaper.

For part of junior high, from 1953 to 1954, Ortiz was sent to St. Catherine's Indian School in Santa Fe, and in one of his poems he writes about leaving his home and family to attend the school. He describes traveling with his parents to Santa Fe and how, when the three of them arrived at the school, he fainted:

> I just fainted, that's all, into the subtle chasm that opens
> and you lose all desire and control, and I fell, very slowly,
> it seemed. I found myself being carried out by my father to
> some steps in front of the boys [sic] recreation hall. He
> talked with
> me for a long time, slowly and gently, and I felt him trem-
> ble
> and stifle his sobs several times. He told me not to worry
> and to be strong and brave.
> I wonder if I have been. That was the first time I ever went
> away from home.

Next, from 1954 to 1956, Ortiz was sent to Albuquerque Indian School, which was closer to home. He went to high school in Grants, New Mexico, at an integrated public school with a mostly "Mericano" student body. He proved to be an outstanding student, winning many honors, both academic and athletic: Boys State, class officer, cocaptain of the football team, allstate in sports, Mr. Grants High, and Senior Honor Boy.

During his high school years he began to think of himself as a writer. He was reading widely, and he came to believe that "as an Acoma person I also had something important, unique, and special to say." In his nascent fiction—in high school he wrote more prose than poetry—the characters were poor, struggling, hardworking, enduring, and caring, but they were not specifically Native American or Indian or Acoma. Ortiz thought of himself as an Acoma person, but his "views and concepts in large part were those of the dominant society," he wrote in *Woven Stone.* "I loved my family, people, community, yet I was also swayed by powerful influences of the outside and even yearned and sought for those 'Mericano ways.'"

By the time of his high school graduation, then, Ortiz knew that he wanted to be a writer, but he had no idea how to proceed. He went to work in the Kerr-McGee uranium mines near Acoma, and the men he worked with, mostly working-class whites, served as the models for characters in his stories and poems. At this period in his life, he also developed a political consciousness, becoming aware of racial and ethnic dis-

Cover for Ortiz's 1981 book of prose and verse, in which he reflects on his experiences while undergoing treatment for alcoholism in a Veterans Administration hospital and on the 1864 massacre of Cheyennes and Arapahos by U.S. troops at Sand Creek in Colorado

crimination, and, as he shows in *Woven Stones,* growing angry at the injustice:

> Like other colonized youth, I had been quietly seething for many years. . . . I recall the anger at my parents and grandparents, blaming them for not warning us and not protecting us from American life and its people, and I was upset at Acoma leadership for not fighting harder to hold our land and water.

During the early 1960s Ortiz began abusing alcohol. A few of his favorite writers—Dylan Thomas, Ernest Hemingway, Thomas Wolfe, and Malcolm Lowry—had been heavy drinkers, and Ortiz was undeterred by any thought that "alcohol might have done them in. I believed in their greatness and in drinking as a part of that." Eventually, he spent time in the Veterans Administration hospital in Ft. Lyons, Colorado, for treatment of his alcoholism.

After a year in the uranium mines, Ortiz enrolled in Fort Lewis College in 1962, planning to be an organic chemist. He soon discovered that he had little affinity for chemistry and in 1963 left college to enlist in the U.S. Army. While in basic training in Louisiana, he encountered overt racism for the first time and suffered the humiliations of having to use the "Colored Only" drinking fountains and restrooms. After serving three years in the army, Ortiz returned to the University of New Mexico, from 1966 through 1968. For one year, beginning in 1968, he attended the University of Iowa, where he was a Fellow in the International Writing Program. Although he considers himself first and foremost a writer, Ortiz has enjoyed a varied career. He has been a teacher—chiefly of creative writing and Native American literature—at the following institutions: San Diego State University and the Institute of American Indian Arts in 1974; Navajo Community College in Tsaile, Arizona, from 1975 to 1977; the College of Marin in Kentfield, California, from 1976 to 1979; the University of New Mexico in Albuquerque from 1979 to 1981; Sinte Gleska College in Rosebud, South Dakota, from 1985 to 1986; and at Lewis and Clark College in Portland, Oregon, in 1990. He served as official tribal interpreter and lieutenant governor of the Acoma Pueblo community and worked as a consulting editor for Acoma Pueblo Press. He has also been a journalist, public relations director, and newspaper editor. He has had four marriages, each ending in divorce: to Agnes Goodluck, from 1967 to 1971; to Joy Harjo, from 1971 to 1974; to Roxanne Dunbar, from 1976 to 1980; and to Marlene Foster, from 1981 to 1984. He has three children—a son and two daughters: Raho Nez, Rainy Dawn, and Sara Marie.

Ortiz has received many awards and honors. In 1969 the National Endowment for the Arts (NEA) honored him for his work in journalism with a Discovery Award; in 1981 the NEA also awarded him a fellowship. In 1980 he and other poets were recognized at the White House Salute to American Poetry and Poets. His *From Sand Creek: Rising in This Heart Which Is Our America* (1981), a book of largely political verse, won the Pushcart Prize in 1981, and in 1989 the New Mexico Humanities Council recognized him for his contributions to literature with a Humanities Award. In 1993 he received a Lifetime Achievement Award for literature at the third annual "Returning the Gift" Festival of Native American Writers and Storytellers.

In his first major book of poems, *Going for the Rain,* Ortiz explores the theme of the journey in the context of a traditional Acoma ceremonial journey to the home of the Shiwana, or Cloud People. Shiwana are the deities who bring the rain necessary for survival in the arid, western New Mexico climate of Acoma—also known as the Sky City for its location at the top of a high mesa. Yet, as he says in *Woven Stone,* the book is also structured "in the narrative form of an actual journey on the heeyaanih, the road of life, and its experience." In the prologue to *Going for the Rain,* he compares the traditional journey to the Cloud People's home for rain to his journey—his search for inspiring words with which to heal his people. The traditional journey involves four distinct stages: preparation, leaving, returning, and the coming of the rain itself. Each stage is played out in the successive sections that divide the book.

In the first stage, known as preparation, the poet-persona makes prayers, sings songs, and considers what is important to him—his home, children, language, and "the self that he is." In the thirteen poems of the first section, Ortiz deals with themes analogous to the physical and spiritual preparations needed before the journey itself can begin. Several of the verses—"Forming Child," "Four Poems for a Child Son," "The Expectant Father," "To Insure Survival"—concern both the birth, in 1973, of his first daughter, Rainy Dawn, and the idea of language, a topic that he examines in all his writings. In a poem titled "Language," he listens to the sounds that Rainy Dawn makes as an infant, connecting her human sounds to sounds in nature—"the wind searching hillside ledge." For him the natural language of the infant is akin to a "language of movements—sights— / possibilities and impossibilities— / pure existence." The child,

> upon hearing a sound hears the poem
> of hearing—original motion of it
> is complete—sanctified—the sphere
> of who he or she is who is hearing
> the poetry. . . .

Language is primarily oral, something that is heard. Just to hear language is to hear a poem, according to Ortiz's lyric. Language as verse completes and sanctifies a person; hearing a poem thus establishes identity and a sense of self. At the end of "Language" he concludes that language is central to the self, expressing the core of one's being:

> All language comes forth
> outward from the center. Hits
> the curve of your being. Fits
> —"chiseled" occurs to me
> . . . . . . . . . . . . . . . . . . .
> into thoughts of sound itself,
> the energy it is
> and the motion inherent in it.

According to Ortiz, language provides identity and continuity—not only for the self but also for a culture.

The second section of *Going for the Rain,* titled "Leaving," consists of twenty-four poems depicting Ortiz's travels. These travels include some short trips to

*Dust jacket for Ortiz's 1983 book of short fiction, acclaimed for its depiction of the cultural conflicts between whites and Native Americans*

places such as Spider Springs, Gallup, and Albuquerque in New Mexico, to Many Farms on the Navajo Reservation in Arizona, and others to the West Coast, the South, and New York City. While most of the poems in "Leaving" concern the alienation that a traveler sometimes experiences in an unfamiliar place, a few also delve into a traveler's sense of wonder at the diversity and beauty encountered on a trip. Significantly, in the poem titled "Many Farms Notes" and dated spring 1973, Ortiz, in response to a question regarding the main theme of his verse, replies, "To put it as simply as possible, / I say it this way: to recognize / the relationships I share with everything."

The twenty-six poems of the third section, titled "Returning," relate as well to his travels, but—as the title suggests—focus, in addition, on the poet's return to Acoma; these poems represent his gifts and blessings to his people. For example, "Leaving America" is set in the Kansas City bus depot, where the persona—surely Ortiz himself since the poems are autobiographical—meets another Indian, Roy, who is from Arizona and also returning home. "Just got paid," Roy says,

> laid off by the Rock Island Line.
> Going home.
> It's got red and brown land,
> sage, and when it rains,
> it smells like piñon
> and pretty girls at a Squaw Dance,

to which Ortiz replies "I know." As the title "Leaving America" evokes, the journey home bespeaks a cultural journey: Ortiz goes from the alienating American culture of white people back to the land and traditions of the Indian people—who, he suggests, are not "American."

"The Rain Falls" is the title of the fourth section of *Going for the Rain*. Like the rain that the journey to the Shiwana has engendered, the twenty-five poems of "The Rain Falls" constitute the fruits of the poetic journey that Ortiz has now completed. Launching the fourth section and bearing the dedication "for Joy"

(Ortiz's first wife), the poem "Earth Woman" shows how woman embodies the earth itself:

> How gentle
> her movements, her hands,
> soft wind,
> warm rain,
> the moving pain
> of pleasure
> we share.

In the second poem, "Spreading Wings of Wind," about a plane ride from Rough Rock to Phoenix, Ortiz reminds himself that he belongs to a community—the Eagle Clan into which he was born:

> I must remember
> that I am only one part
> among many parts,
> not a singular eagle
> or one mountain.

The lyric ends by addressing non-Indians with a question, "What the hell are you doing to this land? / My grandfather hunted here, prayed, / dreamt. . . ." In "Four Deetseyamah Poems," a title that alludes to the Acoma name of McCartys, Ortiz finds himself absorbed into the land:

> when I have needed
> to envision my home, when loneliness
> for myself has overcome me,
> the Mountain has occurred.
> Now, I see it sharing its being
> with me, praying.

Storytelling, identity, and the journey are bound up in his work. As Andrew Wiget points out in the *Dictionary of Native American Literature* (1994), Ortiz's journey in all directions establishes Acu, "the point of origin as well as the destination of what otherwise appear to be pointless wanderings—as the geographical as well as spiritual center of the storytelling person's identity. . . ."

Ortiz's next book of verse, *A Good Journey,* encompasses more than fifty poems, mostly narrative, based on the oral tradition—especially "the oral voice of stories, song, history, and contemporary experience," as he elaborates in *Woven Stone.* The poems chronicle the writer's experiences and the people he has met in his travels, which took place in the late 1960s and early 1970s. Some lyrics have precise dates, while others mention the event motivating a particular poem. Many of the lyrics are about his children or are addressed to them; indeed, he titles the second of the five sections, "Notes to My Child." In the preface he quotes from an interview in which he was asked why he writes:

> Because Indians always tell a story. The only way to continue is to tell a story. . . . Your children will not survive unless you tell something about them—how they were born, how they came to this certain place, how they continued.

Ortiz goes on to explain that he writes for his children, wife, mother, father, and grandparents "and then reverse order that way so that I may have a good journey on my way back home." He suggests that the "good journey" of the title is the journey of return—these poems bring him back to his origins and identity within the Acoma community and culture.

Perhaps the growing political awareness of Ortiz's verse at this point also indicates that poetry returns him home. As in *Going for the Rain,* the poems in *A Good Journey* are personal and autobiographical, yet—unlike in the earlier book—they also display his response to history and to the dominant culture of white Americans. For example, in the fifth poem of the book, "A San Diego Poem: January–February 1973"—about an airplane flight to California—Ortiz discloses his resentment of Catholicism:

> I look below at the countless houses,
> row after row, veiled by tinted smog.
> I feel the beginnings of apprehension.
> Where am I? I recall the institutional prayers
> of my Catholic youth but don't dare recite them.
> The prayers of my native selfhood
> have been strangled in my throat.

The poem concludes when the persona arrives at Los Angeles International Airport and tries to find his way through the tunnels of its "innards":

> I am under L.A. International Airport,
> on the West Coast, someplace called America.
> I am somewhat educated, I can read and use a compass;
> yet the knowledge of where I am is useless.
> . . . . . . . . . . . . . . . . . . . . . . . . . . . . . .
> America has obliterated my sense of comprehension.
> Without this comprehension, I am emptied
> of any substance. America has finally caught me.
> I meld into the walls of that tunnel
> and become the silent burial. There are no echoes.

In "Blessings," which concerns a civil rights fund-raising function in 1969, he writes that Native Americans are not hungry for money or for "carefully written proposals." Rather,

> We are hungry for the good earth,
> the deserts and mountains growing corn.
> We are hungry for the conviction
> that you are our brothers and sisters
> who are willing to share our love. . . .

Storytelling as a theme also informs *A Good Journey:* the first section of the book is titled "Telling," and several of the poems stress the importance of the oral tradition. In dedicating *A Good Journey* to his children, Raho Nez and Rainy Dawn, Ortiz says:

> The stories and poems come forth
> and I am only the voice telling them.
> They are the true source themselves.
> The words are the vision
> by which we see out and in and around.

Stories are, in the words of his dedication, "the true source"—not just of themselves but of everything in one's consciousness, because they shape the consciousness of who people are and of what the world is. According to him, words are the eyes through which people see and know themselves—as well as the world outside and around them. In "I Tell You Now," the final poem in *A Good Journey,* Ortiz addresses an Indian woman he has seen on the street:

> I really have no words to match your stride.
> . . . . . . . . . . . . . . . . . . . . . . . . . . . . . . . .
> Even the sheaf of written stories
> I am carrying under my arm to the printers
> because as I watch you, the stories
> which I did work carefully at lack the depth
> and the meaning of your walk.

He then acknowledges the political ideas that he has incorporated with increasing frequency in his writing:

> Oh I guess the words are adequate enough—
> they point out American depredations,
> the stealing of our land and language,
> how our children linger hungry and hurt
> on street corners like the ones I just passed,
> but then I get the feeling that these
> words of my youth are mere diatribes.
> They remain useless and flat when what I really wish
> is to listen to you and then have you listen to me.
> I've been wanting to tell you for a long time.
> I tell you now.

He implies that political diatribes are lifeless and flat, because they do not entail stories. "I Tell You Now" ends with a series of stories that Ortiz has been wanting to tell,

> because I want you to know
> and in that way
> have you come to know me now.

He shows that through stories people come together—not just Ortiz and the Indian woman to whom he is ostensibly speaking in "I Tell You Now," but also all Native American people and, indeed, his readers.

*Cover for Ortiz's 1999 book, which collects stories from his* Howbah Indians *(1978) and* Fightin' *(1983)*

A third significant component to *A Good Journey*— besides the two themes of travel and storytelling—is the character of Coyote, a combination of culture hero and trickster in the oral tradition. Coyote is prominently featured "in the origin and all the way / through" the stories in the oral tradition and the history of the people. Often Ortiz identifies himself with Coyote—the trickster, the troublemaker, the constant victim of his own pranks. Yet, Coyote is also ancient, present at the creation of the world, and he is not only a source of disorder and sorrow but also brings good things to the people. In *A Good Journey,* Ortiz occasionally shows Coyote in the role of ragged wanderer—a lonely outsider—such as in "Two Coyote Ones"; while the lyric begins in the first person, suggesting Ortiz as the wandering persona, it ends with the assertion that the poem was really told in Coyote's voice.

At this early stage in his career as a writer, Ortiz was writing short fiction as well as poetry. Five of his short stories appear in Kenneth Rosen's 1974 anthology *The Man to Send Rain Clouds: Contemporary Stories by American Indians,* including four of his best: "The San Francisco Indians," "Kaiser and the War," "The Killing of a State Cop," and "The End of Old Horse." "The San Francisco Indians" captures with irony an old Indian man's encounter with members of a hippie "tribe" in San Francisco. The hippies seek a "genuine Indian" to show them how to conduct a peyote ceremony—a rite about which the old man knows nothing. Both "Kaiser and the War" and "The Killing of a State Cop" depict the difficulties that confront Native American veterans when they return to the reservation. "The End of Old Horse" recounts, simply yet profoundly, a young boy's first encounter with the futility of death—in this case the death of a dog named "Horse."

In 1978 Ortiz published four additional short stories in *The Howbah Indians,* a collection that takes its title from that of the first story. "Howbah," as the narrator of the story explains, means "you all Indians—like you Oklahoma folks say: yo'all." Eagle, an army veteran who served in Korea, returns to the reservation and buys a gas station. He puts up a sign that is "a couple of hundred yards long," "like it was a high board fence." In red letters on a bright yellow background, so they can be discerned from ten miles away, the sign reads "Welcome Howbah Indians." The sign makes the Indians proud of Eagle. After a couple of years, however, Eagle loses his way and is found dead in a dry rainwash. "He had what looked like bruises from falling on his face or a stone, but the government police from the Bureau of Indian Affairs never bothered very much." Because the Indians still remember the sign, laughing and laughing "for the important memory and fact that it is," the futility of Eagle's aspirations becomes somewhat muted. As it turns out, the narrator of "Howbah Indians" has awakened suddenly one night, the memory of the sign having entered his sleep. "I felt good for remembering," he says, "and I wrote it down on a notepad. *Howbah Indians.*" The irony of the sign seems to escape the narrator, who does not recognize the fact that the "welcome" that "you all Indians" will receive will be the same quashed aspirations and the same end that "welcomed" Eagle. The story strongly implies that Eagle was murdered because he dared to aspire to a position of ownership, and because he dared to welcome all Indians to his station. Apparently, someone tried to teach Eagle a lesson—that Indians are not welcome and should stay in their place.

For *Fight Back: For the Sake of the People, For the Sake of the Land* (1980), Ortiz set the story, told in both lyric and narrative forms, in the context of the uranium boom of the 1960s. The focus of the book is on the injustice, discrimination, and bigotry that befell Indians as the "boom" flourished on land stolen from the Acoma people. In "What I Mean," a poem from *Fight Back,* he writes:

We didn't talk much.
Some people say Indians are just like that,
shy and reserved and polite,
but that's mostly crap. Lots of times

we were just plain scared
and we kept our mouths shut.
I mean Grants and Milan and the mines
between Haystack and Ambrosia Lake,
all that area used to be Indian land—
Acoma land—but it was surveyed
by the government and stolen
at the turn of the century
and there was plenty to say
but we didn't say it.

The book is divided into two sections—titled, respectively, "Too Many Sacrifices" and "No More Sacrifices." The first section features eighteen poems, mostly about people and incidents that he remembers from working in the mines and in the processing mills around Grants and Milan, towns in the vicinity of Acoma. The second section embodies a lengthy work—a piece mixing prose with poetry and titled "Our Homeland, A National Sacrifice Area"—and a concluding lyric called "A New Story." In the prose sections of *Fight Back,* he recounts the history of the land that surrounds Acoma, from the time that white people arrived on the land until the present. The interspersed poems make up his more personal responses to the prose story that he tells. The story recounts four hundred years of exploitation and injustice, and how the mining and processing industry has depleted and contaminated the water upon which Acoma depends. As he describes in *Fight Back,* Ortiz feels that

Only when we are not afraid to fight against the destroyers, thieves, liars, exploiters who profit handsomely off the land and people will we know what love and compassion are. Only when the people of this nation, not just Indian people, fight for what is just and good for all life, will we know life and its continuance.

Ortiz sets his next book, *From Sand Creek,* in the Veterans Administration Hospital in Ft. Lyons, Colorado, where he underwent treatment for alcoholism in 1974 and 1975. The book takes its title from the site of Colonel John M. Chivington's massacre of more than a hundred peaceful Cheyenne and Arapaho people on 29 November 1864; the Sand Creek massacre is one of the most infamous episodes in the history of the conflict between the white man and the Indian. *From Sand Creek* consists of brief prose comments, often only a single sentence, on roughly one page and somewhat longer poems—though never longer than a single page—on the facing page. As he notes in the preface, Ortiz analyzes himself in *From Sand Creek* "as an American, which is hemispheric, a U.S. citizen, which is national, and as an Indian, which is spiritual and human." He juxtaposes history with his own experience, presented as fragmentary, traumatic, and confined largely to Colorado in the vicinity of the site of the massacre. Many of the poems center on his experiences in the hospital or in the nearby town of La Junta, alluding to fellow patients such as Toby, Billy, Nez, W., the Texan, Dusty, the Colonel, Danny, Larry, and the Oklahoma Boy. In other poems the speaker imagines the scene of the massacre: "It almost seemed magical / that they had so much blood. / It just kept pouring, / like rivers, / like endless floods from the sky." He frames *From Sand Creek* with poems of hope and reconciliation, particularly his hope that "we will all learn something from each other. We must. We are all with and within each other." The opening poem suggests that instead of dwelling on the victimization and the guilt of the massacre, the "burden of steel and mad death," one must now look to the "flowers and new grass and a spring wind rising from Sand Creek." America, as the concluding poem says, must "not be vengeful but wealthy with love and compassion and knowledge." *From Sand Creek* is Ortiz's most cryptic, most difficult work.

In 1992 the University of Arizona Press published *Woven Stone,* which brings together *Going for the Rain, A Good Journey,* and *Fight Back. Woven Stone* includes an excellent autobiographical introduction by Ortiz, in which he discusses the events and issues that have influenced his life and poetry.

In *After and Before the Lightning* (1994), a collection of 133 short poems, with interspersed prose passages, Ortiz reflects on the events of the winter of 1985–1986, which he spent working among the Lakota people and teaching at Sinte Gleska College on the Rosebud Sioux Indian Reservation in South Dakota. He dates the poems, beginning 18 November and ending 21 March–a span of time denoting the season, as he says in his preface, between the last thunder and lightning in the fall and the first thunder and lightning in the spring. He divides the collection into four approximately equal sections: "The Landscape: Prairie, Time, and Galaxy," "Common Trails: Every Day," "Buffalo Dawn Coming," and "Near and Evident Signs of Spring."

*After and Before the Lightning,* like Ortiz's other works, develops the theme of the interrelatedness between people and the land, and–especially–his experiences driving on Highway 18 between the towns of Okreek and Mission, with the wind and snow fiercer than anything he had known at Acoma. As he writes in "Driving, the Snowy Wind," dated 19 November,

The snowy wind is fierce,
insistent, unrelenting,
picking up dry snow
off the hills, turning the hills
into churning clouds and the sky,
blending everything
into one cold surging,
exhaling, forceful breath.

In the preface to *After and Before the Lightning,* he explains the origin of these poems:

I've felt I have never been very good at facing reality nor at dealing with it. And when I lived in South Dakota . . . I needed a way to deal with the reality of my life and the reality in which I lived. The winter prairie surrounded me totally; it was absolutely present in every moment. . . . The reality of a South Dakota winter demanded to be dealt with. So I was compelled the write the poetry in *After and Before the Lightning.*

The book concludes with "Lightning IV," a poem that encompasses the themes found not only in *After and Before the Lightning* but also in Ortiz's work as a whole: memory, life as a journey, man's relationship with the land, the significance of place, and the stories that sustain a people.

Why we should keep riding
toward the storm, we don't know.
. . . . . . . . . . . . . . . . . . . . . . . . . .
It is perhaps way past questioning,
past the moment when it's too late.
Our only certainty, when the horizon
is no longer clear, is our memory
of how the journey has been till now.
. . . . . . . . . . . . . . . . . . . . . . . . . . .
How completely we feel the tremoring
and shuddering pulse of the land now
as we welcome the rain-heart-lightning
into our trembling yearning selves.

For Simon J. Ortiz, memory and the storytelling inspired by memory provide his people with a sense of continuity. Together, memory and storytelling comprise a blueprint for the survival of Native American culture.

**Interview:**

Laura Coltelli, *Winged Words: American Indian Writers Speak,* edited by Laura Coltelli (Lincoln: University of Nebraska Press, 1990), pp. 103–119.

**References:**

Robert M. Nelson, "Simon J. Ortiz," in *Dictionary of Native American Literature,* edited by Andrew Wiget (New York: Garland, 1994), pp. 483–489;

Patricia Clark Smith, "Coyote Ortiz: *Canis Latrans Latrans* in the Poetry of Simon Ortiz," in *Studies in American Indian Literature,* edited by Paula Gunn Allen (New York: Modern Language Association, 1983), pp. 192–210;

Wiget, *Simon Ortiz,* Boise State University Western Writers Series, no. 74 (Boise, Idaho: Boise State University, 1986).

# Eugene Manlove Rhodes

*(19 January 1869 – 27 June 1934)*

Sanford E. Marovitz
*Kent State University*

BOOKS: *Good Men and True* (New York: Holt, 1910); enlarged as *Good Men and True; and Hit the Line Hard* (New York: Grosset & Dunlap, 1920; London: Hodder & Stoughton, 1923);

*Bransford in Arcadia; or, The Little Eohippus* (New York: Holt, 1914); republished as *Bransford of Rainbow Range* (New York: Grosset & Dunlap, 1920; London: Hodder & Stoughton, 1921);

*The Desire of the Moth* (New York: Holt, 1916; London: Hodder & Stoughton, 1921?); enlarged as *The Desire of the Moth; and, The Come On* (New York: Grosset & Dunlap, 1920);

*West Is West* (New York: H. K. Fly, 1917; London: Hodder & Stoughton, 1921);

*Say Now Shibboleth* (Chicago: Bookfellows, 1921);

*Stepsons of Light* (Boston: Houghton Mifflin, 1921; London: Hodder & Stoughton, 1922);

*Copper Streak Trail* (Boston: Houghton Mifflin, 1922; London: Hodder & Stoughton, 1923);

*Once in the Saddle, and Pasó por Aquí* (Boston: Houghton Mifflin, 1927);

*The Trusty Knaves* (Boston: Houghton Mifflin, 1933; London: Wright & Brown, 1934);

*Beyond the Desert* (Boston & New York: Houghton Mifflin, 1934; London: Wright & Brown, 1935);

*The Proud Sheriff,* introduction by Henry Herbert Knibbs (Boston: Houghton Mifflin, 1935; London: Wright & Brown, 1935);

*The Little World Waddies* (El Paso, Tex.: W. H. Hutchinson, 1946);

*The Best Novels and Stories of Eugene Manlove Rhodes,* edited by Frank V. Dearing, introduction by J. Frank Dobie (Boston: Houghton Mifflin, 1949; enlarged edition, with foreword by Hutchinson, Lincoln: University of Nebraska Press, 1987);

*The Rhodes Reader: Stories of Virgins, Villains, and Varmints,* edited by Hutchinson (Norman: University of Oklahoma Press, 1957);

*Eugene Manlove Rhodes*

*The Line of Least Resistance,* edited by Hutchinson (Chico, Cal.: Printed by Hurst & Yount for W. H. Hutchinson, 1958);

*The Brave Adventure* (Clarendon, Tex.: Clarendon Press, 1971);

*Recognition: The Poems of Eugene Manlove Rhodes* (Alamogordo, N.Mex.: Friends of the Alamogordo Public Library, 1997).

**Editions:** *Beyond the Desert,* introduction by W. H. Hutchinson (Lincoln: University of Nebraska Press, 1967);

*The Proud Sheriff,* preface by Hutchinson (Norman: University of Oklahoma Press, 1968);

*Stepsons of Light,* introduction by Hutchinson (Norman: University of Oklahoma Press, 1969);

*Copper Streak Trail,* introduction by Hutchinson (Norman: University of Oklahoma Press, 1970);

*Pasó por Aquí,* introduction by Hutchinson (Norman: University of Oklahoma Press, 1973);

*Bransford in Arcadia: or, The Little Eohippus,* introduction by Hutchinson (Norman: University of Oklahoma Press, 1975).

SELECTED PERIODICAL PUBLICATIONS—
UNCOLLECTED: "The Hour and the Man," *Out West* (January 1902): 43–52;

"The Bar Cross Liar," *Out West* (June 1902): 619–625;

"On Velvet," *All Story* (September 1906);

"Wildcat Represents," *All Story* (March 1907);

Eugene Manlove Rhodes and Henry Wallace Phillips, "The Punishment and the Crime," *Saturday Evening Post* (20 April 1907): 14–15, 29–30;

"A Beggar on Horseback," *Out West* (November 1907): 406–414;

"The Star of Empire," *Saturday Evening Post* (4 September 1909): 8–9, 40–41.

Regarded by many of his contemporaries as the best Western fiction writer of the early twentieth century, Eugene Manlove Rhodes had a mystique that made him almost a cult figure for devotees of his work. From 1907 until his death on 27 June 1934 he contributed fiction, poetry, and essays regularly to *The Saturday Evening Post* and occasionally to *McClure's, Cosmopolitan,* and *Redbook;* book publication usually followed serialization within two years. Although Rhodes's fiction has been read in recent years chiefly for its "historical interest," it engages readers as much now as it did early in the century for its thrills, regional authenticity, commitment to truth, and distinctive style.

Although Rhodes devoted most of his life to writing fictional narratives set in the Southwest, specifically in New Mexico, he was a son of the Great Plains and thus a Westerner by birth. Rhodes was born in Tecumseh, Nebraska, on 19 January 1869. His father, Colonel Hinman Rhodes, was a veteran of both the Mexican and Civil Wars; a hero committed to fairness and justice, and a noted raconteur, he constituted a model in character and ability for his children. Julia May Manlove Rhodes, the author's mother, was a forceful, industrious woman from a well-to-do family; college educated and sensitive to the arts, especially music, she served as a moral guide for Rhodes and his siblings. Seeking a better life, the family moved to Cherokee, Kansas, in 1874—by which time a second child, Clarence Edgar, had been born. The youngest, Helen Mabel, arrived five years later. Rhodes gained most of his early formal education in Cherokee and received limited additional schooling after the family moved in 1881 from Kansas to Engle, New Mexico, where miners were in demand.

Rhodes lived in New Mexico from 1881 to 1906. At sixteen he helped the army search for Chief Nana's band of Apache fighters who had ridden up from Mexico in May 1885, but Rhodes saw no action. On many other occasions he did fight, however, for although he was relatively small, Rhodes was a wiry, fierce, and determined scrapper; he rarely carried a pistol but fought readily with anyone who insulted a woman or himself—and he seldom lost. His extreme defensiveness may be attributed partly to an early self-consciousness because of a cleft palate that caused him to mispronounce *g* and *r*. From 1888 to 1890, two of his most rewarding years, Rhodes attended the University of the Pacific in San Jose, California. The broad range of readings he had completed earlier under his mother's guidance proved its value as a base for his more rigorous course of study at the university.

Rhodes's years with the Bar Cross, a ranch that appears in many of his stories, were equally valuable and memorable; for a while in the 1890s he owned a small horse farm that he leased to the Bar Cross outfit. Although he wrote most of his Western fiction in New York and California, he was a Westerner at heart. While riding for the Bar Cross and other spreads, he voraciously read books often acquired with coupons from packs of tobacco. Because of his excellent retentive memory, Rhodes could instantaneously recall lines he had read long before, which partly explains the enrichment of his texts with literary echoes from the works of dozens of authors, both the enduring and the now forgotten.

His career as an author commenced in April 1896 with the publication of "Charley Graham," a poem inspired by a rancher for whom Rhodes worked in the early 1890s. The poem appeared in the periodical *Land of Sunshine*—later called *Out West* and *Sunset.* In the subsequent three decades this periodical published more than two dozen additional pieces by Rhodes, and its editor, Charles F. Lummis, also became Rhodes's mentor. Before his first story, "The Professor's Experiment," came out in 1901, Rhodes published five more poems, including "A Blossom of Barren Lands"—a lyric on the yucca flower—and "A Ballade of Gray Hills." Both verses echo William Cullen Bryant's romantic depiction of moral insight gained through visions of nature.

On 9 August 1899 in Apalachin, New York, Rhodes married May Davison Purple, a recent widow whom he had met and courted by correspondence. In addition to her two children, Jasper—"Jack"—and Frederick, they had two of their own: Alan Hinman, born

*Dust jacket for Rhodes's 1916 novel, in which a corrupt sheriff facing election defeat tries to frame his opponent for murder*

on 12 June 1901, and Barbara, born on 18 February 1909. The couple named Alan and Barbara after characters in stories by Robert Louis Stevenson, one of Rhodes's favorite authors. Barbara's death before her second birthday affected Rhodes for the rest of his life. In 1906, wanting to be with May and the children—who had been staying for a time with her family in New York—he left New Mexico to live and farm in Apalachin, where he also wrote most of his best-known works. Allegedly, he was also fleeing as a man wanted for either killing or stealing a yearling that belonged to someone else. The crime is unclear because no official record of it has been found. In 1928 Governor Richard C. Dillon of New Mexico supposedly pardoned Rhodes of the crime in a humorous personal letter to the writer.

Rhodes set most of his fiction in the area roughly between Alamogordo and Tularosa to the east and the Black Range Mountains to the west, and from San Antonio in New Mexico—a small town about ten miles

south of Socorro—on the north Rio Grande, south to El Paso in Texas. Mountain ranges both lace and surround much of the diversified landscape as the Rio Grande flows through the center of Texas down to Mexico. Between ranges east of the river is the grassy Jornada del Muerto, and west is the area that Rhodes called in his fiction the "Little World"—"El Mundo Chico"—of contiguous ranches owned and operated by the somewhat idealized cowmen who provided mutual support against threats to themselves or their community.

A careful observer of everything around him, Rhodes was lauded for his authentic depiction of people and places. He often used the names of actual local figures in his narratives and allocated among various characters some of his own features and characteristics. Western critics who knew Rhodes and admired his writing—including W. H. Hutchinson, Walter Prescott Webb, Bernard DeVoto, and J. Frank Dobie—praised his authenticity, and DeVoto added that "Rhodes was an artist" in terms of "the painful care" with which he treated both the structure and plot of a work. Rhodes's stories also warrant consideration for their high moral tone, allusive style, combined romantic and realistic elements, simultaneously typed yet credible characters, and intricate, often suspenseful plots. Although not all his early works take place in the American West, most fall into that category.

Even Hutchinson, who takes an historical approach to Rhodes, commended the tight plotting of "The Fool's Heart" (1909), the kind of Western mystery fiction at which Rhodes excelled. In 1951 this tale was presented on television as an episode of *Suspense*. The detective plot bears a trace of what Hutchinson termed the "Godawful frontier-Gothic," which he perceived in Rhodes's second story, "The Hour and the Man," published in *Out West* (January 1902). Little of frontier Gothic remains, however, in "The Line of Least Resistance" (1907), a story that recalls an Apache raid by Chief Nana. Three years after the story first appeared in *Out West, The Saturday Evening Post* serialized an extended version of "The Line of Least Resistance"; the story was published later as a novel under the same title.

In "The Trouble Man" (20 November 1909), the circumspect John Wesley Pringle contrasts with the impulsive Jeff Bransford. Jeff prevails in a conflict between cowmen and sheepherders—Anglos and Mexicans, respectively—by outwitting a lynch mob. Pringle calls Jeff a "trouble man" because Jeff often overcomes trouble without fighting. Watching Jeff cow the mob without shooting teaches a young novice how the moral code works among honorable Westerners on either side of an issue. The novice also learns that surfaces are deceptive—that an easygoing attitude does not necessarily indicate the truth of a man's character. Rhodes later developed this theme of initiation more fully in *The Trusty Knaves* (1933).

Attracted by Rhodes's early fiction in *Out West,* Henry Wallace Phillips–creator of the humorous "Red Saunders" and "Agamemnon Jones" stories–met the author, and they collaborated on several works between 1905 and 1908. Typically, Rhodes supplied the plot, scene, and characters, while Phillips combined all three into marketable fiction. One of their best stories together was Rhodes's first contribution to *The Saturday Evening Post,* the magazine that serialized most of his best work until his death. "The Numismatist" appeared in the periodical on 3 February 1907 and was based on an incident related to the presidential election of 1884. The story describes a gambling spree that culminates in an election bet, in which the devious houseman loses to a shrewder man with quicker hands. The first-person narrative, uncharacteristic of Rhodes's work, resembles the post–Civil War humor of Mark Twain and his colleagues on the lecture circuit. During the 1910s Rhodes also collaborated with Lawrence Yates–of *The Oswego Gazette*–and Agnes Morley Cleaveland on several stories.

With the publication of his novelette, *Good Men and True* (1910), the Gothic style of Rhodes's early work succumbed to plots governed by ratiocination and intrigue–plots resembling, for example, Edgar Allan Poe's Dupin tales, such as "Murders in the Rue Morgue" (1841) and "The Case of the Purloined Letter" (1845), and Stevenson's mystery narratives about "The Suicide Club" (collected in the first volume of *New Arabian Nights,* 1882). *The New York Times* review of *Good Men and True* described the novel as a fast-paced, vivid tale about the Mexican border that mixes both drama and humor in a broadly appealing way. The novelette exemplifies Rhodes's use of codes and logic to resolve problems, of literary allusion as a component of plot, and of an engaging hero to oppose a wealthy villain. Because his villains are usually identified early, the mystery is generally a matter not of who is guilty but how the questions that are answered prove guilt and how the problems are resolved.

In *Good Men and True* the main character, Jeff Bransford, is kidnapped by syndicate leader S. S. Thorpe when Jeff inadvertently becomes involved in a botched assassination. Impressed with Jeff's fighting ability, Thorpe invites him to join the gang, holding him a comfortable prisoner while Jeff contemplates his decision. Jeff uses literary passages for encoded communications between himself and the "good men and true" among his associates; by working out the code, his friends trace and release him, then capture the crooks. *Good Men and True* is one of Rhodes's brightest stories;

apart from a violent scene near the beginning in which Jeff is almost killed, a scintillating humor brightens the dialogue. Similarly ratiocinative and entertaining is "Consider the Lizard" (*Saturday Evening Post,* 1913), in which a train is hijacked by bandits whom the hero of the story, Johnny Dines, exposes as the sheriff, railroad detective, and posse.

Rhodes usually wrote in the oral tradition of his father rather than according to tight, formal guidelines. Although he worked out the story before putting anything on paper, he revised extensively–thus drafting according to oral tradition but refining with a commitment to art and craft. The pressure he imposed on himself as an artist distressed him to the extent that he hated writing for money yet readily drafted essays and editorials for little pay. He was also fond of sending long letters to admirers and fledgling authors.

Stylistically, Rhodes has no peer among Western authors, and given his limited formal education, his command of language and erudition were extraordinary. Allusions to the Bible and to authors ranging from Geoffrey Chaucer and William Shakespeare to Henry James and William James typically season his writings. This intertextual allusiveness and irony, however, escaped those of Rhodes's reviewers, who criticized him for being too literary. In hindsight his fiction reflects a technique similar to that employed by Ezra Pound and T. S. Eliot, whose reputations in poetry made them unlikely peers for a Western writer such as Rhodes. Indeed, Rhodes's literary allusions were no more a matter of esoteric decoration than those used by avant-garde poets, such as Pound, in the 1910s and 1920s. Rhodes's abundant references–whether explicit or covert–carry charged, complementary meaning from the originals into his own texts. Yet, as the Eastern professor in *The Line of Least Resistance* (1958) tells Westerner Don Kennedy after Kennedy quotes from Robert Browning, "A cowman who quotes Browning–and quotes so very much to the point–is properly the object of suspicion" among Easterners like the professor.

The eclectic Rhodes knew that his stories had little in common with the formulaic "shoot-'em-ups" of Zane Grey, Clarence Mulford, and other popular authors who exploited the myth of the Wild West in romances printed in the tens of thousands of copies. While Rhodes considered himself a Western author, not a writer of "Westerns," few publishers distinguished his fiction from the pulp romances, and they consequently sought corresponding sales–which Rhodes could not achieve after his works progressed from serials to books. He resented that his books in the United States were poorly marketed and had merely modest sales, while abroad the British editions of his first few novels sold extremely well.

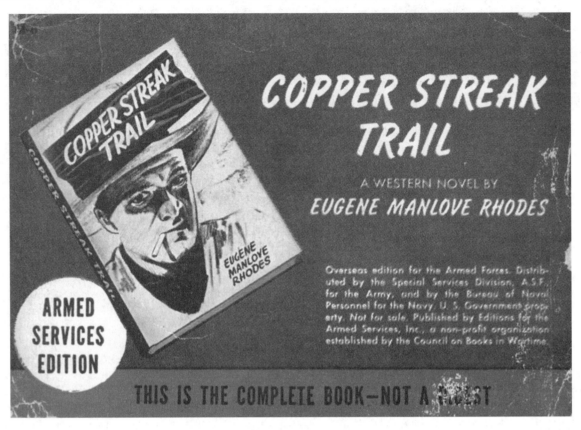

*Cover for the 1943 edition, published for armed forces personnel in World War II, of Rhodes's 1922 novel about two partners who are almost cheated out of their Arizona copper mine (Bruccoli Collection, Thomas Cooper Library, University of South Carolina)*

Because he accurately described the life he knew, Rhodes was identified as a realist by prominent Western authors and critics. According to DeVoto in "The Novelist of the Cattle Kingdom," his introduction to May D. Rhodes's book about her husband, *The Hired Man on Horseback: The Life and Personal Writings of Eugene Manlove Rhodes* (1938), Rhodes's authenticity pertains not only to externals but also to "the beliefs and aspirations" that gave a short, vivid period of American history its vitality. In *A Bar Cross Man: The Life and Personal Writings of Eugene Manlove Rhodes* (1956), Hutchinson noted that Rhodes could depict these truths well because

> Every major tile in the whole mosaic of frontier development . . . was laid down at Engle–so compressed in time and physical compass that one man could see and be a part of it all. It was this happenstance of history that was recorded, firsthand, in Rhodes' writings. They were always regional, . . . but they were innately true to a much greater area.

At the same time, although Rhodes strived to be authentic in his fiction, he detested literary realism. He believed that one should not confuse the historical and topographical accuracy of his novels with the critical realism of William Dean Howells and Sinclair Lewis, the naturalism of Upton Sinclair and Theodore Dreiser, or the psychological "nightmares" of Sherwood Anderson. Nor should one connect Rhodes's penchant for authenticity with the derisive pessimism–the "bilge and poisonous stuff" in his own words–of writers whom he called the mostly humorless, anti-American "Young Intellectuals" in personal letters and in signed editorials written in the 1920s. Among this latter group, Rhodes admired H. L. Mencken for his writing but condemned Mencken's social and political observations. Rhodes expressed his hostility toward all these writers–who were, in his view, modernists–in vehement letters, in published commentaries, and occasionally in fiction. For Rhodes, the ideas of these authors emphasized the shortcomings of American culture instead of the promise and glory of the nation, and they were promoted by well-to-do complainers rather than doers. These realists proselytized that "man is mastered by circumstances; it is the business of a man to prove that he will be damned first," he wrote in a long digression in *Stepsons of Light* (1921), expressing his critical views. Equally damning from his perspective was how the realists consider "culture as an end in itself, and not as a means for service." As Hutchinson suggested in his introduction to the University of Nebraska Press edition (1967) of *Beyond the Desert*–which first appeared in 1934 and is different from the story of the same name that was published in 1914–Rhodes "made real the ideal values" of the "Westering" legacy.

Although some readers at the time had difficulty accepting Rhodes's characters as authentic, the author insisted that most personages in his fiction were based on either acquaintances or a composite of them and that he had portrayed them accurately. In addition, Rhodes said that the actual people from whom he derived his characters were even more interesting and witty in the flesh than in his representations. To Vincent Starret he wrote in 1928, "Sez you, my cowboys were purely imaginary. Sez I–they are actual people." In *Stepsons of Light,* acknowledging complaints that he would "pick the best at their best, and shield with silence their hours of shame and weakness," Rhodes said, "it is true. I take my own risk by that; but for them, it is what they have deserved."

As C. L. Sonnichsen observed in his essay "The Bard of the Tularosa" for *Tularosa: Last of the Frontier West* (1960), Rhodes's "basic belief" was that

> the cowman is a rough and ready frontier citizen, and he lives by a set of principles which the town dweller does not understand. Often this puts him outside the formal codes of law; but when the chips are down, he is ready to sacrifice himself for a woman, a friend, or a principle.

For Rhodes, these high principles constitute an unwritten code, a formulation of moral order in the West. Sonnichsen adds that Rhodes consistently isolated "the core of good in the 'bad' man" and "pictured him calmly choosing death so that a woman or a child might not suffer."

This moral code represents the foundation of order in Rhodes's life and stories as well. According to Hutchinson in his essay about Rhodes for *Twentieth-Century Western Writers* (1982), "Rhodes limned in fiction the values that he held to be those held by the best of the humans he had known as well as by himself–truth, honor, valor, communion with God, fortitude, and magnanimity." Rhodes rarely drank liquor, which he considered the cause of most violence and killings, and he always felt "a passion for the underdog." Cleaveland, a writer and an admiring longtime acquaintance, described him as "a truly noble character" and pointed out that he treated women and their reputations with courtly respect. To Rhoda Williams, a librarian with whom he maintained a lifelong correspondence after

meeting her in Los Angeles, he wrote on 30 December 1921 that any

> book which *may*–not will but may or might–make it easier or more probable for some girl to "go over the edge"–well it is a heavy responsibility to leave it lying around the house in the name of art.

In Rhodes's stories, sexual activity is barely implicit; to him, love was "high enchantment," while "the moderns" saw it as "an affair of the jungle or the barnyard." He refused to read some of Jack London's fiction because he suspected it would be "off-color."

In contrast to his virtuous cowpunchers, Rhodes's villains are judges, lawmen, lawyers, bankers, or large-scale ranchers who rarely manifest a redeeming feature and exploit the law for their own advantage. According to Hutchinson in his introduction to *The Rhodes Reader* (1957), Rhodes typically drew his villains from the East because "the salient truth about the west-that-was" is "that the West was the captive, exploited province of the financial, political, and industrial East." These malicious types should not be confused with the essentially benign figures who occasionally operate outside the law but fall into the tradition of bad men who are good, such as Ross McEwen in *Pasó por Aquí,* translated as *He Passed by Here.*

Both during and after his first stay in New Mexico, Rhodes anticipated its statehood, but despite repeated promises from the U.S. government New Mexico had not become a state by 1910–four years after he had left for New York. For Rhodes, the omission of New Mexico from the union still rankled, and on 6 May 1911 he exposed his anger and disappointment in "The Barred Door," an essay published by *The Saturday Evening Post.* The essay ends with an ironic request not for statehood but for protection against more unkept promises. Perhaps Rhodes's sustained pressure toward statehood was indirectly influential in hastening it, for New Mexico became the forty-seventh state less than a year later in January 1912.

Rhodes's second novelette, *Bransford in Arcadia; or, The Little Eohippus* (1914) again features Jeff Bransford, the hero of *Good Men and True.* Serialized in *The Saturday Evening Post* two years before book publication, critics reviewed *Bransford in Arcadia* favorably for its action, authenticity, and its protagonist–although they acknowledged occasional gaps in credulity. *Bransford in Arcadia* incorporates a change of identities, including a gender switch. Adhering to the Western code, Jeff refuses to implicate Ellinor Hoffman, whom he adores, when he is unjustly tried for murder, although he could legally regain his freedom by explaining that they were together when the murder occurred. Framed by a char-

Published Weekly

The Curtis Publishing Company

Cyrus H. K. Curtis, President

George H. Lorimer, First Vice-President
John B. Williams, Second Vice-President
Walter D. Fuller, Second Vice-President
and Secretary. Philip S. Collins, Second
Vice-President and Treasurer
Fred A. Healy, Second Vice-President
and Advertising Director

Independence Square, Philadelphia

# THE SATURDAY EVENING POST

### Founded A°D¹ 1728 by Benj. Franklin

Copyright, 1932, by The Curtis Publishing Company in the United States and Great Britain. Title Registered in U.S. Patent Office and in Foreign Countries. Entered as Second-Class Matter at the Post-Office Department, Ottawa, Can.

George Horace Lorimer
EDITOR

Thomas B. Costain, A. W. Neall,
Wesley Stout, W. Thornton Martin,
Graeme Lorimer,
Associate Editors

Entered as Second-Class Matter, November 18, 1879,
at the Post Office at Philadelphia. Under Act of
March 3, 1879. Additional Entry at Columbus, O.,
St. Louis, Mo., Chicago, Ill., Indianapolis, Ind.,
Saginaw, Mich., Des Moines, Ia., Portland, Ore.,
Milwaukee, Wis., St. Paul, Minn., San Francisco,
Cal., Kansas City, Mo., Savannah, Ga., Denver, Colo.,
Louisville, Ky., Houston, Tex., Omaha, Neb., Ogden,
Utah, Jacksonville, Fla., New Orleans, La., Portland,
Me., and Los Angeles, Cal.

Volume 205    5c. THE COPY    PHILADELPHIA, P.A., OCTOBER 1, 1932    $2.00 By Subscription (52 issues)    Number 14

# THE PROUD SHERIFF

*"We'll Make a Try of it Together, Then—Fifty-Fifty," Said Spinal. "I've Got More Men Coming"*

## By Eugene Manlove Rhodes

THE gray dump of the Echo mine clung desperately to a red hill in a tangle of wild red hills, lost between tangled ranges; the enormous black crest of the Continental Divide overhung and dwarfed them; and all the world was hills. So, in mid-ocean, all the world is sea.

Against a sheltering face of rock beside the tunnel mouth, heaped sotol made a mattress, gold and black, with the ground for a bedstead, and a thin and tarpaulined bed roll spread out to top it. The brown stock of a rifle showed at the end of the canvas. Then came the kitchen—three flat rocks for fireplace; a neat stack of split cedar, coffeepot, frying pan, bake oven. A ten-pound lard can which was a teakettle, and a ten-pound lard can which was a bean pot. Oaken kegs stood in the shade—the water system. A battered old McClellan saddle hung in a juniper tree beyond, with saddle blankets, bridle, a sawbuck packsaddle, pack sacks and rope. Under the juniper stood the smallest of portable forges and a sack of charcoal.

Such was the Echo outfit. The owners sat upon two stones—Dad Wilson and Otey Beach—a bent old man and a slender boy, each with a tin cup of hot black coffee. They were in conference, really. But this was long ago, and they called it "making medicine" in that time and place.

Dad Wilson sighed. "My specs is real spotted," he said. He breathed upon them, polished them with a dingy blue bandanna, readjusted them, and peered again at the list of supplies he was making with a stubby pencil on the back of an old location notice. He crossed out one item, substituted another and sighed again. "Not enough *dinero* for tobacco and coffee both. And we both use coffee. I'll have to smoke wild grapevine leaves till the fourth. They ain't so bad. Otey, I do wish we could make out to get a box of ca'tridges. Then we'd live high."

Otey nodded. He was a slim, awkward and freckled towhead of twenty, who wore a faded blue shirt and faded blue overalls, a shapeless hat and

3

*First page of the serialization of Rhodes's only novel in which a lawman is the hero (reprinted with permission of The Saturday Evening Post, © 1932 [Renewed] BFL&MS, Inc.)*

acter named Lake, another powerful, wealthy thief like Thorpe, he flees to Mexico and leaves others to expose the banker's guilt. Unknowingly, Jeff is aided in his escape by Ellinor, who disguises herself as a man—a play on gender that Shakespeare often employed to comic effect and that unites the dual crime-love plots of *The Little Eohippus.*

Literary allusions abound in this novelette. Rhodes re-creates one of Topsy's dialogues from Harriet Beecher Stowe's *Uncle Tom's Cabin; or, Life among the Lowly* (1852) and alludes to additional works such as Shakespeare's *Hamlet* (circa 1600–1601) and Lewis Carroll's *Alice's Adventures in Wonderland* (1865). *The Little Eohippus* also invokes Alfred Tennyson, Charlotte Perkins Gilman, Albion W. Tourgée, and Poe. Many devotees of Rhodes read his narratives for their accurate depiction of the Tularosa region, and readers who delve more deeply into them for themes and patterns appreciate their authenticity as a convincing context for a different mode of literary truth.

Rhodes's next novelette, *Hit the Line Hard,* first appeared in 1915 in serial form in *The Saturday Evening Post* and was published as a book—accompanied by a reprint of *Good Men and True*—in 1920. *Hit the Line Hard* tells the story of Neighbor Jones and how he outwits a group of thieves who have stolen a young Easterner's inheritance. By inciting dissension and distrust among them, Jones provokes one member into stealing from the others, whereupon Jones in turn robs the thief with all the loot. *The Desire of the Moth* (1916) followed the periodical publication of *Hit the Line Hard* and boasts two of the writer's most admirable figures, Christopher "Kitty" Foy and John Wesley Pringle. Because Foy is likely to defeat the crooked Sheriff Lisner in a forthcoming election, Lisner and his men plot to kill him in a barroom fight; when that plan fails Lisner frames him for murder, but Foy escapes to a mountain cave. Pringle rescues him and tricks Lisner's men into admitting that the sheriff himself is the killer.

Pringle's pictorial language harks back to the style of speech used by tall-tale heroes, such as the legendary keelboatman, Mike Fink, of early nineteenth-century frontier folklore. "You are a rhomboidinaltitudinous isosohedronal catawampus, George!" Pringle tells one of Lisner's men after overcoming him. Later, Pringle adapts lines from *Hamlet*—"Men are but dust, they tell us. Magnificent dust!"—when, expressing Rhodes's own optimism, he tells the trapped sheriff that the world, "in the long run, is going right. You can't beat the Game!" This Emersonian sense of essential right and good also exposes Rhodes's religious viewpoint, laid bare in Pringle's explanation:

I don't bother much about a blue tin heaven or a comic-supplement hell, but I'm right smart interested in right here and now. It's a right nice little old world, take it by and large, and I like to help out at whatever comes my way.

Reviewers favored *The Desire of the Moth* chiefly for Rhodes's humor and light narrative style. The novelette was republished in 1920 with *The Come On,* a complementary shorter work of decidedly lightweight fare. In *The Come On,* which reflects Rhodes's passion for poker, a gang of Eastern confidence men are outwitted by a presumed yokel from New Mexico who, before heading for New York, had bluffed his way into winning a high-stakes poker game with experienced players.

In April 1916 *Redbook* magazine brought out "The Bird in the Bush," which Hutchinson called "one of the most readable yarns that Rhodes ever wrote"; the author himself regarded the story as "ultra-whimsical." The narrator, Andrew Jackson Aforesaid Bates, speaks in a picturesque Western vernacular and tells his story quite some time after it has occurred. Despite a staged robbery and bungled killing, "The Bird in the Bush" is essentially a comedy in which coincidence protects Bates from being murdered, provides him with half the money that was to be paid to his assassin, and enables the daughter of the man behind the plot to elope with her sweetheart.

The longest and most complex of Rhodes's novels is *West Is West* (1917). His only title published by the H. K. Fly Company, *West Is West* was marred by hundreds of typographical errors upon its first appearance. *West Is West* consists of eight tales loosely joined by transitions to sustain a vaguely unifying love story. While love themes recur in Rhodes's longer narratives, sensuality and illicit sex are rarely even suggested—yet two examples of the latter appear in the book. Sandy MacGregor sacrifices his life to protect Bennie May Morgan from losing her honor through a fake marriage arranged by her villainous would-be seducer; later in the novel, a professional gambler saves another young woman from losing her virtue in a bawdy house. An account of Sandy's sacrifice is the central issue of the story "Beyond the Desert," which Rhodes had published in *McClure's* three years earlier in 1914. In *The Proud Sheriff* (1935), adultery in the background of the narrative motivates a character to murder.

While inscribing a copy of *West Is West* to Eugene Cunningham, the author of *Triggernometry* (1934), Rhodes acknowledged, "this is all short stories—only I *called* it a novel." In *Eugene Manlove Rhodes: Cowboy Chronicler* (1967), Edwin W. Gaston Jr. identi-

*Illustration for the final installment, published in* The Saturday Evening Post *on 9 June 1934, of Rhodes's novel about a greedy landowner and a crooked deputy who try to cheat the hero out of his ranch (reprinted with permission of* The Saturday Evening Post, *© 1934 [Renewed] BFL&MS, Inc.)*

fies seven plots in Rhodes's novel—a structure comparable to the labyrinth of Daedelus. *The New York Times* recognized its conglomerate nature but praised the book as one that will fulfill the expectations of Rhodes's readers for excitement.

In May 1919 Rhodes addressed current international events in "No Mean City," published in *The Saturday Evening Post*. Set during World War I, which had formally ended late in the preceding year, the story is based on a German plot to destroy the huge Elephant Butte Dam near Engle in order to release enough water to flood the vast region surrounding it and drown thousands of inhabitants. Seventy-two-year-old Uncle Ben Teagardner and a young former convict foil the plot and kill the disguised Germans. Teagardner draws the leader into a quicksand trap, watches him sink to the hips, then leaves him to die slowly—an unusually grim conclusion in Rhodes's canon.

In late 1919 he traveled alone to Los Angeles, where he spent three years visiting his mother and arranging for motion-picture rights to his novels but wrote little fiction. During Rhodes's stay in Los Angeles, *Stepsons of Light*—which had been serialized in *The Saturday Evening Post* in the autumn of 1920—came out as a book the following year. Years later, in

a letter from January 1930 to Antoinette Mar Buchanan, Rhodes said that of all his fiction *Stepsons* is "by far the best—beyond all comparison." In the book, when Deputy Sheriff Big Ed Caney and Jody Weir murder a man to steal his claim before it is registered, Johnny Dines—also the main character of "Consider the Lizard"—is framed for the crime. As his own defense attorney against an arrogant prosecutor in the closing courtroom scene, he dominates the proceedings in a scenario reminiscent of the melodramatic performance given by the title character in Mark Twain's *Pudd'nhead Wilson, A Tale* (1894). In *Stepsons of Light* Rhodes attacks lawyers in general through the outspoken judge, who criticizes them for "browbeating witnesses and prisoners" and complains that they "take a mean advantage" of their "privileged position to be overbearing and arrogant." When Johnny exposes Caney's guilt, Caney draws and fires in court, but Charlie See of the Little World is faster, and the deputy is killed. Reviewers typically found the novel authentic and exciting, and the extended digression on realism in the third chapter was noted without comment.

After *Stepsons of Light* Rhodes's next published work was a collection of three essays, *Say Now Shibbo-*

*leth* (1921), which takes its title from the first one. In the book he denounces elitism in language and, especially, the way that class-conscious snobs employ vernacular American speech to deride the habits and appearance of those who use it. Rhodes implies throughout that he himself is a Westerner with minimal formal education yet nonetheless displays erudition, wit, and artful language skills.

*Copper Streak Trail* (1922) was Rhodes's next published novel; it first appeared as a serial in April 1917 in *The Saturday Evening Post* under the title "Over, Under, Around or Through." The most unusual feature of this novel is its double setting in the East and the West. Stanley Mitchell, a young man on the verge of disinheritance by his wealthy Uncle McClintock, leaves the East Coast for Arizona, where he meets Pete Johnson. Together they decide to develop a copper mine, and, seeking capital, Pete travels to Vesper, New York, the home of Stanley's well-to-do cousin, Oscar, a devious attorney. Neither Pete nor Stanley realizes that Oscar is conspiring against them with C. Mayer Zurich, a Tucson-based financial mogul who knows about the copper lode but not its location. The conspirators frame Stanley in Arizona and Pete in Vesper so that both are temporarily jailed, but when the plot is exposed, Uncle McClintock backs the mine and leaves his estate to Stanley.

A distinctive twist at the end of *Copper Streak Trail* shows that however distasteful Zurich may be, as a Westerner he conforms to the code when he refuses to take unfair advantage of Pete and Stanley by jeopardizing a child. *The New York Times* praised Rhodes's authenticity and Western sympathy, but the *Boston Transcript* strangely found the novel rambling and dull. In London the *Times* lauded its realism and considered the New York scenes a lively, entertaining farce and thus a welcome respite from the usual Western format.

Upon his return to Apalachin from Los Angeles in 1922, Rhodes and his wife entered a period of increasing weakness and ill health that continued on and off for the rest of their lives. Rhodes's chronically weak lungs were readily subject to bronchitis, which seriously debilitated him for long periods, and he suffered from heart disease that worsened with time. May, too, was frail and worn, largely from her constant and devoted care of her husband. Between the serialization of "No Mean City" in mid 1919 and the publication of *Once in the Saddle* in April 1925, Rhodes brought out no new fiction—although works that appeared previously in serial form came out as books during this period. He did, however, publish essays on diverse topics—most notably "The West That Was" (*Photodramatist,* September 1922), in which he praised

serious Western writing; criticized the popular horse-opera and movie conception of the West as loaded with gunfighters but devoid of day-to-day cowpunchers; and attacked "The Young Intellectuals," who have "declared war" on America. In "The West That Was" Rhodes suggests that ordinary readers should see actual cowboys as the readers see themselves. The similarity between his suggestion and Eliot's address to the hypocritical reader as "mon semblable,–mon frère!" in *The Waste Land* (also published in 1922) should be recognized, even if in a different light, by all who insist that Rhodes and other serious Western authors of his day–such as Owen Wister and Andy Adams–were writing of a different world. Rhodes also commenced publishing poetry again, including "A Song of Harvest" (*Sunset,* June 1923), which celebrates the work ethic and independence fostered in the grateful poet by his father–"my warrior-sire"–and pictures Rhodes offering the fruits of his toil to the "Master of Harvests."

In November 1923 Rhodes became embroiled in a controversy generated by Stuart Henry in a review of *North of 36* (1923) by Emerson Hough, who had died the previous year. When Hough had visited New Mexico in 1904, he met and encouraged Rhodes, then still unknown, and Rhodes defended him two decades later, partly on the grounds of loyalty to a deceased friend. Henry praised *North of 36* as a thriller but scorned the book for its historical inaccuracy. On reading the review Rhodes challenged him, drawing powerful support from such noted Western authors as Webb, William MacLeod Raine, and Charles A. Siringo, but Henry held firm, and the squabble ended in a draw.

In heart and spirit Rhodes had never left New Mexico, but he had maintained excellent relations with May's family and agreed to remain in Apalachin while her parents lived. With the death of her mother on 1 April 1925, however, both of her parents were gone, and Rhodes was eager to return to New Mexico. By the time they left New York in the late summer of 1926, *The Saturday Evening Post* had serialized two more short novels, later published jointly: *Once in the Saddle, and Pasó por Aquí* (1927). Rhodes thought little of *Once in the Saddle,* but along with action and authenticity, the work manifests unusual social concern. Pliny Mullins seeks land for himself and plans to establish a new community for the coal miners working nearby, a story line that resonates more with the critical realism that Rhodes condemned than with Western romance. When Pinky Ford, a young rancher whom Pliny knows, is thrown from his horse and killed, Cal Pelly–boss of a much larger spread– sees the accident but leaves the corpse alone; it is unlikely to be found. Pelly robs the paymaster on his way to the mines, intending to frame Pinky with the robbery, but Mullins determines where the guilt lies, captures Pelly, and prepares to charge him with robbery and murder. Because rain has erased all the tracks, Pelly cannot establish his innocence in Pinky's death. The *Saturday Review of Literature* praised the melodramatic ending and unity in this story but preferred its companion.

*Pasó por Aquí* has been called Rhodes's finest work. In the narrative Ross McEwen evades capture after robbing a bank by riding into a sparsely populated mountainous region. He reaches Lost Ranch, where a Hispanic family is suffering desperately from diphtheria. Disregarding his own safety, he remains there to nurse the family until Sheriff Pat Garrett notices his distress signal. On arriving and recognizing the weary outlaw, Garrett conceals his identity as an officer of the law after seeing what McEwen has done for the sick family. After more aid arrives, Garrett helps Ross leave the region and avoid capture. As its Spanish title suggests, *Pasó por Aquí* ennobles the Hispanic people of New Mexico and highlights their kindliness and courtesy rather than the malicious, vulgar features for which convention at the time called. Furthermore, the author's sensitivity to imaginative language and his application of it in both literary and vernacular styles are evident throughout. Rhodes effectively uses the regional setting in *Pasó por Aquí* yet transcends it to expose universal truths. Years later, Rhodes published "In defense of Pat Garrett" in *Sunset* (July 1927), a spirited defense of the actual Pat Garrett in response to Walter Noble Burns's quasi-historical account in *The Saga of Billy the Kid* (1926). Burns had romanticized Billy as a heroic outlaw and implicitly maligned Garrett as unfair for shooting the gunman without warning when he came upon Billy unexpectedly in the dark. Rhodes argued that Garrett's only choices were to kill or be killed.

When the Rhodeses returned to New Mexico late in 1926, they discovered that additional roads and construction had altered the face of the region dramatically since twenty years before. The change was not to his taste, but he was ecstatic to be back home. Rhodes and his wife settled first in Santa Fe—where the social life proved excessive, the altitude was too high for his precarious health, and their cost of living became too expensive. Money for the couple was almost always tight. The earnings from Rhodes's writing went mostly into paying bills and repaying debts. He was so generous at times that he gave away what he could not afford to lose, and too often he wrote for little or nothing.

After a year he and May moved to Alamogordo. In March 1928 he agreed to collaborate with Clement Hightower on an autobiographical account, to be published by Houghton Mifflin, of old-time New Mexicans whom Rhodes had known. Rhodes received occasional advances from the publisher, but despite substantial and continuing work on the project, the book was never completed. A few months later Rhodes suffered a nearly fatal heart attack while May was visiting back East, and afterward his condition steadily weakened. Because their delicate health and the normal exigencies of rural living made their existence too risky in New Mexico, they immigrated to California early in 1931.

During his last few years in New Mexico, however, Rhodes published five stories and several more poems. "The Tie-Fast Men," "Aforesaid Bates," "Trail's End," "Shoot the Moon," and "Maid Most Dear" all appeared in *Cosmopolitan* between July 1927 and August 1930 and focused on the Little World cattlemen and their foes. In "Aforesaid Bates" a banker plots to force Bates into relinquishing his ranch for the mortgage due, but Bates outwits him, saves the ranch, and regains financial stability. The story recalls the Old Southwestern frontier tales with their emphasis on duplicitous horse swaps and the down-home art of swindling the swindler. Rhodes was spending his last summer in New Mexico when the fifth story, "Maid Most Dear," was published. Although it has many violent passages, the story appeals partly because of its central figure, the seemingly frivolous Eddie Early, but chiefly by virtue of its amusing dialogue—which includes Eddie's rendition of a courting song from Shakespeare's *Measure for Measure* (1604). The outlaws of the "K P" outfit are based on Butch Cassidy's Wild Bunch during the period when their activities centered in Alma, New Mexico—which Rhodes renames Shard in the story.

Rhodes published more than a dozen poems between 1928 and early 1932, including "The Hired Man on Horseback," which appeared in *Adventure* (1 February 1928) and is probably the best of all his poetry; the lyric laments how the public demeans—or, at best, disregards—the heroic service rendered by ordinary cowpunchers driving herds up the trail. Similarly, "Pegasus at the Plow" (*Saturday Evening Post*, 20 July 1929) implicitly compares a steady, hardworking plow horse with a man who labors persistently and well. *The Saturday Evening Post* also published "Engle Ferry" (10 August 1929), a poem that nostalgically memorializes the ferry crossing of the Rio Grande when the waters were too high to ford—a site now covered by the lake created by Elephant Butte Dam:

Engle Ferry is lost and gone,
 Engle Ford and Ferry.
The owl hoots over Babylon,
Deep over Ur the sand is blown,
Carthage city is sown with salt,
And never again will wagons halt
 At Engle Ford and Ferry—————
Silence and darkness keep watch and ward
On Engle Ferry and Engle Ford.

By the time that Rhodes's next short novel appeared in *The Saturday Evening Post* on 18 April 1931, he and May had moved to Pacific Beach, near San Diego. *The Trusty Knaves* was published in book form in 1933 and again featured an actual notorious outlaw, Bill Doolin of the Wild Bunch fame, as a principal figure. In Rhodes's book, Doolin's criminal nature is suppressed by a noble desire to drive out the prosperous thieves who are passing as honest men and controlling the town of Target—historically, Deming—New Mexico. "Here is Bill Doolin to the life," Rhodes said about the character, acknowledging "some needful exceptions." Doolin had been hiding out at his ranch in the summer of 1896 after escaping from jail, making plans to start anew with his wife and family; Rhodes believed that Doolin had wanted "to begin life afresh," which probably explains why he was portrayed so favorably in the novel. Having come to Target to case its bank, Doolin—using the alias 'Enry Hawkins—perceives the corrupt community leaders and successfully helps Pres Lewis and "a few trusty knaves" to fight them. Then Doolin leaves, with Pres alone knowing his real identity.

Hypocrisy, trickery, and subterfuge are rife in *The Trusty Knaves* and make the work somewhat more complex than most of his others. Adding to the complexity is a subtheme perhaps derived from Wister's *The Virginian* (1902)—the introduction of a naive young Easterner eager to learn and adopt Western ways. Like Wister's tenderfoot, John Cecil Calvert—also known as Frank John—listens, learns, and acts as tutored by Pres Lewis and 'Enry Hawkins. Perhaps for this reason *The Saturday Review of Literature* compared *The Trusty Knaves* to the "drawling charm" of *The Virginian*. *The New York Times* praised Rhodes's book for its authenticity, liveliness, wit, and humor.

Early in 1932 Rhodes was preoccupied with publishing a ten-volume Bar Cross Edition of his works, but despite a heavy investment of time and energy, he did not manage to generate enough financial support to realize the project. Although his health steadily deteriorated during his last few years, keeping him bedridden part of the time, he never lost the spark that fired his imagination and good humor. In October 1932 *The Saturday Evening Post* serialized

*Rhodes about two weeks before his death in June 1934*

*The Proud Sheriff,* but Rhodes did not live to see its publication as a book.

One of Rhodes's last novels, *Beyond the Desert* (1934), appeared first in serial form in *The Saturday Evening Post* only a month before his death. The title is identical to that of a story he had published in 1914, but the two works are otherwise unrelated. Although Rhodes's original manuscript was rejected as too long, he was ailing and desperate for cash; when the editors offered to accept it for $4,500 if they could cut it, he quickly agreed. In the novel Jake Fowler is a greedy landowner, who, in anticipation of a fortune, attempts to squeeze Bud Copeland—a recreation of Rhodes in his twenties—out of Bud's ranch, because Fowler knows that the incoming railroad will want to buy fresh water for its steam locomotives from whomever owns the land. Bat Cremony, a deputy working for Fowler, helps to burn down Bud's ranch house and to steal his best stock. Then Bat attempts to kill Bud, but the latter shoots first, and Bat appears destined to hang for murder. After he pays his mortgage, Bud makes a citizen's arrest of Fowler, who heads for prison.

Rhodes died on 27 June 1934. His body was returned to his spiritual home of New Mexico, where May arranged for his burial in Rhodes Pass, high in the San Andres Mountains near his old homestead.

Rhodes's last work adapted from serialization for publication as a novel was the posthumous *The Proud Sheriff*, which departs from his other narratives because its hero is a lawman. When an innocent youth is framed for murder, Sheriff Spinal Maginnis allows himself to be ambushed and kidnapped. While in control, the outlaws mockingly address Maginnis with names of famous Western lawmen, subjecting him to ridicule over his apparent cowardice. He overcomes his guard, however, gaining his own opportunity for sarcasm, and addresses the disarmed man by using the names of Shakespearean characters equally appropriate to the situation. Ultimately, Maginnis shoots the killer, who draws on him. According to *Readers News*, *The Proud Sheriff* shows Rhodes rebuilding the "lost Western soul" of America through "swift imagery, simple and heartfelt."

In 1938 May Rhodes published an anecdotal biography of her husband. She portrays him as careful in his writing yet impulsive in his behavior; as good-humored and compassionate yet quickly and violently confrontational; as a bronco-busting, baseball-playing hero incongruously devoted to books, the pen, principles, and herself. May Rhodes died in Apalachin on 21 March 1957.

Throughout his career Rhodes depicted a romantic past on which he looked back with reverence and nostalgia. As a person Rhodes was no moral relativist. With few exceptions, his heroes are young, lithe, and handsome, and his heroines—all lovely maidens of twenty—are bright, witty, and independent. In 1930, regarding his female characters, he admitted: "I am not fortunate with my ladies. In my day this was a masculine world." Rhodes's malicious figures usually look and speak like villains, and they are evil to the core, yet by the end of the story, good inevitably and undoubtedly triumphs over evil. Although the structure and plot of Rhodes's works are occasionally hampered by digressions, the action in them is nonetheless often breathtaking. He hints that in the dialogue and in narrative style alike guns are subordinate to wit. Moreover, as he wrote in *Stepsons of Light*, a cowboy "working for the brand" during roundup trusted and depended upon his fellows, and he "joyed in their deeds. And to forget self in the thought of others is for so long to reach life at its highest." For Rhodes, cowpunchers held to a code mutually understood and accepted by all, and each was responsible for maintaining it. In Rhodes's fiction, those who dissent are the villains. For him, there was no middle ground.

Indeed, Eugene Manlove Rhodes stands in the light of Ralph Waldo Emerson, not in the shadow of Karl Marx, Sigmund Freud, or Jean-Paul Sartre. Goodness was fundamental in Rhodes's personal code and art—along with justice, generosity, and compassion. May Rhodes recalls in *The Hired Man on Horseback* that, nearing the end of his life at the height of the Great Depression, in poor health and with little money, her husband declared: "Hard times—but . . . I see ground for a thinking man to hope for a decent world—in time. I recommend this planet as a good place to spend a lifetime."

## Bibliographies:

Vincent Starret, "The Published Writings of Eugene Manlove Rhodes," in May D. Rhodes, *The Hired Man on Horseback: My Story of Eugene Manlove Rhodes,* May D. Rhodes (Boston: Houghton Mifflin, 1938), pp. 257–264;

W. H. Hutchinson, "Check List of Eugene Manlove Rhodes' Writing," in his *A Bar Cross Man: The Life and Personal Writings of Eugene Manlove Rhodes* (Norman: University of Oklahoma Press, 1956), pp. 392–407;

Hutchinson, *A Bar Cross Liar: Bibliography of Eugene Manlove Rhodes Who Loved the West-That-Was When He Was Young* (Stillwater, Okla.: Redlands Press, 1959);

Hutchinson, "Rhodes, Eugene Manlove," in *Twentieth-Century Western Writers,* James Vinson, ed., with a preface by C. L. Sonnichsen (Detroit: Gale Research, 1982), pp. 635–639;

Richard W. Etulain, "Eugene Manlove Rhodes," in *A Bibliographical Guide to the Study of Western American Literature* (Lincoln: University of Nebraska Press, 1982), pp. 228–229;

Etulain and N. Jill Howard, eds., *A Bibliographical Guide to the Study of Western American Literature,* revised (Albuquerque: University of New Mexico Press, 1995), pp. 345–346.

## Biographies:

May D. Rhodes, *The Hired Man on Horseback: The Life and Personal Writings of Eugene Manlove Rhodes* (Boston: Houghton Mifflin, 1938);

Agnes Morley Cleaveland, *No Life for a Lady* (Boston: Houghton Mifflin, 1941), pp. 278–287;

B. F. Day, *Gene Rhodes, Cowboy: (Eugene Manlove Rhodes)* (New York: Messner, 1954);

W. H. Hutchinson, *A Bar Cross Man: The Life and Personal Writings of Eugene Manlove Rhodes* (Norman: Oklahoma University Press, 1956);

Henry Herbert Knibbs, "Gene Rhodes," in Rhodes's *The Proud Sheriff* (Norman: University of Oklahoma, 1968);

Frank M. Clark, *Sandpapers: The Lives and Letters of Eugene Manlove Rhodes and Charles Fletcher Lummis* (Santa Fe, N.Mex.: Sunstone Press, 1994).

**References:**

Mark Busby, "Eugene Manlove Rhodes: Kesey Passed by Here," *Western American Literature,* 15 (Summer 1980): 83–92;

Bernard DeVoto, "The Novelist of the Cattle Kingdom," introduction to *The Hired Man on Horseback: The Life and Personal Writings of Eugene Manlove Rhodes,* by May D. Rhodes (Boston: Houghton Mifflin, 1938), pp. xix–[xliv];

J. Frank Dobie, "Introduction" in *Little World Waddies* (El Paso, Tex.: W. H. Hutchinson, 1946), pp. xiii+; revised as "A Salute to Gene Rhodes," in *The Best Novels and Stories of Eugene Manlove Rhodes,* edited by Frank V. Dearing (Boston: Houghton Mifflin, 1949), pp. xi–xxii;

Jim Lawrence Fife, "Eugene Manlove Rhodes: Spokesman for Romantic Frontier Democracy," dissertation, University of Iowa, 1965;

Edwin W. Gaston Jr., *Eugene Manlove Rhodes: Cowboy Chronicler,* Southwest Writers Series, no. 11 (Austin: University of Texas Press, 1967);

W. H. Hutchinson, "I Pay for What I Break," *Western American Literature,* 1 (Summer 1966): 91–96;

William A. Keleher, *The Fabulous Frontier: Twelve New Mexico Items,* revised edition (Albuquerque: University of New Mexico Press, 1962), pp. 160–174;

Lawrence Clark Powell, *Southwest Classics: The Creative Literature of the Arid Lands, Essays on the Books and Their Writers* (Pasadena, Cal.: Ward Ritchie Press, 1975), pp. 160–174;

Richard Skillman and Jerry C. Hoke, "The Portrait of the New Mexican in the Fiction of Eugene Manlove Rhodes," *Western Review,* 6 (Spring 1969): 26–36;

C. L. Sonnichsen, "The Bard of the Tularosa," in *Tularosa: Last of the Frontier West* (New York: Devin-Adair, 1960), pp. 202–227, 316–318.

**Papers:**

Although Eugene Manlove Rhodes's papers are dispersed among the holdings of numerous libraries and museums, the more substantial collections are at Stanford University and at the University of New Mexico. In addition, occasional manuscripts and at least several dozen letters are variously housed at Brigham Young University, Knox College, New Mexico State University, and the Southwest Museum Library of Los Angeles.

# Richard Rodriguez

*(31 July 1944 –    )*

Gary Layne Hatch
*Brigham Young University*

See also the Rodriguez entry in *DLB 82: Chicano Writers, First Series.*

BOOKS: *Hunger of Memory: The Education of Richard Rodriguez* (Boston: Godine, 1982);
*Days of Obligation: An Argument with My Mexican Father* (New York: Viking, 1992);
*Brown: An Erotic History of the Americas* (New York: Viking, 2002).

OTHER: Ken Light, *To the Promised Land,* introduction by Rodriguez (New York: Aperture, 1988);
Lauren Greenfield, *Fast Forward,* afterword by Rodriguez (New York: Knopf, 1997);
Geoff Winningham, *In the Eye of the Sun,* introduction by Rodriguez (New York: Norton, 1997);
Stephanie Barron and others, *Made in California* (Berkeley: University of California Press, 2000)—includes "Where the Poppies Grow" by Rodriguez;
Richard B. Stolley, *Life: Century of Change: America in Pictures, 1900–2000* (Boston: Little, Brown, 2000)—includes an essay by Rodriguez.

SELECTED PERIODICAL PUBLICATIONS–
UNCOLLECTED: "Leo Carillo as Andy Hardy and Other Losses of White Liberalism," *Columbia Forum* (Summer 1973): 35–40;
"Going Home Again: The New American Scholarship Boy," *American Scholar,* 44 (Winter 1974): 15–28;
"The Achievement of Desire: Personal Reflections on Learning 'Basics,'" *College English,* 40 (November 1978): 239–254;
"Aria: A Memoir of a Bilingual Childhood," *American Scholar,* 50 (Winter 1980): 25–42;
"A Minority Scholar Speaks Out," *Forum* (November 1982): 2–5;
"California Christmas Carols," *California,* 8 (December 1983): 99;
"Success in U.S., Stranger in Land of His Roots," *U.S. News & World Report,* 99 (19 August 1985): 41;

*Richard Rodriguez (photograph by Christine Alicino; courtesy of the author)*

"The Head of Joaquin Murrieta," *Nuestro,* 9 (November 1985): 30–36;
"The Mexicans Among Us," *Reader's Digest,* 128 (March 1986): 171–176;
"Mexico's Children," *American Scholar,* 55 (Spring 1986): 161–167;
"Across the Borders of History," *Harper's,* 274 (March 1987): 42–49;
"Literature and the Nonliterate," *Literature of the Oppressed,* 1 (Fall 1987): 6–19;
"What Is an American Education?" *Design for Arts in Education,* 89 (November–December 1987): 44–46;

"The Fear of Losing a Culture," *Time,* 132 (11 July 1988): 84;

"I Will Send for You or I Will Come Home Rich," *Mother Jones,* 13 (November 1988): 26–33;

"Oh, Ireland," *Wilson Quarterly,* 13 (Winter 1989): 136;

"Late Victorians: San Francisco, AIDS, and the Homosexual Stereotype," *Harper's,* 281 (October 1990): 57–61;

"Mixed Blood," *Harper's,* 283 (November 1991): 47–56;

"La Raza Cosmica," *New Perspectives Quarterly,* 8 (Winter 1991): 47;

"L.A. Watching the Riots," *TV Guide,* 40 (23 May–29 May 1992): 18–21;

"The Birth Pangs of a New L.A.," *Harper's,* 287 (July 1993): 20–21;

"Our Neighbors, Ourselves," *New York Times,* 14 December 1993, A 25;

"Luck Ends, Heroism Begins," *U.S. News & World Report,* 116 (31 January 1994): 37;

"Gang Stats: Hard Truths from the Streets of East L.A.," *Mother Jones,* 19 (January 1994): 46;

"Gangstas," *Mother Jones,* 19 (January–February 1994): 46–54;

"Is It Really Because O. J. Simpson Is Black?" *U.S. News & World Report,* 117 (4 July 1994): 6–7;

"The Assassination of Luis Donaldo Colosio," *Hispanic Law Journal,* 1 (1994): 73;

"Go North, Young Man," *Mother Jones,* 20 (July–August 1995): 30–35;

"America Has No Secrets Anymore," *Utne Reader* (November–December 1995): 72–73;

"Illegal Immigrants: Prophets of a Borderless World," *New Perspectives Quarterly,* 12 (Winter 1995): 61–62;

"True West," *Harper's,* 293 (September 1996): 37–46;

"A Community of Dreams," *Historic Preservation Forum,* 10 (Winter 1996): 9;

"Growing Up Old," *U.S. News & World Report,* 122 (7 April 1997): 60–69;

"The Other '60s," *The American Enterprise,* 8 (May 1997): 34;

"Crossing into El Futuro," *Forbes* (30 November 1998): 278–279.

Richard Rodriguez's life and writing are about balance and paradox–the joining together of seemingly irreconcilable differences. In his life as a writer he balances between journalism, particularly broadcast journalism, and essay writing, particularly memoir. The straightforward, argumentative style of his journalistic prose contrasts with the lyrical and highly rhetorical style of many of his essays. He is most famous for his autobiographical writing, but he considers his autobiographical works collections of essays rather than extended autobiographical narrative. He is an impor-

tant regional writer but conceives of a national audience. Although he is well known as an Hispanic author who writes extensively about the issues facing Hispanic Americans, he also wonders about his ability to speak for his race. He has been an outspoken opponent of Affirmative Action programs, particularly in higher education, but he also recognizes that he is a beneficiary of these programs.

Rodriguez was born in San Francisco on 31 July 1944, the son of Leopoldo and Victoria Moran Rodriguez. His father worked at several jobs before becoming a successful dental technician and introducing his family to middle-class life in California. His mother worked as a clerk-typist. Both parents emigrated from Mexico at a young age and met and married in the United States. Richard moved with his family to Sacramento as a child, where he graduated from Sacred Heart, a Catholic private school. He graduated with a B.A. degree in English from Stanford University in 1967 and received an M.A. degree in religious studies from Columbia University in 1969. Rodriguez did graduate work at the University of California, Berkeley (1969–1972, 1974–1975), and at the Warburg Institute in London (1972–1973) as a Fulbright fellow. He was awarded a fellowship from the National Endowment for the Humanities for 1976–1977. Rodriguez left a promising career as a university professor to become a writer and has written full-time since 1981, both as an essayist and as a journalist. When his autobiography, *Hunger of Memory: The Education of Richard Rodriguez,* appeared in 1982, Rodriguez was awarded a gold medal from the Commonwealth Club, the Christopher Award for autobiography, and the Anisfield-Wolfe Award for Race Relations. His second book, *Days of Obligation: An Argument with My Mexican Father* (1992), was selected as a finalist for the Pulitzer Prize in 1993. Rodriguez is an editor for Pacific News Service, which distributes stories focusing on California on the news wire, and contributing editor for *Harper's, U.S. News & World Report,* and *The Los Angeles Times Sunday Perspective.* In addition to his many published essays, he has made significant contributions to broadcast journalism. In 1992 he won an Emmy Award for his short historical piece "Pearl Harbor Anniversary." In 1997 Rodriguez received the George Foster Peabody Award for his essays on American life as part of the PBS "News Hour with Jim Lehrer." His awards include the Frankel Medal from the National Endowment for the Humanities and the International Journalism Award from the World Affairs Council of California. He has also contributed to two BBC documentaries. Recently, Rodriguez has expanded his writing into a new medium, the Internet. He frequently contributes to *Jinn,* the on-line magazine of the Pacific News Service. Many of his

*Dust jacket for Rodriguez's first book (1982), which he describes as "essays impersonating an autobiography"*

essays have also been translated into Spanish and made available online. Rodriguez currently lives in San Francisco.

Rodriguez's first published writing focuses on his responses to Affirmative Action programs in higher education and bilingual education programs in primary schools, issues that also occupy much of his attention in his first book, *Hunger of Memory*. In his introduction to *Hunger of Memory* Rodriguez characterizes his book as a collection of essays, not an autobiography in the traditional sense. He describes the collection as "essays impersonating an autobiography; six chapters of fugue-like repetition." The major theme of this "fugue" is language. Rodriguez writes, "I write about poetry; the new Roman Catholic liturgy; learning to read; writing; political terminology. Language has been the great subject of my life." Rodriguez's interest in language drew him to the study of English language and literature in college, particularly the literature of the English Renaissance, but his interest in language began much earlier. "From

my first day of school," he states, "I was a student of language. Obsessed by the way it determined my public identity. The way it permits me here to describe myself, writing. . . ."

"Aria," Rodriguez's first essay in *Hunger of Memory,* deals directly with the problem of language and identity, particularly how language helps one to establish a "public" identity. Probably because it focuses on the intersection of language, identity, and schooling, "Aria" is also one of the most frequently anthologized essays in college writing textbooks. In this essay Rodriguez describes his first encounter with schooling, a private Catholic school where he first learned English. From this moment, he gradually began to lose his intimate relationship with his family, his parents in particular, not because he spoke more English than Spanish but because he had formed a public identity apart from his private identity. He writes that "while one suffers a diminished sense of *private* individuality by becoming assimilated into public society, such assimilation makes possible the achievement of *public* identity." For Rodriguez, this diminished sense of self, the "hunger of memory," is tragic, not only because of the loss of self, of intimacy, and of innocence, but also because this loss is a necessary part of growing up. In response to supporters of bilingual education, Rodriguez contends that it is learning public discourse rather than learning English that separates Hispanic children from their origins.

In his second essay, "The Achievement of Desire," Rodriguez describes his encounter in the British Library with a book that changed the direction of his life, Richard Hoggart's *The Uses of Literacy* (1957). Approaching the end of his graduate education, Rodriguez had been awarded a Fulbright fellowship to finish his dissertation on Renaissance poetry at the British Library. Frustrated with the progress of his research and reflecting on his twenty years of schooling, Rodriguez began to read anything he could find in the library on education and literacy. Hoggart's book introduced him to the "scholarship boy," the working-class English student who finds success in school. Seeing himself in Hoggart's description, Rodriguez realized something for the first time: "A primary reason for my success in the classroom was that I couldn't forget that schooling was changing me and separating me from the life I enjoyed before becoming a student." He had finally realized that although his education had separated him from the intimate world of his parents, it had also given him the language he needed to think about this separation and to care about it. What had initially separated him from his family also allowed him to return (though transformed) "unafraid to desire the past" and to achieve "the end of education."

To express this paradox, Rodriguez draws upon his study of Renaissance literature. In the first line of *Hunger of Memory* Rodriguez describes himself in terms of Caliban: "I have stolen their books," he writes, "I will have some run of this isle." Education–the stealing of Prospero's books–has allowed Rodriguez to move from "a childhood of intense family closeness" and "extreme public alienation" to his current position as "a middle-class American," fully assimilated into American society. Because of his separation from what he desires, Rodriguez is able to describe his set of essays as a "pastoral," but a pastoral quite different from the classical and Renaissance genres. Rodriguez describes the Renaissance pastoral as a "high, courtly genre." He argues that "upper-class pastoral can admit envy for the intimate pleasures of rustic life as an arrogant way of reminding its listeners of their difference–their own public power and civic position." Rodriguez describes his work as "middle-class pastoral"; it is "a more difficult hymn" because "the middle class lives in a public world, lacking great individual power and standing." As a result of its lack of power, in the pastoral he conceives, the middle class is "tempted by the pastoral impulse to deny its difference from the lower class–even to attempt cheap imitations of lower-class life." The literary path Rodriguez has laid out for himself not only requires him to portray his past and his desire for that past but also to define what separates him from that past.

In "Credo," Rodriguez describes a progression in his religious identity similar to his progression as a scholar. He writes, "I was *un católico* before I was a Catholic." In this brief line Rodriguez describes the contrast between the private religious life of his Hispanic family and the public religious community of the gringo church they attended down the street. The Mexican Catholicism of his family was part of the "intense family closeness" that he felt as a child, and the gringo church represented the American public life reinforced in his schooling. Like the institution of school, the institution of the church increased the distance Rodriguez felt from his family, but like school, the church also allowed him to return, but not to the same state. His devotion to the church includes a sense of loss, partly because of changes in the church and partly because of changes in himself. The church changed the mass from Latin to English and eliminated much of the ritual and ornament. "It has been 'modernized,'" Rodriguez explains, "tampered with, demythologized, deflated. . . . No longer is the congregation moved to a contemplation of the timeless. Rather it is the idiomatic one hears. One's focus is upon this place. This time. The moment. Now." In many ways, he argues, the American Catholic Church has become more Protestant, but Rodriguez admits that he has,

too, even though he persists in claiming his Catholicism. As Catholics such as he find themselves "increasingly alone in their faith," Rodriguez argues that they become more like seventeenth-century Protestant reformers who "were attempting to form through their writings a new kind of Christian community–a community of those who share with each other *only* the experience of standing alone before God." Although he longed for the intimate Catholic world of his family, Rodriguez also realized that he could not be a traditional Catholic in a world that was no longer Catholic. In another instance of his use of paradox, Rodriguez shows his belief in the face of disbelief and argues that his realization of his position as a "Protestant" allows him to adhere more strongly to Catholicism.

In "Complexion" and "Profession" Rodriguez addresses how his education in public language has separated him from those people who share his same skin color. "Complexion" is the best example from this collection of a middle-class pastoral, for in it Rodriguez describes his fascination with *los braceros* (manual laborers, literally "men who work with their arms"). These poor but powerful field laborers replace the shepherds in the Renaissance pastoral. Rodriguez's mother had encouraged Rodriguez to seek an education in order to escape the world of hard labor, but as a senior at Stanford, Rodriguez felt the desire to experience the world of *los braceros,* so he worked as part of a construction crew for the summer. At first, Rodriguez enjoyed the hard physical work, but eventually he came to understand that he was idealizing the world of the laborer, just as Renaissance poets had idealized the world of the shepherd. He writes, "The adventure of the summer seemed suddenly ludicrous. I would not shorten the distance I felt from *los pobres* (the working poor) with a few weeks of physical labor. I would not become like them. They were different from me." Despite the similarities in skin color and racial heritage, Rodriguez's education favored him. He had learned to speak with a public identity that left him less vulnerable and alienated than working-class Hispanics and poor Mexican laborers. Like the pastoral poet, he could sing as a shepherd, but his position insured that he could never really be one.

In "Profession," Rodriguez describes the role of race in higher education, both from his experience as a student and from his experience as a scholar and teacher. Although he benefited from Affirmative Action programs, Rodriguez felt uneasy in his position as a "highly-rewarded minority student." He argues, "I was not–in a *cultural* sense–a minority, an alien from public life. . . . The truth was summarized in the sense of irony I'd feel at hearing myself called a minority student: The reason I was no longer a minority was because I had become a student." The paradox is that those people

*Dust jacket for Rodriguez's second book, a collection of essays published ten years after* Hunger of Memory

his cultural and public identity and were disappointed to find that he was more interested in talking about John Milton. Rodriguez also felt increasingly uncomfortable with professional success—the many offers extended to him as a "Chicano" intellectual. "The contradictions of affirmative action" had finally caught up with him, and the only response he could make was to leave higher education.

"Mr. Secrets," Rodriguez's final essay in *Hunger of Memory,* may be the most paradoxical of all and the most revealing of how his public education had alienated him from his intimate family identity. He confesses, "I am writing about those very things my mother has asked me not to reveal." The paradox is that although he can share his most intimate thoughts and reflections with a public audience, Rodriguez is uneasy sharing them directly with his family. He writes, "One must sometimes escape to the company of strangers, to the liberation of the city, in order to form new versions of oneself." His choice to be a writer, to give full voice to the public language that he has acquired, has alienated him even further from his family—to the extent that when his mother objected to his discussing family matters publicly, she wrote to him in English, and Rodriguez answered in English. But Rodriguez acknowledges that his public self is his own creation and not the same as his private self. "In the company of strangers," he admits, "I do not reveal the person I am among intimates. My brother and sisters recognize a different person, not the Richard Rodriguez in this book." But then he argues that the closeness of family gatherings precludes the careful examination of self that Rodriguez attempts in these essays. Paradoxically, he must alienate himself from those people most intimate with him, through the public act of writing, to allow others to understand him most intimately.

Rodriguez ends *Hunger of Memory* with the silence of his father. At an intimate family Christmas party—conducted in English, the public language the children and grandchildren have acquired—Leopoldo Rodriguez is a "silent witness" to the events. His uncertain command of English has been compounded by a loss of hearing, but his silence also symbolizes his alienation from the culture his children have been assimilated into.

In his second collection of essays, *Days of Obligation: An Argument with My Mexican Father,* Rodriguez begins where he left off in *Hunger of Memory,* with his father—an attempt to understand something about his parents by visiting Mexico. In writing this book, Rodriguez had worked with two other titles, "The Color Brown" and "Mexico's Children." In a way, the title he chose demonstrates his interest in responding to his father's silence. This argument is one he never had with his father because it is really an argument with his

who had not been educated well could not really benefit from admission to higher education based on race—they were assured of failure—and those people who had been educated, those who could benefit most from a college education, had lost much of their racial identity through the process of assuming a public identity. For Rodriguez, his skin color was no longer an indicator of his cultural identity. The political term *race* referred to culture, not biology. "All Mexican-Americans certainly are not equally Mexican-Americans," he writes. When Rodriguez became an outspoken critic of Affirmative Action and bilingual education programs, he was popular because of his skin color, because he represented a "minority" view. This reaction occurred despite his argument that *class* plays a more important role in social mobility than race does.

As a teacher and scholar, Rodriguez felt the same uneasiness he had felt as a student. Students came to him for information on Chicano/Chicana literature or to enlist his support on racial issues. They had made the assumption that his skin color indicated

father's Mexico, Rodriguez's attempt to understand what is "Mexican" about Mexican Americans. But although Rodriguez uses his own experience in *Days of Obligation,* this collection of essays is even less of an autobiography than *Hunger of Memory.* Rodriguez is clearly more influenced by his work as a journalist. Rather than "a parable for the life of its reader," one phrase Rodriguez uses to describe *Hunger of Memory,* Rodriguez takes on a broader range of issues. His desire to understand his relation to his parents becomes an opportunity to discuss U.S.-Mexican relations, the future of California, illegal immigration, and gay culture in San Francisco. Rodriguez uses "place" as theme in *Days of Obligation;* he explores a myriad of ideas related to the conflict, balance, and paradox of California, the place where Catholic, tragic, lyric, ancient Mexico mixes with the Protestant, comic, prosaic eastern culture of the United States. Rodriguez's family, the intense focus of *Hunger of Memory,* is just one thread in the larger fabric he weaves in *Days of Obligation.*

The lyrical and copious visual imagery in *Days of Obligation* may also indicate the effect of Rodriguez's journalism on his essay writing, particularly his work in broadcasting. In his print journalism Rodriguez addresses directly many of the issues he addresses indirectly through his essays. And his print journalism is much like that of other writers. But Rodriguez's broadcast journalism shows significant innovation in the medium, particularly the development of the "visual essay," for which Rodriguez won the Peabody Award for excellence in broadcasting. The visual essay allows Rodriguez to play his prose off the images captured by the camera. *Days of Obligation* brings this visual element into his writing, as Rodriguez tries to re-create in writing what the camera captures on tape.

"My Parents' Village" and "India" show Rodriguez's individual struggle to understand who he is by where he came from, his parents' Mexico. But he also uses this struggle to address the broader issue of racial identity. He notes that Americans tend to talk about race in discrete terms—black and white. But for Rodriguez, the best term to describe himself is mestizo, a term used to refer to people of mixed European and Indian descent (most Mexicans). But even the term *Indian* is confused. "Race" helps readers see the complexity of racial categories and also introduces Rodriguez's vision of community achieved through balance and paradox, a vision instantiated in Los Angeles and Mexico City. He writes, "Mexico City is the capital of modernity, for in the sixteenth century, under the tutelage of a curious Indian whore, under the patronage of the Queen of Heaven, Mexico initiated the task of the twenty-first century—the renewal of the old, the known world, through miscegenation."

*Dust-jacket photograph of Rodriguez for* Days of Obligation
*(photograph © Brit Thurston)*

"Late Victorians" shifts the scene to San Francisco, but the theme is similar, the complexity of social categories and the balancing of opposites that must prevail for community to survive. In this chapter, however, the focus is not race but gender and the AIDS epidemic that swept through the city in the 1980s. Rodriguez argues, "Few American cities have had the experience, as we have had, of watching the civic body burn even as we stood, out of body, on a hillside, in a movie theater. . . . San Francisco toys with the tragic conclusion." Rodriguez describes the lives of those people affected by the disease, how those people who loved them took care of them, but, moreover, how these lives affected everyone. He writes, "And if gays took care of their own, they were not alone. AIDS was a disease of the entire city. Nor were Charity and Mercy only male, only gay. Others came. There were nurses and nuns and the couple from next door, co-workers, strangers, teenagers, corporations, pensioners. A community was formed over the city." "Late Victorians" shows Rodriguez's redefinition of "community," not the geographic community of the city but the bringing together of the diverse elements of the city, across traditional social categories, into the delicate balance required to address the needs of the suffering. In typical fashion Rodriguez then leads the reader into paradox as he recalls attending the funeral of an AIDS victim at a Catholic church in the Castro district "at a time in the history of the world when the Roman Catholic Church pronounced the homosexual a sinner."

Throughout the remainder of the collection, Rodriguez takes his reader to various locations tied to California and its history—Berkeley, Sacramento, Los Angeles, Tijuana, the famous Spanish missions, and the nineteenth-century hideouts of legendary Joaquín Murrieta. These places all provide occasions for Rodriguez to explore the complexity of California and both the promise and the peril, what he calls the tragedy and the comedy, presented in its communities. *Days of Obligation* addresses the problem, typified in California, of finding a common core, a common set of American values and beliefs in a society moving toward greater and greater diversity, in which economic and social pressures weaken the common bonds that define communities. But Rodriguez realizes that what brings people together will always be an uneasy balance, a set of paradoxes.

## Interviews:

Scott London, "Crossing Borders: An Interview with Richard Rodriguez," *Sun* (August 1977): 1;

Virginia I. Postrel and Nick Gillespie, "On Borders and Belonging: An Interview with Richard Rodriguez," *Utne Reader,* 68 (March–April 1995): 76;

Elisabeth Sherwin, "Rodriguez Remembers Sacramento in His Books: An Interview with Richard Rodriguez," *Printed Matter,* 4 May 1997;

Paul Crowley, S. J., "An Ancient Catholic: An Interview with Richard Rodriguez," in *Catholic Lives, Contemporary America,* edited by Thomas J. Ferraro (Durham, N.C.: Duke University Press, 1997), pp. 59–65;

Postrel and Gillespie, "The New, New World," *Reason* (April 1999): 14;

Timothy S. Sedore, "Violating the Boundaries: An Interview with Richard Rodriguez," *Michigan Quarterly Review,* 38 (Summer 1999): 424–446.

## References:

Norma Alarcon, "Tropology of Hunger: The 'Miseducation' of Richard Rodriguez," in *The Ethnic Canon: Histories, Institutions, and Interventions* (Minneapolis: University of Minnesota Press, 1995), pp. 140–152;

Jesse Aleman, "Chicano Novelistic Discourse: Dialogizing the Corrido Critical Paradigm," *MELUS,* 23 (Spring 1998): 49–64;

Gerdien Blom, "Divine Individuals, Cultural Identities: Post-Identitarian Representations and Two Chicana / o Texts." *Thamyris,* 4 (Autumn 1997): 295–324;

Jennifer Browdy de Hernandez, "Postcolonial Blues: Ambivalence and Alienation in the Autobiographies of Richard Rodriguez and V. S. Naipaul," *AutoBiography Studies,* 12 (Fall 1997): 151–165;

Martin A. Danahay, "Breaking the Silence: Symbolic Violence and the Teaching of Contemporary 'Ethnic' Autobiography," *College Literature,* 18 (October 1991): 64–79;

Danahay, "Richard Rodriguez's Poetics of Manhood," in *Fictions of Masculinity: Crossing Cultures, Crossing Sexualities,* edited by Peter F. Murphy (New York: New York University Press, 1994), pp. 290–307;

Jeffrey Louis Decker, "Mr. Secrets: Richard Rodriguez Flees the House of Memory," *Transition: An International Review,* 61 (1993): 124–133;

Jerzy Durczak, "Multicultural Autobiography and Language: Richard Rodriguez and Eva Hoffman," in *Crossing Borders: American Literature and Other Artistic Media,* edited by Jadwiga Maszewska (Peoria, Ill.: Spoon River Press, 1992), pp. 19–30;

Laura Fine, "Claiming Personas and Rejecting Other-Imposed Identities: Self-Writing as Self-Righting in the Autobiographies of Richard Rodriguez," *Biography* (Spring 1996): 119–136;

Lauro Flores, "Chicano Autobiography: Culture, Ideology and the Self," *Americas Review,* 18 (Summer 1990): 80–91;

W. Lawrence Hogue, "An Unresolved Modern Experience: Richard Rodriguez's *Hunger of Memory,*" *Americas Review,* 20 (Spring 1992): 52–64;

Monika Kaup, "The Architecture of Ethnicity in Chicano Literature," *American Literature,* 69 (June 1997): 361–397;

Michael Krasny and Ariel Sabar, "What is Community?" *Mother Jones,* 19 (May–June 1994): 22;

Antonio C. Marquez, "Richard Rodriguez's *Hunger of Memory* and New Perspectives on Ethnic Autobiography," in *Teaching American Ethnic Literatures: Nineteen Essays,* edited by John R. Maitino (Albuquerque: University of New Mexico Press, 1996), pp. 237–254;

Marquez, "Self & Culture: Autobiography as Cultural Narrative," *Discurso,* 7 (1990): 51–66;

Julio Marzan, "Richard Rodriguez's *Hunger of Memory* and the Poetics of Experience," *Arizona Quarterly,* 40 (Summer 1984): 130–141;

Kevin R. McNamara, "A Finer Grain: Richard Rodriguez's *Days of Obligation,*" *Arizona Quarterly,* 53 (Spring 1997): 103–122;

Gustavo Perez-Firmat, "Richard Rodriguez and the Art of Abstraction," *Colby Quarterly,* 32 (December 1996): 255–266;

Tomás Rivera, "Richard Rodriguez' *Hunger of Memory* as Humanistic Antithesis," *MELUS* (Winter 1984): 5–13;

Randy Rodriguez, "Richard Rodriguez Reconsidered: Queering the Sissy (Ethnic) Subject," *Texas Studies in Literature and Language,* 40 (Winter 1998): 396–425;

Rolando J. Romero, "Spanish and English: The Question of Literacy in *Hunger of Memory*," *Confluencia,* 6 (Spring 1991): 89–100;

Shirley K. Rose, "Metaphors and Myths of Cross-Cultural Literacy: Autobiographical Narratives by Maxine Hong Kingston, Richard Rodriguez, and Malcolm X," *MELUS,* 14 (Spring 1987): 3–15;

Ramon Saldivar, "Ideologies of the Self: Chicano Autobiography," *Diacritics,* 15 (Fall 1985): 25–34;

Rosaura Sanchez, "Calculated Musings: Richard Rodriguez's Metaphysics of Difference," in *The Ethnic Canon: Histories, Institutions, and Interventions,* edited by David Liu Palumbo (Minneapolis: University of Minnesota Press, 1995), pp. 153–173;

Ada Savin, "La memoire de la rupture: Richard Rodriguez de *Hunger of Memory* à *Days of Obligation*," *Annales du Centre de Recherches sur l'Amerique Anglophone,* 20 (1995): 131–141;

Paige Schilt, "Anti-pastoral and Guilty Vision in Richard Rodriguez's *Days of Obligation*," *Texas Studies in Literature and Language,* 40 (Winter 1998): 424–441;

Bill Shuter, "The Confessions of Richard Rodriguez," *Cross-Currents,* 45 (Spring 1995): 95–105;

Henry Staten, "Ethnic Authenticity, Class, and Autobiography: The Case of *Hunger of Memory*," *PMLA,* 113 (January 1998): 103–116;

Ilan Stavans, "La identidad de Richard Rodriguez," *Torre,* 10 (April–June 1996): 203–208;

Stavans, "The Journey of Richard Rodriguez," *Commonweal* (26 March 1993): 20–22;

Stavans, "Voices of Our Times: Twentieth-Century Prose," *English Journal,* 82 (November 1993): 145–147;

Norma Tilden, "Word Made Flesh: Richard Rodriguez's 'Late Victorians' as Nativity Story," *Texas Studies in Literature and Language,* 40 (Winter 1998): 442–459;

Alfredo Villanueva-Collado, "Growing Up Hispanic: Discourse and Ideology in Hunger of Memory and Family Installments," *Americas Review,* 16 (Fall–Winter 1988): 75–90;

Manfred Wolfe, "Two Cultures," *American Scholar* (Winter 1994): 145–147.

# Leslie Marmon Silko

*(5 March 1948 – )*

Dennis Cutchins
*Brigham Young University*

See also the Silko entries in *DLB 143: American Novelists Since World War II, Third Series* and *DLB 175: Native American Writers of the United States.*

BOOKS: *Laguna Woman: Poems* (Greenfield Center, N.Y.: Greenfield Review Press, 1974);
*Ceremony* (New York: Viking, 1977);
*Storyteller* (New York: Seaver, 1981);
*After a Summer Rain in the Upper Sonoran* (Madison, Wis.: Black Mesa Press, 1984);
*Almanac of the Dead: A Novel* (New York & London: Simon & Schuster, 1991);
*Sacred Water: Narratives and Pictures* (Tucson, Ariz.: Flood Plain Press, 1993);
*Yellow Woman* (New Brunswick, N.J.: Rutgers University Press, 1993);
*Yellow Woman and a Beauty of the Spirit* (New York & London: Simon & Schuster, 1996);
*Rain,* by Silko and Lee Marmon (New York: Library Fellows of the Whitney Museum of American Art, 1996);
*Gardens in the Dunes* (New York: Simon & Schuster, 1999);
*Conversations with Leslie Marmon Silko,* edited by Ellen L. Arnold (Jackson: University Press of Mississippi, 2000).

PRODUCED SCRIPTS: *Running on the Edge of the Rainbow: Laguna Stories and Poems,* video, University of Arizona Radio-TV-Film Bureau, Words and Place Videocassette Series, 1978;
*Estoyehmuut and the Gunnadeyah* (Arrow Boy and the Witches), motion picture, by Silko and Dennis W. Carr, 1980.

RECORDINGS: *The Laguna Regulars and Geronimo,* read by Silko, Akwesasne Notes, 1977;
*Leslie Marmon Silko,* read by Silko, University of Missouri, 1991.

OTHER: "The Man to Send Rainclouds," "Yellow Woman," "Tony's Story," "Uncle Tony's Goat,"

*Leslie Marmon Silko (photograph by Nancy Crampton; from the cover for* Conversations with Leslie Marmon Silko, *2000)*

"A Geronimo Story," "Bravura," and "From Humaweepi the Warrior Priest," in *The Man to Send Rainclouds: Contemporary Stories by American Indians,* edited by Kenneth Rosen (New York: Viking, 1974), pp. 3–8, 33–45, 69–78, 93–100, 128–144, 149–154, and 161–168;
"Replacing Confusion with Equity: Alternatives for Water Policy in the Colorado River Basin," by Silko, Helen M. Ingram, and Lawrence A. Scaff,

in *New Courses for the Colorado River: Major Issues for the Next Century,* edited by Gary D. Weatherford and F. Lee Brown (Albuquerque: University of New Mexico Press, 1984), pp. 177–199;

*Yellow Woman* (New Brunswick, N.J.: Rutgers University Press, 1993);

"Interior and Exterior Landscapes: The Pueblo Migration Stories," in *Landscape in America,* edited by George F. Thompson and Charles E. Little (Austin: University of Texas Press, 1995), pp. 155–169;

"Language and Literature from the Pueblo Indian Perspective," in *Tales Within Tales: Apuleius Through Time,* edited by Constance S. Wright and Julia Bolton Holloway (New York: AMS Press, 2000), pp. 141–155.

SELECTED PERIODICAL PUBLICATIONS–
UNCOLLECTED: "Aaron Yava," *Yardbird Reader,* 3 (1974): 98–103;

"An Old-Time Indian Attack Conducted in Two Parts," *Yardbird Reader,* 5 (1976): 77–84;

"Here's an Odd Artifact for the Fairy-Tale Shelf," *Impact/Albuquerque Journal,* 9 (October 1986): 10–11.

Despite that her most successful work is an early one, Leslie Marmon Silko remains a central voice in Native American literature. Her first novel, *Ceremony* (1977), is taught in colleges and universities around the world. Scholarship on her body of work continues to grow, and sales of *Ceremony* have remained constant, indicating its continuing popularity with readers. Silko seems pleased with the popularity of her writings: in a 1986 interview with Kim Barnes in the *Journal of Ethnic Studies* Silko reported, somewhat jokingly, that she wanted her books to "make it to the wire racks at the check-out stands" of the supermarket. Certainly her work has been received well both by the reading public and by scholarly critics. She is the recipient of many grants and awards, including a National Endowment for the Arts Discovery Grant for short fiction (1974), a Pushcart Prize for poetry (1977), a MacArthur Foundation "genius" grant (1983), and a Lila Wallace *Reader's Digest* Foundation Writer's Grant (1992).

Though considered a Native American writer, Silko's heritage is mixed. Her great-grandfather, Robert G. Marmon, was a white man from Ohio who came to Laguna Pueblo, in New Mexico, in 1871 as a teacher. He married Maria Anaya, a Pueblo woman, and spent the rest of his life on or near the Laguna reservation. Silko's mother, Mary Virginia Leslie, was part Cherokee, and her father, Leland Howard Marmon, a photographer, was a mixed-blood Laguna Pueblo Indian. In

her writing and speaking Silko has chosen to focus on her Native American ancestors and seldom, if ever, mentions non-Indian relatives. Since the themes of her writing often center on the struggle of those with mixed blood to find acceptance, an understanding of this mixed racial and cultural heritage is crucial to an understanding of her work. In the biographical note to the 1973 edition of *Laguna Woman: Poems,* Silko wrote, "the core of my writing is the attempt to identify what it is to be a half-breed or a mixed-blooded person; what it is to grow up neither white nor fully traditional Indian." Moreover, much of her work–including *Storyteller* (1981), *Sacred Water: Narratives and Pictures* (1993), *Yellow Woman and a Beauty of the Spirit* (1996), and *Rain* (1996)– has self-consciously explored her own familial and cultural roots.

Silko was born Leslie Marmon in Albuquerque on 5 March 1948 and raised near the Laguna Pueblo, northwest of Albuquerque. Because of her mixed cultural and racial heritage, she often found herself on the fringe of Pueblo life. In *Rain* Silko observes that she "grew up in an old house at the foot of the village where the people put Presbyterians and mixed bloods like the Marmons." Per Seyersted, in his 1980 biography of Silko, points out that "the family was included in clan activities, but not to the same extent as full bloods," and that "the young Leslie helped out at ceremonial dances, but did not dance herself." Despite her family's marginal attachment to the Pueblo, both the Laguna lifestyle and the landscape surrounding the pueblo made an indelible impression on her. Perhaps the most important influences on her childhood were those exerted by her great-grandmother Maria, or "A'mooh," and her great-aunt Susie, both graduates of the Carlisle Indian School. From these women Leslie learned the value of a "white" education as well as the importance of traditional and family stories. The importance of her early experiences listening to clan and family stories cannot be overestimated; through them she received her first sense of belonging. Silko reported to Laura Coltelli in 1990 that "the best thing you can have in life is to have someone tell you a story." That sentiment seems to be a result of Silko's view of storytelling as being not so much an event as a paradigm. In the interview with Barnes, Silko called storytelling "a whole way of seeing yourself, the people around you, your life, the place of your life in the bigger context, not just in terms of nature and location, but in terms of what has gone on before, what's happened to other people." The desert climate and the harsh and beautiful landscape of New Mexico also made an indelible impression on Silko's storytelling style. In a letter to poet James Wright dated 17 October 1978 she wrote, "Laguna narratives are very lean because so much of the stories are

*Silko's great-grandmother, Maria Anaya Silko, known as "A'mooh"
(photograph by Lee H. Marmon)*

shared knowledge—certainly descriptions of the river and the river willows are not included in the narratives because it is assumed the listeners already know the river and the willows." Much of Silko's professional career has been spent making these lean Laguna narratives accessible to people who have never heard of Laguna Pueblo.

Education was important to Marmon's family, and because the small school at Laguna did not have a good reputation, her mother arranged for her to attend a private school in Albuquerque, though it meant a one-hundred-mile round trip every day. This emphasis on education sent Leslie on to college at the University of New Mexico. There she met Richard Chapman, and in 1966 the two were married. That same year she gave birth to her first son, Robert William. The couple separated in 1969 and divorced sometime later. In 1969 Silko also graduated summa cum laude in English from the University of New Mexico and published her first short story, "The Man to Send Rainclouds," in the *New Mexico Quarterly*. This story, originally drafted in a creative-writing class, was based partly on a short newspaper story of a funeral and partly on the characters and stories she had grown up with.

Though she had managed to publish her story with relative ease, Silko did not instantly envision a literary career. She had other plans. After graduation she desired to do something for the Laguna people and began law school in the American Indian Law School Fellowship Program at the University of New Mexico. She completed three semesters of law school before dropping out of the program in 1971. Later, in her collection of essays titled *Yellow Woman and a Beauty of the Spirit* (1996), she expressed her frustration with a legal system that "was designed by and for the feudal lords," and that, she lamented, continues to deliver "'justice' only to the rich and powerful." In 1971 she married John Silko, a lawyer, and began to think seriously about a career as a writer. Her second son, Cazimir, was born in 1972.

Silko's first published book was a collection of poetry titled *Laguna Woman* (1974). The poems in this collection are structured by a powerful evocation of landscape and a distinctly Pueblo view of life. Most of them are set, through the use of epigrams, in northeastern Arizona, in Navajo country. Silko begins "Slim Man Canyon" with the note: "early summer, Navajo Nation, 1972, for John." She then describes the canyon "with sandstone rising high above / The rock the silence tall sky and flowing water / sunshine through cottonwood leaves / the willow smell in the wind." In perhaps the central line of the poem Silko declares "Where I come from is like this," implying that the desert landscape helped to shape her identity. The strong emphasis on landscape suggests that any knowledge of self is predicated on a knowledge of the land.

Silko views her poems as "translations" of Laguna myth and folklore, and the verses in *Laguna Woman* seamlessly blend traditional oral mythology and contemporary narratives. With interviewer Barnes, Silko noted, "I use 'translate' in the broadest sense. I don't mean translate from the Laguna Pueblo language to English, I mean the feeling or the sense that language is being used orally." In short, Silko seeks to translate not Pueblo language but a Pueblo worldview. The act of "translation" is clear in "Toe'osh: A Laguna Coyote Story," dedicated to Simon Ortiz, another Pueblo writer. In the poem Silko relates several traditional Coyote trickster tales. In Pueblo and Navajo mythology Coyote is often portrayed as a kind of foolish hero, prone to make humiliating mistakes but also capable of the clever manipulation of other characters. Silko uses Coyote's actions as a metaphor for Ortiz's otherwise inexplicable behavior. She briefly relates a narrative in which a "coyote" (Ortiz) purposefully bumps into people in Wisconsin bars until they say "excuse me." Silko adds, "And the way Simon meant it / was for 300 or maybe

400 years," suggesting that the apologies of the bar patrons should include regret for the colonization of the Americas. Through the juxtaposition of mythology and contemporary events Silko creates a clear analogy between Ortiz's behavior and that of the mythological trickster, Coyote, and she offers at least one model, that of the trickster, for how Indians should deal with whites. Silko also richly illustrates the text with her own drawings; they are not simply decoration but serve to reinforce the metaphors of the poems. Immediately below "Toe'osh: A Laguna Coyote Story," for example, Silko includes a stylized drawing of an American flag with a distinctly Pueblo flavor. The implied criticism of American colonialism is both pointed and humorous.

The publication of *Laguna Woman* marked a change in Silko's life. She began to think of herself not as a failed lawyer but as a successful writer. Twenty-two years after publishing *Laguna Woman* Silko created a somewhat autobiographical character in *Almanac of the Dead: A Novel* (1991) named William Weasel Tail, a poet-activist who, like Silko, dropped out of law school to write poetry. As if explaining her own abandonment of law through this character, she writes, "The people didn't need more lawyers, . . . the people needed poetry. . . . All that is left [for Native Americans] is the power of poetry." By "poetry" she means more than "literature": poems are, for her, part verse, part personal statement, part sacred text, and part legal document.

In 1973, after completing *Laguna Woman*, Silko traveled with her husband, John Silko, to Alaska, and there, a thousand miles from the desert where she grew up, she wrote *Ceremony* (1977). The novel was well received. Frank MacShane, writing for *The New York Times Book Review* (12 June 1977), called Silko "the most accomplished Indian writer of her generation" and suggested that *Ceremony* was "one of the most realized works of fiction devoted to Indian life that has ever been written in this country." Charles Larsen, writing for *The Washington Post* (24 April 1977), added, "*Ceremony* is an exceptional novel–a cause for celebration." In writing this powerful story of a mixed-blood Pueblo war veteran, Silko was certainly influenced by other Native American authors. This novel is, for example, frequently compared to N. Scott Momaday's *House Made of Dawn* (1968). LaVonne Brown Ruoff, in *American Indian Literatures: An Introduction* (1990), calls *Ceremony* "a response to Momaday's ambivalence about his protagonist's future." Silko, though, downplays Momaday's influence. When Barnes, in a 1986 interview for *Journal of Ethnic Studies,* asked Silko about the similarities between *Ceremony* and *House Made of Dawn*, Silko partially avoided the question by responding, "I like *The Way to Rainy Mountain* [another of Momaday's books]

very much, but I would have been doing what I was doing regardless of what Scott had done or not, written or not written."

As does *Laguna Woman, Ceremony* shows the influence of traditional oral literature. Silko had heard many of these stories since childhood; her father was a collector of Laguna folklore and myth and was one of the first people to tape-record Laguna storytellers. Traditional tales and legends often appear in Silko's short stories and poetry, but in *Ceremony* they serve as the central unifying element. Throughout the main narrative of the novel Silko weaves a second, parallel story, a clan myth that concerns the loss and restoration of fertility in the world. In the myth the people become bewitched by an evil magician who leads them away from their traditional religious practices. By the time the people discover their mistake, it is too late: the Corn Mother, the source of fertility and growth, has left them and gone below to the fourth world. In order to restore the fertility of the land the people must lure the Corn Mother back by completing a complicated healing ceremony that cleanses and purifies the land. This myth serves both as a commentary on Tayo's situation and as a model of behavior for him to follow. Silko's mixing of these two genres creates a novel that is distinctly Pueblo. Though set in the recent historical past, much of the action in *Ceremony* seems to take place in a kind of mythical time in which gods and humans coexist. The mixing of genres and the mythic tone are arguably the most important achievements of the novel. They allow Silko to revise history convincingly from a Pueblo point of view. Events that include the arrival of Europeans in the Americas and the invention of the atomic bomb become part of a rich and complex Pueblo story. This literal revision of history in the form of a Pueblo narrative is the heart of the work. Silko begins the novel with two of her own short poems. One of them reads:

> They aren't just entertainment.
> > Don't be fooled.
> They are all we have, you see,
> > all we have to fight off
> > > illness and death.
>
> > You don't have anything
> > If you don't have the stories.

Narratives, Silko suggests, are the way Pueblo peoples understand who they are and control reality. By circumscribing history within the context of Pueblo myth, *Ceremony* gives Native American readers a powerful tool for controlling their own reality and challenges white readers to see the world from a new and different perspective. These accomplishments are, perhaps, the most important ones of the novel.

*Silko in the Cottonwood Wash below Wasson Peak in the Tucson Mountains of Arizona
(photograph by Denny Carr; from Silko's* Storyteller, *1981)*

Like most of Silko's other works, *Ceremony* is difficult to treat critically because of its eclectic, reflexive nature. It resembles the home of Betonie, one of the characters in the novel. A Navajo healer, Betonie lives in a hogan that is stuffed with items ranging from old phone books and out-of-date railroad calendars to ritual items from several different tribes. Betonie's explanation for this odd collection is that "All these things have stories alive in them." They allow Betonie to keep "track of things" in the larger world. The narrative structure of *Ceremony* incorporates a variety of literary materials. Silko weaves traditional Laguna myths and folklore, revisionist American history, and a powerful third-person narrative into an intricate story that defies any simple explanations.

The central character of the novel, Tayo, is a mixed-blood Laguna Indian prodded into volunteering for service during World War II by his cousin Rocky. The two end up serving in the same U.S. Marine outfit in the South Pacific. In the course of their patrols Tayo's squad captures and kills a Japanese soldier. Tayo becomes convinced, however, that

the dead man is actually his Uncle Josiah. Eventually both Tayo and Rocky are captured and are forced to participate in the Bataan death march. Rocky, who has been wounded, must be carried by Tayo and another soldier. During the march through the fly-infested, muddy jungle, Tayo curses the rain and prays that it will end. The rain does not stop, however, and Tayo and the other soldier finally drop Rocky in the mud, where he is killed by a Japanese guard.

Tayo returns to the United States, after having spent a good deal of the war in Japanese prisoner-of-war camps. Upon his homecoming he is transferred directly to a veterans' hospital in California to be treated for mental instability. After his release from the hospital, Tayo returns home and discovers that his Uncle Josiah has, indeed, died while he was away and that his prayers, while they did not stop the rain on the islands, did cause a drought back in New Mexico. Although Rocky had coerced Tayo into joining the army with him, Tayo feels guilt for Rocky's death, for the death of his Uncle Josiah, and for the drought. Wracked with these feelings of guilt, Tayo rarely leaves his bed.

Whereas Tayo has returned from the war a veritable recluse, several of his Pueblo acquaintances have returned emotionally jaded by the violence in which they have taken part and impressed by the affluence of the white world and the former status they enjoyed as soldiers. The unofficial leader of these other veterans is Emo, a sadistic killer who enjoyed torturing and mutilating Japanese prisoners. He carries a bag of human teeth as a trophy and brags to Tayo and the other men that while he was in the army he could make Japanese prisoners "talk fast, die slow." Tayo and Emo exemplify a range of reaction to the war.

Tayo's condition does not improve as time goes by, and eventually his grandmother sends him to Ku'oosh, the local healer. Ku'oosh, unable to help Tayo, sends him to Betonie. The bulk of the novel concerns Tayo's quest, guided by his mentor, Betonie, to find a healing ceremony that will somehow form a bridge between the awful violence and destruction to which he and the other veterans were exposed and the traditional Pueblo life that seems quite pointless in the face of atomic warfare. Silko emphasizes that Tayo's ceremony is performed not only for himself but also for all of the veterans, as well as for all of the Laguna people.

Tayo's retelling of his story at the end of the novel is important because it reflects the power stories have to heal and restore both individuals and cultures. Since Silko feels that stories have an important, living power that is not quantifiable, she uses the power of stories as a common theme in much of her work. In a 1992 interview with Donna Perry, Silko suggests that "there's a kind of living spirit in stories that can't be seen." This spirit is found throughout *Storyteller* (1981), Silko's second book-length work. Although considered a collection of short stories, *Storyteller* is much more complex. In this book she mixes genres—including poetry, short story, myth, autobiographical essay, and photography—in an attempt to re-create a storytelling experience. All of these texts are interrelated. If there is a key to understanding this work it is *context*. In *Storyteller* Silko consciously dismantles the distinction between text and context. In one sense Silko places her poetry, fiction, and essays in an autobiographical, historical, and social context. In another sense, if someone reads *Storyteller* to understand Silko and her Laguna upbringing, then the stories and poems provide unusual insights into the way a writer, a storyteller, thinks.

Although it defied genre conventions by mixing poetry, short stories, essays, myths, and family photos, *Storyteller* received generally good reviews. In a review for *The New York Times* (24 May 1981) Momaday said of the book: "At her best, Leslie Silko is very good indeed. She has a sharp sense of the way in which the profound and the mundane often run together in our daily lives.

And her sense of humor is acute." The photos included in the text are part of the mundane historical and social context Silko strives to re-create. In a letter to Wright, Silko expresses concern over her decision to use several family photographs in the book:

> I suppose that is the nature of the snapshot—it needs words with it. Photographs which speak for themselves are art. I am interested now in the memory and imagination of mine which come out of these photographs.

Silko includes the photos in the book as artifacts of her life and memory, not as art.

The interplay of the different genres included in *Storyteller* is exemplified in the short story "Yellow Woman." The title of the story comes from a Pueblo myth in which the mythical Yellow Woman is seduced and led away from the pueblo to live with Whirlwind Man. Later she returns to her people and gives birth to twin sons, heroes who eventually save the people. The story is preceded by a brief reminiscence in which Silko notes that her great-great-grandfather "had married an Indian woman, Rhonda Touchstone, and then had left Indian country (Oklahoma)." The story of his migration with his Indian wife is parallel to the myth of Yellow Woman. In "Yellow Woman," a Pueblo woman goes walking outside the pueblo and meets a stranger. She is seduced by the man, Silva, and returns with him to his home in the mountains. Throughout the story he calls her "Yellow Woman" in reference to the myth. The woman, who is given no other name in the story, initially refuses to accept his mythical explanation for her abduction. She reasons,

> I will see someone, eventually I will see someone, and then I will be certain that he is only a man—some man from nearby—and I will be sure that I am not Yellow Woman. Because she is from out of time past and I live now and I've been to school and there are highways and pickup trucks that Yellow Woman never saw.

She is unable, though, to find any other explanation for Silva's existence. During a violent encounter between Silva and a white rancher who has accused him of cattle rustling, Yellow Woman leaves and makes her way back to the pueblo. On her way home she decides to lie and tell her family that she was kidnapped by a Navajo. "But," she laments, "I was sorry that old Grandpa wasn't alive to hear my story because it was the Yellow Woman stories he liked to tell best." This short story is followed by a two-part poem called "Cottonwood" that again concerns the abduction of Yellow Woman. The mixing of myth and "reality," as well as the parallels drawn from Silko's own family history, make all of these narratives resonate on several different levels. In mixing

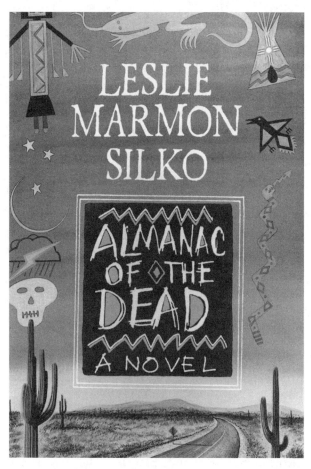

*Dust jacket for Silko's epic 1991 novel, which deals with four hundred years of U.S. history from a Native American perspective*

these genres Silko offers a mythical explanation for Rhonda Touchstone's marriage and migration at the same time that she creates a contemporary, realistic context for an ancient myth.

*Storyteller* reflects many of the themes that dominate Silko's later works. One of the most prominent of these is the exploitation of Native American peoples and lands and the ultimate end of white domination in the Americas. In "Storyteller," the title story, an old Yupik man tells the protagonist that whites "only come when there is something to steal. The fur animals are too difficult for them to get now, and the seals and fish are hard to find. Now they come for oil deep in the earth. But this is the last time for them." The story ends as a murderous white storekeeper, driven by his lusts, chases an Indian woman out into the Arctic winter. She lures him onto a frozen river where he falls through the ice to his death. His fate, Silko suggests, is symbolic of what will happen to all whites bent on the exploitation of Native American lands and peoples.

In 1978 Silko and Wright, whom she had met at a writer's conference in Michigan, began a rich literary

correspondence that was eventually collected and published as *The Delicacy and Strength of Lace* (1985). The letters, written between August 1978 and March 1980, after Wright had read *Ceremony,* touch many different subjects, including Silko's painful divorce from John Silko, the ways in which poetry and fiction are structured and created, and the common things of daily life. Wright's untimely death in 1980 abruptly ended the correspondence. The title of the collection alludes to Wright's mention of lace in a letter dated 14 March 1979. Wright and his wife were visiting Bruges, Belgium, where handmade lace is still created, and he observed that lace had not been much help to the Belgians when they were invaded by Germany. Silko replied, revealing much of her philosophy about art and literature, that its very vulnerability is "the 'good' of the lace–that it is *no good* against bullets." This short exchange suggests that for Silko, art is important because of its weaknesses, not in spite of them.

This very "literary" collection of letters offers interesting insights into Silko's life as well as important contexts for reading her other works. During their correspondence, Silko was in the midst of writing *Storyteller* and was also struggling through divorce. Wright's continued encouragement and praise offered her a much-needed lift at a low time in both her personal life and her professional career. Silko's candor in the letters is revealing. In her first letter she thanks Wright for his praise of *Ceremony* and expresses her own doubts about her place as an American writer: "I feel so much an outsider and alien to mainstream poetic style." Wright's reply reveals his recognition of Silko's genius: "I think it is astonishing to see your mastery of the novel combined with a power of poetry within it." In two letters written in the fall of 1978 Wright praises Silko's evocation "of the landscape of the Southwest." In reply Silko acknowledges that when writing *Ceremony* "it was as if the land was telling the stories in the novel." Such details offer important cues for understanding Silko's writings.

Silko's next novel, *Almanac of the Dead* (1991), did not appear for ten years. Although she wrote many essays (collected in *Yellow Woman and a Beauty of the Spirit*) and book reviews, much of that time was actually spent drafting the novel. In 1988, three years before its publication, Silko noted in the interview with Coltelli that "*Almanac of the Dead* has dominated my life since 1981." *Almanac of the Dead* is a stunning and complex work. The term "epic" is often used loosely, but this novel, truly epic in both its subject matter and its scope, could be subtitled "The Fall of the American Empire." *Almanac of the Dead* covers hundreds of years of history and has more than sixty characters, most of whom are not people with whom most readers will empathize. They include drug dealers and addicts, corrupt policemen and judges, murderous homeless men, dealers in child pornography, and brutal mafiosi. *Almanac of the Dead* catalogues the worst that twentieth-century America has to offer. Much of this catalogue focuses on the treatment of indigenous peoples by the U.S. government. When asked by Donna Perry–for an essay that appears in *Backtalk: Woman Writers Speak Out* (1992)–why she wrote the book, Silko answered, "This is my 763-page indictment for five hundred years of theft, murder, pillage, and rape." Silko's training as a lawyer, though abandoned, was not wasted. She "never lost track of Indian law decisions," and much of the prose of *Almanac of the Dead* is filled with a lawyer's eye for detail. Silko sees her writing, at least in part, as a tool for social and political reform. In a 1985 interview with Coltelli, Silko–who at the time was deeply involved in writing *Almanac of the Dead*–noted that her works were meant to bring about political and social change: "Certainly for me the most effective statement I could make is in my art work. I believe in subversion rather than straight-confrontation. . . . I don't think we're numerous enough, whoever 'we' are, to take them by storm."

*Almanac of the Dead* was not well received by critics. For many reviewers the novel was simply too much; it was too violent, too graphic, and too long. In a review for the *Los Angeles Times* (2 February 1992) Paul West declared, "Here is an excellent work of myth and a second-rate novel, full of lacunae because there are just too many people in it." In a review that appeared in *The Washington Post* (26 November 1991) Larsen added, "In trying to convince readers of the seriousness of her cause, Silko too often resorts to overkill." In *The Christian Science Monitor* (3 February 1992) Brad Knickerbocker, although he praised the prose and ambition of the novel, mused, "one wonders why Silko's characters (Indians, as well as Anglos and those of mixed race) should be so dark, indeed perverted to the point where some passages are exceedingly painful to read." Some reviewers, to be sure, liked the novel. In *The New York Times* (22 December 1991) Elisabeth Tallent wrote, "there is genius in the sheer, tireless variousness of the novel's interconnecting tales." Most reviewers, however, agreed more or less with Alan Ryan, who said in *USA Today* (21 January 1992), "although Silko introduces a teetering truckload of politically correct themes, from racial oppression to ecology, even the most sympathetic reader will grow impatient."

As with *Ceremony,* one of the major accomplishments in *Almanac of the Dead* is the total revision of American history. Silko mentions to Perry that "the way time is calculated in western European cultures is completely political." In *Almanac of the Dead* Silko begins with the premise that history is culturally constructed and works to reconstruct the last four hundred years of American

history from a Native American perspective. For instance, 1929, the year of the stock market crash, was mild and wet at Laguna and is remembered by characters in the novel "as a Year of bounty and plenty for the people." In another part of the novel one of the characters discovers that the 1983 crash of a Korean Air Lines flight was actually caused by an Eskimo woman's magic. The chapters on Geronimo–"Mistaken Identity" and "Old Pancakes"–further illustrate Silko's manipulation of history. In those chapters an old Yaqui named Mahawala describes that there were really four different men called Geronimo. He argues that the man who eventually surrendered to the army had nothing to do with any of the "real" Geronimos but was an alcoholic named Old Pancakes.

This revision of history is one of the main themes of the novel. In a 1985 interview with Coltelli, Silko noted that *Almanac of the Dead* was "about time, and what's called history, and story, and who makes the story, and who remembers." The history of the West, and in particular the history of Tucson, serves in the novel as a microcosm of the persecution of Native Americans by mainstream America. Silko retells much of the story of the American West from a Native American perspective. The results suggest that the significance of historical events lies not in the events themselves but rather in their interpretation. Time constantly twists and laps over itself in the course of the narrative. The logic of the novel is not, therefore, the cause-and-effect logic of linear time. Silko's method is also her message: time and history are malleable.

The novel is structured loosely around a fictional Meso-American codex or almanac that is in the possession of Zeta, a Native American psychic. Zeta has been translating and transcribing the pages of the almanac and has discovered that they include criticisms of the Euroamerican government. One such remark is

> There was not, and there never had been, a legal government by Europeans anywhere in the Americas. Not by definition, not even by the European's own definitions and laws. Because no legal government could be established on stolen land.

Other pages of the almanac confirm this attitude:

> War had been declared on the first day the Spaniards set foot on Native American soil, and the same war had been going on ever since: the war was for the continents called the Americas.

The most startling messages of the almanac, though, concern the end of the world. One section, the "Spirit Snake's Message," concludes,

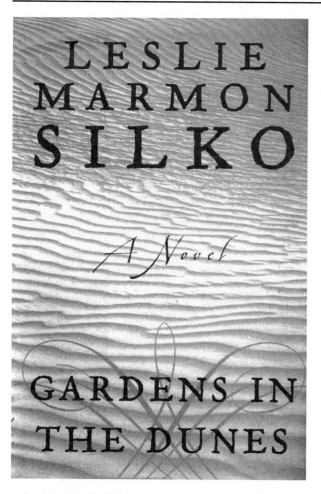

*Dust jacket for Silko's 1999 novel, about the divergent path taken by two orphaned Native American sisters as they try to make their way in the white world of nineteenth-century America*

What I have told you has always been true.
What I have to tell you now is that
this world is about to end.

These themes of the almanac parallel the themes of the novel. The decadence of Euroamerican culture and the repression and eventual resurgence of indigenous cultures are reiterated throughout. Silko's record of Euroamerican decadence is horrifying in its detail and scope. She describes, for instance, a corrupt judge who has a penchant for sex with his basset hounds. This judge is bribed by gangsters to ensure that water rights are obtained for a huge, wasteful housing development in the desert. There is a Mexican police chief who videotapes the torture and murder of suspects, and then sells the tapes as black market pornography. There is a real estate developer who uses his chain of crooked plasma centers to "harvest" organs from unwilling–and still living–donors. Perhaps the worst offenders are two

rich aristocrats named Serlo and Beaufrey. Serlo is a neo-Nazi who belongs to a "multinational organization" that created the AIDS virus to help depopulate the world. Beaufrey, with his love of sadomasochistic torture videos and his own brand of psychological torture for his many lovers, is Silko's epitome of Euroamerican selfishness. At one point in the novel the narrator observes that

> The most bloody spectacles of torture did not upset him; because he could not be seriously touched by the contortions and screams of imperfectly drawn cartoon victims. Beaufrey knew only he could truly feel or truly suffer.

This brutal self-centeredness, to one degree or another, is a common trait in most of the Euroamerican characters in the novel.

Many of the characters also share a perverse fascination with death that Silko seems to see as another common thread in contemporary America. As one of the characters in the novel notes, Europeans and Euro-Americans are "fascinated with death and decay." This preoccupation may be considered a metaphoric representation of American social "decay." Perhaps the best example of this perversion is the "art" of David, one of Beaufrey's lovers. When Eric, one of David's lovers, commits suicide, David discovers the body. With methodical care, David sets up his photo equipment and makes a series of photographs of the naked and bloody body. The photos become an instant collector's item, and David's reputation as a photographer is assured. Only a culture fascinated with death and violence, Silko seems to suggest, not only would tolerate these photos but also would welcome them.

The novel closes as diverse groups of people simultaneously plan the overthrow of the U.S. government. Mexican revolutionaries, led by twin brothers who receive revelations from a parrot and a large gem, march north, toward the border. Radical eco-terrorists blow themselves up to destroy the Glen Canyon Dam. Homeless veterans plot the takeover of U.S. military bases. A genius computer hacker arranges the complete shutdown of every power grid in the country. All of these story lines, carefully developed in the novel, foretell the doom of the United States.

*Yellow Woman and a Beauty of the Spirit* is a collection of twenty-three of Silko's wide-ranging personal essays, originally published between 1981 and 1994 in such places as *The Los Angeles Times, The Nation,* and the magazine *Mother Jones.* Critical response to the collection was generally positive. Judith Gaines in *The Boston Globe* (19 April 1996) called Silko's writing "breathtaking at points and often enlightening" but added, "those who reach the end of her essay collection may find themselves yearning for nothing so much as a good editor—who would have eliminated duplication and overlap in recurring sentences and even entire paragraphs."

The subject matter and tone of the essays ranges from political invective to touching personal revelation. In "Tribal Councils: Puppets of the U.S. Government" Silko attacks tribal councils as "an alien form of government that was forced upon the Indian people by the U.S. government." She adds that these councils "usually consist of so-called progressives, or acculturated individuals of the Indian communities, persons who had been brainwashed in Bureau of Indian Affairs schools or missionary schools." Silko's inflammatory language is aimed specifically at political reform, and she hints that the tribal council form of government should be challenged in court. This short essay ends, as do many of the essays in the collection, with a passage concerning the importance of land. In response to various tribal councils' decisions to allow logging, mining, and other industries to operate on tribal lands Silko asserts, "No part of the earth is expendable; the earth is a whole that cannot be fragmented, as it has been by the destroyers' mentality of the industrial age." The "destroyers" she refers to here are the witches fictionalized in both *Ceremony* and *Almanac of the Dead*. In this essay, however, Silko moves them from fiction to the real world of tribal politics and ends the essay with a call to battle: "There can be no compromises with these serial killers of life on earth because they are so sick they can't stop themselves."

Other essays in the collection are less politically blunt. The title essay, "Yellow Woman and a Beauty of the Spirit," is a touching essay in which Silko yearns for a place to "fit in." Near the beginning of the essay Silko recalls a childhood event that hurt her deeply. During recess at her kindergarten she, along with the other children in her class, posed for pictures being taken by a white tourist. Just before the picture was snapped, the man with the camera asked her to leave. She knew that, because of her green eyes and light-colored skin, she did not look the same as the other Pueblo kids. "Something about my appearance was not acceptable to some people, white and Indian." This rejection by both groups is juxtaposed in the essay with the acceptance Silko felt from her great-grandmother A'mooh. "Her love and her acceptance of me as a small child were so important." She also describes, with more than a little nostalgia, the egalitarian nature of the Pueblos before they had contact with whites. "In the old Pueblo world," she asserts, "differences were celebrated as signs of the Mother Creator's grace." Silko seems to long for this precontact world when "beauty was manifested in behavior and in one's relationships with other living beings," not simply in one's appearance. In this pre-contact world, the reader is left to assume that having green eyes and light skin would not have been a mark of shame for a Laguna child. As Silko pointed out to Barnes in 1986, "One should be able to see one's own life and the lives of other beings as a part of something very sacred and special." It is, no doubt, a quest for this sacred space that continues to drive Silko's writings.

Silko's novel *Gardens in the Dunes* (1999) concerns a Native American girl, Indigo; her sister, Sister Salt; and an array of characters who touch the lives of the two. Through these characters Silko explores the religious, cultural, and gender-related connections among Euroamericans, African Americans, Native Americans, and Europeans. Not as politically strident as *Almanac of the Dead* nor as mythic and mystical as *Ceremony, Gardens in the Dunes* is more mature than either of these earlier novels. This maturity is most evident in Silko's careful character development: these characters move and act like real people. The white characters in particular are not the cardboard cutouts of *Ceremony* nor the archetypal villains of *Almanac of the Dead*.

The novel begins as Indigo and Sister Salt participate in a Ghost Dance meeting with their mother and grandmother. The dance is violently dispersed by government representatives, and the girls' mother disappears in the confusion. The grandmother dies shortly thereafter, and the two sisters are forced to fend for themselves. They decide to leave their desert home in the dunes in search of their mother, but they soon find the wrecked remains of homes of white people who had participated in the dance. Seeing fruit trees that have been chopped down by the soldiers sent to stop the dances and punish the dancers, Salt laments, referring to herself, "If this was what the white people did to one another, then truly she and the sand lizard people and all other Indians were lucky to survive at all. These destroyers were out to kill every living being, even the Messiah and his dancers." This sentiment is certainly familiar from its expression in *Ceremony* and *Almanac of the Dead*.

Salt and Indigo are eventually captured by government authorities and separated—Salt is sent to work at a construction camp and Indigo to school. From this point the novel follows the substantially different lives the two sisters lead. Salt becomes a laundress and a prostitute whose story is played out against the brutally violent backdrop of frontier boomtowns. Indigo, on the other hand, escapes from the school and is taken in by an Eastern couple, Hattie and Edward Palmer. Her life with the Palmers puts her in the circle of the socially elite. Edward Palmer's self-absorbed quest for wealth eventually destroys both his health and his personal relationships. The destructive nature of this "American Dream" becomes a repeated motif in the novel.

Edward's wife, Hattie, must come to terms with her own failures. Her quest, quite different from Edward's, is to understand the nature of God in her own femininity. Her graduate thesis, rejected by her Harvard professors, concludes "that Jesus himself made Mary Magdalene and other women apostles in the early church." Her quest for feminine religious knowledge is another motif in the novel.

In the conclusion of the novel, the lives of Hattie, Indigo, and Sister Salt are drawn together as they approach their common goal of feminine spirituality. The controlling metaphor of the novel is the garden. Silko compares the literal garden in the dunes tended by Indigo, Sister Salt, their mother, and their grandmother, to the artificial and highly "cultured" garden owned by Edward's family in New York, the mystical garden kept by Aunt Bronwyn in England, and a primitive and sexually charged garden in Italy. In each of these gardens Indigo collects seeds and bulbs that are eventually used to create a new, eclectic garden in the dunes. In this new garden, readers are led to hope, a feminine spirituality will be allowed to blossom.

Silko's place in the canon of Western writers has been assured since she published her first novel. A prize-winning poet, short-story writer, essayist, and novelist, Silko has written major works that have been groundbreaking in their revision of literary conventions. Her portrayals of the Laguna Pueblo and the desert Southwest as a whole create a literary landscape matched by only a handful of writers, such as Edward Abbey and Wallace Stegner. Like the work of those writers, her work is often marked by its strong political overtones, but Silko is not merely a political writer. Her work, especially *Ceremony*, moves people. Wright, in a 28 August 1978 letter to Silko, wrote of that novel,

> In some strange way it seems inadequate to call it a great book, though it is surely that, or a perfect work of art, though it is one. I could call *Ceremony* one of the four or five best books I have ever read about America and I would be speaking the truth. . . . My very life means more to me than it would have if you hadn't written *Ceremony*.

Silko currently lives on a ranch near Tucson, Arizona, with Gus Nitshe, her companion since 1988. She continues to write and is deeply involved in state and local politics. She is a frequent contributor to *The New York Times Book Review*.

## Letters:

*The Delicacy and Strength of Lace: Letters Between Leslie Marmon Silko and James Wright,* edited by Anne Wright (St. Paul, Minn.: Greywolf Press, 1985).

## Interviews:

Lawrence J. Evers and Dennis W. Carr, "A Conversation with Leslie Marmon Silko," *Sun Tracks: An American Indian Literary Magazine,* 3 (Fall 1976): 33–38;

James Fitzgerald and John Hudak, "Leslie Silko: Storyteller," *Persona* (1980): 21–38;

Dexter Fisher, "Stories and Their Tellers: A Conversation with Leslie Marmon Silko," *The Third Woman: Minority Women Writers of the United States,* edited by Fisher (Boston: Houghton Mifflin, 1980), pp. 18–23;

Elaine Jahner, "The Novel and Oral Tradition: An Interview with Leslie Marmon Silko," *Book Forum: An International Transdisciplinary Quarterly,* 5, no. 3 (1981): 383–388;

Per Seyersted, "Two Interviews with Leslie Marmon Silko," *American Studies in Scandinavia,* 13 (1981): 17–33;

Kim Barnes, "A Leslie Marmon Silko Interview," *Journal of Ethnic Studies,* 13, no. 4 (1986): 83–105;

Laura Coltelli, "Leslie Marmon Silko," in *Winged Words: American Indian Writers Speak* (Lincoln: University of Nebraska Press, 1990), pp. 135–153;

Donna Perry, "Leslie Marmon Silko," *Backtalk: Woman Writers Speak Out* (New Brunswick, N.J.: Rutgers University Press, 1992), pp. 313–340;

Coltelli, "*Almanac of the Dead:* An Interview with Leslie Marmon Silko," in *Native American Literatures,* edited by Coltelli (Pisa, Italy: SEU, 1994), pp. 65–80;

Stephen Pett, "An Interview with Leslie Marmon Silko," *Short-Story,* 2 (1994): 91–96;

Florence Boos, "An Interview with Leslie Marmon Silko," *Speaking of the Short Story: Interviews with Contemporary Writers,* edited by Farhat Iftekharuddin, Mary Rohrberger, and Maurice Lee (Jackson: University Press of Mississippi, 1997), pp. 237–247.

## References:

Paula Gunn Allen, "The Feminine Landscape of Leslie Marmon Silko's *Ceremony,*" in *Studies in American Indian Literature: Critical Essays and Course Designs,* edited by Allen (New York: Modern Language Association, 1983), pp. 127–133;

Allen, "Special Problems in Teaching Leslie Marmon's *Ceremony,*" *American Indian Quarterly: A Journal of Anthropology, History and Literature,* 14, no. 3 (Fall 1990): 379–386;

Thomas E. Benediktsson, "The Reawakening of the Gods: Realism and the Supernatural in Silko and Hulme," *Critique: Studies in Contemporary Fiction,* 33, no. 2 (1992): 121–131;

Susan Blumenthal, "Spotted Cattle and Deer: Spirit Guides and Symbols of Endurance and Healing in *Ceremony,*" *American Indian Quarterly: A Journal of Anthropology, History and Literature,* 14, no. 3 (Fall 1990): 367–377;

Laura Coltelli, "Leslie Marmon Silko's *Sacred Water,*" *Studies in American Indian Literatures: The Journal of the Association for the Study of American Indian Literatures,* 8, no. 4 (1996): 21–29;

William Dinome, "*Laguna Woman:* An Annotated Leslie Silko Bibliography," *American Indian Culture and Research Journal,* 21, no. 1 (1997): 207–280;

Lawrence J. Evers, "The Killing of a New Mexican State Trooper: Ways of Telling a Historical Event," *Wicazo Sa Review,* 1, no. 1 (1985): 17–25;

Michael Hobbs, "Living In-Between: Tayo as Radical Reader in Leslie Marmon Silko's *Ceremony,*" *Western American Literature,* 28, no. 4 (1994): 301–312;

Helen Jaskoski, *Leslie Marmon Silko: A Study of the Short Fiction* (New York: Twayne, 1998);

Jaskoski, "Teaching with Storyteller at the Center," *Studies in American Indian Literatures: The Journal of the Association for the Study of American Indian Literatures,* 5, no. 1 (1993): 51–61;

Linda J. Krumholz, "'To Understand This World Differently': Reading and Subversion in Leslie Marmon Silko's *Storyteller,*" *ARIEL: A Review of International English Literature,* 25, no. 1 (1994): 89–113;

Arnold Krupat, "The Dialogic of Silko's *Storyteller,*" in *Narrative Chance: Postmodern Discourse on Native American Indian Literatures,* edited by Gerald A. Vizenor (Albuquerque: University of New Mexico Press, 1978), pp. 55–68;

Toby C. S. Langen, "*Storyteller* as Hopi Basket," *Studies in American Indian Literature: The Journal of the Association for the Study of American Indian Literatures,* 5, no. 1 (1993): 53–58;

Carol Mitchell, "Ceremony as Ritual," *American Indian Quarterly: A Journal of Anthropology, History and Literature,* 5 (1979): 27–35;

Robert M. Nelson, "A Laguna Woman," in *Leslie Marmon Silko: A Collection of Critical Essays,* edited by Louise Barrett and James Thorson (Albuquerque: University of New Mexico Press, 1999), pp. 15–22;

Nelson, "Place and Vision: The Function of Landscape in Ceremony," *Journal of the Southwest,* 30, no. 3 (1988): 281–316;

Christopher Norden, "Ecological Restoration as Post-Colonial Ritual of Community in Three Native American Novels," *Studies in American Indian Literatures: The Journal of the Association for the Study of American Indian Literatures,* 6 (1994): 94–106;

Elsie Clews Parson, *Notes on Ceremonialism at Laguna,* Anthropological Papers of the American Museum of Natural History (New York: The Trustees, 1920), XIX: part 4;

Susan Perez Castillo, "Postmodernism, Native American Literature and the Real: The Silko-Erdrich Controversy," *Massachusetts Review: A Quarterly of Literature, the Arts and Public Affairs,* 32, no. 2 (1991): 285–294;

LaVonne Brown Ruoff, *American Indian Literatures: An Introduction* (New York: Modern Language Association, 1990);

Ruoff, "Ritual and Renewal: Keres Traditions in the Short Fiction of Leslie Silko," in *American Women Short Story Writers: A Collection of Critical Essays,* edited by Julie Brown (New York: Garland, 1995), pp. 167–189;

Gregory Salyer, *Leslie Marmon Silko* (New York: Twayne, 1997);

Kathleen M. Sands and others, "A Discussion of *Ceremony,*" *American Indian Quarterly: A Journal of Anthropology, History and Literature,* 5 (1979): 63–70;

Per Seyersted, *Leslie Marmon Silko* (Boise, Idaho: Boise State University Press, 1980);

Janet St. Clair, "Death of Love/Love of Death: Leslie Marmon Silko's *Almanac of the Dead,*" *MELUS: The Journal of the Society for the Study of the Multi-Ethnic Literature of the United States,* 21, no. 2 (1996): 141–156;

Edith Swan, "Laguna Prototypes of Manhood in Ceremony," *MELUS: The Journal of the Society for the Study of the Multi-Ethnic Literature of the United States,* 17, no. 1 (1991–1992): 39–61;

Swan, "Laguna Symbolic Geography and Silko's Ceremony," *American Indian Quarterly,* 12, no. 3 (1988): 229–249;

Joan Thompson, "Yellow Woman, Old and New: Oral Tradition and Leslie Marmon Silko's *Storyteller,*" *Wicazo Sa Review,* 5, no. 2 (1989): 22–25;

Alan R. Velie, *Four American Indian Literary Masters: N. Scott Momaday, James Welch, Leslie Marmon Silko, and Gerald Vizenor* (Norman: University of Oklahoma Press, 1982);

Shamoon Zmir, "Literature in a 'National Sacrifice Area': Leslie Silko's *Ceremony,*" in *New Voices in Native American Literary Criticism,* edited by Krupat (Washington, D.C.: Smithsonian Institution Press, 1993), pp. 396–415.

# William V. Studebaker

*(21 May 1947 – )*

## Keith Browning
*Lewis-Clark State College*

BOOKS: *Everything Goes Without Saying: Poems* (Lewiston, Idaho: Confluence, 1978);

*Trailing the Raven: Poems,* Limberlost Review, no. 12 (Pocatello, Idaho: Limberlost, 1982);

*The Cleaving* (Lewiston, Idaho: Confluence, 1985);

*The Rat Lady at the Company Dump* (Boise, Idaho: Limberlost, 1990);

*Falling from the Sky* (Twin Falls, Idaho: Redneck Press, 1994);

*River Religion* (Boise, Idaho: Limberlost, 1997);

*Travelers in an Antique Land* (Moscow: University of Idaho Press, 1997);

*Short of a Good Promise* (Pullman: Washington State University Press, 1999).

OTHER: *Idaho's Poetry: A Centennial Anthology,* edited by Studebaker and Ronald McFarland (Moscow: University of Idaho Press, 1988);

*Backtracking: Ancient Art of Southern Idaho,* edited by Studebaker and Max G. Pasevic (Pocatello, Idaho: Idaho Museum of Natural History, 1993);

*When the Morning Light's Still Blue: Personal Essays about Idaho,* edited by Studebaker and Rick Ardinger (Moscow: University of Idaho Press, 1994).

*William V. Studebaker (courtesy of the author)*

As a sixth-generation Westerner and a fourth-generation Idahoan, William V. Studebaker has lived his entire life in the "antique land." Using this phrase from Percy Bysshe Shelley's poem "Ozymandias" (1818) in a Western context, Studebaker conveys the antiquity of Western lands in terms of both time and space. Spatially, the antique land refers to contiguous portions of Idaho, Oregon, Nevada, Utah, and Wyoming—acres and acres of mountains, hills, river valleys, and ranch and farm lands as well as great stretches of high desert. Temporally, the antique land encompasses the prehistorical as well as the historical and the eventual that together evoke the past and the present. As might be expected, this thoroughly regionalist perspective has cost the poet the renown of a broader readership. Absorbed in his own geographical and cultural

territorial imperatives, he has not actively sought recognition beyond the confines of his Western locales and, consequently, has not enjoyed the wide literary acclaim he deserves.

Studebaker's regional preoccupation, however, has led to a richly poetic sense of place. As Ford Swetnam notes in his essay for *Tough Paradise: The Literature of Idaho and the Intermountain West* (1995), "Cultures may change landscape, as a successful irrigation project might do; landscape can also change cultures, as a failed irrigation project might do. Poetry records these changes to animals, vegetables, minerals and spirits, and presents our region as something like a poem, something both still and moving."

Born in Salmon, Idaho, on 21 May 1947, the youngest of three children, William Vern Studebaker experienced a remarkable Western childhood and youth. In 1942 his parents, Robert Studebaker and Betty Silbaugh Studebaker, spent their wedding night in a snowstorm, moving their stranded band of sheep out of the mountains and down to the shelter of the Lemhi Valley ranch that Robert and his father, Vern, owned and worked as partners. In 1944 Robert began a tour of duty in the navy, and Betty moved back to Salmon to live with her parents. Discharged in 1946, Robert came home to find that his father had decided that their "partnership" never existed; his father's decision forced Robert to work at various ranch jobs. From 1948 to 1952, Robert and Betty–who by then had three children, Dennis, Penny, and William–lived wherever the Forest Service or the location of Robert's job afforded them: camps, tents, "lookouts," cabins–even the back of a stock truck. They moved according to the seasons and to places with names such as Red Rock Peak, Yellow Jacket, and Beetle Creek. The family's largely outdoor life was hardly comfortable, and it had its dangers: Dennis was kicked in the head by a horse, Penny was almost stung to death by band-headed hornets, and William was saved by his mother from drowning in a raging creek.

This prolonged frontier existence no doubt had a major influence on all three of the Studebaker youngsters, who–like their parents and grandparents–were forced to rely on themselves. "I was born to pioneers whose families had been pioneers for centuries," the poet asserts in his introduction to his memoir, *Short of a Good Promise* (1999). "My life has been lived on the fringe, on the edge of towns and woods and high desert foothills. Physical demands were genuine. Injuries were commonplace." Consequently,

I became accustomed to my own company and guided myself through the fits and starts of my parents' seasonal rounds as they gathered up a living. In winter we were in the lowlands, in the bigger valleys where the eye could stretch out for a mile or two and where there was an abundance of relatives. The other seasons were spent in the high country, in the tight corridors and creek bottoms where the eye seemed to stop at arm's length. This was hill country–really mountains, ranging from a few sloping feet above my head to ten or eleven thousand feet. Everything I wanted to do as a child was up: up the road, up the hillside, up the tree, up the river, up at Grandma's and, yes, up the creek. It became obvious to me that observing had its rewards. When I dropped out of the race as youngest, slowest, last . . . I tuned in. It wasn't that I chose to become an observer, I was merely allowed to do it.

Another part of Studebaker's childhood that informed his development as an artist was his experiences at the "Big House," the "old folks' home" operated by his maternal grandparents, Grandpa and Grandma Silbaugh. The home was the assisted-living establishment of its day, a place where the elders were treated more as boarders than as poor folk or patients. According to Studebaker in *Short of a Good Promise,* he learned from those days "that no one knows what's good for an old man or woman" and that "tolerance is the best teacher." As a boy, with his big eyes and open ears, he spent a lot of time at the home and found he could learn much "just by watching"–the hours of observation also meant silently coming to terms with mortality.

Vivid memories of the old folk in the Big House occasionally enter Studebaker's poetry. Two elders, Mrs. Cassell and Old Fisher, who appear in *Everything Goes Without Saying: Poems* (1978), show in the memoir how useful the earliest of recollections can be to a poet's sensibility. In *Short of a Good Promise* Mrs. Cassell is an elderly eccentric who passes a good deal of time picking river moss, sometimes in the nude, from the bottom of a mill ditch that runs past the Big House. When Mrs. Cassell was not in the mill ditch,

. . . she kept her knee-high rubber boots full of water, sloshing around the Big House. No one cared. The rule was if it's not hurting anyone, let it go.

Harmless? I don't know. I sat for hours on the bridge that crossed the Mill Ditch between the Big House and the outbuildings. I sat there staring into the water. It was clear Lemhi River water, flowing westward toward the Salmon River–the River of No Return. The moss leaned as far as it could after the water, waving a hypnotic goodbye. There were stretches of the ditch that were bald, barren, without moss. Mrs. Cassell saw to that. Moss gathering was her principal business.

The other elder, Old Fisher, plays music that entrances the young Studebaker. Old Fisher was

. . . blind and played a fiddle. It may have been his tunes that attracted me, that got me to allow myself to be transported upstairs. Or it may have been his tunes that introduced us as I stood outside his door staring into his black glasses. But from the first moment he knew who I was. His greetings were friendly and wise, 'Hey, Billy, you're really quiet today.' I never questioned why or how he knew who I was or how I felt, but because he knew, he gave me the greatest sense of importance.

*Short of a Good Promise* concerns Studebaker's parents and grandparents as much as it concerns himself. In his mind these people constitute a direct link to the "pio-

*Studebaker with his older brother, Dennis, circa 1953*
*(courtesy of the author)*

neer" past of the whole region—a past that, in turn, has obvious historical relevance for the Indian population that the poet's forebears helped to displace. He is interested in how both the white and Indian populations have had to cope with the land. For the "pioneers" the land was all too often "short of a good promise," whereas, as Studebaker writes in *Backtracking: Ancient Art of Southern Idaho* (1993), for the Indians the land was sometimes an opportunity to make use of the "spirituality of place." Two poems that are grounded in this difference in perspective are "Wind Sickness" and "The Wind's Ecclesiastical History of Utah." In "Wind Sickness," which appears in *Short of a Good Promise,* the wind is a local environmental force that curses the "carriers" of its sickness, such as the poet's father, Robert, for whom "the wind's no good. / Half a chance and it'll steal / the breath from / under your nose." In "The Wind's Ecclesiastical History of Utah," which is collected in *Travelers in an Antique Land* (1997), the wind, an itinerant who has frequented this territory for ages, is the speaker: "Before the Mormons came, there was just

/ enough / Utes, Paiutes, traders and trappers to keep / this place from getting lost." For Studebaker, the wind sounds like the only spiritual voice worth listening to.

While *Short of a Good Promise* enables the reader to understand Studebaker and his poetry, the book sheds little, if any, light on his married life, his academic background, or his professional development—beyond the mention that he started writing poetry as early as his junior year in high school and that he realized, after two semesters at Idaho State University, his life would be at once "considerably" different from the lives of his parents and yet much the same. He pictured himself constructing his "own house" and adding "Idaho's latent literary culture" to his "fringe-filled experience." Studebaker married his high-school sweetheart, Judy Infanger, on 23 August 1969; they had two daughters and two sons—Tona, Tyler, Robert, and Eric. The Studebakers did build their own house, paying for it as it was constructed over a period of seven years.

Studebaker's academic background includes a B.A. in history, which he received in 1970 from Idaho State University in Pocatello, and a M.A. in English, completed in 1972, also at Idaho State. After a year in law school at the University of Idaho in Moscow, between 1974 and 1975, he returned to Twin Falls, Idaho, to teach in the English Department at the College of Southern Idaho (CSI), where he had been an instructor from 1972 to 1973. He has been at CSI ever since, becoming an assistant professor in 1977. He has also taught, beginning in 1981, graduate and undergraduate courses in the teaching and writing of poetry at the Idaho State University Residency Center. At both schools Studebaker's teaching and literary pursuits have continued to focus on the "latent literary culture" of Idaho.

According to James H. Maguire of Boise State University, until the 1960s native writers of any consequence totaled scarcely half a dozen in Idaho: Vardis Fisher, Norman McLeod, James Stevens, Carol Ryrie Brink and Grace Jordan. In the last section of *The Literature of Idaho: An Anthology* (1986), Maguire suggests that an Idaho literary renaissance of sorts took place between 1960 and 1985, a rejuvenation that was spurred by increased funding from federal and state arts and humanities programs and private foundations in general, and by college and university creative writing programs, literary magazines, and small presses in particular.

Surely the influx of writers from out of state—writers who have lived in Idaho long enough to make a difference—also contributed to the Idaho literary renaissance. As a member of the Idaho Commission on the Arts, from 1979 to 1985, Studebaker represented the interests of the literary community in the state—an advocacy that Idaho had not enjoyed previously. He initiated funding for an Idaho writer-in-residence program as well as for many literary fellowships. Since 1996 he has been a member of the Idaho Humanities Council. The literature of Idaho has been as important to Studebaker as the landscape that enriches it so consistently, for he has been an integral part of a generation of Idaho poets–including the late Charles David Wright, Robert Wrigley, Gary Gildner, Ronald McFarland, Margaret Aho, Neide Messer, and William Johnson. These writers admired and, in some cases, studied under several key Northwest poets: Richard Hugo, William Stafford, David Wagoner, Carolyn Kizer, and John Haines; most of these writers, in turn, studied with Theodore Roethke. In a letter written to Keith Browning on 23 April 2001, Studebaker mentions the individuals who have had the most impact on his poetic growth, such as Stafford, Haines, and Hugo–whose *Triggering Town: Lectures and Essays on Poetry and Writing* (1979) especially affected Studebaker.

Five days in the poet's life that merit particular attention are those he spent as a participant in a 1977 symposium held in Twin Falls by Joseph Campbell, the eminent scholar of comparative mythology and religion. Studebaker interpreted Campbell's invitation to participate in this symposium as *buha*–Shoshone for "inexplicable luck"–and has vivid memories of the event. At the symposium Professor Campbell talked about "mandalas," some of which Campbell had "gleaned" from Carl Gustav Jung and others from a tour of the Orient. Studebaker and the other symposium participants

> were given the assignment to use our individual art form (I don't recall that he asked if we had one.) to construct a mandala. Usually, mandalas are drawn, painted visual expressions. But he encouraged us to strive for mythic/psychological articulation in whatever–In my case it was poetry.

Mandalas–or circles with centers that hold–do appear occasionally in Studebaker's poetry, beginning with his first collection. *Everything Goes Without Saying* encompasses the fairly typical, high modernist verse of allusions and ambiguities, reflecting the poet's fondness for opacity. The three sections of the book–"Squatter's Rights," "Old Folks," and "Shadows"–exemplify the poet's earliest and most enduring lyric preoccupations: place; landscape, in particular, as an inherent value; people as itinerants; and grace as a positive psychic individuation. In much of his poetry, in fact, he juggles these central preoccupations with a kaleidoscopic mind, pursuing the all-embracing mandala: an inclusive, coherent worldview, or weltan-

schauung. In particular, Studebaker's first collection of verse as a whole introduces his strongest poetic suit: an ability to present many of his observations in unexpected, even startling, ways.

The first section, "Squatter's Rights," makes an excellent introduction to Studebaker's poetic methods and materials. The poet deliberately uses a casual, conversational tone, enhanced by short, spare–almost desiccated–lines and a pattern of imagery that demands close examination:

> As I stoop
> beneath an old sage,
> a ring of dust
> shook by the wind
> growls in its sleep.
> . . . . . . . . . . . . . .
> We have had our times
> the dust and I,
> and the old gray lizard
> watching from the hollow
> of an ox's skull.
>
> And I have arranged
> bouquets of time,
> until my wrists have hands
> like brown blossoms
> and my fingers rattle,
>
> seeds in the mouth
> of the wind's den.

Studebaker infuses these lines with imagery that animates the elemental forces of the desert, where he sets the lyric. The wind that creates a circle of dust around a sage sounds like the growling of a dog curled in sleep. After a dust storm an old, gray lizard sees through the remains of an animal, and many other natural events have taken place. Like the watchful, old, gray lizard, the speaker knows his way around the desert and how to arrange events to his advantage. Yet, the wind and the desert dust have also left their mark on the speaker. Not just another landscape poem, "Squatter's Rights" is as dramatic as it is descriptive. The desert is no country for an old man or a place for blundering about. The old itinerant squats in the shadow of a sage, and the wind encloses all three–sage, shadow, and squatter–in a mandala of dust. Studebaker suggests that while squatters may have no rights, they do have the "rites" that a given location allows them. To perform the rites well, the poet implies, means to interpret them spiritually and thus creatively.

The poet, who created "The Bruneau Desert," a poem that also appears in *Everything Goes Without Saying*, believes in a god who created the land, rather than man, in his own image. In "The Bruneau Desert" God

TRAILING THE RAVEN

POEMS BY WILLIAM STUDEBAKER

*Cover for Studebaker's second collection of verse, published in 1982 as a special issue of* The Limberlost Review

versa. Salmon or steelhead are on their way to their spawning beds "up the clear stream / of death." "Everything goes without saying," muses the poet,

> Like my fish
> these lines will turn belly-up
> in the headwaters at the glacier's foot.

The generation of anadromous fish and the generation of poetry are not too far removed from each other in the overall scheme of things. Both fish and verse signify a creative endeavor—both embody mystery.

"Old Folks," the second section of *Everything Goes Without Saying,* shows how much the poet learned as a boy by "just watching" the inhabitants of the Big House, the assisted-living establishment owned and operated by his grandparents; he observed enough, indeed, to recall and transmute the observations into verse years later. A couple of the dozen poems in this section are portraits of certain people who appear in *Short of a Good Promise.* Old Fisher in the memoir has become "Old Blind Pretchit" in a poem of the same title, and Mrs. Cassell has become "The Woman Who Thought She Was Water," also the title of the lyric. Both poems demonstrate Studebaker's ability to catch the reader unaware. The last three lines of "Old Blind Prechit" startle the reader: "and the only light / he ever saw / was death." Studebaker must have written "The Woman Who Thought She Was Water" expressly for the unwary:

> With the conviction
> of an old heron,
> you stood
> kneeing the water.
> Nothing moved
> but what you were watching:
> you had seen her before
> like an old trout weaving herself
> up stream;
>
> when you reeled
> your hand in,
> it was hooked
> to a line of moss &
> mud bled between your legs.
> . . . . . . . . . . . . . . . . . . . . . .

Moss gathering is not this poor woman's "principal business"—rather, it is fishing for her own image in ditch water. The line "mud bled between your legs" resounds with a heavy material beat and a pronounced assonance; Lemhi mud is an awful substitute for the normality of menstrual blood.

"Shadows," the final section of the book, obviously pivots on Studebaker's knowledge of Jung. The

is personified as a "spirituality" that "spent a day, / rough-framing the canyons, / troweling the flats. / Said he'd be back. / Hasn't been, except at night." At night, the poem notes, God can be heard "settling down in the King's Chair." "Winter Climb" alludes to T. S. Eliot's "The Love Song of J. Alfred Prufrock" (1911), especially at the point in Studebaker's poem when the speaker reaches a summit from "where the whole world / is etherized below me, / waiting for the scalpel of my eye." The rest of the poems in this section are similar, in that they mark observations generated by values that are inherent in one place or another. These observations result in images that are typical of Studebaker, such as "The cold nose of night / drops to the ground."

The first line of the last stanza in another of Studebaker's lyrics, "Ars Poetica," inspires the title of the book, *Everything Goes Without Saying.* "Ars Poetica" meditates on the ironies of art imitating life and vice

"shadow" aspect of a person's soul constitutes one of Jung's major "archetypes," or psychic potentials for significance. Jung's "shadow" is, simply stated, the "dark" side of human nature, the potential for evil that one sometimes tries to project onto something or someone else. Yet, the shadow can also be a potential for good when it becomes an integrated and thus positive part of the human personality. In "Sister," Studebaker constructs an allegory of psychic individuation–of learning to live with oneself. The sister of the poem "keeps a shadow" and "feeds it fresh air" in various ways: "In this way / she works her- / self-forgiveness." "Black Cat" illustrates an even better lesson in learning to live with others and features a house cat, who "watches from [its] own darkness." The speaker knows "of a strangeness / never shared," and he asks no more than the cat can tell. "That's what keeps the cat coming back." "First Wife" tells the sad story of a marriage that fails, because one of the spouses or, perhaps, both of them are too busy projecting their own shadows on the other. Despite their Jungian motifs, these fascinating poems do not demand a scholarly acquaintance with Jung. The old folks in the Big House, for example, whom Studebaker writes about in the first section of the book, "Squatter's Rights," provide background material in the titular lyric, "Shadows," as much as does Jung's complex archetype:

> I know death, and
> because I do, I wish
> the old man in me could step out.
> . . . . . . . . . . . . . . . . . . . . . . . .
>
> The old man would be
> memory and I would know my place
> and be there tomorrow
> as the sun rises.
>
> And the feeling I have
> of living behind
> venetian blinds
> would surely end.
>
> And my shadow would have
> its place beside me.

The old folks in the Big House afforded the nascent poet a definite sense of his own mortality–enough at least for him to claim that he knew death from a young age. From Campbell and Jung, Studebaker learned the value of intelligent, systematic introspection and the relationship of introspection to creativity. "Shadows" itself responds to the feeling that one has at times of "living behind venetian blinds."

*Trailing the Raven: Poems* (1982) was Studebaker's first chapbook and initiated his connection with Lim-

berlost Press, started by Rick and Rosemary Ardinger; the Ardingers also founded the literary journal, *Limberlost Review*. *Trailing the Raven* encompasses the twelfth issue of *Limberlost Review* and includes many of the noteworthy poems about mining culture from the poet's first letterpress chapbook, *The Rat Lady at the Company Dump* (1990). Several landscape poems found in *Travelers in an Antique Land* are also in this earliest limited edition. *Trailing the Raven* anticipates some of the new directions that Studebaker's poetry takes in his later collections.

The title poem of the collection, "Trailing the Raven: After Her Kill" represents a different use of landscape than seen previously in Studebaker's verse. Here, he regards the "flip" side of place, which for him is usually a location where one can take a dependable bearing–psychically, geographically, or spiritually. In this poem, a place is where someone can get lost as well.

> I look for the wind still disturbed
> a parting where the air
> will not quite close
> . . . . . . . . . . . . . . .
> I decipher blood, on this rock
> on his leaf, on this sage
> always the same, *dying*.
>
> Often I must heed little hunches
> from the brain stem we share . . .
> . . . . . . . . . . . . . . . . . . . . . . . . . .
> she is feeding her young
> the headless half of the rattle snake
> and they, a claw a piece, are holding
> its headless body at leg's length
> while I, miles away from nowhere
> hold its head
> like a pocket watch toward the sunset–
>
> its dead face striking
> the hour I was lost.

The two couplets in the poem signify interesting shifts into the suggestive: whereas the first couplet yokes the scientific–the brain stem anatomies–with the mystical–the heeding hunches–the second yokes the biological with the mechanical. Together the couplets highlight a pattern of interaction between the natural and the supernatural, a relationship that often occurs in Studebaker's landscape poetry. Two other poems in the chapbook also explore the theme of becoming lost: "In Hell's Canyon" and "Drawing a Map to the Wilderness."

With respect to Studebaker's second book-length collection of poetry, *The Cleaving* (1985), Karyn Riedell states in a review for *Western American Literature* (Winter 1986) that "Like other poets of the American West,

Slightly Delirious in a Super-Market
in Salt Lake City

At Ruby's Delicatessen and Catering Corner,
I order a belly-full of rice                                    *half-bowl*
*browse*  and read through the Salt Lake Tribune
and chant a caffeine mantra:  coffee, coffee--
From where I sit, I can see
*uc*  all the signs/on isle Thirteen:          *13*

Garden
Salad Dressing  →
Imported Cheese
Pickles  →                        *2 columns
Salad Bar                          (on isle)*
Catsup  →
Fresh Squeeze
Kosher Foods  →

This must be where SLC Jews          *Salt Lake City*
*lc*  and Vegetarians hangout.

Where are you to night Allen Ginsberg?
Old image maker.
Is that you down at the Meats,
fumbling the pork chops?
How's your macro-biotic diet?
How's your diabetes?
How are the young boys
on the Lower Eastside?

*Walk*  I wander up and down the isle:
fat apples and bananas;
cabbage, cauliflower, broccoli,
and lettuce heads;
red, russet, and sweet potatoes;
onions, turnips, parsnips;
cucumbers, carrots,
green tomatoes,
and a vacancy for watermelon.
I finger the frozen foods,
the instant breakfasts,
the Manwich dinners.
The girls at the check-out counters click
their Funner-Than-Real Nails

*Corrected typescript for a poem by Studebaker that was published in* Atom Mind, *no. 18, in 1996 (Collection of William V. Studebaker)*

Studebaker combines Zen Buddhist philosophy with reverence for the still vast and uncorrupted landscape." The poet considers *The Cleaving* his "mandala of love," a book that he dedicated to "those who know the daughters of Desire"; these "daughters" also turn out to be the titles of the three sections that compose the book: "Yearning," "Heartache," and "Fulfillment." In his letter discussing the Campbell symposium, however, he calls these three divisions "a section on 'lust,' a section on 'amor,' and a section on 'agape'–or Yearning, Heartache, and Acceptance." For the poet Carolyne Wright, whose brief assessment appears on the back cover of the book, the verses in *The Cleaving* are "quiet, deeply-felt poems–poems of love and loss, of separation and of 'crossing the distance between.'" Wright adds that Studebaker's craft "is less on the artfulness of trope than on the thing itself, the dramatic nexus and personae at the center of his work, with a harmony of purpose and natural interaction we have come to seek in poets of the Northwest."

Harmony of purpose and natural interaction are precise expressions for the centrality of place in Studebaker's poetics–even when he is focused on a mental, as opposed to a physical, landscape, as in the opening lines of "A Letter to a Woman, Dead Some Twenty Years," which is also a prologue:

> When I think of you, images pile up
> in my head like a hive about to swarm,
> driving me between old and new faces.

These lines encompass more than a tidy simile; the poet presents an accurate understanding of what this person still means to him:

> No, there can be no love between us,
> but when you get up
> from some gray place in my head
> and walk toward me, hand out,
> lips moving, I want to say
> how I have grown,
> how I have tried to think of you,
> how I have followed the instructions
> of the bee-dancer,
> how I have returned with a little less
> as the years bloomed between us.
>
> And what I am able to remember
> I put down here, as it were
> honey and this were our nest.

An epistolary poem, "A Letter to a Woman, Dead Some Twenty Years" is a tribute to the poet Richard Hugo, whose form–if not also style–Studebaker has borrowed. Studebaker hints at the poem as a letter to his anima, or inner female self. Most powerfully, the lyric evokes the harmony

that Wright has in mind: the formality of a head or mind dancing with mental activities rendered as familiar as a hive or nest of dancing honey bees. In the poem the dancers and the dances are one.

At its core, *The Cleaving* harbors a polarity that demands some kind of resolution, since "cleaving" can allude to both severance and adherence. Yet, the poet dedicates the collection to the "daughters of desire," who are threefold and thus provide a dialectical way out of this semantic dilemma. Because one cannot know one of these daughters without knowing the other two, the poems in Studebaker's second book embody ways of getting to know all three of these daughters in a holistic sense. Each section includes at least one lyric that conveys the essence of knowing each daughter of desire. "In The Fields," from the first section, depicts yearning, which is the first daughter: "In the house / a child waits to hear her name. / You know her the way you know / when she chokes in the night / she must have your care." In the second section, "Staying Alone" encapsulates heartache, the second daughter: "I stand as if stalled forever in the middle of no place." In the third section, "The Need" reflects fulfillment, the third daughter of desire, by alleviating a pain or privation: "The way a dog tends to his wounds, / the way a creek tends to her stones / rolling them with the soft tongue / of her water, I tend my need."

In *The Rat Lady at the Company Dump,* Studebaker's first letterpress chapbook, he takes the same careful look at the mining culture in Southeast Idaho that he has taken with everything else he has observed. "A Meditation on Mining," which first appeared in *Trailing the Raven,* is a Hugoesque apostrophe to–or a third person dramatic monologue by–a miner, who knows the extent to which his inner landscape mirrors his outer landscape: "Your personality is gone / blasted and mucked out years ago." In a review essay that appeared in *Western American Literature* (Fall 1992), John C. Dofflemeyer finds the poems in *The Rat Lady at the Company Dump* depressing, "with only the poet's introspective light to sustain the reader through his black claustrophobic labors within the bowels of earth." Dofflemeyer correctly understands these poems as bleak even when they are humorous, as in "Jumping Claims," which Studebaker compares to "raping a skeleton / a lot more story than thrill. / They're usually deadends / that petered out anyway." The title piece, "The Rat Lady at the Company Dump," epitomizes bleakness and humor. Studebaker portrays two hellish landscapes in the lyric: the empty, interior landscapes of the mines and miners alike and the symbolic, cultural landscape of the midden, or refuse, heap that is the company dump. The speaker tells about himself and old Norma Jean: "I come here to shoot rats / and I do, but when

*Dust jacket for a 1997 collaborative volume celebrating the Western desert landscape*

the ratting / is slow, I think of shooting / old Norma Jean. She's not dead yet / but I can tell she will be." In the last stanza the speaker gets what he has come for: "I squeeze the trigger / The cartridge unloads itself / of death's heavy weight. / The rat, hit in the head, jumps / straight out of its shadow / as if it wanted a larger bite / of life than it had been given."

Studebaker wrote about the feminist movement of the 1980s and 1990s in the form of the eleven poems that constitute *Falling from the Sky* (1994). Feminists of those decades probably did not view the fall of Icarus as a tragic event, yet the person who wrote *The Cleaving* is hardly a male chauvinist. In "Grounds for Divorce," which appears in *Falling from the Sky,* the poet lends a

twist to the theme of becoming lost, which he explores in *Trailing the Raven:*

> How can you be so nonchalant?
> Squat here pissing on the ground
> Right beside where we are lost.
>
> And why doesn't the landscape
> Show a difference?
> A rock give a hint?
> The grass lean some other way?
> Or the hill rise to some height—more or less?
>
> This is the trouble
> you don't care about:
> searching for the end of things,
> for the beginning of another.

Studebaker implies that interruptions—the "cuttings" of life—fascinate men more than the continua that women seem to be so busy living. In "The Point of Being from Nowhere," dedicated to "the women patients at State Hospital South," the poet reveals what chauvinism does to men as well as to women: "Crazy as nervous does, / we chew the hollow of our hands too." Chauvinism deprives men of the women that are committed to the hospital. In his review of *Falling from the Sky* in *Western American Literature* (Fall 1995), Jim Harris notes that the poem "The Phantom Female" comments on the sense of loss that the passage of time brings about—an idea that runs throughout several of the other poems in the collection. Hence, "The Phantom Female" ends with an allusion to the mother, suggesting not only a return to the beginning of life—which parallels the beginning of time—but also the notion that a mother is someone who keeps others from becoming lost:

> I must, every now and then,
> Wear the mask of my own placenta
> And find the mother in me again.

Everyone has a mother inside. Jung called this part of one's psyche the anima.

In his "Ars Poetica," from *Everything Goes Without Saying,* Studebaker treats the river not as an object or a subject but, rather, as a setting that is as ripe for poetic development as any other. *River Religion* (1997), in which he explores the symbolism of the river, evolved in the wake of a 1995 automobile accident that nearly killed the poet; his injuries led to several long and debilitating major surgeries. In the preface titled "Introduction: Born Again" he explains how he had become an avid whitewater kayaker, concluding that "These poems are histories of adrenalin rushes, elliptical memoirs of whitewater I have waltzed through or limboed under. They are but a sample of the good times, good friends, and rapid adventures I've had. They are allegorical, symbolic journeys through physical and emotional therapy. I give thanks and pray for more."

Moments of truth seemingly occur often enough in whitewater adventures, but there is nothing Hemingwayesque about these poems. They are written not only for other "whitewater folk" but also for anyone else who finds that rivers can be as spiritually or ontologically revealing as mountains and deserts. For the reader—or listener—there are many moments when the rivers sing the music of their own "hydraulics," as in "Floating":

> I rode rapids, rapids'
> wavetrains. I bodysurfed
> broiling boulderholes.
> I fisheyed the sun.

*Cover for Studebaker's 1999 memoir, which combines
poetry and prose*

> Pea gravel filled my shoes
> with limps & pains.
> My knees were knocked
> raspberry sore
> sore raspberry head.

Studebaker provides a glossary for those who do not understand whitewater lingo, but any careful reader should enjoy the sly puns on and allusions to religious fundamentalism. The poet's saints are whitewater survivors; his sinners are not.

*Travelers in an Antique Land* is a collection of photographs by Russell Hepworth as well as of verse by Studebaker; and while the photographs and lyrics were intended to be published together, each is able to stand on its own. Pictures and poems come together so that the former provides a place that the latter can turn into a dramatic setting. Some examples of verses in juxtaposition with photos are "The Bruneau Desert" and "Thousand Springs, Idaho: Outlet for Lost Rivers." This book collects much of Studebaker's best landscape poetry. In addition, useful commentaries on *Travelers in an Antique Land* appear in an article by Bert Almon for *Western American Literature* (Fall 1999) and in John Sollers's review of the book for *The Idaho Librarian* (February 1999). Both Almon and Sollers comment from the standpoint of the three sections of the book: "Desert Passage," which concerns just the desert wilderness; "Remains of Time," which focuses on the antiquity of the desert; and "Practice Range," which addresses the contemporary uses of the antique land by intruders. Almon and Sollers also comment on how the organization of these sections relates to Percy Bysshe Shelley's poem "Ozymandias." Almon compares Studebaker's craftsmanship to that of Gary Snyder, while Sollers concludes his review with the notion that *Travelers in an Antique Land* is for "those who wish to hold a part of the world in their hands and minds and to comprehend and become a part of that place."

*Travelers in an Antique Land* develops further the ecological concerns expressed in *Trailing the Raven* and *The Rat Lady at the Company Dump*. The latter limited editions left few doubts about the extent to which the mining culture intruded upon the interior and exterior landscapes of the miners and their families living in the company towns. Alternatively, *Travelers in an Antique Land* takes the theme of intrusion and displays how people can sully yet not destroy the high desert with the refuse and discarded articles they leave there. Studebaker's book compels Sollers to assert that the

*spiritus loci* (spirit of the place) remains intact in the antique land.

William V. Studebaker's work as a whole reflects his native background, in that he tends to operate from his own pronounced sense of place. This sense of place has always included an equally pronounced tendency toward self-reliance, something the poet learned early in life, and the desire to write his own way. Whether such tendencies will take him far professionally, especially in terms of national–as opposed to regional–recognition, remains to be seen. Yet, his sense of craft, his inventiveness, and his ability to learn from other professionals, indirectly as well as directly, should stand him in good stead.

## References:

Bert Almon, "A Fruitful Emptiness: Poets and Artists in the Great Basin Region," *Western American Literature,* 34 (Fall 1999): 347–354;

James H. Maguire, "REFLECTING: The Literature of Our Time–1960–1985," in *The Literature of Idaho: An Anthology,* Hemingway Western Studies Publications, edited by Maguire (Boise, Idaho: Boise State University, 1986), pp. 253–254;

Ford Swetnam, "Nature and Culture in Idaho's Poetry," in *Tough Paradise: The Literature of Idaho and the Intermountain West* (Boise, Idaho: Idaho Humanities Council, 1995), pp. 30–31.

# Douglas H. Thayer

*(19 April 1929 –  )*

Eugene England
*Utah Valley State College*

BOOKS: *Under the Cottonwoods and Other Mormon Stories* (Provo, Utah: Frankson Books, 1977);
*Greg* (Provo, Utah: Frankson Books, 1979);
*Summer Fire* (Midvale, Utah: Orion Books, 1983);
*Mr. Wahlquist in Yellowstone and Other Stories* (Salt Lake City, Utah: Peregrine Smith, 1989).

SELECTED PERIODICAL PUBLICATIONS–
UNCOLLECTED: "The Brain," *Improvement Era,* 63 (February 1960): 86–87, 100, 102, 104;
"His Wonders to Perform," *Brigham Young University Studies,* 6 (Winter 1965): 101–118;
"The Turtle's Smile," *Prairie Schooner,* 44 (Fall 1970): 190–208;
"The First Sunday," *Ensign,* 1 (May 1971): 58–63;
"Ten Years of Laughter," *Sunstone,* 1 (Autumn 1976): 30–36;
"Germany (1947–48): The Maturing of an Imagination," *Wasatch Review International,* 1 (1992): 78–93;
"The Sparrow Hunter," *Dialogue: A Journal of Mormon Thought,* 32 (Spring 1999): 145–156;
"Brother Melrose," *Dialogue: A Journal of Mormon Thought,* 32 (Fall 1999): 141–154;
"Ice Fishing," *Dialogue: A Journal of Morman Thought,* 33 (Summer 2000): 167–185.

Douglas Thayer conveys the tragic in American experience that comes from what people and the wilderness have done to each other as well as any contemporary Western writer. From his early story "Red-Tailed Hawk" (1969) through two collections and a novel, and into his latest stories and essays, he displays insight into the particular history of the destructive relationship between mankind and the wilderness in the West, from the arrogant, self-defeating mountain men of the 1830s, intruding into lands and cultures they could not comprehend, to modern men and boys who try, at great cost to themselves and others, to recapture the primitive and merge with wilderness. Among Western writers, Thayer's work is comparable in quality and theme to

*Douglas H. Thayer (courtesy of the author)*

that of Levi S. Peterson, whose writing explores the values as well as the dangers of wilderness as a place for modern people to seek salvation.

In addition, Thayer is the father of contemporary Mormon fiction and one of its major voices. He was raised before and during World War II in Provo, Utah, when it was still in many ways a nineteenth-century Mormon village and a boys' paradise. He and his friends had easy access to the fields and marshes, river and lake to the south and west, and the canyons and mountains to the east. He lived constantly in them, imaginatively connecting himself to the romantic violence of the Old West and the heroic violence of World War II–often with the thoughtless destructiveness of some of his protagonists, killing whatever wildlife he could, running wild, and swimming naked–living, as he later said, like a "barbarian." Right after World War II he spent two years as a rather lonely, morally isolated but patriotic, volunteer soldier in the U.S. Army of Occupation in Germany–images of the limbless men who survived the war and the women prostituting themselves to stave off the postwar starvation haunt his stories–and then another two years as a Mormon missionary in the same land. After graduating with a major in English from Brigham Young University in 1955, he started work on a Ph.D. in American literature at Stanford University in California, but left in 1957 to begin teaching at Brigham Young University. Thayer was at the University of Maryland from 1960 to 1961 working on a Ph.D. in American studies. However, finally realizing that he wanted to write fiction and not literary criticism, he then enrolled in the Iowa Writers' Workshop, where he studied under R. V. Cassill, Vance Bourjailly, and Phillip Roth. He received an M.F.A. degree from Iowa in 1962. He currently teaches creative writing as Professor of English at Brigham Young University and has been Freshman Writing Coordinator (1983–1986) and Associate Dean of the College of Humanities (1986–1991).

Though Thayer began early to write stories of great stylistic and intellectual sophistication based in the tension between his developing ethical identity and the seductions of wilderness and authoritative religion, he did not begin publishing regularly until he was almost forty. Then he produced in quick succession some of his finest work, including "The Red-Tailed Hawk" (1969) and "Opening Day" (1970), which led to publication in 1977 of *Under the Cottonwoods and Other Mormon Stories*. He was the first writer to remain centered in Mormon belief and located in Mormon country and to create a fiction deeply grounded in Mormon theology and experience; yet it was also responsive to personal vision and feeling rather than merely to didactic or institutional purposes. Consequently, his influence on a generation of younger Mormon writers continues to be profound. According to John Bennion, whose collection *Breeding Leah and Other Stories* (1991) includes experimental contemporary styles and subjects, "Thayer taught us how to explore the interior life, with its conflicts of doubt and faith, goodness and evil, of a believing Mormon." Levi S. Peterson reports that the example of Thayer, whose work he reread carefully

while writing his masterpiece, *The Backslider* (1986), taught him to write of difficult and complex religious and psychological subject matter with simple, short, highly resonant sentences. Beginning with that outburst of creative energy in the late 1960s, Thayer has regularly received awards for his fiction from *Dialogue,* from Brigham Young University, and from the Utah Institute of Fine Arts. In 1998, when he received an Honorary Lifetime Membership Award from the Association for Mormon Letters, he was credited with having achieved in his work "the remarkable feat of creating the deep human attraction to nature, especially wilderness, that energized the Romantic movement and the myth of the American West–while at the same time portraying the terrible descent into blankness and violence that total surrender to wilderness can bring."

Douglas Heal Thayer was born on 19 April 1929 in Salt Lake City, Utah, and grew up mainly in Provo, a central Utah town that had already experienced ten years of the Great Depression. His mother, Lily Nora Thatcher, with her parents and nine siblings had immigrated to the United States in 1920 from Bath, England, as Mormon converts. Thayer's father, Edward Frank Thayer, was thirty years older than Lily when they married. His parents divorced when Thayer was quite young, and he has never been able to locate his father's relatives or genealogy but remembers hearing that his father was born in Scotland and that his papers had all been destroyed in the San Francisco earthquake and fire in 1906. Thayer occasionally visited his father, who lived in a room behind an old hotel in downtown Provo, until his father died in 1942, when Thayer was thirteen.

Thayer grew up with a single mother who, as he said in an unpublished interview, "was on federal relief and worked scrubbing other women's houses and taking in laundry, so I had to work for what I wanted. Got my first job catching worms for bait and selling them wholesale by the quart." Thayer also worked as a laborer in construction and in a pig-iron plant, as a salvage crewman, driller's helper, janitor, clerk, insurance salesman, and as a seasonal ranger in Yellowstone National Park for three summers. Despite marginal poverty and having to earn every dime, he remembers his youth as a time of remarkable freedom and natural joy. He was sometimes gone whole days, with a few companions and their .22 rifles or shotguns or fishing poles, roaming up the immediately accessible canyons of the Wasatch range or biking out to the marshes to sit in duck blinds with his homemade duck decoys or to fish up and down the Provo River. In those days, before the Army Corps of Engineers channeled out the entire lower Provo River, it contained a large, deep hole known as "The Crusher," forty by sixty yards, dredged out for crushing rocks into gravel; there Doug and his friends swam naked for hours.

Thayer did his graduate work in American literature at Stanford when Yvor Winters taught there and was recognized as the most powerful modern voice against Romantic optimism about nature. Thayer's early stories, written in the 1960s, reveal a constant and increasingly successful effort, as Bruce W. Jorgensen showed in a study published in *Western American Literature* (1987), to adapt the major Romantic lyric form, a self-educative meditation in or upon a wilderness setting–such as William Wordsworth's "Ode on Intimations of Immortality" (1807)–"to western Mormon experience and consciousness, but in ways that also question and undercut this form." Thayer's mature work achieves a similar undermining of the typical Romantic lyrical content: he makes it Christian by turning it from the naturalized supernaturalism of a merely self-imagined interior education or wholeness "back towards the sacred narrative sequence of fall and redemption that it once derived from."

Thayer's characteristic early story form, which Jorgensen describes as following "the introspective and retrospective processes of a male protagonist through some brief, decisive interval in his life," is well illustrated in the title story of *Under the Cottonwoods and Other Mormon Stories*. Paul, a successful dentist in Palo Alto, coming home for a visit to his parents in Provo, stops on the freeway near the place on the river where he swam as a boy and, leaving his pregnant wife and three small children in the car, finds the swimming hole destroyed by dredging for flood control. There he engages in a long meditation focused on the contrasts between his memories of the cool, cottonwood-shaded Eden of the river where he had been "alive there under the trees, full of a kind of freedom, sensation, and pure careless joy he had never known afterward, a sense of being"–and the present destroyed landscape in which for him, as for Wordsworth's lyric speaker, "There hath passed away a glory from the earth." But for Paul this loss reflects a deeper change, from a time when he felt connected to himself, his body, and the natural world, to a present in which he is alienated from all three. He reflects on fulfilling the upwardly mobile expectations of his pious Mormon mother and on the pressures toward "perfection" of a Puritanical strain in Wasatch-front Mormonism:

> All his life he had been an example . . . for his younger brothers and sisters, then for the neighborhood boys, for his classmates. In the army he had to be the example for his whole company. . . . His example was supposed to help other servicemen to become interested in the Church, investigate it, join. And before they would do that they had to find that he was clean,

Cover for Thayer's first collection of short fiction, published in 1977. In the title story the protagonist is launched on a far-ranging reverie by discovering that his boyhood swimming hole has been destroyed by dredging.

wholesome, spiritual, happy, different from them. . . . Now in the Palo Alto Ward he had to be an example for all of the Stanford students. . . . It was as if being an example were more important than being a person.

Indeed, Paul has lost his personhood, not in the sense of Christ's admonition to lose one's life for his sake, in order to find it, but more in the sense of the Romantic loss of wholeness by falling into self-consciousness and alienation from nature and thus into "dejection." But, as Jorgensen says, Romantic dejection is a "secularized and psychologized version of the Biblical fall of man," and Thayer's undermining of his Romantic models lies in a focus on Paul's fall from grace and his precariously hopeful reaching for spiritual salvation–not simply a Romantic self-reflective journey to higher knowledge.

Paul's narrative journey is enriched by powerful symbolic parallels to his fall and possible redemption focused on the now-destroyed river. It was the scene of paradisiacal wholeness with his young body and its eroticism, of an aborted near-wholeness with his father when they once swam naked there together, and the home of trout, now gone from the river. The Romantic "fall" was principally a fall into self-consciousness, into awareness of each person's estrangement from what is "other" to it, particularly nature. The great Romantic nature poems resist and mourn such a fall, though the best finally accept it as a necessary part of the educative journey. Paul's particular Mormon Christian self, alienated from his body and its natural eroticism in his quest for perfection, frantically resists the flawed uncleanliness and self-awareness that means both accepting the Primal Fall of all humans and accepting the contingent perfection in grace made available through Christ's healing atonement. Thayer's story suggests that Paul's Romantic reverie by the ruined river will not heal him—but that a highly symbolic movement of his imagination might. That night at his parents' home, he asks his brother to go fishing with him "up on Strawberry [Reservoir]," and the reader moves back into Paul's central consciousness:

> In the darkness he would stand in the thigh-deep cool water, cast out into the lake, . . . see the beautiful silver rainbow trout leap shining in the moonlight. Mark and his father would kill the trout they caught. . . . But he wouldn't. . . . He would hold the rainbow in the net to see it shining rose-silver, pull the hook from the lip, then release it, see the trout hover then flash back into the deep water, vanish.

This desire is, as Jorgensen points out, as yet only a wish, but if acted out could, in a Jungian reading, let Paul's "lost and ravaged self sink into the dark unconscious, . . . prepare the way a for psychic renewal," or it could, even more subtly, suggest that the Romantic imagination is not enough until fulfilled in a "thing done"—the actual, graceful release of the highly symbolic fish.

Even more powerful critiques of the Romantic and of its secular modes of "salvation" are two other stories—"Opening Day," from *Under the Cottonwoods and Other Mormon Stories,* and "The Red-Tailed Hawk," from Thayer's second collection, *Mr. Wahlquist in Yellowstone and Other Stories* (1989). "Opening Day" is more effectively plotted than "Under the Cottonwoods" and subtly presents an ethically revealing double voice by having an older Mormon recount the story of his first deer hunt after returning from his mission in Germany. There, after seeing the horrors that resulted from World War II, he had vowed, in the terms of a spiritual conversion, never to kill anything again. Thayer gains the reader's full empathy by creating the hunt with the immediacy of the young man's naive voice, but he also informs the narration by details and symbols only possible from the older man's sorrowing, repentant, possibly redeemed, point of view. This blending of points of view includes the final lines, when

the young man, after arrogantly tempting himself by going on the hunt despite his vow, succumbs to temptation and shoots four bucks: "Still trembling, I knelt down by the big buck's head. His pooled blood started to trickle down through the oak leaves. 'Oh, Jesus, Jesus,' I whispered." This is, at once, a profane recognition, half-joy, half-regret, that his self-willed and immature new faith in his Christian pacifism has been found wanting, and, in Jorgensen's words, "perhaps the most earnest prayer he has ever made, in the 'opening' recognition . . . of radical dependence on grace."

"The Red-Tailed Hawk" uses a meditative mode similar to that in "Under the Cottonwoods" but is, like "Opening Day," more fully and effectively plotted. In addition, while many Thayer stories use some form of limited-omniscient central consciousness within the present action in order to gain sympathy and reveal complexity of feeling, this story, also like "Opening Day," has an older narrator looking back in clear-eyed judgment on his unredeemed self—and thus he helps the reader see more clearly the infusion of grace and the completed action that led to his salvation. This dual point of view creates a balance of sympathy and judgment.

The narrator tells of a daylong hunt just before Christmas, more than ten years before, when he was fifteen. But the plot is carefully interspersed with his present versions of his earlier meditations on the seductive freedom and solitude of his life in nature, which he had constantly attempted to fix and preserve through killing and mounting birds, particularly a red-tailed hawk that hangs over his bed. The hunt ends with his killing a Canada goose, swimming out to retrieve it, and then nearly dying of exposure. He loses parts of three fingers but comes to a full awareness of the cost of merging with nature; that insight brings him back into acceptance of his family and thus himself as part of the human community. It brings him to acceptance of both the works—the actions of law and societal structure—and the grace that have saved him.

The boy experiences powerfully the Romantic temptation to deify nature and to attempt to lose alienating self-consciousness by merging with nature—even, if necessary, in death. The mature narrator, clearly a voice for Thayer himself, is able, while giving the boy's meditations sympathetically, to feel deeply the temptation:

> I was always hiding from Glade and the others, the sheriff when he came down to see if we wore swimsuits; always driven, I reached out for something infinite, not knowing what it was, but feeling myself drawn to it, some final feeling beyond the earth in the yellow sun.

> . . . In a wind I rode the trees, the high limbs, heard a million leaves, screamed into the sound. And when I

Douglas H. Thayer
2746 N. 550 E.
Provo, Utah 84604

Thayer--1
9/20/82

The summer I turned sixteen my ~~first~~ cousin Randy and I
left Provo and went to work on the Johnson ranch twenty miles
outside of Silverton, Nevada, on the Battle River. ~~Kmzihamxm~~ My
Uncle Mark got us our jobs. He wanted to get Randy away from
his girl friend, *Lana Baker* ~~Kellie Miller,~~ for the summer, and *he wanted Randy* to learn how
to work. Uncle Mark said that I needed to stop reading books
and practicing the piano ~~for a summer,~~ and *that I needed to* get ~~away~~ away from
~~to little checked, and there was a branch of the Chruch in Silverton,~~
*for a* my grandmother. ~~s~~ My father died when I was three and my mother
*while* ~~so I wouldn't miss my meetings.~~ and I lived with my Grandmother Nelson. My Grandfather Nelson
was dead, too.

~~Yexhafim~~ Randy and I left Provo (on May thirty-first,) on the
Greyhound bus at four-fifteen in the morning. ~~We~~ *At the station we*
all stood back from the bus. ~~Enixinxdmxnxinxkxxnxxxinxxthaxsmallxk~~
~~afmxinxmxikx~~ The smell of diesel *fuel* always nauseated me. Eight of
the through passengers to Los Angeles stood under the sodium
vapor lamp smoking cigarettes. ~~Across the parking lot, Randy t.~~

*Corrected typescript page for Thayer's 1983 novel,* Summer Fire *(Collection of Douglas Thayer)*

297

swung on the rope it was fantastic because I couldn't see where the water started. The tingling went from my crotch clear to my skull, and I reached out to a world I had never known, something inviting me, as in my dreams.

But the narrator is also able, first in imagery and then in action, to give the reader the profound, tragic awareness of the high Romantics, best expressed in John Keats's "Ode to a Nightingale" (1820), that the human mind is finally entirely separate from nature and can only cross the void in death or oblivion; to do so, of course, means losing the ability to perceive and be tempted by nature, to feel or express anything.

Thayer's protagonist in "The Red-Tailed Hawk" finally makes this discovery, expressed as if it were in the young boy's mind as central consciousness, but, as the reader is sufficiently reminded in the actual words and understanding of the future man: he includes images of death in the boy's paradise that were, in his earlier, fallen state, incomprehensible to him and finally uses mainly the language of the mature person when thinking back to his moment of grace and resurrection at the point of near death from freezing:

Snow filled the wrinkles of my coat; I was turning white.

All summer the [dead] cows had been vanishing, the wire-hung birds [I had killed] too, the carp, the little buck. And I had no name for it, only vanishing, knew only that it was not swimming, not running naked in the moonlight, not embracing trees, not soaring. It was not feeling. I grew whiter, saw myself vanishing into the snow. I watched, and then slowly, like beginning pain, the terror seeped into me, the knowing. I struggled up, fled.

But the felt power of such a discovery is earned by the convincing sensual detail and yearning emotional directness of the earlier meditations on the temptation to merge with that world that he has now rejected.

The boy is saved by the sheriff, sent by his parents to look for him. The sheriff–representative of civilized order, society–was earlier seen by the boy merely as an intruder on his natural world, but he becomes now an instrument of grace and a bridge back to the human community. Besides losing his fingers, the boy nearly dies of pneumonia. He comes up into consciousness from the oxygen tent, which "is like being under water," either to his mother or to his father, waiting alternately through the nights by his bed. He is terrified of sleep, that little death, and stops his pain shots so he can use the hurt to keep himself awake, but then he becomes aware that the old man sharing his hospital room has died. The boy is taken home to find his family dressed up for a late Christmas, saved for him, and then lies in his bedroom,

warm with a new oil heater, looking up at the red-tailed hawk. But now, like Keats, he sees the bird with new understanding of death and of the impossibility of entering its realm, and also of the corruption of trying: "The yellow glass eyes looked down, the bird motionless, suspended from a wire, dusty. Out in the barn the hanging birds were dusty too, some of them splotched with pigeon droppings."

In a flash-forward, the narrator tells of the devastation of later seeing his hand for the first time without bandages, of hiding it, quitting gym so others would not see it, crying to God, making promises, awaking afraid to look; and he tells of his father making him start gym again, making him do chores, "no matter how many things I broke or spilled, and although he shouted at me sometimes, swore, he never again hit me." The father tells him, "You can't hide; you have to live with it. . . . That's life." As the narrator who makes that pun has since learned well, such acceptance of limitation and responsibility is in every sense true living–the very opposite of vanishing into cold nature.

An important measure of Thayer's achievement is the extent to which, like Keats, he is able to embody the full Romantic dilemma, as well as to give it a Christian, even a particularly Mormon, resolution. He suggests not only that the central Romantic emotion of attraction to nature and away from the conscious and civilized can be inimical to life itself–but he does so without denying the power of that attraction. Though the narrator is now a new creature, he can evoke with lyric nostalgia the still-precious emotions attendant on his youthful closeness to that realm:

Low, gabbling, three great Canada geese flew out of the greyness below me, shadows, but then blacker, coming right at me in good range. Big, bigger than I had ever thought, beautiful, somebody pounding me over the heart. I watched through a hole in the blind. "Wait, wait," whispering, "not too soon. Big. Wait, wait." The gabbling grew louder–marvelous the wings, the long necks, the rhythmic birds.

The influence of "The Red-Tailed Hawk" has been considerable. It makes possible experiencing with proper emotion the precise nuances of the moral complexity of life. Thayer credits "The Red-Tailed Hawk" with being a superior example, one that changed him into a writer of fiction: "It opened my mind to the nuances of my own life and increased my level of consciousness. . . . I had done a lot of reading . . . , but this was the first *experience* I had ever had. . . . [It] affected me more profoundly and positively than any scripture I ever read or any talk I ever heard."

Thayer married Donlu DeWitt in 1974 when he was forty-five. The couple had six children in nine years, and Thayer gave up killing animals (except for an occasional trout as he became an avid fly fisherman), privately published his first collection of stories, *Under the Cottonwoods and Other Mormon Stories,* and wrote and published a coming-of-age novel. *Summer Fire* (1983) was the first "real" Mormon novel in nearly thirty years–that is, the first to deal seriously with Mormon characters and ideas and to use them to create versions of the central human conflicts that energize good fiction. The protagonist, Owen, is much like Paul of "Under the Cottonwoods," a somewhat self-righteous Mormon raised mainly by his protective mother and grandmother. But Owen leaves his antiseptic Provo home to work for the summer on a Nevada ranch. There the ranch foreman, Staver–one of Thayer's most unusual and powerful fictional creations–rubs Owen's face in dirt, manure, and disgrace. More subtly, Staver attempts to initiate Owen–as he usually does all the summer hands–into error and sin.

Owen is certainly not a Billy Budd, fixed forever in beautiful, amoral innocence; he begins as an offensive prig, but he is also touchingly reflective and determined as a moral being. But Staver is not merely like Melville's Claggart, fixed forever in a mysterious, yearning love/hate for goodness and a compulsion to destroy it. Thayer skillfully unpacks the "mystery of iniquity" in Staver, using the fine symbol of his being wounded in the heart in Korea and evoking his Claggart-like despair in violent midnight rides he takes on a half-wild stallion. Staver's best friend had joined the army to be with him in Korea and was killed there trying to save others the day before Staver himself was wounded, in what seems to have been some desperate, even suicidal, action. Staver will not accept his friend's sacrifice; but through Owen's only partly comprehending vision, the reader sees Staver teaching Owen about work and caring, even about giving, and sees that Staver's flaw is a complex one. There is hope, which even Owen can finally feel, that Staver, too, might be healed.

The main source of that hope is Mrs. Cummings, cook and housekeeper for the ranch, who, besides striving to heal Staver, becomes, in effect, Owen's pastor. Raised a Mormon in Utah but married outside the Latter-day Saints Church, Mrs. Cummings is now a devoted but pragmatic evangelical Christian, faithfully enduring, despite serious illness, a son in jail and the continuing prospect of Staver's evil. In one of her frequent minisermons to Owen, she says:

> We all need the Lord Jesus Christ, son. . . . We need to let him love us and wash us clean with his blood; we all need that. It takes lot of suffering sometimes before most people are willing to let the Lord teach them anything, and some never are. . . . Staver had that terrible

*Cover for Thayer's novel about a young Mormon who comes to self-awareness while spending a summer working on a ranch*

wound in his heart. . . . I tell that boy he's got to let the Lord teach him and love him, but he won't listen. . . . Helping everybody and having party friends ain't enough. A man's got to have the love of a wife and children to make any sense. Staver's got a lot of good in him.

Mrs. Cummings's simple but unsentimental goodness, together with her steady Christian–but non-Mormon–voice for redemptive love, is an important innovation in Mormon fiction. It allows Thayer to place his own moral and spiritual authority firmly within the story without intruding on Owen's first-person naiveté, thus presenting a fine balance of compassion with precise ethical assessment. Mrs. Cummings becomes Thayer's direct agent for saving Owen. Finally pushed too far by Staver's success in corrupting Owen's cousin Randy–the other summer ranch hand–Owen becomes enraged enough to fight Staver and then, after a humiliating defeat, to aim a rifle at him from outside the bunkhouse with intent to kill. But Owen is stopped by Mrs. Cummings's providential appearance:

*Cover for Thayer's second collection (1989), in which stories such as "The Red-Tailed Hawk" deal with his complex understanding of grace*

"Son, son."

I turned. Mrs. Cummings stood under the trees in her long, white nightgown, her white hair down over her shoulders.

This redemptive figure has done much more than prevent Owen from committing a terrible crime; she has helped him toward the essential understanding of himself and Christ that now begins to dawn. On his way home to Utah, Owen looks at a section of famous war photographs in *Life* magazine. Included in the photographs is one of a young German soldier,

> holding a rifle and looking down from a guard tower at the people in a concentration camp. I looked at him. . . . I looked at my hands, and then I looked at Randy and the other people in the bus whose faces I could see. I knew that I wasn't any different from them, and I knew that was part of what I'd learned. But there was something else, something even more important, that I didn't

have a word for yet. But I would. It was a word like *prayer* or *faith* or *love*.

The concept of grace is central to *Mr. Wahlquist in Yellowstone and Other Stories*. In addition to "The Red-Tailed Hawk," the book includes four other stories that explore in detail Thayer's complex understanding of the legitimate attractions and terrible dangers of wilderness as opposed to the saving grace of human community. "The Gold Mine" asks what attracts civilized people to the wilderness edges of life, but this story only hints at a possible answer. The story deals with the preservation and transportation through decomposing heat of the body of a wild young man who has been killed while exploring a mine in the Nevada desert–where his parents have sent him to be rid of him but also in the hope that he might be "saved." Maude Miller, whose humanely garrulous and community-building words make up most of the story, redeems the accidental death by using it to try to save from similar isolation and silence young Carl, the discoverer of the body.

"The Rooster" is Thayer's slightest story in this collection, but it is perhaps his most devastating translation of the brute mountain man into the brute modern suburban American with a similar Romantic view of nature. His protagonist is trying to live out a fantasized wilderness connection on weekend hunts but is so enslaved to habits of drink and self-gratifying eroticism that he not only fails as husband and father but also turns the necessary, even perhaps heroic, hunting rituals of primitive humans into failure and squalor.

In contrast, Mr. Wahlquist, of the title story, turns his hunt in modern Yellowstone Park into the tragic rather than the trivial. The narrator–a young, unconverted version of Thayer–gives a sympathetic, even seductive, view of old Mr. Wahlquist, who has spent most of his life wishing he could have been a mountain man or, better, a Crow Indian.

The storms that darken three of these stories–including the last, "Dolf"–and obscure life as well as vision are supreme symbols of the destructive, life-ending force of wilderness. The mountain men and Crows are real enough–as are the fiercely destructive Blackfeet. Dolf and his cousin Gib leave Providence, Rhode Island, to travel up the Missouri River with one of the early fur-trading companies, just twenty years after Lewis and Clark. Gib, especially, senses a "last chance" to be part of the incredible, raw westering that they have heard about and that is already vanishing, and he goes "native." He kills animals wantonly and kills an Indian savagely, scalping and mutilating the body. He fathers children with Crow women. He pushes for an opportunity to trap beavers over the winter in an untouched valley–untouched because it is too close to dangerous Blackfoot country;

and he refuses to leave immediately when a Blackfoot hunting party comes into the valley.

Gib pays for his arrogance with his life, and the story is about Dolf's heart-pounding run for his own life, his ingenious trapping and killing of most of the Blackfeet, and his ultimate destruction in the wilderness through his own tragic mixture of arrogant strengths and blind weaknesses. Dolf's mistakes include leaving "Providence"–clearly a symbol of the family and of civilized, even sanctified, human community that for Thayer is the only salvation–and eventually succumbing to Gib's temptations of primitivism, violence, and irresponsible sexual behavior. But his more intellectual pretensions of learning the Crow language and "thinking" his way through the adventure with his supposedly superior white man's rationality do not prevent–and may even contribute to–mistakes that combine to tempt him to extreme and violent actions.

Thayer shows himself fully sensitive to the Romantic poets' fearful awareness of a tragic paradox about experience and words–that the very unity with nature they so much yearned for, the very merging into wilderness and the primitive that so attracted them, inevitably meant enormous loss, not only of the higher consciousness that they found so alienating from nature and wished to leave behind but also, as a result, of language, the means for exploring and expressing their yearning. Language, understood and well used, is essential for understanding the values, as well as the dangers, of wilderness.

None of the stories of *Mr. Wahlquist in Yellowstone and Other Stories* are overtly Mormon. Since 1989 Thayer has focused his energies on two novels about Mormon protagonists working out their salvation in fear and trembling in Provo.

One of these novels, the as yet unpublished "A Good Man," explores the inner development of an average middle-aged Mormon as he deals with the death of his overbearing grandmother, the liberation of his wife, and his own introduction, through a funny, cosmopolitan sister, to a much wider world than he had known. The other novel, "A Member of the Church," accepted for publication by Signature Books, is more complex and provides the first extensive fictional look at an important Mormon cultural phenomenon: the development, in the past twenty years, of hundreds of millionaires and a few billionaires in traditionally impoverished Mormon country and in a church that has a radically egalitarian, even antiwealth–at least anticonsumption–theology and a history and

expected future of actually practicing, under church direction, a thoroughly communitarian social order. Thayer looks at what happens when these facts collide in the ethical, social, and aesthetic lives of East Bench Provoans, many of high church position, when suddenly wealthy people build and decorate with huge religious icons multimillion-dollar homes that reflect a new combination of conspicuous consumption with spiritual yearning, artistic uncertainty, and religious aristocracy. All of these new conditions are seen through the wondering, only somewhat naive, eyes of a teenage Mormon from California, who has come to spend the summer with his dying cousin in such a home.

After spending all of his time writing novels, Thayer is starting again to write and publish short stories and story-essays. He remains the contemporary Mormon writer with the longest, and most continuously productive, career. He employs various and weighty themes and, through his sophistication with point of view and sharply honed self-reflection on a long life in the West, ethically challenging and persuasive writing.

**Interview:**

Jerry Johnston, "Doug Thayer's Fiction on the New Frontier," *Deseret News* (7 June 1990), p. E1.

**References:**

Tory Anderson, "Just the Fiction, Ma'am," *Wasatch Review International,* 1, no. 2 (1992): 1–9;

Eugene England, "Douglas Thayer's *Mr. Wahlquist in Yellowstone:* A Mormon's Christian Response to Wilderness," *BYU Studies,* 34, no. 1 (1994): 53–72;

England, "Faithful Fiction," *Dialogue: A Journal of Mormon Thought,* 18 (Winter 1985): 196–201;

Edward Geary, Review of *Summer Fire, BYU Studies,* 24, no. 2 (1994): 250–252;

Geary, Review of *Under the Cottonwoods, Dialogue: A Journal of Mormon Thought,* 11, no. 1 (Spring 1978): 123–127;

Bruce W. Jorgensen, "Romantic Lyric Form and Western Mormon Experience in the Stories of Douglas Thayer," *Western American Literature,* 22 (Spring 1987): 33–49;

Kathleen Lubeck, "Two Mormon Writers: Translating the Peculiar Culture into Words," *Brigham Young University Today* (April 1977): 16–17.

**Papers:**

Douglas H. Thayer's papers are held at the Harold B. Lee Library, Brigham Young University, Provo, Utah.

# David Wagoner

*(5 June 1926 –    )*

Ron McFarland
*University of Idaho*

See also the Wagoner entry in *DLB 5: American Poets Since World War II.*

BOOKS: *Dry Sun, Dry Wind* (Bloomington: Indiana University Press, 1953);

*The Man in the Middle* (New York: Harcourt, Brace, 1954);

*Money, Money, Money* (New York: Harcourt, Brace, 1955);

*A Place to Stand* (Bloomington: Indiana University Press, 1958);

*Rock: A Novel* (New York: Viking, 1958);

*The Nesting Ground, A Book of Poems* (Bloomington: Indiana University Press, 1963);

*The Escape Artist* (New York: Farrar, Straus & Giroux, 1965; London: Gollancz, 1965);

*Staying Alive* (Bloomington: Indiana University Press, 1966);

*Baby, Come on Inside* (New York: Farrar, Straus & Giroux, 1968);

*New and Selected Poems* (Bloomington: Indiana University Press, 1969); republished as *Working Against Time* (London: Rapp and Whiting, 1970);

*Where Is My Wandering Boy Tonight?* (New York: Farrar, Straus & Giroux, 1970);

*Riverbed* (Bloomington: Indiana University Press, 1972);

*The Road to Many a Wonder* (New York: Farrar, Straus & Giroux, 1974);

*Sleeping in the Woods* (Bloomington: Indiana University Press, 1974);

*Tracker* (Boston: Little, Brown, 1975);

*Collected Poems (1956–1976)* (Bloomington: Indiana University Press, 1976);

*Travelling Light* (Port Townsend, Wash.: Graywolf, 1976); enlarged as *Traveling Light: Collected and New Poems* (Urbana: University of Illinois Press, 1999);

*Whole Hog* (Boston: Little, Brown, 1976);

*Who Shall Be the Sun?: Poems Based on the Lore, Legends, and Myths of Northwest Coast and Plateau Indians* (Bloomington: Indiana University Press, 1978);

*In Broken Country: Poems* (Boston: Little, Brown, 1979);

*The Hanging Garden* (Boston: Little, Brown, 1980; London: Hale, 1982);

*Landfall: Poems* (Boston: Little, Brown, 1981);

*First Light* (Boston: Little, Brown, 1983);

*Through the Forest: New and Selected Poems, 1977–1987* (New York: Atlantic Monthly, 1987);

*Walt Whitman Bathing* (Urbana: University of Illinois Press, 1996);

*House of Song* (Urbana: University of Illinois Press, 2002).

PLAY PRODUCTION: *An Eye For An Eye For An Eye,* Seattle, University of Washington Theater, 1973.

RECORDINGS: "*A Valedictory to Standard Oil of Indiana*" *and Other Poems,* read by Wagoner, Western Michigan University, Aural Poems, 1966;

*Today's Poets: Their Poems, Their Voices,* includes readings by Wagoner, volume 2, New York, Scholastic Records, 1967;

*100 Modern American Poets Reading Their Poems,* includes readings by Wagoner, volume 16, New York, Spoken Arts, 1969;

*Carolyn Kizer & David Wagoner,* includes readings by Wagoner, New York, Academy of American Poets, 1995.

OTHER: *Five Poets of the Pacific Northwest: Kenneth O. Hanson, Richard Hugo, Carolyn Kizer, William Stafford, David Wagoner,* edited by Robin Skelton, includes poems by Wagoner (Seattle: University of Washington Press, 1964);

*Straw for the Fire: From the Notebooks of Theodore Roethke, 1943–1963,* edited by Wagoner (Garden City, N.Y.: Doubleday, 1972).

SELECTED PERIODICAL PUBLICATION–
UNCOLLECTED: "The Song of Songs Which is Sheba's," *Slackwater Review,* special David Wagoner issue (1981): 52–87.

*David Wagoner (photograph by Robin Seyfried; courtesy of the author)*

Among the poets who studied with Theodore Roethke, David Wagoner is one of the most prolific and versatile. Few of Roethke's progeny have matched Wagoner's record of publications, which includes more than a dozen books of poetry, ten novels, a novella, several short stories, and a few one-act plays. At the age of seventy-five he still teaches in the English Department at the University of Washington, to which Roethke lured him in 1954, and edits *Poetry Northwest,* which he helped establish in the early 1960s. From 1978 to 1999 he served on the Board of Chancellors of the Academy of American Poets. Wagoner has been preparing a new edition of *Collected Poems (1956–1976)* to reflect his work since the first appearance of the book in 1976; seeking a publisher for his new novel, "Early and Often," which is set in Chicago in 1893; and developing a one-man play based on poems he adapted from the journals of Henry David Thoreau. Although he has maintained his interest in fiction, Wagoner made his reputation initially as a poet. He has been hailed as one of America's premier nature poets, as a visionary poet, and as a master of verbal wit and semantic legerdemain. Yet, Wagoner's many admirers nearly always point out that he deserves broader renown.

In an autobiographical essay for *Contemporary Authors* (1999) Wagoner speculates that there has always been a discrepancy between the apparent ease of his life and its painful actuality. Tall, trim, handsome, and possessed of an athletic build–he played football and basketball while in high school in Indiana, although he makes light of the experience in his poems–his appearance alone might arouse envy in fellow writers. Perhaps because of his early exposure to the excesses of Dylan Thomas, with whom he spent time in 1950 and in 1952, and his years as a colleague of the manic-depressive Roethke, Wagoner has not lived what is popularly regarded as the traditional poet's life–an existence of manic intensity, self-destructive indulgence in drink and drugs, and reckless abandon. While other students of the charismatic Roethke, such as James Wright and Richard Hugo, lived mostly on the edge like their mentor, Wagoner has remained self-controlled, moderate, and low-key. The path of moderation may have kept him alive and comfortable, even prosperous, but his shyness or reticence has sometimes been interpreted as aloofness or arrogance. He is a departure from Hugo, who had a magnetic personality, and from William Stafford, a writer whose congenial affability put people at ease.

Wagoner begins his autobiographical essay with the sentence, "Geography had a lot to do with it." Born on 5 June 1926 to Walter Siffert and Ruth Banyard Wagoner in Massilon, Ohio, where his father worked at a steel mill, Wagoner moved with his older brother Walter and sister Jeanne to the industrial wasteland of Whiting, Indiana, in 1933. Wagoner's first book of poems conveys the sterility of the landscape through its title, *Dry Sun, Dry Wind* (1953). Although Walter worked for most of his life in the mills, he graduated magna cum laude with a B.A. in classical languages from Washington and Jefferson College, in Washington, Pennsylvania, where he played football. As Wagoner recalls in his essay, Walter was "very strong, very short-tempered, very opinionated," and he figures in several of the poet's lyrics. Unlike Wagoner's "deeply uneasy and unhappy" father, his mother was "almost pathologically self-effacing." Both parents were fond of music, and Wagoner has written playful verse on his own marginal success with the trumpet in the school band.

A navy ROTC scholarship brought Wagoner to Pennsylvania State University (Penn State) in 1944, where he met Roethke in a poetry-writing class. He received his M.A. degree at Indiana University in 1949 and then taught for a year at DePauw University before returning to Penn State as an instructor in 1950, the same year that he married Elizabeth Arensman. His first poems appeared in the December 1948 issue of *Poetry* magazine, and his first short stories were published in periodicals such as *Folio* (February 1949) and *Kenyon Review* (Summer 1949). Two years after his marriage ended in divorce in 1952, Wagoner was invited to teach at the University of Washington. At twenty-eight—well advanced in his career as a writer of both poetry and fiction and a newcomer to the Northwest—Wagoner found himself in the process of discovering the region of his new residence. In describing his first experience exploring a rain forest on the Olympic Peninsula, Wagoner writes, "I thought I'd found where God lived."

Wagoner's appointment at the University of Washington followed the publication of his first book of poetry. The poems that make up the two parts of *Dry Sun, Dry Wind* clearly reflect Roethke's influence in both metaphor and cadence—particularly in the short lyrics of the first section. Wagoner's awareness of his mentor's impact may account for the exclusion of these poems from later collections, such as *New and Selected Poems* (1969) and *Collected Poems (1956–1976)*.

In 1954 Wagoner's first novel, *The Man in the Middle,* was published. The book incorporates a plot that, according to William J. Schaefer in his article "David Wagoner's Fiction: In the Mills of Satan," for *Critique* (1966), serves as a paradigm for several of Wagoner's narratives that are set in the urban Midwest: an innocent man, usually a loner, becomes unintentionally

involved with corruption that is connected somehow with money; in the case of *The Man in the Middle,* Charlie Bell is such a man. As Schaefer describes, he is then pursued by "evil forces" and is himself corrupted and either "damaged or destroyed" in the process. In Wagoner's fiction the most significant casualty in the lust for money is love, which is nearly always either undermined or distorted in these novels; even in Wagoner's later and arguably more successful comic Westerns, greed persistently threatens the protagonists. The novel *Money, Money, Money,* which appeared in 1955, features another vulnerable protagonist, the mentally retarded Willy Grier. Grier is beaten up at the end by a mobster and is left hugging a tree in the rain that splashes "on his throbbing head like coins." In a review for *The New York Herald Tribune Book Review* (2 October 1955), Sylvia Stallings referred to the novel as "a morality play for our times."

In 1958 *Rock: A Novel,* Wagoner's third book of fiction to be set in the blighted urban Midwest, and *A Place to Stand,* his second collection of poems, were both published. *A Place to Stand* represents considerable advances over his first poetry volume, in part because of a preference for first-person speakers, which gives the poems greater intimacy. Although some reviewers still detected Roethke's influence, the book was critiqued more widely and positively than *Dry Sun, Dry Wind.* Despite the title of *A Place to Stand,* however, the lyrics did not yet display Wagoner's realization that the landscape of the Northwest was his "place." In his novel *Rock* the twenty-eight-year-old protagonist, Max Fallon, returns home after graduating from college in the East and suffering a divorce. Like most of the lead characters in Wagoner's novels, Max is estranged from his father—often in Wagoner's fiction the father is missing altogether—and he feels uneasy in the world of rock music, of which his brother and sister are avid fans. Yet, Max is forced to return to that world when the only job he can find is working as a lifeguard. He learns that he must not "become a child again" in his regressive journey toward self-discovery but, rather, must experience adolescence once more in order to regain his manhood. Unlike the protagonists of Wagoner's two previous novels, Max also discovers the healing powers of love. While critics were divided in their assessment of *Rock,* Robert Phelps in his critique for *The New York Herald Tribune Book Review* (17 August 1958) ranked Wagoner among "the dozen or so novelists under forty from whom we should expect our most useful novels in the next few decades."

Although Wagoner devoted considerable energy to the writing of novels in the next twenty years, he came into his own as a poet in the 1960s. Significantly, unlike the poems of his contemporaries (including

Robert Bly, Denise Levertov, and W. S. Merwin), the poems from Wagoner's three books of that period— *The Nesting Ground, A Book of Poems* (1963), *Staying Alive* (1966), and *New and Selected Poems*—do not reflect the social and political turmoil of the times, such as racial unrest and the protests against the war in Vietnam. During this decade he also married for a second time; Wagoner and the glamorous Patricia (Patt) Parrott, the addressee of many of his love lyrics, were wed in August 1961. As he notes in his autobiographical essay, the summer of 1961—when he was thirty-five years old—was "a clear demarcation point" for his poems. In submitting "The Nesting Ground"—the title lyric of his 1963 collection—and a commentary about the poem to Paul Engle and Joseph Langland for inclusion in their anthology *Poet's Choice* (1961), Wagoner touches on this point of demarcation. In the commentary he says that he greatly admires poems with open lines, because such verse is "simultaneously free and controlled." He adds that these poems "tend to be dramatic presentation which have to account for themselves with as little author comment as possible."

"A Guide to Dungeness Spit," a powerful piece that appears in *The Nesting Ground,* indeed blends the free and the controlled. A celebration of nature in the Northwest, the lyric recounts a walk that two lovers take along paths in the National Wildlife Refuge, which juts out from the Olympic Peninsula into the Straits of Juan de Fuca. Told in present tense, in a serene, almost meditative tone, the poem is fifty-four sinuous lines long, for Wagoner has described each line as a sort of "sine-wave," operating on roughly a six-beat, five-beat, three-beat, or two-beat sequence:

> If we cross to the inner shore, the grebes and goldeneyes
> Rear themselves and plunge through the still surface,
> Fishing below the dunes
> And rising alarmed, higher than waves. Those are cockleshells.
> And these are the dead. I said we would come to these.
> Stoop to the stones.

Wagoner achieves a tension between line and sentence, creating the paradoxical sensation of freedom and control that he admires in verse. A longtime bird-watcher, he demonstrates throughout this poem, as well as in many others, an awareness of the regional species. Wagoner's nature lyrics bring to mind Terry Tempest Williams's observation in *Refuge* (1991), which could serve as a definition of regionalism: "The birds and I share a natural history. It is a matter of rootedness, of living inside a place for so long that the mind and imagination fuse."

In "Staying Alive," the title poem of Wagoner's second collection, he continues his celebration of the

*Wagoner in 1929 (courtesy of the author)*

Northwest. Instead of a gently instructional lover who intones a message of passion and enlightenment, as in "A Guide to Dungeness Spit," the speaker of "Staying Alive" lectures in a stern voice on survival in the woods, where "The bottom of your mind knows all about zero" and "If you hurt yourself, no one will comfort you." Moreover, in the opening poem of *Staying Alive,* "The Words," Wagoner suggests that he regards himself as a "nature poet":

> Wind, bird, and tree,
> Water, grass, and light
> In half of what I write
> Roughly or smoothly
> Year by impatient year,
> The same six words recur.

*Wagoner (right) with his brother, Walter, in 1944*

Yet, to accept such a self-limiting label uncritically is a mistake, for Wagoner has written delightfully comic poems as well, such as "The Shooting of John Dillinger Outside the Biograph Theater, July 22, 1934," which rambles for more than a hundred witty, pun-filled lines. He has woven autobiography into his lyrics, as shown in "The Man of the House," and fulminated on politics, as in "A Valedictory to Standard Oil of Indiana." Unlike the nature lyrics that predominate in *The Nesting Ground* and *Staying Alive,* most of the new poems in Wagoner's *New and Selected Poems,* such as "At St. Vincent DePaul's," "The Shoplifter," and "The Apotheosis of the Garbagemen," have urban locations.

Wagoner also continued to write fiction during this time, and in 1965 *The Escape Artist* was published;

the novel was adapted as a motion picture of the same title in 1982. The protagonist, sixteen-year-old Danny Masters, is a clever orphan and–like Wagoner himself– a talented amateur magician. Like most of Wagoner's other novels that are set in the urban Midwest, *The Escape Artist* involves political corruption and pursuit of the innocent by the mob. Yet, Danny is the most capable of Wagoner's "good guys"; intelligent, quick-witted, and self-reliant, he is a contemporary, urban Huck Finn. Wagoner's other novel written in the 1960s recalls *Rock,* his third book of fiction. *Baby, Come on Inside* (1968) features an aging singer, Popsy Meadows, who–like Max Fallon–is estranged from his father and finds that he cannot come home again. Comedy mingles with pathos throughout the novel, which Dennis Powers–in an article for *The Saturday Review* (17 August 1968)–referred to as a "comic nightmare." Although at the end the fifty-year-old Popsy takes a young bride, Wagoner suggests that the marriage only temporarily relieves Popsy's lonely life of dreary hotel rooms and gigs in smoky nightclubs.

Upon the death of Roethke in 1963 and the departure of poet Carolyn Kizer to Washington, D.C., in 1966 for a position with the National Endowment for the Arts, Wagoner was left as the senior writer in residence at the University of Washington, which granted him tenure and the rank of full professor. He produced no fewer than six books of poems during the 1970s– including *Collected Poems (1956–1976)* and a chapbook, *Travelling Light* (1976), which was his first poem sequence. This poem sequence continued the tradition established by Roethke in his lyric "North American Sequence," which appeared in his posthumous verse collection, *The Far Field* (1964). Wagoner also edited his mentor's notebooks, titled *Straw for the Fire: From the Notebooks of Theodore Roethke, 1943–1963* (1972).

In the 1970s Wagoner also found a new dramatic voice through the writing of his four comic Westerns: *Where Is My Wandering Boy Tonight?* (1970), *The Road to Many a Wonder* (1974), *Tracker* (1975), and *Whole Hog* (1976). Featuring adolescent protagonists in the mold of Danny Masters, these novels appeal especially to teenage or young adult males and are written in what might be described as a rural American dialect or country-western English, as in the following passage from *Where Is My Wandering Boy Tonight?:*

> Back in them days–in the 1890's–in Slope, Wyoming, they thought they was going to amount to something, being on a railroad and a junction at that, but it sort of went sour and ran downhill and frittered out, and you won't find it on most maps unless you look hard, and you can just barely find it if you go there in the flesh on a dim day.

*Dust jacket for Wagoner's first poetry collection, published in 1953, shortly before his mentor, the poet Theodore Roethke, invited him to teach at the University of Washington*

a style of writing that recurs throughout much of his poetry. The poem locates the speaker in a natural world that, typically for Wagoner, is equally alluring and threatening:

> To be here, in the first place, is sufficiently amazing:
> The flat, tough, gray-green, prickly, star-shaped weeds
> Are the sole proprietors . . .

In most of his poems Wagoner employs loose, rambling syntax. For example, although "The Middle of Nowhere" has forty-two lines, it is composed of just four sentences. Wagoner often creates line endings that momentarily mislead the reader, a technique that might be described as the disruption of idiomatic expectation. In this poem the cracks in the clay "follow directions / Not yet invented–north / By South, upright by easterly, northwest by nothing." The poet plays with the reader's expectations at the end of the following passage:

> This patch may have a name and coordinates
> By Sextant out of Star
> Or out of Map by Compass, but the problem of being . . .

The reader is suddenly confronted with a metaphysical issue, but the next line quickly undercuts the ontological problem: "Here is not deducible." "The Middle of Nowhere" ends with a flurry of idioms or clichés:

> This is the place where we must be ready to take
> The truths or consequences
> Of which there are none to be filched or mastered or
>    depended on,
> Not even, as it was in the beginning, the Word
> Or, here, the squawk of a magpie.

All four novels, none of which has literary pretensions, disclose coming-of-age themes; a youthful protagonist outwits the "lunkhead" bad guys in a world corrupted by greed. In *The Road to Many a Wonder* the main character, Millie Slaughter, sets up a sting operation in the Pike's Peak goldfields of 1859. Her nineteen-year-old boyfriend, Ike Bender, is honest, courageous, and excessively upbeat. Yet, to succeed in the fallen world that Wagoner depicts in all of his novels, even the most innocent—including Ike—must resort to some form of chicanery. The last of these "moral comedies," *Whole Hog,* is also the darkest. It displays considerable violence, some sexual depravity, and a villain who is considerably more sinister than those in Wagoner's other Westerns.

Wagoner made his mark, however, through the poetry he wrote in the 1970s. In "The Middle of Nowhere," which is collected in *Riverbed* (1972), he writes in pulsating lines that operate almost like tercets—

Wagoner's next book of poems, *Sleeping in the Woods* (1974), was the first to be divided into sections since *Dry Sun, Dry Wind,* which he had organized into two parts. He prefaces each of the four sections of *Sleeping in the Woods* with a lyric about poetry; the first poem, "The Singing Lesson," also serves as an introductory piece for the entire collection. Whereas love poems dominate the first part, which reaches a climax with "An Offering for Dungeness Bay," the second part approaches miscellany—although its poems often appear in pairs or clusters that enhance each other thematically. The most important poems in the third section demonstrate Wagoner's commitment to environmental politics. These poems, arranged in a group of three, challenge the wisdom of clear-cut logging in general and take on the Weyerhaeuser Company in particular. In "Elegy for a Forest Clear-Cut by the Weyerhaeuser Company" he notes that only one of ten fir seedlings survives "Below the small green struggle of the weeds." Wagoner con-

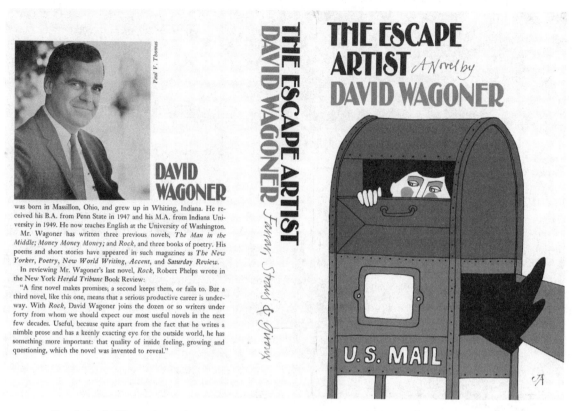

*Dust jacket for Wagoner's 1965 novel, about the adventures of a quick-witted sixteen-year-old amateur magician*

cludes, "As selective as reapers stalking through wheatfields, / Selective loggers go where the roots go." The last section of *Sleeping in the Woods* is titled "Seven Songs for an Old Voice"; this section of poems was incorporated later into *Who Shall Be the Sun?: Poems Based on the Lore, Legends, and Myths of Northwest Coast and Plateau Indians* (1978).

*Collected Poems (1956–1976)*, which was nominated for a National Book Award in 1977, brings together lyrics that Wagoner wrote over a span of twenty years. The most celebrated new lyrics by the then fifty-year-old poet were included in the nine-poem sequence titled *Travelling Light*. Although relatively few of Wagoner's poems have been subjected to close analysis, Laurence Lieberman offers a thorough commentary on the sequence as "survival lessons" in love, for—as Wagoner observes in his autobiographical essay—his private life was in shambles at that time. His wife, Patt, was diagnosed with cancer in 1974, and the illness caused her much psychological distress. Shortly thereafter, Patt began an affair with a younger man, and after 1978 Wagoner found himself alone for the first time in twenty years; they were officially divorced in 1982. Wagoner views his intense productivity of the late 1970s, during which he also resumed writing short fiction, as his way of coping with personal problems.

In an author's note to *Who Shall Be the Sun?* which comprises seventy-eight poems, Wagoner terms most of the Native American narratives as "retellings"; these stories, preserved by turn-of-the-century ethnologists such as Franz Boas, serve as the basis for his poetic versions in the book. Wagoner's sensibility has much in common with the Indian reverence for nature, and he particularly admires the trait of animism. Yet, events such as the occupation of Wounded Knee by militants of the American Indian Movement—an incident that occurred five years after the publication of *Who Shall Be the Sun?*—and the increasing productivity of Native American poets, have rendered the writing of Indian poems by non-Indians quite suspect.

Wagoner's next book, *In Broken Country: Poems* (1979), constitutes a return to verse and thus more familiar ground. The opening poem, "After the Speech to the Librarians," shows Wagoner at his best; he also opens *Through the Forest: New and Selected Poems, 1977–1987* (1987) with the same lyric. In "The Junior High Band Concert," in which he and his classmates become "A lesson in everything minor, / Decomposing our first composer," Wagoner harks back to autobiography, an especially prominent characteristic of *In Broken Country*. The lyrics, "For a Woman Who Dreamed All the Horses Were Dying" and "Love

*Dust jacket for Wagoner's 1999 verse collection, an enlargement of his 1976 chapbook with the same title*

Song After a Nightmare," for instance, refer to his estranged wife's emotional turmoil. *In Broken Country* also includes poems of environmental protest aimed at Weyerhaeuser. The book closes with a twelve-poem sequence, which Wagoner later titled "The Journey" in *Through the Forest,* in which is heard the familiar voice of the instructor, who is leading an unspecified "you" out of a harsh desert past the point of no return. This sequence does not celebrate the visionary love or enlightenment of the poems that encompass *Travelling Light* but instead leads the reader through an ordeal to a "worn-down, hard, incredible sight / Called Here and Now." What the second-person addressee of the sequence attains, however, is not a hard-won goal, but "another / Journey without regret . . . being your own unpeaceable kingdom." Here, as often in Wagoner's poems, the second person might apply to some anonymous subject, to a specific person–perhaps his wife–to himself, or to the reader. The ambiguity, of course, is intentional.

Wagoner's last published novel to date is *The Hanging Garden* (1980), which the author describes in his autobiographical essay as "a grisly gothic story full of dead animals." While one may argue that the novel simply takes the ominous implications of *Whole Hog* a

step further and apparently shifts the locale to a contemporary city in the Midwest, *The Hanging Garden* nonetheless lacks the thematic focus of his other fiction. The novel departs from most of Wagoner's other fiction, in that it features a successful romance. Moreover, besides the character of Millie Slaughter in *The Road to Many a Wonder,* Diane Lee in *The Hanging Garden* is the only other female protagonist in Wagoner's fiction that is not merely one-dimensional.

*Landfall: Poems* came out in 1981, the year before he and Patt divorced, and the book is the last one he dedicated to her, "downstream and upstream, with love." The poetry spanning the five sections of the book is quite diverse. The poems range from predictable autobiographical fare such as "My Fire" and "My Father's Garden" to "garden poems" such as "Cutworm" and "Nuthatch"–both of which are short and abound in imagery. *Landfall* also includes playful, witty descants such as "In Distress," which Wagoner calls a "found poem," and "Applying for a Loan with the Help of the *Dictionary of Occupational Titles.*" He incorporates serious, visionary poems such as "Return to the Swamp" and "Wading in a Marsh," in which the speaker is alone in nature, as well as a section of ten love poems, including "Note with the Girl of a Bird's

SENTRY

Attention. You'll begin right here on the ~~spot~~ dot
    Of midnight and, till dawn, you'll ~~march along~~ wear
        A ~~line~~ path between this place and that other place
Over there.  Then you'll pause and about-face
    And come back here and do likewise, always
        On the alert, your ears and your rifle cocked
For something not in the book.  You're looking out
    For suspicious forms.  You see one, you say,
        *Halt! Who goes there?*  And tonight's password
Is silence.  Nothing at all, since no one
    Is supposed to be up or [even] out or about
        But you and the enemy.  You do your part
At the outer line of defense. Your purpose is
    To keep ~~the~~ there people lying there behind you
        Safe in their ~~sleep~~ sheets.  Most of them have fallen
~~Asleep by now. Remember,~~ they're depending
    On you and others like you to let them go
        On and on ~~drowsing without imagining~~ drowsy + slumbering
~~Or dreaming~~ about anything
    Too ugly creeping up over the edge
        Of the mattress across the sheets to the ~~limp land~~ craters
Of their pillow slips and into the privacy
    Of their semicircular canals.  Your aim
        Is to stay awake at all costs.  Of course you may
Relax once in a while, sit down and take your time
    To mull things over.  The most creative men
        Don't ~~waste~~ their energy pacing back and forth, and
Isn't the ~~final~~ goal of all armed conflict
    The achievement of equilibrium?  Just think
        Of peace and quiet.  The voice of the enemy
Can be surprisingly restful.  ~~Wouldn't you rather~~ why not and
  ~~End~~ all hostilities by laying down
        The law ~~in~~ for the soothing pax romana of sleep?

*Corrected typescript for a poem by Wagoner (Collection of David Wagoner)*

Nest" and "Sleeping on Stones." *Landfall* also features a six-poem sequence, "Sea Change," which concludes with the title poem of the book.

Two years after the publication of *Landfall,* on 24 July 1982, Wagoner married Robin Heather Seyfried, his former student and editorial assistant at *Poetry Northwest;* he dedicated his next book of poems, *First Light* (1983), to his new wife. *First Light* may simply appear to follow what had become for Wagoner a successful "genre"–the autobiographical lyric. Verses in the book that are based on the poet's life, such as "The Bad Uncle" and "The Best Slow Dancer," strike one as familiar, especially because they have stylistic traits typical of a Wagoner poem–such as the lack of punctuation, through which he implies the inherent nature of language to deconstruct itself. Yet, however familiar the autobiographical poems of *First Light* may seem, they also rank among the best in the book. Certainly "The Bad Uncle" and "The Best Slow Dancer" constitute two of his most delightful comic poems, and his elegiac verse to his parents, "Their Bodies," is one of his most moving poems in the autobiographical vein. Other poems in *First Light* are important for their implicit ecological themes, such as "The Author of *American Ornithology* Sketches a Bird, Now Extinct" and "To a Farmer Who Hung Five Hawks on His Barbed Wire." Every new book by a poet or novelist offers something different from the previous works, however, and Wagoner's cynical, free-form villanelle, "Canticle for Xmas Eve," might be the most singular case in point. Like all of his books since *Collected Poems (1956–1976), First Light* includes a sequence encompassing nine love poems and titled, "The Land Behind the Wind." In these love poems the point of view is generally third-person plural. In the concluding poem of the sequence the lovers, having slept all night exposed to the wind and dreaming of "a place to stand behind the wind," turn around in circles "As predictably as all lost travellers"–a recurrent metaphor in Wagoner's poems–and find themselves embraced by the air. The poem ends, "There lay the wind at their feet like a pathway."

*Through the Forest: New and Selected Poems, 1977–1987,* in which thirty-one new poems appear, is in part a thematic reorganization of Wagoner's verses into "a summa of his life and work," as *Publishers Weekly* said in its review (26 June 1987). While several of the new poems are central to the book as a whole, the arrangement of *Through the Forest* into five carefully measured sections, with four sequences acting as dividers, is its most significant achievement. Of greater pertinence to Wagoner's present status, however, is his most recent collection of verse, *Walt Whitman Bathing* (1996), which features forty-four new poems–including a nine-poem sequence titled "Landscapes." The opening section has

autobiographical poems such as "My Father Laughing in the Chicago Theater" and "My Passenger," which cast a backward glance to Wagoner's adolescence, as well as "Walking around the Block with a Three-Year-Old," which reflects on his new role as a father of two adopted children. The section concludes with a familiar scenario in "At the Mouth of a Creek": two lovers lying beside a creek–an osprey, salmon, and a wren nearby– all "Transfixed by the play of light." Although light imagery has always played some part in Wagoner's poems, beginning with *First Light,* he employs references to light with increasing intensity; "At the Mouth of a Creek" ends with the hope for a "morning knowledge / At last to fight our frail, permanent love." In fact, light and sight may be the keys to these poems, one of the most powerful of which is "My Vision," concerning his experience with laser surgery on his eyes.

Through his verse David Wagoner has encompassed a remarkable range of voices and modes, establishing himself as a supreme master of the poetic craft. His sharp eye, his attention to the nuances of colloquial or conversational English, and his feeling for the pulse of the line are unerring. Wagoner counts among his students such accomplished poets as Tess Gallagher, Mary Ann Waters, and Laura Jensen. As an editor for the Princeton University Press and the University of Missouri Breakthrough Series, he has promoted the work of acclaimed poets such as Jorie Graham, Robert Pinsky, and Pattiann Rogers. Whether he will receive the attention that so many of his admirers–including fellow poets such as Maxine Kumin, Dave Smith, Stanley Kunitz, and Stephen Dobyns–believe he deserves will be decided by readers in the next century.

**Interviews:**

"An Interview with David Wagoner," *Crazy Horse,* 12 (Autumn 1972): 38–46;

"Conversation with David Wagoner," *Yes* (1973): 21–28;

Ron McFarland, "An Epistolary Interview with David Wagoner," *Slackwater Review,* special David Wagoner issue (1981): 11–18;

Phil Dacey, "David Wagoner," in *American Poetry Observed: Poets on Their Work,* edited by Joe David Bellamy (Urbana: University of Illinois Press, 1984), pp. 266–274;

Nicholas O'Connell, "David Wagoner," in his *At the Field's End: Interviews with Twenty Pacific Northwest Writers* (Seattle: Madrona, 1987), pp. 39–57.

**References:**

Justin Askins, "Mild Delight," *Parnassus,* 12 (Fall 1984): 331–341;

Robert Boyers, "The Poetry of David Wagoner," *Kenyon Review,* 32 (1970): 176–181;

Richard Howard, "David Wagoner," in his *Alone with America: Essays on the Art of Poetry in the United States Since 1950,* enlarged edition (New York: Atheneum, 1980), pp. 619–638;

Richard Hugo, "David Wagoner: A Poet of Elizabethan Wisdom and Wit," *The Weekly's Reader* (November 1979): 1+;

X. J. Kennedy, "Pelting Dark Windows," *Parnassus,* 5 (Spring/Summer 1977): 133–140;

Laurence Lieberman, "David Wagoner: The Cold Speech of the Earth," in his *Unassigned Frequencies* (Urbana: University of Illinois Press, 1977), pp. 152–181;

Karl Malkoff, "Wagoner," in his *Crowell's Handbook of Contemporary American Poetry* (New York: Crowell, 1973), pp. 313–316;

Sara McAulay, "'Getting There' and Going Beyond: David Wagoner's Journey Without Regret," *Literary Review,* 28 (Fall 1984): 93–98;

Ron McFarland, *David Wagoner,* Western Writer's Series, no. 88 (Boise, Idaho: Boise State University Press, 1989);

McFarland, "David Wagoner's Comic Westerns," *Critique,* 28 (Fall 1986): 5–18;

McFarland, "David Wagoner's Dynamic Form," *Contemporary Poetry,* 5 (1983): 41–50;

McFarland, "David Wagoner's Environmental Advocacy," *Rocky Mountain Review of Language and Literature,* 44 (1990): 7–16;

McFarland, "Learning to Laugh at Being a Flop: David Wagoner's Poems of Adolescence," *California English,* 28 (January/February 1992): 6–7, 30–31;

McFarland, *The World of David Wagoner* (Moscow: University of Idaho Press, 1997);

McFarland, ed., *Slackwater Review,* special David Wagoner issue (1981): 100–108, 109–118, 119–123;

Robert Peters, "Thirteen Ways of Looking at David Wagoner's New Poems," *Western Humanities Review,* 35 (Autumn 1981): 267–272;

Sanford Pinsker, "The Achievement of David Wagoner," *Connecticut Review,* 8 (October 1974): 42–47;

Pinsker, "On David Wagoner," in *Contemporary Poetry in America,* edited by Robert Boyers (New York: Schocken, 1974), pp. 360–368;

Pinsker, *Three Pacific Northwest Poets: William Stafford, Richard Hugo, and David Wagoner* (Boston: G. K. Hall, 1987), pp. 99–124;

William J. Schaefer, "David Wagoner's Fiction: In the Mills of Satan," *Critique,* 9 (1966): 71–89;

Hyatt Waggoner, *American Visionary Poetry* (Baton Rouge: Louisiana State University Press, 1982): 179–197.

**Papers:**

Collections of David Wagoner's manuscripts are housed at the Olin Library, Washington University, St. Louis, and at the University of Washington, Seattle.

# James Welch
## *(18 November 1940 – )*

### Jane Helm Maddock
*University of Montana, Western*

See also the Welch entry in *DLB 175: Native American Writers of the United States.*

BOOKS: *Riding the Earthboy 40* (New York: World, 1971; revised edition, with additions, New York: Harper & Row, 1976);

*Winter in the Blood* (New York: Harper & Row, 1974; Toronto & London: Bantam, 1975);

*The Death of Jim Loney* (New York: Harper & Row, 1979; London: Gollancz, 1980);

*Fools Crow* (New York: Viking, 1986);

*The Indian Lawyer* (New York: Norton, 1990);

*Killing Custer: The Battle of the Little Bighorn and the Fate of the Plains Indians,* by Welch and Paul Stekler (New York: Norton, 1994);

*The Heartsong of Charging Elk* (New York: Doubleday, 2000).

PRODUCED SCRIPT: "Last Stand at Little Bighorn," television, by Welch and Paul Stekler, *The American Experience,* PBS, 20 November 1995.

OTHER: William E. Farr, *The Reservation Blackfeet, 1882–1945: A Photographic History of Cultural Survival,* foreword by Welch (Seattle: University of Washington Press, 1984), pp. vii–viii;

Mildred Walker, *Winter Wheat,* introduction by Welch (Lincoln: University of Nebraska Press, 1992), pp. ix–xiii;

Drex Brooks, *Sweet Medicine: Sites of Indian Massacres, Battlefields, and Treaties,* foreword by Welch (Albuquerque: University of New Mexico Press, 1995), pp. xi–xii;

Walker, *If a Lion Could Talk,* introduction by Welch (Lincoln: University of Nebraska Press, 1995), pp. vii–xiii;

David Fitzgerald and Linda Hasselstrom, *Bison, Monarch of the Plains,* foreword by Welch (Portland, Ore.: Graphic Arts Center, 1998), pp. 10–12.

SELECTED PERIODICAL PUBLICATION–
UNCOLLECTED: "The Loose Screw," "Flight," *Weber Studies,* 12, no. 3 (Fall 1995): 6–14.

*James Welch (photograph © Keith Buckley; from the dust jacket for* The Heartsong of Charging Elk, *2000)*

James Welch–poet, novelist, documentary scriptwriter, and historical essayist–has long been acknowledged as a major voice in the Native American Renaissance. His book of poems, *Riding the Earthboy 40* (1971), and his first two novels–*Winter in the Blood* (1974) and *The Death of Jim Loney* (1979)–brought him wide acclaim. Welch's third novel, *Fools Crow* (1986), earned him an American Book Award, the *Los Angeles Times* Book Prize, the Pacific Northwest Book Award, and commercial success as well. Subsequent novels, *The Indian Lawyer* (1990) and *The Heartsong of Charging Elk* (2000), and the nonfiction *Killing Custer: The Battle of the Little Bighorn and the Fate of the Plains Indians* (1994) have enjoyed high critical praise and wide readership. Welch received a Lifetime Achievement Award, Native Writers Circle in 1997, and for *The Heartsong of Charging Elk* he won a Pacific Northwest Book Award in 2001.

Welch's works, which have been translated into several foreign languages, are read and praised worldwide. He has received honorary doctorates from the University of Montana and Rocky Mountain College and is a Chevalier de l'Ordre des Arts et des Lettres of France. In December 1998 he was invited to address the Institute of Letters in Milan, Italy. William W. Bevis has praised Welch's contributions to the current Native American movement, the honesty and quality of his writing, and "his graceful sense of what is important in ordinary lives."

James Philip Welch Jr. was born 18 November 1940 in Browning, Montana, on the Blackfoot Reservation near Glacier National Park to James P. Welch Sr. and Rosella O'Bryan Welch, predominantly Blackfoot and Gros Ventre respectively. Welch grew up on Montana's Blackfoot and Fort Belnap Reservations and is an enrolled member of the Blackfoot tribe. After attending Northern Montana College in Havre, he transferred to the University of Montana, Missoula, receiving a B.A. degree in 1965. He then entered the M.F.A. program in creative writing at Missoula under the direction of the poet Richard Hugo. Since 1968 he has been married to Lois Monk Welch, professor of English at the University of Montana, Missoula.

In an interview with Ron McFarland and M. K. Browning in February 1984, Welch claimed distant kinship on his father's side with a Spanish explorer named Sandoval as well as with Malcolm Clarke, the white man whose murder led to the Baker Massacre on the Marias River in January 1870, an event that haunts Welch. The Massacre on the Marias is memorialized in at least three of his books and his introduction to *Sweet Medicine: Sites of Indian Massacres, Battlefields, and Treaties* (1995), a collection of photographs by Drex Brooks.

Welch has taught both creative writing and contemporary Native American literature at Cornell University in 1985 and at the University of Washington during several summer sessions. He also served on the Montana State Board of Pardons from 1979 to 1990, making good use of the experience in his contemporary urban novel, *The Indian Lawyer*.

Welch's knowledge of Blackfoot life, history, and traditions comes from a combination of close observation and personal experience on and off the reservation, family history, and research. Research was especially important in *Killing Custer* and *The Heartsong of Charging Elk*, in which Welch moved beyond Montana and the Blackfeet.

*Riding the Earthboy 40*, Welch's volume of poems published in 1971, was his first published book. It takes its name from the forty-acre ranch of the Earthboy family, as the title poem suggests: "Earthboy farmed this land / and farmed the sky with words." The poems reach far beyond that farm in both subjects and poetics. In *Understanding James Welch* (2000), McFarland says that he sees Richard Hugo as the clearest and strongest influence on Welch's poetry, followed by Cesar Vallejo and James Wright. *Riding the Earthboy 40* remains in print, and many of the poems continue to be anthologized. When the book was republished in 1976, Welch rearranged the sections and added poems. The most abstract, those in the section called "Knives," are now at the beginning of the book.

Welch's poems–ironic, abstract and surrealistic–are sometimes as puzzling and fragmented as the dreams some pieces resemble. At other times, they are direct, clear, and simultaneously mournful and funny, with witty internal rhymes such as "Disgusted, busted whites," and stale phrases reworked, as "in the dead of spring." "The Man from Washington" becomes "a slouching dwarf with rainwater eyes."

Names and phrases first found in Welch's poems occur in his novels as well. The Earthboy place turns up at the beginning of the 1974 publication *Winter in the Blood*. The title of that novel appears in the poem "In My Lifetime":

> the buttes are young to look
> for signs that say a man could love his fate,
> that winter in the blood is one sad thing.

McFarland comments that the poem "may provide something of a gloss on the novel or at least one key to its unnamed protagonist."

The man in "Grandma's Man" aspires to art. He paints pictures, but not very good ones. He is inspired when Grandma, cross with a goose, which has bitten her, flings it over the barn. Welch writes of the fowl's fate: "that silly goose / is preening in her favorite pillow." Frustrated in his painting, the artist "got a bigger brush and once painted the cry / of a goose so long it floated off the canvas / into thin air."

"Christmas Comes to Moccasin Flat" is set in the unpromising place where Sylvester Yellow Calf, protagonist of Welch's fourth novel, *The Indian Lawyer*, was reared by his grandparents. The poem has its dark side, as in "warriors down in wine sleep," but it offers touches of humor as well:

> Medicine Woman, clay pipe and twist tobacco,
> calls each blizzard by name and predicts
> five o'clock by spitting at her television.

The uneasy relationship of Eurocentric religion to native culture is a theme in *Winter in the Blood,* in which the narrator's mother, Teresa, has embraced Catholicism and is a drinking buddy of the priest in Harlem, Montana, who refuses to bury Indians on their land. The narrator describes him as having "feuding eyes." In "The Last Priest Didn't Even Say Goodbye," Welch writes, "the priest has decorated the one pink church with hate." Welch used to say that he intended to return to poetry, but he has continued to write novels and nonfiction and the two stories originally intended as chapters for his latest novel.

*Winter in the Blood,* Welch's first novel, nearly died in embryo. In the 1985 American Audio Prose Library interview with Kay Bonetti and in the 1991 *Bloomsbury Review* interview with Tom Auer, Welch tells how he wrote a draft and then had writer William Kittredge look at it. Devastated by the plethora of suggestions that followed, Welch was ready to give up. After letting the manuscript rest, however, he revised it and turned a series of vignettes into a novel. Welch also credits Kittredge with teaching him to write convincing dialogue.

All of Welch's novels, especially the first two, are marked by the density and depth of poetry; they are linguistically and philosophically rich. In "American Indian Fiction, 1968–1983," in *A Literary History of the American West* (1987), Paula Gunn Allen suggests reading each of Welch's first two novels four times, once for each of the four stories united in them, which reflect human loss, alienation and grief, the world of spirits, the natural world, and interrelationships among these.

The humorous scenes, characters, and, most of all, the witty twists of language in *Winter in the Blood* were initially missed by readers, who found the work dark and bleak. In *Four American Indian Literary Masters* (1982), however, Alan R. Velie called *Winter in the Blood* a comic novel:

> Welch's humor varies from raucous farce to subtle satire, and it informs every corner of the novel. The broadest humor occurs in scenes like the one in which the unknown man dies face down in his oatmeal, or the one in which the hero and the airplane man march through the streets of Havre, the hero carrying a teddy bear and the Airplane Man carrying five boxes of chocolate-covered cherries under his arm.

Most of the humor, however, is verbal. Welch makes masterful use of ironic diction to undercut the dignity of his characters.

Welch has expressed satisfaction that readers have noticed the humor, remarking that people too often expect all Indian fiction to be dismal. Nonetheless, much about *Winter in the Blood* is sad, even tragic. The unnamed first-person narrator is thirty-two years old

*Dust jacket for Welch's partly surrealistic 1986 novel, about three years in the lives of the title character and his fellow Blackfeet*

and lives on a farm near Dodson, Montana, with his mother, Teresa; her Blackfoot mother, who is nearly a century old and has long since ceased speaking; and Lame Bull, Teresa's second husband. He also lives with the memory of his father, First Raise, who could repair all sorts of machines, who could make people—white or Indian—laugh, who lovingly made breakfast for the narrator and his older brother Mose, and who had frozen to death ten years earlier by the abandoned Earthboy place as he was coming home drunk.

The other memory haunting the narrator but kept submerged by guilt is the death of his brother twenty years earlier when Mose was fourteen and the narrator was twelve. The details of Mose's fatal accident emerge slowly, first in fragments of memory and finally in an entire re-creation. The narrator drinks too much and spends too much time in the bars of Malta, Havre, and other small towns on Montana's Highline. He also occupies his time chasing women, getting beaten up by men, and trying to remember what happened both the night before and in his partially repressed childhood.

At the beginning of the novel, Agnes, the woman who has been living with him, has run away, taking his rifle and his electric razor. He alternately denies that he wants her and his belongings back and laments that he feels nothing but an immense distance from everyone and everything, especially himself: "I was as distant from myself as a hawk from the moon."

His language, strikingly funny in sharply observed details and offbeat juxtapositions throughout much of the novel, is remote and abstract at this point. He refers to Agnes as "the girl who was thought to be my wife," although he eventually calls her by name. The mysterious Airplane Man and the barmaid from Malta with whom the narrator is *almost* certain he has spent the night, continue to turn up but remain as nameless as the narrator himself.

The Airplane Man enters the novel proclaiming that he has just torn up his plane ticket and tries to get the narrator to drive him to Canada, insisting that since the border guards like to harass Indians, they will pick on the narrator and let Airplane Man slip through. Like some of William Shakespeare's nincompoops who offer needed comic relief, the Airplane Man, with his purple teddy bear and boxes of chocolate-covered cherries—won in frenetic bouts at the punchboard—distracts readers from the narrator's angst, at least temporarily.

The narrator's two visits to the aged blind man, Yellow Calf, result in his discovery that his silent grandmother, once a beautiful young widow, survived the Starvation Year of 1883–1884 through Yellow Calf's hunting, and with that knowledge comes the recognition that the old man is his grandfather. Soon after, the narrator is able to endure reliving Mose's death. At the end of the novel, the narrator throws his grandmother's tobacco pouch with its arrowhead, her "medicine," into her grave, in a gesture that may be an acknowledgment of her Indian identity and his own.

Critics ask whether the narrator has really made any progress. Will he go on drinking, wandering, and getting into fights? At his grandmother's funeral, one of the great humorous funerals of literature, he thinks he will go find Agnes and "maybe offer to marry her on the spot." The ending is ambiguous.

The searches for identity and survival of one sort or another—physical, cultural, or spiritual—are recurrent themes in Welch's fiction. The second novel fits into that thematic category as did the first, but no one calls *The Death of Jim Loney,* published in 1979, a comic novel. Loney is a half-breed for whom that designation means a weak sense of self. He has a collection of basketball trophies from an earlier time, but no real connections. Like the narrator of *Winter in the Blood,* he searches for his past, but he finds no one who is willing to provide answers. His Indian mother is dead, in prison, or in an asylum. His white father, Ike, wants nothing to do with him. His sister, Kate, has solved the half-breed dilemma by moving away from it physically and mentally. She calls Ike "your poor father" and urges Loney to move to Washington, D.C. Rhea, Loney's white Texas girlfriend, has had enough of Harlem, Montana, and wants Loney to move with her to Seattle, Washington. Both want him to make something of himself, something neither Montanan nor Indian.

Some readers see the end of novel as affirmation, since Loney takes definite action, rejects adapting to white expectations, and dies on reservation land, having yearned vaguely toward it all his life. Others see the ending as only a sad finish to a useless life and as a reinforcement of the stereotypes about bright but doomed and drunken Indians. Bevis sees in the novel two plots, white and Indian, working in opposition.

*Fools Crow,* published in 1986, broke entirely fresh ground for Welch. Covering a three-year period from 1867 to 1870, the novel follows the lives of a fictional band of Pikuni (Piegan, or Blackfoot, Indians), the Lone Eaters. The novel is written, as Welch described it in a 1986 interview with McFarland and M. K. Browning, "from the inside-out." Robert Gish, in "Word Medicine: Storytelling and Magic Realism in James Welch's *Fools Crow*" (Fall 1990), says of the novel:

> Alternating between realism and surrealism, states of consciousness and subconsciousness, dreamscape reality and everyday waking reality, Welch makes the tried and true, now conventional techniques of steam-of-consciousness narration seem rather antiquated if not naive.

In *Fools Crow,* Welch has crafted a linguistic universe in which names, concepts, and the making of meaning nudge readers into an alternative reality where they initially feel disoriented. The title *Fools Crow* is puzzling until the meaning finally appears: Fools Crow is the new name given to the hero, initially called White Man's Dog. He has apparently "fooled" a Crow warrior into thinking he was dead. The opening paragraph is baffling:

> Now that the weather had changed, the moon of the falling leaves turned white in the blackening sky and White Man's Dog was restless. He chewed the stick of dried meat and watched Cold Maker gather his forces.

The reader may wonder why the main character is called White Man's Dog but must wait for the explanation. Other mysteries are the identity of Cold Maker and the time, place, and culture. Welch expects non-Indian readers to intuit or deduce the identities of

*Dust jacket for Welch's 1994 nonfiction work, which presents the 1876 Battle of Little Bighorn from the Indian point of view*

Napikwans, Seven Persons, Real-bear and the Seizers, and other representations of Blackfoot (Pikuni) terms.

Old connotations of color are useless. White Man's Dog has no ties to Caucasians. Black suggests neither death nor evil, nor does white mean purity. Sometimes Welch puts the familiar English phrase near the translated Pikuni one, but more often readers learn this language as they learned their own, through immersion and context.

Names are not merely new words for old ideas; they bring with them fresh possibilities. Eurocentric thought personifies winds and seasons, but only as a poetic device. In *Fools Crow,* Cold Maker is a force to be courted and placated. His daughters need robes for warmth and coals for their eyes so they can see, and when the rebel Fast Horse fails to give these to Cold Maker as promised, the Pikunis suffer. The warrior Yellow Kidney comes home mutilated and dispirited. Ways of knowing for Welch's Blackfeet are markedly different from the empiricism of advanced societies in the late twentieth century. Although Fast Horse betrayed Yellow Kidney by loud boasting during the

horse-stealing raid, prematurely alerting the Crows, the Pikunis know that breaking one's vow to Cold Maker is a serious matter. In almost all of Welch's writing, dreams, visions, and information from animals are valid ways of knowing.

The narrator of *Winter in the Blood,* for example, hears from old Yellow Calf that his grandmother's beauty caused the people's long-ago suffering, as they learned from Fish, the Many Faces man. When the narrator asks whether they could really have believed that, Yellow Calf says, "It wasn't a question of belief, it was the way things were." In the 1994 *Killing Custer,* the dreams and visions of Crazy Horse and Sitting Bull are important and treated as valid information. In "Seeing with a Native Eye: How Many Sheep Will It Hold?" in *Seeing with a Native Eye: Essays on Native American Religion* (1976) Barre Toelken says,

Through our study of linguistics and anthropology we have learned that different groups of people not only think in different ways, but that they often "see" things in different ways. Good scientific experiments can be provided, for example, to prove that if certain ideas are offered to people in patterns which they have not been taught to recognize, not only will they not understand them, they often will not even see them.

*Fools Crow* gives the reader two ways of seeing the death of Malcolm Clark–spelled in the novel without the final *e*. The soldiers who report the killing and threaten the Lone Eaters see Clark as a good man murdered by savages. The Lone Eaters see his death as Owl Child's private vengeance and not their business or the army's. To them, Clark was "a two-faced man, a bully, a dangerous fool."

A third view of Clark's death appears in *The Indian Lawyer*. Driving north from Helena, Sylvester Yellow Calf muses that the Prickly Pear Valley was once called Many Sharp Points. Yellow Calf "knew it was not far from here where a small group of Blackfeet killed Malcolm Clark, which led to the eventual Massacre on the Marias and the subjugation of his people."

The omniscient narrator of *Fools Crow* expands the definition of omniscience: he enters the thoughts of the hero; his wife, Red Paint; other Lone Eaters, Fast Horse, and even a few whites, whose inner reflections pull the reader into a world of clocks, calendars, and Indian-hating. The narrator can speak from the center of white culture or Blackfoot culture–observing the definitions of reality belonging to each, while seeing everything that occurs in Montana from 1867 to 1870. He even speaks from the point of view of Raven as he visits the Bad Napikwan, who is wantonly killing animals in the mountains. In this scene the bird perches on a bedpost in the sleeping hunter's cabin and inspires him to dream about Fools Crow's wife, so that the hunter will stalk her and Fools Crow will shoot him.

One might call this scene a dream, but Fools Crow is not in the cabin, and everything follows as Raven has proposed. A real Napikwan shoots and leaves animals to rot, stalks Red Paint, and is killed by Fools Crow in a scene that is not dream-like. The dream/reality dichotomy belongs to white culture, not to the Blackfoot universe of this novel.

At one point, two characters have intertwining, overlapping dreams: White Man Dog's dream about his father's youngest wife, Kills-Close-to-the-Lake, coincides with hers about him. She sacrifices a finger, which, she says, was exchanged by Fools Crow's animal helper, the wolverine, for a small stone. On waking, she finds the stone and gives it to Fools Crow, who puts it in his war medicine pouch.

One of the best-crafted scenes in the book is also one of the most troubling for anyone still trying to understand what happened from a rational-empiricist standpoint. In a long journey sequence, interspersed with scenes back at the Lone Eaters' village, Fools Crow travels to a strange realm and meets So-At-Sa-Ki, Feather Woman, a character from a traditional Pikuni story. Feather Woman shows Fools Crow a blank buffalo skin on which he suddenly sees moving images of his people's suffering since he has been away: the smallpox plague, the impending massacre on the Marias River, and a scene from a more distant future–of Blackfoot children isolated and sad at a school where other children play happily.

Fools Crow really has made a journey somewhere. His wife and parents worry about him and wonder when he will return. The narrator later says he has been "between earth and sky." Readers from non–Native American backgrounds may want to know exactly where he went and whether he was gone for hours or weeks. Clearly this journey is a different one from the ones marked on the map in the back of the book showing raids on the Crow village, Many Sharp Points, and other locations of events in the novel. The journey to Feather Woman is missing, but the visions are valid. Fools Crow returns to find the smallpox and the massacre. The sad schoolchildren are a matter of history. Fools Crow evolves from warrior to "Many-Faces Man," a healer and seer, with a new purpose in life–preserving intact his people and their culture in an increasingly hostile environment.

In various interviews Welch has said that in writing *Fools Crow* he wanted to get the small details of daily life right–the process of tanning a deer or buffalo hide, for example. He also says that he wanted to grant his nineteenth-century Pikunis their own reality. In the process, Welch goes far toward disclosing the tribal pasts and lost identities of the protagonists of his first two novels.

"The Indian Lawyer" is what Jim Loney might have become had either of his female missionaries succeeded in converting him to white success. Reared by grandparents on Moccasin Flat, Sylvester Yellow Calf is a dazzling basketball star, who, unlike Loney, does not fade away after high school. He becomes alienated from his Blackfoot friends when a sportswriter singles him out for extravagant praise and indicates that Sylvester, unlike them, will do great things. A degree from the University of Montana at Missoula and his playing more basketball are followed by his attending law school at Stanford, serving (like Welch) on the Montana State Board of Pardons, finding a trophy girlfriend, and being encouraged from leaders of the Montana Democratic Party to run for Congress. Yellow Calf seems to have a brilliant future.

The omniscient narrator begins in the consciousness of Jack Harwood, a white prisoner in the Montana State Prison at Deer Lodge. Knifed by one of the many incarcerated Indians, Jack wants out and devises a blackmail scheme calling for his wife, Patti Ann, to seduce the sole Indian on the parole board, Blackfoot lawyer Sylvester Yellow Calf. He also involves two more criminals in his plot.

Emotionally and physically entangled with Patti Ann and suddenly filled with questions about his own identity, Yellow Calf goes to his grandparents' home on the reservation in an upscale version of the traditional Native American "homing plot." There he sees his great-grandfather's war medicine, an ancient leather pouch containing what feels like a small stone, similar to Fools Crow's war medicine, and though he has previously felt no interest in his Indian heritage, he takes the pouch with him, to his grandmother's joy. The little pouch fills him with courage and a fighting spirit as he goes back to Helena to confront and defeat the three criminals.

A major theme of *The Indian Lawyer* is the dilemma of the successful Indian in a white world. Despite his great intelligence, his star-athlete status, his Stanford law degree, and his promising political career, Yellow Calf feels conspicuous in Helena's Montana Club and barely averts an altercation with drunken racists at a resort. His name has echoes in other novels. Yellow Calf is the narrator's Blackfoot grandfather in *Winter in the Blood*. The name is also the one old Yellow Kidney had chosen for Fools Crow's baby shortly before Yellow Kidney was murdered.

The ending of *The Indian Lawyer* is as ambiguous as the endings of earlier novels. Observed by his friend and former teacher, Lena Old Horn, Sylvester, now out of the running for Congress, is back on the reservation, shooting baskets all alone in the sleet. Welch presents the lawyer through Lena Old Horn's eyes. Whether this scene represents for Yellow Calf personal growth, self-realization, and happy escape from politics or only capitulation and defeat depends on the reader's own values. Welch said in the *Bloomsbury Review* interview that this character had "always felt guilty about leaving his people behind . . . and wanted to get involved in weightier matters, water rights or whatever." At the end, he is free to do that.

Growing out of Welch's experience with Paul Stekler and the making of the PBS documentary "Last Stand at Little Bighorn," *Killing Custer: The Battle of the Little Bighorn and the Fate of the Plains Indians* is a personal treatment of events before, during, and after June 1876, largely from the Indian point of view. In the book, as in the movie, Custer himself and the events of the much-celebrated battle are secondary.

Covering far more than the Battle of the Little Bighorn, the book is enhanced by excellent photographs of sites, historical Indian and white participants, ledger drawings by Indian survivors, and maps. One of

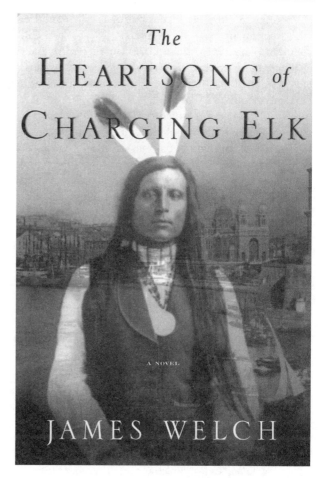

Dust jacket for Welch's 2000 novel, about a Sioux performer in Buffalo Bill's Wild West Show who is stranded in France after he becomes ill with the flu

the points that Welch makes in this book is that, contrary to the traditional white version of the story, there were survivors of that June battle, many of whom lived for decades afterward. Members of the various tribes that came together at Sitting Bull's invitation reported the battle from a variety of vantage points. Because they were Indians, their stories were often mistranslated and discounted.

A highly selective chronology lists Indian battles, massacres, treaties, and other important events—such as the Lewis and Clark expedition—starting with the arrival of the Lakotas in the Black Hills in 1775. For 1868, along with the treaty of that year, Welch writes, "Massacre on the Washita River in Indian Territory, in which Black Kettle is killed. This act establishes George Armstrong Custer as a great Indian Fighter." While the prologue relates how Welch's collaboration with Stekler came about, details of the making of the movie emerge throughout the book.

The first chapter largely ignores Custer to retell the major events of *Fools Crow*—the murder of Malcolm

Clarke in 1869 by the Pikuni renegade Owl Child and the subsequent massacre in January 1870 of a friendly band of Blackfeet by the drunken Colonel E. M. Baker. The chapter also records Welch's 1985 quest, as part of his research for *Fools Crow,* of the unmarked site of the massacre on the Marias River.

Welch had a reason for wanting to visit the place. His great-grandmother, Red Paint Woman, a child in 1870, was a survivor of the massacre. Her stories told to Welch's father and passed on to him had given him a sense of life and death in that camp struck first by a raging smallpox epidemic and then, just before dawn that cold January night, by Baker's merciless soldiers. Reading *Killing Custer* yields insight into many events, names, and themes in Welch's other writings and into his discovery of the meaning and value of his own Indian heritage. All his writing is so connected that each work illuminates the others. In an earlier draft of *Fools Crow,* the hero's wife is named Killdeer. In the published version, she is Red Paint.

Families are fragmented in Welch's novels, with the exception of *Fools Crow.* Jim Loney's father wants nothing to do with him; his mother is dead or crazy; and his sister cannot understand what his girlfriend sees in him. The narrator of *Winter in the Blood* has lost a father and a brother, and he finds his grandfather almost by accident. Sylvester Yellow Calf has been raised by his grandparents.

In *Killing Custer* Welch writes about the aftermath of the Battle of Little Bighorn—broken treaties, fragmentation of tribal lands, and the establishment of Indian boarding schools with the object of separating Indian children from tribes and culture. Without the modeling of parents to teach children how to create whole families like the ones in *Fools Crow,* that knowledge was often lost.

Perhaps the most striking personal revelation in *Killing Custer* is Welch's description of how Indian children on the reservation watched Western movies and cheered for the U.S. cavalry when it arrived to save the settlers from the Indians. Another notable scene occurs when the reservation children, in playful reenactments of "Custer's Last Stand," choose Welch to play Custer.

Welch's 2000 novel, *The Heartsong of Charging Elk,* set chiefly in France, was originally intended to combine contemporary and historical points of view, but on the advice of his editor, Welch eliminated the narrative frame, leaving the action entirely in the nineteenth and early twentieth centuries. On the dust jacket are plaudits from distinguished American writers. Kittredge calls *The Heartsong of Charging Elk* "wonderfully readable, a romance, a fable, and a sternly realistic story about salvaging emotional victory." Ivan Doig says, "James Welch, who long has been one of our finest American voices, here reaches the goal of all great literature: to transform worlds into words." Reviewing the book on-line for the Aboriginal Multi-Media Society of America (<http://www.ammsa.com/bookreviews/Heartsong-review.html>), Suzanne Methot wrote,

> Charging Elk's experiences as a refugee allow Welch to explore three major themes: the notion of exile, the reinvention of self, and the idea of cultural identity. He begins by describing the differences between Aboriginal and European cultures—the things that confuse Charging Elk at first, such as language, institutions and religious celebrations—but he soon draws readers into a complex examination of culture that goes far beyond simple comparisons.

Methot suggests that because Charging Elk has escaped the ravages of reservation life and education, he may be the sole surviving true Lakota.

The most obvious source of *The Heartsong of Charging Elk* is *Black Elk Speaks* (1932), John G. Neihardt's true account of the Lakota mystic who witnessed the Battle of the Little Bighorn as a child, went to Europe with Buffalo Bill's Wild West Show, was stranded in England, and later returned to witness the Wounded Knee Massacre. A second inspiration was an oddly dressed Frenchman who approached Welch in Marseilles, claiming to be descended from an Indian permanently stranded in France by the Wild West Show. Because of sensational elements in the plot—for example, Charging Elk murders a homosexual chef in a brothel—readers could easily miss the deeply spiritual core of this work.

The novel begins in the American West, just after the Battle of Little Bighorn, which the title character, like Black Elk, has watched as a child; also like Black Elk, Charging Elk has cut off a dead soldier's finger to get his ring. Welch's Charging Elk is a young Sioux who refuses to move to the reservation. He lives as a wild Indian—riding, hunting, and hiding out with his friend Strikes Plenty at the Stronghold, where life is hard but the two boys, good with bows and arrows, have food when others lack it because they have no bullets.

On a visit to his family, Charging Elk is recruited for Buffalo Bill's Wild West Show. At a performance in Marseilles, Charging Elk, sick with influenza, falls and is injured and hospitalized, as is another Sioux, Featherman, who dies. Frightened, Charging Elk runs away from the hospital. A death certificate is erroneously issued in his name, an error that cannot be corrected, given the depth of French bureaucracy. Legally dead, Charging Elk cannot leave France to rejoin the show, which has gone to Rome. He is jailed for vagrancy, rescued, and turned over to a genuinely religious French fishmonger, René Soulas, to house and employ as best he can.

Soulas is the second devout Catholic whom Charging Elk encounters. Earlier, in Paris, a young girl had given him a holy card and befriended him. In this novel, the old dichotomy of real native religion versus insincere Christianity is replaced by the view that real spirituality transcends cultures. Not all of Charging Elk's contacts are spiritual or kind. Spotting him on the quay with Soulas, the most famous chef in Marseilles conceives a desire for the exotic stranger. Charging Elk is also betrayed by the prostitute Marie Colet, whom he wants to marry. Between betrayal and bureaucracy, he spends a long time in a French prison, but is freed when someone realizes that he is not a U.S. citizen. Time blunts the edges of his isolation. Encountering the Wild West Show once more, Charging Elk chooses to remain in France.

Welch, still living in Missoula, Montana, with his wife, Lois, is currently working on a sequel in which Charging Elk will return to America. Meanwhile, James Welch's reputation as a major American writer continues to grow, both because of his writing and because of his influence on younger writers.

**Interviews:**

Kay Bonetti, audiotape, "James Welch Interview with Kay Bonetti" (Columbia, Mo.: American Audio Prose Library, 1985);

Ron McFarland and M. K. Browning, "An Interview with James Welch," in *James Welch,* edited by McFarland (Lewiston, Idaho: Confluence Press, 1986);

Tom Auer, "The Indian Writer: An Interview with James Welch," *Bloomsbury Review,* 11 (March 1991): 11, 25;

William W. Bevis, "Wylie Tales: An Interview with James Welch," *Weber Studies,* 12, no. 3 (Fall 1995): 15–32.

**References:**

Paula Gunn Allen, "American Indian Fiction, 1968–1983," in *A Literary History of the American West* (Fort Worth: Texas Christian University Press, 1987), pp. 1058–1066;

William W. Bevis, "James Welch," *Western American Literature,* 32, no. 1 (Spring 1997): 33–53;

Bevis, *Ten Tough Trips: Montana Writers and the West* (Seattle: University of Washington Press, 1990);

Peter Donahue, "New Warriors, New Legends: Basketball in Three Native American Works of Fiction," *American Indian Culture and Research Journal,* 2, no. 2 (1997): 43–60;

Karsten Fitz, "Bridging the Gap: Strategies of Survival in James Welch's Novels," *American Indian Culture and Research Journal,* 20-21 (1996): 131–146;

Robert Gish, "Word Medicine: Storytelling and Magic Realism in James Welch's *Fools Crow,*" *American Indian Quarterly,* 14 (Fall 1990): 349–354;

Ake Hultkrantz, "The Contribution of the Study of North American Indian Religions to the History of Religion," in *Seeing with a Native Eye: Essays on Native American Religion,* edited by Walter Holden Capps (New York: Harper & Row, 1976), pp. 86–106;

Kenneth Lincoln, "Blackfeet Winter Blues," *Native American Renaissance* (Berkeley: University of California Press, 1983), pp. 148–182;

Jane Helm Maddock, "Napikwans, Lone Eaters and the Stone in the War Medicine: Language and Epistemology in James Welch's *Fools Crow,*" *This is Just to Say,* report of the National Council of Teachers of English, Assembly on American Literature, 7, no. 2 (Spring 1996): 1–4;

Ron McFarland, "'The End' in James Welch's Novels," *American Indian Quarterly,* 17 (Summer 1993): 319–327;

McFarland, ed., *James Welch* (Lewiston, Idaho: Confluence Press, 1986);

McFarland, *Understanding James Welch* (Columbia: University of South Carolina Press, 2000);

John G. Neihardt, *Black Elk Speaks* (New York: Morrow, 1932);

Stephen Tatum, "Distance, Desire, and the Ideological Matrix of *Winter in the Blood,*" *Arizona Quarterly,* 46, no. 2 (Summer 1990): 73–100;

Barre Toelken, "Seeing with a Native Eye: How Many Sheep Will It Hold?" in *Seeing with a Native Eye: Essays on Native American Religion,* edited by Capps (New York: Harper & Row, 1976), pp. 9–24;

Alan R. Velie, "Blackfeet Surrealism: The Poetry of James Welch" and "*Winter in the Blood:* Welch and the Comic Novel," *Four American Indian Literary Masters: N. Scott Momaday, James Welch, Leslie Marmon Silko and Gerald Vizenor* (Norman: University of Oklahoma Press, 1982), pp. 65–103;

O. Alan Weltzien, "George Custer, Norman Maclean, and James Welch: Personal History and the Redemption of Defeat," *Arizona Quarterly,* 52, no. 4 (Winter 1996): 15–133.

**Papers:**

James Welch's papers are at the Beinecke Library at Yale University.

# Laura Ingalls Wilder

*(7 February 1867 – 10 February 1957)*

## Alison M. Wilson

See also the Wilder entry in *DLB 22: American Writers for Children, 1900–1960*.

BOOKS: *Little House in the Big Woods* (New York & London: Harper, 1932; London: Methuen, 1956);

*Farmer Boy* (New York & London: Harper, 1933; London: Lutterworth, 1965);

*Little House on the Prairie* (New York & London: Harper, 1935; London: Methuen, 1957);

*On the Banks of Plum Creek* (New York & London: Harper, 1937; London: Methuen, 1958);

*By the Shores of Silver Lake* (New York & London: Harper, 1939; London: Lutterworth, 1961);

*The Long Winter* (New York & London: Harper, 1940; London: Lutterworth, 1962);

*Little Town on the Prairie* (New York & London: Harper, 1941; London: Lutterworth, 1963);

*These Happy Golden Years* (New York & London: Harper, 1943; London: Lutterworth, 1964);

*On the Way Home: The Diary of a Trip from South Dakota to Mansfield, Missouri, in 1894* (New York: Harper & Row, 1962);

*The First Four Years* (New York: Harper & Row, 1971; London: Lutterworth, 1973).

SELECTED PERIODICAL PUBLICATION–
UNCOLLECTED: "Notes from the Real Little House on the Prairie," *Saturday Evening Post,* 250 (September 1978): 56–57, 104–105.

*Laura Ingalls Wilder in 1937*

Once upon a time, sixty years ago, a little girl lived in the Big Woods of Wisconsin, in a little gray house made of logs.

So begins the fascinating chronicle of Laura Ingalls Wilder, one of the best-loved American writers of the twentieth century, who grew up with the young country, following the Western trails in a covered wagon with her remarkable family. At the age of sixty-three, Wilder began writing her "Little House" books, a fictional series that reflects the essential truth of the pioneer experience and of the Ingalls family who lived it. "I wanted the children now to understand more about the beginning of things, to know what is behind the things they see–what it is that made America as they know it," Wilder said in a 1937 Bookweek address. "I had seen the whole frontier; the woods, the Indian country of the great plains, the frontier towns, the building of railroads in wild, unsettled country, homesteading and farms coming in to take possession. I realized that I had seen and lived it all–all the successive phases of the frontier, first the frontiersman, then the pioneer, then the farmers, and the towns."

Laura Elizabeth Ingalls was born in the "Big Woods" near Pepin, Wisconsin, on 7 February 1867, to Charles Philip and Caroline Lake Quiner Ingalls, a young homesteading couple. Charles's family had moved to Wisconsin from New York state when he was a boy; Caroline's family were originally from Connecticut, though she herself was born in Wisconsin. Charles had grown up in the Wisconsin woods near the Oconomowoc River and had learned the frontiersman's skills: hunting, trapping, farming, felling trees, and building dwellings and crafting their furnishings. In addition to these practical abilities, Charles Ingalls was also an accomplished violinist and singer, enlivening many gatherings with his music making and good spirits.

Caroline Quiner received her teaching certificate at the age of sixteen; she loved reading and writing poetry and other compositions and, in the words of her daughter Laura, "was proud and particular in all matters of good breeding." Charles and Caroline raised the close, affectionate family that was later immortalized in the Little House books, written in loving tribute by their daughter Laura many years after the pioneering adventure ended.

The shortest book in the Little House series—except for *The First Four Years* (. . . [1971]), which was found among Wilder's papers and published posthumously—is the first, *Little House in the Big Woods* (1932), which deals with the life of the Ingalls family when they lived in the cabin in the Wisconsin woods where Laura and her older sister Mary were born. The Little House books are not strictly autobiographical, nor even chronological, in a purely factual sense. For example, the Ingalls family left the Big Woods in 1868 and went first to Missouri, then to Kansas, where their daughter Carrie was born in 1870. Too late they discovered that they had built their homestead on Indian land, and to avoid problems with the government, the family returned in 1870 to their Wisconsin cabin before moving still farther west. Wilder sets her first novel in the year 1862, just after the Civil War began and following the passage of the Homestead Act, though Charles Ingalls did not actually build the cabin in the woods until 1863.

In addition, Wilder combined the Ingalls family's two separate sojourns in the cabin into one continuous stay and made Carrie, who was actually born in Montgomery County, Kansas, in 1870, a part of the family from the beginning of the story. The story of the family's stay in Kansas is told in *Little House on the Prairie* (1935). Because Laura Ingalls was a young child during most of the family's stay in the Big Woods, she obviously had to rely on family recollections for much of the detail. Thus, the Little House books are "true to

life" but not necessarily "factual," and the "Laura" of the novels is based on the youthful Laura Ingalls Wilder and her experiences but is not exactly the same person.

Wilder cleverly writes the books in a style and reading level appropriate to the child heroine, Laura; the books become more sophisticated and stylistically complex as Laura matures. Laura is a child of five when the story opens, and she thinks and reacts like a child.

> So far as the little girl could see, there was only the one little house where she lived with her father and mother, her sister Mary and baby sister Carrie. A wagon track ran before the house, turning and twisting out of sight in the woods where the wild animals lived, but the little girl did not know where it went, nor what might be at the end of it. . . . Sometimes, far away in the night a wolf howled. Then he came nearer, and howled again. It was a scary sound. Laura knew that wolves would eat little girls. But she was safe inside the solid log walls.

Laura feels safe because Pa's gun hangs over the door, and Jack, the brindled bulldog, is on guard. In actual fact, Laura is perfectly secure because she and her sisters are blessed with parents who are clever, competent, resourceful, and altogether admirably suited for life on the frontier.

*Little House in the Big Woods* covers a year in the life of the Ingalls family, starting and ending with autumn. Every season is defined by the chores necessary to keep the family safe, well fed, and happy. Wilder describes in meticulous detail many of the tasks involved in running a pioneer household: the reader learns about salting fish, making and storing cheese, and crafting a smoke house from a hollow log to smoke venison and other meat for storage. Butchering a pig involves curing its hide; making lard, cracklings, head cheese, and sausage; pickling pork; and, for fun, playing with a balloon made from the animal's bladder and sharing a deliciously greasy, crunchy, roasted pig's tail.

Laura and Mary help with all the chores—picking and storing the garden vegetables for winter use, washing, ironing, mending, churning, cleaning, and baking. They help their father tend the livestock, work at carpentry projects, and clean and maintain his gun, which includes making bullets. The children love working with their parents as useful and responsible members of the family. There is also plenty of fun—songs, stories, games, looking at pictures in an animal book or in the big family Bible, many visits with relatives, and a chance to romp with their cousins on holidays and other occasions.

Laura is the focus of the story and is probably the key to the success of the series with young readers; she is

*The Ingalls family in the early 1880s: Caroline, Carrie, Laura, Charles, Grace, and Mary*

not the perfect little lady her sister Mary is but an independent, curious, sometimes "naughty" tomboy, occasionally jealous of Mary's beautiful golden curls and decorous behavior. Pa calls Laura his "little half-pint of sweet cider half drunk up," and they share a love for adventure, the outdoors, and animals, while Mary and Ma prefer domestic duties and working indoors. The family animals—the bulldog, Jack, and a cat named Black Susan—are also favorites with child readers; in fact, Wilder received many queries from children when she neglected to tell what happened to Black Susan after the family left the Big Woods.

Biographer William Anderson reports in *Laura Ingalls Wilder, a Biography* (1992) that when *Little House in the Big Woods* was a big success when it was published in 1932, with pen-and-ink illustrations by Helen Sewall, "despite the fact that the Depression had slowed the sale of books. . . . Children and their parents immediately loved Laura's storytelling." Perhaps the message of the brave, hardworking, and self-sufficient Ingalls family triumphing over difficulties to make a secure home was one the Depression-weary readers needed to bolster their own confidence.

Encouraged by Harper and Brothers to write another book, Laura decided to write the story of her husband's boyhood in Malone, New York. Anderson writes that it was difficult for Laura to get her husband Almanzo James ("Manly") Wilder, whom she married 25 August 1885, to talk about his early years. "He said he was 'not much of a hand to tell a story' and was so modest that he did not like to be the focus of attention." Wilder persevered, however, and gathered enough information to tell the story *Farmer Boy* (1933), which chronicles Almanzo's ninth year on the family farm, when he was desperately trying to prove to his father that he was responsible enough to drive the family horses and to care for his own colt.

The Wilders are portrayed as much more prosperous than the Ingalls family, making a good living from a well-established farm. The Wilder parents are as hardworking, competent, and resourceful as Laura's parents. Once again, Wilder includes marvelously detailed descriptions of many routine chores of the period. Mother spins, dyes, and weaves the wool from their own sheep and makes the family's clothes. Father is skilled at carpentry, among other jobs; he helps Almanzo make a yoke for his little oxen team and then helps him train his little calves gently and patiently, so they will grow to be good and willing workers. Children who love animals find Almanzo and his father especially congenial because they are gentle and caring with their livestock just as the grown-up Almanzo and Laura are.

Pa and his helpers harvest ice from the nearby lake and store it in an icehouse; Wilder describes the process in meticulous detail. She also chronicles the family's careful husbandry–making soap; cleaning and whitewashing the family root cellar so their root vegetables will be properly stored and command good prices; making the "best butter in New York" to sell profitably; and harvesting and preserving the many crops from the farm.

Thanks to Wilder's engrossing descriptions, a reader is transported into this long-vanished world. She recounts the operation of the one-room schoolhouse that the Wilder children attend, including the teacher's victory over a gang of rowdy bullies bent on disrupting the class and driving the teacher away. Another high point for the Wilders and for the reader is the local Independence Day celebration; Garth Williams's superb illustrations make the occasion still more graphic. Almanzo's milk-fed pumpkin wins a prize, and he enjoys the parade of beautiful horses, the patriotic readings, the bands, the firing of the town cannons, the lemonade vendors, and the other excitements of the day. Excitements at home include an itinerant tin peddler, who makes an overnight visit, bringing "treasures" for everyone, and a cobbler who comes to the house once a year to make the family boots and shoes. He sets up shop right in the Wilder dining room and stays as an honored guest until all the family feet are shod.

Finally, on a long-awaited day, Almanzo is permitted to ride to town with his father to sell their baled hay. He finds a lost pocketbook with $1,500 in it, and when the stingy old miser who lost it offers Almanzo only a nickel reward and questions his honesty as well, the burly owner of the local wagon shop forces the old man to give Almanzo a $200 reward. The boy puts his windfall in the bank to save for his own colt; Father is so impressed with his son's new maturity that he gives him the family's beautiful colt Starlight for his own.

The best known of the Little House books is probably *Little House on the Prairie* (1935), after which the television series was named. The series ran from September 1974 to March 1983 and introduced a new generation of young readers to the books. The pilot movie covered the Ingallses' trek from the Big Woods to Kansas; in fact, the opening episode includes the terrifying fording of the flood-swollen creek where the family almost drowns and the dog, Jack, disappears, only to reappear miraculously a few days later. However, most of the subsequent programs are set in Walnut Grove, Minnesota, and though they feature characters from the later books, the plots wander far afield from the originals.

*Little House on the Prairie* begins with the Ingalls family leaving their comfortable home in the Big Woods because "Pa said there were too many people in the Big Woods now." They cross the frozen Mississippi River in a covered wagon and camp on the prairies as they make their way westward. Not realizing that he is encroaching on Indian land, Pa chooses a spot near the Verdigris River where he builds a log house for the family and a shelter for the horses. A wonderful neighbor, Mr. Edwards, helps Pa build the cabin and shelters for the animals and dig a well. Later in the story, in a memorable show of friendship, Edwards travels many miles to Independence to buy gifts, then fords the creek in the freezing December night in order to arrive at the Ingalls cabin with a bundle of clothes and gifts and to play Santa for the girls so they can have a proper Christmas.

Indians come to visit the house, sometimes when Pa is not there. Ma feeds them corn bread, and they take all of Pa's tobacco. Ma does not like Indians, and Jack must be chained to keep him from attacking them and precipitating a crisis. Laura's descriptions of the "wild men" whose faces were "bold and fierce and terrible," with eyes that "were black and still and glittering, like snake's eyes," or of others, "dirty, scowling and mean," who later invade the house and try to steal Pa's furs have made *Little House on the Prairie* unwelcome in some politically correct classrooms.

A serious health crisis threatens the entire family when they come down with the "ague" (malaria). Fortunately, they are saved by a visit from a neighbor, Mrs. Scott, who brings Dr. Tan, a black physician, who prescribes a bitter powder–probably quinine–for them, then nurses them back to health. They had all been bitten many times by the swarms of mosquitoes that lived near the creek, but they do not connect the insects with their illness; in fact, Mrs. Scott is convinced it has come from eating watermelon!

As the months go by, the rumblings from the Indian camp grow more ominous. Fortunately, Pa has established a good relationship with the Indians, and later the Osage chief, Soldat du Chene, prevents a planned massacre of the white "intruders" by more-militant Indian tribes, persuading them to leave the settlers in peace. In a memorable scene, Laura watches the Indian retreat. At first excited by all the beautiful ponies, she then begins to look at their riders, some of them children no older than Mary or herself:

> The ponies did not have to wear bridles or saddles, and the little Indians did not have to wear clothes. All their skin was out in the fresh air and the sunshine. Their straight black hair blew in the wind and their black eyes sparkled with joy. . . . Laura looked and looked at the Indian children, and they looked at her. She had a naughty wish to be a little Indian girl. Of course she did not really mean it. She only wanted to be bare

*Laura Ingalls Wilder and her husband, Almanzo Wilder. The scenery is a photography-studio backdrop.*

naked in the wind and the sunshine, and riding one of those gay little ponies.

Then Laura sees an Indian mother riding by, with her baby in a basket beside the pony. "Laura looked straight into the bright eyes of the little baby. . . . Its hair was as black as a crow and its eyes were black as a night when no stars shine." Laura begs her Pa to get her the Indian baby and cries bitterly when it disappears from view. In response to Ma's baffled question, "Why on earth do you want an Indian baby, of all things," Laura can only sob, "'It's eyes are so black. . . .' She could not say what she meant."

In her perceptive study of Wilder's work, Janet Spaeth suggests in *Laura Ingalls Wilder* (1987) that Laura's response to the Indian baby signals that Laura has begun

to be aware of the complexity of language, particularly its inadequacy as a means of relaying one's innermost feelings . . . ; the baby is, to her, a symbol of a part of herself that she does not know how to acknowledge. She has discovered an aspect of her own being that is

inexpressible through language: it cannot be touched by the intellect, only by the heart.

When Pa finds out that "the government" is planning to send soldiers to warn the settlers off Indian territory, he decides to pack up and leave. Laura goes to sleep in the wagon to the sound of Pa's singing:

Row away, row o'er the waters so blue,
Like a feather we sail in our gum-tree canoe.
Row the boat lightly, love, over the sea;
Daily and nightly I'll wander with thee.

They were all there together, safe and comfortable for the night, under the wide, starlit sky. Once more the covered wagon was home.

*On the Banks of Plum Creek* (1937) carries on the saga of the Ingalls family, but again, not precisely as it happened. Wilder depicts the family's arrival at Plum Creek, using Jack, the dog, to introduce the new setting. "All day long for many, many days, Jack had been trotting under the wagon. He had trotted all the way from the little log house in Indian Territory, across Kansas, across Missouri, across Iowa, and a long way into Minnesota." In reality, the Ingalls family found their way from Wisconsin to Plum Creek, near the town of Walnut Grove, Minnesota, after their second stay in the Big Woods. But what happens to them in *On the Banks of Plum Creek* is based on real events. The family settles into a sod house acquired from a Norwegian settler, Mr. Hanson, in exchange for their Indian ponies and a mule colt. Pa dreams of a big wheat crop, which will make them prosperous. True to form, Ma soon has the dugout trim, neat, and attractive, and the girls enjoy playing in the creek and caring for the pretty white milch cow Pa gets from a neighbor in exchange for work during the harvest.

Pa does not understand when people tell him that the warm weather is "grasshopper weather," and he plants a magnificent wheat crop, borrows money, and builds the family a splendid house with glass windows and a "lordly" cookstove for Ma. Laura and Mary begin going to school and Sunday school in town, and Laura has her first contact with "Nellie Oleson," the snobbish storekeeper's daughter who appears in subsequent books and whose infamy lives on via the television series. Nellie is actually a composite of two girls Wilder disliked during her growing-up years, but the name Nellie is fictitious.

Just when the wheat crop is at its best and Pa's hopes are highest, a huge cloud covers the sun and the sky, and a plague of grasshoppers descends to destroy everything in their path. Pa cannot pay his loans, so he walks two hundred miles across Minnesota to find farmwork, leaving Ma and the girls to manage for themselves, under the watchful care of the Nelsons and other kindly neighbors. Pa comes home for Christmas, with money to pay bills and to repay the Nelsons for helping out, and over the winter he traps animals for fur trading and does carpentry work. At the church Christmas celebration, Mary gets a new Christmas coat, and Laura receives a beautiful white china jewel box with a tiny teapot and cup and saucer on it, as well as a little brown fur cape and muff, all from people back East whom the minister had told about "his little country girls."

As in Wilder's previous books, most of the characters in the story are based on real people. The Nelson family were prominent Walnut Grove citizens who stayed on in the town and prospered after the Ingalls family had moved on. "Brother Alden," the kindly minister who called Laura and Mary "his little country girls," was the Reverend E. H. Alden, a traveling missionary preacher who helped to establish the Congregational Church in Walnut Grove and who was present at the dedication of the church building on 20 December 1874. The church bell for which Pa helped to raise money was saved when the old church building was demolished in the 1950s and now rings in the bell tower of the English Lutheran Church in Walnut Grove; the tiny jewel box Laura received that day is now on display at the Laura Ingalls Wilder Home and Museum in Mansfield, Missouri.

During the second summer beside Plum Creek, the grasshopper eggs hatch, and the grasshoppers eat every green thing in sight. They finish their foraging with a terrifying three-day walk through the ruined fields, the stables and other outbuildings, and through the house, climbing over everything in their path.

> No grasshopper turned out of its way for anything. They walked steadily over the house. They walked over the stable. They walked over Spot [the cow] until Pa shut her in the stable. They walked into Plum Creek and drowned, and those behind kept on walking in and drowning until dead grasshoppers choked the creek and filled the water and live grasshoppers walked across on them.
>
> Finally, on the fourth day, the grasshoppers suddenly mount to the sky and fly away. Though the crops begin to grow again, Pa is once more forced to go East for work to pay off his loan and buy supplies for winter. With the help of Mr. Nelson and their own pluck and ingenuity, Ma and the girls manage. They survive a prairie fire and a fierce blizzard, and they keep the cattle from starving by feeding them turnip tops, until Pa comes home again to sing and play his fiddle and to settle in with the family for a cozy, warm winter.

*By the Shores of Silver Lake* (1939) opens on the banks of Plum Creek, but many changes have taken place, some of which are chronicled and others not mentioned by Wilder in the Little House books. The real Pa rented a little house in Walnut Grove during the winter of 1875 so that the girls could attend school without risking dangerous treks through blizzards or treacherous weather. There a son, Charles Frederick, was born on 1 November 1875. When spring came, the family moved back to their home beside Plum Creek, but the grasshopper eggs hatched, and once again the grasshoppers ate everything in sight. Though Laura's fictional family coped and triumphed in *On the Banks of Plum Creek,* the real Pa Ingalls actually decided to leave the "blasted country" and try his luck elsewhere. A new settler offered to buy the farm along Plum Creek, and Pa and Ma planned to move the family to Burr Oak, Iowa, to help run a hotel there. On the way to Iowa, they stayed for several months with relatives near South Troy, Minnesota; there, on 27 August 1876, baby Freddie, who had never been robust, died. The baby was buried in eastern Minnesota, and shortly thereafter the Ingalls family loaded up their wagon and headed for Burr Oak, Iowa, to take up their duties at the Master's Hotel.

Anderson calls the time at Burr Oak "The Missing Era of Laura's Books" and suggests several reasons for its omission. The Burr Oak era dealt with what the settlers called "back-tracking," in other words, going back East,

*Wilder's daughter, Rose, at nineteen. Her suggestion led
her mother to write the "Little House" books.*

and Wilder's series stresses the westward movement of
Laura and her family. But most interesting is the problem
of Laura's chronological age as the books unfold. Anderson explains.

> Laura had no idea when she wrote *Little House in the Big
> Woods* that she was commencing a series of books that
> readers would follow carefully from one volume to
> another, with full attention to dates, time, and details all
> coinciding with the previous story. When she com-
> pleted *On the Banks of Plum Creek,* she needed to account
> for two years she had earlier added to Laura's age.

Anderson adds that Wilder's daughter, Rose Wilder
Lane, told him that Wilder wanted her fictional character
to be three years old in the Big Woods book, but Harper
adamantly refused to publish the book unless Wilder
agreed to make Laura five years old, maintaining that a
child of three was too young to have "credible memories."
Lane added, "So she left out the two years spent in Burr
Oak, partly to make her age correct and partly because
Burr Oak was not too different from the Little Town [De
Smet, South Dakota] that she wrote about later."

Grace Ingalls was born in Burr Oak on 23 May
1877. Pa worked at the hotel and later as a carpenter and

as a laborer at a grinding mill; the older girls attended
school. Before long, Pa grew restless and decided it was
time to move west again. The family returned to Walnut
Grove in the fall of 1877, where they were warmly welcomed by the townspeople. Pa quickly found work as a
carpenter, and the girls resumed their schooling. In 1878
Pa opened a butcher shop, though he continued to work
at building and carpentry as well when his skills were
needed.

Suddenly, in the winter of 1879, Mary became seriously ill and shortly thereafter lost her sight. *By the Shores of
Silver Lake* begins at this point in the Ingalls history; however, Wilder puts her fictional family back in their Plum
Creek home, weak and exhausted after a bout with scarlet
fever that has affected Ma, Mary, Carrie, and "Baby
Grace." Though Laura attributes Mary's affliction to scarlet fever, and the doctors called it "brain fever," Anderson
suggests it was most likely spinal meningitis that caused
her blindness.

*By the Shores of Silver Lake* opens with the visit of Pa's
sister, Aunt Docia, to the convalescent family. She has married, and her new husband is a contractor working on a
railroad in the Dakota Territory. She wants to take Pa west
with her to work as a storekeeper, bookkeeper, and time-
keeper at the railroad camp for wages of $50 a month and
a chance to homestead. Though Ma is reluctant to uproot
the family again, she agrees that Pa should leave immediately; she and the girls plan to follow later on the train,
when Mary is well enough to travel. In the midst of preparations, as poor old Jack looks on forlornly, Laura makes
Pa promise that Jack can ride to their new home in the
wagon, but the next morning the old dog is dead. Pa tells
Laura that good dogs go the Happy Hunting Grounds,
and Laura imagines Jack "running gaily in the wind over
some high prairie, as he used to run on the beautiful wild
prairies of Indian Territory."

After months of separation, Ma and the girls have
an exciting train ride to join Pa; they stay at the railroad
camp where Laura's "boisterous" cousin Lena teaches her
to ride the Indian ponies. Then they move on to the Silver
Lake camp, where Pa is working and where they will
homestead a claim. Pa has put up a shanty on the shores
of Silver Lake, and Laura, Mary, and Carrie explore the
Big Slough and other wonders, though they heed Ma's
warning to stay away from the rough railroad men. Ma
said that "she wanted her girls to know how to behave, to
speak nicely in low voices and have gentle manners and
always be ladies." One day, however, Pa takes Laura to see
the men working on the railroad; once again, Wilder
makes an almost forgotten era live with her descriptions of
the preliminary plowing and grading, the laying of the
track, and the way the men who did this vital work lived.
Pa proves to be a good paymaster and supervisor at his
company store and, with the help of a huge Indian named

Big Jerry, is able to thwart a band of roving horse thieves and avert a possible riot over late pay.

Pa moves the family into town for the winter; they stay in the Surveyor's House, which has been provisioned and proves to be comfortable and warm. Pa files his claim on his chosen homestead before the crowd heading west comes out in the spring. The Reverend Alden makes a surprise visit and tells the Ingalls family that a new town called DeSmet will be growing up around them when spring comes. When, as predicted, strangers start arriving, Ma and the girls begin running a boardinghouse, housing and feeding a steady stream of strange men, and saving as much as they can toward Mary's fees for the College for the Blind. As Laura watches the town grow, she becomes more and more anxious to move out to the homestead, and when they hear of a friend's murder at the hands of a claim jumper, the Ingalls family decide it is time to move back to the claim. On the way back to the prairie home, they pass a young man with a beautiful horse; the man turns out to be Almanzo Wilder, who has recently moved to the Dakota Territory and who later becomes Laura's husband.

*The Long Winter* (1940) was originally titled "The Hard Winter," but the publishers feared such a negative title might discourage young readers, so they insisted that Wilder change it. But the story of the way the Ingalls family and their fellow citizens of DeSmet, Dakota Territory, survived the winter of 1880–1881 is based on historical fact.

In spite of the mild fall, Pa has read Nature's warnings: the thick walls on the muskrat houses and an early blizzard, which freezes some poor cattle's heads to the ground, seem ominous to him, and an old Indian warns the townsfolk that "heap big snow" is coming and that the blizzards will last seven months. Though Ma laughs at Pa's misgivings, he moves the family to town, and Laura and Carrie begin attending school until a big blizzard effectively shuts down the town. The townspeople get along all right until the snow becomes so deep that the railroad is forced to suspend service. For months, they exist on the small amount of food they have left and are at last reduced to burning hay sticks and going to bed early because they have no oil for their lamps. Nineteen-year-old Almanzo Wilder and his friend Cap Garland are credited with saving the town from starvation: at extreme danger to themselves, they travel more than twenty miles through trackless snow to buy wheat from a settler. When spring comes, everyone in the town has survived the long winter.

When *Little Town on the Prairie* (1941) opens, the Ingallses are established on their claim, but Pa finds Laura a job in town, which she reluctantly takes so she can help raise the tuition for Mary to attend college. Though Laura misses the beauty of the prairie, she spends the entire month of June helping the town seamstress make shirts for the men in the town; for this work Laura earns 25¢ a day plus dinner.

Pa makes the shanty into a proper home; Ma and the girls make the house livable and attractive; and the family acquires a kitten and some chickens. The activity of the new town is described in fascinating detail, including a Fourth of July celebration at which Almanzo Wilder's team of beautiful Morgan horses wins a race. Hordes of blackbirds, which come to eat the crops, find they have met their match in Ma, who devises many ways to serve blackbirds as culinary delicacies. Mary goes off to college, and Laura survives an unpleasant school year with Almanzo's sister, Eliza Jane, as her teacher. Laura soon becomes the center of a group of young friends, and both Pa and Laura help to organize town activities, including spelling bees, literary evenings, and music school. Laura works hard at school and earns her third-grade certificate. The book ends with her looking forward to her first teaching job on a claim twelve miles away.

*These Happy Golden Years* (1943), the last book in the series, begins with Pa driving Laura to her first teaching job, at Brewster Settlement. Laura is not quite sixteen and is nervous about taking the position, but Pa advises, "Have confidence in yourself, and you can lick anything." The Brewsters' claim shanty, where Laura is to stay, is cold and bleak; Mrs. Brewster is unfriendly; and their child is hostile and bad tempered. Laura is given a tiny room with only a couch for a bed and a hook to hang her coat and clothes on. Calling Laura a "hoity-toity snip," Mrs. Brewster refuses to talk to her; instead, when Laura is around, Mrs. Brewster either fights with her husband or sits silent.

The small schoolhouse is about a mile away, and two of Laura's pupils are older than she. The school is short of books, and both teacher and students suffer greatly from the cold. Though at first Laura has some trouble with discipline, tips from Ma and Pa help her gain control and carry out a successful school term. However, the situation at the Brewsters does not improve; one horrifying day, Mrs. Brewster threatens her husband with a butcher knife. The only bright spot turns out to be the weekends, when Almanzo Wilder faithfully appears with his crack team to take Laura home to her family for the weekend. Laura survives her ordeal and is gratified by the $40 she earns, which she gives to Pa and Ma for Mary's education. The Brewster job is based on one of Wilder's actual experiences; she changed the name of the place because of the unpleasant details connected with the incident.

When Laura arrives home, she and Almanzo begin keeping company, and she enjoys working with a new teacher, who encourages her talent for composition. Laura finds a job helping a dressmaker and later takes her teacher's examination, earning a second-grade certificate.

2

covered it with an armful of the wilting, cut grass.

"This sun almost makes a fellow wish for a bunch of sprouts to make a shade," he said to Laura. But his teeth gleamed out between his mustache and his beard as he smiled. Laura knew that he didn't want any sprouts; he had grubbed out so many from the little cleared field in the Big Woods, and they always grew again and he had to grub them out again, every summer.

were no sprouts/ There was not
because
Here on the Dakota prairies there~~was not a single thing that grew~~ a single tree, ~~nothing~~ Nothing made the smallest bit of shade from the burning sun, nothing gave any coolness to the scorching wind.

"Well, well. A man works better when ~~shm~~ he's warmed up, anyway!" Pa said cheerfully. He chirruped to start the horses.

Laura sat down in the uncut grass, to watch Pa go once
the stubble-field.
around, ~~the horses~~ Sam and David, the Christmas horses,
light mowing machine. The long,
plodded solemnly, pulling the ~~long~~
thin                                   whirring
~~thin~~ blades, notched with/steel teeth, went steadily against the waving tall grass and laid it down in a wide
sat on the high mowing machine seat
swath. Pa ~~seated behind~~, watching and guiding.
It smelled
Where Laura sat in the grass the heat was pleasant, ~~like~~
as good as the
~~the~~ heat in an oven when bread is baking. She sat so still that little brown-and-yellow striped gophers came out of their holes and hurried about their affairs all around her.
gripping
Tiny birds flew from grass stem to grass stem, ~~they gripped~~ the bending stems with wee claws and balanced lightly. A
came flowing      over the ground,
striped gopher snake ~~swung her long, brown body~~, curving and rippling through the forest of grass. It came to Laura, where she sat hunched with her chin on her drawn-up knees and the sunshine burning on her back. She felt suddenly very big, as big as a mountain, when the snake lifted up its head with a curving of its neck and stared at the high, high wall

*Page from the second draft of Wilder's 1940 novel,* The Long Winter, *typed by her daughter, Rose, with handwritten corrections by Wilder (from John Miller,* Becoming Laura Ingalls Wilder, *1998)*

She soon finds another teaching job, which is much more enjoyable than the Brewster one had proved to be.

Laura and Almanzo become inseparable and decide to marry. When they get an inkling that Almanzo's meddling sister, Eliza Jane, is heading to DeSmet to put on a big wedding for them, they quietly seek out the local minister and are married, and, as the story ends, move to "their own little house," which Almanzo has built and furnished for them. It was, as Laura records, an idyllic time:

> All this was theirs; their own horses, their own cow, their own claim. The many leaves of their little trees rustled softly in the gentle breeze. Twilight faded as the little stars went out and the moon rose and floated upward. Its silvery light flooded the sky and the prairie. The winds that had blown whispering over the grasses all the summer day now lay sleeping, and quietness brooded over the moon-drenched land. "It is a wonderful night," Almanzo said. "It is a beautiful world," Laura answered, and in memory she heard the voice of Pa's fiddle and the echo of a song, "Golden years are passing by, These happy golden years."

The first years of Laura and Almanzo's married life do not remain idyllic, however. Though the young couple bring hard work, determination, and considerable pioneer experience to their new homestead, Fate and Nature conspire to defeat their best efforts.

*The First Four Years* (1971), which describes the early years of Laura's marriage to Almanzo, was not published during Wilder's lifetime. The manuscript was found among her papers after her death, and after her daughter's death in 1968 it came into the possession of Roger Lea MacBride, Lane's lawyer, executor, and heir. MacBride took the manuscript to Harper and Row, who published the original draft as written, in 1971, as a welcome addition to the Little House series.

Though MacBride suggests in his introduction that Wilder had written this account in the 1940s, then probably lost interest in revising it after Almanzo died, subsequent research by Anderson makes a strong case for an earlier date, perhaps around 1933. The story, titled in manuscript "The First Three Years and a Year of Grace," chronicles the discouraging early years of the Wilders' marriage, which ultimately led to their leaving South Dakota and moving to Missouri. With high hopes and enthusiasm, Almanzo and Laura move into the trim little house on the tree claim on their 320-acre homestead. But a hailstorm destroys their first wheat crop, and Almanzo is hard-pressed to keep up the mortgage payments, as well as payments on the various loans he has taken out to buy farm machinery and livestock. The young couple are forced to rent out the tree-claim cottage and move into the shanty on their homestead, but they are soon comfortably established once again.

Daughter Rose is born the second year, and though the crops are not abundant, because of sparse rainfall, the Wilders manage to make ends meet. However, during the third year, a heat wave literally cooks the wheat crop in the field, and an attack of diphtheria leaves Laura weak and Almanzo permanently impaired. Whether Almanzo's paralysis was caused by diphtheria, a subsequent stroke, or possibly by polio, he remained physically challenged for the remainder of his life. Almanzo acquires a flock of sheep, hoping that the sale of their wool will help their shaky financial situation, and Laura's cousin Peter helps to manage them. The renter leaves the tree-claim house, so Laura and Almanzo move back in and soon thereafter sell the homestead property where they had been living.

In the fourth year Almanzo buys oxen to help with the sod-breaking on his claim. His first seeding is blown away by a dust storm, and subsequent plantings are ravaged by hot winds and drought. An infant son is born to the Wilders but dies only a few weeks after birth. Then, while Laura is still weak from childbirth, a fire destroys their home. In spite of these ordeals, the book ends on a positive note: "It would be a fight to win out in this business of farming, but strangely she felt her spirit rising for the struggle."

In reality, the Wilders finally decided to abandon the struggle in South Dakota and to move to a new, more promising part of the country. They sold their sheep and set off in a covered wagon for Spring Valley, Minnesota, where the elder Wilders had a thriving farm. They spent more than a year there, until Almanzo decided to try a warmer climate to improve his health. Almanzo auctioned off his remaining livestock, and in the fall of 1891 the family boarded a train for a trip south to Westville, a village in the Florida Panhandle, where Laura's cousin Peter was living. Florida proved uncongenial to the Midwesterners, however, and Anderson reports,

> When the Wilders were settled, the neighbors viewed them with suspicion. Laura was seen as a haughty "up-North gal" and disliked even by Cousin Peter's wife, a Florida backwoods girl. The atmosphere made Laura so uneasy that she carried a revolver in her skirt pocket for safety. The hot, humid climate made her tired and listless, and Manly's health was not improved as much as they had hoped.

Years later, Lane used the memories of that Southern sojourn as the background for a short story published in *Harper's* magazine in April 1922. "Innocence" is a chilling tale of a northern family caught in an uneasy alliance with a sinister band of moonshiners in the Florida backwoods. The story suggests the tensions and ominous undercurrents that drove the Wilder family north again, to the familiar surroundings of South Dakota.

*Wilder signing books at Brown's Bookstore in Springfield, Missouri, in October 1952*

The Wilders stayed in DeSmet, first living with Laura's parents, then renting a home nearby. Almanzo worked as a painter or carpenter and helped his brother Royal and Pa Ingalls, who both owned stores, and Laura worked for a dressmaker. But lured by the promise of "The Land of the Big Red Apple," the Wilders soon began planning and carefully saving for a journey to Mansfield, Missouri, which proved to be their last stopping place. Ingalls hid a $100 bill in her writing desk as they prepared for the long journey, which they undertook with another pioneering family. Laura's diary of the trip was published by Harper and Row in 1962 as *On the Way Home: The Diary of a Trip from South Dakota to Mansfield, Missouri, in 1894.* Lane's "setting" supplied her own memories of the trip and of their subsequent life in Mansfield; period photographs further enrich the account.

At the end of the six-week journey, the Wilders found their farm on a rocky forty acres not far from the town of Mansfield. Thus began a love affair with "Rocky Ridge Farm" that lasted throughout the rest of their long lives. Under their willing and capable hands, this unpromising, abandoned little farm ultimately became the showplace of the countryside. The farm also led, indirectly, to Wilder's career as a writer. Her reputation as a successful poultry raiser led to invitations to speak and share ideas at farmers' gatherings. According to Anderson, she was too busy at home one day to present a talk in person, so she sent her speech to be read in her absence. The speech so impressed John Case, the editor of the farm weekly the *Missouri Ruralist,* that he invited her to submit articles to the paper. She began her long career as a writer for that publication with her first article, "Favors the Small Farm Home," which appeared in the February 1911 issue. Later, the *Missouri Ruralist* made her a columnist, and she served also as Household Editor. In addition, from time to time she contributed articles and feature stories to the *St. Louis Star,* the *St. Louis Globe-Democrat,* and the *Kansas City Star.*

Meanwhile, Rose Wilder had become a career woman, starting as a Western Union telegrapher, then working as a newspaper writer. She eventually settled in

San Francisco, where she married Gillette Lane and began to encourage her mother to try her hand at writing for a more lucrative market than the *Missouri Ruralist*. Wilder visited Rose in San Francisco, and the letters she wrote to Almanzo about the visit were later edited by MacBride and published by Harper and Row in 1974 as *West from Home: Letters of Laura Ingalls Wilder, San Francisco 1915*.

Lane became a world traveler when she took a job in the Paris publicity office of the American Red Cross, and her magazine and newspaper articles made her a celebrity. Her novel *Peaks of Shala* (1922) increased her prestige, and on her occasional visits home to Rocky Ridge she became the "celebrity in residence" and certainly strengthened Wilder's resolve to make her own writing more profitable. When Lane became prosperous, she was able to help her aging parents make their farm less physically demanding. The house was wired for electricity; a Buick helped them travel about the countryside; and they sold off the sheep, which had kept Almanzo busy but were too physically demanding. Laura decided to work on her autobiography. Her manuscript, titled "Pioneer Girl," did not find a publisher, in spite of Lane's best efforts, but eventually it found its way to Harper and Brothers, and at their suggestion Wilder rewrote her material, adding many of Pa's stories, which were, in her words, "much too good to be lost." The result was *Little House in the Big Woods*, which proved to be "the miracle book which no depression could stop," according to Virginia Kirkus, then an editor at Harper. "That book was a labor of love and is really a memorial to my father," Wilder said during a lecture to a local group. "I did not expect much from the book but hoped that a few children might enjoy the stories I had loved."

Wilder's efforts have succeeded far beyond anything she could have envisioned. There are museums and memorial sites in nearly all the places where she and her family once lived, and a succession of Little House songbooks, guidebooks, recipe books, trivia books, newsletters, biographical reflections in national magazines, and miscellaneous memorabilia testify to her continued popularity with old and new generations of readers.

Almanzo Wilder died 23 October 1949. Garth Williams, who was asked to illustrate the new edition of the Wilder books that were published in 1953, had little knowledge of the West. Before undertaking the illustrations, Williams visited Wilder in Mansfield, Missouri, and then spent weeks following by automobile the route her family had taken in their covered wagon so many years before. In an article in the *Horn Book Magazine* for December 1953 Williams characterized Wilder and her appeal

with insight and understanding. "She understood the meaning of hardship and struggle, of joy and work, of shyness and bravery. She was never overcome by drabness or squalor. She never glamorized anything; yet she saw the loveliness in everything." Laura Ingalls Wilder died 10 February 1957 in Mansfield and was buried in the Mansfield Cemetery.

In a world in which old values are being challenged and the past seems a closed book to many, Wilder continues to find new disciples who respond to her goodness, her sense of adventure, her love for nature and its creatures, her sturdy self-reliance, and her joy in living. She speaks to many fundamental American beliefs: the importance of family, the reliance on one's own abilities, and the promise of tomorrow and of "the sweet, simple things of life which are the real ones after all."

**Letters:**

*West from Home: Letters of Laura Ingalls Wilder, San Francisco 1915,* edited by Roger Lea MacBride (New York: Harper & Row, 1974).

**References:**

William Anderson, *Laura Ingalls Wilder, a Biography* (New York: HarperCollins, 1992);

Anderson, *Laura Ingalls Wilder: The Iowa Story* (Burr Oak, Iowa: Laura Ingalls Wilder Park & Museum, 1990);

Anderson, *The Walnut Grove Story of Laura Ingalls Wilder* (Walnut Grove, Minn.: 1987);

*The Horn Book's Laura Ingalls Wilder: Articles about and by Laura Ingalls Wilder, Garth Williams, and the Little House Books,* edited by Anderson (Boston: Horn Book, 1987);

*A Little House Sampler: Laura Ingalls Wilder, Rose Wilder Lane,* edited by Anderson (Lincoln: University of Nebraska Press, 1988);

Janet Spaeth, *Laura Ingalls Wilder* (Boston: Twayne, 1987);

Donald Zochert, *Laura: The Life of Laura Ingalls Wilder* (Chicago: Regnery, 1976).

**Papers:**

Laura Ingalls Wilder donated several of her original manuscripts, including *The Long Winter* and *These Happy Golden Years,* to the Detroit Public Library, which named a branch after her. Other papers can be found at the various memorial sites, particularly at Mansfield, Missouri, and among the Rose Wilder Lane papers housed at the Herbert Hoover Presidential Library in West Branch, Iowa.

# Robert Wrigley

*(27 February 1951 –    )*

Ron McFarland
*University of Idaho*

BOOKS: *The Sinking of Clay City* (Port Townsend, Wash.: Copper Canyon, 1979);
*The Glow* (Missoula, Mont.: Owl Creek Press, 1982);
*Moon in a Mason Jar: Poems* (Urbana: University of Illinois Press, 1986);
*In the Dark Pool* (Lewiston, Idaho: Confluence, 1987);
*What My Father Believed: Poems* (Urbana: University of Illinois Press, 1991);
*In the Bank of Beautiful Sins* (New York: Penguin, 1995);
*Moon in a Mason Jar; and, What My Father Believed* (Urbana: University of Illinois Press, 1998);
*Reign of Snakes* (New York: Penguin, 1999).

SELECTED PERIODICAL PUBLICATION–
UNCOLLECTED: "Making Music of Sense," *Writing's Chronicle,* 32 (May/Summer 2000): 15–18.

Robert Wrigley has so far achieved a goal that is dear to the heart of nearly every writer–to have each succeeding book improve upon the one before it. His awards and honors have kept pace with his evolution as a poet, from his first National Endowment for the Arts Grant in 1978 to the Kingsley Tufts Poetry Award for 2000 for *Reign of Snakes* (1999), an "endowed cash award of $50,000 . . . presented annually, after an open competition, for a new work by an American poet who is past the beginning but has not yet reached the pinnacle of his or her career."

Additional recognitions include the Cecil B. Wagner Award from the Poetry Society of America (1985); a two-year appointment as Idaho's State Writer in Residence (1986–1988); the Frederick Bock Award from *Poetry* magazine (1988); two appointments as the Richard Hugo Distinguished Poet in Residence at the University of Montana (1990, 1995); Pushcart Prizes for poetry in 1991 and 1992; a Guggenheim Fellowship (1996); the San Francisco Poetry Center Book Award (1997); the Theodore Roethke Memorial Prize from *Poetry Northwest* magazine (1997); and the J. Howard and Bar-

*Robert Wrigley (courtesy of the author)*

bara M. J. Wood Prize from *Poetry* (1998). In 1987 he was selected by James Dickey to read at the Library of Congress as part of the "Legacy of American Poetry" celebration in honor of the nation's first poet laureate, Robert Penn Warren.

Born in East St. Louis, Illinois, on 27 February 1951, Robert Wrigley grew up near a coal-mining town and was the first male in several generations of his family never to work in the mines. His father, Arvil William Wrigley, was a miner and his mother, Betty Ann Feutsch Wrigley, was a church librarian. Robert and his twin sister, Kathryn (Kitty), graduated in 1969 from high school in Collinsville, Illinois, where he sang and played lead guitar for a rock-and-roll group. Music appears frequently in his poems, not only in their euphony and carefully controlled assonance but also as a subject. A quick scan of his books turns up singers as various as Mario Lanza and Bessie Smith, but jazz musicians predominate: Dave Brubeck, George Gershwin, Frank Sinatra, Art Pepper, Charlie Parker, John Coltrane, Billie Holiday, and Tommy Dorsey. Some of the musicians are personal acquaintances unfamiliar to the reader; many are not humans at all—bees, birds, and crickets. Wrigley's titles also reflect his love of music—"Harmony," "Torch Songs," "Sinatra," "A Cappella," and "Night Music," to name just one title from each of his five books. In an essay, "Making Music of Sense," Wrigley asserts that a crucial element of his "writing ritual" involves listening to a compact disc: "I prefer something instrumental—wordless, that is; no distractions from the province of *what*." "I prefer something mournful," he continues, "letting the music wash over me. I enter into it, and I long. I envy the musician's utter abandon to sound."

Wrigley was drafted into the army on 12 March 1971 and married Vana Berry on 29 May 1971. He served four months before filing for a discharge as a conscientious objector. After serving an additional five months in a special training detachment at Fort Sam Houston in San Antonio, Texas, he received an honorable discharge and began studies at Southern Illinois University (SIU) in Edwardsville, from which he graduated with honors in 1974, majoring in English. While at SIU he served as editor of the literary magazine, *Sou'wester*. At the University of Montana, where he pursued a Master of Fine Arts (MFA) degree in poetry, he helped to revive *CutBank*, the literary magazine of the university. In 1976 he completed an MFA, studying the craft of poetry with Madeline DeFrees and Richard Hugo. His first child, Philip, was born 31 January 1977, the year he moved to Lewis-Clark State College in Lewiston, Idaho, where he was to teach for the next twenty-two years, except for stints as Visiting Professor of Poetry and Acting Director of the MFA program at the University of Oregon (1990–1991) and as the Richard Hugo Distinguished Poet in Residence at the University of Montana in 1990 and 1995.

When Wrigley's first book of poems, *The Sinking of Clay City,* was published in 1979 by Copper

Cover for Wrigley's first poetry collection, published in 1979. The title poem deals with the decline of a town when its only industry, a coal mine, is closed.

Canyon, a small press in Port Townsend, Washington, he was only beginning to discover the West. The book was ignored by reviewers, but its origins are his MFA thesis and the influence of Richard Hugo. Although Wrigley makes some overtures to the West among the eighteen poems in the opening section, "Migratory Habits," as in "In the Great Bear, Flathead Range, August 1976," his world remains more than half Midwestern, as in the cornfields of "The Midwest" and the crappie and catfish of "Survival." Overall, he takes few risks in these poems, and he tends toward miniatures. The metaphor from painting, rather than music, is apt: Wrigley's early poems testify to his sense of image and, occasionally, of narrative, rather than of music. Only one of the seventeen poems that make up the first section is longer than thirty lines, and thirteen poems consist of twenty lines or fewer. In the seven-poem sequence titled "Slides," Wrigley's fascination with the image continues, as does his inclination to look back at his life in Illinois, despite that one of the "slides" is labeled "Carlton Lake, Bitterroot Range, 1976." The longest of the seven poems runs only twenty-four lines.

The focus of the best poems from Wrigley's first book, those in the title section, are on the miner's life. They also concern death, a subject that has retained its fascination for Wrigley over the years. Dedicated to his grandfather William H. Wrigley, a coal miner who died in 1970, the section opens with an elegy of sorts to the man whose "great lode of arteries / has turned diamond and ice." The title poem of the section and of the book begins with the closing of the last mine and the town and its inhabitants going under, as well. One of the most powerful poems in the book, "Song of the Trapped Miners," begins, "A miner sees in the dark: a trapped / miner sees beyond." Identifying himself with the trapped miners, the speaker seems to "see" their weeping families and friends, "the owner's / fierce impatience," and the approaching rescuers, but finally the miners "see the crowd breaking up," and as darkness comes, "the churchbell / sends a shock through the violet air, / and all the world goes blur." The last three poems in the book survey the reactions of the newly made widows, offer a coroner's report, and present a "legacy" from one of the miners: "all I have to pass on / is the wisdom of darkness." Such paradoxical wisdom is in keeping with that of Theodore Roethke: "In a dark time, the eye begins to see."

Wrigley and his wife, Vana, divorced in December 1981. On 20 July 1983 Wrigley married Kim Barnes, a talented student he met in one of his poetry-writing classes, who has since become well known for her two memoirs, *In the Wilderness* (1996) and *Hunger for the World* (2000), both of which concern her coming of age in northern Idaho. They have two children—a daughter, Jordan, born 24 October 1987, and a son, Jace, born 9 December 1989. In 1982 Owl Creek Press in Missoula, Montana, published Wrigley's chapbook *The Glow*, the title poem of which is arranged in five sections and is 180 lines long. The poem is densely textured both aurally and thematically, and it illustrates his fusion of narrative and lyric modes. The opening lines of the first poem, "The Collection," offer some sense of the rich interplay of imagery and music that has come to be indicative of Wrigley's style, which verges on the baroque:

Imagine a rack under glass, thin silver
pins and iridescent confections.

Nestled to the knuckle, a bluebottle fly
could be flossy aquamarine, an opal
on fire in its jeweled husk.

The assonantal short *a* (*ae*) sound of "imagine," "rack," and "glass" shifts to the short *i* (*ih*) of "thin," "silver," "pins," and "iridescent," then quickly shifts yet again to the short *e* (*eh*) of "iridescent," "confections," and "nestled," only to be capped once more by the liquid *l* (*ul*) sounds of "nestled," "knuckle," "bluebottle," "opal," and "jeweled." Wrigley's fascination with all creaturely life lies at the heart of the dozen poems in the chapbook, which reflect on such biota as bees, wasps, butterflies, nightcrawlers, fireflies, and termites. As David Baker concluded in a review of *The Glow* for *Western American Literature* (February 1984), the poems "are about our lives and our place, both marginal and fragile, in the natural world."

By the time his third book, *Moon in a Mason Jar: Poems* (1986), was published by the University of Illinois Press, Wrigley was placing his poems in such magazines as *American Poetry Review, Georgia Review, Kenyon Review,* and *Quarterly West.* The opening poem of *Moon in a Mason Jar,* "Moonlight: Chickens on the Road," one of his most memorable and most powerful poems, is seventy lines long; it thus affirms Wrigley's use of narrative in his poetry, an impulse he had from the outset but which he seemed reluctant to exploit in his first book. About half of the poems from *The Glow* are included in the full-length volume, which has fewer poems, thirty-four, but is about ten pages longer than *The Sinking of Clay City.* The opening poem of *Moon in a Mason Jar* is set in the Ozarks; a child speaks in the first person after a wreck in which his parents have been killed. "Called out of dream by the pitch and screech," the child awakens to the painful yet darkly comical world of life and death heralded by "the bubbling of chickens." Wrigley's deft use of images and verbal music suggests that the child's confrontation with pain—including his own—and death somehow acquires special value, as the reader finds the child "ambling barefoot through the jeweled debris, / glass slitting little blood-stars in my soles." One critic, M. K. Browning, writing for *Connections* in 2000, has suggested that a character's confrontation with "quotidian creatures that can have an unpleasant or even painful side" usually leaves the person "richer for the experience." Fred Chappell notes in *The Georgia Review* (Winter 1991): "Wrigley is very good at shading his poems with apprehension, with intimations of mortality."

Although such poems as "Pheasant Hunting" and "The Skull of a Snowshoe Hare" from *Moon in a*

*Mason Jar* suggest some receptivity of his new home west of the Rockies, Rick Ardinger, the reviewer for *Western American Literature* (August 1987) detects no significant indications of Western regionalism in the poems. In *What My Father Believed: Poems* (1991) the bulk of the poems pertain to Wrigley's awkward relationship with his father in the context of the Vietnam War and the poet's experience as a draftee and conscientious objector in 1971. Suggesting Philip Levine as a parallel, Steven Cramer in his review of *What My Father Believed* for *Poetry* (December 1992) describes the poems as "melancholy recollections of growing up American, working-class, and male." Had the book appeared twenty years sooner, Wrigley might have been recognized with Robert Bly and others as one of the militant Writers Against the War, but in fact the book is confessional and apologetic, particularly for Wrigley's own adolescent self-righteousness. In something of a paternal role now with respect to his bored students, Wrigley's first-person speaker concludes in the title poem, "My father believed in the nation, I in my father, / a man of whom those students have not the slightest notion." The first-person viewpoint predominates, figuring in twenty-five of the thirty-three poems, and when the third person appears, the character often bears a similarity to the persona who elsewhere speaks as "I."

Throughout the book Wrigley presents himself as a husband and father in implicit counterpoint to his own father. Consequently, although he focuses on events that occurred in Illinois about twenty years before the poems were composed, at least a dozen of the poems are located "Here, in the empty West" among mountains "heavily timbered and ripped again and again / for their logs" or "peering / into the northern sky over the emptiness / of central Idaho." The book concerns the difficulties of being an adolescent male in the United States, not just during the Vietnam War but any time. It also concerns the challenges of fatherhood, and it concerns war, which is the subject of the last poem, probably the finest in the book. Although several of the poems bear testimony to Wrigley's experimentation with form, mainly with alternating rhyme scheme loosely distributed in nonmetered lines, this one, "The Wishing Tree," adheres to the more-casual, open (enjambed) free-verse line employed without rhyme. The forty-two lines vary in syllabic count from seven to sixteen, and more than half of the lines are marked with no terminal punctuation, so the narrative of the father and son fishing and camping together flows freely.

Cover for Wrigley's 1999 collection, in which all of the poems deal in some way with serpents

"The Wishing Tree" is something of a companion poem, or an antitype, to the one just before it, "Camping," in which the poet recalls camping with his father "twenty-seven years / ago grappling inside the canvas gullet of a tent." The opening section is a sprawling twenty-one-line sentence. His memory is of camping trips cluttered with gear, of "my father raging toward fun," and of little communication. In "The Wishing Tree" the poet investigates his son's notebook while the boy is fishing, and he finds an assortment of "great trout and sheer unclimbable mountains" and tales, including one of "an old Indian man who found a tree for wishes." Although he regrets not having followed his son to the river, he turns his attention back to the drawings, where he finds a "picture of rockets" and around them signs of destruction, "everywhere flame and smoke, / ruins and rubble." But in a "white sphere of peace" at the bottom of the page he discovers two people playing catch. Their mouths are drawn as straight, unsmiling lines, in "strictest concentration," as if "they could / never let the ball be caught, as though everything / depended on them, everything– / and in the picture, it did, it did." The reader realizes that important communication has passed between father and son in this poem of healing.

Wrigley's fourth full-length book, *In the Bank of Beautiful Sins,* published by Penguin in 1995, drew considerable acclaim and made him a finalist for the Lenore Marshall Award of the Academy of American Poets. The thirty-five poems begin with a section titled "Believing Owl, Saying Owl," a line from "Majestic" that seems to bring together the references to one of the most symbolically significant of the creatures from his poems. Seeing himself as a boy in "The Owl," near the end of *Moon in a Mason Jar,* the first-person speaker reflects, "When the owl lit, I knew it was God," and at the end he is pulled into dream "on great white wingbeats." In "In the Dark Pool, Finding You," a love poem from *What My Father Believed,* the first-person speaker sees himself as a muskrat but would like to be the owl with his eyes and his voice "to stir the night with": "This is love's skill and power, as real as the owl, / high in the pine, and dining on imaginary mice."

Wrigley is a Western poet in *In the Bank of Beautiful Sins,* or as Calvin Bedient said in a review of the book for *Southern Review* (Winter 1997), "Most of the poems are set in hell-canyoned, eagle-and-lion-feral Idaho." Bedient admired the "ferocity" of the poems and found the book "lightning-rimmed by the sublime." The first-person speaker in "Majestic" joins a mill hand from Orofino and a prison guard, probably from the same town on the Clearwater River, in a futile effort to resuscitate a drowned priest. None of the three sees the owl sweep past in the night, but all believe it to be that traditional Indian bird of death, and the speaker blesses the owl because it brings back to the natural world "breathable air." In "Little Deaths" the speaker reflects, as he watches moths immolate themselves in a candle,

> How easy it is to live with
> little deaths–mostly bugs,
> the less musical birds, the cats
> and rabbits we can't avoid in our cars.

His meditation remains domestic and somewhat playful as he reflects on his son poking at an injured grasshopper and on how his children dispatched crawdads, except for one, the previous summer. The one they released, however, was promptly gobbled up by a "huge, shadowy bass." In "Meadowlark" the bird is not so much the focus of attention as a neighbor's dog, apparently killed by a mountain lion. The

"neatly eviscerated" carcass causes the dog's owner to think of his daughter, the speaker to think of his three-year-old son, and the other neighbor to reflect on "his youngest boy. . . coked out / in the Tenderloin, cross-dressing and bound / for something worse than any easy death." What distinguishes the "crazy" meadowlark as it sings a sort of eulogy in its "sad, ineffectual key" is that it is a "sweet die-hard."

Not all of the poems of *In the Bank of Beautiful Sins* concern death, and the focus of so many of them on that deep subject does not necessarily mean that they are "sublime"; but they are serious. In the words of Browning, in *Connections* (Summer 2000), Wrigley "makes the natural world the seat of his search for spiritual insight." His most mature, thoughtful, and musical collection to date, *Reign of Snakes,* published in 1999, the year he began teaching at the University of Idaho, is constructed in four sections, each of which is prefaced with substantial poems from a sequence that ends with an envoy. The five titles suggest something of these poems in which the narrative gives way to a more meditative mode: "The Afterlife," "Amazing Grace," "Meditation at Bedrock Canyon," "Night Music," and "The Name." The first of three quotations Wrigley attaches as epigraphs to the book is from Theodore Roethke, his and Richard Hugo's mentor: "Beautiful my desire, and the place of my desire." The other epigraphs are from Dante and Ernest Hemingway. The writers make for an unusual trinity. Roethke more than any other poet popularized the poem sequence, and Wrigley's sequence is reminiscent of those written by another of Roethke's students, David Wagoner.

Occasionally, Wrigley's playfully lyrical exuberance echoes Roethke both in content and in sound, as in the first stanza of "The Afterlife," in which the speaker declares, "I would enter the sky through the soil"–presumably, that is, the infinite through the finite, or, as Roethke expresses in "The Far Field," "All finite things reveal infinitude." The rich sound-play in the closing two lines of that stanza are resonant with references to Roethke: "Licked by filaments, I would lie, / a billion love-mouths to suckle and feed." Animal life floods the opening poem–from maggots to eagles and from frogs to herons–and it figures in most of the poems in *Reign of Snakes,* but the serpent is ubiquitous. The title poem is actually a nine-poem sequence, the individual poems ranging in length from the seventeen lines of "Glossolalia" to the sixty-four lines of "Deliverance." Wrigley may have drawn on the Pentecostal upbringing of his wife, Kim Barnes, for some of the language and imagery in these poems; in the first,

AFTER THE COYOTES' SONG

Now night is a little darker than before *clearly*

and it smells more still, the star wick trimmed *its*

audibly down.  Now all rodents are made brave, *emboldened*

all owls through their talons knowing,

down the limb-bones and capillary fretwork

of roots and holes, that every living thing's

about to bolt,

        even the tiny dumb animal

of my sleep, having for how many hours now

cowered under the rock of dreams— *possible*

look, there it goes, a whip of tail

running for its life, and the owl soars up

as silent on its nightmare wings as sleep's breath is

to the sleeper.

*Corrected typescript for a poem to be included in Wrigley's collection "Lives of the Animals," scheduled for publication by Penguin Books in 2003 (Collection of Robert Wrigley)*

"Revival," the speaker tells of coming upon snake handlers one summer evening in Arkansas, and the sequence draws on personal encounters with snakes that have an aura of mythic truth about them. In the fifth poem of the sequence, "Fellowship," he tells of a worker's detonating explosives in an area where rattlesnakes abound and witnessing "a bloody rain of snakes."

The sequence culminates in "Resurrection," in which the speaker places a frozen rattler in a burlap bag and takes it into his home, where one Sunday he finds himself waiting, presumably for the snake to be resurrected. But as he has said earlier in the poem, "this is fabulous"—punning on the etymology, which implies that what follows is a fable, but also that it is somehow wonderful or remarkable. The stance of the speaker in this poem is representative of Wrigley's personae: dazzled by the natural world, the speaker—essentially identifiable with Wrigley himself—feels tempted to become a believer in some transcendent Other, but he never quite takes that final step. In addition to human love, an increasingly common theme in his later poems, what Wrigley believes in finally is what most poets believe in—language, "the purity of one voice saying beautiful sounds."

**Interview:**

Buddy Levy, "Writing Their Way Home: An Interview with Kim Barnes and Robert Wrigley," *Poets & Writers,* 27 (May/June 1999): 26–31.

**References:**

Calvin Bedient, Review of *In the Bank of Beautiful Sins, Southern Review,* 33 (Winter 1997): 138–141;

M. K. Browning, "Robert Wrigley's Canon–Earlier Works," *Connections,* no. 2 (Spring 2000): 33–37;

Browning, "Robert Wrigley's Canon–Poems and Parables," *Connections,* no. 3 (Summer 2000): 29–36;

Fred Chappell, Review of *Moon in a Mason Jar, Georgia Review,* 45 (Winter 1991): 772–775;

Steven Cramer, Review of *What My Father Believed, Poetry,* 161 (December 1992): 171–176;

Ron McFarland, Review of *Moon in a Mason Jar, Northwest Review,* 25, no. 2 (1987): 152–156;

McFarland, Review of *Reign of Snakes, Northwest Review,* 38, no. 1 (2000): 128–133.

# Checklist of Further Readings

Bold, Christine. *Selling the Wild West: Popular Western Fiction, 1860 to 1960.* Bloomington: Indiana University Press, 1987.

Cawelti, John. *The Six-Gun Mystique.* Bowling Green, Ohio: Bowling Green University Popular Press, 1984.

Etulain, Richard W. *The American West in the Twentieth Century: A Bibliography.* Norman: University of Oklahoma Press, 1994.

Etulain. *Re-Imagining the Modern American West: A Century of Fiction, History, and Art.* Tucson: University of Arizona Press, 1996.

Etulain, and N. Jill Howard, eds. *A Bibliographical Guide to the Study of Western American Literature,* second edition. Albuquerque: University of New Mexico Press, 1995.

Everson, William. *Archetype West: The Pacific Coast as a Literary Region.* Berkeley, Cal.: Oyez, 1976.

Ganewere, Robert J., ed. *The Exploited Eden: Literature on the American Environment.* New York: Harper & Row, 1972.

Goetzmann, William H., and William N. Goetzmann. *The West of the Imagination.* New York: Norton, 1986.

Kowalewski, Michael, ed. *Reading the West: New Essays on the Literature of the American West.* Cambridge: Cambridge University Press, 1996.

Lamar, Howard R., ed. *The New Encyclopedia of the American West.* New Haven, Conn.: Yale University Press, 1998.

Lee, Robert Edson. *From West to East: Studies in the Literature of the American West.* Urbana: University of Illinois Press, 1966.

Limerick, Patricia Nelson. *The Legacy of Conquest: The Unbroken Past of the American West.* New York & London: Norton, 1987.

Lyon, Thomas J., and others, eds. *Updating the Literary West.* Fort Worth: Texas Christian University Press, 1997.

Maguire, James H. "Fiction of the West," in *The Columbia History of the American Novel,* edited by Emory Elliott and others. New York: Columbia University Press, 1991.

Maguire, ed. *The Literature of Idaho: An Anthology.* Boise, Idaho: Boise State University, 1986.

Malone, Michael P., and Etulain. *The American West: A Twentieth-Century History.* Lincoln: University of Nebraska Press, 1989.

Milner, Clyde A. II, Carol A. O'Connor, and Martha A. Sandweiss, eds. *The Oxford History of the American West.* New York & Oxford: Oxford University Press, 1994.

Morgan, Ted. *A Shovel of Stars: The Making of the American West, 1800 to the Present.* New York: Simon & Schuster, 1995.

Nash, Gerald D. *The American West in the Twentieth Century: A Short History of an Urban Oasis.* Englewood Cliffs, N.J.: Prentice-Hall, 1973.

Nash. *The American West Transformed: The Impact of the Second World War.* Bloomington: Indiana University Press, 1985.

Nash, Roderick. *Wilderness and the American Mind,* third edition. New Haven, Conn.: Yale University Press, 1982.

Peavy, Linda, and Ursula Smith. *Women in Waiting in the Westward Movement.* Norman & London: University of Oklahoma Press, 1994.

Sadler, Geoff, ed. *Twentieth-Century Western Writers.* Chicago: St. James, 1991.

Savage, William W. Jr. *The Cowboy Hero: His Image in American History & Culture.* Norman: University of Oklahoma Press, 1979.

Slotkin, Richard. *Regeneration through Violence: The Myth of the American Frontier, 1600–1860.* Middletown, Conn.: Wesleyan University Press, 1973.

Smith, Henry Nash. *Virgin Land: The American West as Symbol and Myth.* Cambridge, Mass.: Harvard University Press, 1950.

Sonnichsen, C. L. *From Hopalong to Hud: Thoughts on Western Fiction.* College Station: Texas A&M University Press, 1978.

Starr, Kevin. *Americans and the California Dream: 1850–1915.* New York: Oxford University Press, 1973.

Stauffer, Helen Winter, and Susan J. Rosowski. *Women and Western American Literature.* Troy, N.Y.: Whitston, 1982.

Steckmesser, Kent L. *The Western Hero in History and Legend.* Norman: University of Oklahoma Press, 1965.

Stegner, Wallace. *The American West as Living Space.* Ann Arbor: University of Michigan Press, 1987.

Stegner. *The Sound of Mountain Water.* Garden City, N.Y.: Doubleday, 1969.

Stegner. *Where the Bluebird Sings to the Lemonade Springs.* New York: Random House, 1992.

Steiner, Stan. *The Waning of the West.* New York: St. Martin's Press, 1989.

Stevenson, Elizabeth. *Figures in a Western Landscape: Men and Women of the Northern Rockies.* Baltimore & London: Johns Hopkins University Press, 1994.

Stewart, Frank. *A Natural History of Nature Writing.* Washington, D.C. & Covolo, Cal.: Island Press/Shearwater Books, 1995.

Taylor, J. Golden, Thomas J. Lyon, and others, eds. *A Literary History of the American West.* Fort Worth: Texas Christian University Press, 1987.

Thacker, Robert. *The Great Prairie Fact and the Literary Imagination.* Albuquerque: University of New Mexico Press, 1989.

Tomkins, Jane. *West of Everything: The Inner Life of Westerns.* New York: Oxford University Press, 1992.

Tuska, Jon. *A Variable Harvest: Essays and Reviews of Film and Literature.* Jefferson, N.C.: McFarland, 1990.

Tuska, and Vicki Piekarski, eds. *Encyclopedia of Frontier and Western Fiction.* New York: MacGraw-Hill, 1983.

White, Richard. *"It's Your Misfortune and None of My Own": A History of the American West.* Norman & London: University of Oklahoma Press, 1985.

Wiget, Andrew. *Native American Literature.* Boston: Twayne, 1985.

Work, James C., ed. *Prose & Poetry of the American West.* Lincoln & London: University of Nebraska Press, 1990.

Wrobel, David M. *The End of American Exceptionalism: Frontier Anxiety from the Old West to the New Deal.* Lawrence: University Press of Kansas, 1993.

# Contributors

Keith Browning . . . . . . . . . . . . . . . . . . . . . . . . . . . . . . . . . . . . . . . . . . . . *Lewis-Clark State College*

Russell Burrows . . . . . . . . . . . . . . . . . . . . . . . . . . . . . . . . . . . . . . . . . *Weber State University*

Mark Busby . . . . *Center for the Study of the Southwest, Southwest Texas State University, San Marcos*

Lawrence Clayton . . . . . . . . . . . . . . . . . . . . . . . . . . . . . . . . . . . . . *Hardin-Simmons University*

Dennis Cutchins . . . . . . . . . . . . . . . . . . . . . . . . . . . . . . . . . . . . . . *Brigham Young University*

Eugene England . . . . . . . . . . . . . . . . . . . . . . . . . . . . . . . . . . . . . . *Utah Valley State College*

David L. Evans . . . . . . . . . . . . . . . . . . . . . . . . . . . . . . . . . . . . . . . *Brigham Young University*

Gary Layne Hatch . . . . . . . . . . . . . . . . . . . . . . . . . . . . . . . . . . . . . *Brigham Young University*

Dennis R. Hoilman . . . . . . . . . . . . . . . . . . . . . . . . . . . . . . . . . . . . . . . *Ball State University*

Arthur R. Huseboe . . . . . . . . . . . . . . . . . . . . . . . . . . . . . . . . . . . . . . . . *Augustana College*

B. W. Jorgensen . . . . . . . . . . . . . . . . . . . . . . . . . . . . . . . . . . . . . . *Brigham Young University*

Suzanne Evertsen Lundquist . . . . . . . . . . . . . . . . . . . . . . . . . . . . . . . *Brigham Young University*

Jane Helm Maddock . . . . . . . . . . . . . . . . . . . . . . . . . . . . . . . *University of Montana—Western*

Sanford E. Marovitz . . . . . . . . . . . . . . . . . . . . . . . . . . . . . . . . . . . . . *Kent State University*

Ron McFarland . . . . . . . . . . . . . . . . . . . . . . . . . . . . . . . . . . . . . . . . *University of Idaho*

John J. Murphy . . . . . . . . . . . . . . . . . . . . . . . . . . . . . . . . . . . . . . *Brigham Young University*

Zina Petersen . . . . . . . . . . . . . . . . . . . . . . . . . . . . . . . . . . . . . . . *Brigham Young University*

Marty Priola . . . . . . . . . . . . . . . . . . . . . . . . . . . . . . . . . . . . . . . . *Cormac McCarthy Society*

Rena Sanderson . . . . . . . . . . . . . . . . . . . . . . . . . . . . . . . . . . . . . . . . *Boise State University*

David Stevenson . . . . . . . . . . . . . . . . . . . . . . . . . . . . . . . . . . . . . . *Western Illinois University*

Paul Varner . . . . . . . . . . . . . . . . . . . . . . . . . . . . . . . . . . . . . . . *Oklahoma Christian University*

Alison M. Wilson . . . . . . . . . . . . . . . . . . . . . . . . . . . . . . . . . . . . . . . *Pittsburgh, Pennsylvania*

# Cumulative Index

*Dictionary of Literary Biography,* Volumes 1-256
*Dictionary of Literary Biography Yearbook,* 1980-2000
*Dictionary of Literary Biography Documentary Series,* Volumes 1-19
*Concise Dictionary of American Literary Biography,* Volumes 1-7
*Concise Dictionary of British Literary Biography,* Volumes 1-8
*Concise Dictionary of World Literary Biography,* Volumes 1-4

# Cumulative Index

**DLB** before number: *Dictionary of Literary Biography,* Volumes 1-254
**Y** before number: *Dictionary of Literary Biography Yearbook,* 1980-2000
**DS** before number: *Dictionary of Literary Biography Documentary Series,* Volumes 1-19
**CDALB** before number: *Concise Dictionary of American Literary Biography,* Volumes 1-7
**CDBLB** before number: *Concise Dictionary of British Literary Biography,* Volumes 1-8
**CDWLB** before number: *Concise Dictionary of World Literary Biography,* Volumes 1-4

# C

# F

# I

# J

# L

# O

# P

# S

# U